Fourth Edition

Lee Anne Phillips

Contents at a Glance

Using HTML 4, 4th Edition

International Standard Book Number: 0-7897-1562-7

Library of Congress Catalog Card Number: 97-80845

Printed in the United States of America

First Printing: March 1998

00 99 98 4 3 2

Trademarks

Credits

Publisher
Jordan Gold

Executive Editor
Beverly Eppink

Managing Editor
Patrick Kanouse

Acquisitions Editor
David Mayhew

Development Editor
Bob Correll

Project Editor
Andrew Cupp

Copy Editor
Pat Kinyon

Technical Editors
Bill Vernon
Kelly Murdock

Cover Designer
Dan Armstrong

Book Designer
Nathan Clement

Indexers
Greg Pearson
Bruce Clingaman

Production
Carol Bowers
Mona Brown
Ayanna Lacey
Gene Redding
Elizabeth San Miguel

Contents

About the Author

Lee Anne Phillips is one of the old hands in the networking business, having skipped straight from the University of California at Berkeley into the mainframe world in 1977. Since that time, she's worked for a variety of companies, dabbling in one aspect of networking or another. She finally stumbled onto the World Wide Web itself in 1994, after a brief flirtation with ARPAnet during her carefree student days and a long-term romance with the Internet. After many years in exile and on the road, she now resides in her place of birth, the San Francisco Bay area. She holds a bachelor's degree in computer science and is a card-carrying computer nerd. Her current interests are electronic mail systems, user interfaces, and the continuing development of HTML and SGML as universal communications media.

About the Technical Editors

Bill Vernon (`vernon@4omega.com`) holds a bachelor's degree in computational physics from Purdue University. He is currently on site at Eli Lilly and Company (Pharmaceutical) where he is helping develop the company's intranet, code-named ELVIS. Bill owns Omega Design, an Indianapolis-based Web development studio. He enjoys mountain biking, skiing, snowboarding, soccer, and inline hockey. Bill spends the remainder of his time with his lovely wife Karly (whom he adores) and his two Siberian Huskies, Kivi and Bailey.

Kelly Murdock (`murdocks@itsnet.com`) works for Corel in their Web Products Group. He spends much of his spare time exploring the graphics frontier. He especially enjoys dabbling in 3D. He is the lead author of *Laura Lemay's Web Workshop: 3D Graphics and VRML 2* and has contributed to several other titles, including *HTML 4 Unleashed, Professional Reference Edition*. He also writes software reviews for `www.3dreview.com`.

Dedication

For Alison Eve Ulman, dear friend, who showed me that blindness is not a loss of vision but merely of sight, that impairments can be doorways into new experiences, and that human courage is as beautiful as roses.—Lee Anne

Acknowledgments

I'd like to thank Molly Holzschlag and Heather Guylar, who have been sources of inspiration, help, and advice to me for what seems like forever, as well as for supplying a warm shoulder to lean on when I needed advice or someone to complain to. Thank you. Thank you both from the bottom of my heart.

I'd also like to thank the wonderful people at Macmillan Computer Publishing, who have been not only helpful and professional, but friendly and thoughtful as well, going beyond the call of duty more than once to help me when I needed it. Thank you all, especially David Mayhew and Bob Correll, who are among my many editors and certainly among my favorites.

Many, many thanks to Claire Fedoruk, Martin Fedoruk, and Jill Funamoto, proud Canadians and very cool people. You know who you are.

Grateful thanks to Ryan Powers for the use of a screen shot of his Speller applet; Lee Oades for permission to use a screen shot of the Lee's Oil applet; Nathan Arora for permission to use a screen shot of his Tic Tac Toe applet; and David Griffiths for his blanket permission to use his Lake applet, provided that his own acknowledgment to the Beyond Photography applet from Stanford is mentioned. All these excellent Java programs were used in preparation of the chapter on Java, a very cool environment for cross-platform development from the good people at Sun Microsystems.

Thanks also to Rick Darnell, Kelly Murdock, Rob Falla, Bruce Campbell, Dennis Jones, Eric Ladd, and Bill Vernon, who offered much-welcomed technical assistance during the development of this book.

And of course, thanks to my mother, Eleanor, who has been a source of inspiration and admiration to me all of my life. Thanks, Mama.

We'd Like to Hear from You!

Que Corporation has a long-standing reputation for high-quality books and products. To ensure your continued satisfaction, we also understand the importance of customer service and support.

Tech Support

If you need assistance with the information in this book or you have feedback for us about the book, please contact Macmillan Technical Support by phone at **317-581-3833** or via email at `support@mcp.com`.

Orders, Catalogs, and Customer Service

To order other Que or Macmillan Computer Publishing books, catalogs, or products, please contact our Customer Service Department:

Phone: 1-800-428-5331
Fax: 1-800-835-3202
International Fax: 1-317-228-4400

or visit our online bookstore:

`http://www.mcp.com/`

Comments and Suggestions

We want you to let us know what you like or dislike most about this book or other Que products. Your comments will help us to continue publishing the best books available on computer topics in today's market.

Mark Taber
Executive Editor
Macmillan Computer Publishing
201 West 103rd Street
Indianapolis, IN 46290 USA
Fax: 317-817-7070
Email: `mtaber@mcp.com`

Please be sure to include this book's title and author as well as your name and phone number or fax number.
We will carefully review your comments and share them with the author. Please note that, due to the high volume of mail we receive, we might not be able to reply to every message.

Thank you for using Que!

INTRODUCTION

THIS BOOK IS designed for the busy woman or man with a job to do that does *not* entail becoming some sort of computer guru who can tell charming anecdotes about the interesting history of the World Wide Web and the fascinating history of markup languages all night long. Or even longer.

It's designed for the nonspecialist; it's designed for anyone who needs to know "a little of this" and "a little of that" to do the job he or she was hired to do, or for the average user at home who wants to create a family home page or host a page for a social club or professional organization. Everyone's on the Web these days, so almost everyone can benefit from a working, as opposed to theoretical, knowledge of how to get there.

People might have told you that creating a Web page is hard and that HTML is an arcane language best left to the sort of truly dedicated programming guru who has seven differently colored pens stuffed into a pocket protector meant for five at most. Nothing could be further from the truth. HTML is *easy*, and you'll make your first page in about two minutes flat, once you get started.

Anyone who has ever taken a yellow highlighter to a textbook or even a newspaper article; anyone who has ever circled an important word or drawn lines under a memorable phrase; or anyone who has ever made a note in a margin has already grasped the basic concept of HTML, which is marking up words and phrases to add emphasis or special meaning. The very name means

(Hyper)Text Markup Language; it's a language (symbols really) you use to mark up text. The proofreader's marks you might have used or seen revising printed text are part of a markup language, as are the special tags you might have seen if you turn on the Reveal Codes option in WordPerfect.

The "Hyper" part means simply that you can also mark words with pointers to other words or even other documents, as if you had drawn an arrow extending off the page and pointing to another page.

A hyperlink is sort of like a marginal note or footnote; you'll be reading along and see a mark that points to other information that might expand on what you've just read, or just tell you where you might find more references. That's HTML in a nutshell—marking the text on the page with special symbols to show that they're important, should be treated in special ways, or should point to other words in a different location. It's really a piece of cake.

This book is designed to help you with practical advice and techniques that work in the real world and will help you create your first Web pages quickly and with minimum fuss. I'll give you enough background so you can understand what's going on, but won't bury you in mystical phrases and technical details that only a graduate student in advanced programming concepts could understand and love. We'll use real-world examples, the sorts of pages you might be interested in actually doing, and will stay away from detailed explanations of how to represent your high-speed atom-smasher experiments in particle physics, for now anyway.

And each short example, illustrating a single task clearly, will link with others to allow you to easily branch to related tasks, or to follow the thread of a complete project from start to finish.

Que's *Using* series is designed to present information in a uniform way, so you can pick up any book in the series and find a familiar way of looking at things. As part of the series concept, we'll describe things in the most easily-understandable way in the text and then include technical names in sidebars, the glossary, and in the index, so you'll be able to translate between the technical jargon often spoken by specialists and the language of the everyday world.

I hope you have as much fun reading this book as I had writing it, because I tried to keep you, the reader, in mind at every step. If I succeeded, please let me know! If not, well, let me know that too and I'll try and do a better job next time. I can be reached through Que via what we sometimes call snail-mail today, or through their Web site. Contact information can be found on the "We'd Like to Hear from You!" page just prior to this introduction.

And speaking of keeping people in mind, I'd especially like to thank the many people who helped bring this book into existence. If you look at the title page overleaf, you'll notice a long list of names, all of whom did a lot, but they are only some of the people who helped, including the people who laid out and printed this book, the truck drivers who delivered the book to the bookstores, and the bookstore employees or owners themselves, who looked at this book and thought, "Hey! Our customers would really like to read this!" And of course you, dear reader, who may be thinking of buying this book right this minute, I hope! So thank you all, readers, editors, bookstores, printers and everyone. This is the work of many hands and now rests in yours.

Why This Book?

Have you ever purchased a *Using* book from Que? The *Using* books have proven invaluable to readers both as learning guides and as references for many years. The *Using* series is an industry leader and has practically become an industry standard. We encourage and receive feedback from readers all the time, and we consider and implement their suggestions whenever possible.

Using HTML 4, 4th Edition incorporates fresh new ideas and approaches to the *Using* series. This book is not a compiled authority on all the features of HTML. Instead, it is a streamlined, conversational approach for using HTML productively and efficiently. New features include:

- *Improved index to help you find information the first time you look!* What do you call tasks and features? Every possible name or description of a task was anticipated and cross-referenced in the index.
- *Real life answers.* Throughout the book you will find real life examples and experiences. *How* to perform a task is only one question you may have, and perhaps the bigger questions are *why* and *what for*?
- *Relevant information written just for you!* The features and tasks have been carefully scrutinized, and only those that apply to your everyday use of HTML have been included.
- *Reference or tutorial.* You can quickly learn to perform a task using step-by-step instructions, or you can investigate the why and wherefore of a task with discussions surrounding each task.
- *Wise investment.* Lastly, pay the right price for the right book. Don't waste your valuable bookshelf real estate with redundant or irrelevant material. You don't have to "know it all" to be productive. Here is what you need, when you need it, how you need it, with an appropriate price tag.
- *Easy to find procedures.* Every numbered step-by-step procedure in the book has a short title explaining exactly what it does. This saves you time by making it easier to find the exact steps you need to accomplish a task.
- *SideNote elements with quick-read headlines save you time.* Small tips or notes about how to make something work best are given here. Or perhaps a caution or warning about a problem you may encounter. By giving these SideNotes precise titles that explain their topic and by placing them in the margins, each one is easy to skip if you don't need it and easy to find if you want to read it.

Who Should Use This Book

Anyone who wishes to create Web pages with HTML and needs to accomplish a specific task or solve a problem or wants to learn a technique that applies to something they need to get done. Basically, anyone who

- Wants to create Web pages using HTML.
- Uses HTML, but wants to become more proficient.
- Uses HTML at work.
- Uses HTML at home.
- Needs a handy reference of HTML tasks and how to perform them.

How This Book Is Organized

Using HTML 4, 4th Edition has task-oriented, easy-to-navigate tutorials and reference information presented in a logical progression from simple to complex tasks. It covers the features of HTML you use everyday. You can work through the book chapter by chapter or you can find specific information when you need to perform a job quickly. Everything needed to create powerful, interactive, and practical Web pages is here!

Using HTML 4, 4th Edition is divided into seven parts:

Part I: Creating the Basic Web Page
This section provides a quick start to creating Web pages and covers the basics of HTML. If you are new to HTML you should begin here.

Part II: Including Images and Multimedia
Spruce up your Web pages by adding images, animated graphics, sound, video, and Java applets.

Part III: Controlling Presentation
Effectively control how your Web pages will look online by using Cascading Style Sheets, tables, and frames.

Part IV: Adding Interactivity
Offer more than a static Web page through forms and scripting. Dynamic HTML, which builds on style sheets and scripting, is covered here as well. By using Dynamic HTML, you can change the style and content of your pages.

Part V: Advanced Topics
Maximize your site's chances of being indexed correctly by search engines; this section offers tips on how to create Web pages that most people can access.

Part VI: HTML Publishing
Validate your HTML against the current standard, publish your pages to the Web, and finally, maintain your site as it grows and changes.

Part VII: Appendixes
The appendixes provide a quick reference to the HTML language, Cascading Style Sheets, Web color, and Web entities and characters.

Conventions Used in This Book

Commands, directions, and explanations in this book are presented in the clearest format possible. The following items are some of the features that will make this book easier for you to use:

- *Menu and dialog box commands and options.* You can easily find the onscreen menu and dialog box commands by looking for bold text like you see in this direction: Open the **File** menu and click **Save**.
- *Hotkeys for commands.* The underlined keys onscreen that activate commands and options are also underlined in the book as shown in the previous example.
- *Combination and shortcut keystrokes.* Text that directs you to hold down several keys simultaneously is connected with a plus sign (+), such as Ctrl+P.
- *Cross-references.* If there's a related topic that is requisite to the section or steps you are reading or a topic that builds further on what you are reading, you'll find the cross-reference to it after the steps or at the end of the section like this:

SEE ALSO

➤ *Changing the appearance of text in other ways, see pages 230 and 402*

- *Glossary terms.* For all the terms that appear in the glossary, you'll find the first appearance of that term in the text in *italic*, along with its definition.
- *SideNotes.* Information related to the task at hand, or "inside" information from the author, is offset in sidebars so as not to interfere with the task at hand and to make it easy to find this valuable information. Each of these sidebars has a short title to help you quickly identify the information you'll find there. You'll find the same kind of information in these that you might find in notes, tips, or warnings in other books, but here the titles should be more informative.

Your screen may look slightly different from some of the examples in this book. This is due to various Web browsers, HTML editors, and hardware configurations.

PART I

Creating the Basic Web Page

CHAPTER

1

What You Need to Get Started

Getting started with computers

Getting started on the Internet

Choosing an HTML editor

Choosing an application to create or modify graphics

Learning HTML

Understanding design

Providing "content"

Uploading your new page to the Web

Get Started

New to the Net? Don't touch that credit card yet! Quite simply, you don't *really* need anything more than the tools that are sitting on your computer right this minute. You don't need a special editor, or graphics programs, or fancy gadgets of any sort. All you need is an Internet account (you *do* want to *see* your brand new pages, don't you?) and a computer of almost any sort with the simple text editor that most likely came with it. On the Macintosh that'll be Simple Edit, and on the PC it'll likely be Notepad, but even DOS Edit will work.

Getting started

1. You'll need a computer, any kind at all! If you don't have a computer, see the "Brand New to Computers?" section in this chapter.
2. Obtain Internet access of some sort, either through work or with a dial-up PPP or SLIP connection from an Internet service provider (ISP).
3. Get a modem compatible with your Internet access provider's dial-up lines.
4. Set up your computer to access the Web.
5. Find an HTML editor that suits you.
6. Find a graphic tool that suits you.
7. Learn a little about HTML.
8. Learn a little about design. Know what you like and try to design your pages to reflect your sense of propriety and taste.
9. Think about and then choose what resources you want to make available on the Web and why.
10. Put your page on the Web!

PCs with Windows or OS/2 are great, Macintoshes are wonderful (this is pure prejudice on my part) and UNIX is just fine, not that UNIX is a likely thing to find on an average desktop. You can even build pages on the Amiga you got yourself for your birthday five years ago, you know, the one you put in the closet and never touched again because computers weren't as much fun as you'd thought they would be? Well, take it back out of the closet. The Internet is almost as good as chocolate, far less fattening, and *way* fun! And making your own pages is *totally* cool.

That said, let's look at some of the tools you might want to have eventually, as well as a few things you might want to understand in slightly greater detail before going on.

Requirements for Using HTML

Any computer system will work, no matter what anyone may tell you. *HTML* is a *text* markup language and any system and any editor that lets you edit text (which is all of them) will let you edit and publish your pages to any *server* in the world. You'll need a modem on the machine, either built-in or attached, or some other sort of network connection, possibly through work.

Brand New to Computers?

Computers are not at all hard to buy. The trouble is that it's difficult to say exactly what sort of a machine you really need before you buy one. It's a little like buying your first car. It's very easy to get talked into far more than you will ever really use. Any computer will work, and you can often find real bargains in the used market because people trade up for the latest and greatest hardware and software and become tired of "older" models. Buying a used computer can be a great way to experiment without a major investment.

Buying your first machine

Try not to be oversold on features you may not ever use, and be conservative in your first purchase. If you can, try out several machines at a local service shop where you can rent time by the hour, or take a hands-on class before laying down your credit card or check.

Tables 1.1 and 1.2 list very rough retail prices for the sorts of machines people are buying now, from entry-level (but still very powerful) machines that will run almost any home software on the market today, through mid-range systems suitable for a graphic artist or someone who does a lot of detail work at a terminal, to dream machines that most people can only drool over when they see them in the stores but sit toward the upper end of machines available for the home or small office.

Platform costs

Macintoshes run a little bit more than PCs and their software is sometimes more expensive, but many people feel they're more productive on a Macintosh and, if you're dealing with graphics arts professionals (who most often use Macintoshes), the convenience of being on the same platform can far outweigh the slight extra cost.

TABLE 1.1 **Recommended PC hardware**

Type	Class	Speed	Memory	Disk	Monitor	Approximate Cost
Starter	Pentium	166MHz	16MB	2GB	15"	$1500
Graphics	Pentium	233MHz	32MB	4GB	17"	$2500
Dream	Pentium II	300MHz	64MB	8GB	20–21"	$5000

Check newspaper or magazine listings regularly for special pricing. Closeout bargains and special incentives often result in sales prices substantially lower than those listed here.

TABLE 1.2 **Recommended Macintosh hardware**

Type	Class	Speed	Memory	Disk	Monitor	Approximate Cost
Starter	603e	225MHz	16MB	2GB	15"	$2000
Graphics	603e	266MHz	32MB	4GB	17"	$3000
Dream	604e	350MHz	64MB	8GB	20–21"	$6000

Check newspaper listings regularly for special pricing. I've seen a new PowerMacintosh 6500/250 with 15" monitor and printer for as little as $1600. It pays to shop around and take your time.

Modern computers

Today's computers are fast and cheap. You can easily buy a fabulous system with almost any budget at all. See the Recommended Hardware tables in this chapter.

Buying a modem

Before you buy any modem, check with your service provider to make sure that it's usable on their lines, especially if you buy one of the 56Kbps modems. If ISDN intrigues you, make sure that your provider allows for digital access and what options are needed to make it work.

Modems and Modem Speeds Made Simple

Modems are the gadgets that let you connect your computer over ordinary telephone lines to the Internet. They work by converting the electrical signals a computer understands into sounds that the telephone network understands and then back again. They come in many speeds and generally cost more in high speeds and less in low speeds.

Usually they're measured in kilobits-per-second (Kbps), which means thousands of bits per second. Typical speeds are 14.4Kbps or 14,400 bits per second (a bare minimum for use on the Web), 28.8Kbps or 28,800 bits per second, all the way up to the current maximum, 56Kbps. If you use ISDN lines or other digital options from your telephone company, you can get either 56Kbps or 64Kbps on a single line, and many services allow you to double up by using two lines (which comes standard with ISDN) for a maximum rate of 128Kbps or 128,000 bits per second. So the range of readily-available speeds is enormous, more than a factor of ten, and depends only on what you want to spend.

If you don't have dedicated network access through your job and need a modem, you could scrape by with a barely usable *modem speed* of 14.4Kbps but, if you're on the Web for any length of time and use graphics, you'll want more—28.8Kbps minimum, and preferably as much more than that as you can afford. Lower speed modems cost much less and are perfectly suitable for text-mode access, but the typical range is from a few tens of dollars to a few hundred, so even a fancy model won't require mortgaging the house for most people. Usually the speed is part of the modem name or is prominently mentioned on the package. If your modem is slower than 14.4Kbps, you should definitely replace it with the fastest modem you can reasonably afford, at least 28.8Kbps, and preferably one of the newer 56Kbps or 64Kbps models.

56Kbps modems

There are currently two "standards" for very high-speed modems, X2 and K56flex, which are incompatible for technical reasons that really aren't terribly important. The final standard for high speed modems is very unlikely to be either, so make sure that any 56Kbps modem you buy is easily upgradable to the eventual standard, preferably with a free software download.

Internet Service

You'll also need an Internet connection, which can be through your local phone company, an *Internet service provider (ISP)*, your school or employer, or even your local cable TV company in some areas. At the present writing, you can expect to pay about twenty U.S. dollars per month for the connection, although it can easily vary up or down. In my own case, I have one account that costs about thirty dollars a month, but that includes a lot of extras that most people don't need and won't use. Of course, if you need dedicated high-speed access, the cost may go up, but we'll assume that you're either satisfied with lesser speed or have access through your work and don't have to worry about it.

Buying Internet access

Make sure your provider has the services you need. If you think you'll need nationwide or worldwide access, you should start with national providers. You may be able to find quicker response times and more personalized service through a local provider, though, so there are tradeoffs in any decision you make.

Your First (or Next) Internet Account

When you ask about Internet accounts, you'll run into a lot of people whose business it is to sell you their own particular brand of access, so it's good to know a little something about it before you start. To begin with, any Internet connection will work, but some are better than others.

Basic Internet access

In almost all cases, you'll want graphical access to the Web, which means a SLIP or PPP account if you're using dial-up lines. Make sure when you talk to the salesperson that this is what you're getting.

If you've been provided with Internet access through your school or work, you can skip this section unless you also want a private account.

The basic access you'll want is what's called *PPP* or *SLIP* access, which lets you see graphics. There is another kind, usually called a *shell account*, which can be very inexpensive (or even free, since they are sometimes available through a local library) but which has no graphics capability. You won't want that type unless you are comfortable with cryptic and hard-to-use command line interfaces or become a real HTML hound and want to do your own programming.

Space on the Web

Space is relatively cheap to find, running from two or more megabytes (millions of bytes) for free at Geocities to ten megabytes or more from your provider. Extra space is usually available for a small extra charge per month. In characters, a byte is roughly equivalent to a character. A Danielle Steel novel might push a million characters, or one megabyte. Graphics can fill up a megabyte rather quickly but will be correspondingly tiresome to load. For a typical home page, a couple of megabytes is usually ample space unless you want to include lots of pictures.

If you'll be putting up your own pages, you'll also want to make sure that you can put pages on the Web from your account using storage and a Web server maintained by your provider. There are other options, including free pages from places like Geocities, `http://www.geocities.com`, but it's much simpler if you have your own space on your own account. If your pages will go on a server owned by your business, you don't have to worry about this.

Other than that, the main thing to look for is *bandwidth*, the faster the connection the better, all other things being equal. As you progress in using the Internet, you may find that your needs change, so a good thing to look for in a provider is the ability to change your account as time goes on. Are there differing speeds available? Levels of access? Disk storage space? All these things can mean the difference between simply upgrading an existing account and changing providers (and email IDs and Web addresses) when it comes time to change.

Getting Connected to the Web

OK. You've got the computer, you've got the account. Now what do you do?

If you're on the Net through a *dedicated access line*, you're already there, so you can skip the rest of this section.

Assuming that you're on a Windows 95 machine, you simply run the Connection Wizard by opening the My Computer folder and then the Dial-Up Networking folder inside that; select and run Make New Connection; follow the instructions given to you by your provider or local system administrator and you're ready to go. The connection you just made will dial the phone for you and log on to your Internet service provider and from there to the Internet when you double-click it, and usually when you request an Internet service.

On the Macintosh, at least after System 7.5, it's about as easy and more reliable, in my experience. You'll access the Control Panel for the older MacTCP or the far better and more stable replacement, Open Transport, and enter values provided by your system administrator or ISP. Once these are set up correctly, your Internet software, Web browser, email program, and the like will automatically connect to the Web on demand. In OS 8, just use the Internet Setup Assistant to have it run through all the setup steps with you.

Warning: Bandwidth is always limited

Providers share access to the Internet among their many customers. If they're skimping on their own access while signing up too many customers, you can find your access throttled, no matter what your own connection speed is. Always ask what real bandwidth will be available during peak hours, the hours most people use the Net, from late afternoon through the evening.

Finding an HTML Editor That Fits Your Needs

Any editor can create HTML. Don't let anyone tell you differently. But there are specialized editors than can speed the creation of your pages, or automatically check to make sure you didn't make too many mistakes. That's very convenient because it's all too easy to misspell a keyword or *tag* and create a hard-to-find error that hides very nicely when you go looking for it.

On the other hand, almost all the helpers are not complete; they don't let you use certain tags, or the standards change and they go out of date so you have to buy an upgrade.

HTML editors

An HTML editor is just a text editor with the possible addition of special features to support HTML through tag templates, help files, or even more specialized "helpers." Many perform validation of your tags to make sure you haven't made a mistake in spelling or syntax.

Many real HTML coders use more-or-less simple text editors like Notepad on the PC, or Simple Text on the Macintosh, because the knowledge they have in their heads beats any page-building "environment" hands down. It's also a lot easier and better to learn using a simple text editor. Many of the helper applications hide so much from you that you never really learn anything but how to use that one program.

So before you rush out and buy something, think about what you want to do. Buying this book, as opposed to a book dedicated to Adobe Page Mill (a very fine product, by the way), sort of implies that you want to know what's really happening, so I'd definitely avoid any of the completely WYSIWYG (What You See Is What You Get) environments for now. But you're the boss; it's up to you.

Warning: Visual or graphic HTML editors

Learning HTML is very difficult using visual design tools that don't let you type in code directly or see what the code really looks like as you type. If you're tempted, remember that none are perfect and the worst force you into non-standard ways of doing things that break many of the browsers being used on the Web today.

Let's look at a very few low-cost or free options out of many.

For the Windows PC, you always have Notepad, which will work just fine and is available straight out of the box. On the Macintosh, you could try Simple Text or any of the equivalents. And on UNIX, if there are any of you out there, either Vi or Emacs is a superb editing environment, and PICO is usually available as well and a little more user friendly to people used to onscreen menus. You could even use your regular word processor, Corel WordPerfect, or Microsoft Word, for example, as long as you remember to save your file as plain text and not as a formatted document.

Free (or nearly so) editors

An ordinary text editor like Simple Text (Macintosh) or Notepad (PC) is perfectly adequate for HTML editing. Start there and work up slowly instead of trying to get the best and most versatile of everything before you even know what exactly it is you want to do.

There are lots of more specialized options available, either as shareware on the Web or in your local computer or software store. The boxes will usually promise you the world, so please take your time before rushing in. Try out the simple free things first, so you'll have a better idea of what you want later.

Professional HTML editors

Using a professional tool can be great fun. Tags get automatically completed, pages get automatically uploaded, code gets validated, and many of them come with fun little gadgets to add Javascript or Java toys to the page. But they make it harder to learn and are overkill if you're going to make a simple page and update it once a month or so.

Among professional HTML environments, a lot of people are very fond of either Hot Dog Pro, `http://www.sausage.com/`, or HoTMetaL Pro, `http://www.softquad.com/`. Both have error checking built in and both do a great job. People who prefer one or the other are usually swayed more by user interface than capability, since HoTMetaL Pro has a semi-WYSIWYG interface available (plus a unique keyboard interface for disabled persons) while Hot Dog Pro does not but has more gadgets built in. Hot Dog Pro lets you see the code in a separate window as you're editing, which is sort of WYSIWYG, but you can't tweak the picture and have it show up in the code like Dorian Grey's wrinkles.

On the Macintosh, BBEdit Lite is great and free. You can find it on almost any download site. Here's one that I like because it has so many mirrors and rates the software it carries: TUCOWS—`http://www.tucows.com/`. The commercial version of BBEdit is more powerful, but the freeware version is a great way to get started. And Page Mill, although more graphically oriented, does allow viewing the code and has wonderful site design tools available with it as well. Page Mill is also available on the Windows PC, but not all the site manager tools have been ported.

For Windows PCs, Hot Dog Express is a very easy WYSIWYG jump start, although it will only put up a quick page and won't let you fool with the code, and the list of great tools is very long. Some are even free or ask for a donation of "caring." Looking through the Advanced HTML Editors section of TUCOWS will find lots of five-gold-cow titles (their highest rating), all of which are very good and have strong followings. 1-4-All, Aardvark Pro, Anawave CoolCat, Arachnophilia, ATRAX Web Publisher, Coffeecup HTML Editor, FlexED Pro, Hippie 97, HomeSite, Nachos HTML Editor, Net-It Now!, TC-director, WebEditor Pro, ...well, you get the idea.

Arachnophilia may be of particular interest if you're on a tight budget, since it includes an FTP site updater and is the "careware" program I mentioned above. The owner asks that you stop "whining" for a day (assuming that you do) and appreciate all the good things around you. Not a bad price for a good editor, if slightly presumptuous, even for a programmer.

In addition, you can use a "real" programmer's editor like American Cybernetics' Multi-Edit (`http://www.amcyber.com/`) or MicroEdge's Visual SlickEdit (`http://www.slickedit.com/`). These are uncompromising text editors with tremendous power and were designed by and for people used to creating great chunks of raw text every day. I use Visual SlickEdit mostly, and it does everything I want, including automatic indentation so I can

Shareware HTML editors

Here is where you can find real bargains and some are even free. This is an excellent way to start trying things out, once you have the basics well in hand, to see what features and gadgets you'll really use before springing for an expensive professional editor of any sort.

Programmer's editor

A programmer's editor is an uncompromising tool for editing text. Many have special help files and modes available for editing HTML, but they're not intrusive as a rule. Most let you cut and paste among multiple windows, create special keyboard macros to speed repetitive tasks, and flip back and forth between a viewer and the editor so you can see what you've coded on-the-fly.

format my code easily as I type, although Multi-Edit has slightly more specialized support for creating Web pages.

There are many others but those are the two I'm fondest of and am most familiar with. I've also heard from people who use Helios Software Solutions' TextPad (`http://www.textpad.com/`), Premia's CodeWright (`http:/www.premia.com/`), Zeus by Jussi Jumppanen (`http://ourworld.compuserve.com/homepages/jussi/zMain.htm`), and IDM's UltraEdit (`http://www.idmcomp.com/`), so those are other possibilities. Most of the programmer's editors also support Vi and Emacs emulation, so they can be very good for people who have to work in both the UNIX environment and on a PC because it's easier to flip back and forth.

There are undoubtedly many more wonderful editors out there, but the point is that all of them will work. If and when you choose an editor, you'll choose based on features you can use, so before you invest a lot of money in some fancy editor, spend some time discovering what you really do. That way you'll have a much better idea how an editor can help you. Table 1.3 lists some of the editors previously mentioned and some related information about them.

TABLE 1.3 Representative editors

Editor	Ease of use	Preview	HTML help	Project help	Cost
Notepad	Yes	No	No	No	N/A
Simpletext	Yes	No	No	No	N/A
BBEdit Lite	Yes	Yes	Yes	No	Free
SlickEdit	Yes	Yes	No	Yes	>$100
HotDog Pro	Yes	Yes	Yes	Yes	>$100
TextPad	Yes	No	Yes	No	<$50

This is just a small sample of the many editors available but sufficient to show the wide range of features and prices available.

Choosing an Application to Create or Modify Graphics

First of all, you don't have to create graphics. There are lots of places to find graphics for your pages on the Web. You can buy inexpensive collections of images at your local computer store as well. There are even services available at many camera or film developing shops that will automatically convert your own rolls of film into computer-formatted pictures.

Kodak, for example, will take your roll of film and save it to either a floppy disk, or, at slightly higher cost (and with much better resolution possible), to a CD-ROM. They have several formats available, but the cheapest version on floppy disk will set you back much less than ten U.S. dollars for a roll. It comes with a little viewer program included so you can do a screen capture from the viewer and plug it into whatever graphics program you have laying around and go from there.

On the other hand, it can be very useful, even fun, to crop and manipulate your pictures, to add other elements into a picture, or make your own animations. There are special tools for this purpose on every platform and in every price range, from free or nearly so to design and graphics suites costing hundreds or even thousands of dollars.

The premiere graphics applications for the Web, of course, are Adobe Photoshop and Illustrator, available on both Macintosh and Windows 95 PC platforms. You should give serious consideration to Adobe products, especially Photoshop, if you'll be dealing with outside graphics vendors and professionals; there's just no other real choice in a professional graphic arts context. But people whose pocketbooks are not quite deep enough for the power toys that the big girls and boys play with can find loads of real functionality, more than enough for a simple home page or even a small business or departmental Web site, for much less money.

In many cases, they're easier to use as well, being designed for the express purpose of creating Web pages rather than general-purpose tools equally at home preparing artwork for major

Graphics on the Web

Graphics can help make a page more interesting and help identify it as a unique destination. But if drawing your own artwork isn't in the cards, you can do a fine job with your own photos or with art made available as freeware on the Web. Collections of graphic images can also be found at your local computer store for reasonable prices.

Professional graphics

There's a real sense of pleasure when using the latest tools available to the professional artist to create your own artwork. But that pleasure comes at a fairly high cost. If you not sure you're going to be using a graphics tool for a long time to come, or if freehand artwork isn't your strong point, you might want to start slow with an inexpensive tool and work up.

Shareware and low cost tools

You can get real bargains for editing your own graphics, from Photo Soap, which lets you easily crop and repair photographs, to Paint Shop Pro, which is well suited to the beginning artist and even accepts Photoshop plug-ins, for well under a hundred dollars.

CorelDRAW! suite

The Corel graphics suite is worth mentioning separately. Although it's not as widely supported by professionals as the Adobe tools, for about the cost of one Photoshop you get a paint program, a drawing program, and a three-dimensional rendering program. It's a real bargain.

national magazines as taking the "red-eye" out of Cousin Emma's snapshot. Adobe support is also not quite as responsive as it could be, so you may well get more and better service from smaller companies that try harder.

On the Windows PC, there are very inexpensive programs like Alchemy Mindworks' GIF Construction Set for Windows, whose owner asks only twenty U.S. dollars if you use the program after trying it (`http://www.mindworkshop.com/alchemy/alchemy.html`); the more capable Graphic Workshop for Windows from the same company, which is also shareware and not terribly expensive; PaintShop Pro, again shareware at `http://www.jasc.com/` and very popular among people who are not graphics arts professionals; and the Corel Draw and Paint programs from `http://www.corel.com`. Take your pick.

Corel is a very powerful tool kit containing several complementary programs roughly equivalent to the Adobe Photoshop/Illustrator combination but for much less money. Both Adobe and Corel have strengths, and many professional designers use both, swapping files back and forth to take advantage of the best each program has to offer. You probably won't need quite that much power, though.

In rough order from the most powerful to the least, and roughly from the most expensive to the least, I'd go for Adobe, Corel, PaintShop Pro, Graphic Workshop, and then GIF Construction Set, although GIF Construction Set excels at making animations, so I'd probably get that one too. If I were you, that is, and money were no object.

I use Photoshop almost every day, but find Corel very handy from time to time, and when I need an animation, even if I created the artwork in another program, I use GIF Construction Set. If I couldn't afford either of the top two, I'd definitely go for PaintShop Pro. It's a powerful tool and accepts Photoshop plug-ins, which are add-on programs that extend the functionality of the base graphics program.

If you just want something for tweaking your own photographs, MetaCreations Kai's Photo Soap is excellent (`http://www.metatools.com/`) and fairly cheap at around $50 U.S. It lets you crop images, correct for color, and do simple photo retouching to repair damaged pictures. This is a particularly fine tool in combination with Kodak Photo-CD images, because it supports them directly. MetaCreations also makes Painter, a simply fabulous painting program that many artists really like a lot. Table 1.4 lists some of the previously mentioned graphics programs with some of their features and prices.

Table 1.4 Representative graphics programs

	Retouch	Draw	Effects	Masks	Animate	Layers	Cost
Photoshop	Yes	Yes	Yes	Yes	No	Yes	< $600
PhotoPaint	Yes	Yes	Yes	Yes	Yes	Yes	< $500
Photo Soap	Yes	No	Yes	No	No	No	~ $50
Painter	Yes	Yes	Yes	Yes	No	Yes	< $300
Paint Shop Pro	Yes	Yes	Yes	Yes	No	Yes	< $100
GIF Construction Set	No	No	No	No	Yes	No	< $50

Of course this simple table can't capture the complexity of the tradeoffs you make with different programs, but the range of prices is very clear. In general, you get roughly what you pay for. On the other hand, why pay for more than you need?

Understanding More About HTML

HTML is a *markup language*, the Hypertext Markup Language. In everyday life you use markup language all the time but probably don't call it that. Figures 1.1 through 1.3 have a few familiar examples.

All of these examples are pretty much self explanatory. We add emphasis in a handwritten note by underlining (sometimes several times), mark direct quotes with quotation marks, and show special meaning or feelings with symbols.

Markup languages

Markup languages have been in use for thousands of years, from musical notations added to words to tell you what note to sing them on to punctuation marks that tell you where to pause or emphasize a word. It's just a new word for an old tradition, adding extra symbols to a text to add information that can't be easily or quickly described in words.

George,

Please take Lille

Cat to the Vet!!!

Don't forget!!!

♡ Bess

FIGURE 1.1
Examples illustrating common use of markup language.

Our firt real accompplishment was

understanding spell words right.

s

how to correctly

FIGURE 1.2
Examples illustrating common use of markup language.

Mission Statement ctr

In the words of our founder and CEO:

Insistence on perfection is the

beginning of failure. Success

is measured by "good enoughs."

What does this mean for our

quality control program?

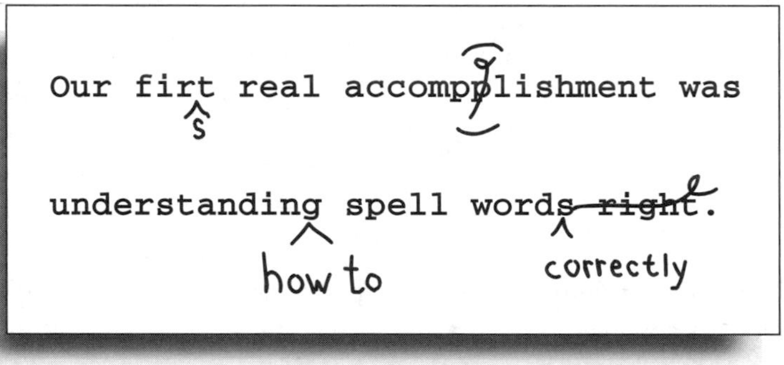

FIGURE 1.3
Examples illustrating common use of markup language.

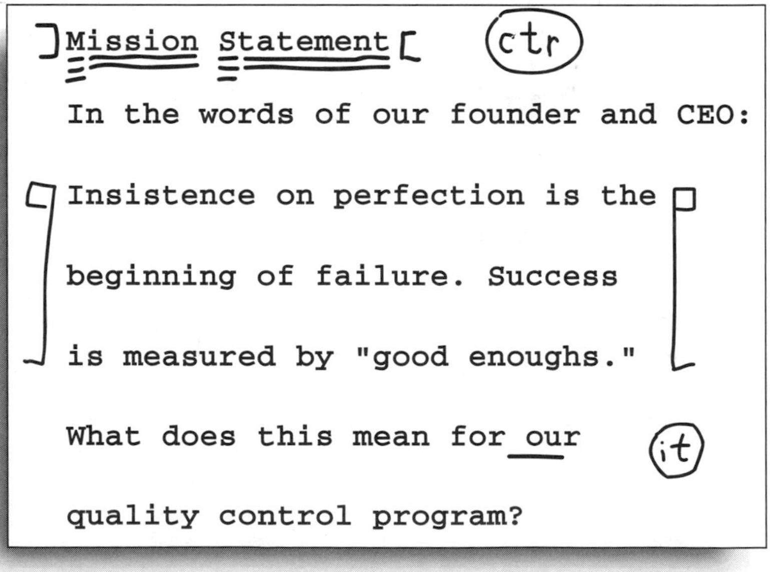

In the printed example, we mark insertions and deletions with a special visual code, make notes on how to treat certain sections with special symbols, and give hints on formatting to the person who'll create the final printed version. But that person has the responsibility for what the document looks like in the end. You've probably dealt with both sides of these conventions before, if you've ever turned in homework in school that was less than perfect or ever had work turned in that needed some changes before it was "ready for prime time."

Proofreader's marks

The editing marks used to control the appearance of printed text are the closest to what HTML is at its heart. In our example, almost every mark on the page shown in the illustration has an exact equivalent in HTML.

HTML is just that simple, once you get beyond the sometimes confusing way it's been presented in books written by and for computer programmers who may think that the words, "n-ary nodes on a weakly-directional connected graph" are actually a good way to describe Web pages.

HTML is a clear way of describing the context of words and how they should be used in a document. Just as in our examples, the exact way in which the meaning is rendered is often left up to the judgment of the program responsible, usually a browser.

Champagne Design on a Beer Budget

Design for yourself first

Design is making things look appropriate for their surroundings. It's a sense of proportion and balance. Most people who can arrange a room or a vase of flowers have no trouble seeing what looks good and what doesn't. You're the one you should try to please first, since you'll be living with that page as your calling card and representative for a long time to come.

Design is another subject, like HTML itself, that gets mystified by people with axes to grind. Basically, it's just a matter of making things look attractive. There are some basic rules to follow, like "Avoid visual complexity," that are really as simple to understand as not wearing plaids with stripes, or saving the florescent yellow tie with the radioactive purple polka dots for parties unless you work in a wild and crazy sort of office. Those rules can be broken freely, as long as you're pleased with the results and the people you're interested in attracting are pleased as well.

We're all different, thank heavens, and some people like raggedy flannel shirts with faded jeans every bit as much as others like *haute couture* fashions by Paris designers. Don't let people intimidate you into making a page that doesn't fit your own image of what you want your page to look like. This is your chance to distinguish your page from the millions of pages out there on the Web and your business from the many competitors who're also getting interested in the Internet as a commercial medium.

Style is relative

Style makes sense only in context. Creating a style for your page requires an understanding of what your page means and how its appearance will help it or hurt it on the Web.

Formal pages for traditional businesses

A formal page tends to be symmetrical, linear, formal, and low-key. Of course any rule can be broken just a little to good effect, but overall the effect is one of conservative restraint.

A page that says "Cool, kicky, hip" might be just the thing for a personal page or an advertising office, while a bank or stock broker might want to say "Stable, conservative, honest" on theirs. Just like the clothes you wear, what a page looks like says a lot about the person or company responsible creating it. If you want warm and fuzzy, go for it! If you want sophisticated and sleek, right on!

Some general guidelines might help you plan your Web site.

Traditional businesses: If the usual attire in your office is Brooks Brothers and skirted suits with heels, you're probably more interested in a solid look of dependability and professional competence than "glitz." Use the following suggestions:

- Symmetrical—Neat, typeset pages work best in a traditional environment. Keep off-center elements to a minimum or make the off-centeredness a subtle component of the site by maintaining the same layout on every page. A left-margin navigation bar, for example, shouldn't jump to the right, bottom, or top margin depending on what page you're on.
- Linear—Straightforward presentation works very well for most professional sites. No-nonsense bullet lists, clear and logical navigation elements, and no surprises all help contribute to an atmosphere that looks safe when you're thinking of trusting your money, your legal affairs, or your health to a firm or individual.
- Formal—This isn't the place for chatty pages. You probably wouldn't want to have an animated cowboy saying "Howdy Pardner!" at the top of your page, or embedded links, or any element that looks unplanned or unstudied. Black or at least dark print on a white or very light creme-color page would probably work well. Trendy light text on dark or black backgrounds is probably out.
- Low key—Think of any ad you've ever seen for a financial service company; have you ever seen your banker riding a hippopotamus? Probably not. Used car salesmen ride

strange beasts to attract attention. Your banker tries to attract attention by pointing out how dull but friendly he or she is. Family leisure or hearthside images, calm color-schemes, and gentle vistas of serene landscapes all help project the image of friendly but businesslike safety. A picture of a terrifying plunge down a roller coaster might not be the happiest association to put on a stockbroker's page.

Informal pages for non-traditional businesses

An informal page breaks rules to make a statement about creativity or down-home friendliness. They tend to be asymmetrical, non-linear, informal, daring in color scheme, and high energy.

Non-traditional businesses or home pages: If your regular business attire is jeans and a sweatshirt or polo top, or you're making your own home page, you may want to create a friendly, down-home atmosphere, or a fashion-conscious high-tech page that makes you buzz with excitement just to look at it. This is the place to experiment with images and effects to mirror your own unique outlook on life and business. You don't want to wimp along with the cookie-cutter look that less cool places have, but thrust your own ideas and concepts out there where everyone can see them.

- Asymmetrical—Here's the place for radically off-center bleeds off the page and unbalanced elements that suggest motion and change. A *bleed*, if you've never seen the term, is a picture or color that runs off the edge of the page, the sort of thing you see in fashion magazines and trendy publications—not usually in *Scientific American* or *The New Yorker*.
- Non-linear—Some degree of confusion may help create a friendly cluttered look, but don't let your visitors get lost! A bewildering array of links that entwine without logic can discourage the people you may want to attract.
- Informal—A "just us" approach works well in some cases, although you have to balance between your intended audience and your personal style here. It's one thing to be trendy and quite another to be flaky! Ornamental fonts and geegaws may also be appropriate, where in a more formal setting they would be distracting.
- Alternative page colors and backgrounds—White text on Black? Purple text on a background of yellow daisies? You go! The rules are made to be broken, and only you can decide what works and what doesn't for what you want to do.

- High Energy—Animations and cool effects can really make a high-tech page or fashion page look great! A slide show of designs or a changing element on the page can add movement to the design and graphically reflect the forward look of the site's owner. On the other hand, if homey little whirligigs on the front lawn or those little glass birds that perpetually bob their beaks into a glass of water make you smile, an animation or two on your page can give the same effect to every visitor.

With no hard-and-fast rules, you'll have to rely on your own taste and eye when looking at your page to judge how well the design works. Just as you might want to ask a friend about your outfit, you'll probably want to get the opinion of other people as well, incorporating their comments and suggestions into your page as it evolves.

Good luck!

Content is the key to attracting repeat visitors

The most carefully-designed page won't be worth a bookmark if it doesn't contain good content that attracts visitors and changes regularly enough to keep them coming back for more. A Web page is not like a billboard; people don't see it while driving by on the information highway. There is no highway and every page is a destination. Your page has to be a great place to visit or people will truck on through and never look back.

Provide Excellent Resources to Attract the People You Want

This is really part of design, but it warrants a special section because this is where most pages succeed or fail. With millions of pages out there, how do you get people to visit yours? Assuming that you're not a rock star or celebrity in your own right (and if you are, can I have your autograph?), you'll need to provide a reason for people to visit your page in the first place, and to keep them coming back for more.

There's only one answer and that's content, the stuff that people read your pages for. Some people think they can just put up a sort of billboard on the information highway and people will see it as they're driving by; that isn't the case. People don't usually read magazines for the ads, they read the articles and are attracted by an ad while engaged in more important (to them, if not to you) things.

Your page has to offer something unique and interesting or no one will bother to stop by. The best pages are labors of love, but that isn't as hard to do as you might think. If you don't love your job (even a little), it's probably time to do something else, and if you do you probably know lots about it that other people might be interested in.

Sharing that knowledge provides your content, whether it's an informative discussion of what makes products like yours useful, how they've developed over the past hundred years, simply what the full range and features are, or how you fix them if they break.

Providing unique information

Mine what you know or have access to in order to create unique and valuable content that others will be interested in. The more esoteric the better because most of the easy clichés have already been done.

Each type of content attracts a different user: An online support site is a feature for present and past customers, a history site might be attractive to nostalgia buffs, and discussion would attract people who might be interested in buying. Figure 1.4 shows a non-commercial site with a very specialized subject matter that attracts an audience of scholars and historians.

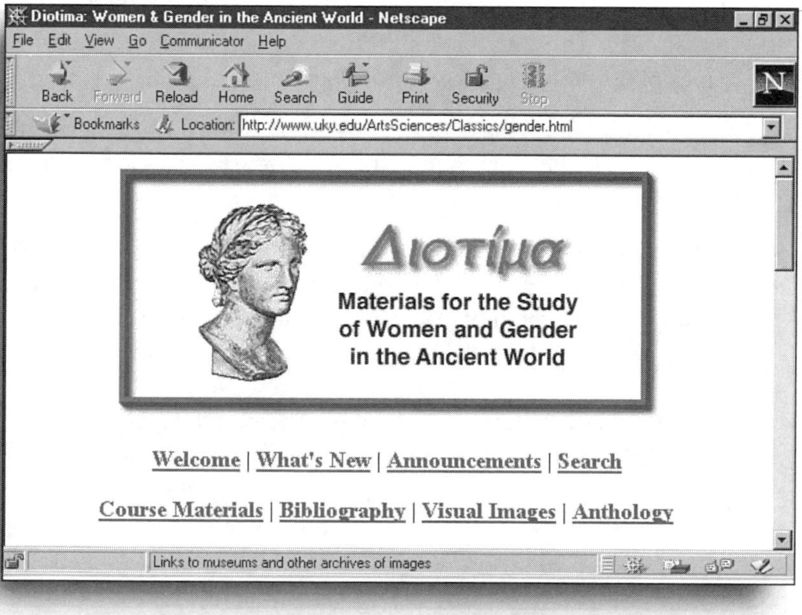

FIGURE 1.4

Diotima: Women's Ancient History Site `http://www.uky.edu/ArtsSciences/Classics/gender.html`

What you do with your site will determine who visits. If you want to attract people who are athletic and interested in the outdoors, you could have ski reports and updates on mountain climbing expeditions. If you're interested in attracting TV viewers, you might try a daily report on the developments of ongoing shows. Or pick your own audience and find something that interests you both.

Getting Your Page Up There (Wherever That Is)

Using FTP or a Web utility page to upload your pages.

The easiest way to upload pages is to use a Web utility page and a browser that supports file uploads. The most recent versions of Netscape Navigator and Internet Explorer allow file uploads, but many ISPs don't supply an upload page. So you'll most often be stuck with the default upload method, almost always FTP, the File Transfer Protocol.

OK. You've got your page, it's filled with wonderful content and seasoned with great design, but where do you put it so other people can find it? The answer is you have to give it to what's called an HTTP server, which is a fancy way of saying you have to give it to a machine running a server program that hands out copies of your page when people ask for them.

Your business may have a server online already, in which case the usual procedure is to hand it to your local system administrator or Webmaster and it will be taken care of for you. Or you may be given a location on your internal network that you just copy the files to. Voilà! Done!

If you're using dial-up access, the situation is a little more complicated. Some providers have a special update page, which works only with recent browsers, that lets you simply type in the names of your files and they upload automatically.

But most Web sites have to be updated by using a special program called *FTP*, which stands for *File Transfer Protocol*, which may not be installed on your machine.

To get it, you can point any recent browser to a location where they keep such things. TUCOWS is a great resource for downloading many of them or you can go right to the source.

For Macintoshes:

FTP on the Macintosh

There are two popular FTP programs for the Macintosh: Anarchie (named after an obsolescent search engine called Archie) and Fetch. Each has legions of fans, and you should try both to see which one you like before settling on one or the other.

- Peter Lewis's Stairway Software's Anarchie FTP software is superb, and a very good Net citizen as well, since it only accesses the FTP connection when it's actually transferring data. It has all the Macintosh goodies like drag-and-drop file transfer and Finder-style searches. It's great software and can be found at `http://www.share.com/peterlewis/`.
- Dartmouth University's Fetch FTP software is very good as well. It's a little simpler than Anarchie, is free to noncommercial users, and some people like it better. This software can be found at `http://www.dartmouth.edu/pages/softdev/fetch.html`.

For Windows platforms, I like WS-FTP, a low-cost shareware program that automatically connects to your favorite FTP destinations (if you have more than one) and also keeps track of which directories are used at both ends of the connection. So if one of your projects is in the /jones directory while another is in the /smith directory, and both have different Internet destinations, this great program keeps track of them for you and places you in the right directories on both ends with no work on your part except to tell it where you want to go in the first place. I really like its ability to decipher which files should be sent in binary form based on their file extension because this saves a lot of time and helps prevent mistakes. This program can be found at `http://www.ipswitch.com/`.

FTP on Windows

There are many more FTP programs available for Windows platforms, but the quality is more uneven. Of particular interest is WS-FTP from Ipswitch, but your own work habits may make another program easier to learn and use.

There are many, many more, including a no-frills version that comes standard with Windows 95. Do yourself a favor and get another one, because it's tiresome interacting with FTP from a command line unless you're used to doing it on a daily basis.

More FTP programs

There are lots of FTP programs available, and you should try several if you don't like WS-FTP, whose interface seems very intuitive and logical to me. The only trouble with it is that it comes with a whole bunch of destinations predefined that make it hard to find your own. The easiest way to fix this is to delete the default addresses. I've never used but one of them and that as a model for filling in the fields of the first one I ever did.

All the programs I've mentioned have easy-to use graphical interfaces that simplify using FTP to the point where literally anyone can do it with few hassles. If you're using a UNIX shell account and have to use the manual version of FTP, type `man ftp` for a short description. It's not really too hard, but it takes a while to describe it.

And that's all for this introductory chapter. You know where to get everything you need and what to do with it all once your pages are done. It's time to get cracking and make some pages. So let's start now!

CHAPTER

2

Building the Foundation

Using HTML in a nutshell, first text, then tags

Why use the *<HTML>* tag

Keeping the main sections straight, separating heads and bodies

Putting a title on your page

Change the default text and background colors

Your First Web Page

We're ready to start writing our first page, and because we're using a text-oriented and task-centered approach, we won't start with the "Hello, World" two-word pages you may have seen elsewhere, but with real words that might make up a real home page. We'll find out first how to turn words into pages with simple tags, not memorize the rituals of an esoteric programming rite and fit the text around them.

Although we'll pay attention to *standards* and *specifications*, we won't be bound by them either. When it's simpler and easier to use older tags that are widely supported, we'll use them, and we definitely won't get caught up in the *browser wars*.

Warning: Standards aka specifications

The most current official standards and specifications are always available from the World Wide Web Consortium at `http://w3c.org/`, and their recommendations should be a part of your reading eventually, but not right now. Few of the browser manufacturers pay close attention to what they say and none of the commercially-available browsers are free of non-standard and sometimes ill-advised ways to do things. We have to live with what we have, not what we wish for, but you should strive to follow the HTML 4.0 recommendation promulgated by the world standards body, the World Wide Web Consortium. Adherence to these standards is part of the recommendation itself, and is the only way to opt out of the Browser Wars.

Create Your Text First!

Starting building your HTML page by writing solid text:

1. Make an outline first!

```
The Fayne Family Page
  Who We Are
  Where We Live
  Our Special Interests
  Fun Places We've Been
```

2. Add text to your outline and edit until you have a page that sounds good when read aloud.

```
The Fayne Family Page
  Who We Are
    Hi! You've discovered the home page of Bess and
George Fayne, and of our wonderful children, Nancy,
five, and Mikey, who's only six months old right now
but already loves the computer, at least to eat! This
is an experiment for us, the first time we've really
done much of anything on a computer for ourselves,
although both George and I use one at work. We hope
```

you'll enjoy reading our page and looking at our pictures, which are like any family photo albums, except that you can set them aside as soon as you want without hurting our feelings!

Where We Live

We're both natives of the Midwest, born in a little suburb of Chicago, "hog butcher to the nation," but moved to California shortly after we were married. Both our children were born here and this is home for us now, although we both enjoy going "back home" to visit the folks on holidays. Right now we're living in Walnut Creek, California, which is right over the hills from the beautiful San Francisco Bay Area. We love our adopted home and really enjoy being only a few hours drive from the ocean to the west and not so very far to some of the most spectacular mountains in the world to the east.

Our Special Interests

I'm a gourmet chef and George is a budding helicopter pilot (at least the model airplane variety) so our weekends are often spent out at the local model airfield, where George can tell "war stories" to all the other ace pilots over an ice cold soft drink or two. Nancy's favorite hobby right now is her bicycle (the training wheels came off last week!) and her stuffed animal collection while Mikey's favorite activity is still eating the computer!

Fun Places We've Been

Since we've been living in California, we just had to go to Disneyland (especially since Nancy discovered that it was only 450 miles south of us), although it seemed like a lot longer with a five year old and a nursing infant all piled into one little car. We've also been to the simply spectacular Point Reyes National Seashore and, of course, San Francisco!

Warning: Browser incompatibilities

Not all browsers pay close attention to the official specifications, and bugs are quite common, even in the latest versions from major corporations. We'll warn you when this is the case with special notes like this one.

Warning: Bug note

Microsoft Internet Explorer and NSCA Mosaic for Windows ignores the HTML tag we're about to discuss and depends on the file extension to display the HTML file properly. HTML files *must* use an .htm or .html suffix or the file will be treated as plain text by these browsers. You should always use one of these file extensions to avoid problems with both browsers and servers.

Warning: Sanity check

Whichever suffix you use, apply it consistently. Keeping track of files is much easier if they all use the same suffix. The only reason you'd want to use .htm instead of .html is if you often transfer files to or from older DOS or Windows 3.x systems, which were terribly limited in filename choices. They only permitted an eight-letter name plus a three-letter suffix, which encouraged cryptic and hard-to-understand filenames.

Indenting

Indenting your words as you write can make it easier to go back and tag them correctly later. HTML is a logical language and the more organized your thoughts are the easier it will be to mark them for the Web.

Starting from text is important, especially for people just starting out. HTML is a text markup language that works best when used to mark up data *after* it's been created. Going the other way around, trying to create HTML and then hanging text on your tags, is possible, once you have the basics down really pat, but at first you'll want to be sure that your page reads well, and, only then, start tagging to make it look good as well.

A good place to start is with an *outline*. Professional writers use them all the time. In fact, this book started life as an outline. You needn't follow your outline slavishly, but HTML has some tags that are especially suited for outlines, so it's a very good place to start.

As an example, we'll do a simple family home page, nothing complicated, just the bare facts about one family at one point in time. We'll start with an outline, opening the file with our favorite editor and calling it homepage.html, to remind us that it's an HTML file.

That's enough to start with, maybe not as much as you'd want to say on your own page, but typical of the sort of information you might want to put on your home page. It's the sort of informal letter you might write to a friend when you send some photos, or the entry you might make in a family history—the things that will interest your own friends and family and serve as a snapshot of your life at one particular time. I like to test my words by reading them aloud, which will help you identify awkward phrases and help spot typographical errors as well. Always spell check your pages by eye as well as with automatic spell checkers. The latter often miss errors (like "two" for "too" or "form" for "from") that will be apparent if you read the page aloud.

Creating a Page Skeleton

Setting up the HTML framework

1. Place an `<HTML>` tag at the start of your text to tell the browser that this is HTML and not plain text.

```
<HTML>
The Fayne Family Page
  Who We Are
    Hi! You've discovered the home page of Bess and
George Fayne, . . .
```

2. Now place a closing tag at the end of your text.

```
    . . . all piled into one little car. We've also
been to
    the simply spectacular Point
    Reyes National Seashore and, of course, San
Francisco!
</HTML>
```

Now we start turning the words into a page. As it is, the words have a structure that we can see on the page, but, in order to display correctly on the Web, we have to start making marks on it by adding what are called tags, special marks that tell the browser when to turn on and off certain effects or treatments of the text. This is necessary because a browser can't really see at all, and ignores what it thinks of as excess *whitespace*, carriage returns, and spaces, when rendering our text. Unless we tell it differently with tags, browsers will display all our text as one long paragraph with a single space between each word, no matter how many carriage returns and spaces we put in.

The first tag to add is a special tag pair at the beginning and end to tell the browser that the enclosed text is HTML. Logically enough, the tag looks like this:

```
<HTML>
```

We'll put that tag on a line by itself at the very start of our words. While we're at it, we'll add what's called a *closing tag* at the end of our text. It's not really necessary in this case, but it makes a neater-looking file and helps us identify problems if the file gets broken for any reason, so let's get in the habit of doing that.

Style

A personal home page can have a personal style. Think of it as a holiday newsletter that anyone can read. You'll include the things that are important to you, pictures of you and your friends and family, special interests, and maybe some tips about places you've found that seem interesting.

Tagging

Marking up your text is often referred to as tagging, like you'd tag items at a yard sale. HTML *elements* are usually called tags as well.

Identify your text as HTML

All HTML files should be enclosed in an opening/closing pair of HTML tags. This is mainly a human convenience, but has some useful real-world consequences as well.

```
</HTML>
```

That's it. We now have an HTML page that will actually display, although we probably won't be happy with the result. HTML is only text, and any text surrounded by <HTML> tags is really HTML. This is what we have so far:

```
<HTML>
   ...(our text)...
</HTML>
```

And Figure 2.1 shows what it looks like all run together in one paragraph, as I warned you.

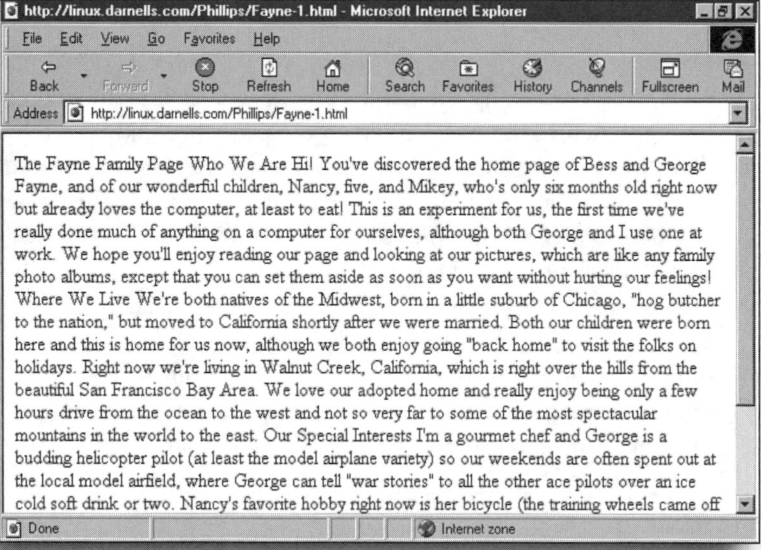

FIGURE 2.1
The Fayne Home Page in a jumble.

Identifying the Major Sections

Identifying and adding major sections to the page

1. Add the <HEAD> tags right under the beginning <HTML> tag.

```
<HTML>
   <HEAD>
   </HEAD>
      ...(our text)...
</HTML>
```

2. Then surround the text with the <BODY> tags like this:

```
<HTML>
   <HEAD>
   </HEAD>
   <BODY>
      ...(our text)...
   </BODY>
</HTML>
```

There are more tags that we'll need to turn our raw text into a formatted page, first comes the *head* section—which we'll use in just a minute to contain some housekeeping information—and then the *body* section, which contains the actual text of the page. The head and body sections are identified with <HEAD> and <BODY> tags, and you should always use them because it helps make the structure of the page more visible, just like the frame on a picture. Without the frame, the raw image is still there, but a good frame sets off the picture and makes it more attractive to the eye.

```
<HTML>
   <HEAD>
   </HEAD>
   <BODY>
      ...(our text)...
   </BODY>
</HTML>
```

"Extra" tags

Always use the <HEAD> and <BODY> tags, even though some books advise against it because "the browser will (probably) fill them in for you." In the first place, some older browsers become confused if they don't see them, and, in the second place, some people may become confused when looking at your code even if the browser doesn't.

Major HTML page sections

Every HTML page is divided into head and body sections. Placing the tags helps keep those sections distinct and easy to find.

Titling the Page So Users Can Find It in a Bookmark List

Creating a page title

1. Add <TITLE> tags between the <HEAD> tags.

```
<HTML>
   <HEAD>
      <TITLE>
      </TITLE>
   </HEAD>
   <BODY>
```

Indenting to make structure clear

Did you notice how I indented the tags and the text under them? This is a very important technique that will help keep you from getting confused later, although it's not required and, indeed, most HTML examples you'll see in other books don't use it. It's just like the structure of an outline, the sort of outline we started out with when we wrote this example. It's worth repeating here, HTML has a lot of tools that were created especially for dealing with outlines, and keeping to an outline structure will almost always help you understand your page better and help keep you from getting lost while you're adding tags.

Document titles

Every Web document must have a title to conform to the HTML specification. Titles are used to create bookmark list entries and are displayed above the menu bar in graphical browsers. Also, when you use a search engine like Yahoo! or AltaVista, the title is used to title each listing.

```
      ...(our text)...
    </BODY>
  </HTML>
```

2. Next to the opening <TITLE> tag, add a title that describes the HTML page succinctly.

```
<HTML>
  <HEAD>
    <TITLE>The Fayne Family Page</TITLE>
  </HEAD>
  <BODY>
    ...(our text)...
  </BODY>
</HTML>
```

What do we use the head section for? We just made one and it seems to be going to waste! Never fear, we're going to use it now and it's very important. In fact, every page is supposed to have a head section and there's one element that is theoretically mandatory, although nobody forces you to do it. It's one of the things that sets off amateurs from professionals though, so you'll always want to do it. It's the <TITLE> tag. In our case, because we have a title on our outline, we can simply copy that into the head section like this:

```
<HTML>
  <HEAD>
    <TITLE>The Fayne Family Page</TITLE>
  </HEAD>
  <BODY>
    ...(our text)...
  </BODY>
</HTML>
```

Having a title on the page means that if Grandma, or anyone else, wants to add a bookmark in her browser so she can go back to the page later, it will have a description built into it and she won't see the embarrassing "No Title" or blank space on her list. It also means that it will be nicely titled so people can see it in a search list, as we'll talk more about in Chapter 28, "Publishing Your Web Pages." It will be well worth your while to spend some time thinking of the best title for any page, putting your best foot forward in a way, because it will often be the first thing people see when they run across your page on the Web.

Setting Background and Other Colors for the Document

Setting background and text colors

1. Use the bgcolor attribute of the <BODY> tag to change the color of the page background.

```
<BODY bgcolor="FFFFFF" text="000000">
```

2. Change the text and link colors using the text and link attributes.

```
<BODY bgcolor="FFFFFF" text="000000" link="0000FF">
```

3. Set the active link and visited link text colors with the alink and vlink attributes.

```
<BODY bgcolor="FFFFFF" text="000000" link="0000FF"
alink="FF0000" vlink="800080">
```

Tags, like the <BODY> tag, are not just placeholders marking the beginning and end of important sections; they can also be used to specify important properties that might affect the entire scope or the text contained within the tags through the use of *attributes* (extra information that can alter the effect of a tag on the display) contained within the initial tag. The <BODY> tag is no exception.

Among the important attributes the <BODY> tag can take are several that affect the overall appearance of the page. Let's talk about them a little first, because this part can get confusing if you try to do too much at once. If you think back to our first discussion of what tags do in Chapter 1, "What You Need to Get Started," you'll recall that I compared a tag to a yellow highlighter. You start at one location and end up at another and everything in between is changed somehow. Well, that's true as far as it goes, but highlighters also come in many colors and attributes are sort of like different-colored versions of the same

Background colors

Change the background color of your page with the `bgcolor` attribute of the <BODY> tag.

Specifying color

Although it's possible to use plain English to specify colors, it's not easy. Just as it's hard to go to the paint store and explain exactly what you mean by "peach," the names of the colors are not at all consistent across browsers. One browser's aqua may be another's cyan. The most accurate way is to use numbers, even though they are hard to understand. I've included a table of numeric "safe" colors in Appendix C, "Colors," at the back of this book, together with a more detailed explanation of what colors are safe and what that means. For this exercise, we'll just use some color values that are very commonly seen on the Web.

Colors are specified by numbers representing differing levels of red, blue, and green light, the same colors as the little dots or lines you can see if you look at your monitor screen with a powerful magnifying glass. Zero is no light of that color at all, while the higher the number is, the more of that color light is present. Since this system was invented by computer geniuses, they used a special type of number called *hexadecimal* (base 16) which is very convenient for computers, even though it's a little hard for people to understand. They also ran the three sets of numbers together so they're all bunched up in a glop, called a *hexadecimal triplet or hexadecimal pairs*, so black (no color at all) looks like 000000, while white (all the colors) looks like FFFFFF. Each pair of numbers represents one primary color, first red, then green, then blue, `rrggbb`. I explain that in Appendix C as well.

tag. They mean almost the same thing as the bare tag but the exact meaning can be changed slightly, just as you might reserve yellow highlighting for things you want to remember and blue highlights for important dates.

As it happens (and this is purely accidental), some of the attributes that can affect the `<BODY>` tag have to do with color. There are five of these and they each affect the color of a different part of your page.

TABLE 2.1 Color attributes of the *<BODY>* tag

Attribute	Description
`bgcolor=`	Sets the background color for the entire page
`text=`	Sets the color of ordinary (non-linked) text on the page
`link=`	Sets the color of ordinary links on the page
`alink=`	Sets the color of active links, in the process of connecting
`vlink=`	Sets the color of visited links (links that have been followed)

The most important attributes are `bgcolor=` and `text=`, since they determine the background color and default text color of your page. For our example, we'll start with black text on a white background, just like a regular printed page. Black is `000000` and white is `FFFFFF`, so our attributes will look like this:

```
<BODY bgcolor="FFFFFF" text="000000">
```

We'll also want to set the other colors, because if we set even one, we have to set them all or run the risk of some of our text becoming invisible, white text on a white background for example. Traditionally, for a white background, we'd set `link=` to blue, `alink=` to red, and `vlink=` to purple. We'll translate those into numeric color values using the safe colors table in Appendix C and fill them in as well.

```
<BODY bgcolor="FFFFFF" text="000000" link="0000FF"
alink="FF0000" vlink="800080">
```

That completes the attributes for the `<BODY>` tag, so our complete template (with enclosed body text) will look like this:

```
<HTML>
```

```
<HEAD>
  <TITLE>The Fayne Family Page</TITLE>
  </HEAD>
<BODY bgcolor="FFFFFF" text="000000" link="0000FF"
alink="FF0000" vlink="800080">
  ...(our text)...
  </BODY>
</HTML>
```

Adding Content to Your Page Template

As you can see, the steps involved in creating the basic skeleton of an HTML page are quite regular. You'll perform exactly the same steps each time you make a page, so many people like to keep a template—like the one given earlier—and just paste their outline into it when they want to start tagging. But it's a good idea to do it at least once to start with, because the concept of adding tags to text instead of vice versa is central to making an error-free Web page. When you cut and paste, you have to remember to go back and change things—for example, you should copy the title from your outline title.

Adding text to a code template can be a real time saver if you're careful. You can even buy books with predefined page layouts to speed development time. But you should write your text first and then cut and paste it into the template afterwards. It's just too confusing for most people to try to write decently and keep track of HTML tags at the same time.

As you update your page you may want to reference an actual printout of the page as displayed in a browser. The tags and attributes can cause the page to appear far more complicated than it really is sometimes, while the browser hides the tags and just shows the text. This can make it much easier to rewrite or add to a section without worrying about the tags. You can then go to the edit file and insert the new or changed content with less fear of losing your place or forgetting what the words actually say.

In the next chapter, we'll add the last block structure tags needed to actually display the text on the Web, almost exactly as we generated it in raw text.

Important compatibility tip

The latest version of HTML 4.0 has declared that the use of these attributes is *interim*, which means that they are slated for eventual removal from the official HTML standard and are no longer recommended for use. However, these tag attributes are still compatible with more than half the browsers in use on the Web today, and it would be a mistake not to use them at this point in time. The new standard has given us a way to set these values that is (or will be) much easier, style sheets, which we talk about in Chapters 13, "Using Cascading Style Sheets to Define Appearance," and 14, "Controlling Layout with Cascading Style Sheets," but support for style sheets is still very uneven and incompatibilities are common.

Warning: Set text and link colors

Always set the text and link colors when setting a background color. Users can override all these values on their browsers, and if a user has set defaults to blue text on a white page and changes the background color to blue, the text will seemingly vanish, even though it would be visible if the text were the normal black.

Making low-contrast text visible

As a quick workaround, if you run across a page where the text is difficult to see, select the entire page using **Edit**, **Select All**. The text will usually appear highlighted in a different and more contrasting color. In many browsers, **Ctrl+A** or **Apple+A** does the same thing.

CHAPTER

3

Providing Structure

- Use headings to outline your pages
- Create paragraphs of text
- Format quotations
- Center and align text

Adding Visual Structure

So far, the page is still a jumble because we haven't told the browser what our visual structure means. Browsers don't pay any attention at all to the visual cues that we can read easily. We have to provide the markup language that tells the browser, so it, in turn, can render our text the way we want it to be shown.

Outlining Your Page with Headings

Format your outline with heading tags

1. Place level 1 headings at each end of the top level headings.

```
<H1>The Fayne Family Page</H1>
  Who We Are
  ...our text...
  Where We Live
  ...our text...
  Our Special Interests
  ...our text...
  Fun Places We've Been
  ...our text...
```

   Quick usage tip: Tag syntax

```
<Hx> ...paragraph heading text... </Hx>
```

   where `Hx` is a heading level from `H1` to `H6`.

2. Add `<H2>` tags around any secondary headings in your outline like this:

```
<H2>Who We Are</H2>
```

So far, we've outlined our text and formatted our page visually, but the browser doesn't understand our visual cues. So now we begin to tell the browser what the visual cues really mean. Of course, we do that with more tags.

First, we'll look at the outline headings; HTML has quite a few tags that translate directly into outline conventions. The one used to make a heading is called (again logically) the heading tag. Since headings can occur at multiple levels there are a total of six heading tags, `<H1>`, `<H2>`, `<H3>`, `<H4>`, `<H5>`, and `<H6>`. These tags must be followed by their closing tags. Unlike the basic foundation structure we talked about in Chapter 2, "Building the Foundation," there are no optional parts.

Dedicated HTML editors

Although I think it's not the best way to learn, some people feel more comfortable using a dedicated editor. In many cases, these types of editors work exactly backwards from the way I recommend, inserting empty tag containers that you then fill in with text. It's a good idea to cut and paste text from a simple editor into the dedicated editor rather than trying to keep track of the literary structure of your page and the tagging structure at the same time.

Our original outline had two levels, so we'll only be using two of the heading tags, <H1> and <H2>, to represent the elements of the outline on our page. Here's the outline with the text left out so you can see the structure more clearly.

```
The Fayne Family Page
  Who We Are
  Where We Live
  Our Special Interests
  Fun Places We've Been
```

Inserting the tags is a completely mechanical process, since our text retains the visual structure of the original outline.

```
<H1>The Fayne Family Page</H1>
  <H2>Who We Are</H2>
  ...our text...
  <H2>Where We Live</H2>
  ...our text...
  <H2>Our Special Interests</H2>
  ...our text...
  <H2>Fun Places We've Been</H2>
  ...our text...
```

It's a good idea to start at <H1> and then go up one number at each successive indent, although many people also use the heading tags to choose a particular font size, especially when they want to give the effect of fine print, since many browsers render <H6> in a very small size. It's a bad idea, even though you see it a lot. Quite a few browsers don't render it as small print but at normal size, which can be confusing to say the least. As a compromise between logic and looks, if the <H1> tag seems to render the heading in too large a font, you could start at <H2> and continue from there.

Tagging intrudes on your thinking, do it last!

Structuring your thoughts and words at the outset is very important. It's hard enough to write coherently without juggling dozens of tags and thinking about the visual appearance of your words at the same time.

Indentation is never guaranteed

Outline indentation structure may not carry over to the page, since many browsers align everything on the left margin by default. We'll see several techniques to affect the indent levels in the chapters on style sheets later on.

SEE ALSO

➤ *Learning better ways to control indentation, see page 254*

Structuring with Paragraphs

Separating your text into paragraphs with the <P> tag

1. Place a <P> tag at the start of every paragraph, like this:

```
<P>
...our text...
```

2. Do not include a closing paragraph tag; it's not a good idea to use it because there are complex rules about what tags can be used inside a paragraph.

   Quick usage tip: Tag syntax

   ```
   <P> ...paragraph text...
   ```

We're really on a roll now, and almost done with the basic structure of our family home page. Although for complex reasons it will actually display correctly in many browsers, some browsers will do funny things to the text so there's one last tag we'll need to use, the paragraph tag, `<P>`. This is a really simple one to use because the closing tag is not only optional, but most browsers actually ignore it. So you can safely forget about the closing tag completely, which is nice because it saves typing and makes for cleaner code. Also, paragraphs obey confusing rules about which elements can go inside which others, so leaving off the closing tag means one less thing to worry about; the browser will close the paragraph on its own when appropriate.

Ignoring bugs

Some people prefer to close every paragraph with a closing `</P>` tag, because of a bug in Microsoft Internet Explorer that caused it to ignore style sheet commands if this tag was not closed. On the other hand, using the closing tag is a potent source of error in your code because you have to be very careful to close out the tag at the proper level. It's easy to make a mistake. You can decide about this for yourself but in my opinion it's crazy, and a never-ending source of trouble, to try and code around browser bugs. Your text will always be readable, even if a particular browser doesn't behave properly, and you'll remain sane and happy.

All we have to do is insert a `<P>` tag at the start of every paragraph and we're done.

```
<H1>The Fayne Family Page</H1>
  <H2>Who We Are</H2>
    <P>
    ...our text...
  <H2>Where We Live</H2>
    <P>
    ...our text...
  <H2>Our Special Interests</H2>
    <P>
    ...our text...
  <H2>Fun Places We've Been</H2>
    <P>
    ...our text...
```

That's it! We now have a complete page that displays correctly in any browser using a mere handful of tags. It isn't all that complicated, and almost all the tags used so far are pretty logical, not really hard to memorize when you use them for any length of time. Here's the complete code with the paragraph text omitted for clarity.

```
<HTML>
  <HEAD>
```

```
  ...
</HEAD>
<BODY bgcolor="#FFFFFF" text="#000000" link=...>
  <H1>The Fayne Family Page</H1>
    <H2>Who We Are</H2>
      <P>
      ...our text...
    <H2>Where We Live</H2>
      <P>
      ...our text...
    <H2>Our Special Interests</H2>
      <P>
      ...our text...
    <H2>Fun Places We've Been</H2>
      <P>
      ...our text...
</BODY>
</HTML>
```

Seven tags and five attributes and we have a completely correct home page. Of course there are things we can add, like pictures, links, and other goodies to make the page look prettier. We'll add those new tags to the existing page, building up logically from the original text, which is almost guaranteed to eliminate most causes of confusion and poor rendering in the browser.

Figure 3.1 shows the display as it is after these last edits. It's quite a change.

There's still a lot that needs to be done, but we'll wait until later.

Formatting Large Quotations

Formatting lengthy quotations

1. Write the text to be included as a quotation.

```
The Friends of Hypatia Home Page
Life is an unfoldment, and the farther we travel the
more truth we comprehend. To understand the things that
are at our door is the best preparation for understand-
ing those that lie beyond.
- Hypatia of Alexandria
```

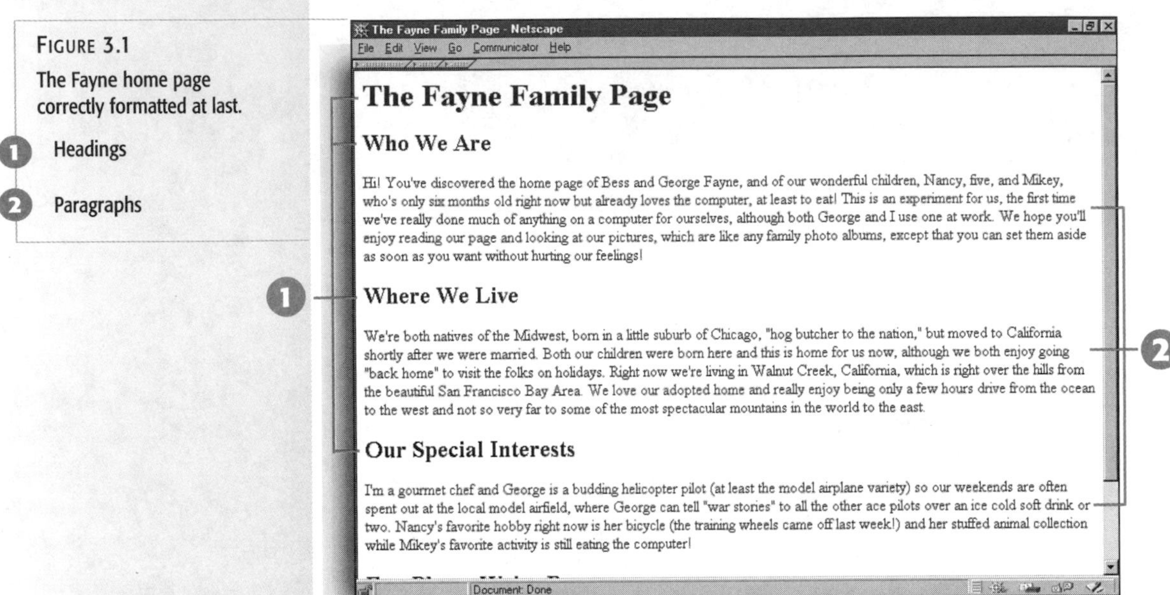

FIGURE 3.1
The Fayne home page correctly formatted at last.

1. Headings
2. Paragraphs

2. Use the <BLOCKQUOTE> tags to create a margin on the left and right margins that can make a page look more finished and attractive. This use is not approved by the standards body, but is often seen.

```
<H1>The Friends of Hypatia Home Page</H1>
  <BLOCKQUOTE>
    Life is an unfoldment, and the farther we travel
    the more truth we comprehend. To understand the
    things that are at our door is the best prepara-
    tion for understanding those that lie beyond.
    - Hypatia of Alexandria,
    </BLOCKQUOTE>
...
```

3. To further indent text, nest the <BLOCKQUOTE> tags.

```
  <BLOCKQUOTE>
...quotation...     <BLOCKQUOTE>
...text to be indented further...        </BLOCKQUOTE>
    </BLOCKQUOTE>
...
```

Quotations are very popular on the Web, and people expect long quotations to be handled slightly differently than a regular paragraph, usually by offsetting both the left and right margins toward the center of the page slightly. In everyday life, we'd call this a block quote, and the corresponding tag is `<BLOCKQUOTE>`. It takes a mandatory closing tag because you can put many other things inside `<BLOCKQUOTE>` tags.

Many people actually use `<BLOCKQUOTE>` tags for formatting the page with a margin by starting a `<BLOCKQUOTE>` tag at the top of the page and continuing straight down until they close the page with a `</BLOCKQUOTE>` tag. Strictly speaking, you're not supposed to do this, but life is full of compromises and the technique has the advantage of working on almost all browsers, whereas others we'll meet later don't.

SEE ALSO

➤ *Creating margins in another way, see page 240*

We've used the family page quite a bit already, and we'll come back to it later, but for our quotation let's start a new page. As before, we'll start with some text. To give us an excuse for a long quotation we'll make this page the sort of thing an interest group or fan club might want to put up on the Web. So the outline fragment is as follows.

```
The Friends of Hypatia Home Page

Life is an unfoldment, and the farther we travel the more
truth we comprehend. To understand the things that are at
our door is the best preparation for understanding those
that lie beyond.

- Hypatia of Alexandria
```

We already know how to make this fragment into a page, so we'll concentrate on turning the quote into a block quote. It's not hard. Like almost all tags, the `<BLOCKQUOTE>` tag simply surrounds its contents so the quote would be tagged as follows:

```
<H1>The Friends of Hypatia Home Page</H1>
  <BLOCKQUOTE>
    Life is an unfoldment, and the farther we travel the
    more truth we comprehend. To understand the things that
    are at our door is the best preparation for understand-
    ing those that lie beyond.
```

```
    - Hypatia of Alexandria,
    </BLOCKQUOTE>
...
```

which results in the display shown in Figure 3.2.

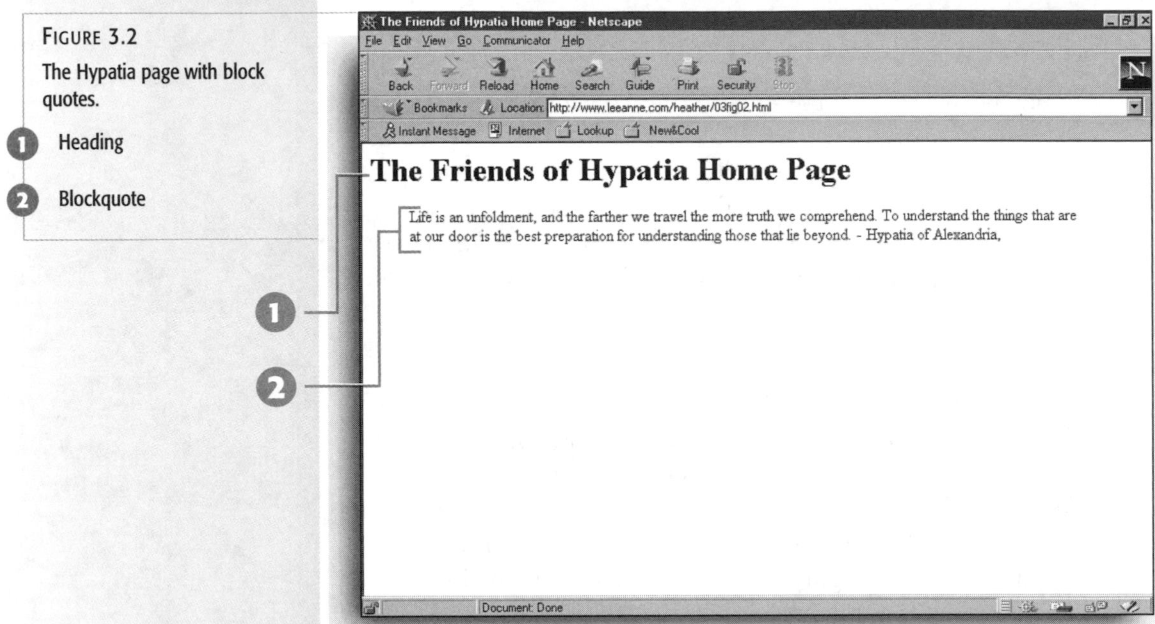

FIGURE 3.2
The Hypatia page with block quotes.
1 Heading
2 Blockquote

Each nested level of <BLOCKQUOTE> offsets the margins by another level, so it's possible to achieve interesting layout effects by nesting <BLOCKQUOTE> tags.

```
<H1>The Friends of Hypatia Home Page</H1>
  <BLOCKQUOTE>
    Life is an unfoldment, and the farther we travel the
    more truth we comprehend. To understand the things that
    are at our door is the best preparation for understand-
    ing those that lie beyond.
    <BLOCKQUOTE>
      - Hypatia of Alexandria,
      </BLOCKQUOTE>
    </BLOCKQUOTE>
...
```

We'll look at this after we've made further changes later in this chapter.

Using Pre-Formatted Text

Pre-formatting text with the <PRE> tag

1. Create text that shouldn't be re-flowed into paragraphs by using extra spaces and line feeds.

```
                Triangles

         Triangles    rearrange
          silently    stealing
           through    deepest
            shadow    slants
             light    fades
              into    dark
               you    and
                we    to
                 I    .
```

2. Surround this text with <PRE> tags to maintain the formatting.

```
<PRE>
                Triangles

         Triangles    rearrange
          silently    stealing
           through    deepest
            shadow    slants
             light    fades
              into    dark
               you    and
                we    to
                 I    .
</PRE>
```

Sometimes, when displaying poetry or arranging data in a particular format for a form, you want to control the exact placement of every letter on the page. Ordinarily, an HTML browser will gobble up any extra spaces and linefeeds you may throw in to make it easier to read. When you want to pre-format the text, however, the <PRE> tag really comes into its own.

```
<PRE>
                Triangles


          Triangles   rearrange
           silently   stealing
            through   deepest
             shadow   slants
              light   fades
               into   dark
                you   and
                 we   to
                  I   .
</PRE>
```

Every space in the above fragment will be rendered exactly as written, which is probably exactly what you want as well. The result can be seen in Figure 3.3.

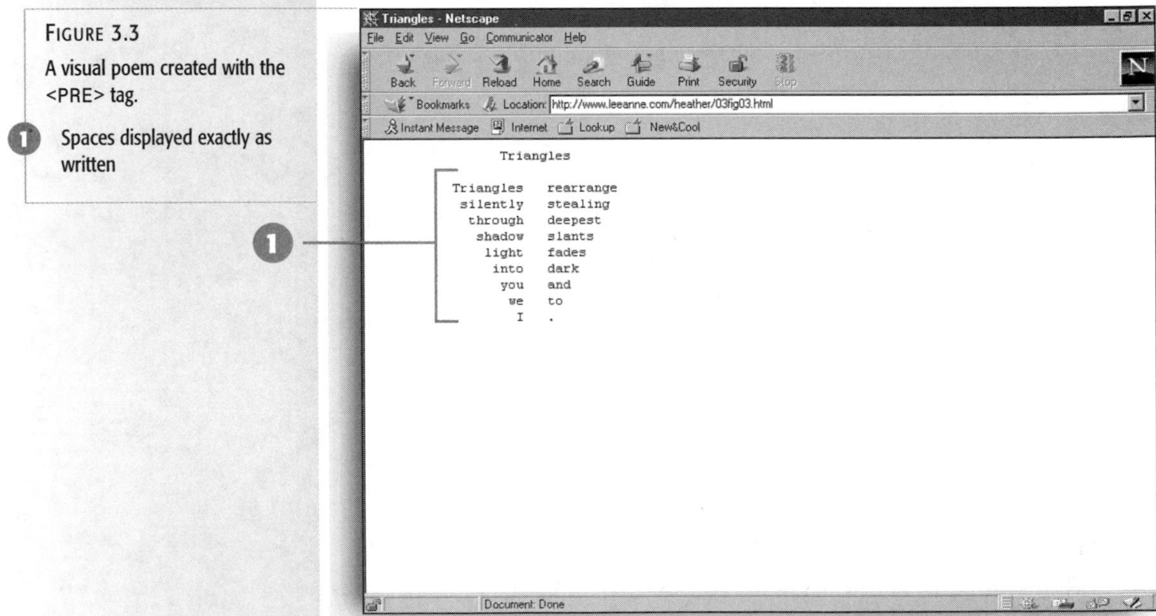

FIGURE 3.3
A visual poem created with the <PRE> tag.

1 Spaces displayed exactly as written

Centering and Other Paragraph Alignments

Centering text

1. Identify text that needs to be centered.

```
<H1>The Friends of Hypatia Home Page<H1>
```

2. Add the <CENTER> tags to either end.

```
<H1><CENTER>The Friends of Hypatia Home Page
</CENTER></H1>
```

Quick usage tip: Tag syntax

```
<CENTER> ...
centered text, headings, and/or other elements...
</CENTER>
```

3. Other alignment choices can be made with the `align=` attribute on the <P> and several other tags, including heading tags, although the use of this attribute is also an interim solution.

```
<H1 align=CENTER>The Friends of Hypatia Home Page</H1>
```

Quick usage tip: Tag syntax

```
<P align="value"> ...paragraph text...
```

where *value* can be `left`, `right`, `center`, `justify`.

SEE ALSO

➤ *Using style sheet commands to center in the approved way, see page 264*

We use centering all the time in ordinary life. Book titles are usually centered on the title page, we set our tables with a centerpiece, and we often admire the center of attention. So it comes as no surprise that there are special tags and attributes just to arrange things in relationship to the center of the page.

The most familiar and widely supported is the <CENTER> tag, which has a mandatory closing tag and does just what you'd think, taking any enclosed text and forcing it to the center of the page. This tag is recognized by many browsers so you'll want to know and use it even though it's officially an interim measure until style sheets become widely supported. Style sheets are supposedly more general methods that work consistently across multiple elements, if they work at all, which is not at all certain across multiple browsers.

SEE ALSO

➤ *Using other methods to align text, see page 242*

For our example, we'll center the `<H1>` heading on our Hypatia page.

```
<H1><CENTER>The Friends of Hypatia Home Page</CENTER></H1>
  <BLOCKQUOTE>
    Life is an unfoldment, and the farther we travel the
    more truth we comprehend. To understand the things that
    are at our door is the best preparation for understand-
    ing those that lie beyond.
    <BLOCKQUOTE>
      - Hypatia of Alexandria,
       </BLOCKQUOTE>
    </BLOCKQUOTE>
...
```

We'll wait to show it until we've done more.

We could have done the same thing with an `align` attribute on the heading tag itself, like this:

```
<H1 align="center">The Friends of Hypatia Home Page</H1>
  <BLOCKQUOTE>
    Life is an unfoldment, and the farther we travel the
    more truth we comprehend. To understand the things that
    are at our door is the best preparation for understand-
    ing those that lie beyond.
    <BLOCKQUOTE>
      - Hypatia of Alexandria,
       </BLOCKQUOTE>
    </BLOCKQUOTE>
...
```

Using this option would have given us the ability to choose `left`, `right`, and `justify` in addition to `center`. The choice is up to you. If your primary audience is using browsers that have been updated in the past year or so, you can probably use `align` safely and gain many more options at the same time. If you want to reach the widest possible audience, `<CENTER>` might be safer, or you can use both.

Creating Other Document Divisions

Creating other document divisions

1. Surround the section of text that you want to separate with <DIV> tags.

```
<DIV>- Hypatia of Alexandria, </DIV>
```

2. Control the alignment by adding the `align` attribute where the values can be `left`, `right`, `center`, or `justify`.

```
<DIV align="right">- Hypatia of Alexandria, </DIV>
```

Officially, the <CENTER> tag is only a special case of the division tag defined as <DIV align="center">. Unfortunately, the division tag is not nearly as useful since many browsers don't support it today. When it works, though, it can be used to create arbitrary divisions of your text and apply alignment values to them such as `left-justified`, `right-justified`, `centered`, and `justified` (spaced out to the left and right margins). Justified text is rarely used on the Web except for special effects because the typographical control of letter spacing on most browsers is imprecise and the justified text often looks amateurish.

We'll use a division tag to move the author line over toward the right margin and under the quote because that's the way you usually see them.

```
<H1><CENTER>The Friends of Hypatia Home Page</CENTER></H1>
  <BLOCKQUOTE>
    Life is an unfoldment, and the farther we travel the
    more truth we comprehend. To understand the things that
    are at our door is the best preparation for understand-
    ing those that lie beyond.
    <BLOCKQUOTE>
      <DIV align="right">- Hypatia of Alexandria, </DIV>
       </BLOCKQUOTE>
       </BLOCKQUOTE>
```

We're going to do one more thing to this text, so we'll wait to show it until the very last.

Using Horizontal Rules to Create Major Separations

Adding horizontal rules

1. Create a major division in your text by adding a horizontal rule, but avoid overuse. No closing tag is needed.

   ```
   <HR>
   ```

2. Modify the horizontal rule by using its attributes, `align` and `width`.

   ```
   <HR align="left" width=80%>
   ```

   Quick usage tip: Tag syntax

   ```
   <HR align="value" width="lengthvalue">
   ```

   where *`value`* can be `left`, `right`, `center` and *`lengthvalue`* is a percentage of the available display width or a fixed pixel length.

Horizontal rules are sometimes controversial. There have certainly been many pages that overused them, resulting in "beautiful" displays of rule patterns that reminded me of the scarification rituals of some tribal people in the Amazon. On the other hand, a simple rule can sometimes add a certain finished look to the page, at least when rules themselves are used sparingly and reserved for just the right moment. As a model, look at a pictorial magazine you read and enjoy. If its use of rules, or lack of rules, appeals to you, you can safely imitate it on your pages until you figure out what your own taste in horizontal lines might be.

As an example of a legitimate use of a horizontal rule, we'll add a rule under the quotation, since the heading and the quotation together could represent the masthead (the paper's name and logo) of our Hypatia special interest page.

```
<H1><CENTER>The Friends of Hypatia Home Page</CENTER></H1>
<BLOCKQUOTE>
  Life is an unfoldment, and the farther we travel the more
  truth we comprehend. To understand the things that are at
  our door is the best preparation for understanding those
  that lie beyond.
```

```
<BLOCKQUOTE>
  <DIV align="right">- Hypatia of Alexandria, </DIV>
   </BLOCKQUOTE>
<HR>
</BLOCKQUOTE>
```

The final result is seen is Figure 3.4.

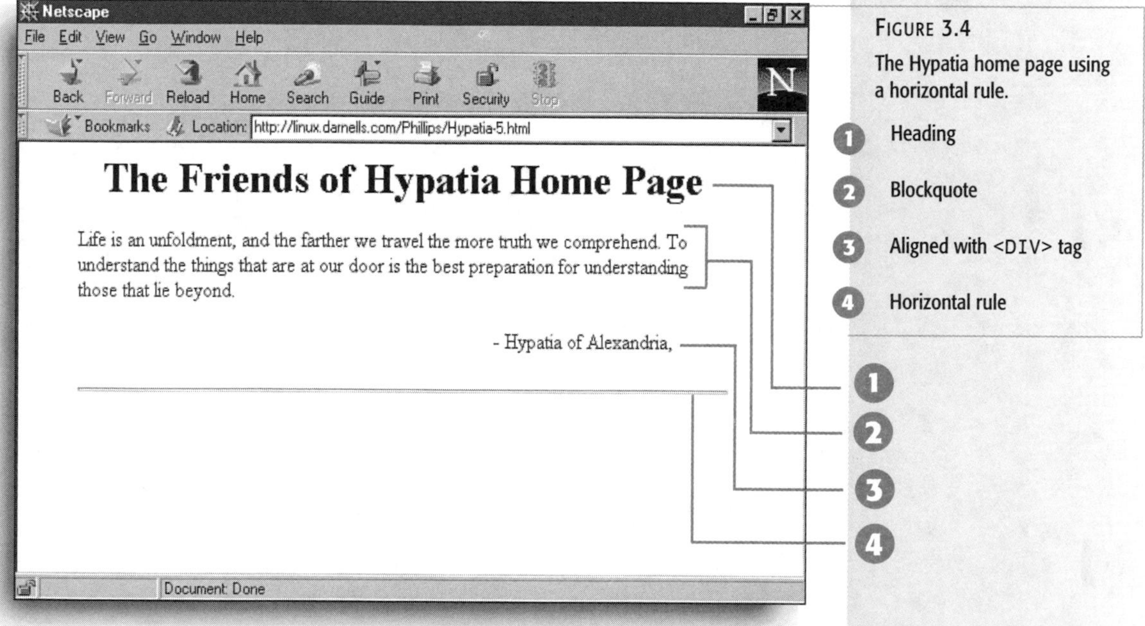

FIGURE 3.4

The Hypatia home page using a horizontal rule.

1. Heading
2. Blockquote
3. Aligned with <DIV> tag
4. Horizontal rule

CHAPTER 4

Adding Context

- Emphasize text
- Use abbreviations and acronyms
- Mark human-machine interactions
- Use quotations

Browser dependencies

Browsers are not precise machines that flawlessly track your code and do exactly what you tell them to do. Quite the opposite; they're quirky, stubborn little beasts that sometimes have to be persuaded by clever tricks to act the way they *ought* to act. Some HTML tags are ignored by most browsers and some are treated differently by each. Part of the art and fun of learning this stuff is figuring out how to coax the best performances out of the feuding divas the browsers (or their makers) sometimes remind one of.

Use logical tags for Dynamic HTML

Logical tags are at their most powerful with style sheets and Dynamic HTML because you can define arbitrary treatments of their enclosed text and be assured that you won't accidentally affect text with similar physical appearance but different logical function in the text.

Describing Text Function

This chapter covers logical text tags and is a companion to Chapter 5, "Using Basic Style," which cover physical tags. Logical tags describe the function of the text in the document rather than exactly what you want the text to look like, so any special treatment depends on what your own browser decides to do about them. They have the great advantage that they can be replaced or modified automatically, either by style sheets or simply by searching for them, and the contents can even be usefully extracted to a database.

At the present time, many of these tags don't actually change the appearance of the text they surround by themselves. You'll have to combine their descriptive precision with the power of cascading style sheets and possibly Dynamic HTML to make full use of the tags that don't have a default text treatment in your browser. All of these will be identified in the sections that follow and are placed toward the end of the chapter.

SEE ALSO

➤ *Changing the appearance of text in other ways, see pages 230 and 402*

But folks, I have to tell you this, the next two chapters are *boring*. That's right, even the combined narrative power of Shakespeare and Marcel Proust couldn't dredge these tags out of the depths of *sameness*, much less *my* lesser (but still sparkling) wit. My best advice, and I say this because I have your interests at heart, is to look at two or three of the ones that interest you most and then skip straight to Chapter 8, "Adding Images to a Web Page," where we start to talk about images and pictures, the really *good* stuff. Believe me, you won't miss much, because all these tags work the same way; once you've seen one you've seen them all. Which is not to say they aren't important—they're the absolute foundation of HTML text treatments. But do yourself a favor and come back to them when you need to use them rather than trying to slog through them all in one sitting.

So flip through the pages to see what's in there and come back when you want to use a particular tag but can't remember exactly how it looks or works. The index at the back of the book will help you find the tags quickly. The index, by the way, is the finest money can buy and makes the competition look silly.

Creating Different Levels of Emphasis

Highlighting text

1. Identify words and phrases that you want to highlight.
2. Surround these words within their context with `<EM>`, `<STRONG>`, or `<I>` tags for emphasis, strong emphasis, or italics, respectively.

   `<EM>`*`Emphasized text`*`</EM>` is usually rendered in italics. `<STRONG>`*`Strongly emphasized text`*`</STRONG>` is rendered in bold. `<I>`*`Italicized text`*`</I>` is obviously italicized.

   Quick usage tip: Tag syntax

   ```
   <EM> ...emphasized text...</EM> or <STRONG> ...strongly
   emphasized text...</STRONG>
   ```

One of the best things about logical tags is that they separate logical roles in the text of your page from physical expression, so if you later decide to change the way you want to show a particular type of text, you can separate just those elements and affect only those. This can save a huge amount of time over using physical tags, which are explored in the next chapter, as well as making it possible to easily apply style sheets, which we talk about in Chapter 14, "Controlling Layout with Cascading Style Sheets," and Chapter 22, "Dynamically Changing Style," and which are incredibly cool.

As an example, let's think about the emphasis tag, `<EM>`, which is usually rendered with an italic font by default; why not just use a tag that says "italic"? The answer is that we use italics for all kinds of things—book titles, words we think are special, words we want to emphasize, even words in a foreign language. It's an awful lot for one font type to bear! But when you use a logical tag, you know that it will be used only for words or phrases you want to emphasize in some way, so later, if you want to display them in red for example, they'll be easy to find and modify in various ways.

The strong emphasis tag, `<STRONG>`, is most often rendered as boldface, but by using a logical tag you can change the way you think about emphasizing words. Perhaps you want them in different colors, different sizes, or both.

So let's start by creating some that can be emphasized for our Hypatia page. Since the example is basically simple, we'll show only the tagged version, with the understanding that it was created from text that was typed in first and read for syntax and clarity before sticking in tags. It can be amazingly difficult for the eye to see problems once an awkward phrase is buried in tags.

Tribon, *chiton*, *peplos*, and *himation* are Greek terms usually shown in italics in English sentences as they are here. We'll show them in italics using physical tags from Chapter 5 to better show how they are contrasted with the logical emphasis tags used to put strong emphasis on Hypatia's name as the first word of the paragraph and regular emphasis on the word "very" in the second sentence. They could also have been tagged with definition tags, as we do in the next section.

```
<P>
  <STRONG>Hypatia</STRONG> is often depicted in the
  <I>tribon</I>, a poor working-class garment made of coarse
  materials that was the traditional attire of philosophers
  and ascetics. However, this is a <EM>very</EM> controver-
  sial idea in many ways and some scholars believe that she
  would have been gowned in the style of the upper class
  Greek women of a Late Roman Alexandria still very much
  influenced by Hellenistic Greece, the typical
  <I>chiton</I> and girdled <I>peplos</I> with
  <I>himation</I>. In this viewpoint the poor quality of
  clothing in which she is shown would be a sort of pious
  fraud by her latter-day admirers, to exalt and exemplify
  her scholarship, selflessness, and purity. She was by all
  credible accounts a lifelong virgin who had dedicated her
  life to science and mathematics; her partisans have been
  many and vocal through the centuries since that murderous
  day in 415 CE.
```

Figure 4.1 shows the text as it appears on the page. Normal emphasis is rendered exactly the same way as italics, but the distinction between the two text types is clear in the codes embedded in the text.

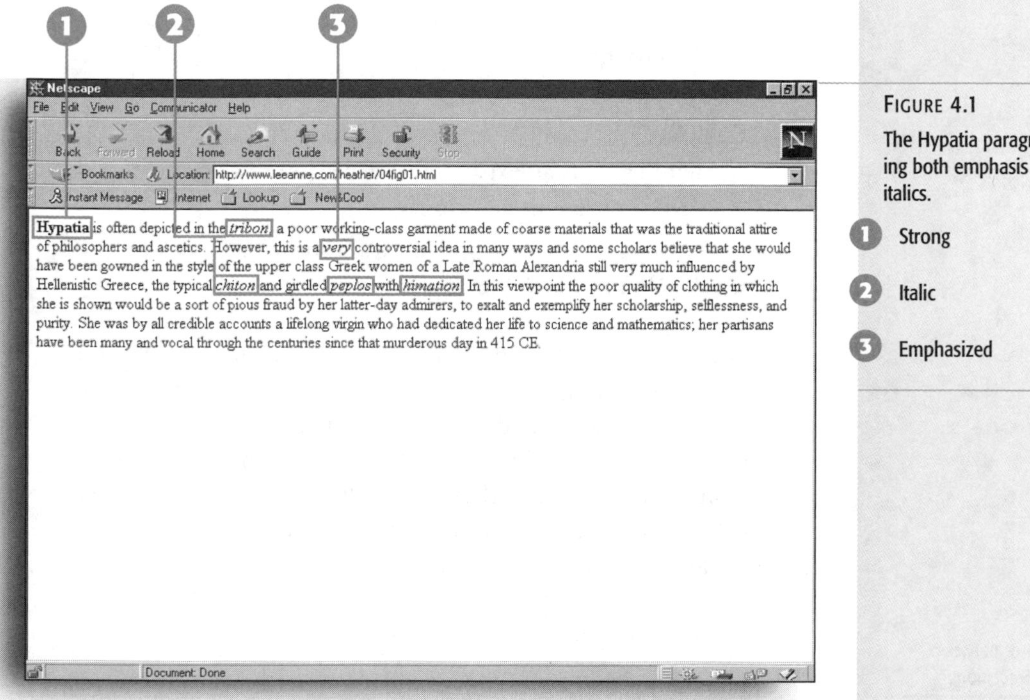

FIGURE 4.1
The Hypatia paragraph showing both emphasis types and italics.

1. Strong
2. Italic
3. Emphasized

Identifying Abbreviations and Definitions

Marking acronyms, abbreviations, and definitions

1. Tag all acronyms with the `<ACRONYM>` tag and insert the expanded name in the `title` attribute.
2. Follow step 1 for all abbreviations and definitions using the `<ABBR>` and `<DFN>` tags, respectively.

```
<ACRONYM title="Spell the acronym out
here">STAOH</ACRONYM>
```

```
<DFN title="The definition goes here">Obscure or techni-
cal phrase that needs to be defined</DFN>
```

Quick usage tip: Tag syntax

```
<ABBR title="value"> ...abbreviation...</ABBR>
```

where *`value`* is the expanded name or phrase the abbreviation refers to;

```
<ACRONYM title="value"> ...acronym...</ACRONYM>
```

where `value` is the expanded name or phrase the acronym refers to; or

```
<DFN title="value"> ...term requiring explanation or
definition...</DFN>
```

where `value` is an expanded explanation or definition of the word or phrase in question.

These three tags are odd men out right now, since most browsers don't actually do anything with them on their own. They are very well suited for special treatment with style sheets and Dynamic HTML though, so we'll learn when to use which and what they're good for and then extend their capabilities with style sheets and Dynamic HTML in Chapters 14 and 22. In addition, browser technology will shortly catch up to the specifications, and all three of these tags will be useful in ways we can hardly imagine today. Learning when and how to use these tags is an investment in the future at the very least, and browsers are evolving so fast that by the time you read this, the following "futuristic" features I describe may be commonplace.

What's the difference between acronyms and abbreviations?

An acronym is usually made up from the initial letters of a phrase, although the phrase itself may be lost to memory. So IBM stands for International Business Machines, although many people no longer know or remember this. An abbreviation is a shortened word or phrase like etc., which stands for the Latin *et cetera* and means roughly "and so forth." Sometimes it's difficult to say which is which, but acronyms are usually spelled out and abbreviations are usually spoken. So NASA would probably be tagged as an abbreviation since one usually says NASA rather than "En Ay Ess Ay." It's a complicated problem and each shortened word or phrase is a puzzle that should be resolved on its own.

The *acronym* tag, for example, will allow audio browsers to recognize an acronym, treating it according to special rules so that IBM can be spelled out rather than pronounced as a pseudo-word, "ibbem." The *abbreviation* tag can be used similarly to ensure that etc. isn't pronounced "etkuh." For difficult technical material, the *definition* tag might even make it possible to set one's browser to automatically expand the condensed jargon writers sometimes use into a more readable, but longer, layperson's version. And all three tags may allow us to create the text for a little pop-up "help balloon" in a visual browser, so anyone puzzled by an acronym, abbreviation, or difficult word could point to it and have an expansion appear on the screen without fooling around with hyperlinks.

For this example, we'll use the previous text and add information about some of the more puzzling or unfamiliar words. First, we'll use definition tags, `<DEF>`, to add some information to the Greek words mentioned in the text—*tribon* in the first sentence and *chiton*, *peoplos*, and *himation* in the second, all various types of clothing—and then use an acronym tag, `<ACRONYM>`, to expand the acronym CE—the very last word in the paragraph—to its English equivalent.

Again, since we always assume that the text comes first with tags added after we're happy with the text, we won't show the unmarked text in the interest of saving space.

```
<P>
  <STRONG>Hypatia</STRONG> is often depicted in the
  <I><DFN title="tunic">tribon</DFN></I>, a poor working-
  class garment made of coarse materials that was the tradi-
  tional attire of philosophers and ascetics. However, this
  is a <EM>very</EM> controversial idea in many ways and
  some scholars believe that she would have been gowned in
  the style of the upper class Greek women of a Late Roman
  Alexandria still very much influenced by Hellenistic
  Greece, the typical <I><DFN title="sleeveless shift">
  chiton</DFN></I> and girdled <I><DFN title="ankle-length
  gown">peplos</DFN></I> with <I><DFN title="draped
  mantle">himation</DFN></I>. In this viewpoint the poor
  quality of clothing in which she is shown would be a sort
  of pious fraud by her latter-day admirers, to exalt and
  exemplify her scholarship, selflessness, and purity. She
  was by all credible accounts a lifelong virgin who had
  dedicated her life to science and mathematics; her
  partisans have been many and vocal through the centuries
  since that murderous day in 415 <ACRONYM title="of the
  Common Era - i.e. AD">CE</ACRONYM>.
```

Note that we didn't take out the physical italics tags, even though we'll later find out how to use style sheets to duplicate this text treatment. Style sheets are not widely supported yet, while italics are. In order to reach the widest audience, it sometimes pays to tag things in several ways. If you use the more advanced logical tags inside the more widely supported physical tags, whatever level of HTML is supported will take effect in the correct order and you can easily see the logical precedence.

Figure 4.2 shows the text as it appears on the page.

Using logical and physical tags together

Logical tags and physical tags are often used together to reach the broadest audience. In general, you should probably use physical tags outside the logical ones, so you can easily see that you can override their effect if the physical tag was a second choice. See Chapters 13, 14, and 22 for more information on style sheets and Dynamic HTML.

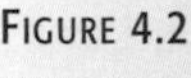

FIGURE 4.2

The Hypatia paragraph showing the addition of explanations for unfamiliar words and abbreviations.

1 Pop-up definition

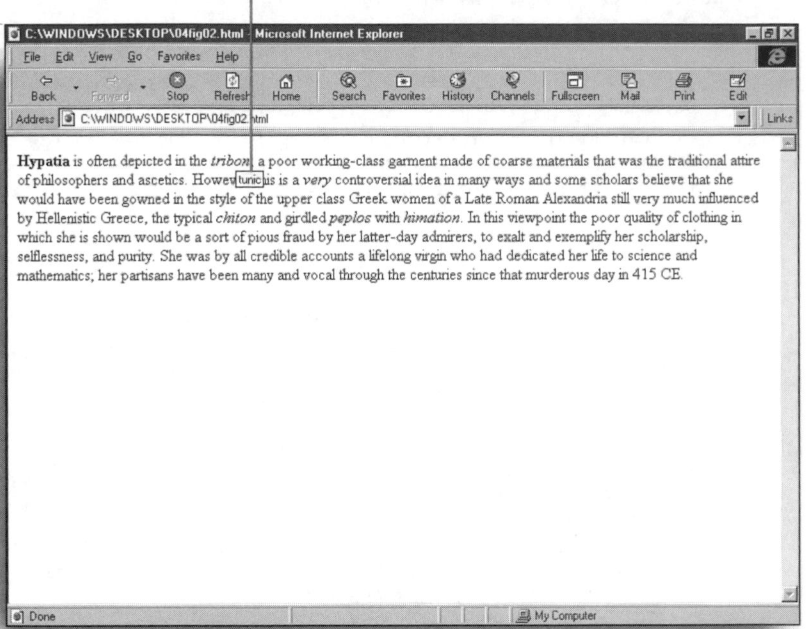

Marking Variables, Input, Output, and Code

Marking human-machine interactions with the *<VAR>*, *<KBD>*, *<SAMP>* and *<CODE>* tags.

1. Use the <VAR> tag to identify all program or table variables.

```
<VAR>outputline</VAR>
<VAR>outputline</VAR>
<VAR>xlatbuffer</VAR>
```

2. Mark all keyboard input with the <KBD> tag and all program output with the <SAMP> tag.

```
<KBD>This identifies text a user should enter via the
keyboard </KBD> <SAMP>This tag identifies sample output
to the computer screen or printer</SAMP>
```

3. Identify actual program code with the <CODE> tag.

```
<CODE><VAR>outputline</VAR> := uppercase(<VAR>xlat-
buffer</VAR>);</CODE>
```

Quick usage tip: Tag syntax

```
<VAR> ...program or table variables... </VAR>
```

or

```
<KBD> ...user or keyboard input...</KBD>
```

or

```
<SAMP> ...program screen or printer output...</SAMP>
```

or

```
<CODE> ...actual code from a program...</CODE>
```

We'll start a new task thread here to use these tags to their best advantage. They logically mark the components of an instruction manual, such as this one, any online document describing things you'd type at the keyboard, the data or messages displayed on the screen or on paper, variables that you might use in a program or table, or the code itself. We'll describe a page that could be used by a small workgroup to make the status of a project available to members of the group, who might be working in widely-separated locations. The page could even be available to customers so they can see an "instant update" of current project status without calling by telephone—which may be difficult if the customer is half the world away from the developers.

First, let's look at a simple project report that describes the current status of a company development product, the same sort you may have written and distributed in your own workplace or to your own customers.

```
Aristotelian Logical Systems, Ltd.
Intelligent Translation Prototype
Project Status - July 21, 1999
Overall project status is good, with code modules AUD123,
AUD124, and AUD125 delivered to QA yesterday. Preliminary
testing is very encouraging and shows no significant
problems although the tester did note that when he typed in
any sentence in English for translation into the target
language, the output was rendered entirely in uppercase.
Thus, for the following inputs:
The early bird catches the worm.
Slow but steady wins the race.
Two wrongs don't make a right.
Italian outputs resulted that were idiomatically correct but
improperly capitalized:
CHI DORME NON PIGLIA PESCI.
```

```
CHI LA DURA LA VINCE.
DUE TORTI NON FANNO UNA RAGIONE.
QA suspects that the problem lies in the outputline
variable, because whitebox inspection revealed the code
fragment:
outputline := uppercase(xlatbuffer);
towards the end of the routine. The code has been sent back
for minor rework.
```

The first items requiring special treatment are the inputs that the tester typed in. The keyboard tag, <KBD>, is used to mark up text that a user types in. Secondly, the machine displays some output for which we can use the sample text tag, <SAMP>, to make it stand out from the rest.

After that come two specialized tags, the variable tag, <VAR>, which changes the display of a program variable, or whatever else you want to call a variable, including row and column headings in a table. The <CODE> tag is used to mark up any code meant to be read by a computer. All these tags have mandatory closing tags.

Note that tags are cumulative, so the two variables inside the code fragment receive both treatments.

```
<H1>Aristotelian Logical Systems, Ltd.</H1>
<H2>Intelligent Translation Prototype</H2>
<H3>Project Status - July 21, 1999</H3>
<P>
  Overall project status is good, with code modules AUD123,
  AUD124, and AUD125 delivered to QA yesterday. Preliminary
  testing is very encouraging and shows no significant
  problems although the tester did note that when he typed
  in any sentence in English for translation into the target
  language, the output was rendered entirely in uppercase.
<P>
  Thus, for the following inputs:
<OL>
  <LI><KBD>The early bird catches the worm.</KBD>
  <LI><KBD>Slow but steady wins the race.</KBD>
  <LI><KBD>Two wrongs don't make a right.</KBD>
</OL>
<P>
  Italian outputs resulted that were idiomatically correct
  but improperly capitalized:
```

```
<OL>
  <LI><SAMP>CHI DORME NON PIGLIA PESCI.</SAMP>
  <LI><SAMP>CHI LA DURA LA VINCE.</SAMP>
  <LI><SAMP>DUE TORTI NON FANNO UNA RAGIONE.</SAMP>
</OL>
<P>
  QA suspects that the problem lies in the <VAR>output-
  line</VAR> variable, because whitebox inspection revealed
  the code fragment:
<BLOCKQUOTE>
  <CODE><VAR>outputline</VAR> := uppercase(<VAR>xlat-
buffer</VAR>);</CODE>
</BLOCKQUOTE>
<P>
  towards the end of the routine. The code has been sent
  back for minor rework.
```

For explanations of other tags in the above fragment, see the cross references listed.

Figure 4.3 shows the text as it appears on the page. Normal emphasis is rendered exactly the same way as italics, but the distinction between the two text types is clear in the codes embedded in the text.

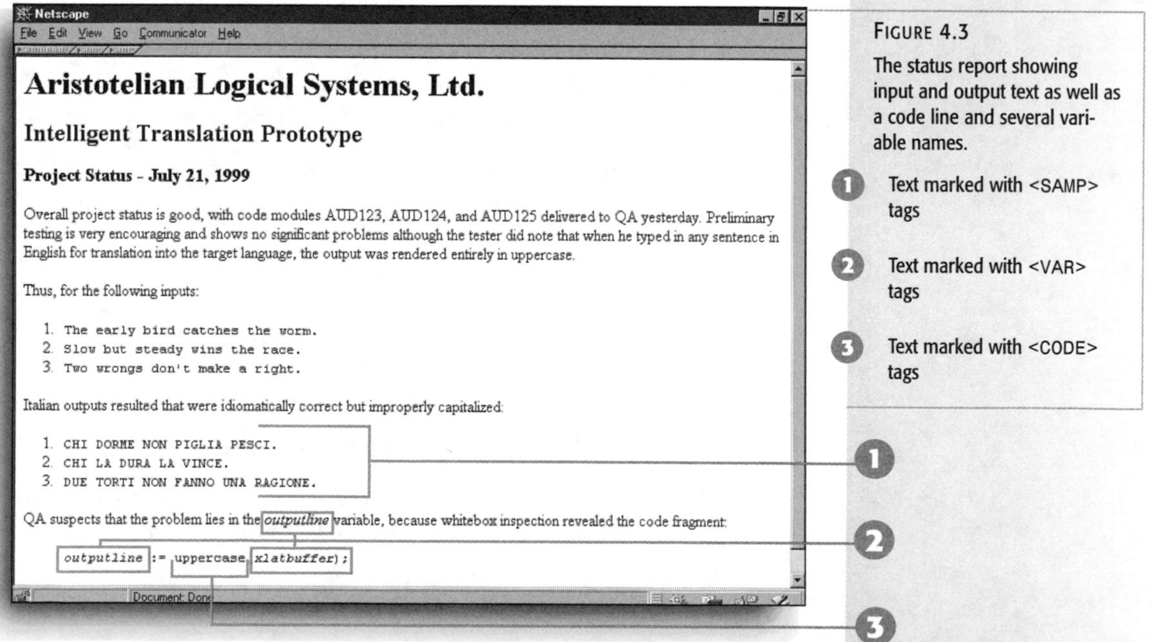

FIGURE 4.3

The status report showing input and output text as well as a code line and several variable names.

1. Text marked with <SAMP> tags
2. Text marked with <VAR> tags
3. Text marked with <CODE> tags

Inserting Quotes in the Text

Marking short inline quotes

1. Mark an inline quotation in the text with a quote tag, <Q>.
2. Add the cite attribute within the <Q> tag and include a URL to help identify the quote.

```
Jael is considered to be the original source for that
famous quote, <Q cite="http://www.jael.org">"Fear
not,"</Q> and is perhaps the least likely to have meant
it seriously.
```

Quick usage tip: Tag syntax

```
<Q cite="url">...quoted text... </Q>
```

where *url* is the address of an explanatory note or source document.

The quote tag, <Q>, is another of those things that ought to work and will work someday soon but doesn't really right now. It's meant to serve two purposes: to give a reference for the quote, so you know where it came from by means of the cite attribute, and also to end the messy problem of showing quotation marks in various languages.

In English, we use inverted commas, while in French one often sees double angle brackets surrounding a quote. There are others. This is a rendering problem, something browsers are designed to do, and the <Q> tag is meant to tell the browser that it should insert the preferred quotation mark form for the user.

The only trouble is that it doesn't work, at least not without help. Few browsers support the tag directly, but with the aid of style sheets and Dynamic HTML, one can do quite a lot to beautify the page. In the meantime, you should add explicit quotation marks inside the <Q> tags, assuming that future browsers will be clever enough to hide them if they put in their own versions. By identifying the quote as we do, we tell these future browser prodigies that we're using the enclosed text as a quotation, so there should be no problem doing just that.

In the meantime, it makes a handy place to keep a reference citation in the code and will eventually be supported by modern browsers.

This example is not part of any thread, but just a short tidbit to show how it works. <Q> tags are inserted into a pre-drafted passage to allow the browser to make its best guess as to what quotation marks to use and how deeply they're nestled.

```
<P>
  Jael is considered to be the original source for that
  famous quote, <Q cite="http://www.jael.org">"Fear
  not,"</Q> and is perhaps the least likely to have meant it
  seriously.
```

Figure 4.4 shows the text as it appears on the page.

Always include explicit quotation marks inside quote tags

Many browsers don't understand <Q> tags and ignore them, so you should always include quotation marks inside <Q> tags. Smarter browsers that do understand them should also be smart enough to remove the extra marks.

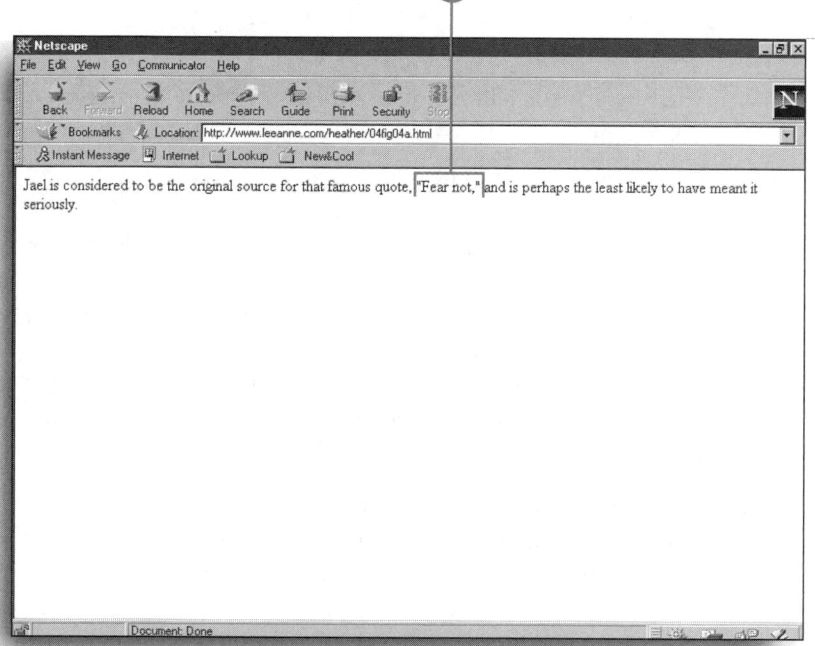

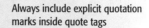

FIGURE 4.4
Short passage showing quoted text.

1 Text quoted with the <Q> tag

Documenting Inserted or Deleted Text

Marking inserted or deleted text

1. Show inserted text by marking it with the <INS> tag.
2. Mark deleted text with the <DEL> tag.

3. For both inserted and deleted text, include the source attribute along with a URL to an explanation or source document, or deleted text with insert and delete tags.

```
<INS cite="codes/sec230/p12-3.html"><U>except that meters
   will not be operational on weekends, or on National
   or State holidays</U></INS>. <DEL cite=
   "codes/sec230/p12-3.html"><S>Parking meters in a
   one block radius of City Hall are operational 24
   hours on each and every day.</S></DEL>
```

Quick usage tip: Tag syntax

```
<INS source="url"> ...inserted text...</INS>
```

where *url* is the address of an explanatory note or source document, or

```
<DEL source="url">...deleted text...</DEL>
```

where *url* is the address of an explanatory note or source document.

Well, here we go again. The inserted text tag, <INS>, and the deleted text tag, <DEL>, are meant to replace the physical tags sometimes used to render inserted and deleted text explicitly. Most current browsers don't display the enclosed text any differently by default, so these are still more tags whose real value can be appreciated in combination with style sheets and Dynamic HTML. If you're not planning on using style sheets, you may want to supplement these tags with physical tags from Chapter 5, such as <U> and <STRIKE>.

For our example, let's use a law, since lawyers and legislators are often the ones most interested in displaying inserted and deleted text. Most of us get by with change bars, which is, by the way, something you might do with style sheets.

We'll just mark up the text, since few of us are likely to want to read through the law twice—or even once. Inserted text is surrounded by (surprise!) inserted text tags (<INS>), while deleted text is shown by (you guessed it!) deleted text tags (<DEL>). I've also added physical tags from Chapter 5 so you can see one possible effect without style sheets.

```
<H3>Proposed Revision to Municipal Code 230.12.3</H3>
<H4>Hours of Parking Meter Operation</H4>
<P>
  230.12.3.3 Parking meters will be operational between the
  hours of 10:00 A.M. and 6:00 P.M. daily <INS
  cite="codes/sec230/p12-3.html"><U>except that meters will
```

```
not be operational on weekends, or on National or State
holidays</U></INS>. <DEL cite="codes/sec230/p12-3.html">
<S>Parking meters in a one block radius of City Hall are
operational 24 hours on each and every day.</S></DEL>
```

Figure 4.5 shows the law as amended. Additional words are underlined while deleted words are rendered in strikeout letters. Although I don't usually like using underline because it can be easily confused with a hyperlink in some browsers, it's clear enough here, and both physical tags have the advantage that they're deprecated, so you could override their effect later with a style sheet and not hurt anything serious.

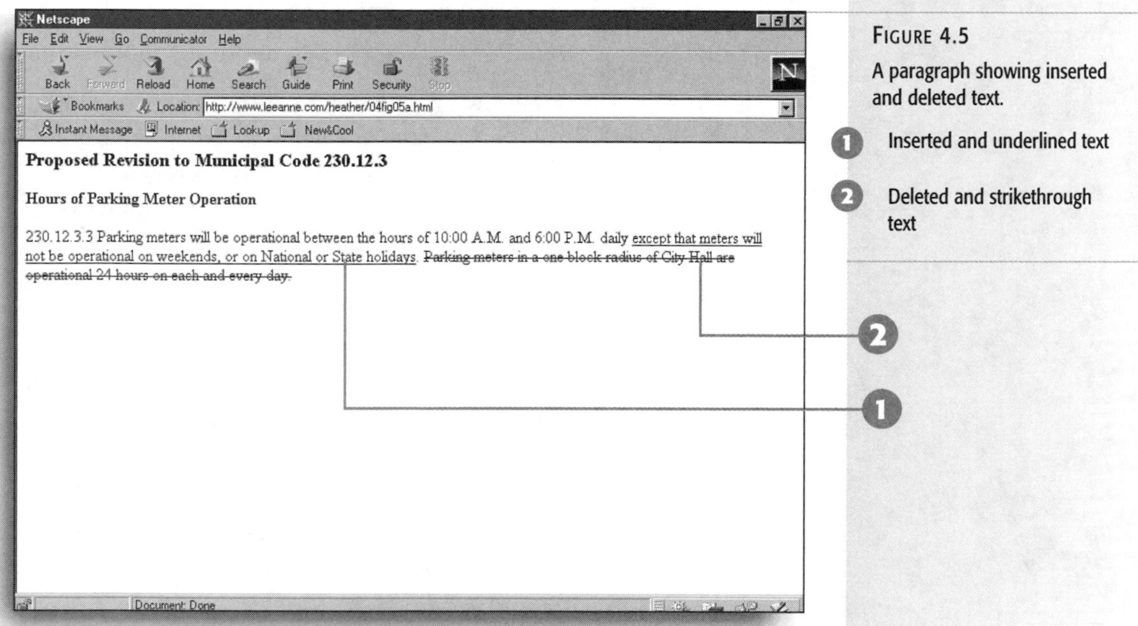

FIGURE 4.5
A paragraph showing inserted and deleted text.

1. Inserted and underlined text
2. Deleted and strikethrough text

Changing Text Direction

Changing text direction for non-Latin scripts

1. Override the default text direction and language using the bidirectional override tag, `<BDO>`.
2. Use the `dir` and `lang` attributes of the `<BDO>` tag to change the text direction and/or the document language.

```
<BDO dir="rtl"  lang="en">BACKWARDS<BDO></B>
```

Quick usage tip: Tag syntax

```
<BDO dir=
"textdirection" lang="language code"> ...
directional inline text...</BDO>
```

where *textdirection* can be `ltr`, `rtl` (left-to-right, right-to-left) and where *language code* is any valid language code.

Why on earth would anyone want to change the direction of the text on the page? So they can print the word AMBULANCE backward in an instruction manual for sign painters? Well, actually it makes a great deal of sense if you happen to speak one of the many languages that uses a different directionality on the page. In Hebrew and Arabic, to choose two better-known examples, text flows from right to left and begins on the right margin.

Hebrew and Arabic browsers know this and take it into account, but what if they want to include an English word on the page, say in a glossary? Or if you wanted to place a Hebrew or Arabic word on your own page? Most browsers don't currently let you do that easily, other than by placing a graphic image of the desired text on the page. But that's so inconvenient. Well, that's what the bidirectional override tag, `<BDO>`, is for, to change the text direction temporarily, so you can include a few reverse-order words in the middle of the sentence. Since we don't actually have a browser available that supports the tag, we'll simulate a display using a trick, the same sort of trick you actually have to use to do this currently.

We'll show the code and then show a prototype display that looks like it would have worked, although we'll have to show it using slightly different techniques.

```
<P>
This is a sample of text that includes a <B><BDO dir="rtl"
  lang="en">BACKWARDS<BDO></B> word printed
  in the reverse direction to the normal left to right flow
  in most European languages. The same
  technique could be used to include a Hebrew word, or an
  Arabic word, although this requires special
  fonts installed on your machine.
```

Figure 4.6 shows a might-have-been that browsers in the future will be able to accomplish simply. Immediately after, we'll show you what had to be done to make it work.

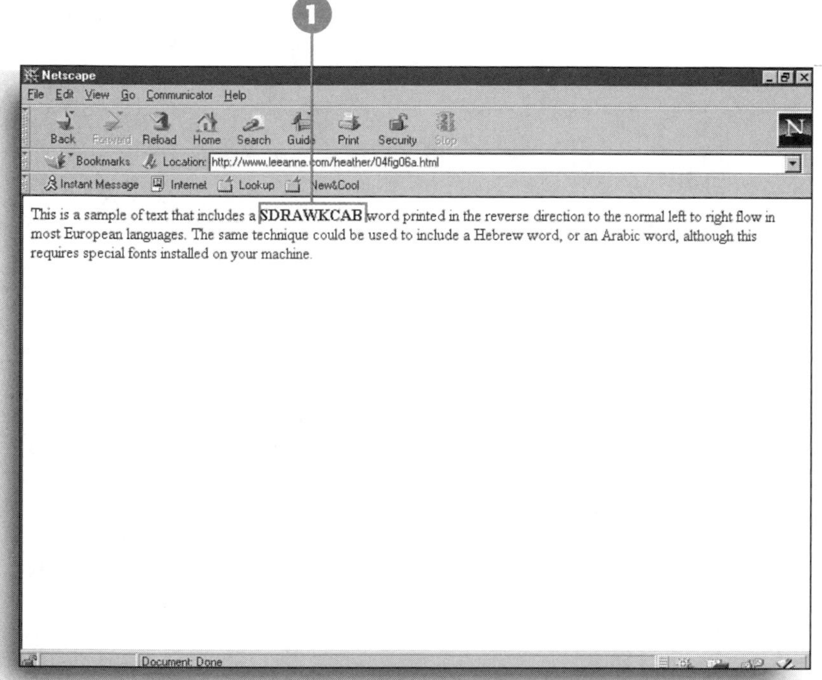

FIGURE 4.6
The backward text displayed by an imaginary supporting browser.

1 Backward text

This is how it was done.

```
<P>
  This is a sample of text that includes a <B>SDRAWKCAB</B>
  word printed in the reverse direction to the normal left
  to right flow in most European languages. The same
  technique could be used to include a Hebrew word, or an
  Arabic word, although this requires special fonts
  installed on your machine.
```

As you can see, we had to delete the `<BDO>` tags and type the letter in backwards by hand. Not a very satisfactory way to create bidirectional content, but one used by many sites out there on the Web. When the browsers support it, there'll be dancing and singing in the streets for many Web designers trying to maintain two languages on one site.

Using Basic Style

Make your text bold

Underline text

Use line breaks

Change font size

Italicize text

Creating Physical Markup

This is the second chapter on text markup, covering physical text tags as opposed to the logical tags discussed in Chapter 4, "Adding Context." Physical text tags change the look of the text explicitly by specifying exactly what you want done, while logical text tags identify text types and leave it up to the browser to decide the most appropriate way to display them. In general, logical text markup should be preferred because it's a timesaver overall, but some things need physical tags.

Making Text Bold and Italicized

Emphasizing text with italics and boldface

1. Create italic text by placing the `<I>` tag to either side of the text.

   ```
   <I>Hypatia of Alexandria</I>
   ```

2. Boldface text is created using the `<B>` tag and these tags can be combined.

   ```
   <B><I>Hypatia of Alexandria</I></B>
   ```

   Quick usage tip: Tag syntax

   `<I> ...italicized text...</I>` or `<B> ...boldface text...</B>`

Probably the simplest text treatment you can think of is either italic or boldface. Almost every printed document uses both to mark special words or phrases like book titles, words that would receive strong emphasis in speech, parenthetical or *sotto voce* comments made as asides to an audience, and other special meanings. The newest versions of HTML sometimes discourage their use in favor of stylesheets and content-based tags, but these two in particular have the advantage of working exactly as advertised in almost every browser. That's a significant advantage.

Using them is really simple; you just put matching opening and closing tags around each word or phrase you want to turn into italics or boldface. The closing tags are always mandatory, and most browsers will render nested text markup correctly, so it's possible to mark a word as bold *and* italic and see the difference on the screen. We'll do a couple of examples, so you can see what might come up in the normal way of business.

Here's a little chunk of text already marked (on a typewriter) with appropriate markings that won't mean anything in an HTML page. Our mission is to replace the informal markup in Figure 5.1 with correct HTML.

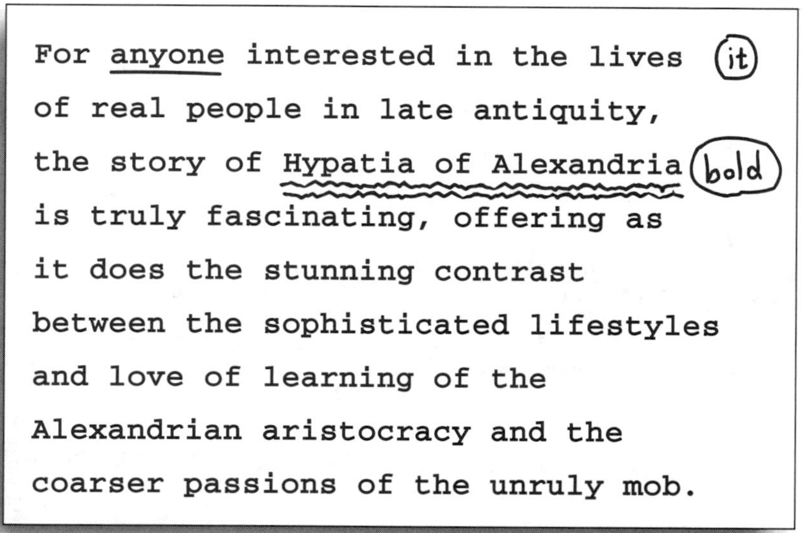

For anyone interested in the lives (it)
of real people in late antiquity,
the story of Hypatia of Alexandria (bold)
is truly fascinating, offering as
it does the stunning contrast
between the sophisticated lifestyles
and love of learning of the
Alexandrian aristocracy and the
coarser passions of the unruly mob.

FIGURE 5.1
Informal markup to be replaced.

First of all, since Figure 5.1 shows a paragraph, we should insert a <P> tag before the text. Next, we see that the word "anyone" is underlined, which usually means that it should be set in an italic font. Knowing that this is true (since I wrote it and there's a marginal notation) we should place an opening <I> at the beginning of the word and the mandatory closing tag, </I>, at its end. That will cause browsers to render the enclosed text in an italic font if possible. Audio browsers may read the text in a higher pitch, or make other changes to the normal reading strategy to indicate that the word is specially marked.

The next word is the name Hypatia of Alexandria, which has a wavy underline, indicating that it should be in boldface, as well as the underline indicating italics. First, we'll surround the name with <I> </I> tags, just as we did on "anyone," and then surround those in turn with an opening <B> and the mandatory closing </B>. The order in which this in done—which set of tags surrounds which—is unimportant, but some browsers are

Physical styles are limiting

Although no one has yet called most of the basic text style tags bad things to use, the trend is away from all physical markup in favor of using style sheets (Chapters 14, "Controlling Layout with Cascading Style Sheets," and 22, "Dynamically Changing Style") with logical tags (Chapter 4). Be aware that some tags are going out of favor, but these very same tags are among the most widely supported and consistent. On the other hand, with the addition of style sheets, they can be used in an almost logical manner.

sensitive to improperly nested tags, so you wouldn't want to type `<B><I>phrase</B></I>`, closing one set of tags before the other tag is closed.

As a general rule, it's safer to follow a last-in, first-out rule when nesting tags, so the better way to nest the tags would be `<B><I>phrase</I></B>`. Of course we could have set a word in plain boldface simply by enclosing it in the bold tags, but we'll leave that as an exercise for your imagination.

Here's what the text looks like when marked up correctly, and Figure 5.2 shows the page on the NSCA Mosaic browser.

```
<P>
  For <I>anyone</I> interested in the lives of real people
in late antiquity, the story of <B><I>Hypatia of
Alexandria</I></B> is truly fascinating, offering as it does
the stunning contrast between the sophisticated lifestyles
and love of learning of the Alexandrian aristocracy and the
coarser passions of the unruly mob.
```

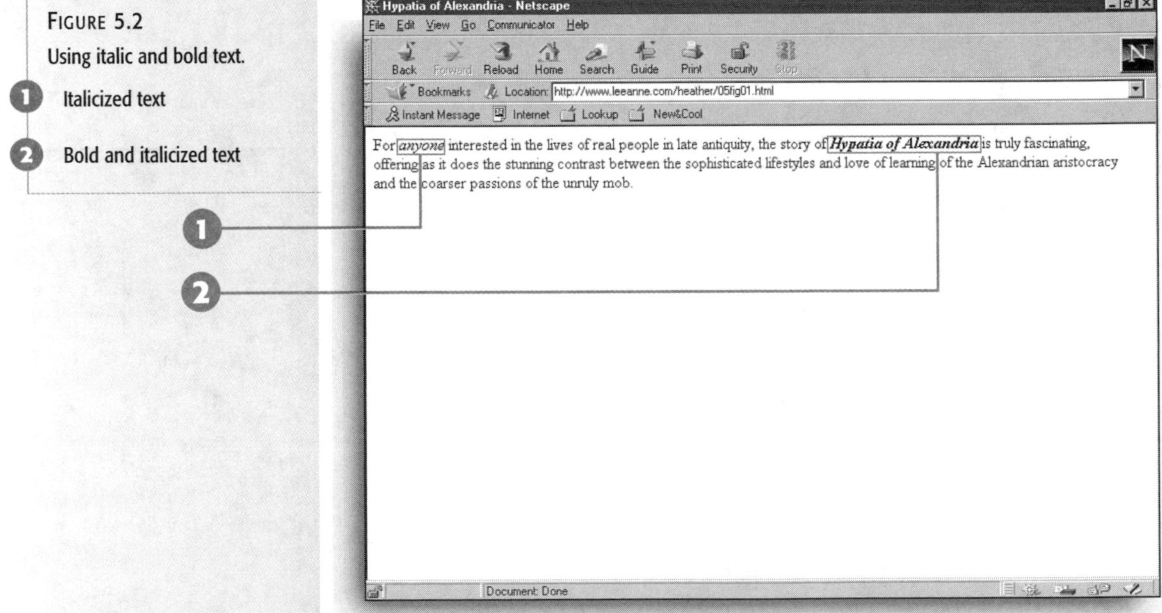

FIGURE 5.2
Using italic and bold text.
1. Italicized text
2. Bold and italicized text

Striking Out Text

Marking strikeout text

1. Create strikeout text with the `<STRIKE>` tag.

```
Retail Price: <STRIKE>$159.95</STRIKE>
```

2. Alternatively, you could use the `<S>` tag to accomplish the same result.

```
Retail Price: <S>$159.95</S>
```

Quick usage tip: Tag syntax

`<S>` *...strikeout text...* `</S>` or
`<STRIKE>` *...strikeout text*
...`</STRIKE>`

There are two tags that render strikeout text, and there's little difference between them. The shorter version is easier and quicker to type (`<S>`), while the longer version is self explanatory. Take your pick. `<STRIKE>` is perhaps more widely supported, but one uses the tag so rarely that I'm not sure it matters. Both versions of the tag are considered *interim* (advised against but allowed) in the newest version of HTML, version 4.0, and they may conflict with or duplicate the rendering of the new deleted text tag, `<DEL>`.

The only people who usually care about strikeout text are lawyers and legislators, who use it to show portions of legal language that have been repealed or deleted, and used car salesmen, who use it to prove that their prices are slashed, falling through the floor, and ridiculously cheap.

Here are two examples in one; the first part is a simulated Municipal Ordinance revision, and the second is the sort of display you see in a corner of the screen on the shopping channels on TV:

Section 1923.1 The Municipal Planning Commission authority to conduct public meetings regarding the implementation of the Shaker Village Draft Proposal is hereby repealed. ~~extends to April 21, 1998, at which time a~~ A completed plan will be prepared and presented to the full City Council no later than October 1, 1998.

Item Number:Q-13221

Retail Price: ~~$159.95~~

Acme Price: $29.95

Quantity On Hand: 23

Both of the examples are marked for strikeout text already, so the task consists on putting <P> tags at the start of each paragraph and then surrounding the text to be rendered in a strikeout font with the <STRIKE> tag and its mandatory closing tag.

```
<P>
  Section 1923.1 The Municipal Planning Commission authority
to conduct public meetings regarding the implementation of
the Shaker Village Draft Proposal is hereby
repealed.<STRIKE>extends to April 21, 1998, at which time
a</STRIKE> A completed plan will be prepared and presented
to the full City Council no later than October 1, 1998.
<P>
  Item Number:Q-13221
<P>
  Retail Price: <STRIKE>$159.95</STRIKE>
<P>
  Acme Price: $29.95
<P>
  Quantity On Hand: 23
```

Figure 5.3 shows how both examples look onscreen.

We'll revisit this example in the next section, "Underlined Text," to finish marking it up with underlines to show insertions or emphasis.

Underlined Text

Underlining a word or phrase

Create a homey sort of emphasis in your text by underlining with the <U> tag.

Quick usage tip: Tag syntax

```
<U> ...underlined text...</U>
<U>Shoppers!</U> Act Now For <U>BIG</U> Savings On Acme
Orange Juice!
```

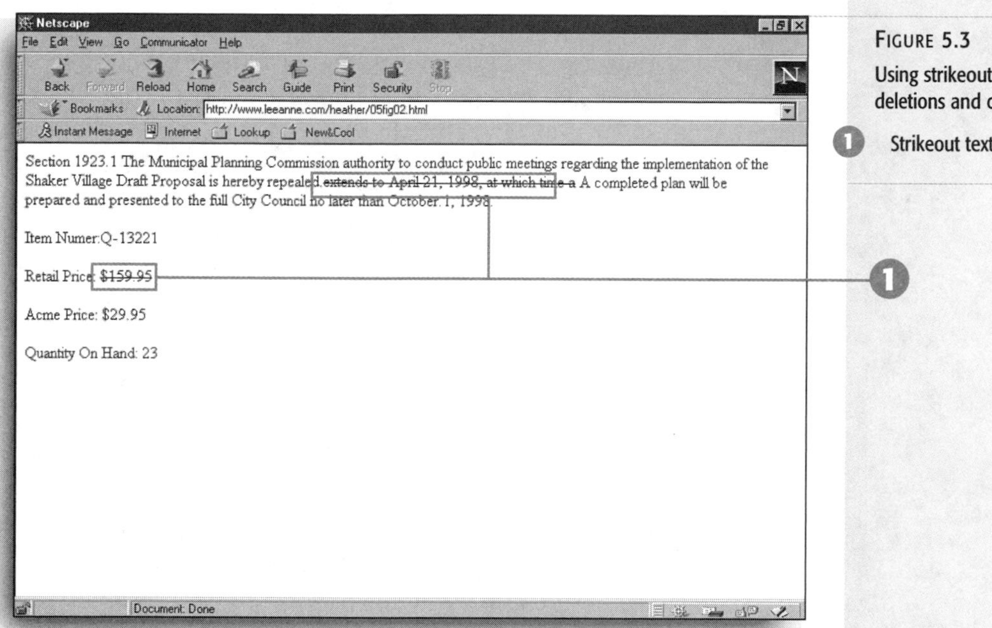

FIGURE 5.3
Using strikeout text to show deletions and changes.

1 Strikeout text

Underline text is another of those tags that isn't really used all that much. It's a homey sort of emphasis, though, and it might be useful on a personal home page or anywhere that traditional typographic emphasis styles might seem too polished. It's sometimes used to show inserted text, so it can make a good companion for the strikeout tags in the previous section, "Striking Out Text."

Underlined text has some problems though, in my opinion at least. For many people it may look like a hypertext link and be confusing, since that's the default method of indicating a link in most browsers. In addition, the rendering of underlined text may conflict with the new inserted text tag, `<INS>`, since rendering of inserted text is often done in underline or sometimes bold or italic. The new HTML 4.0 standard calls the underline tag *deprecated*, which means they advise against using it or think that there are better ways to do the same thing.

On the other hand, everyone recognizes underlining as a naive or hand-drawn way to make words stand out, so it may be a good way to make your page look informal and folksy. If you don't mix hyperlinks and underlining in the same location on the page, it ought to be easy enough to figure out anyway. Here's an example you might see on a supermarket page. It's so simple that I've shown the HTML code immediately following it. Surrounding the text that should be underlined with the <U> tag and its mandatory </U> tag will render correctly in most recent browsers.

```
Shoppers! Act Now For BIG Savings On Acme Orange Juice!
<P>
  <U>Shoppers!</U> Act Now For <U>BIG</U> Savings On Acme
Orange Juice!
```

While we're at it, let's update the strikeout text from the previous example in the "Striking Out Text" section as well, since inserted text is often shown in an underlined font.

```
<P>
  Section 1923.1 The Municipal Planning Commission authority
to conduct public meetings regarding the implementation of
the Shaker Village Draft Proposal <U>is hereby
repealed.</U><STRIKE> extends to April 21, 1998, at which
time a</STRIKE><U> A completed plan will be prepared and
presented to the full City Council no later than October 1,
1998.</U>
<P>
  Item Number:Q-13221
<P>
  Retail Price: <STRIKE>$159.95</STRIKE>
<P>
  Acme Price:<U>$!29.95</U>
<P>
  Quantity On Hand: 23
```

Figure 5.4 shows the completed display of both examples.

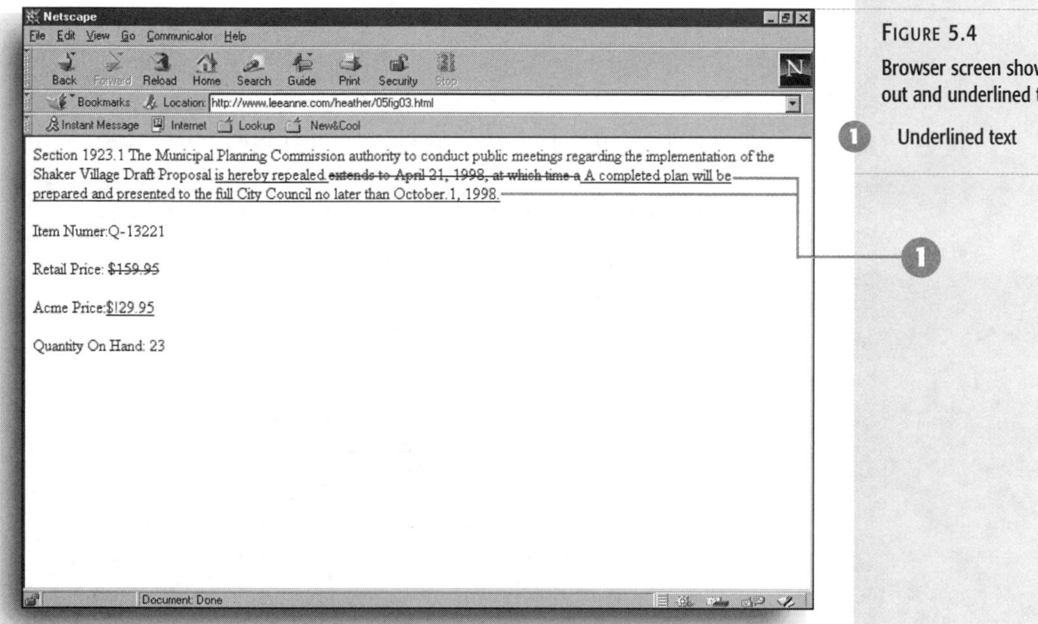

FIGURE 5.4
Browser screen showing strike-out and underlined text.

1 Underlined text

Big Text, Small Text: A Safe Way to Change Font Size

Making big text or small text

1. Change the size of the enclosed text with the <BIG> tag.
```
<BIG>ACME CORPORATION</BIG>
```
2. Use the <SMALL> tag to make the text size small.
```
<SMALL>This text will be smaller than the rest</SMALL>
```

Quick usage tip: Tag syntax

```
<BIG> ...big text...</BIG> or <SMALL> ...small
text...</SMALL>
```

There are several ways to change the size of text in your document. The `size` attribute of the <FONT> tag is one, style sheets are another, and the two tags discussed in this section are a third. Like most of the physical tags, their use is very intuitive. You put the opening tag at the beginning of the text you want to make bigger or smaller and then place the mandatory closing tag at the end of that text.

A little later in this chapter, we'll use one of these tags, the <SMALL> tag, in combination with another to create a true superscript and a subscript. But for now let's use them in isolation.

Here's one I'm sure you'll recognize.

```
ACME CORPORATION
LIMITED WARRANTY
Whereas, that in consideration of the payment of goods or
specie in the form of cash payment or credit card transac-
tion, the party of the first part, known herein as SELLER,
transfers all title, claim and possibility of recourse...
```

And so on, and so on. We usually call this sort of quasi-legal gobbledygook fine print, so our first inclination, to get this stuff out of our sight, isn't all that far off. While we may not be able to render it completely invisible, we can at least make it a little harder to see by shrinking the text size with the <SMALL> tag. Hooray!

But the Board of Directors will want the name of the company to remain visible. In fact it might be wise to make it even bigger, so we'll use the <BIG> tag to do that.

```
<P>
  <BIG>ACME CORPORATION</BIG>
<P>
  LIMITED WARRANTY
<P>
  <SMALL>Whereas, that in consideration of the payment of
goods or specie in the form of cash payment or credit card
transaction, the party of the first part, known herein as
SELLER, transfers all title, claim and possibility of
recourse...</SMALL>
```

Figure 5.5 shows the result.

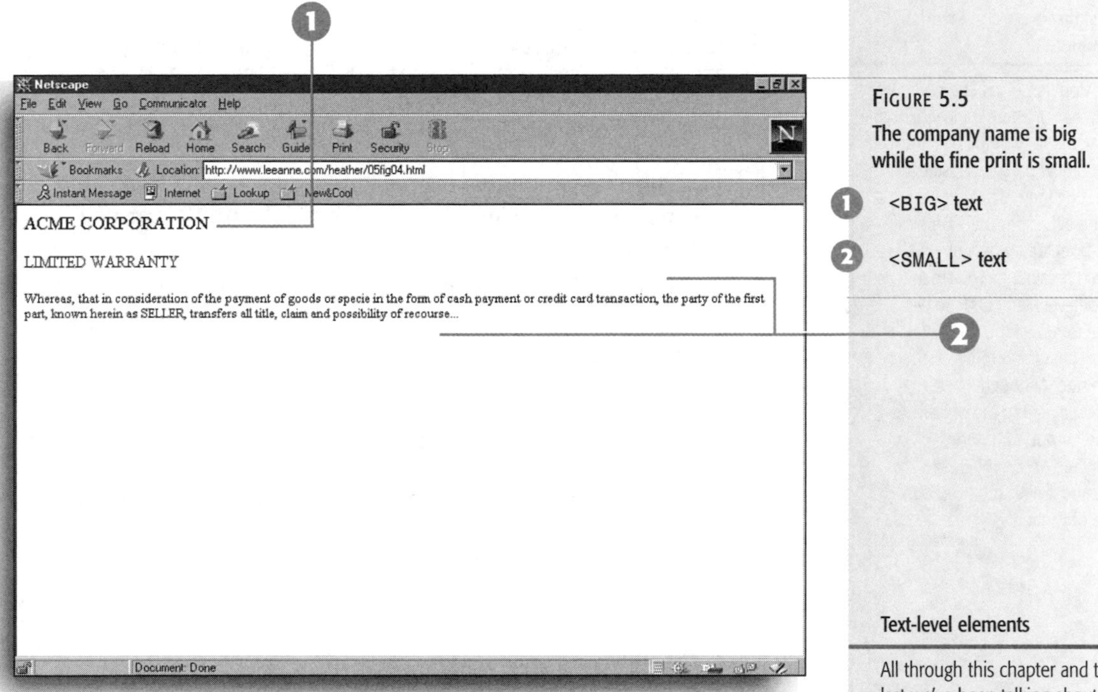

FIGURE 5.5
The company name is big while the fine print is small.

1. <BIG> text
2. <SMALL> text

Simulating Typewriter Text

Simulating typewriter text

1. Simulate typewriter-style text with the typewriter text tag, `<TT>`.

   ```
   <TT>Hi Joe,</TT>
   ```

   Quick usage tip: Tag syntax

   ```
   <TT> ...typewriter text...</TT>
   ```

Actually, the name of the tag should be Teletype, since that's the actual machine the tag is designed to emulate, but hardly anyone has heard of those antique clattering monsters in today's world. There are quite a few who've probably never used a typewriter. I know it's been a while since I've seen one, although I think I used to have one in a box somewhere in the garage. This physical style can be used for anything that one would expect to find written or typed by hand. It's usually rendered in Courier or another monospaced font. The closing tag is mandatory.

Text-level elements

All through this chapter and the last we've been talking about text treatments that you can put anywhere in your code and the text just keeps flowing, changed in appearance maybe, but still the same paragraph or whatever. That kind of tag can go almost anywhere without a problem. The only trouble is that there are other kinds of tags, called block-level elements, that can't go inside a text-level element, in theory at least. A `<P>` tag is a block-level element; it cuts off the flow of text, inserts a blank line, and starts over. This sounds way more complicated than it is, but basically, both physical and logical text markup should end at the paragraph boundary, just like the text itself. When you start a new paragraph you *should* start all over again. Most current browsers are not so finicky, but future browsers may be.

Most browsers don't work like they should

The trouble begins and ends with the <P> tags. Since they break the flow of the text and start a new paragraph, strictly speaking they're not allowed inside either physical or logical text-level tags, which operate within paragraphs (or other block-level elements). So we have to repeat the <TT> tag in every paragraph to be on the safe side. Although most browsers ignore the official content models, future browsers may not be as forgiving, and it pays to err on the side of caution.

```
Hi Joe,
This is just a quick note to remind you to finish up the
contract for the Jones account, Our meeting with their nego-
tiating team is this coming Friday!
Adam
```

This example is going to show a special rule as well that quite often applies when using HTML. You might think that you could just put a <TT> tag at the beginning of the selection and then another when you come to the end. Unfortunately, although this may work in some browsers, strictly speaking it's against the rules.

```
<P>
  <TT>Hi Joe,</TT>
<P>
  <TT>This is just a quick note to remind you to finish up
the contract for the Jones account, Our meeting with their
negotiating team is this coming Friday!
  </TT>
<P>
  <TT>Adam</TT>
```

Figure 5.6 shows the result.

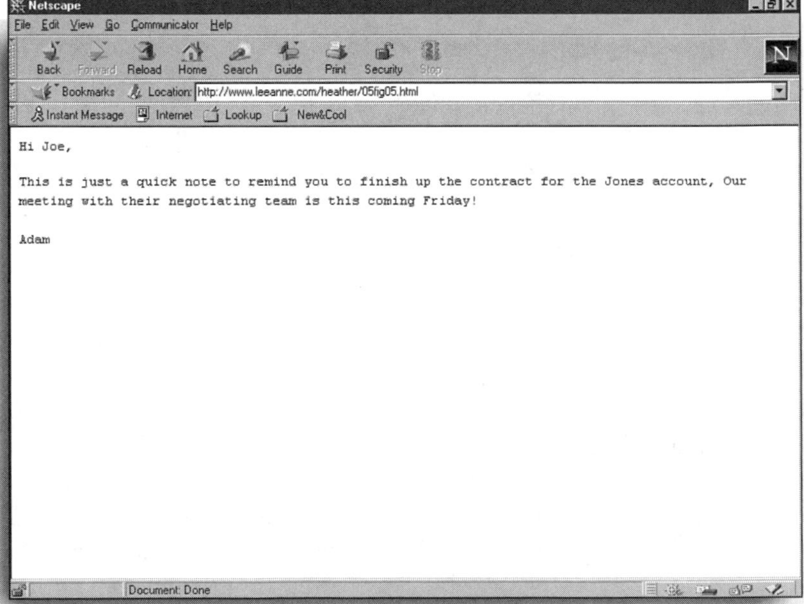

FIGURE 5.6
A memo represented in a typewriter (Teletype) font.

Adding Subscripts and Superscripts

Adding superscripts and subscripts

1. Create superscripts in your text with a simple <SUP> tag.

```
Principal Author: M<SUP>lle</SUP> Sophie Robards, PhD
```

2. Subscript text is created with the <SUB> tag.

```
Oxygen Isotope Exchange Between CO<SUB>2</SUB> and
H<SUB>2</SUB>O
```

3. Reduce the size of the superscript and subscript text with the <SMALL> tag.

```
H<SUP><SMALL>2</SMALL></SUP>O in the Lower Atmosphere
```

Quick usage tips: Tag syntax

```
<SUP> ...superscript text...</SUP>
```

or

```
<SUB> ...subscript text...</SUB>.
<SMALL>sub or superscript text</SMALL>
```

The smaller font size can also be set by means of style sheets.

Subscript and superscript tags should enclose a smaller font

<SUP> and <SUB> tags are often annoyingly obtrusive. Whenever possible, you should make the enclosed subscript or superscript smaller, so that the visual line of the text is well ordered. Do this with the <SMALL> tag or with style sheets.

Superscripts don't sound like much until you realize that we use and see them every day in abbreviations on street signs, for one common example. In almost every town in America there's a street sign that looks like this: Main S^{t}—and probably a church named St Stephen's, or something very like it.

They're also the way we usually show footnotes, an obvious application on the Web, and other handy things. You don't know how much you miss them until you run across the need to use them and can't. Subscripts aren't used as much in English, unless you're a chemist or mathematician, but you need them badly when you are. Almost everybody recognizes at least one subscripted chemical formula, good old H_2O, water. It's just not the same if you write it as H2O.

Until fairly recently, many browsers didn't support either text treatment. Support is still not universal, but it's common enough that we can safely use it in our pages, since the text is usually quite understandable even if the position and size of the character aren't changed.

Quite often, you'll want to use other tags in tandem with the subscript and superscript tags, since we usually expect the text to be in a smaller size. You can use any of several ways to do this: the deprecated <FONT> tag, <SMALL>, or style sheets. In our example, we'll try it both ways so that you can see the difference it makes on the page.

```
Oxygen Isotope Exchange Between CO2 and H2O in the Lower
Atmosphere
Principal Author: Mlle Sophie Robards, PhD
Graduate Assistant: Thomas Franz, MS
St Francis Xavier School of Meteorology
Bldg G1, 245 Therapod St, St Paul, MN
Oxygen Isotope Exchange Between CO2 and H2O in the Lower
Atmosphere
Principal Author: Mlle Sophie Robards, PhD
Graduate Assistant: Thomas Franz, MS
St Francis Xavier School of Meteorology
Bldg G1, 245 Therapod St, St Paul, MN
```

Walking through the text, we can see several opportunities to tag for both super- and subscripts. The 2 in CO2 and H2O should be subscripted, as should the lle in the French abbreviation for Mademoiselle, Mlle; the t in St Francis and the two t's in the St that abbreviates both Street and Saint in the last line could be superscripted. The first time through, we'll just tag the superscripts and subscripts in both copies of the text, and then we'll take the second and add <small> tags to each of them so we can judge what appeals to our own eye.

```
Oxygen Isotope Exchange Between CO<SUB>2</SUB> and H<SUB>2
  </SUB>O in the Lower Atmosphere<BR>
Principal Author: M<SUP>lle</SUP> Sophie Robards, PhD<BR>
Graduate Assistant: Thomas Franz, MS<BR>
S<SUP>t</SUP> Francis Xavier School of Meteorology<BR>
Bldg G1, 245 Therapod S<SUP>t</SUP>, S<SUP>t</SUP> Paul,
  MN<BR>

Oxygen Isotope Exchange Between CO<SUP><SMALL>2</SMALL>
  </SUP> and H<SUP><SMALL>2</SMALL></SUP>O in the Lower
  Atmosphere<BR>
Principal Author: M<SUP><SMALL>lle</SMALL></SUP> Sophie
Robards, PhD<BR>
```

```
Graduate Assistant: Thomas Franz, MS<BR>
S<SUP><SMALL>t</SMALL></SUP> Francis Xavier School of
  Meteorology<BR>
Bldg G1, 245 Therapod S<SUP><SMALL>t</SMALL></SUP>,
  S<SUP><SMALL>t</SMALL></SUP> Paul, MN<BR>
```

Looking at Figure 5.7, I think you'll agree that making the abbreviation elements smaller helps make them less obtrusive on the page and is an improvement.

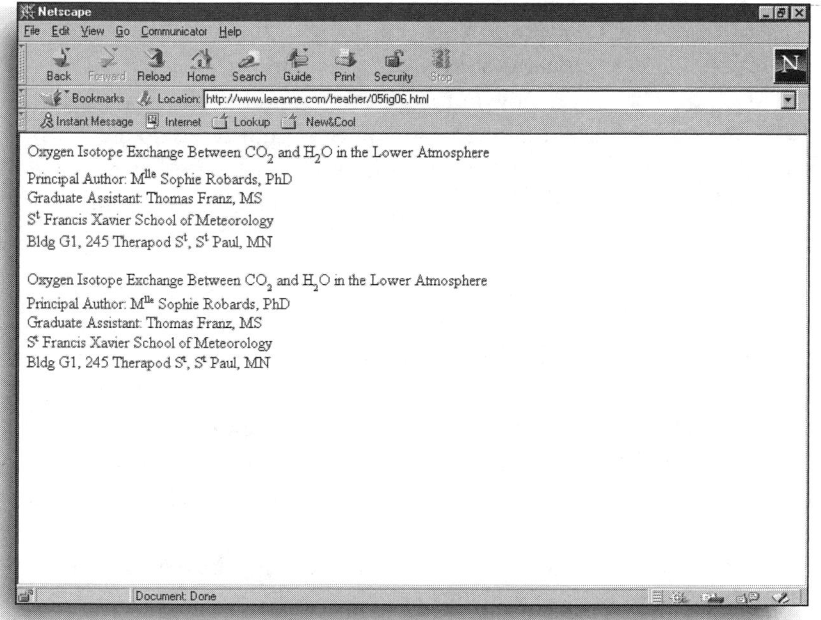

FIGURE 5.7
The listings as they appear with super- and subscript.

Using Line Breaks

Using a line break to alter text flow

1. Create a break in the flow of text with the break tag, `<BR>`.

   ```
   Though they are only breath,<BR>
     words that I speak are immortal.
   ```

   Quick usage tip: Tag syntax

   ```
   <BR clear="clearvalue">
   ```

   where *`clearvalue`* can be `left`, `all`, `right`, or `none`. The default value is `none`.

2. Set the clear attribute to left, all, right, or none to stop the text from flowing around an image.

```
<IMG src="picture.gif" height="50" width="50" vspace="8"
hspace="8" align="left">
  This text will appear beside the image but by using
the clear attribute we<BR clear="left"> make this line
start after the image on the left side of the page<BR>
```

Break is as handy a tool as you're likely to use on your pages, as it does basically one thing and does it very well. The <BR> tag does an immediate carriage return and takes the text cursor back to the current margin, whatever that is, so the next line starts immediately below the start of the previous line. Unlike most tags that break the flow of text, it doesn't add any line spacing and is a text-level treatment, so you can use it freely to control the layout of text on the page without closing out other tags. It acts just like a typewriter carriage return and has no closing tag because it acts immediately.

If you want to present a link directly below a description, for example, a break will bring you back to the margin without adding an extra blank line, which a <P> tag would do whether you wanted it to or not. Using the <BR> tag is so intuitive that it doesn't really need much in the way of an example, but it does have one attribute that can be a little confusing, the BREAK attribute. This attribute is deprecated by the newest version of HTML, version 4.0, but can be handy, so we'll use it once or twice to show how it works and then sum up, since we're nearly at the end of this chapter.

**
 tags look like paragraph tags visually**

You can use two <BR> tags in a row to simulate a paragraph break without losing the scope of other text-level tags. That's really convenient in many cases, and you see it done all the time.

First, let's put some breaks in a stanza of poetry, which must be chopped at exact line lengths but shouldn't have extra line spaces added—a perfect use for <BR> tags.

```
Though they are only breath,
words that I speak are immortal.
```

Turning those into a legal HTML fragment is easy. Just put a <P> tag in front and a <BR> tag after the first line:

```
<P>
  Though they are only breath,<BR>
  words that I speak are immortal.
```

If your text is formatted the way you want it to look on the page, almost always a good idea if possible, putting in the tags is a mechanical process. No problem at all. See the result in Figure 5.8.

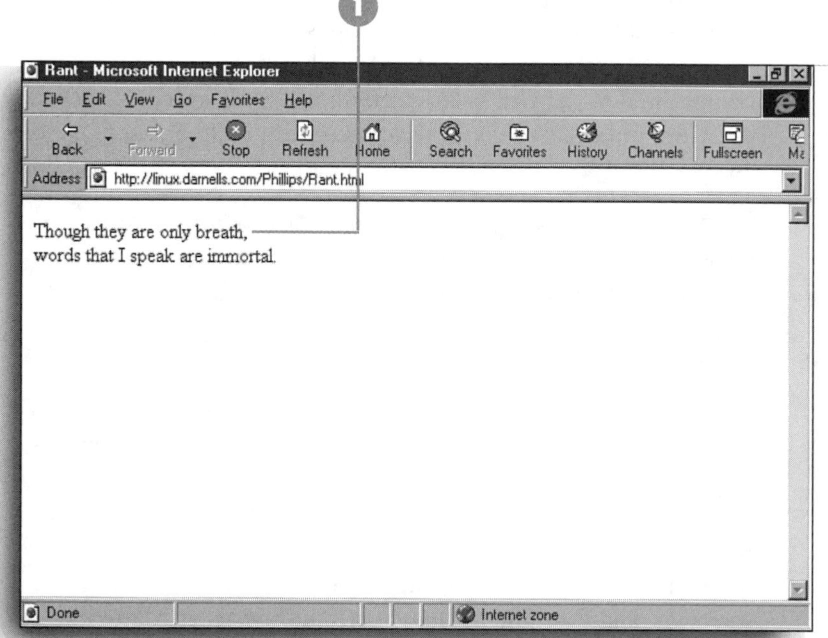

FIGURE 5.8
The <BR> tag allows a line to break without the extra space added by paragraphs.

1. Line break added here with <BR> tag

But people are never satisfied with one capability and are always fiddling around trying to do different things with it. Someone noticed that you couldn't easily use this trick to make text behave next to pictures. Drat! For complex historical reasons, text behaves differently around pictures, and if you wanted to put some text, but not all, around a picture, things didn't work well. So they added two attributes, one to the `<IMG>` tag to make the text flow around the picture as if it were a bump on the margin (which I explain fully in Chapter 8, "Adding Images to a Web Page") and one to the `<BR>` tag, to turn off the flowing behavior they just created with the `<IMG>` tag attribute. The attribute on the `<BR>` tag is called `clear`, and it takes four possible values, `left`, `right`, `all`, and `none`.

left says to break (or move) the text down to the real left margin beyond the image. right says break down to the real right margin. all says to break until you clear all images on both the left and right. And none, the default, says to behave normally, which is to do whatever the browser would do if you hadn't written the tag attribute in the first place. Of course this means you usually won't actually use none. This attribute is deprecated in HTML 4.0, so use it with caution, but it does things that are rather more complicated to do with style sheets and is more widely supported. More information about style sheets can be found in Chapter 14.

Now comes the tricky part, especially since we'll have to use something you may not be familiar with yet, a graphic image. You can refer to Chapter 8 if you want more depth, but for now we'll just use one without talking too much about it. Pay no attention to that woman behind the curtain.

In the following bit of code, which might represent an ordinary sort of business letterhead with a logo and address in the upper-left portion of the page, we're telling the browser that we want an image to line up on the left side of the screen and then flow text down the edge of it as if it were a new margin. We then insert three lines, spaced one after the other with two ordinary <BR> tags, and finish by breaking with the special attribute that says we want to break all the way to the bottom of the image and over to the real margin again. Whew! It's easier to show than to describe.

```
<P>
  <IMG src="wr-logo.gif" height="100" width="100" vspace=
    "10" hspace="10" align="left">
  4200 Avenida Alvarez - Suite 250<BR>
  Los Madres, CA  92000<BR>
  USA<BR clear="left">
  Dear Customer,
<P>
  Welcome to the Los Madres page of...
```

Figure 5.9 shows the result.

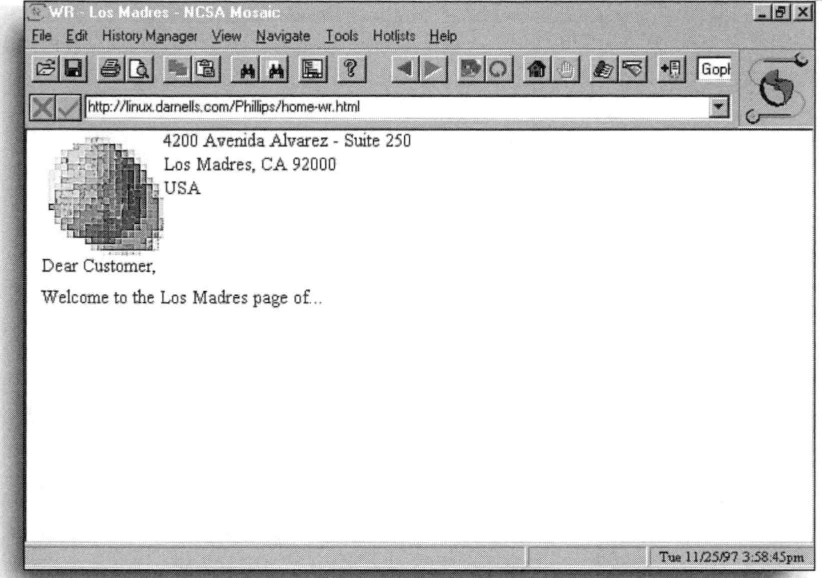

FIGURE 5.9
An image inserted into the letterhead with line breaks to flow the address down the side of the logo.

CHAPTER

6

Creating Lists

Organizing your data with lists

Using numbered lists

Using bulleted lists

Other list types

Lists Organize Information

Lists! They say that the people who need lists can never find them, but obviously they didn't put them on the Web. You can always find things on the Web, even if you never lost them in the first place. Lists are a basic way of organizing data in a linear way, one item after another, and are very valuable for formatting data in an easy-to-use-and-understand way.

Making a Numbered List for Ordered Items

Make a numbered list

1. Create a numbered list with the ordered list tags.
2. Include list items with a single `<LI>` tag.
3. Nested lists can be created by starting another list, which can be of any type, immediately after a list item.

   Quick usage tip: Tag syntax

   ```
   <OL> ... list items... </OL>
   <LI>list item
   ```

Making a numbered list is probably the first thing you do when you have any complex task to perform, so naturally HTML allows us to make lists with numbers. A numbered list makes sense for any list where there is a logical order to the individual items or where you want to keep count of the total number easily. As an example, putting on your shoes and socks is easy as long as you remember to reverse the order they're usually said in, but try doing it shoes first and then socks! That would make a good numbered list, first socks, second shoes.

Or you might want to list all the people who've been invited to your birthday party. You know that you can only fit ten people into your living room, so a numbered list would be good for them as well.

Let's make a numbered list for the task of putting on shoes.

As usual, we'll start with plain text and then put tags around the words to make our example.

Shoe Installation Procedure

Insert left or right foot into one sock.

Insert opposite foot into another sock, preferably matching in color and type.

Insert left or right foot into a corresponding shoe and tie laces. Warning! Pain and difficulty walking can result if foot/shoe congruence is not carefully maintained.

Insert opposite foot into the other shoe (hopefully still maintaining color, style, and type) and tie laces.

To turn the text into valid HTML, we'll first put header tags, any level will do, around the title of the procedure. Then we'll precede the list itself with an <OL> tag and follow the list with the mandatory closing </OL> tag. Then the only thing that remains to do is to put <LI> in front of every item. The <LI> can take an optional closing tag but I don't like to, because it clutters your code and makes it harder to read. It's up to you though; some people prefer to close every tag, cross every t, and dot every i. As usual, I like to indent the list to show the structure of the code more clearly.

```
<H1>Shoe Installation Procedure</H1>
<OL>
  <LI>Insert left or right foot into one sock.
  <LI>Insert opposite foot into another sock, preferably
      matching in color and type.
  <LI>Insert left or right foot into a corresponding shoe
      and tie laces.
      Warning! Pain and difficulty walking can result if
      left and right foot/shoe congruence is not carefully
      maintained.
  <LI>Insert opposite foot into the other shoe and tie
      laces.
</OL>
```

Figure 6.1 shows how this list will look using the Netscape browser.

Using nested lists

Nested lists are a good way to break down a main task into subtasks, and HTML allows you to nest lists of any type as deep as makes sense. It's a good idea not to go too far down that road, though, because the list level gets very confusing, and each sublist is indented from the outer list, so the text of your list can easily get jammed up against the far margin. As a rule of thumb, two or three sub-levels is probably enough. We'll talk about nested lists in the "Nested Lists" section in this chapter, when we have more tools to work with.

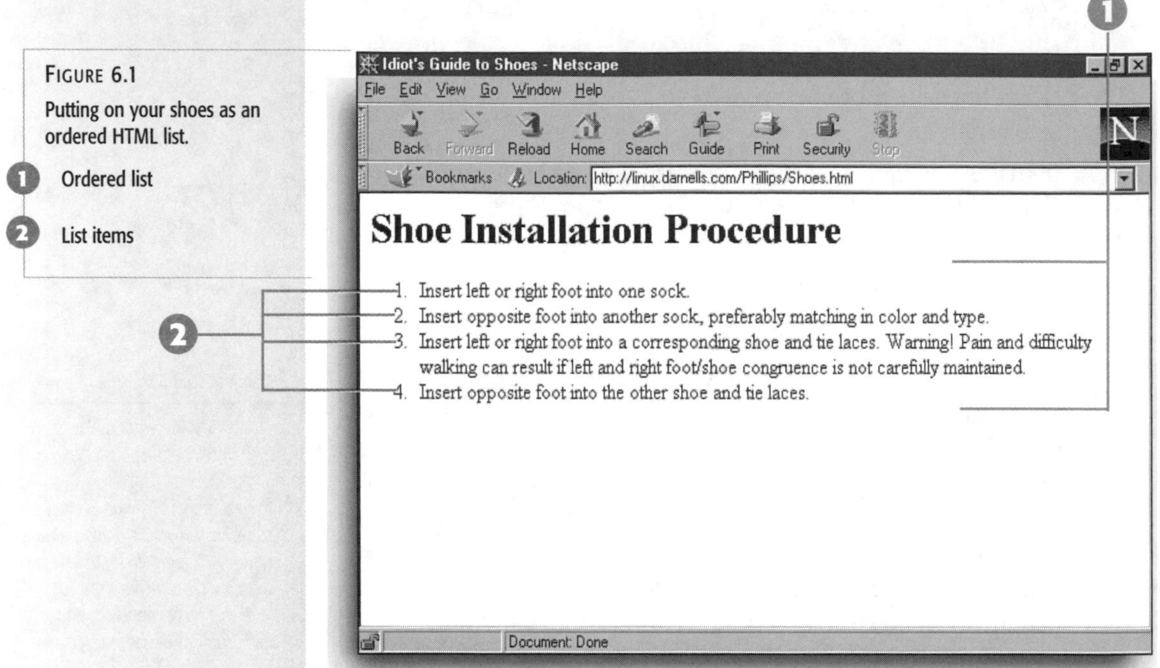

FIGURE 6.1
Putting on your shoes as an ordered HTML list.

1. Ordered list
2. List items

Using Different Numbering Systems

Changing the default numbering on an ordered list

1. Create an ordered list with the ordered list tags.

   Quick usage tip:Tag syntax

   ```
   <OL> ...list items... </OL>
   ```

2. Include list items with a single <LI> tag, selecting the numbering type and starting number.

   Quick usage tip:Tag syntax

   ```
   <LI type="listtype" start="number">list item
   ```

   where *listtype* is: A (capital letters), a (lowercase letters), I (capital Roman numerals), i (lowercase Roman numerals), or 1 (Arabic numbers), the default. *number* is always an Arabic number that changes the starting point of that item and all after.

3. Nested lists can be created by starting another list, which can be of any type, immediately after a list item.

By using optional attributes on the list tag, you can change the way the list looks. If you want your list to read A, B, C instead of 1, 2, 3, the `type=` attribute allows you to do that. You can even change the starting point of the list items at any point in the list, so you could use an ordered list to show a list with missing steps or one that starts out in midstream. This might be a valuable technique if you want to start a list at one point in your document, break off to discuss something more thoroughly, and then take up where you left off some time later.

Not every browser supports changing these default values, although most do, so it's a good idea to avoid talking about Item A, for example, since some people may see Item A as Item 1. If the list is small enough, you can say "the first item," "second item," and so on, without danger of confusing anyone.

Changing the numbering type is a good idea for lists involving numbers, or when the order isn't quite as important, as on a multiple-choice mathematics test.

As an example, we'll make an ordered list using letters instead of numbers. You guessed it, we start with text.

Question 1. What is the cube root of 27?

2.27950...

6

3

5.196152...

9

We'll use an ordinary paragraph to create the question, but we'll put it in boldface to make it stand out a little by preceding the question with a `<P>` tag and surrounding it with `<B>` and `</B>` tags. Then create the list by preceding the list of items with `<OL>` and following it with the mandatory `</OL>` tag.

Now comes the tricky part. You'll put an `<LI>` tag in front of every item, as usual, but you'll have to include a `type=` attribute on at least one to start the ball rolling. Of course that one is usually the first. Since we want our answers to be lettered instead of numbered, we should make the first list item tag look like this: `<LI type="A">`.

Change the default ordering marker

As an alternative, the `type` attribute can also be included with the `<OL>` tag. The powers that be, that is the W3C, would prefer us to use style sheets for all this, but this attribute is far more widely supported.

Numbering types have significance

The numbering type says a lot about the items on the list. Arabic numbers imply the greatest amount of order in the list, while Roman numerals and letters are not quite as strong. Upper- and lowercase say something about the importance of the items as well, so it pays to think about what makes sense for your own list.

There are several options we can use for the `type=` attribute. `A` selects uppercase letters, `a` is lowercase letters, `I` is uppercase Roman numerals, `i` is lowercase Roman numerals, and `1` is the default Arabic numbers. The only reason you'd have to use that last one is if you wanted to change the numbering from one of the other choices into numbers.

The rest of the items can use `<LI>` tags without attributes, because the browser will "remember" what numbering scheme is in use until the list ends.

```
<P><B>Question 1. What is the cube root of 27?</B>
<OL>
  <LI type="A">2.27950...
  <LI>6
  <LI>3
  <LI>5.196152...
  <LI>9
</OL>
```

This will look like Figure 6.2.

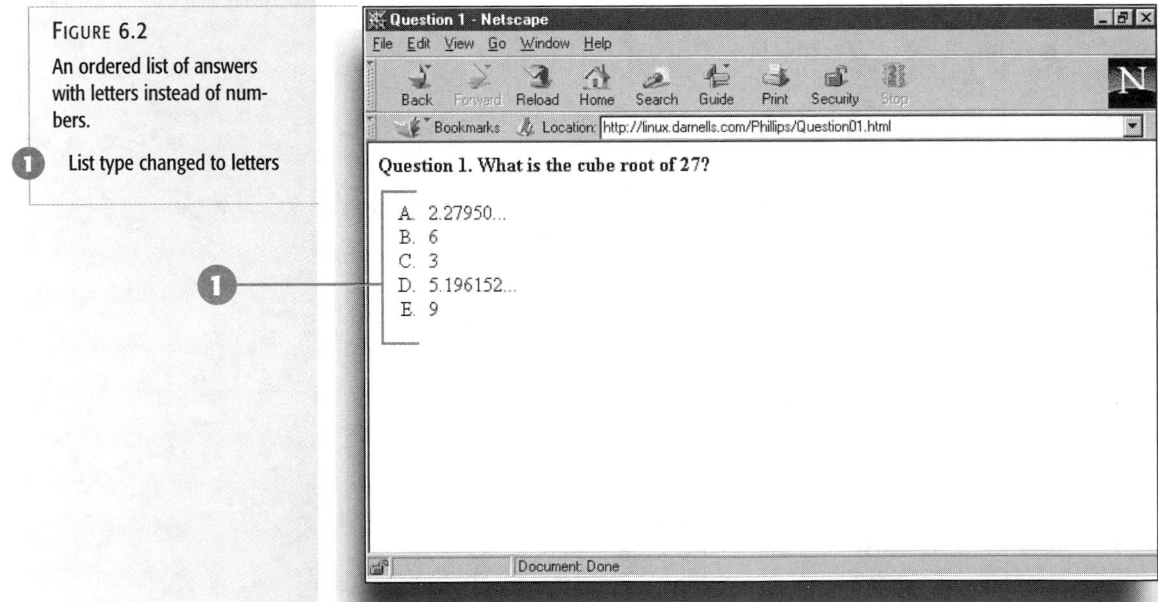

FIGURE 6.2

An ordered list of answers with letters instead of numbers.

1 List type changed to letters

If you want to change the starting number for a list, you use the `start=` attribute. You have to use an Arabic number for this attribute, even if the list type is alphabetic or Roman numerals, which can be confusing for those of us who don't remember exactly what Roman numeral XLIV really means. Let's see, if L is 50.... (This only sounds like a radio station; it's really 44, but then I cheated by looking it up in a dictionary.)

Creating a Bulleted List for Items Without a Logical Order

Create a bulleted list

1. Create a bulleted list with the unordered list tags.
2. Include list items with a single `<LI>` tag.
3. Nested lists can be created by starting another list, which can be of any type, immediately after a list item.

   Quick usage tip: Tag syntax

   ```
   <UL> ...list items...</UL>
   <LI>list item
   ```

Some lists have no order at all, or an order so weak that a numbered list doesn't really make sense. A good example might be important points about a product in a brochure, or a list of important historical figures. The bulleted list is made just for those kinds of displays, and they're even easier to use than numbered lists; since there are fewer options, a bullet is pretty much a bullet.

Let's jump right in and make a bulleted list.

Historical Figures in Mathematics and Geometry

Archimedes

Euclid

Hypatia

Plato

Pythagoras

Thales

Zeno of Elea

These names are alphabetized, but no particular order is necessary, so a bulleted list is perfect for them. Start by surrounding the title with a heading tag; the level doesn't matter. Then place an unordered list tag, <UL>, at the start of the list and the mandatory closing </UL> tag at the end. Put a list item tag, <LI>, in front of each item and we're done. My example is indented to show the actual structure of the text and this is a good idea in your own code as well. Here's what it looks like.

```
<H1>Historical Figures in Mathematics and Geometry</H1>
<UL>
  <LI>Archimedes
  <LI>Euclid
  <LI>Hypatia
  <LI>Plato
  <LI>Pythagoras
  <LI>Thales
  <LI>Zeno of Elea
</UL>
```

The display in Microsoft Internet Explorer is shown in Figure 6.3.

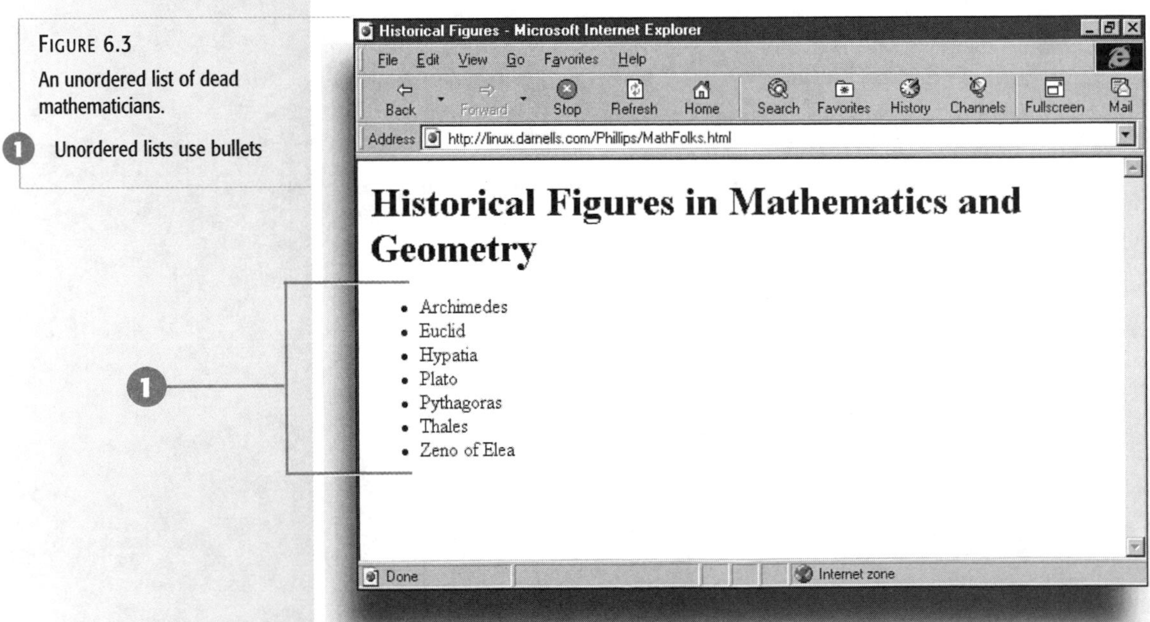

FIGURE 6.3
An unordered list of dead mathematicians.

1 Unordered lists use bullets

Changing Bullet Types

Create other document divisions

1. Create a bulleted list with the unordered list tags.

   Quick usage tip: Tag syntax

   ```
   <UL> ...list items...</UL>
   ```

2. Include list items with a single `<LI>` tag, selecting the bullet type.

   Quick usage tip:Tag syntax

   ```
   <LI type="listtype">list item
   ```

   where *listtype* is `circle` (a small open circle), `square` (a small solid square), or `disk` (a small solid disk), the default.

3. Nested lists can be created by starting another list, which can be of any type, immediately after a list item.

There are only three different types of bullets that can be selected by means of an attribute. Complicating the issue, though, is the fact that if you're using nested lists, most browsers cycle through a list of bullet types that may or may not be related to these types. See the section immediately following for more information on nested lists.

It's hard to imagine why one would actually want to change the default bullet type, unless it doesn't fit with a theme perhaps. The Four Square Marketing Seminar might want to use square bullets instead of circles to avoid sending a mixed message, for example. In ordinary use this is sort of a waste of time and can lead to confusion as well, since there is no inherent or logical order to the different types of bullets.

For the sake of completeness, we'll create a bulleted list with different bullets for each item, just for the exercise. Start with text.

Strange Ways

Circles Are Number One!

Squares Are Only Second Best

Disks Are Always Last

Because there's a logical relationship between the names of the items and the available bullet types (and you'd be surprised how rarely this happens in real life), we can use an appropriate dingbat for each.

Start by making a heading out of the title; then place a `<UL>` tag at the start of the list and the mandatory closing `</UL>` tag after. Then we'll place `<LI type="circle">` in front of the first item, `<LI type="square">` in front of the second item, and `<LI type="disc">` in front of the last. Please note that there is no way to make the bullet type revert to the default; once you start controlling it you have to continue if you want to change back. Because you don't really know what type of bullet the browser chooses in a nested list, this can be quite confusing unless you're very careful. But we'll talk about that in the very next section. Here's what the code looks like:

```
<H1>Strange Ways</H1>
<UL>
  <LI type="circle">Circles Are Number One!
  <LI type="square">Squares Are Only Second Best
  <LI type="disc">Discs Are Always Last
</UL>
```

Figure 6.4 shows what the display looks like in Internet Explorer.

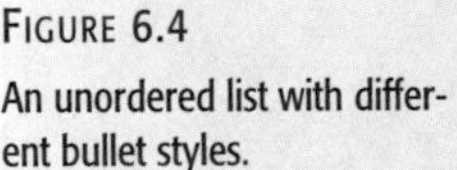

FIGURE 6.4
An unordered list with different bullet styles.

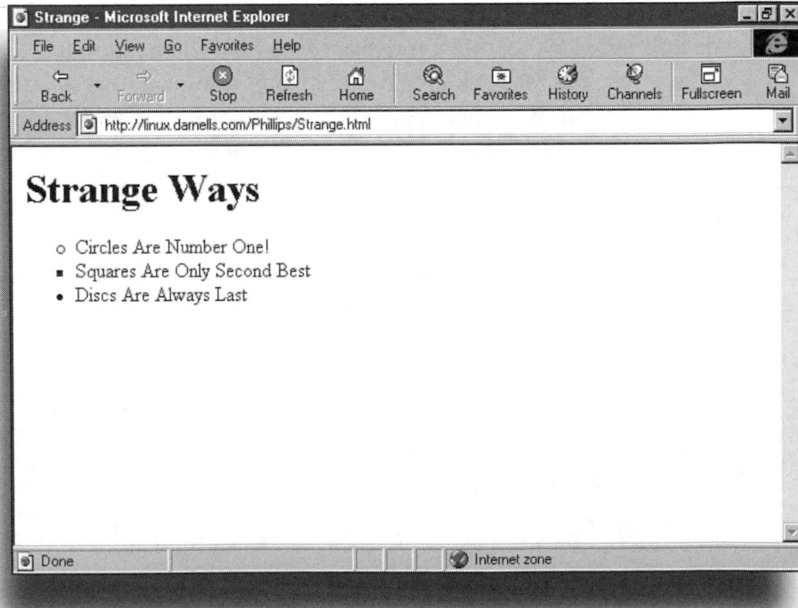

Nested Lists

Creating nested lists

1. Create an ordered or unordered list with the appropriate list tags.

   Quick usage tip: Tag syntax

   ```
   <OL> ...list items...</OL> or <UL> ...list items...</UL>
   ```

2. Include list items with a single `<LI>` tag, selecting the numbering type and starting number if appropriate.

   Quick usage tip: Tag syntax

   ```
   <LI type="listtype" start="number">list item
   ```

   where *`listtype`* is `A` (capital letters), `a` (lowercase letters), `I` (capital Roman numerals), `i` (lowercase Roman numerals), or `1` (Arabic numbers), the default, in an ordered list, or `circle` (a small open circle), `square` (a small solid square), or `disk` (a small solid disk), the default, in an unordered list. *`number`* is always an Arabic number that changes the starting point of that item and all after but has no purpose or effect in an unordered list.

3. Nested lists can be created by starting another list, which can be of any type, immediately after a list item. Go back to step one and repeat until finished with the nested list.

Lists can be quite complex when you stop to think about it; a task may be made of several smaller tasks that can be broken down into still smaller ones. It would be nice to be able to show this as clearly and automatically as possible, and HTML allows multiple levels of both ordered and unordered lists. Some combination can show almost any relationship one wants, from components to wholes.

To show how one such list might work, we'll use a familiar example, a travel itinerary. While the order of the trip is probably fixed, the individual activities available in a given location probably have no special order, so we'll use a combination of an ordered list and unordered sublists to show available activities in each of three cities on our trip.

Using nested lists

Nested lists show complex levels of authority or importance clearly, so they work well in any linear solution. But when items relate to more than one category, or the relationship between categories may change as time goes by, lists may not be the best choice. Consider using a table instead (see Chapter 15, "Creating Tables for Data").

Southwest Vacation

Phoenix

Golf

Sightseeing

Hot Air Balloon Festival

San Diego

Planetarium

Historic District

Harbor Cruise

Long Beach

Spruce Goose

Disneyland

Goodyear Blimp

The steps to create the outer list are very familiar by now, so we'll go over them quickly and then a little more slowly on the inner lists. First, make the title into a heading, then surround the entire list with opening and closing `<OL>` tags and insert list item tags in front of each first-level item.

Now insert unordered list opening and closing tags around each inner list, immediately after the list item that marks the outer list element and before the next first level item or the end of the list. Then, add a `<LI>` tag before each second level item. If you follow the steps carefully and work from one end or the other, it's not really too hard, especially if you leave the indents visible to keep from getting lost. Here's what the code should look like:

```
<H1>Southwest Vacation</H1>
<OL>
  <LI>Phoenix
  <UL>
    <LI>Golf
    <LI>Sightseeing
    <LI>Hot Air Balloon Festival
  </UL>
  <LI>San Diego
  <UL>
```

```
    <LI>Planetarium
    <LI>Historic District
    <LI>Harbor Cruise
  </UL>
  <LI>Long Beach
  <UL>
    <LI>Spruce Goose
    <LI>Disneyland
    <LI>Goodyear Blimp
  </UL>
</OL>
```

And you can see the result in Figure 6.5.

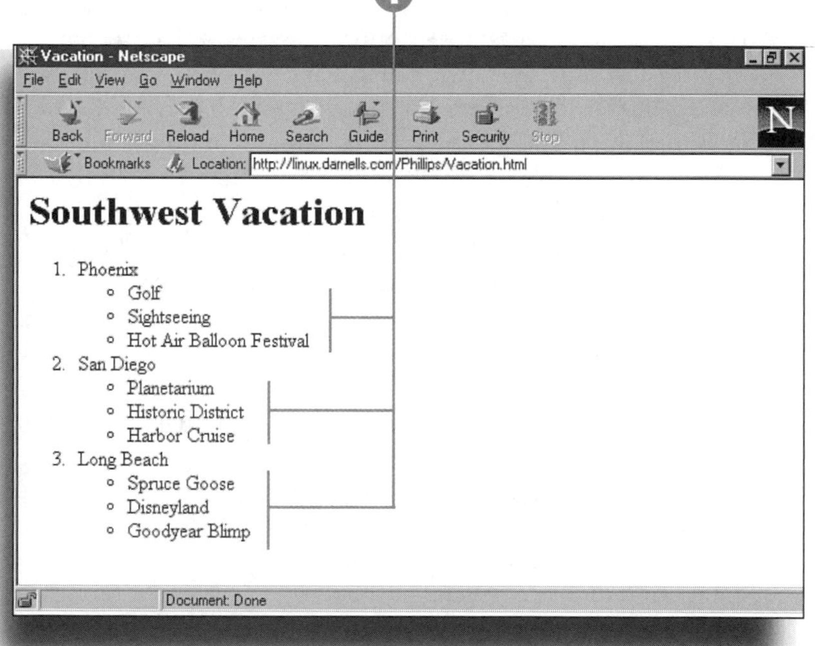

FIGURE 6.5
Unordered lists nested within an ordered list.

1 Nested unordered lists

This is cool stuff, and I'm sure you'll be able to see ways to use these techniques to format your own data in attractive and meaningful ways.

Using Definition Lists to Create a Glossary or Link List

Create a glossary or link list

1. Create a definition list with matching <DL> and </DL> tags; everything in between is part of the list.
2. Insert each definition term with a single <DT> tag.
3. Follow each definition definition with a single <DD> tag.

   Quick usage tips: Tag syntax

   <DL> *...terms and definitions, or other logically-related items...*</DL>

   <DT>*term* or *phrase*

   <DD>*definition*

Definition lists are ideal for creating glossaries, of course, but they are also very valuable for almost any list where you want a list of names or descriptive phrases to be followed by a value or other definition. Among the most useful ways of organizing a link list, for example, is simply using a definition list to format the name of each resource as the definition term and the Web location as a hyperlinked URL. Let's see how that could be done using our Friends of Hypatia page. As usual, we start with indented text.

Using definition lists to create glossaries

Glossaries are simple lists of terms and their meanings, which is what definition lists were designed for. But like so much in HTML, this element can be used as a powerful formatting tool to create many types of list in which every term or phrase is followed by another related term or phrase.

```
Friends of Hypatia Link List
  Biography of Hypatia
    http://www.lib.virginia.edu/science/parshall/hypatia.html
  Hypatia
    http://hypatia.ucsd.edu/~kl/hypatia.html
  Hypatia of Alexandria
    http://cosmopolis.com/people/hypatia.html
  The Martyrdom of Hypatia
    http://www.chewable.com/hypatian/hypatia.htm
  Hypatia of Alexandria
    http://www.polyamory.org/~howard/Hypatia/
  Harvard University Press Books
    http://www.hup.harvard.edu/F96Books/F96Long/hypatia.html
  A Review of Maria Dzielska's Hypatia of Alexandria
    http://www.cybergrrl.com/review/gb0796.html#Hypatia
```

This is the only type of list that doesn't use the list item tag for its members. Instead there are two item tags, one of which marks a definition term, <DT>, and the other of which marks a definition definition, <DD>. I apologize for the ungainly name for the <DD> tag, but they didn't ask me about it when they chose the name.

The process of tagging a definition list is just the same as any list really, except that there are two type of items: terms and definitions. We'll use terms as the name of the resource and definitions as the actual Web address of the link. We'll also make the addresses "clickable," so we'll use information from Chapter 7, "Adding Links," to create the hyperlinks, in addition to the three types of definition list tags themselves.

Let's skip over the process of tagging the hyperlinks, although you can familiarize yourself with the process in Chapter 7 if need be, and assume that we know how to do that. To tag the list itself, surround the entire list with the definition list open and mandatory closing tags, <DL> and </DL>, and then simply step down the list, tagging the items with definition term and definition definition tags based on their indentation levels. The first-level indents all get <DT>, while the second-level indents all get <DD>. It's really quite simple when the text is formatted beforehand.

SEE ALSO

➤ *Adding links, see page 117*

Here's what the finished code looks like:

```
<H1>Friends of Hypatia Link List</H1>
<DL>
  <DT>Biography of Hypatia
    <DD><A href="http://www.lib.virginia.edu/science/
    parshall/hypatia.html"
    >http://www.lib.virginia.edu/science/parshall/hypatia.html</A>
  <DT>Hypatia
    <DD><A href="http://hypatia.ucsd.edu/~kl/hypatia.html"
    >http://hypatia.ucsd.edu/~kl/hypatia.html</A>
  <DT>Hypatia of Alexandria
    <DD><A href="http://cosmopolis.com/people/hypatia.html"
    >http://cosmopolis.com/people/hypatia.html</A>
```

```
    <DT>The Martyrdom of Hypatia
      <DD><A href="http://www.chewable.com/hypatian/hypatia.htm"
      >http://www.chewable.com/hypatian/hypatia.htm</A>
    <DT>Hypatia of Alexandria
      <DD><A href="http://www.polyamory.org/~howard/Hypatia/"
      >http://www.polyamory.org/~howard/Hypatia/</A>
    <DT>Harvard University Press Books
      <DD><A href="http://www.hup.harvard.edu/F96Books/F96Long/
       hypatia.html"
      >http://www.hup.harvard.edu/F96Books/F96Long/
       hypatia.html</A>
    <DT>A Review of Maria Dzielska's Hypatia of Alexandria
      <DD><A href="http://www.cybergrrl.com/review/
      gb0796.html#Hypatia"
      >http://www.cybergrrl.com/review/gb0796.html#Hypatia</A>
</DL>
```

The page itself is shown in Figure 6.6.

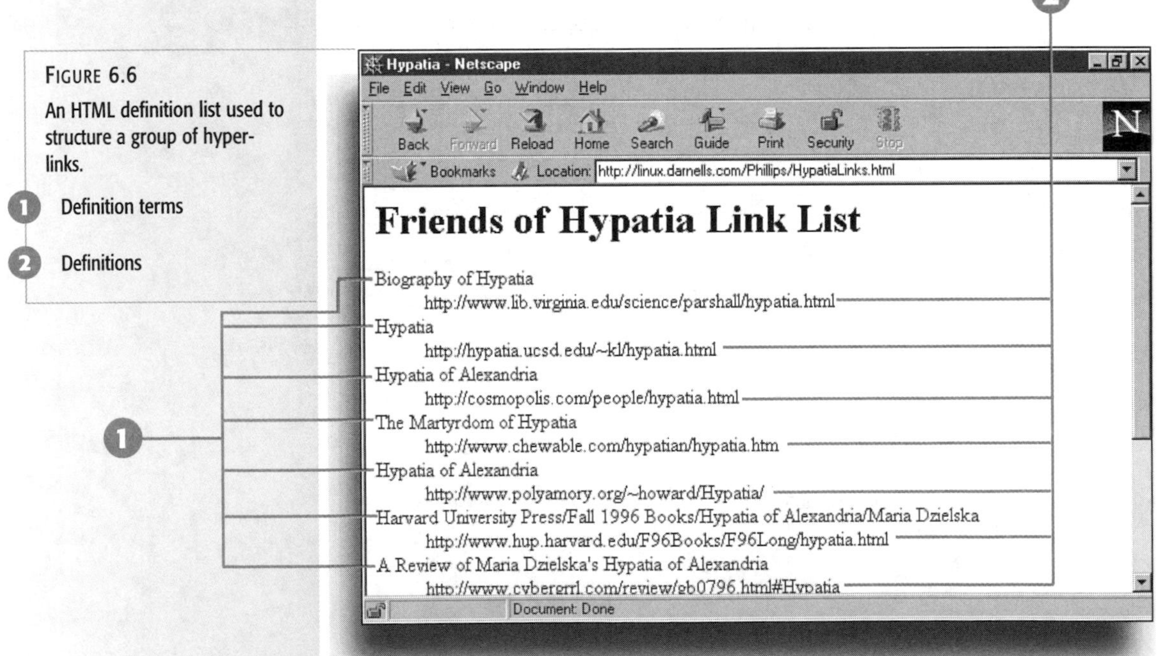

FIGURE 6.6
An HTML definition list used to structure a group of hyperlinks.

1 Definition terms

2 Definitions

Using Other List Types

Create menu and directory lists

1. Create a menu or directory list in your text with the menu and directory tags.
2. Include list items with a single `<LI>` tag.

   Quick usage tip: Tag syntax

   ```
   <MENU> ...list items...</MENU>
   ```

   or

   ```
   <DIR> ...list items...</DIR>
   ```

   Both of these elements are now considered interim measures and their use is discouraged.

   ```
   <LI>list item
   ```

The other list types are not much used anymore, although you still see them every once in a while. You should know how they're used so you can maintain them if you run across them, but avoid them in your own pages if possible. They're both rendered in exactly the same way in most browsers. In fact, most browsers render them as an unordered list, so there's really not much point in having two special tags.

Unlike the regular unordered list, however, the menu and directory elements should never include nested lists, or anything else really. We'll do one type, but the same steps apply to both. In fact, you could use the directions in the "Creating a Bulleted List for Items Without a Logical Order" section earlier in this chapter without harm as long as you don't try to include a sublist.

Store Directory

Ground Floor—Perfumes and Toiletries

First Floor—Soft furnishings

Second Floor—Women's Fashion Apparel

As usual, we'll tag the title with a heading and then surround the list with directory tags, <DIR> and </DIR>. Then we use our old standbys, the list item <LI> tags, to mark each item in our short list. That's it! Presto! Finito! Here it is as tagged:

```
<H1>Store Directory</H1>
<DIR>
  <LI>Ground Floor—Perfumes and Toiletries
  <LI>First Floor—Soft furnishings
  <LI>Second Floor—Women's Fashion Apparel
</DIR>
```

Figure 6.7 shows the result.

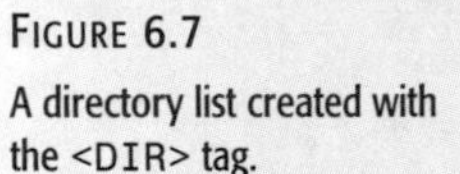

FIGURE 6.7
A directory list created with the <DIR> tag.

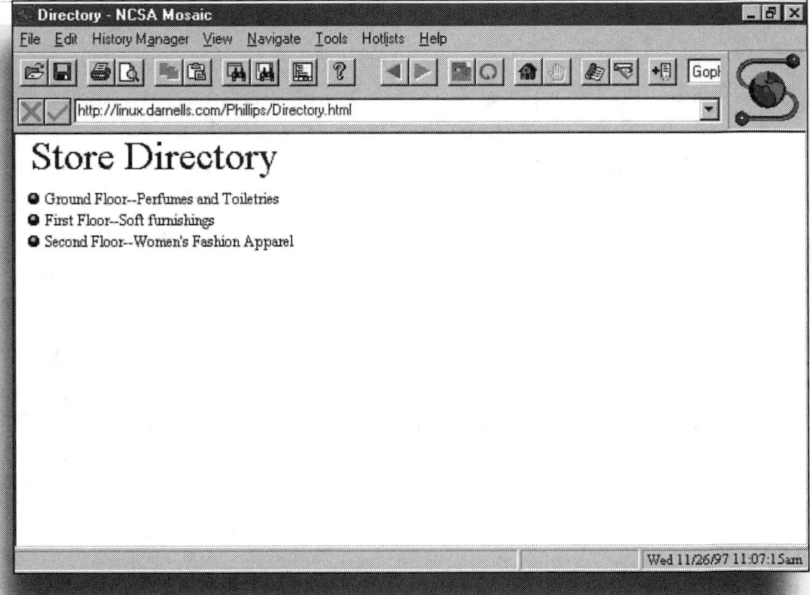

CHAPTER 7

Adding Links

Expand your site into the entire world!

Organize your site logically

Use smaller pages to improve load times

Using Links to Expand Your Page

Using links to connect to other pages

1. Create a link by surrounding the descriptive text or image with <A> tags.

```
<A> Link to Page 2 </A>
```

2. Identify the target of the link with the `href` attribute.

```
<A href="page2.html"> Link to Page 2 </A>
```

Quick usage tip: Tag syntax

```
<A href="target">...descriptive text and/or image...
</A>
```

where *target* is the location of the destination of the jump made from this link.

Pages should usually be kept small. People don't like scrolling, many browsers will bounce you out to the previous site if you try to page down while the cursor is in the location box, and long pages mean long load times, all of which are almost guaranteed to create problems for your users and encourage them to stay away in droves.

But if you have a lot of information to offer, you'll need to have lots of text! Catch-22! The answer of course is to break up long chunks of text into many pages. Before we do that though, let's think about how information is usually organized.

In a book, we have lots of text arranged in a very linear structure, one page after another in a long list of hundreds of pages. You can look at the table of contents and quickly flip through to the page you want. Or, if the table of contents doesn't give you enough detail, you can use an index to search out important words.

A Web page isn't like that. It has no sense of location (unless we choose to give it one) and no memory of things past. When we're on a particular page we can't flip forward or backward easily, and going through a hundred pages or more to find the one we want would try the patience of a saint. We need a new model.

As it happens, we don't have to look very far. When you open a book, the first thing you see after the title page is the table of contents. Although we use the table of contents in a linear manner in a book, one page after another, we don't have to do that in a Web site. We can jump directly to the start of the "chapter" we want using a hyperlink. Cool! And if the chapter needs to be subdivided into even smaller pages, all we have to do is provide another table of contents for the chapter. If we have 12 main headings and 12 subheadings under each, we can reach 144 pages in two jumps. Not bad. Not bad at all.

In the following sections we'll explore different kinds of links, but all will follow the same general pattern and use the same tag, the anchor tag, `<A>`. For now, we'll be concerned with only a few of the attributes the anchor tag can take, since we can do lots of things with just two. First we'll look at the `href` attribute, since that's the one we use all the time. In fact it almost defines the Web.

Using Formal Links to Define a Businesslike Site Structure

Create a list of list of links

1. Start with tags for a definition list.

```
<DL>
</DL>
```

2. Next add the text for your list items inside the `<DL>` tags.

```
<DL>
    Company Fact Sheet
    Product Information
    Contact Sales and Marketing
    Intelligent Translation Prototype Product Status
    24-hour by 7-day Customer Support
    The History of Machine Translation
</DL>
```

3. Create the links for each item by adding the `<A>` tags along with an `href` attribute.

```
<A href="faq.html">Fact Sheet</A>
<A href="prods.html">Product Information</A>
```

For a business or professional site, a formal presentation of external links, like a table of contents or an index, presents a thoughtful and well-organized image. You don't want your readers to have to wade through text looking for mysterious highlighted words to click and wonder where they're going to wind up. You need a disciplined navigation system that reflects the discipline of the workplace, with everything nicely organized and nothing out of place.

We already have a nice status report for our workgroup, so let's put that into the context of a workgroup home page. We'll link to the status report (without worrying too much about how that works) to show you the sorts of simple layouts that can be done right now, with only the very most basic tools available. We'll expand on this page later.

```
<H1>Aristotelian Logical Systems, Ltd.</H1>
<P>
  <STRONG>ALS</STRONG> is a world leader in machine
  translation software and offers the most comprehensive
  suite of translation engines with the best recognition
  of idiomatic constructs in the known universe.
<P>
  We want to help you, our present customers, as well as
  others interested in seeing how ALS products can power up
  international businesses as well as improve communications
  between the far-flung offices of global and trans-national
  businesses.
<P>
  Explore our site:
<DL>
  <DT><DD><A href="alsfaq.html">Company Fact Sheet</A>
  <DT><DD><A href="alsprods.html">Product Information</A>
  <DT><DD><A href="alssales.html">Contact Sales and
    Marketing</A>
  <DT><DD><A href="alsitpstatus.html">Intelligent
    Translation Prototype Product Status</A>
  <DT><DD><A href="alssupport.html">24-hour by 7-day
    Customer Support</A>
  <DT><DD><A href="alshistory.html">The History of Machine
    Translation</A>
```

```
</DL>
<ADDRESS>
  Contact the Webmaster: <STRONG>Webmaster@ALSLtd.com</STRONG>
</ADDRESS>
```

We used a definition list because they look very clean, without numbers or bullets cluttering the page. They also allow a second level of indentation below each term, which is exactly the effect I wanted for the list. Each of the links in the definition list uses the same format, a blank definition term followed by a definition that includes a link. The link is just an anchor tag with an `href` attribute pointing to a file. Between the anchor tag and its mandatory closing tag is the text we want to display that people can select to jump to that portion of the site. Folks, this isn't rocket science; these are just bookmarks that have a mind of their own. Ordinary book marks tell you where to open a book to find your information. Hypertext bookmarks open themselves when you select them. Figure 7.1 shows the code result onscreen.

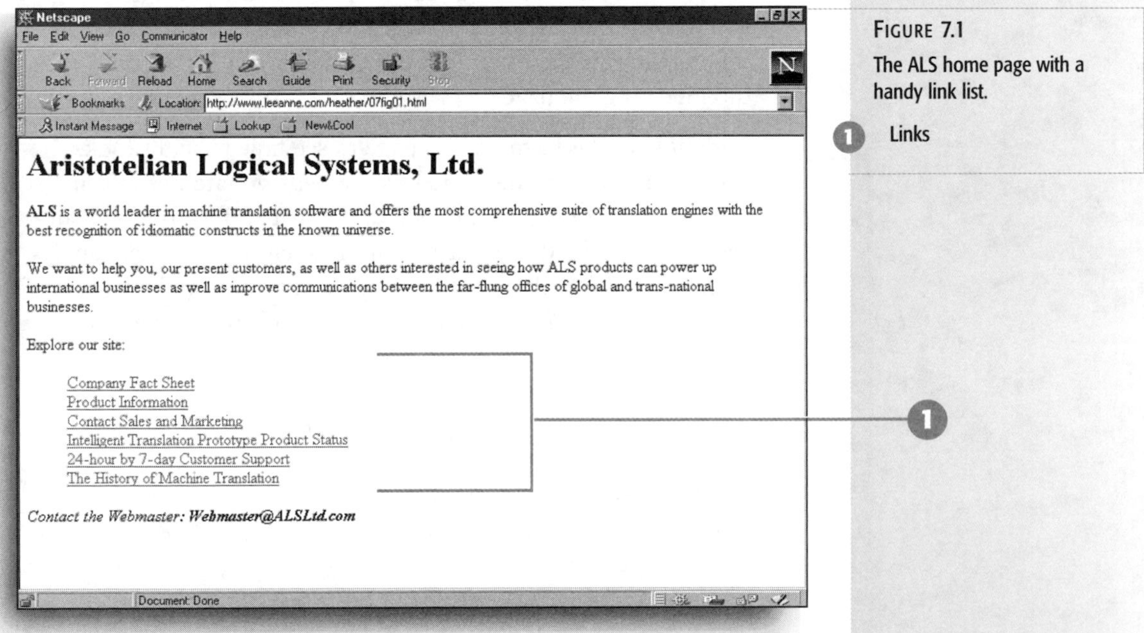

FIGURE 7.1
The ALS home page with a handy link list.

1 Links

Using Informal Links Inline to Create a Homelike Structure

Creating informal inline links

1. Start by identifying text that defines the links you wish to build.
2. Put hyperlink anchors, `<A>`, inline to avoid breaking the flow of the text.

```
Hi! You've discovered the home page of <A href=
"marriage.html"> Bess and George Fayne</A>, and of our
wonderful children, <A href="nancy.html">Nancy</A>,
five, and <A href="mikey.html">Mikey </A>, who's only
six months old right now but already loves the computer,
at least to eat!
```

For a home page, the order and discipline of a professional site can be intimidating. The rigid logic and neat little lists that we often find on corporate pages might seem affected or silly on a personal page.

Using inline links can be a real boon to a home page, allowing you to keep the text friendly and "down home" while still presenting your information in an accessible way without putting too much on one page.

Let's link up the Fayne home page to see how it might look. We'll worry about where the links actually go later. For each keyword in the text, we'll choose a file that relates to it and surround the keyword or phrase with the anchor tags. Then we'll fill in the `href` attribute with the name of the file and we're done. This is *totally radical*, as they say on California beaches.

```
<HTML>
  <HEAD>
    <TITLE>The Fayne Family Page</TITLE>
  </HEAD>
  <BODY bgcolor="FFFFFF" text="000000" link="0000FF"
  alink="FF0000" vlink="800080">
    <H1>The Fayne Family Page</H1>
      <H2>Who We Are</H2>
        <P>
```

```
Hi! You've discovered the home page of <A
href="marriage.html"> Bess and George Fayne</A>, and of our
wonderful children, <A href="nancy.html">Nancy</A>, five,
and <A href="mikey.html"> Mikey</A>, who's only six months
old right now but already loves the computer, at least to
eat! This is an experiment for us, the first time we've
really done much of anything on a computer for ourselves,
although both George and I use one at work. We hope you'll
enjoy reading our page and looking at our pictures, whichare
like any family photo albums, except that you can set them
aside as soon as you want without hurting our feelings!
      <H2>Where We Live</H2>
        <P>
We're both natives of the <A href="backhome.html">Midwest</A>,
born in a little suburb of Chicago, "hog butcher to the
nation, " but moved to California shortly after we were
married. Both our children were born here and this is home
for us now, although we both enjoy going "back home" to
visit the folks on holidays. Right now we're living in<A
href="walnutcreek.html">Walnut Creek</A>, California, which
is right over the hills from the beautiful San Francisco Bay
Area. We love our adopted home and really enjoy being only a
few hours drive from the ocean to the west and not so very
far to some of the most<A href="yosemite.html">spectacular
mountains</A> in the world to the east.
...
  </BODY>
</HTML>
```

Figure 7.2 shows the full text (well, part of it anyway) with the hyperlinks underlined.

Linking Within the Page

Creating links within a page

1. Start by creating destination names using the `<A>` tag with the `name` attribute, and position them at the place where you wish to jump.

   Quick usage tip: Tag syntax

   ```
   <A name="destination"> ...descriptive text and/or
   image... </A>
   ```

   where *`destination`* is the name that other links can jump to directly.

   ```
   <A name="index"></A>
   ```

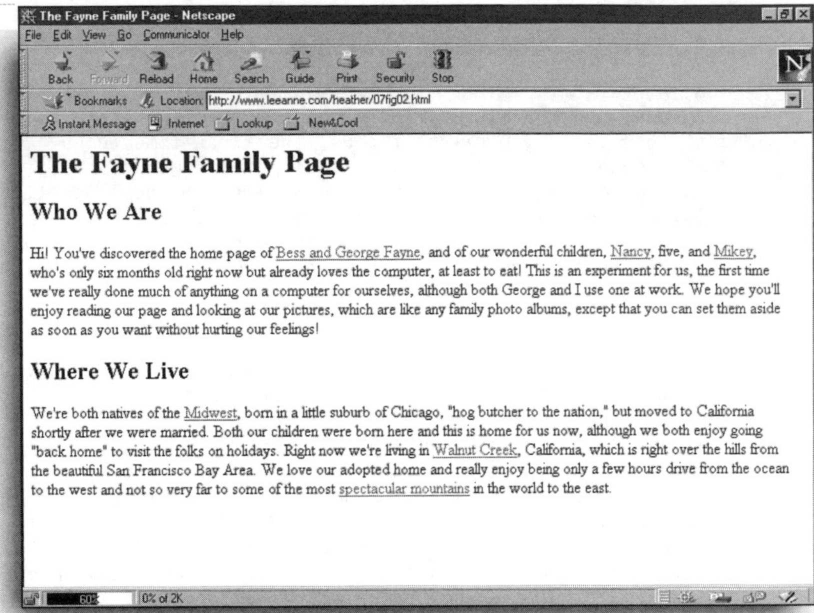

FIGURE 7.2
The Fayne family home page with some downhome hyperlinks.

2. Create links within a page as normal using the `<A>` tag with the `href` attribute, but, instead of an URL, include an `#` symbol followed by the name of the destination defined earlier.

```
<A name="index"></A>
  More text...
<A href="#index">Back to the index</A>
```

Creating a hyperlink within a page requires one extra step, naming the destination. We'll use the same anchor tag we've been using for links but with a different attribute, `name`.

By creating a name on an anchor, we make a spot in our document that we can jump to directly by using a secret bit of extension on the normal link. All you do is add a pound (crosshatch) sign to your URL and type the name after it. Within the page, of course, you won't have a URL, but will have only crosshatch and the name as a destination.

These are often used to jump quickly back up to the top of the page or to an index after reading text far below. It requires a big page to show this in action though, which I don't want to display here, so we'll just imagine that there are huge masses of text in between the target and destination anchors. In fact, we have to imagine there are huge masses of text since the display won't actually change unless there's enough room to move around. And the browser will "round off" to the bottom of the page if a target is too close to the bottom, so the actual line jumped to may not be at the top of the page.

```
<A name="index"></A>
<DL>
  <DT><DD><A href="#target1">Target One</A>
  <DT><DD><A href="#target2">Target Two</A>
</DL>
<BLOCKQUOTE>
  Masses of text...
</BLOCKQUOTE>
<A name="target1"></A>
<P>
  More text...
<A href="#index">Back to the index</A>
<A name="target2"></A>
<P>
  Still more text...
<A href="#index">Back to the index</A>
```

Displaying this as a figure would be a waste of time, since you can't see where the links take you on a static page. Either obtain the code from our Web site or type it in and try it. It works quite well.

Linking to Other Pages on the Same Site

Working with relative and absolute links

1. Link to other pages on your site using relative path names by including the path within the `href` attribute of an `<A>` tag.

   ```
   <A href="workfiles/index.html">Workfiles</A>
   ```

2. Link to a page anywhere on the Web by including the full URL for the page within the `href` attribute of the `<A>` tag.

   ```
   <A href="http://www.netcom.com/~leeph/workfiles/
   index.html"
   >Workfiles</A>
   ```

So far, all of our links have been in the same directory or in the same document, so naming the links has been very easy. The browser will assume that any links are relative to the current page unless you tell it differently, which we won't right now.

But what about dealing with complex directory structures like you might have on your own site? Can you do *that* in HTML?

Sure can. It's easy and you use exactly the same syntax you may be familiar with in dealing with your directory structure now. You can either use directories relative to your own page or absolute directory names based on where they are in relation to the root or base directory of the Web server.

A relative entry might look like

```
<A href="workfiles/index.html">Workfiles</A>
```

or even

```
<A href="../workfiles/index.html">Workfiles</A>
```

The first entry says that there is a file named index.html in a folder called workfiles immediately below the directory where the page you're viewing files. The second says that there is a directory named workfiles at the same level in the directory tree as mine and tells you how to get there. Go up to the directory immediately above mine (my parent) and then select a folder called workfiles that contains an HTML file called index.html.

An absolute entry would look like this, including the full path from the root of the directory tree:

```
<A href="/webfiles/workfiles/index.html">Workfiles</A>
```

Or, in the case of an exterior file where you wanted to go to a specific place within a larger file:

```
<A href="/webfiles/workfiles/index.html#index">Workfiles
Index</A>
```

When you enter a URL, you're specifying an absolute entry in many cases, although exceptions do exist. For example, the following URL references a file that actually exists at the end of a rather more complex path. The special ~ syntax tells the server that you want to start your "root" directory at the home directory of the username specified, `leeph`, which happens to be my own.

```
<A href="http://www.netcom.com/~leeph/workfiles/
index.html">Workfiles</A>
```

Without giving too much away, the actual path might be

```
http://www.netcom.com/users/le/leeph/workfiles/index.html
```

All this means is that you aren't restricted to a single directory, so you could load all your graphics files, for example, into one location where they'd be easy to find and reuse for other projects or to maintain consistency of design across multiple pages and page designers.

Again, displaying a figure doesn't make much sense, as the actual physical action of the link is invisible for the most part, or at least very inconspicuous. In many browsers you'll see a little prompt in the status bar telling you where a link is going to take you. This is a good idea sometimes, as there's no point going to a related destination if you've already discovered that the server seems to be down this time.

Linking to Other Sites

Linking to other Internet resources

1. Linking to FTP resources requires that you replace the `http` designation with `ftp` using the `<A>` tag.
   ```
   <A href="ftp://resources/library/file74.txt" >Link to
   text file, number 74</A>
   ```
2. Links to other such resources, such as Gopher or WAIS, are made in a similar manner.
   ```
   Hagith S. Sivan's review of Dzielska's book
   <A href="gopher://gopher.lib.virginia.edu:70/0R0-18115-/
   alpha/bmcr/v95/95-7-7" >gopher://gopher.lib.virginia.edu:
   70/0R0-18115-/alpha/bmcr/v95/95-7-7</A>
   ```

We visited this problem once before in the Hypatia Interest Page thread. At that time we didn't look closely at how we were making the actual links, so let's look at them again now.

SEE ALSO

➤ *Learn about creating link lists, see page 112*

Links offsite have to call a server directly, and each type has its own particular way to communicate. Most of your pages will link to an HTTP (Hypertext Transfer Protocol) server because they are now the most common type of file on the Web. But there are others, made in the pre-Web days before hypertext, and a lot of them are still around.

All of them use the same type of address, the URL or Uniform Resource Locator. So when you construct a link offsite using an anchor tag, the `href` attribute will point to the same kind of address and the same sorts of filenames. Only the access method changes.

FTP (File Transfer Protocol) is one access method, and prefixing a URL with `ftp:` tells the browser to go get a page using FTP.

Another is Gopher, an older scheme for serving files, or WAIS, the Wide Area Information Server. Both of these are slightly antique, but there was so much out there that needed to be altered to fit nicely into the Web using HTTP that people looked around and discreetly decided not to.

After whichever protocol name is used come two forward slashes that tell the browser that a machine name is expected next, either a regular name or those strings of numbers you sometimes see. Both work pretty much the same way. And then comes the name of the file, index.html by default.

So in the first address, we're asking the browser to find an HTTP server on a machine named `www.lib.virginia.edu`. Once there, we'll ask that server to look for a file like this:

`/science/parshall/hypatia.html`

Which, of course, it does. We then duplicate the entire address in the descriptive text, enclosed by the anchor tags so people will know where they're going when they select that link.

The rest of the links are constructed in exactly the same way.

```
<H1>Friends of Hypatia Link List</H1>
<DL>
  <DT>Biography of Hypatia
    <DD><A href="http://www.lib.virginia.edu/science/
    parshall/hypatia.html">
    http://www.lib.virginia.edu/science/parshall/hypatia.html</A>
```

```
<DT>Hypatia
  <DD><A href="http://hypatia.ucsd.edu/~kl/hypatia.html">
  http://hypatia.ucsd.edu/~kl/hypatia.html</A>
<DT>Hypatia of Alexandria
  <DD><A href="http://cosmopolis.com/people/hypatia.html" >
  http://cosmopolis.com/people/hypatia.html</A>
<DT>The Martyrdom of Hypatia
  <DD><A href="http://www.chewable.com/hypatian/hypatia.
  htm">
  http://www.chewable.com/hypatian/hypatia.htm</A>
<DT>Hypatia of Alexandria
  <DD><A href="http://www.polyamory.org/~howard/Hypatia/">
  http://www.polyamory.org/~howard/Hypatia/</A>
<DT>Harvard University Press Books
  <DD><A href="http://www.hup.harvard.edu/F96Books/
  F96Long/hypatia.html">
  http://www.hup.harvard.edu/F96Books/F96Long/hypatia.html</A>
<DT>A Review of Maria Dzielska's Hypatia of Alexandria
  <DD><A href="http://www.cybergrrl.com/review/gb0796.
  html#Hypatia">
  http://www.cybergrrl.com/review/gb0796.html#Hypatia</A>
<DT>Hagith S. Sivan's review of Dzielska's book
  <DD><A href="gopher://gopher.lib.virginia.edu:70/0R0-
  18115-/alpha/bmcr/v95/95-7-7">
  gopher://gopher.lib.virginia.edu:70/0R0-18115-/alpha/bmcr/
  v95/95-7-7</A>
<DT>Hypatia: A journal of Feminist Philosophy
  <DD><A href="http://www.indiana.edu/~iupress/journals/
  hyp.html">
  http://www.indiana.edu/~iupress/journals/hyp.html</A>
<DT>Hypatia's Web
  <DD><A href="http://kalypso.cybercom.net/~hypatia/
  index.html">
  http://kalypso.cybercom.net/~hypatia/index.html</A>
<DT>The Hypatia Trust
  <DD><A href="http://www.hypatia-trust.org.uk/">
  http://www.hypatia-trust.org.uk/</A>
</DL>
```

Using our new appreciation for the intricacies of links, we see that most are HTTP-style links. In other words, they return a regular Web page. But there's an oddball there called Gopher, which uses an older protocol. What's *that* about? Who cares actually? The browser takes care of all that stuff for us so we don't have to worry about it. Figure 7.3 shows the result of this code.

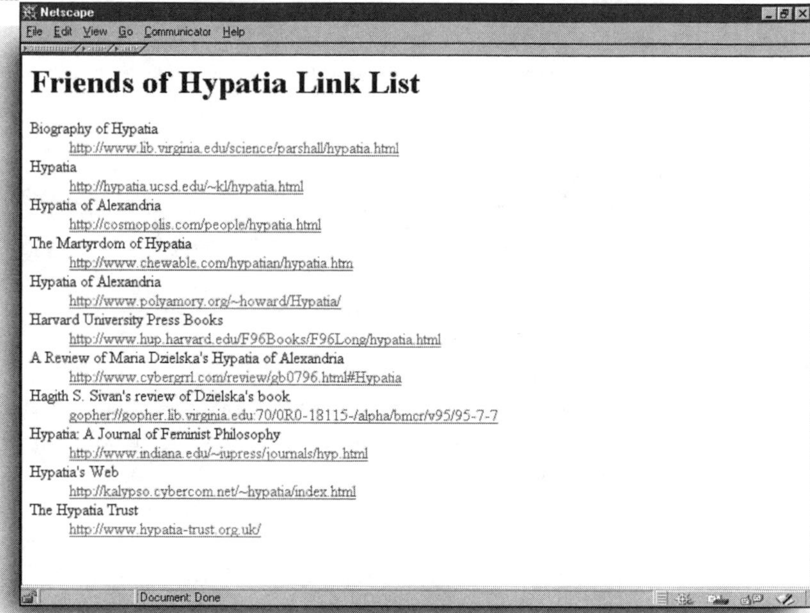

FIGURE 7.3

The Hypatia page with hypertext links.

PART

II

Including Images and Multimedia

CHAPTER 8

Adding Images to a Web Page

Using pictures on your pages to add life and interest

Establish brand recognition with unique graphic elements

Provide navigation clues with logo variations

Creating Visual Impact

Although not every page *needs* a picture, visual impact and appearance are so ingrained in our culture that we sometimes describe a person's character, personality, and public behavior as his or her *image*. For a page to achieve a personality of its own, it often needs a picture or two to let you know what the page is about and the sort of things you might find here.

So a site featuring racing cars might show a picture of a racer screeching around a corner, or a gardener's Web paradise might display the fruits of a bounteous harvest. We don't have any way of really appealing to most of our senses on the Web, just sight, most easily, and hearing to a lesser extent, so we have to overload those senses with far more meaning than they may carry in real life.

Marcel Proust's experience of the odor of Madeline's baking is one we are not likely to ever experience on the Web; the warmth of the warm summer sun on our shoulders and the smell of freshly turned earth are things we can only imagine with words and pictures as cues.

If your words don't tell a story, pictures are unlikely to carry it off on their own, but just as gestures and expression make the difference between a master storyteller and an amateur, the images we use to set the atmosphere for a page can make the difference between a ho-hum experience and an engaging sense of immediacy.

Adding Images

Adding pictures to your page

1. Add images to your pages with the image tag, `<IMG>`. Use the `src` attribute to identify the image file.

```
<IMG src="hypatia.gif">
```

2. Use the `alt` and `longdesc` attributes to present additional information about the image.

```
<IMG src="hypatia.gif" alt="[Hypatia as a young woman]"
        longdesc="hypatia-description.html">
```

Quick usage tip: Tag syntax

```
<IMG src="imgurl" height="imgheight" width="imgwidth"
alt="alttext" longdesc="alttexturl" hspace="gutter"
vspace="gutter" border="linkborder" align="alignment">
```

where `imgurl` is the location of the image source; `imgheight` is the height of the image in pixels; `imgwidth` is the width of the image in pixels; `alttext` is a short description of the image—significant or null if it can be ignored by non-visual browsers; and `alttexturl` is the location of a longer description of the image. Gutters are the horizontal or vertical empty space surrounding the image; `gutter` is the width of the border in pixels when an image is used as a link; and alignment is `left`, `right`, `top`, `middle`, or `bottom` and alters the relative position of text and images on the page.

Let's start out by adding one picture to our Hypatia page, a portrait of the woman herself as she probably appeared in her youth. So many centuries and miles of distance separate us from her times that even a glimpse of who she was can help bring her home to us. We can see that she was like ourselves, our sisters, our mothers; she grew up with hopes and ambitions and yet her fate was as shadowed as her face appears to be, sad and contemplative, not laughing and wild, although the young woman we see surely had days of joy as well.

All images usually carry the same tag, the image tag (`<IMG>`) with a mandatory `src` attribute to tell the browser where to get the image itself. In addition, almost every image should carry a short text description in the `alt` attribute to make the page more easily accessible to people with vision difficulties or for those who merely *prefer* browsing with an audio browser, perhaps a motorist tooling down the highway. If the image is purely decoration, this value should be explicitly set to null by typing `alt=""`. These are the only attributes you really need for any image, but there are a lot that will sneak in for one reason or another and we'll talk briefly about the most common here in this chapter, introducing them a few at a time.

The most recent HTML 4.0 draft added the `longdesc` attribute that lets you list a URL a browser can go to for more information about a picture. You could use this feature to provide a complete narrative description of the image or even a catalog listing of a picture's history, its history and origin, and a short biography of the artist.

Let's begin, taking the time to fill out the page with a proper title as well as the image we want to use. We evoke the image with the `<IMG>` tag, adding the `source` attribute as well as the two descriptive attributes. We'll do more later, but look at what it reads like now.

```
<HTML>
  <HEAD>
    <TITLE>Hypatia: A Notable Woman of Science</TITLE>
  </HEAD>
  <BODY>
    <IMG src="hypatia.gif" alt="[Hypatia as a young woman]"
         longdesc="hypatia-description.html">
    <H1>Hypatia</H1>
    <H2>A Personal Relationship with History</H2>
    <P>
      <STRONG>Hypatia</STRONG> is often depicted in the
      <DFNtitle="tunic"><I>tribon</I></DFN>, a poor working-
      class garment made of coarse materials that was the
      traditional attire of philosophers and ascetics.
      However, this is a <EM>very</EM> controversial idea in
      many ways and some scholars believe that she would
      have been gowned in the style of the upper class
      Greek women of a Late Roman Alexandria still very
      much influenced by Hellenistic Greece,the typical
      <DFNtitle="sleeveless shift"><I>chiton</I></DFN> and
      girdled <DFN title="ankle-length gown"><I>peplos</I>
      </DFN> with <DFN title="draped mantle"><I>himation</I>
      </DFN>. In this viewpoint the poor quality of clothing
      in which she is shown would be a sort of pious fraud
      by her latter-day admirers, to exalt and exemplify
      her scholarship, selflessness, and purity.  She was
      by all credible accounts a lifelong virgin who had
      dedicated her life to science and mathematics; her
      partisans have been many and vocal through the
      centuries since that murderous day in 415 <ABBR
      title="of the Common Era - i.e. AD">CE</ABBR>.
  </BODY>
</HTML>
```

The display is still not what we truly want, but we're getting there. If you study Figure 8.1, you'll see a few problems; she's looking away from the page for one, and the size of the image seems large for the page. There are more issues to be addressed, but we've done a good job for now. We can see what she looked like and get a better sense of who she was.

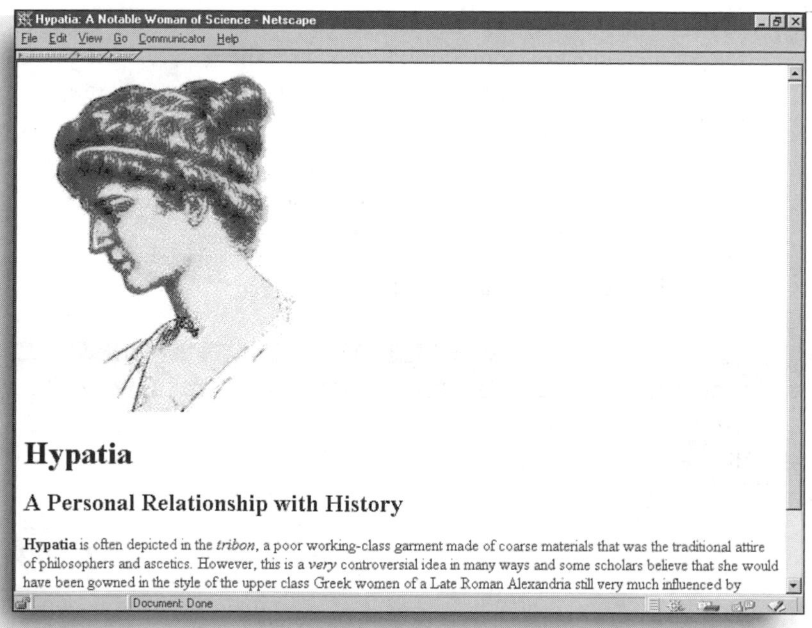

FIGURE 8.1
The Hypatia page with a portrait of the scientist as a young woman.

Controlling Image Size

Control the size of images on the page with simple attributes

1. Use a graphics program to determine the size and width of your image.
2. Use the `height` and `width` attributes to control image size on the page.

```
<IMG src="hypatia.gif" alt="[Hypatia as a young woman]"
        longdesc="hypatia-description.html"
        height="243" width="200">
```

The attributes flow thick and furious now, and most images require nearly all of them because images are among the most complex features on the page and need a lot of coaxing to obtain the best results. We're just going to fiddle with the `<IMG>` tag itself, to find the best size for the image before we actually make

Save space and time by "blowing up" images in code

Working in reverse, taking a small image and enlarging it by doubling its size or more, can save quite a lot of download time. In fact, you can fill an area with a solid color by using a one-pixel image of that color and arguing the size of the area you want filled.

changes in it, so I'll just list the lines with the <IMG> tag by itself, to avoid wasting space. First, we make it smaller by shrinking the numbers in height and width. The browser will override the actual size of the image and force it to take the size you say it is. Ultimate power. Note that this is a temporary method, just to see what the image would look like at a smaller size. In our production version we'll resize the image so we don't waste time loading more image than we need.

```
<IMG src="hypatia.gif" alt="[Hypatia as a young woman]"
     longdesc="hypatia-description.html"
     height="243" width="200">
```

results in the display shown in Figure 8.2.

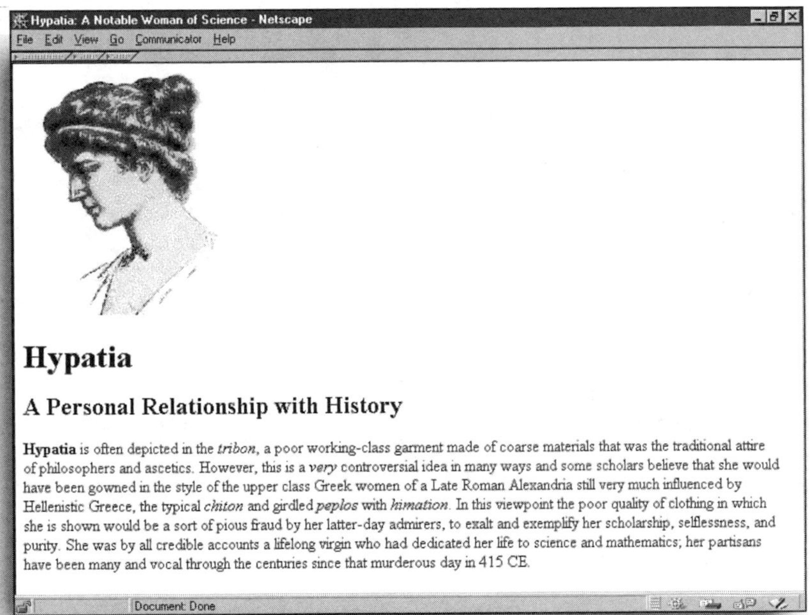

FIGURE 8.2
The Hypatia page with a resized image.

I like it like that. How about you? I'm going to resize the image to the size we set it to directly in the browser, calling it hypatia2.gif to distinguish it from the first version, and we can go on to the next step, making her look into the page instead of away from it. Pardon me for doing the resize behind the scenes, but this is a book on using HTML, not on how to use a graphics program. Pay no attention to that woman behind the curtain....

Whew! It's done and is about half the size to boot. Not a bad few minutes work.

Flowing Text Around Images

Formatting your pages so text flows around images

1. Determine where you wish your text to be aligned in relation to the image.
2. Use the `align` attribute to move the graphic relative to the text to the `left`, `right`, `top`, `middle`, or `bottom`.

```
<IMG src="hypatia2.gif" alt="[Hypatia as a young woman]"
        longdesc="hypatia-description.html"
        height="243" width="200" align="right">
```

There one more thing we need to do before leaving Hypatia for a while; she's still looking off the page, which focuses attention away from our page and sort of implies that she's saying, "Hey guys! I'm outta here!" Not the best feeling for a page we want people to look at. We feel happier (and don't ask me why this is) when the people in pictures on the page seem to be relating to it. Maybe we all played with dolls and action figures so much as children that we think everything is real on some level. Whatever, face single profiles toward the page if you have a choice, and we do.

We're going to tell the browser to place our portrait against the right margin and then treat her as if she were part of the margin, flowing the text down the side of the image until it clears at the bottom and flows out to the real right margin again. That's the way things behave in every book and magazine you've likely ever read, so I don't really know why the original browsers chose a simpler march-everything-in-sequence-along-the-left-margin approach.

Figure 8.3 shows the result, and it's looking pretty good if I do say so myself.

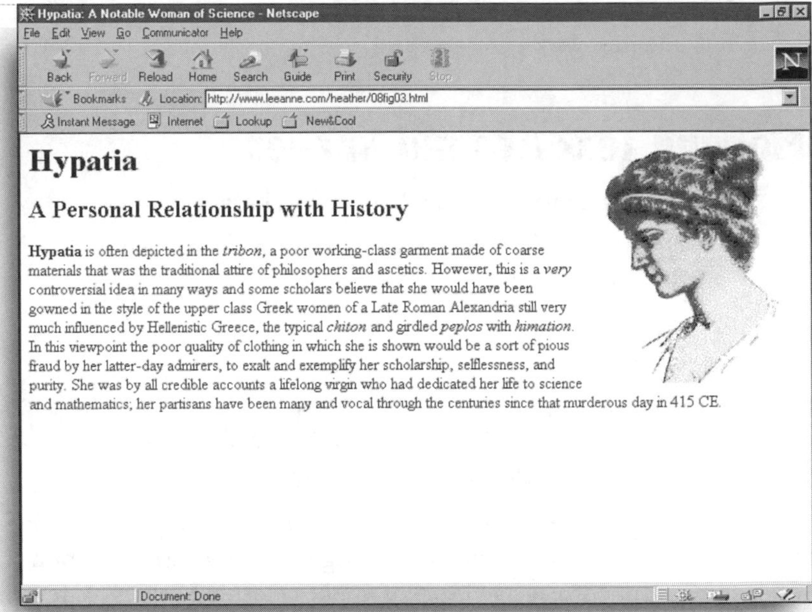

Hypatia: A Notable Woman of Science - Netscape
File Edit View Go Communicator Help
Back Forward Reload Home Search Guide Print Security Stop
Bookmarks Location: http://www.leeanne.com/heather/08fig03.html
Instant Message Internet Lookup New&Cool
Hypatia
A Personal Relationship with History
Hypatia is often depicted in the tribon, a poor working-class garment made of coarse materials that was the traditional attire of philosophers and ascetics. However, this is a very controversial idea in many ways and some scholars believe that she would have been gowned in the style of the upper class Greek women of a Late Roman Alexandria still very much influenced by Hellenistic Greece, the typical chiton and girdled peplos with himation. In this viewpoint the poor quality of clothing in which she is shown would be a sort of pious fraud by her latter-day admirers, to exalt and exemplify her scholarship, selflessness, and purity. She was by all credible accounts a lifelong virgin who had dedicated her life to science and mathematics; her partisans have been many and vocal through the centuries since that murderous day in 415 CE.
Document: Done

FIGURE 8.3
The Hypatia page with a perfectly-sized and oriented portrait at last!

Using Images as Links

Making images into links

1. Include the image in your page.

```
<IMG src="alslogo.gif" alt="[ALSLogo]">
```

2. Turn an image into a link simply by including it in the descriptive content of the anchor tag (<A>).

```
<A href="developers.html"><IMG src="alslogo.gif"
alt="[ALS Logo]"
          longdesc="als-description.html" border="0"
          height="100" width="100" align="left"></A>
```

Quick usage tip: Tag syntax

```
<IMG src="imgurl" height="imgheight" width="imgwidth"
alt="alttext" longdesc="alttexturl" hspace="gutter"
vspace="gutter" border="linkborder" align="alignment">
```

where `imgurl` is the location of the image source; `imgheight` is the height of the image in pixels; `imgwidth` is the width of the image in pixels; `alttext` is a short description of the image—significant or null if it can be ignored by non-visual browsers; and `alttexturl` is the location of a longer description of the image. Gutters are the horizontal or vertical empty space surrounding the image; *gutter* is the width of the border in pixels when an image is used as a link; and *alignment* is `left`, `right`, `top`, `middle`, or `bottom` and alters the relative position of text and images on the page.

Using images as links can be fun and helps overcome language barriers as well. We recognize and grasp pictures, in most cases, much quicker than we do words, especially unfamiliar words. It's also a way of hiding little "Easter Eggs" in your page, where people who are curious and explore the page can find interesting surprises.

Let's go back to our workgroup page and put in a graphic logo, which would be nice anyway, and make a link from the logo to display the names of the developers and a little project history. We'll clean it up in a few other ways as well, turning it from a code fragment into a well-formed page.

After putting a head section and title on the page, we wrap an anchor around the image of the logo. The image tag sits inside the anchor tag, just like the text links we've used before, and it's possible to use both. As always with images, but especially those that do something, we've used clear alternate text to tell people using non-visual browsers what the picture is. I like to put alternate text inside square brackets—although that's just me—because it is visually different from ordinary text that way, if you look at it in Lynx.

```
<HTML>
  <HEAD>
    <TITLE>Aristotelian Logical Systems, Ltd.</TITLE>
  </HEAD>
  <BODY>
    <A href="developers.html"><IMG src="alslogo.gif" alt="
     [ALS Logo]"
          longdesc="als-description.html" border="0"
          height="100" width="100" align="left"></A>
    <H1>Aristotelian Logical Systems, Ltd.</H1>
      <BR clear="left">
      <BR>
      <P>
```

```
        <STRONG>ALS</STRONG> is a world leader in machine
        translation software and offers the most
        comprehensive suite of translation engines with the
        best recognition of idiomatic constructs in the
        known universe.
      <P>
        We want to help you, our present customers, as
        well as others interested in seeing how ALS
        products can power up international businesses as
        well as improve communications between the far-
        flung offices of global and trans-national
        businesses.
      <P>
        Explore our site:
      <DL>
        <DT><DD><A href="alsfaq.html">Company Fact Sheet</A>
        <DT><DD><A href="alsprods.html">Product
          Information</A>
        <DT><DD><A href="alssales.html">Contact Sales and
          Marketing</A>
        <DT><DD><A href="alsitpstatus.html">Intelligent
          Translation Prototype Product Status</A>
        <DT><DD><A href="alssupport.html">24-hour by 7-day
          Customer Support</A>
        <DT><DD><A href="alshistory.html">The History of
          Machine Translation</A>
      </DL>
      <ADDRESS>
        Contact the Webmaster:
          <A href="mailto;Webmaster@ALSLtd.com"><STRONG>
            Webmaster@ALSLtd.com</STRONG></A>
      </ADDRESS>
  </BODY>
</HTML>
```

The preceding code results in the display shown in Figure 8.4.

Are Pictures Worth a Thousand Words? Navigating with Icons

Using navigational icons

1. Start by creating the icons.
2. Use the <IMG> tags to place the icons on your page.

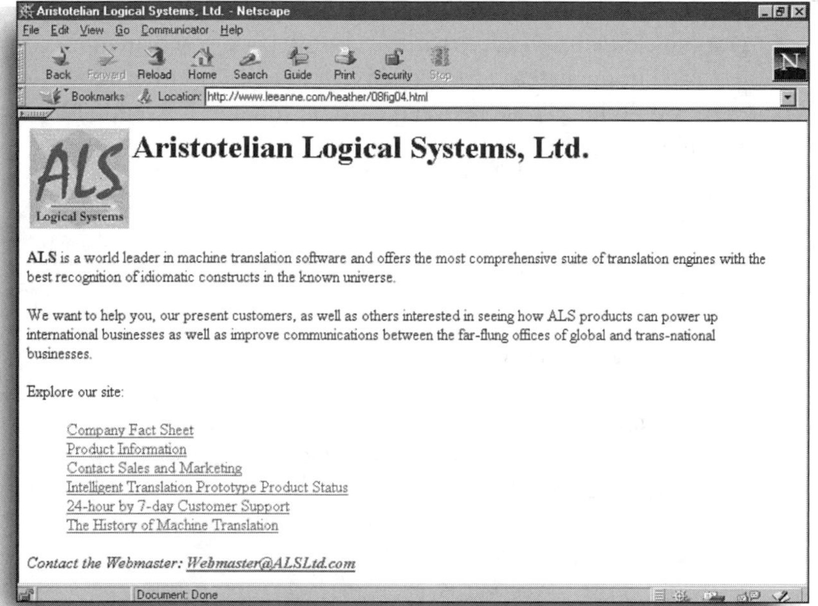

FIGURE 8.4

The workgroup page with an "Easter Egg" in the logo.

3. Surround the icons' descriptions with anchor tags, <A>, that link to the location where the icon should take the user.

```
<A HREF="index.html#Index"><IMG src="bb3back.gif" alt="
[Back to Entry] "
          width="40" height="25" vspace="0" hspace="0"
            border="0"></A>
```

Navigation bars are almost a cliché today, although they are the Cadillac of interfaces and the sort you see on *Star Trek*—collections of symbols that you press to make things happen. Ordinary navigation bars have been partially replaced by fancier ones that flicker scifi changing lights at you with more and better features, but the old ones are still very useful in most situations. The tendency now is toward more subtle and free flowing shapes, as opposed to the hard-edged buttons of some years ago, but for our example, I'll use the hard buttons, because it's easier to see what's happening.

Each of the navigation elements is a little rectangular 3D button, and the links are repeated in order as text links immediately below. The buttons have the same alternative text as the text links, so they have their own little help balloons built in on most modern browsers.

There is no text in the navigation bar proper, just a series a graphic elements. Notice that the closing tag of each anchor is followed immediately by the opening of another. Otherwise there would be a space between each button and it wouldn't look as self contained.

```
<HTML>
  <HEAD>
    <TITLE>Navigation Bar Example</TITLE>
  </HEAD>
  <BODY>
    <H1>Navigation Bar</H1>

    <CENTER>
      <A href="index.html#Index"><IMG src="bb3back.gif"
      alt="[Back to Entry] "
         width="40" height="25" vspace="0" hspace="0"
           border="0"></A><A
         href="#Top"><IMG src="bb3index.gif"
           alt="[Main Index] "
         width="40" height="25" vspace="0" hspace="0"
           border="0"></A><A
         href="thanx.html"><IMG src="bb3thanx.gif"
           alt="[Thank You] "
         width="40" height="25" vspace="0" hspace="0"
           border="0"></A><A
         href="index.html"><IMG src="bb3query.gif"
           alt="[About This Site] "
         width="40" height="25" vspace="0" hspace="0"
           border="0"></A><A
         href="contact.html"><IMG src="bb3mail.gif"
           alt="[Contact Me] "
         width="40" height="25" vspace="0" hspace="0"
           border="0"></A><A
         href="about.html"><IMG src="bb3in2.gif"
           alt="[Continue to Next Page]"
         width="40" height="25" vspace="0" hspace="0"
           border="0"></A>

    <P>

      <A href="index.html#Index">[Back to Entry]</A><A
         href="#Top">[Main Index]</A><A
         href="thanx.html">[Thank You]</A><A
```

```
        href="index.html">[About This Site]</A><A
        href="contact.html">[Contact Me]</A><A
        href="about.html">[Continue to Next Page]</A>
    </CENTER>
  </BODY>
</HTML>
```

This code results in the display shown in Figure 8.5.

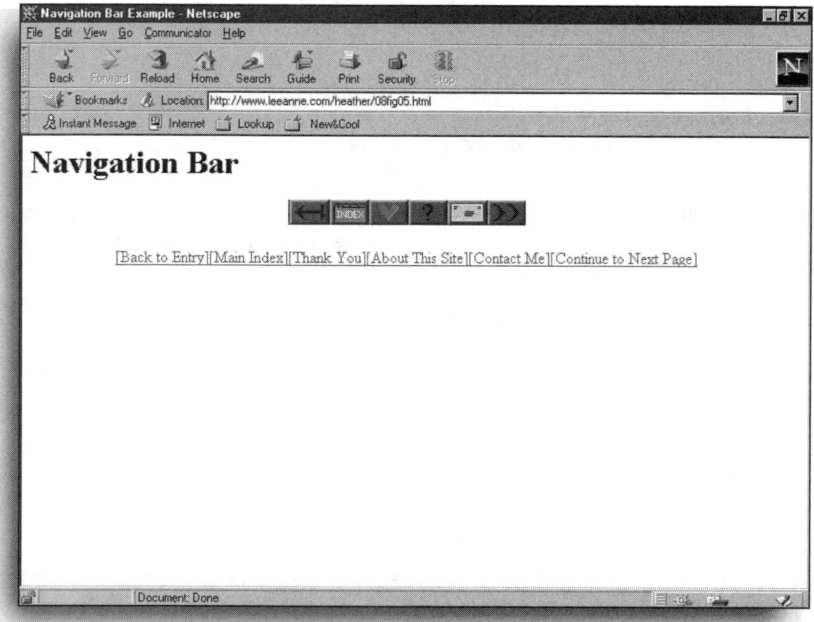

FIGURE 8.5
A sample navigation bar.

Displaying Thumbnail Images to Improve Load Times

Using thumbnail images

1. Using an image editor, decrease the size of large images and save them as separate thumbnails.
2. Place these smaller thumbnail images on your Web pages and link them to pages containing the larger version.

```
<A href="hypatia.gif"><IMG src="hypatia-thumb.gif"
alt="[Hypatia Thumbnail Image]"
         longdesc="hypatia-description.html" border="2"
         height="49" width="40"></A>
```

The logical culmination of these techniques for navigation is to make an icon that refers to a larger version of the picture itself. This sort of self-referential icon is usually called a thumbnail because it's so small you might paint it on your thumbnail.

We won't make any special deal out of this, since you already know how to do navigation with icons. Here's a simple example using our famous picture of Hypatia. I've chosen to load the GIF directly but could just as easily have loaded an HTML page with information about the portrait.

```
<HTML>
  <HEAD>
    <TITLE>Hypatia en large</TITLE>
  </HEAD>
  <BODY>
    <A href="hypatia.gif"><IMG src="hypatia-thumb.gif"
      alt="[Hypatia Thumbnail Image]"
          longdesc="hypatia-description.html" border="2"
          height="49" width="40"></A>
    <H1>Link to large portrait of Hypatia</H1>
  </BODY>
</HTML>
```

This results in the display shown in Figure 8.6.

Simulating Exotic Fonts with Graphics

Including non-system fonts on your site as graphic images

1. Using a paint or drawing program, create your text in the desired font with the Text tool and save it as a graphic.
2. Use the `<IMG>` tag to load the graphic into your Web page.

```
<IMG src="greek-font.gif" alt="[Greek saying]">
```

On our Hypatia page, it would be nice to give a little more of a Greek flavor to the image by including her name as it would appear in the Greek alphabet. (I just made this up to give us a good reason to do it, but it sounds like a really good idea now that I said it.) Since it's safe to assume that few browsers, other than those of native speakers of the Greek language, will have such a font available. We'll have to set the words as type in a graphic.

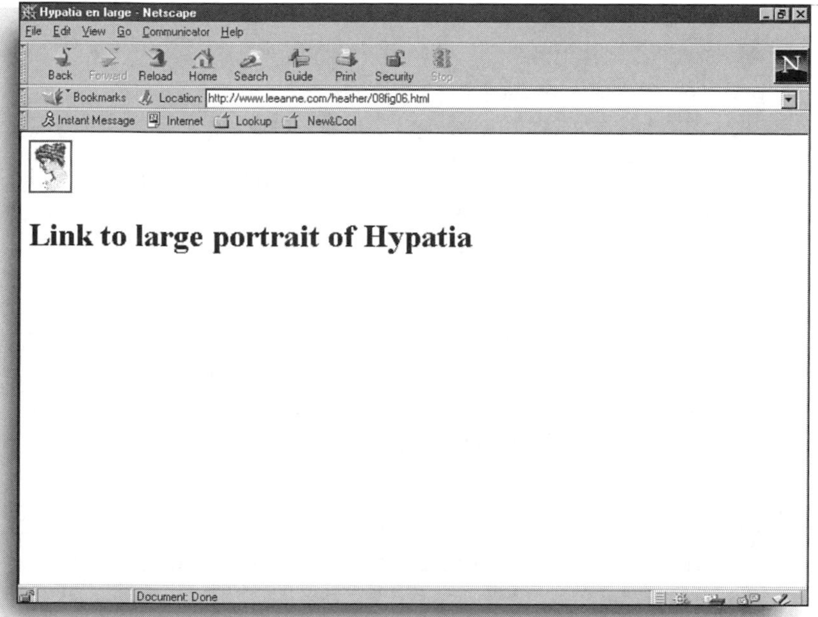

FIGURE 8.6
The Hypatia portrait in miniature, with a link to the large version.

The exact procedure for doing that will vary between graphics packages, but generally you'll need to have whatever font you want to use available on the machine, create a new graphics file big enough to hold the amount and size of text you need, use the text paintbrush—or whatever it's called in your own program—to insert the text (and hope we know what we're doing), and then do any fiddling with the image needed.

One of the things you'll often have to do is fix up visual spacing between letters, a process called kerning, because you're knocking the visual corners off the white space in which the letter is embedded. Typical candidates for kerning are W and A, A and V, and any other letter combination that looks a little spread out in comparison to the rest of the letters. You can see it in the following example.

WAVEHUNVowHowTelMel

You can see how letters with strong diagonal elements leave more empty space between letters than those that are more vertical. The degree of difficulty this causes varies from words that have severe kerning problems to those that will usually pass without notice. In the old days of wooden type, you'd fix the problem by taking a saw and whacking off the lower corner of the first W in WAVE and the upper corner of the A so you could slide them together slightly, and so on down the line. Now we do it all with electrons.

WAVE HUN Vow How Toll Moll

When we're happy with the result, we'll save it as a GIF file usually—or in any other graphics file type—and then we're ready to use it in a page.

The same technique can be used to add text to a logo or letterhead, or even to create text that stands out from the rest of the page because it has a different background or font type. This is one way to insert Hebrew, Chinese, or Arabic elements into a page. You don't have to worry about whether a font is available because you rendered it once and for all.

For the Hypatia page, now that we've tweaked our Greek text until it looks pretty, we'll insert it into the side of her portrait so it's one of the first things we see on the page. The two images together, Greek text and ancient portrait, combine to give a flavor of Alexandrian antiquity to our page. You can see the results in Figure 8.7.

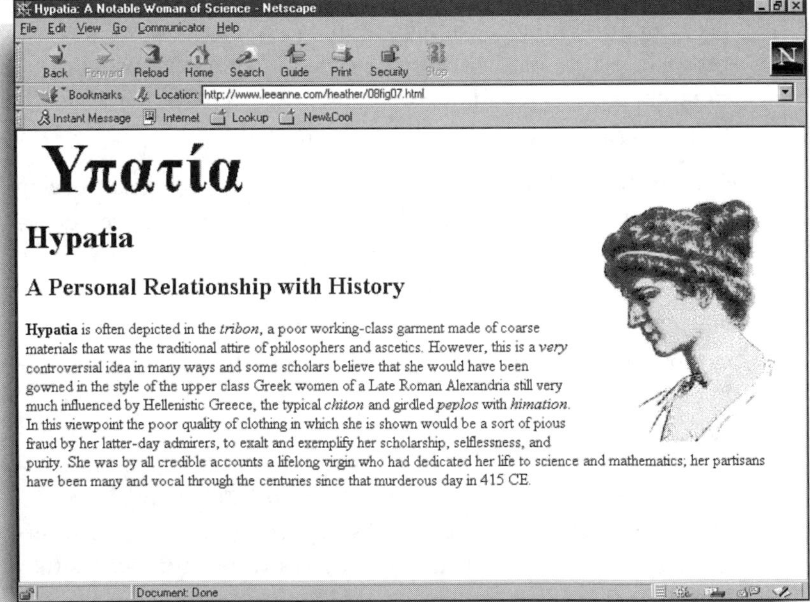

FIGURE 8.7
The Hypatia page with Greek text.

Using Background Images Effectively

Making background images work effectively on your page

1. To add a background image to your page, use the `background` attribute on the `<BODY>` tag.

   ```
   <BODY background="parchment.jpeg">
   ```

2. Usually, you should use both the `background` and `bgcolor` attributes, since choosing a background color close to the overall tone of the image helps improve the appearance of the page while loading, and also helps prevent problems on browsers that don't load images. The background color will be displayed first and then the background image will overlay it.

   ```
   <BODY background="parchment.jpeg" bgcolor="F7F1F2">
   ```

   Quick usage tip: Tag syntax

   ```
   <BODY background="imgurl" bgcolor="color">
   ```

   where *`imgurl`* is the location of the image source, and *`color`* is a related color to lessen visual snap as the background image loads.

Background images can add textures to the page like linen or sandstone, as well as allow you to create a very subtle corporate watermark visible on every significant page of your Web site. You also see them used to create borders down the left margin, bleeds (visual elements that spill over the edge of the page), and other typographical elements on the page.

There should always be good contrast between the text and the background, and they're usually made to be very pastel and light in overall tone unless there will be no text in the neighborhood of any darker or more contrasting portions.

Let's look at some of these techniques in the context of our corporate workgroup page. For this example, we'll use a background I happened to have lying around, but you can find many wonderful backgrounds on the Web that you can use freely in exchange for a thank you and a link back somewhere on your pages. Among the better sites is Cool Graphics at `http://www.geocities.com/SiliconValley/Heights/1272/index.html`. It has links to hundreds of sites.

We'll use a neutral background on our corporate page, almost white but not quite, so it looks a little distinctive. I have one that fits that description fairly well, called parchment.jpeg. When loading a background image, it's a good idea to set a background color explicitly as well, since it will make the visual "snap" when it loads less noticeable. And whenever you set background colors, set all the other `color` attributes as well, so you don't inadvertently make someone's text disappear against your cool new background.

SEE ALSO

➤ *For information on* `color` *attributes of the* <BODY> *tag, see page 42*

```
<HTML>
  <HEAD>
    <TITLE>Aristotelian Logical Systems, Ltd.</TITLE>
  </HEAD>
  <BODY background="parchment.jpeg" bgcolor="F7F1F2"
        text="000000" link="0000FF" alink="FF0000"
        vlink="800080">
    <A href="developers.html"><IMG src="alslogo.gif"
    alt="[ALS Logo]"
         longdesc="als-description.html" border="0"
         height="100" width="100" align="left"></A>
    <H1>Aristotelian Logical Systems, Ltd.</H1>
      <BR clear="left">
      <BR>
      <P>
        <STRONG>ALS</STRONG> is a world leader in machine
        translation software and offers the most
        comprehensive suite of translation engines with
        the best recognition of idiomatic constructs in the
        known universe.
      <P>
        We want to help you, our present customers, as well
        as others interested in seeing how ALS products can
        power up international businesses as well as
        improve communications between the far-flung offices
        of global and trans-national businesses.
      <P>
        Explore our site:
      <DL>
        <DT><DD><A href="alsfaq.html">Company Fact Sheet</A>
        <DT><DD><A href="alsprods.html">Product
```

```
          Information</A>
        <DT><DD><A href="alssales.html">Contact Sales and
          Marketing</A>
        <DT><DD><A href="alsitpstatus.html">Intelligent
          Translation Prototype Product Status</A>
        <DT><DD><A href="alssupport.html">24-hour by 7-day
          Customer Support</A>
        <DT><DD><A href="alshistory.html">The History of
          Machine Translation</A>
      </DL>
      <ADDRESS>
        Contact the Webmaster:
          <A href="mailto;Webmaster@ALSLtd.com"><STRONG>
            Webmaster@ALSLtd.com</STRONG></A>
      </ADDRESS>
  </BODY>
</HTML>
```

The preceding code results in Figure 8.8.

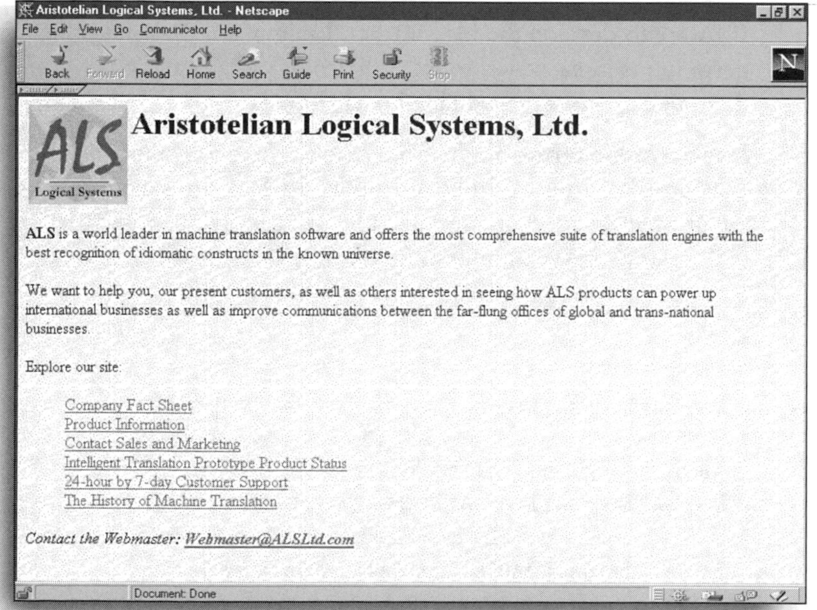

FIGURE 8.8
The workgroup page with a parchment background.

Using Images to Provide Visual Landmarks

Visual cues make it easy to remember where you are and what you were doing when you walked in. This may seem facetious, but it's terribly easy to get lost on the Web, because every place seems to lead almost directly to every place else. Some sites are like the famous maze of twisty passages, all alike, so it's hard to know where you are at any given moment. Consistent labeling and navigation will help keep visitors from becoming confused, especially when they wander in through the back door.

The code below illustrates the concept of putting in signposts to let people know where they are in the workgroup site. I just put everything together to save space, but each logo and header belongs at the top of its own page. The little bottom bars are very efficient to load and, when combined with the main logo, give a nice continuity between pages as well as differentiation between sections.

If I were to develop the idea further, I might want several other decorations in each area to echo the color of its bottom bar, and then create a color-coordinated navigation bar.

It's impossible for me to describe exactly what your imagination, as opposed to mine, could come up with when you start thinking about what makes a site unique. That very individuality is what will make your Web home stand out from the crowd with its own personality and charm.

```
<HTML>
  <HEAD>
    <TITLE>Aristotelian Logical Systems, Ltd.</TITLE>
  </HEAD>
  <BODY background="parchment.jpeg" bgcolor="F7F1F2">
    <IMG src="alslogo.gif" alt="[ALS Logo]"
         longdesc="als-description.html" border="0"
         height="100" width="100" align="left">
    <H1 align="center">ALS Support</H1>
    <BR clear="left">
    <IMG src="alssupport.gif" alt="[ALS Support]"
         longdesc="als-description.html" border="0"
         height="20" width="100" align="left">
```

```
<BR clear="left">
<BR>
<HR>
<P>
<IMG src="alslogo.gif" alt="[ALS Logo]"
      longdesc="als-description.html" border="0"
      height="100" width="100" align="left">
<H1 align="center">Machine Translation History</H1>
<BR clear="left">
<IMG src="alshistory.gif" alt="[ALS History]"
      longdesc="als-description.html" border="0"
      height="20" width="100" align="left">
<BR clear="left">
<BR>
<HR>
<P>
<IMG src="alslogo.gif" alt="[ALS Logo]"
      longdesc="als-description.html" border="0"
      height="100" width="100" align="left">
<H1 align="center">ALS Special Projects</H1>
<BR clear="left">
<IMG src="alsprojects.gif" alt="[ALS Projects]"
      longdesc="als-description.html" border="0"
      height="20" width="100" align="left">
<BR clear="left">
<BR>
<HR>
<P>
<IMG src="alslogo.gif" alt="[ALS Logo]"
      longdesc="als-description.html" border="0"
      height="100" width="100" align="left"></A>
<H1 align="center">Aristotelian Logical Systems,
Ltd.</H1>
<BR clear="left">
<BR>
<P>
<ADDRESS>
  Contact the Webmaster:
    <A href="mailto;Webmaster@ALSLtd.com"><STRONG>
    Webmaster@ALSLtd.com</STRONG></A>
```

```
        </ADDRESS>
    </BODY>
</HTML>
```

Due to a bug in Netscape 4.0, each of the graphic elements had to be aligned left to prevent a slight misalignment. Fiddling with things like that is very typical of the sorts of things you'll run into every day when you start working with browsers. Test everything; you can't trust anything.

Figure 8.9 shows the browser rendering for the previous code.

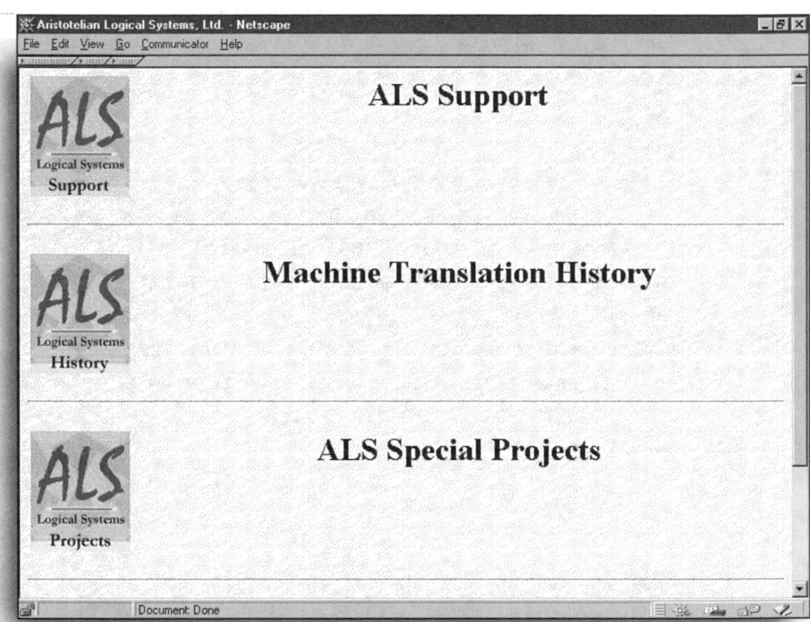

FIGURE 8.9
Combined logos and signposts for three representative sections in the workgroup site.

Establishing Brand Recognition with Unique Elements

As previously demonstrated, it really doesn't take a great deal of effort to render a site unique. You have to spend some time thinking and then a little time working. The end of it all is a site you can be truly proud of, because it didn't come out of a box, but out of your own imagination and labor.

To show how small the elements were that I added to the basic logo to make the section logos, I've included Figure 8.10, which displays the four elements on the same screen in Photoshop. Paintshop Pro, Corel Paint, or any of a dozen graphics programs could have done the same thing so please don't panic, thinking you have to have a professional tool like Photoshop.

I'd encourage you to put together your own graphic elements, either by taking a snapshot of some "found art" and having it processed to Kodak Photo-CD-ROM or disk, or by using any graphics program you can get your hands on to put together something of your own. Although clip art is very nice and handy for many jobs, it does tend to be used over and over again. So go for the gold if you can, and never be ashamed of the best that you can do.

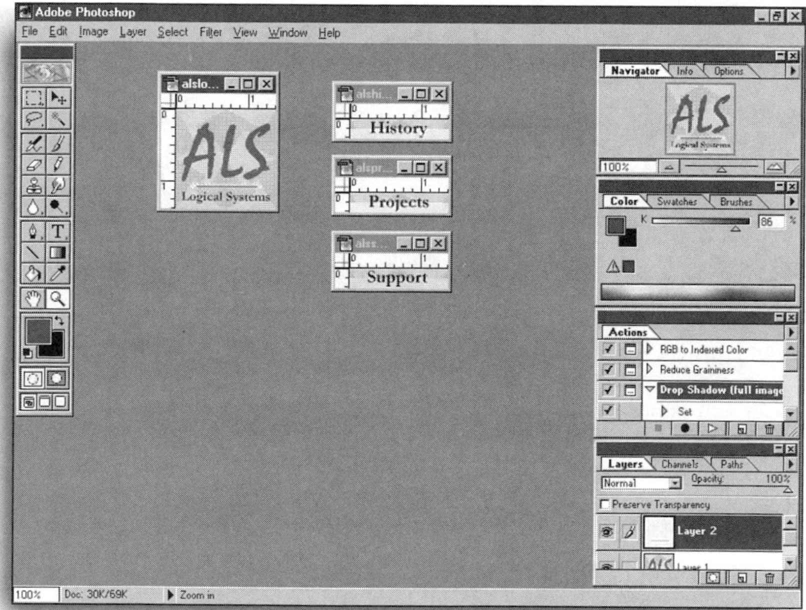

FIGURE 8.10
Photoshop screen showing all the elements of the workgroup logos.

CHAPTER

9

Using Imagemaps for Navigation

Getting started with imagemaps

Defining significant areas on the map

Creating alternatives to images

Pulling it all together

Imagemap utilities

Creating a remote control

Imagemaps can be used to create a "remote control" by making the buttons on the control hyperlinked hotspots. Be sure that the controls make sense or correspond to some familiar object to make them maximally useful.

Navigating an actual map

The most intuitive use of an imagemap is to make one out of an actual map. This can be an easy way to locate the nearest service center or showroom, for example, by asking the user to click their own location.

Navigating with Images

Whenever you're faced with a *navigation* problem too complex to explain in a few words, you may be looking at something that could be solved by an *imagemap*. Remember that a picture can be worth a thousand words if chosen or created carefully. A successful map visually corresponds to the site itself, or a portion of it, so that navigation is as quick and intuitive as driving to your favorite grocery store.

An unsuccessful map is the opposite: a hard-to-understand mess of incomprehensible icons, or an awkward *metaphor*, strained at best and confusing at worst.

Think of the times when you wished you had a picture to explain what you needed. If you don't know the correct terminology, a clear picture will let you point at "that thingamajig" with some degree of confidence that you're getting the right thing. If the range of possibilities is huge or amorphous, being able to get into the general areas with an intuitive pointing finger can be a huge time saver. How many people can look at a list of U.S. cities, for example, and identify exactly where in their respective states they're located?

Imagemaps can be *very* cool but are also overused on the Web. You get the impression sometimes that the designer sat down and decided to use a map whether it was needed or not, and just shoved a map into the site by brute force. What a waste! Imagemaps are often fairly expensive to load because they can be pretty big. Make sure your site really needs an imagemap before you decide to add one.

Finding an Appropriate Visual Metaphor

Creating imagemaps

1. Start by loading the graphic to be used as an imagemap. Specify the name of the map coordinates to use with the `usemap` attribute.

```
<IMG src="09fig01-kansasfarm-1913.jpg" alt="[Granddad on
a threshing crew in Kansas, 1913]"
longdesc="kansasfarm-1913.html"
usemap="#kansasfarm" width="450" height="321"border="0">
```

2. Define the map with a map tag, <MAP>. Use the name attribute to define the map for reference. The name should match the usemap attribute in the <IMG> tag, except for the # symbol.
   ```
   <MAP name="kansasfarm"></MAP>
   ```
3. Use your graphics program to identify coordinates on your image. Record these coordinates to be used by the coords attribute in the <AREA> tag.
4. Identify the areas in the imagemap with <AREA> tags, including a nohref to cover the entire area and be overridden by the areas chosen.
   ```
   <IMG src="image.jpg" usemap="imagemap">
       <MAP name="imagemap">
           <AREA shape="rect" coords="0, 0, 50, 50"
           href="firstarea.html">
           <AREA shape="rect" coords="60, 0,  80, 50"
           href="secondarea.html">
       </MAP>
   ```
   Quick usage tip: Tag syntax
   ```
   <AREA shape="areashape" coords="coordlist" href="mapurl"
   nohref>'
   ```
   where *areashape* is circ, rect, or poly; *coordlist* is a comma-delimited list of coordinates that define the shape; *mapurl* is the destination linked to by the map; and *nohref* is a default value that has no effect.

Imagemap tip

Almost every graphics editing program has an indication of where the cursor is located. That's good enough for an imagemap as it doesn't pay to be too finicky. The people clicking your map are going to select "somewhere close," and your measurements can be just that loose. For rectangular areas, select a rectangular area on the picture. There's usually a display showing the top left and bottom right locations.

For our first example, we're going to choose a subject for which there is no clear terminology. I've *scanned* in an old photograph of a farm scene in 1913 about which I happen to know a little. We'll pretend that it's out of a family album owned by Bess Fayne, and that she wants to start organizing her genealogical information on the Web so her many relatives can see it, too. It happens to be a picture of her paternal great-grandfather and one of the only ones that shows him as a young man, so it's important to her and she wants to share everything she knows.

Here she confronts a problem. How does she explain the photograph to someone who doesn't know the individuals involved? She could use the awkward reading-from-right-to-left convention used in actual photo albums, but there's almost always a potential for confusion in those sorts of directions. People aren't terribly good at judging whether we meant to start at the back row and read the people like lines in a book, or jump back and forth between front-row people and back based on actual horizontal displacement along an imaginary axis. Dang!

Photographs as maps

A photograph is often very complex to explain in words. Using an imagemap to allow the user to point at objects they want further information on is an excellent way of simplifying a difficult task.

Using metaphors

Many of the best imagemaps embody a metaphor. The natural act of pointing at something and asking what it is can be directly modeled in a map. Other metaphors might be borrowed from elevator buttons, television remote controls, and so on.

Luckily she figures that an imagemap will be a perfect solution. Her visitors can look at her picture and point at people they don't know and she'll tell them who it is and everything she knows about them with perfect clarity, just as if she were in the room.

So her visual metaphor is pointing at a picture and asking the question "Who's that?," which seems very natural for the subject matter.

Here's the resulting code:

```
<HTML>
  <HEAD>
    <TITLE>Fayne Family: Granddad on a farm in Kansas -
    1913</TITLE>
  ...
    <CENTER>
      <H1>Near Belle Plaine, Kansas - 1913</H1>
        <H2>A threshing crew poses by their tractor</H2>
          <IMG src="09fig01-kansasfarm-1913.jpg"
          alt="[Granddad on a threshing crew in Kansas,
          1913]" longdesc="kansasfarm-1913.html"
          usemap="#kansas farm" width="450" height="321"
          border="0">
          <MAP name="kansasfarm">
            <AREA shape="rect" coords="0,112   , 80,320"
              href="09fig01-neal-phillips.html">
            <AREA shape="rect" coords="88,118  , 154,320"
              href="09fig01-jay-phillips.html">
            <AREA shape="rect" coords="167,106 , 216,320"
              href="09fig01-crew-one.html">
            <AREA shape="rect" coords="217,106 , 259,320"
              href="09fig01-crew-two.html">
            <AREA shape="rect" coords="275,132 , 324,297"
              href="09fig01-frankie-phillips.html">
            <AREA shape="rect" coords="333,120 , 372,292"
              href="09fig01-crew-three.html">
            <AREA shape="rect" coords="373,130 , 415,266"
              href="09fig01-crew-four.html">
            <AREA shape="rect" coords="120,76  , 167,139"
              href="09fig01-albert-fayne.html">
```

```
            <AREA shape="rect" coords="260,83  , 373,249"
              href="09fig01-tractor.html">
            <AREA shape="rect" coords="355,60  , 384,117"
              href="09fig01-tractor.html">
            <AREA shape="rect" coords="269,298 , 302,320"
              href="09fig01-jay-phillips-hat.html">
            <AREA shape="rect" coords="326,296 , 405,320"
              href="09fig01-kansasfarm-location.html">
            <AREA shape="rect" coords="418,279 , 440,303"
              href="09fig01-kansasfarm-photographer-
              boyer.html">
            <AREA shape="rect" coords="0,0     , 449,320"
              nohref>
          </MAP>
          <H3>The photographer of this charming rural scene
          is Boyer, of whom I know nothing more</H3>
    </CENTER>
      <BLOCKQUOTE>
This picture was taken by a professional photographer
outside Belle Plaine, Kansas, in 1913. Many of the names of
the men and boys in the picture are unknown to me and anyone
having any information about them is invited to write and
let me know whatever they know in addition to what dim
family memories can provide. Three of the threshing crew are
members of the Phillips family, all brothers, and long-time
friends and acquaintances of the Faynes. Shown are William
Neal Phillips, Aden Jay Phillips, and Benjamin Franklin
Phillips, III. The man seated on the tractor is Edward
Albert Fayne, the head of the crew and owner of the tractor
which was bought from Hildebrandt's Hardware in Oxford,
Kansas. This hardware store is still in business in Oxford.
      </BLOCKQUOTE>
  ...
  </BODY>
</HTML>
```

For the sake of simplicity, I used rectangular *coordinates* for everything. For most purposes this is all that's really needed, because people will generally do a good job of pointing at what they want, and if their aim is a little off there will be some leeway. Each of the destination pages will have a small blowup of the person in the picture, if possible, so we've allowed for some error recovery as well. The destinations are very plainly labeled in the filenames, which will help people using text-mode browsers to select interesting destinations.

Rectangular coordinates

The simplest shapes to describe are rectangular, because you can pick them directly from the image without much calculation or estimation.

Figure 9.1 shows the edit screen of Paint Shop Pro displaying, in the lower-left status bar, the coordinates of the rectangle selected using the box tool.

FIGURE 9.1
The Kansas farm photo displayed in Paint Shop Pro, a relatively low-cost graphic editor with many advanced features.

Imagemap areas can overlap

You don't have to worry about overlapping your areas as long as you list them in order from the foreground to the background. A `nohref` default should always be the last area entry to account for any missing areas.

Provide feedback to the user

On a client-side imagemap, the destination will appear in the status bar as you move the pointing device. If you use meaningful names, this can help the user choose the right area.

Notice that people behind other people are listed last. That's because the browser will select the coordinates it finds first and go down the list until it finds a match. The `nohref` entry, which includes the entire picture, is dead last and behind everything, so it's the default choice. That's also what makes it easy to select the areas; you don't have to fiddle with trying to make sure that areas don't overlap, just do the best you can, starting with the foreground, and everything will sort itself out all right.

One huge advantage of client-side imagemaps is that the browser provides feedback in the status line to show what file you're pointing at. If the file names are meaningful, this can tell you who it is and let you know if you're a little off.

Figure 9.2 shows the page as built so far with the Albert Fayne destination selected with the mouse pointer.

FIGURE 9.2
The Kansas farm photo displayed in the browser.

Creating the Imagemap

Displaying imagemap coordinates

1. You can use the browser to locate the coordinates within any image. Simply use the `ismap` attribute.

   ```
   <A href="junk"><IMG src="09fig01-kansasfarm-1913.jpg"
   ismap border="0"></A>
   ```

   Quick usage tip: Tag syntax

   ```
   <A href="junk"><IMG src="imgurl" ismap></A>
   ```

   where *imgurl* is the location of the image.

2. This code will create a server-side imagemap and display the image coordinates in the browser.
3. Plug these values into the <AREA> tags to complete the imagemap.

Getting the coordinates

Images are measured from the upper-left corner, starting at 0,0 and measuring down and to the right. The horizontal measurement comes first and then the vertical measurement. The maximum measurement in any direction will always be one less than the width and height of the image.

Display image coordinates without special software

Use a temporary server-side imagemap to create your own "no-cost" coordinate finder. It doesn't have to connect with a real server because you're only using it to check coordinates.

Use any image as a map. As long as you can load it into your graphic editor, or even estimate the coordinates using a ruler on the screen image, you can do a decent-enough job of setting the coordinates.

If you don't have a graphic editor you can create a temporary file containing the code to create a server-side imagemap and use the display of coordinates in the browser to obtain coordinates easily. When you pass the mouse over the display, it will show the exact coordinates of the mouse. Estimating circles is easy as they have a center which you find by pointing at it, and a radius which you can estimate by moving the pointer vertically or horizontally—whichever is more convenient—and subtracting to get the value. Rectangles are specified by the upper-left coordinates followed by the lower-right coordinates. Polygons just trace out a path. All you need to do is plug those values into the area parameters and you've got your self a workable map.

Imagemaps aren't rocket science. Although shops sell special programs that capture area coordinates "automatically," they aren't really needed unless you plan to do loads of them. Close enough is good enough for most imagemaps, and you can quickly transfer coordinates into your HTML editor while switching back and forth between the edit file and the image. I never write them down, just flip back and forth until they're done—but then I can never find a pen!

Here's the code for a one-line no-brainer to display coordinates for this imagemap.

```
<A href="junk"><IMG src="09fig01-kansasfarm-1913.jpg"
ismap border="0"></A>
```

which results in the display shown in Figure 9.3.

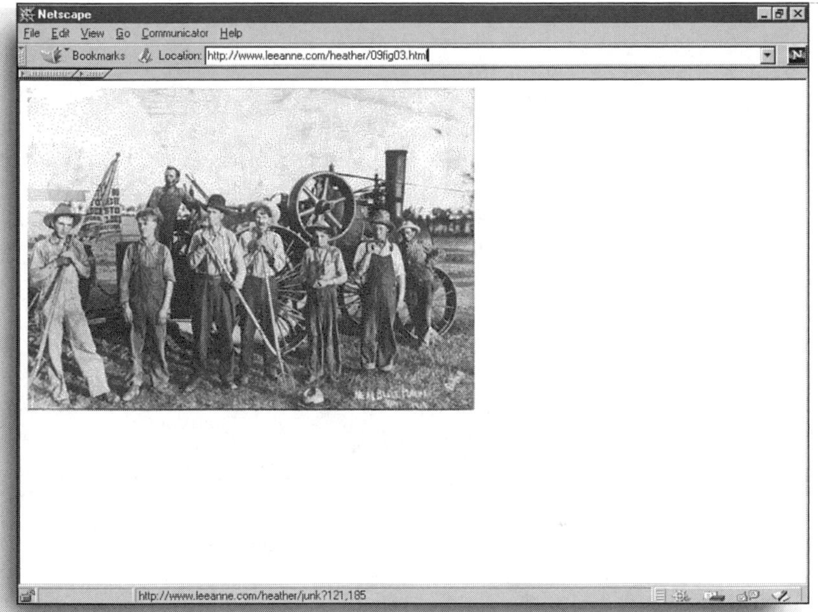

FIGURE 9.3
The farm image by itself, with coordinates visible in the status bar at the bottom of the screen.

Providing Alternative Navigation

Providing textual navigation along with imagemaps

1. Include a text description for each clickable area in the imagemap.
2. Match the links within the imagemap to the textual description.

```
<DT><A href="09fig01-neal-phillips.html">Neal
Phillips</A>
                <DD>Neal is 21 years old in this picture
<DT><A href="09fig01-jay-phillips.html">Jay Phillips</A>
                <DD>Jay is 18 years old here
```

There's one thing missing from our page so far, an alternate method of navigating to the various sub-pages. We really ought to provide this because it will make it a little easier to explain what the links refer to if for any reason they're viewed with images turned off.

Alternatives for text-only browsers

Any time you use an imagemap, you should also provide a navigation method for people who don't use graphical browsers. Many people cannot, and others choose not to load images, so providing an alternative is thoughtful. If there isn't room on the page or if it makes the page cluttered, you can easily link to a page that contains the special navigation selections.

We'll show just the code fragment and incorporate it into the page later.

```
    <H4>Listed in order from left to right and finally
    Albert on the tractor</H4>
  <DL>
    <DT><A href="09fig01-neal-phillips.html">Neal
    Phillips </A>
        <DD>Neal is 21 years old in this picture
    <DT><A href="09fig01-jay-phillips.html">Jay
    Phillips</A>
        <DD>Jay is 18 years old here
    <DT><A href="09fig01-crew-one.html">Unknown</A>
        <DD>Whoever he is, he's tall!
    <DT><A href="09fig01-crew-two.html">Unknown</A>
        <DD>With his mustache, he looks like a real
        character!
    <DT><A href="09fig01-frankie-phillips.html">Frank
    Phillips</A>
        <DD>Frank is 15 years old here and very small
    <DT><A href="09fig01-crew-three.html">Unknown</A>
        <DD>This man seems a little shy, hanging back
        from the group a little
    <DT><A href="09fig01-crew-four.html">Unknown</A>
        <DD>The man leaning against the tractor
    <DT><A href="09fig01-albert-fayne.html">Albert
    Fayne</A>
        <DD>Albert is 28 years old here and very
        proud of his tractor!
    <DT><A href="09fig01-tractor.html">Tractor</A>
        <DD>The tractor is a real monster!
    <DT><A href="09fig01-jay-phillips-hat.html">Hat</A>
        <DD>The hat lying on the ground probably
        belongs to Jay
    <DT><A href="09fig01-kansasfarm-location.html">
    Photo note</A>
        <DD>The note identifies the location and year
    <DT><A href="09fig01-kansasfarm-photographer-
    boyer.html">
    Photographer</A>
        <DD>The photographer identifies himself as
        Boyer </DL>
```

Figure 9.4 shows a page without images.

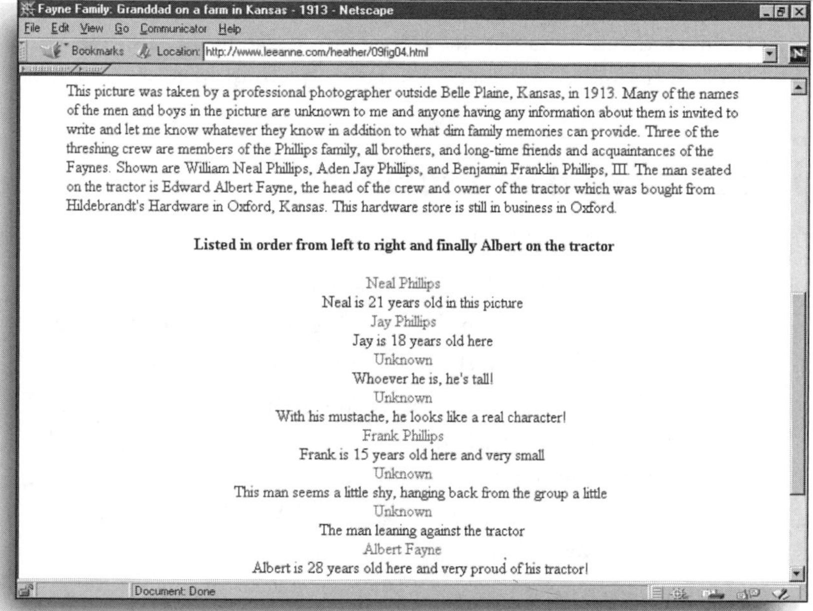

FIGURE 9.4
The Kansas farm page, showing the alternative navigation elements.

Making Link Names Meaningful

Although we provide alternate navigation on this page, sometimes the navigation elements are so numerous that you have to provide just one link to an alternate way of looking at the data. In that case, meaningful names are very important, because people can remember more easily where they've been.

Contrast the following list of names, which is meaningful to me but possibly not to you, with the longer names we used for the actual list:

56270901.html, 56270902.html, 56270903.html, 56270904.html, and so on...

Names with meaning are better

When you navigate through a site, meaningful names are easier to remember and relate to than arbitrary numbers or codes. If there's any chance that people will see a filename, as in the status display at the bottom of the screen, it pays to make the name as clear and self-explanatory as possible.

Naming conventions

If you must use arbitrary codes to organize a very large site, sometimes it makes sense to combine meaningful names with the codes to make a hybrid name, capturing the best of both worlds.

Not very user-friendly is it? These are the sorts of names one encounters on many large sites, but they're almost impossible to remember and type in for most people. It's worth the extra effort to make meaningful names, even if you precede them with a code, to identify their place in a large group of files.

Using Imagemap Tools

Using image mapping tools

1. Locate and download an imagemap utility.
2. Use mapping tools to shorten development time for large projects, or if you just like fooling with little utilities.

   Quick usage tip: The products discussed here work essentially the same way. You use a wizard to set up an initial file and then use point-and-click tools to outline areas you want to map. Both programs build an HTML file for you that contains the code necessary for the map.

Imagemap utilities

If you have a lot of images to make into maps, or if you need very close wrapping of a shape to an irregular image, a utility mapping tool makes a lot of sense. Basically, these tools collect mouse clicks on the image and stuff them into a description of the area you clicked around, making the process of saving the coordinates easy and nearly foolproof.

For our next trick we're going to discard my sage advice from the top of this chapter (how soon we forget!) and use two mapping tools to generate some code automatically. We'll use two programs (CoffeeCup's Image Mapper++ and LiveImage Corporation's LiveImage) to avoid any accusations of favoritism, and to let you see the similarities in both. They're shareware programs with a limited free trial, so you have the opportunity to download them and try them out before you buy them.

Both seem adequate to the task and fairly user-friendly, but I had some trouble importing existing files into LiveImage, so if you have a lot of existing code to maintain the other product might be a better choice. And, of course, by the time you read this the bug may have been fixed. Every program has *some* bugs and there are strengths and weaknesses to both. Overall, I couldn't choose between them and you might well choose to purchase both. They're not terribly expensive. They're both available from TUCOWS at `http://www.tucows.com/`, which is a great site for downloading because there are so many local versions of the site scattered around the world. In general, the closer the site you download from, the faster everything goes. I list their own Web sites later so you can also read about them, but you're usually better off downloading from Tucows.

We'll open our existing file in CoffeeCup's Image Mapper++, discarding a few of the more visually confusing areas so we can clearly see the results of picking areas by hand. It's really not bad, is it? The figures are fairly well contained in their rectangular boxes and there seems to be little opportunity for getting lost without a deliberate effort. We could tweak the settings in Mapper++, or replace them with *polygons*, but let's not and say we did, eh? You'll notice that my file's hrefs have disappeared, which is annoying because the time I save by being able to tweak my areas will likely be lost reinserting the file destinations. On the other hand, it automatically puts in code for mouseovers, so maybe it's a wash either way. You can download CoffeeCup Image Mapper++ from `http://www.coffeecup.com/`.

Warning: Information may be lost!

When you open an existing file containing an imagemap, Image Mapper++ silently discards some of your information, which is an unfortunate tendency in a program supposedly designed to save you time. Always work on a copy of your file and save the original in a safe place.

Next, we'll try creating code from scratch in LiveImage (found at `http://www.liveimage.com/`). Using the wizard, I select the graphic file and make a new HTML file, and then start clicking. By selecting the polygon tool, I can trace the outline of each person in the file, then double-click when I'm done, and it will pop up a menu asking what the destination file is. Very neat! You can see the result after a few outlines, and it's quite impressive how well you can follow the outline, even if you're as impatient as I am. (I tried the same thing in the CoffeeCup program and it works in a very similar way.) On the other hand, every image took more than two dozen mouse clicks, and by the time I finished outlining all the figures in the photo, as well as the umbrella just for the heck of it, my wrist was a little sore from mousing and I was thoroughly bored. But then I wouldn't use polygons normally and would have been excruciatingly bored trying to follow the outlines that closely by hand. Here's a sample of just one of the coordinate lists:

```
<AREA SHAPE=POLY COORDS="140,242,139,261,141,281,146,297,151,
305,146,311,130,302,124,297,118,245,116,273,117,286,114,300,
107,310,99,312,96,308,97,303,104,293,103,265,101,246,104,234,
99,234,93,200,93,190,97,160,103,153,109,150,113,149,111,142,
110,134,110,127,113,122,119,118,133,125,134,133,131,142,128,
144,133,149,140,156,146,166,150,185,150,196,148,205,144,218,
140,242"
HREF="jay-phillips" ALT="">
```

Try *that* by hand, eh? If your project needs close tolerances and image-hugging maps, you'd be crazy not to use one of these tools. In fact, if you're obsessive about precision, you might want to use this tool whether it's crazy or not. My own preference for rectangles is due partly to the fact that they're so easy and partly because they can be easily converted to a collection of discrete images that can be navigated directly.

The one thing I'd really like to change about both programs would be to insert spaces around the inter-pair commas, as I did in the example code. I really like code to be easy to read and self-documenting to some extent. The mashed-together numbers are hard to inspect or fiddle with by hand, something I often do.

Both programs possess the irritating notion that they are the center of the universe and try to open and save files in their home directory first, requiring more tedium and mouse clicks as you click through the directories putting things back where you got them. Oh well, nobody's perfect.

All in all, if I had a *lot* of imagemaps to do, or did them every day, I'd probably use the tools to eliminate some of the possibilities for error using a manual method. But as rarely as I make imagemaps, I don't really see the need. Your mileage may vary, of course, and you may get tired of entering coordinate pairs more quickly. I find it soothing and mechanical and it's soon done, leaving me time to do other things. And of course, I never make mistakes. Did you hear thunder rumble just now?

Figures 9.5 and 9.6 show the same image being edited in the two different mapping packages.

Saving your sanity as well as your time

As the example shows, an imagemap utility program can help make your life a lot easier when the areas defined on your image are complex. Mapping all the coordinates of a freeform polygon like this without making even one mistake is a daunting task without an automated tool.

Go with the flow

Since both programs like their own home directories better than any other place and will rewrite your code if you open it in them, you might consider leaving the skeleton files they create in that location, copying the generated code into your actual page instead of trying to work directly in your Web directories.

FIGURE 9.5

The picture being edited in CoffeCup Image Mapper++ with rectangles.

FIGURE 9.6

The picture being edited in LiveImage with polygons.

CHAPTER

10

Animating Graphics

Add movement and life with simple animations

Create slide shows

Using animation tools

Draw Attention with Animation

Our eyes are naturally attracted to motion, and some of the most successful pages exploit this by means of an easy technique called *animation*. Although the total size and load time of an animated image file is increased, the initial image loads in about the same time as a single image, so the time to load the page to the point that you can see and navigate is not really increased. Animation is a very easy way to add motion to the page in comparison to video, for example, or plug-in techniques, and should be tried first before more exotic means.

Attracting Attention with Animations

Adding movement and life by including GIF animations

1. Create GIF animations yourself or borrow them from the Web.
2. Add them to your pages with the image tag, just like an ordinary image.

```
<IMG src="kitty.gif" height="" width="" alt="[Kitty]>
```

Quick usage tip: Tag syntax

```
<IMG src="imgurl" height="imgheight" width="imgwidth"
alt="alttext" longdesc="alttexturl" hspace="gutter"
vspace="gutter" border= "linkborder" align="alignment">
```

where *`imgurl`* is the location of the image source; *`imgheight`* is the height of the image in pixels; *`imgwidth`* is the width of the image in pixels; *`alttext`* is a short description of the image if `significant`, or `null` if it can be ignored by non-visual browsers; *`alttexturl`* is the location of a longer description of the image; *`gutter`* is the horizontal or vertical empty space surrounding the image; *`linkborder`* is the width of the border in pixels when an image is used as a link; and *`alignment`* is `left`, `right`, `top`, `middle`, or `bottom` and alters the relative position of text and image on the page.

Let's start out by finding an animation ready to load from one of the many sites which offer free animations. This is the simplest way to use animations, because someone else has already done the work. Often, you're free to use the animation in exchange for a credit and a link somewhere on your page. For additional ways to add motion to your Web page, see Chapter 11, "Adding Sound and Video," and Chapter 12, "Including Java Applets."

Here's the URL of Web GraFX-FX, a large site with loads of animations and links to other animation sites available.

```
http://webgrafx-fx.com/pages/archive.html
```

We'll search the site for something Bess might want to use on her page, at least to start out. She finds a little picture of a kitty she thinks might be darling on the page, downloads it from the site, and then inserts it in her home page.

```
<HTML>
  <BODY>
    <IMG src="kitty.gif" height="" width="" alt="[Kitty]>
    ...
  </BODY>
</HTML>
```

The display is still not what she truly wants, but she's getting there. The kitty animation attracts attention, but it doesn't really have anything to do with the Fayne family. It's really just a little piece of random kitsch and distracts from her basic message. If her page had been about "Secrets your cat wishes you knew," it would be very appropriate, but under the circumstances, she resists the temptation to use it, even though it's very cute, as shown in Figure 10.1.

Special Animation Effects

Creating a slide show to inject unique content into your page without special drawing skills

1. Choose the images you wish to include in your slide show.
2. Use an image editing package to crop the image to the same size.

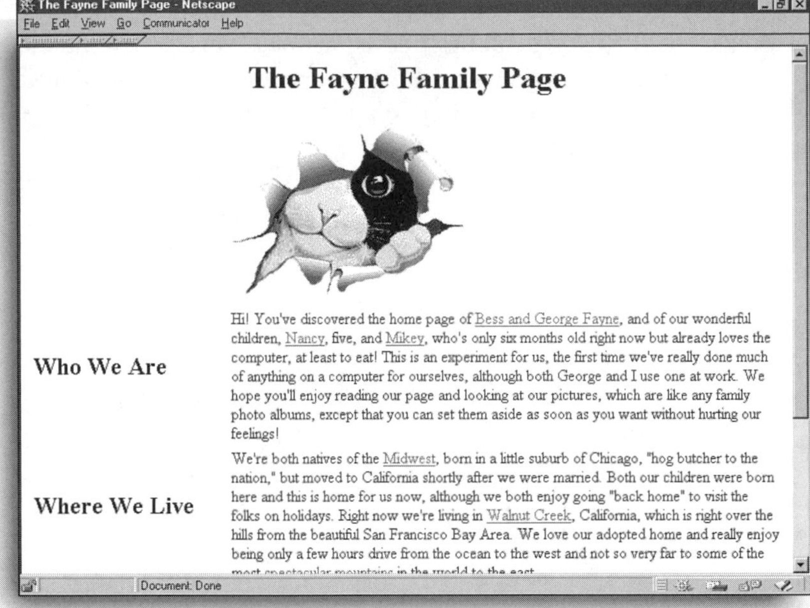

FIGURE 10.1
The Fayne home page with a very cute winking kitty.

3. Create a GIF animation using a tool like the GIF Construction Set for Windows or GIF Builder for the Mac.
4. Place the GIF animation on your Web page using the `<IMG>` tag, just like an ordinary image.

Bess didn't like the "found" animation in the context of her page, but she doesn't have the special skills to draw her own animation, so decides to make a special kind of animation called a slide show. A slide show only requires some pictures, all the same size, with a similar appearance.

Without a scanner, how can she use some of her existing photos to make the slide show? Luckily there are two ways to do it. You can take them to a shop that will scan them for you, turning them into files that you can use on your computer, or you can take them to almost any camera shop or film processing store in the world and have them copied to a Kodak Photo CD-ROM.

Just say "No" to bad art

Don't be afraid to toss out an image that doesn't quite work for your page. You're better off without any image than with one that detracts from your page or sends a different message than the one you want. Just as you (probably) wouldn't decorate a letter to your sweetheart with a skull and crossbones or daggers dripping blood, you want your images to enhance your page, not compete with it.

This is an incredibly cool way to start making your own image library, guaranteed to be royalty-free, and it's pretty cheap as well. If you have a professional do the developing of the exposed film, it costs less than a dollar an image. Scanning existing photos or negatives are slightly more, but not exorbitant. You can make a slide show out of your snapshots on your computer screen as well, so this is one more way to trick your guests into looking at baby pictures.

To edit and crop the images, we'll use several inexpensive tools including Paint Shop Pro (`http://www.jasc.com/`), an image editing tool, and Photo Shop (`http://www.metacreations.com`), a tool specifically designed to make it easy for home users to touch up and crop their photos.

We'll choose three photos out of the many available, one of Bess, one of Nancy, and one of little Mikey. This will make an attractive slide show and relates directly to the point of the page, which is to spotlight the Fayne family. This results in the display shown in Figure 10.2

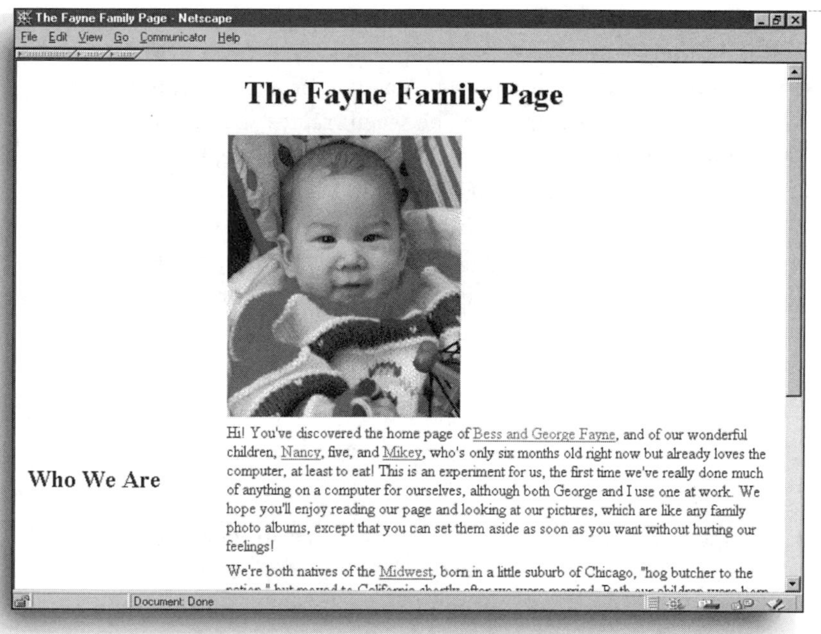

FIGURE 10.2
The Fayne page with a slide show.

Using Animation Tools

Using animation tools to put your graphics together into animations

1. Open a new GIF animation file.
2. Load each individual image into the file.
3. Set any additional attributes like looping values.
4. Save your file as a regular GIF image.

Now that you have a selection of images to animate, you need to put them together into an animated image file. There are a wide variety of tools available, from utilities within larger graphics programs to standalone packages that do only the one thing. Well-known packages include the GIF Construction Set (`http://www.alchemymindworks.com/`) for Windows platforms and the freeware GifBuilder for the Macintosh, but there are lots more. Try out a selection from `http://www.tucows.com/` or other download sites before selecting your favorite. Ulead's GifAnimator has gotten very good reviews, and others may be more user friendly than the most well known.

To use the animation tool, we first crop and size our images so that they're exactly the same size and orientation, and then use the tool to pull them in one-at-a-time or in bulk, adding delays and possibly special effects between frames. Some tools allow you to *optimize the color palette* at the same time, but others assume that the palette is optimized going in. That's just a fancy way of saying that color files save enough room to include many more colors than the typical file uses. By telling your graphics program that you aren't using those extra colors, you may be able to save room in the file and make it faster to download from the server.

Most of the packages work much the same way, so I'll discuss the way GIF Construction Set works, since it's widely used and relatively inexpensive.

Open GIF Construction Set and you see an index of any GIF files in your current directory. You can choose one of these to start your animation, or go look for another. Selecting the images is very straightforward, as you just choose them one at a time from a directory index.

When you're done selecting images, insert control points between each image. These controls let you define the time interval between one frame of the animation and the next. For a slide show choose several seconds, while an animated cartoon may require a few milliseconds. Finally, insert a loop command to tell the browser how many times to look at the animation.

It's a good idea to stop the animation eventually, just to avoid annoying people, so choose a reasonable value for the number of times to loop.

Figure 10.3 shows the result and it looks great, even though we can't show every image in this book.

Select delay times to make the animation look natural

Selecting the delay times is critical to making sure that the animation looks natural and neither looks jerky or hectic nor runs so slowly that people get bored watching it. Most programs have a view selection that lets you see how the image will look without loading it into a browser.

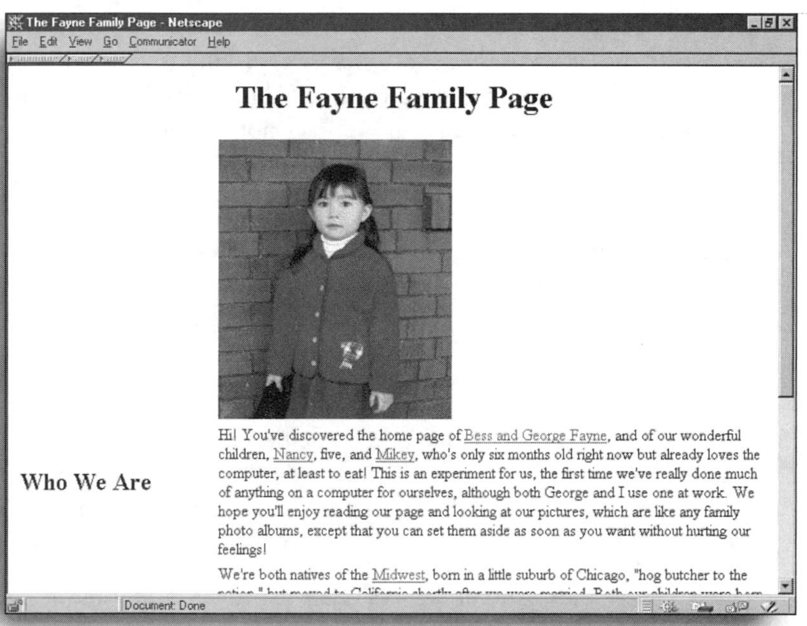

FIGURE 10.3

The Fayne slide show showing one frame of three.

When you create an animated image, it's a good idea to test it using as many different browsers as you can find. There are many formats for animation, and not all of them display well in every browser.

Using Animation to Load Placeholder Images Quickly

Using animation to create a more universal version of the Netscape *lowsrc* attribute

1. If a "quick look" is more important than overall load time, create a very low resolution image.
2. Use the `lowscr` attribute of the `<IMG>` tag to load this low resolution image first. The final version will replace the low resolution version.

```
<IMG lowsrc="kitty-low.gif"src="kitty.gif" height=""
width="" alt="[Kitty]>
```

In Netscape Navigator and Communicator, images have a `lowres` attribute that does an initial load before replacing it with the final version. It's an interesting technique but, although it covers the majority of browsers on the Web, it's not universal and is not a part of the new HTML 4.0 Recommendation.

Of interest, you can use animation to create almost the same effect and with far more coverage. You can't do quite as much in the way of shrinkage since animations have to follow a few more rules than the `lowres` attribute enforces, but the resulting graphic will load the low resolution image first before continuing with the second, just like `lowres`.

Interlacing accomplishes much the same thing, with the familiar blocky blur coalescing gradually into a clear picture. But that effect gets old after a while, and you may want to experiment with this alternative.

First, create a low resolution version of the image you want to load quickly. You can use a graphics editor to reduce the color depth to black and white, for example, or a gray scale. This usually makes the file much smaller and helps the image load faster. So you'll have two images: the first, a low-resolution version, and the second at normal resolution.

Just as with any animation, load the two images into your animation utility program. Since you don't want a delay between the first image and the next, you can eliminate the control block and, because you don't want it to loop, you can eliminate that control block as well.

The result is shown in Figure 10.4.

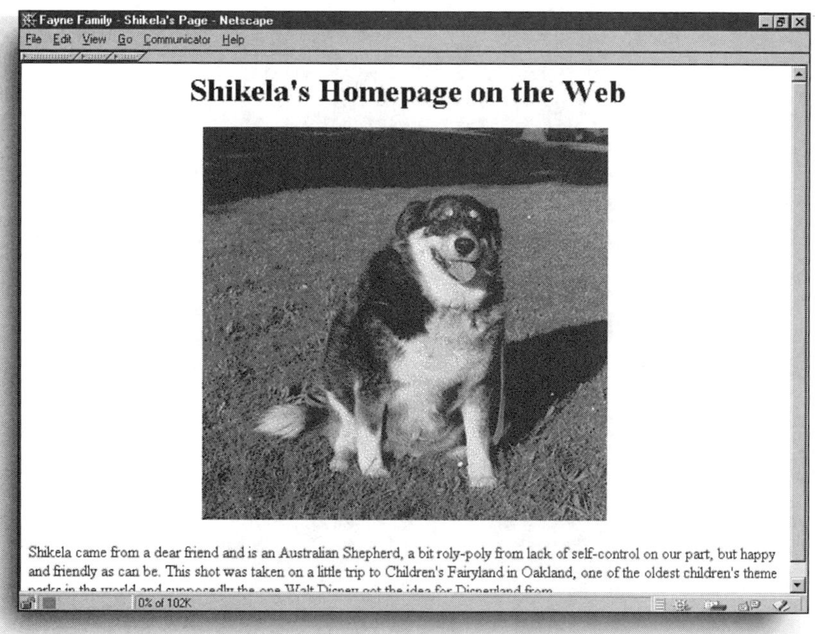

FIGURE 10.4
A low-resolution first image in an animation.

CHAPTER

11

Adding Sound and Video

Use sound to add a new dimension to the browsing experience for visitors

---

Use video to add optional motion and life to a page

Entertain with Sound and Video

Sound and motion are among the most arresting of the sensations that surround most of us. Incorporating these elements into a Web page can make them seem more like real life (or at least TV) and less like something you'd expect from a computer, or at least your parent's computers of years gone by.

Don't let your pages fall behind in this evolution of entertainment values on the Internet if you're aiming your page toward young people or to attract people's attention to amuse or divert them. While sound and video or other multimedia are not necessary for everyone, they can add immeasurably to a site's audience appeal if the sounds and sights are carefully chosen.

The simplest and oldest method is the simple sound file, so we'll look at that first.

Using .WAV and .AU Files

Adding basic sound effects or "sound bites"

1. Add sounds with the object tag, `<OBJECT>`, the general-purpose means of including non-text content. Several options may be offered by nesting object tags.

   Quick usage tip: Tag syntax

   ```
   <OBJECT data="soundurl" type="audio/mimetype"
   height="imgheight" width="imgwidth"> ...alternative
   content for non-supporting browsers, including a nested
   object tag... </OBJECT>
   ```

   where *soundurl* is the location of the sound file; *mimetype* is one of the audio MIME types; and *imgheight* and *imgwidth* are the height and width override values.

   ```
   <OBJECT data="greetings.wav" type="audio/wav" width="145"
   height="60">
   </OBJECT>
   ```

2. Add a little "kickstart" with a `<PARAM>` tag immediately after the opening object tag.

   Quick usage tip: Tag syntax

   ```
   <PARAM name="autostart" value="true">
   ```

where `name` and `value` are Netscape values that make the application start instead of merely loading and waiting for the user to play it.

```
<OBJECT data="greetings.wav" type="audio/wav" width="145"
height="60"><PARAM name="autostart" value="true">
</OBJECT>
```

3. Provide alternate sound content inside the lowest level of object tag with the `<EMBED>` tag.

   Quick usage tip: Tag syntax

   ```
   <EMBED src="soundurl" type="mimetype" height="imgheight"
   width="imgwidth" hidden="value" autostart="autovalue">
   ```

   where *soundurl* is the location of the sound source; *mimetype* is the MIME content type of the data that the plug-in will fetch for itself or contain; *imgheight* and *imgwidth* are the size of the display, if any; and *autovalue* is true if you want the sound to start automatically. Either the `src` or the `type` attribute is mandatory and `height` and `width` are advisable unless the embedded object is hidden. The `hidden` attribute is optional and controls whether the sound player will be visible; *value* is `true` or `false`.

   ```
   <OBJECT data="greetings.wav" type="audio/wav" width="145"
   height="60">
   <PARAM name="autostart" value="true">
   <EMBED src="greetings.wav" type="audio/wav" width="145"
      height="60">
   </OBJECT>
   ```

4. Provide alternate content for browsers that don't support embedded objects or sound with the `<NOEMBED>` tag.

   Quick usage tip: Tag syntax

   ```
   <NOEMBED>...alternative content for non-supporting
   browsers...<NOEMBED>
   ```

   The following is our code so far:

   ```
   <OBJECT data="greetings.wav" type="audio/wav" width="145"
      height="60">
   <PARAM name="autostart" value="true">
   <EMBED src="greetings.wav" type="audio/wav" width="145"
      height="60">
   <NOEMBED>
       <P>
   ```

```
    [Bess and George Fayne speak: Hi ya! Come on
    in!]<BR>
      <A href="greetings.wav">Get the sound file!</A>
<NOEMBED>
</OBJECT>
```

5. Provide alternate sound content for Microsoft Internet Explorer with the `<BGSOUND>` tag.

   Quick usage tip: Tag syntax

   ```
   <BGSOUND src="soundurl" loop="number">
   ```

   where *soundurl* is the location of the sound source and *number* is the number of times to loop, if any. A value of `-1` tells the browser to loop the sound forever. This is usually a bad idea.

   ```
   <OBJECT data="greetings.wav" type="audio/wav" width="145"
      height="60">
   <PARAM name="autostart" value="true">
   <EMBED src="greetings.wav" type="audio/wav" width="145"
      height="60">
   <NOEMBED>
       <P>
       [Bess and George Fayne speak: Hi ya! Come on
       in!]<BR>
       <A href="greetings.wav">Get the sound file!</A>
   <NOEMBED>
   </OBJECT>
   <BGSOUND src="greetings.wav">
   ```

To start with, this set of actions is more complicated than most we've done before. Why tag the sound file twice? There *is* a reason. The `<EMBED>` tag is on its way out, being replaced by the new HTML 4.0 `<OBJECT>` tag, but `<EMBED>` is still widespread while the `<OBJECT>` tag isn't. Learning this technique of tagging twice (or even more) for one effect is an interim measure until the new tags become more widely used.

In fact, because of the way the `<OBJECT>` tag was designed, you can safely use both, one inside the other, to cover the long transition period during which both tags will be needed. That's what we're doing here; starting with the more modern and universal tag and using the non-standard tag within it. Part of the `<OBJECT>`

tag is something we haven't really seen before, an attribute describing its MIME type, which is a fancy way of saying that we're telling the browser what kind of file we're expecting. This attribute is optional but advisable because the browser can look at it to see if it knows what to do with a file before loading it, saving time for users who aren't interested. The other advisable attributes are `height` and `width`, but we don't really know those in advance since the rendering is performed by a browser plug-in. You'll have to make a wild guess, which just happens to be 145×60. Table 11.1 lists the basic MIME types that your browser may support.

Browser plug-in sizes are not standard

In the case of players provided by the browser, it's very difficult to know their size in advance, so you'll have to play with them to allocate enough space for basic audio file players. If you don't mind a little extra gray space or clipping them slightly, a common size is 145 wide by 60 high.

TABLE 11.1 Audio MIME types

Basic Audio MIME Types for Sound		
.wav	audio/wav	Windows platforms
.wav	audio/x-wav	Windows platforms
.au	audio/basic	UNIX and other platforms
.aiff	audio/aiff	Macintosh platforms
.aiff	audio/x-aiff	Macintosh platforms

We'll also use the `<NOEMBED>` tag to provide alternative text content for browsers that don't support sound, or for those in our audience who don't appreciate it. Our text-only content is non-judgmental, unlike so much of what you see on the Web. In the case of deaf or hearing-impaired users, telling them to get a new browser so they can hear is both thoughtless and unkind. In the case of people using other browsers by choice, well, what they use and why is none of our business in any case. If you'll pardon me for climbing on a soap box for just a bit, just as the proper alternative text for images is a simple description, the responsible alternative text for sounds is a plain description, not an arrogant lecture on which browser they *should* be using.

Always use alternate text

Always provide alternate text content for sound files. If the sound is used in any meaningful way, to set a mood or attract attention, see if you can provide a "stage direction" to accomplish the same thing. If the audio file is a short "sound bite," you can simply transcribe the quote as text.

For our first sound file, we'll add a spoken greeting to the Fayne home page to welcome visitors and give us a chance to show off our new sound card. To save space, we won't describe how capturing the voice is done, since every operating system and card can incorporate different methods, and we'll show only the changed text.

Through some sort of magic, then, we have a sound file and want to play it. First, we'll type in the <OBJECT> tag with the attributes needed for a simple sound file and a descriptive content. The data attribute points to the data and the type attribute tells the browser what kind of data it is.

```
<BODY>
    ...
    <OBJECT data="greetings.wav" type="audio/wav"
    width="145" height="60">
      <P>
        [Bess and George Fayne speak: Hi ya! Come on in!]
    </OBJECT>
</BODY>
```

According to the most recent standard, that's all you really need, but no one seems to do it that way. To actually get it to work correctly in Netscape, you'll have to add a parameter tag (<PARAM>) to tell your shiny new object to start working. Since we're trying to be as inclusive as possible, we'll also add an <EMBED> tag, a non-standard way of embedding sounds that's very widely supported on older Netscape browsers. <EMBED> uses an odd <NOEMBED> tag to contain alternative content, so we'll wrap our text with that and add a way for people who are absolutely intent on knowing what the greeting sounds like to download it separately. Presumably they can play it with some sort of external program. We could have done that inside the <OBJECT> tag as well and probably should have, but the nice thing about HTML is you can always go back and add little refinements like that as they occur to you.

```
<BODY>
    ...
    <OBJECT data="greetings.wav" type="audio/wav"
    width="145" height="60">
      <PARAM name="autostart" value="true">
      <EMBED src="greetings.wav" type="audio/wav"
      width="145" height="60">
```

```
            <NOEMBED>
              <P>
                [Bess and George Fayne speak: Hi ya! Come on
                in!]<BR>
                <A href="greetings.wav">Get the sound
                file!</A>
            <NOEMBED>
        </OBJECT>
    </BODY>
```

Well, that's great. Now we have a file that will play almost anywhere, don't we? Is there any thing else we can think of?

In a word, yes. The .wav file we used is a Windows audio format, as we saw in Table 11.1, but what if our viewers are using UNIX or Macintoshes? It depends. They *might* have a helper application that lets them hear .wav files, or they might not. Since we want to make the file audible to the widest possible range of visitors, we can use nested `<OBJECT>` tags, outside the `<EMBED>` tag fallback position and inside the first Windows version, to offer alternatives to still more people.

First we'll have to do more magic to turn our .wav file into the other formats. I used a brand of magic for the Windows PC called Cool Edit from Syntrillium, `http://www.syntrillium.com/`, a shareware program widely available for Windows systems (see Figure 11.1). There are similar programs available for other platforms that cost very little, including Norman Franke's freeware SoundApp, `http://www-cs-students.stanford.edu/~franke/SoundApp/`, for the Macintosh. Of course you can start out with any supported sound format and use these tools to turn it into the others.

We'll use two levels of nesting, the first level for Macintoshes and the second level for UNIX, and hope to accommodate everyone. Please note that every `<OBJECT>` tag will need its own `<PARAM>` tag to set it going. While we're at it, we'll also add tags to allow users to download the files themselves inside the noembed tag pair. For more information on accessibility, see Chapter 26, "Creating Widely Accessible Web Pages."

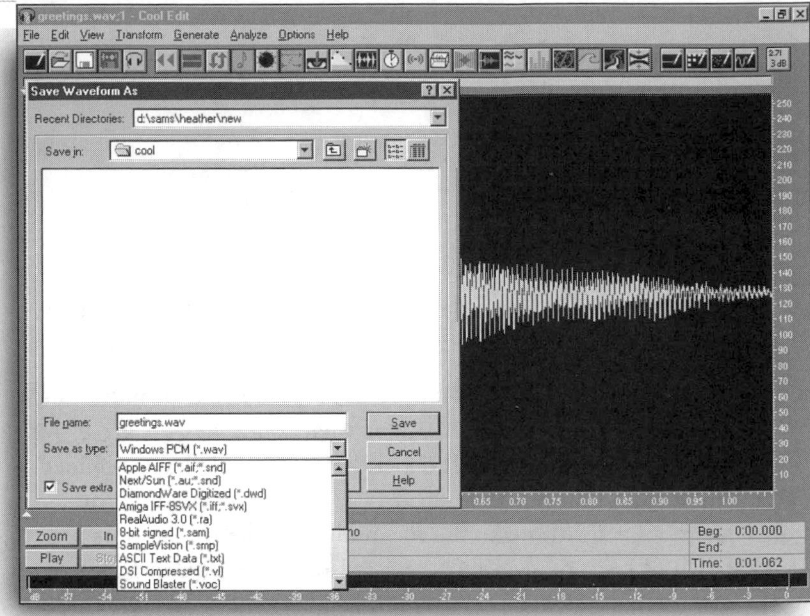

Figure 11.1

The editing screen for Cool Edit 98, a shareware audio file conversion and editing program, showing the Save As possibilities.

```
<BODY>
    ...
    <OBJECT data="greetings.wav" type="audio/wav"
    width="145" height="60">
      <PARAM name="autostart" value="true">
      <OBJECT data="greetings.aiff" type="audio/aiff"
      width="145" height="60">
      <PARAM name="autostart" value="true">
        <OBJECT data="greetings.au" type="audio/basic"
        width="145" height="60">
        <PARAM name="autostart" value="true">
          <EMBED src="greetings.wav" type="audio/wav"
          height="imgheight" width="145" height="60">
            <NOEMBED>
              <P>
                [Bess and George Fayne speak: Hi ya!
                Come on in!]<BR>
              <A href="greetings.wav">Get the Windows
              .wav sound file!</A><BR>
```

```
                <A href="greetings.aiff">Get the Mac .aiff
                sound file!</A><BR>
                <A href="greetings.au">Get the Unix .au
                sound file!</A><BR>
            <NOEMBED>
         </OBJECT>
      </OBJECT>
   </OBJECT>
</BODY>
```

The code looks complex but it really isn't; there's just a lot of it. The resulting screen is shown in Figure 11.2. All the sound object tags nest inside each other and the browser will decide which one it will display based on which it encounters first and recognizes. Many modern browsers will display any or all of the listed file types, so this is slightly excessive if you expect all your visitors to be using the latest and greatest versions of whatever. The reality of the Web, though, is that many people are perfectly happy with the browser they have, even if it's a few years old, and may not be motivated to upgrade anytime soon.

You can't depend on visitors having any particular browser

People won't upgrade their browsers until they feel they need to. If you want your page to be useful and attractive to everyone, you have to take into account the wide variety of browsers on the Web and plan for them. It's not terribly difficult to make pages that will work for almost everyone, so why not do it?

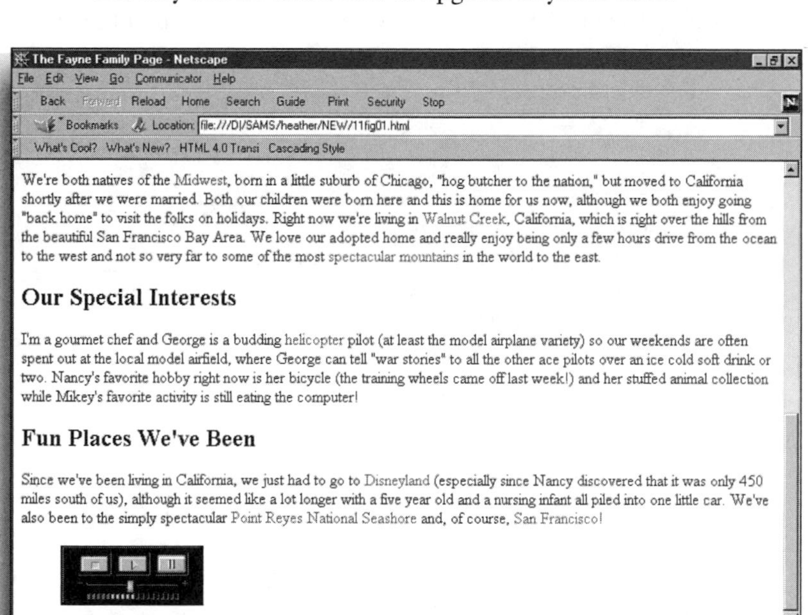

FIGURE 11.2
The Fayne family home page with a sound file player embedded.

There's one last thing we should do to the page to make sure we cover as many bases as possible. Because the Microsoft implementation of object tags wasn't quite what the Internet standards body codified, the previous code won't work for many Microsoft Internet Explorer versions. They use a `<BGSOUND>` tag to do much the same thing as the Netscapism, `<embed hidden="true" ...>`. To make very sure that we cover as many browsers as possible, we should add either a visible link to the audio file or incorporate it in a `<BGSOUND>` tag. Other browsers will ignore it, so it's a pretty safe thing to do. Internet Explorer may show an advisory notice or a broken icon symbol, both of which can be ignored. There's not much you can do about it in any case.

Warning: Browsers often use multimedia in a non-standard way

In the present uncertain mix of features and incompatibilities that plague the browser market, all you can do is your best. Every manufacturer seems intent on hanging on to its own "pet" tags, and, even with all the skill and good will in the world, you're going to make some strange displays on some browsers. You can only do your best and try to affect no one badly, and as few people in a minor way, as you can.

In general, I don't like coding around bugs and extensions to base functionality, figuring that the browser manufacturers have to have some incentive to fix their broken code, but video and audio are so nonstandard and so important to the page that I don't mind spending a little extra time making sure it works for almost everyone. Ask me again in a few years, when the manufacturers have had a chance to fix their code, and I might have entirely different advice and suggest going with the `<OBJECT>` tag to the exclusion of everything else.

```
<BODY>
    ...
    <OBJECT data="greetings.wav" type="audio/wav"
    width="145" height="60">
      <PARAM name="autostart" value="true">
      <OBJECT data="greetings.aiff" type="audio/aiff"
      width="145" height="60">
        <PARAM name="autostart" value="true">
        <OBJECT data="greetings.au" type="audio/basic"
        width="145" height="60">
          <PARAM name="autostart" value="true">
          <EMBED src="greetings.wav" type="audio/wav"
          height=" imgheight" width="145" height="60">
            <NOEMBED>
              <P>
```

```
                    [Bess and George Fayne speak: Hi ya!
                    Come on in!]<BR>
                  <A href="greetings.wav">Get the Windows
                  .wav sound file!</A><BR>
                  <A href="greetings.aiff">Get the Mac .aiff
                  sound file!</A><BR>
                  <A href="greetings.au">Get the Unix .au
                  sound file! </A><BR>
                <NOEMBED>
            </OBJECT>
          </OBJECT>
        </OBJECT>
        <BGSOUND src="greetings.wav">
    </BODY>
```

There are lots of audio types

The range of audio file types is fairly large but three options–.wav, .au, and .aiff–will cover most of the browsers and platforms on the market today. If you have the time, it's thoughtful to provide all three types to account for most of your potential viewers.

Include MIDI Files

Adding music to your page with MIDI files

1. Add MIDI (Musical Instrument Digital Interface) files for lots of sound in a small file. Several options may be offered by nesting `<OBJECT>` tags.

   ```
   <OBJECT data="homesweethome.mid" width="145" height="60">
   </OBJECT>
   ```

2. Add a little "kickstart" with a `<PARAM>` tag immediately after the opening object tag.

   ```
   <OBJECT data="homesweethome.mid" width="145" height="60">
   <PARAM name="autostart" value="true">
   </OBJECT>
   ```

3. Provide alternate sound content inside the lowest level of `<OBJECT>` tag with the `<EMBED>` tag.

   ```
   <OBJECT data="homesweethome.mid" width="145" height="60">
   <PARAM name="autostart" value="true">
   <EMBED src="homesweethome.mid" width="145" height="60">
   </OBJECT>
   ```

4. Provide alternate content for browsers that don't support embedded objects or sound with the <NOEMBED> tag.

```
<OBJECT data="homesweethome.mid" width="145" height="60">
  <PARAM name="autostart" value="true">
  <EMBED src="homesweethome.mid" width="145"
  height="60">
    <NOEMBED>
      <P>
        [Sentimental music plays in the background:
        Home Sweet Home]<BR> <A href="homesweethome.
        mid">Get the MIDI file!</A><BR>
    <NOEMBED>
</OBJECT>
```

5. Provide alternate sound content for Microsoft Internet Explorer with the <BGSOUND> tag.

```
<OBJECT data="homesweethome.mid" width="145" height="60">
  <PARAM name="autostart" value="true">
  <EMBED src="homesweethome.mid" width="145"
  height="60">
    <NOEMBED>
      <P>
        [Sentimental music plays in the background:
        Home Sweet Home]<BR> <A href="homesweethome.
        mid">Get the MIDI file!</A><BR>
    <NOEMBED>
</OBJECT>
<BGSOUND src="homesweethome.mid">
```

A MIDI file is used in just the same way as a WAV or AU file, by enclosing it in the proper tags. The sequence is exactly the same, so we won't go through all the steps in quite the same detail. We insert an <OBJECT> tag describing our MIDI file and, since they don't have a MIME type associated with them in most browsers, we leave off the type attribute. We include an enclosed <EMBED> tag to handle older versions of Navigator and also a freestanding (unenclosed) <BGSOUND> tag to handle the vagaries of Internet Explorer. We could have inserted another set of object tags to offer a standard audio file for those without MIDI cards, but it would take too long to download an entire musical piece as a basic audio file so we'll leave it out in this situation.

```
<BODY>
    ...
    <OBJECT data="homesweethome.mid" width="145"
    height="60">
      <PARAM name="autostart" value="true">
      <EMBED src="homesweethome.mid" width="145"
      height="60">
        <NOEMBED>
          <P>
            [Sentimental music plays in the background:
            Home Sweet Home]<BR><A href="homesweethome.
            mid">Get the MIDI file!</A><BR>
        <NOEMBED>
    </OBJECT>
    <BGSOUND src="homesweethome.mid">
</BODY>
```

The result of this code is seen in Figure 11.3.

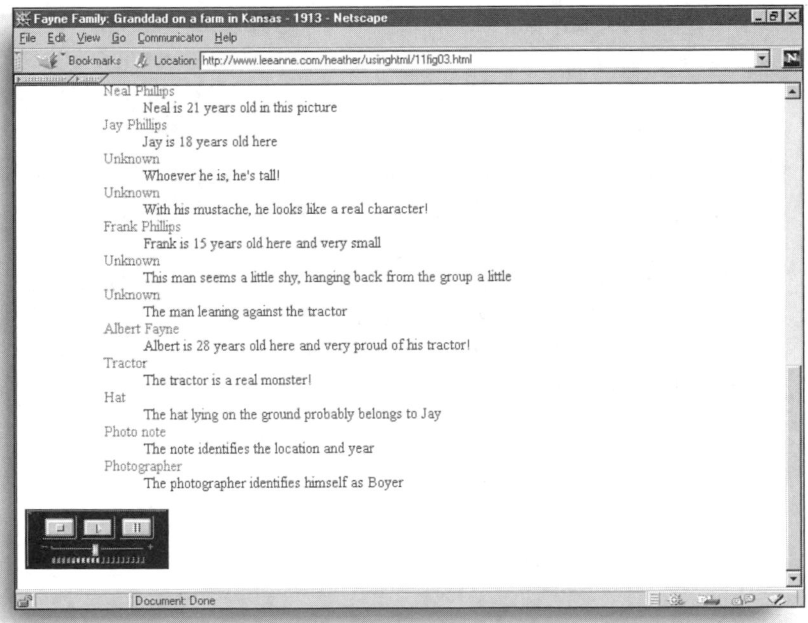

FIGURE 11.3
A genealogy page with an embedded MIDI player.

IDI files save space and download time

MIDI files can be tiny compared to other types of audio files. Use them when you want ambient music that goes on for more than a few seconds.

Warning: Copyright violations are matters of law as well as good taste

Don't fool around with copyright, especially if you're creating a commercial site. The laws in almost all countries take a very dim view of using other people's work without permission, especially so if you're making money, even indirectly, from using a musical work belonging to someone else.

Setting the Atmosphere with Background Music

Let's talk a bit more about MIDI files and why they're so easy to use. Instead of trying to capture every nuance of a musical performance, a MIDI file is like a musical score. It tells your computer what notes to play, but leaves it up to your sound card or music processor to actually perform the notes. This means that a MIDI file can be very small in comparison with a basic audio file. As an example, I have one MIDI file on my own system that plays for about a minute and a half and is less than 20 kilobytes in size. I have a short musical piece, less than thirty seconds, stored as a .wav file and it's 623 kilobytes! You might not want to load it over the Net unless you have *lots* of patience.

That's why background music either is almost always a MIDI file or uses a technique called streaming audio, which allows your computer to start playing an audio file before it finishes downloading. We'll talk about streaming audio in the section entitled "Streaming Audio and Video from a Personal Web Site," later in this chapter, but for this task we'll ignore that possibility.

The first thing you'll want to do is find some music, and luckily there are loads of sites that specialize in things like that. Be sure to read the copyright policies of each site before using any file in your own Web site, but especially if the site is for your business. Most sites have two sets of rules, one for individuals and one for businesses, and the copyright laws are nothing to fool around with in either case.

Clifford E. Odenkirk's MidiCity (`http://www.midicity.com/`) is one nice site that has links to many MIDI sites on the Web.

Once you've found a site with the kind of music you like, whether it be Queensryche or Beethoven, you can start auditioning songs for your site. Many times a composer or arranger is listed with an email address where you can write for permission to use the song, or the composer may have given permission on a blanket basis. Please be aware that someone who performs or arranges a Beatles tune, for example, can't give you permission to use the tune, only his or her arrangement of it. If your site is commercial, you'll also have to contact the ultimate copyright owners for a separate permission and possibly a payment.

```
<BODY>
    ...
    <OBJECT data="inagaddadavida.mid" width="145"
    height="60">
      <PARAM name="autostart" value="true">
      <EMBED src="inagaddadavida.mid" width="145"
      height="60">
        <NOEMBED>
          <P>
            [Rock music plays in the background: In A
            Gadda Da Vida by Iron Butterfly]<BR>
            <A href="inagaddadavida.mid">Get the MIDI
            file!</A>
            <BR>
        <NOEMBED>
    </OBJECT>
    <BGSOUND src="inagaddadavida.mid">
</BODY>
```

Using QuickTime and AVI to Add Video

Adding video with QuickTime or AVI

1. Add video to a Web page with the same tags you use for audio files, but be careful, video files can be huge! Several options may be offered by nesting <OBJECT> tags.

   Quick usage tip: Tag syntax

   ```
   <OBJECT data="videourl" type="video/mimetype"
   height="imgheight" width="imgwidth"> ...alternative
   content for non-supporting browsers, including a nested
   object tag... </OBJECT>
   ```

   where *videourl* is the location of the video file; *mimetype* is one of the video MIME types; and *imgheight* and *imgwidth* are the height and width override values.

   ```
   <OBJECT data="homesweethome.avi" width="300"
   height="200">
     </OBJECT>
   ```

2. Add a little "kickstart" with a <PARAM> tag immediately after the opening <OBJECT> tag.

```
<OBJECT data="homesweethome.avi" width="300"
height="200">
  <PARAM name="autostart" value="true">
</OBJECT>
```

3. Provide alternate video content inside the lowest level of <OBJECT> tag with the <EMBED> tag.

   Quick usage tip: Tag syntax

```
<EMBED src="videourl" type="video/mimetype"
height="imgheight" width="imgwidth" hidden="value"
autostart="autovalue" controller="value" loop="value">
```

   where *videourl* is the location of the video source; *mimetype* is the MIME content type of the data that the plug-in will fetch for itself or contain; *imgheight* and *imgwidth* are the size of the display, if any; and *autovalue* is `true` if you want the video to start automatically. Either `src` or `type` is mandatory, and `height` and `width` are advisable unless the embedded object is hidden. The `hidden` attribute is optional and controls whether the video player will be visible; `controller` regulates the appearance of working pushbuttons on the display; and `loop` controls whether the video will repeat or not; *value* is `true` or `false`.

```
<BODY>
      ...
      <OBJECT data="homesweethome.avi" width="300"
      height="200">
        <PARAM name="autostart" value="true">
        <EMBED src="homesweethome.avi" width="300"
        height="200">
      </OBJECT>
      <BGSOUND src="homesweethome.avi">
  </BODY>
```

4. Provide alternate content for browsers that don't support embedded objects or video with the <NOEMBED> tag.

```
<OBJECT data="homesweethome.avi" width="300"
height="200">
  <PARAM name="autostart" value="true">
```

```
<EMBED src="homesweethome.avi" width="300"
height="200">
  <NOEMBED>
    <P>
      [Sentimental video: Home Sweet Home]<BR>
      <A href="homesweethome.avi">Get the AVI
      file!</A>
      <BR>
  <NOEMBED>
</OBJECT>
```

5. Provide alternate video content for Microsoft Internet Explorer with the `dynsrc` attribute of the image tag. This gives you the option of including a still image for other browsers.

   Quick usage tip: Tag syntax

   `<IMG dynsrc="videourl" ... >`

   where *videourl* is the location of the video source and other attributes are standard for the image tag.

```
<OBJECT data="homesweethome.avi" width="300"
height="200">
  <PARAM name="autostart" value="true">
  <EMBED src="homesweethome.avi" width="300"
  height="200">
    <NOEMBED>
      <P>
        [Sentimental video: Home Sweet Home]<BR>
        <A href="homesweethome.avi">Get the AVI
        file!</A><BR>
    <NOEMBED>
</OBJECT>
<IMG dynsrc="homesweethome.avi" src="homesweethome.gif"
      width="300" height="200">
```

First we need a video. You probably have some laying around, or you can make one especially for your Web page. You do want the video to be rather short, as people usually don't like waiting for downloads that give them ample time to go out to a leisurely dinner and dancing with time to spare for putting the car in the garage at the end of the evening. You should probably aim towards 60 seconds tops, which is a very short clip.

Because it seems logical to do this on our family page, that's where we'll put it. Instead of just loading it whether our guests want to see it or not, though, we'll put it in a link so they can see it if they want to and don't have to bother if they're not interested. We'll show just the code fragment to save space.

```
For a look at Bess and the baby, check out our
<A href="bess.mpeg">movie!</A>
```

It's *really* simple. Table 11.2 lists the basic MIME types for movies that your browser may support.

TABLE 11.2 Video MIME types

Video MIME Types for Movies		
.mpeg	video/mpeg	Motion Picture Experts Group video for any platform
.mpg	video/mpeg	Motion Picture Experts Group video for any platform
.mpe	video/mpeg	Motion Picture Experts Group video for any platform
.mpv	video/mpeg	Motion Picture Experts Group video for any platform
.vbs	video/mpeg	Motion Picture Experts Group video for any platform
.mpa	video/mpeg	Motion Picture Experts Group video for any platform
.mpegv	video/mpeg	Motion Picture Experts Group video for any platform
.mov	video/quicktime	QuickTime video for any platform
.avi	video/avi	Windows video for Windows platforms
.avi	video/x-msvideo	Windows video for Windows platforms

Streaming Audio and Video from a Personal Web Site

Adding streaming multimedia files to minimize initial startup time

1. Eliminate long delay times by using streaming multimedia data files.

   Quick usage tip: Tag syntax

   ```
   <OBJECT data="multimediadiaurl" type="mimetype"
   height="imgheight" width="imgwidth"> ...alternative
   content for non-supporting browsers, including a nested
   object tag... </OBJECT>
   ```

   where *multimediaurl* is the location of the streaming multimedia file; *mimetype* is one of the streaming multimedia MIME types; and *imgheight* and *imgwidth* are the height and width override values.

   ```
   <OBJECT data="homesweethome.rpm" width="200"
   height="168"> </OBJECT>
   ```

2. Add a little "kickstart" with several <PARAM> tags immediately after the opening <OBJECT> tag to control many aspects of the video.

   ```
   <OBJECT data="homesweethome.rpm" width="200"
   height="168">
          <PARAM name="align" value="baseline">
          <PARAM name="border" value="0">
          <PARAM name="controls" value="ImageWindow">
          <PARAM name="autostart" value="false">
          <PARAM name="console" value="Clip1">
   </OBJECT>
   ```

3. Provide alternate multimedia content inside the lowest level of <OBJECT> tag with the <EMBED> tag.

   Quick usage tip: Tag syntax

   ```
   <EMBED src="multimediaurl" type="mimetype"
   height="imgheight" width="imgwidth" hidden="value"
   autostart="autovalue">
   ```

where *multimediaurl* is the location of the multimedia source; *mimetype* is the MIME content type of the data that the plug-in will fetch for itself or contain; *imgheight* and *imgwidth* are the size of the display, if any; and *autovalue* is `true` if you want the multimedia to start automatically. Either `src` or `type` is mandatory, and `height` and `width` are advisable unless the embedded object is hidden. The `hidden` attribute is optional and controls whether the multimedia player will be visible; *value* is `true` or `false`.

```
<OBJECT data="homesweethome.rpm" width="200"
height="168">
        <PARAM name="align" value="baseline">
        <PARAM name="border" value="0">
        <PARAM name="controls" value="ImageWindow">
        <PARAM name="autostart" value="false">
        <PARAM name="console" value="Clip1">
        <EMBED src="homesweethome.rpm" align="base
        line" border="0" width="200" height="168"
        controls="ImageWindow" autostart="false"
        console="Clip1"></OBJECT>
```

4. Provide alternate content for browsers that don't support embedded objects or multimedia with the `<NOEMBED>` tag.

```
<OBJECT data="homesweethome.rpm" width="200"
height="168">
        <PARAM name="align" value="baseline">
        <PARAM name="border" value="0">
        <PARAM name="controls" value="ImageWindow">
        <PARAM name="autostart" value="false">
        <PARAM name="console" value="Clip1">
        <EMBED src="homesweethome.rpm" align=
        "base line" border="0" width="200"
        height="168" controls="ImageWindow"
        autostart="false" console="Clip1">
            <NOEMBED>
              <P>
                [While a fire crackles in the
                fireplace, sentimental music plays
                in the background: Home Sweet
                Home]<BR> <A href="homesweethome.rpm">
                Get the RealVideo file!</A><BR>
              <NOEMBED>
</OBJECT>
```

5. Provide alternate multimedia content for Microsoft Internet Explorer with the `<BGSOUND>` tag or `dynsource` attribute on an image.

Quick usage tip: Tag syntax

```
<BGSOUND src="multimediaurl" loop="number">
```

where *multimediaurl* is the location of the multimedia source, and *number* is the number of times to loop, if any. A value of `-1` tells the browser to loop the multimedia forever. This is usually a bad idea.

```
OBJECT data="homesweethome.rpm" width="200" height="168">
       <PARAM name="align" value="baseline">
       <PARAM name="border" value="0">
       <PARAM name="controls" value="ImageWindow">
       <PARAM name="autostart" value="false">
       <PARAM name="console" value="Clip1">
       <EMBED src="homesweethome.rpm" align="
       baseline" border="0" width="200"
       height="168" controls="ImageWindow"
       autostart="false" console="Clip1">
          <NOEMBED>
            <P>
              [While a fire crackles in the
              fireplace, sentimental music plays in
              the background: Home Sweet Home]<BR>
              <A href="homesweethome.rpm">Get the
              RealVideo file!</A><BR>
          <NOEMBED>
       </OBJECT>
       <IMG dynsrc="homesweethome.rpm" src="
       fireplace.gif" width="200" height="168">
```

All these sound and image tags have one big disadvantage—they can take a long time to load if the file is of any size at all. Streaming techniques allow the browser to start playing the file before the entire file is delivered by saving the first few seconds and then beginning play without waiting for the rest, depending on the few seconds of stored capacity to act as a bank account from which to draw if transmission slows down for any reason.

There are many types of streaming and many require a dedicated plug-in, but one, from RealAudio, is so commonplace that almost everyone already has it. Another type relies on Java to download a custom Java streams player on-the-fly, so no plug-in is needed. That's a very cool way to do it, but is not yet wide spread.

RealAudio has made a simple conversion and publishing utility available at low cost that allows you to convert a simple audio or video file into a special format that can be served by any HTTP server so you can offer streaming audio on your own site. For longer files, like a complete musical selection, or for video where there might easily be several minutes of download time required, this is a great timesaver for your users. RealAudio, available from RealAudio Publisher, can be found at `http://www.real.com/`.

The following code embeds a RealVideo presentation in a table.

```
</table>
 <BODY>
     ...
     <TABLE align="center">
       <TR>
         <TD>
           <OBJECT data="homesweethome.rpm" width="200"
           height=
           "168">
           <PARAM name="align" value="baseline">
           <PARAM name="border" value="0">
           <PARAM name="controls" value="ImageWindow">
           <PARAM name="autostart" value="false">
           <PARAM name="console" value="Clip1">
           <EMBED src="homesweethome.rpm" align="baseline"
           border="0" width="200"
                  height="168" controls="ImageWindow"
                  autostart ="false" console="Clip1">
              <NOEMBED>
                <P>
                  [While a fire crackles in the
                  fireplace, sentimental music plays in
                  the background: Home Sweet Home]<BR>
                  <A href="homesweethome.rpm">Get the
                  RealVideo file!</A><BR>
```

```
            <NOEMBED>
         </OBJECT>
    <TR>
      <TD>
         <OBJECT data="homesweethome.rpm" width="200"
         height="30">
         <PARAM name="align" value="baseline">
         <PARAM name="border" value="0">
         <PARAM name="controls" value="ControlPanel">
         <PARAM name="autostart" value="false">
         <PARAM name="console" value="Clip1">
         <PARAM name="autostart" value="true">
         <EMBED src="homesweethome.rpm" align="baseline"
         border="0" width="200" height="30" controls=
         "ControlPanel" autostart="false"
         console="Clip1">
            <NOEMBED>
              <P>
                [Control panel]<BR><A href=
                "homesweethome.rpm">Get the RealVideo
                file!</A><BR>
            <NOEMBED>
         </OBJECT>
  </TABLE>
  <IMG dynsrc="homesweethome.rpm" src="fireplace.gif"
  width="200" height="168">
</BODY>
```

The result of this code is shown in Figure 11.4.

The Publisher utility does more than just convert files types, although that's its primary task. It will also upload your files automatically and perform a few other site maintenance chores. The Publisher utility is shown in Figure 11.5.

Other options include Vosaic's RadioStudio and VideoStudio, which create files that can be streamed by a Java applet, thereby eliminating the need for any sort of plug-in for modern browsers. RadioStation and VideoStudio are available at `http://www.vosaic.com/`.

FIGURE 11.4
The Fayne family home page using a RealAudio viewer.

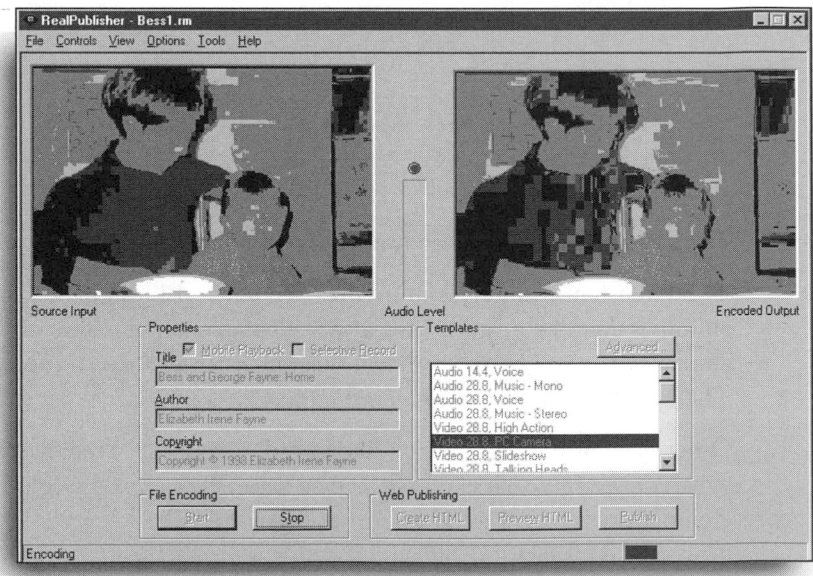

FIGURE 11.5
The RealPublisher main screen.

CHAPTER

12

Including Java Applets

Finding Java applets to enhance your pages

Worried about security? Don't be!

Educational resources in Java

Time for some games? Java for fun!

Understanding What Java Is

Java is either the greatest thing that ever happened on the Web or the most overhyped marketing strategy since the Betamax/VHS wars—you decide who wins. Java is the subject of both legal and theoretical controversy, although the basic principle is both sound and reasonable. It runs on an idealized virtual computer implemented in software instead of hardware, so it can be easily emulated on other machines. The only catch is that the vendor of the other machine's operating system has to agree to provide Java support.

Java is an open standard that, if all vendors support it in good faith, will eventually mean that you can buy an off-the-shelf application that will run on any machine in the world. Exactly what *eventually* means is the real sticking point, since the current situation is far more complex than many Java partisans would have you believe. Dueling standards and incomplete or faulty implementations have changed the "write once, run anywhere" promise of the initial Sun Microsystems vision to "write once, test everywhere," in the opinion of some developers.

Poor browser implementations have meant that Java can be a hindrance and an annoyance to your users, if not carefully done and isolated on a few "splash" pages or in Java "playgrounds" that people who don't feel comfortable with Java avoid.

Among the problems are browsers that allocate system resources for Java applications and never release them, leading to system crashes at worst or sluggishness at best; Java applets that throw confusing error messages onto the screens of your users, over which you have no control and have no way of discovering without exhaustive testing; and browsers, or even systems, that lock up unexpectedly when loading Java applets, requiring a reboot to get back to work. The problems seem worse on Windows 95 due to the antiquity of the environment, but no system is immune to problems. The next release of Windows may solve some of the problems, but it's unclear how supportive Microsoft will be.

On the other hand, Java could eventually mean an end to those annoying plug-ins that hog system resources, slow initial startup of browsers, and generally make life difficult when surfing the Web. But the best part is that you can easily find Java applets on the Web that can be used for free or for a small charge, so you don't need to learn how to program to use Java.

Finding Pre-Written Java

Borrowing Java applets

1. Think about what you want an applet to do before looking for it.
2. Search for Java applets on one of the many Web sites devoted to that purpose, such as `http://www.gamelan.com/`.
3. Make sure you understand the license terms for each applet you want to use. Many are free for non-commercial use but require payment if used commercially.

Stop! Before you hare off after a Java applet for your pages, think about what you want the applet for. Unless you plan to just include applets because you think they're cool, you'll want to have a plan in mind. That plan could very well be to insert an eye-catching visual effect on the page to grab people's attention, but it's good to know that before you start, not just grab something and then try and figure out where to put it.

There are so many places that offer free Java that we couldn't possibly list them all, but we'll start with one of the most popular and then discuss how you can get the applets from the site to your own machine. We'll start with Gamelan, cryptically named after a percussion orchestra that is native to Java and Bali. Gamelan will actually point you to a directory on `http://www.developer.com/`, but it's a convenient shorthand so we'll use that. Gamelan's home page is seen in Figure 12.1.

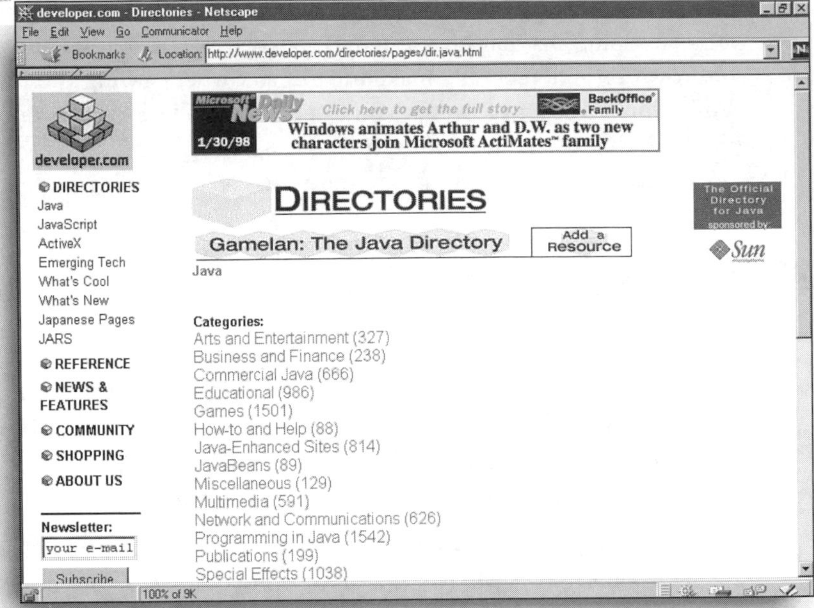

FIGURE 12.1

The Gamelan home page showing the many categories of Java applets available.

For our Java effect, we want something really eye-catching and beautiful, not something practical and boring, because it's for a personal page, the Fayne family page, and because we aren't boring people. On the main Gamelan page we see a list of applet types. Since we know we want an effect, we'll choose that category and scroll down until we see something interesting. Hmmm. Since the Faynes live in the San Francisco Bay Area and spend a lot of time on the ferry commuting, the Lake applet by David Griffiths (`dgriffiths@msn.com`), at `http://www.demon.co.uk/davidg/`, looks interesting. We'll choose an image that will look natural across a watery surface and see what happens. Let's download it!

From Gamelan we can link directly to David's site by clicking his name. Off to the side is a navigation bar that has icons for downloading the file, notes on using it, and other useful information. We'll download it and read the notes first, before inserting his sample code into our own page. We do that by clicking the **Download** button and then saying yes when the browser asks if we want to download a file.

It comes as a compressed file with a .zip extension, so you'll need a utility program to uncompress it before you can use it. Since it uses a compression *algorithm* named *zip*, or pkzip, you'll need an unzip tool to get the file out where you can use it. You'll find an assortment of unzip utilities at TUCOWS, `http://www.tucows.com/`, if you don't have one already. Look in the section labeled Compression Utilities.

We'll assume that you've used WinZip or other unzip package to extract the files from the download file.

Adding Java Applets to Your Pages

Adding motion and interactivity to your site without expensive plug-in servers

1. Study the release notes for the Java applet before using it.
2. Insert an <OBJECT> tag referring to the applet, along with any parameters the applet will need.

```
<OBJECT classid="lake.class"
      align="right" border="0" codebase="/java"
      width="251" height="260">
  <PARAM name="image" value="/images/sfskyline.jpg">
```

3. Also add the <APPLET> tag, along with its parameters to cover as many bases as possible.

```
<APPLET code="lake.class"
        align="right" border="0" codebase="/java"
        width="251" height="260">
    <PARAM name="image" value="/images/sfskyline.jpg">
```

Quick usage tip: Tag syntax

```
<OBJECT classid="classname" codetype="codetype" code-
base="urlbaseforcode" archive="codearchivelist"
data="dataurl" type="mimetype" height="imgheight"
width="imgwidth" standby="text to display when loading
the applet"> ...alternative content for non-supporting
browsers, including a nested object
tag... </OBJECT>
```

where *classname* is the name of the object; *codetype* is the MIME type of the code; *urlbaseforcode* is the base address where this object resides; *codearchivelist* is a space-separated list of archives; *dataurl* is the location of any data file the applet needs; *mimetype* is the data MIME type; and *imgheight* and *imgwidth* are the height and width override values.

```
<APPLET> code="classname" object="serializedapplet"
codebase="urlbaseforcode" archive="codearchivelist"
data="dataurl" type="mimetype" height="imgheight"
width="imgwidth" standby="text to display when loading
the applet" name="name"> ...alternative content for
non-supporting browsers, including a nested object
tag... </APPLET>
```

where *classname* is the name of the applet; *serializedapplet* is the serialized applet file; *urlbaseforcode* is the base address where this object resides; *codearchivelist* is a comma-separated list of archives; *dataurl* is the location of any data file the applet needs; *mimetype* is the data MIME type; *imgheight* and *imgwidth* are the height and width override values; and *name* is a unique name another applet can use to find this applet.

4. Test the applet by using as many browsers, versions, and operating systems as possible.

So, we wind up with a thing called lake.class. Now what do we do? Well, a class is what Java programmers call a program, so that little thing is what we want in the directory with our page. Now we're ready to insert the applet into our own page. In David's notes he tells us what to do very succinctly and gives us some sample code we can play with.

Read applet notes if available

Often an author's notes can save you an enormous amount of time incorporating an applet into your page. In this case, the notes are particularly clear and concise, making the task simple and pleasant.

For our image, we'll choose the San Francisco skyline as seen every weekday by George riding on the ferry across the Bay. Putting it behind a lake gives some of the effect of the Bay itself and is very appropriate for both the subject and the page, while providing a delight for the eye and food for the imagination. Here's the code snippet we insert in the page.

```
<OBJECT classid="lake.class"
      align="right" border="0" codebase="/java"
      width="251" height="260">
  <PARAM name="image" value="/images/sfskyline.jpg">
  <APPLET code="lake.class"
        align="right" border="0" codebase="/java"
        width="251" height="260">
    <PARAM name="image" value="/images/sfskyline.jpg">
        <p align="left">
        <table>
          <td align="center">
          <p>
            <font size="6">
            <font face="Arial,Helvetica">
            [The image shows a picture of San Francisco
            reflected
            in a lake of water]
            </font>
            </font>
          </td>
        </table>
  </APPLET>
</OBJECT>
```

This code has two elements, the new HTML 4.0 <OBJECT> tag and the older <APPLET> tag, both of which argue the name of the class (or program), alignment (right), border (0), and a codebase, a special directory where we put our Java applets. We then feed the applet a parameter that identifies the picture we want to use, which we put into another special directory. This results in the display shown in Figure 12.2.

Pretty cool, eh? You can almost smell the salty air. And it's really not very hard to do. Really, the hardest part is picking what you'd like to use from the thousands of applets available on the Web.

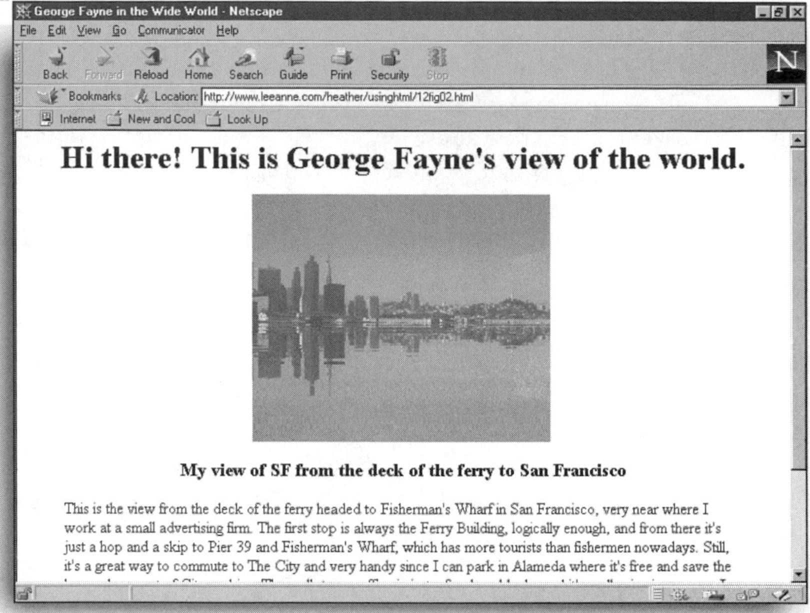

FIGURE 12.2
The San Francisco skyline and the Lake applet.

Providing Interactive Content

Another technique is to use Java to provide true interactivity, either by reacting to mouse clicks or by asking for user input before performing the Java magic. Let's use an example I found on the Web that shows you how to fingerspell words using the American manual alphabet, Ryan Powers' Speller. His URL is `http://members.iquest.net/~powers/speller.html`, and here's how you'd set it up in your code.

```
<OBJECT classid="speller.class" width="400"
height="400">
  <APPLET code="speller.class" width="400" height="400">
     [Fingerspelling Java Applet From Ryan Powers]
  </APPLET>
</OBJECT>
```

Figure 12.3 shows the speller in the process of spelling out my name.

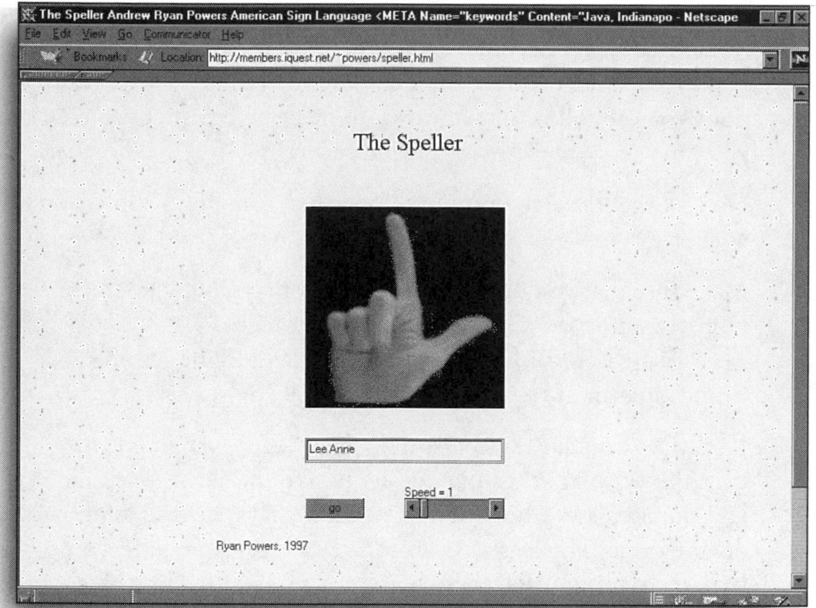

FIGURE 12.3
Ryan's Speller spelling my name in the manual alphabet.

Interactive information may persuade people to come back to your site repeatedly

Interactive elements on your page can help prevent people from seeing your page as more of the same-old-same-old. By providing educational opportunities like the Speller program mentioned here, you give people a reason to come back and learn some more.

Maintaining Security on Your Site

Avoiding security problems with Java applets

1. Always download from sites you trust. It's very unlikely that authors hoping for recognition and fame by distributing their applets for free are going to do anything to jeopardize their reputations for the cheap thrill of imagining your chagrin when the program lets your dog out of the back yard and burns your toast in the morning.
2. Test the applet yourself before showing it off on your pages. By placing it on your own site you're vouching for it, too. Don't be caught short by a little "surprise."
3. Provide some sort of feedback mechanism so a user who does experience a problem, however unlikely that may be, can get back to you with a warning.

I'm sure you've heard stories about evil security flaws in Java that crop up from time to time. Don't obsess about them too much, because Java is actually very secure. The attacks are most often theoretical exercises by people intent on breaking Java rather than your machine, and none has actually been seen in the real world that I'm aware of. That said, there are a few precautions you can follow on your own to make sure that any applet you offer on your pages is safe and secure.

Don't worry too much about Java security

Java is inherently pretty safe to work with. It builds what it calls a sandbox of memory and resources to play with and then releases them all back to your computer when it's done. Real hackers usually have better things to do than try to break into your machine when they could try for major banks or the CIA. In more than 20 years of full-time computing and network exposure, I've only had one computer virus infection, and that was more of an annoyance than a threat, since I had to buy an expensive anti-virus package to get rid of it. And the lowly route it chose to enter my computer on was a floppy disk from my publisher.

Don't forget these important points when using Java applets on your site.

Make sure that you download applets from a reputable site. Don't be surprised if something from `http://www.evilhackers.com/` turns out to have problems, but anything from Gamelan or other large sites is probably very safe.

It's always a good idea to test the applet before sending it out over the Web. Your testing doesn't have to be exhaustive, but you should play with it enough to know that it doesn't appear to do any damage or crash. As an added safeguard, provide a feedback mechanism somewhere on your site. By providing an easy way for visitors to get in touch with you if they have problems, you may find out about bugs before hundreds of people are affected.

Games and Other Crowd Pleasers

Using games to generate repeat visits

1. Add a game room to attract game-playing visitors.
2. Study the release notes for the Java applet before using it.
3. Insert an `<OBJECT>` tag referring to the applet.

```
<OBJECT class="Tic_Tac_Toe.class" width = "230"
height = "250"></OBJECT>
```

4. Also include the `<APPLET>` tag and alternate content to cover as many bases as possible.

```
<OBJECT class="Tic_Tac_Toe.class" width = "230"
height = "250">
       <APPLET code="Tic_Tac_Toe.class" width = "230"
       height = "250">
         [Nathan Arora's Multimedia Java Tic Tac Toe]
       </APPLET>
     </OBJECT>
```

4. Test the applet using as many browsers, versions, and operating systems as possible.
5. Be aware of the demographics about games.

Games are always popular with some visitors, and there are literally hundreds of Java games, some of which can be customized to include your own images or messages. Since loading Java applets sometimes takes a while, it's thoughtful to place games and other non-essential content on pages of their own with a clearly-labeled link to the game page from elsewhere in your site.

We'll choose tic-tac-toe for its simplicity rather than the likelihood that anyone other than children will really want to play it for more than a few games. Here's a nice one from Canada, Nathan Arora's Multimedia Java Tic Tac Toe found at `http://etude.uwaterloo.ca/~nathan/Tic_Tac_Toe.html`.

It talks to you, so it will probably be popular with younger children in your family. Nice safe entertainment for the kids without making you crazy playing Chutes and Ladders. This is very simple to include. All you have to do is argue the height and width and tell it the name of the class. Drop it into your code and you're done!

```
<OBJECT class="Tic_Tac_Toe.class" width = "230"
height = "250">
  <APPLET code="Tic_Tac_Toe.class" width = "230"
  height = "250">
    [Nathan Arora's Multimedia Java Tic Tac Toe]
  </APPLET>
</OBJECT>
```

This code results in the display shown in Figure 12.4.

Java's not hard at all! Don't be nervous! Have a cup of coffee and relax!

Most Java applets use only a few of the many attributes available in the tags that call them. They're really not hard to use once you become familiar with them, and they're very cool fun to fool with!

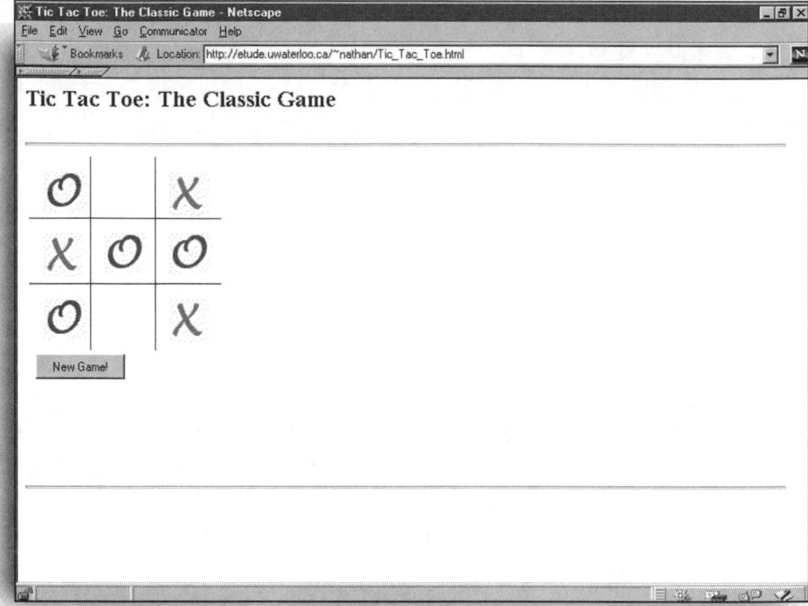

FIGURE 12.4
A simple game of Java Tic Tac Toe written by Nathan Arora.

Fun Stuff and Kitsch

Adding Java animations

1. Use Java applets to provide more complex animations than an animated GIF can provide or content that goes further than a Web page can provide.
2. Study the release notes for the Java applet before using it.
3. Insert an <OBJECT> tag referring to the applet.

```
<OBJECT CLASS="wisemansay.class" WIDTH="600"
HEIGHT="64">
             <PARAM NAME="File"
             VALUE="quotes.wms.9.utf8">
             <PARAM NAME="FontSize" VALUE="12">
</OBJECT>
```

3. Also add the <APPLET> tag and alternate content to cover as many bases as possible.

```
<OBJECT CLASS="wisemansay.class" WIDTH="600"
HEIGHT="64">
```

```
              <PARAM NAME="File"
              VALUE="quotes.wms.9.utf8">
              <PARAM NAME="FontSize" VALUE="12">
    <APPLET CODE="wisemansay.class" WIDTH="600"
    HEIGHT="64">
                <PARAM NAME="File"
                VALUE="quotes.wms.9.utf8">
                <PARAM NAME="FontSize" VALUE="12">
      [Michael Imamura's WiseMenSay Java Applet]
    </APPLET>
  </OBJECT>
```

4. Test the applet using as many browsers, versions, and operating systems as possible.
5. Be aware that many people don't like Java, for whatever reason. Balance the cool appearance of the applet with how interested you are in keeping your visitors happy.

Sometimes you don't want to have to justify doing something on your page, but want to add waving text or bouncing balls just because they're kicky and fun. There's nothing wrong with that; the Web is the last and best bastion of rugged (some would say flamboyant) individuality there is, and if you can't have fun there what's the point? Really.

So here's an applet just for fun, a pop-up quote server. You'll notice that we've used two parameters to specify the location of the quote file and the text size. There are other things that can be changed, but that's enough to show how it's done.

One of the cool things about this applet is that you can feed it your own quote file saying anything you want. So if you've always dreamed of writing the *Collected Sayings of Me*, this is your opportunity to really shine. Or if you think that Alfred E. Newman was sadly underrated as a philosopher, you now have the chance to right this historic wrong by telling the world what Alfred would say at any given moment. Go for it!

```
<OBJECT CLASS="wisemansay.class" WIDTH="600" HEIGHT="64">
            <PARAM NAME="File" VALUE="quotes.wms.9.utf8">
            <PARAM NAME="FontSize" VALUE="12">
  <APPLET CODE="wisemansay.class" WIDTH="600" HEIGHT="64">
              <PARAM NAME="File" VALUE="quotes.wms.9.utf8">
```

```
                <PARAM NAME="FontSize" VALUE="12">
    [Michael Imamura's WiseMenSay Java Applet]
  </APPLET>
</OBJECT>
```

This code results in the display shown in Figure 12.5.

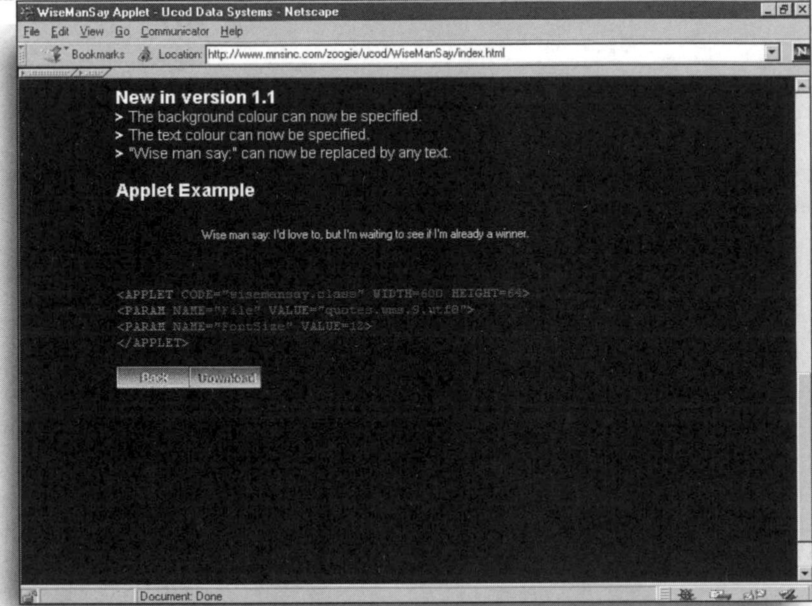

FIGURE 12.5
A fine example of Web kitsch, a Java applet used purely for decoration and entertainment.

Another super toy is Lee's Oil, a lovely doodling tool from Lee Oades, which has no purpose but to amuse as far as I can tell. The metaphor is dropping bits of colored paint into a swirling tub of oil and watching them spin down into oblivion. It's easy to spend an idle hour or two playing with the variations available in swirl rate and direction, as well as drop size and the ability to splash a handful of drops at once to see how it affects your fleeting composition. This would be popular with children as well, if I remember my own experiences with my daughter. In fact, the only thing it lacks to make a young girl's joy complete is a way to hang the great art it produces on the refrigerator!

To use the Oil applet, you'll reference it in your code and set the size, really very simple.

```
<OBJECT CLASS="leesoil.class" WIDTH="600" HEIGHT="400">
            <PARAM NAME="x" VALUE="500">
            <PARAM NAME="y" VALUE="400">
  <APPLET CODE="leesoil.class" WIDTH="600" HEIGHT="400">
              <PARAM NAME="x" VALUE="500">
              <PARAM NAME="y" VALUE="400">
    [Lee Oades' Lee's Oil Java Applet]
  </APPLET>
</OBJECT>
```

This code results in the display shown in Figure 12.6.

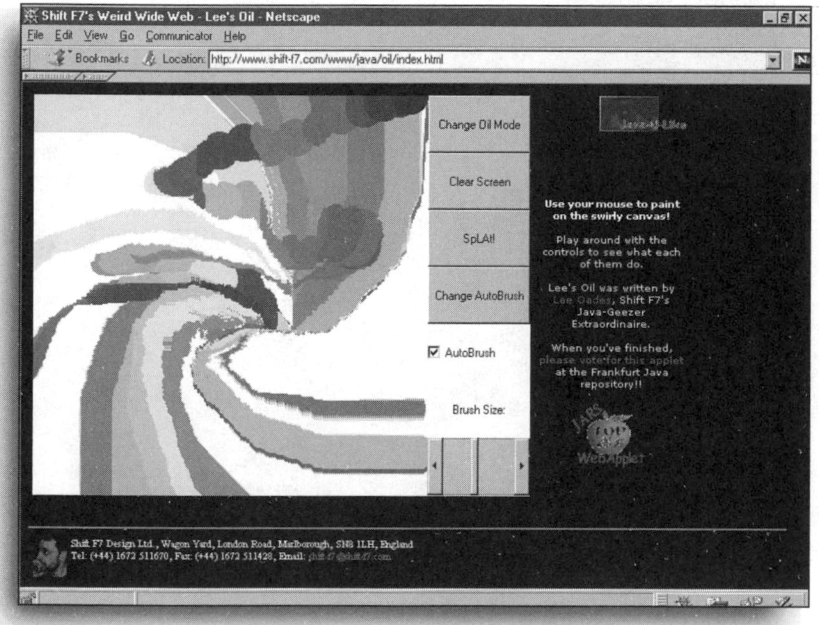

FIGURE 12.6
Lee's Oil, another Java applet used to amuse and delight.

PART III

Controlling Presentation

Using Cascading Style Sheets to Define Appearance

Create a corporate look

Use style to define yourself

Choosing fonts and colors with style

Why Use Cascading Style Sheets?

Cascading style sheets (CSS1) are one of the most exciting things to come down the road in a very long time. They make it possible to really take control over the design of your page without breaking the page when viewed in other browsers, and without performing the sort of *kludgey* tricks that have been necessary up to now in order to make any kind of complex design possible. While they're not perfect yet, mainly because none of the major browser makers has installed full support for them, they're functional enough that you can use them. By the time you read this, the situation will be better (or getting better) because Netscape is making a major release right around the time this book hits the stores and Microsoft will continue to improve Internet Explorer. Style sheet improvements are bound to be high on their respective agendas.

Inserting Style Sheet Information in Your Pages

Using basic style sheet techniques

1. Add styles to your pages with the <STYLE> tag, which goes between the <HEAD> and <BODY> tags.

```
<STYLE>
</STYLE>
```

2. Add a selector to which the properties are applied.

```
<STYLE>
   BODY { }
</STYLE>
```

3. Add properties and values to define the styles. Separate properties with a semicolon.

```
<STYLE>
   BODY { background: #FFFFFF; color:#000000;
   margin-left: 0.4in; margin-right: 0.4in; }
</STYLE>
```

4. Test the style before releasing it to the Web.

   Quick usage tips: Tag syntax

```
<STYLE type="mimetype" media="mediatype"
title="title"> ...style selectors and {property/value
pairs}... </STYLE>
```

   where *mimetype* is the MIME type of the style: `"text/css"`; *mediatype* is the media the style is designed for; and *title* is the title of the style element.

```
<LINK href="linkurl" rel="linktype" type="mimetype"
media="mediatype" title="title"> ...style selectors and
{property/value pairs}... </STYLE>
```

   where *linkurl* is the location of the external stylesheet; *linktype* is the type of link: `"stylesheet"`; *mimetype* is the MIME type of the style `"text/css"`; *mediatype* is the media the style is designed for; and *title* is the title of the link element.

```
<htmltag style="style property: value; pairs" ... >
```

There are three ways to include style sheet information on your pages: by including an embedded `<STYLE>` tag in the head, referencing an external style sheet with a `<LINK>` tag, and using the `style` attribute on almost any HTML tag to create inline styles. The most reliable method is to include the information in the head, since external links are not universally supported, and adding the `style` attribute to a tag is inherently local and hard to update when maintenance is needed.

All these methods use the same general syntax: a *selector*, which describes the scope of the style effect, and one or more *property/value* pairs that describe the *typographic* effect desired across that scope.

A selector is basically the name of a tag, although these can be modified in various ways to limit the scope to a subset of the tags or even a single tag.

Styles in brief

Every style command uses three parts: the selector, which tells the browser which elements the style applies to, and one or more property/value pairs that make up the style.

The *properties* and *values* are the physical treatment the visible text and graphics within scope of that tag should have, from color, font, and placement, to borders and background color. The full specification is very flexible, even as it stands, and there's already a CSS2 in the wings that offers even more power and control.

We'll start by defining a corporate style sheet for the ALS page. Since we want to use the same style sheet for every document, we'll place it in a file ready to be linked into every page.

Open a new file in your favorite word processor and call it als-style.css. Since we don't know any styles yet, we'll use the following code, which I swear is a style sheet.

```
BODY { background: #FFFFFF; color:#000000; margin-left:
0.4in; margin-right: 0.4in; }
  H1 { font-size: 18pt; }
  H2 { font-size: 14pt; }
  H3 { font-size: 12pt; }
  P ( font-size: 10pt; }
```

Save your work and we're ready to link to it in our HTML code.

Now we'll open the ALS home page and enter the following code in the head section.

```
<HTML>
  <HEAD>
    <META http-equiv="Content-Style-Type"
    content="text/css">
    <LINK type="text/css" rel="stylesheet"
    href="als-style.css">
    ...
  </HEAD>
  <BODY>
    ...
```

The results can be seen in Figure 13.1.

There's another way of importing an external style sheet, although it's not widely supported yet, which is to import it into an embedded style sheet. To do the same thing we just did with a link, we'd insert the following alternate code into the header.

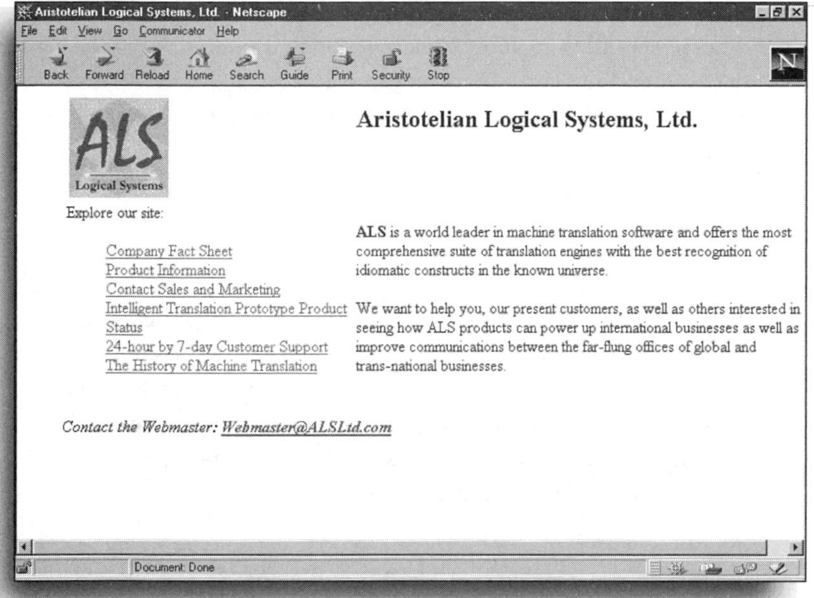

FIGURE 13.1
The ALS page with some styles applied.

```
<HTML>
  <HEAD>
    <META http-equiv="Content-Style-Type"
    content="text/css">
    <STYLE type="text/css" >
      <!--
      @import als-style.css
      -->
    </STYLE>
    ...
  </HEAD>
  <BODY>
    ...
```

Notice that we enclosed the style commands in a comment tag. That's to prevent problems with browsers that don't support style sheets and would otherwise start displaying the style commands as text in the body. The comment tags prevent that and are ignored by browsers that support style sheets.

The same commands we used in the embedded style command can be used to modify individual tags. To add the same commands to the `<BODY>` tag, as in the previous example, all we have to do is argue them to the `style` attribute in the `<BODY>` tag. Note that we shouldn't include a selector, since the tag itself is the selector, and the curly braces are not included either, because the quotation marks surrounding the `style` attribute value take their place.

```
<BODY style="background: #FFFFFF; color:#000000;
margin-left: 0.4in; margin-right: 0.4in">
```

Which comes first? Inline, embedded, or external styles?

When the browser reads style information, it first tries to apply an external style sheet, then an embedded one, and then style information found inline. Whatever information appears last in that list is what appears on the page. Actually, the browser may also attempt first to apply a default style sheet and then a user style sheet registered with the browser.

The natural order of applying styles can be altered by describing certain information as important. You do this by prefixing the keyword `! important` to the property. There are few times that you as a Web author would be justified in doing this. For persons with special visual needs, it's the primary way to override your style sheet to provide better contrast or type size selection to meet their unique requirements.

So a user who requires high contrast and large type size could make a personal style sheet like the following:

```
BODY { ! important background: #FFFFFF; ! important
color:#000000;
       ! important margin-left: 0.2in; ! important
       margin-right: 0.2in;
       ! important font-size: 24pt; }
  H1 { ! important font-size: 64pt; ! important color:
  #000000 }
  H2 { ! important font-size: 48pt; ! important color:
  #000000 }
  H3 { ! important font-size: 32pt; ! important color:
  #000000 }
```

Unless you've improperly argued an `important` property in your own code, the user's values will take effect and leave the page legible.

Changing Font Faces and Sizes

Changing font face and size

1. Use the `font-family` property to change the default font used to display your page.

```
<STYLE>
BODY { font-family: verdana, garamond, palatino, times
roman, serif; }
</STYLE>
```

2. Use the `font-size` property to change the size of the fonts used on your page.

```
<STYLE>
BODY { font-family: verdana, garamond, palatino, times
roman, serif; font-size: 12pt; }
</STYLE>
```

Table 13.1 provides a list of font properties and their values.

TABLE 13.1 Table of font properties and values

Property	Values
`font-family`	`<family-name>` (Specify a font family name like `Garamond` or `Beppo`)
	`<generic-family>` (`serif`, `sans-serif`, `cursive`, `fantasy`, `monospace`)
`font-style`	`normal, italic, oblique`
`font-variant`	`normal, small-caps`
`font-weight`	`normal, bold, bolder, lighter, 100-900`
`font-size`	`<absolute-size> (xx-small, x-small, small, medium, large, x-large, xx-large)`
	`<relative-size> (larger, smaller)`
	`<length>`
	`<percentage>`
`font`	`<font-family values>`
	`<font-style values>`
	`<font-variant values>`
	`<font-weight values>`
	`<font-size values>`
	`<line-height values>`

We'll start by creating a style sheet for the Fayne Family page. They're pretty basic "salt-of-the-earth" type people from the Midwest so they don't want to be too hip; a nice font like Verdana would suit them fine. But not every machine will have Verdana installed, so we'll argue several alternate values to cover all bases. We'll use the <BODY> tag as a selector, since we want all the text to use the same font unless stated otherwise.

```
BODY { font-family: verdana, garamond, palatino, times
roman, serif; }
```

Since George has a slight vision impairment, we'll want the base font size to be slightly larger than normal, and we'll argue this with the `font-size` property. Twelve points ought to be adequate, while not looking too huge for most people.

```
BODY { font-family: verdana, garamond, palatino, times
roman, serif; font-size: 12pt; }
```

That's all for now, although we'll finish up this style in the next section.

Changing Background and Text Colors

Changing text colors

1. Use the `color` property to change text colors.

```
<STYLE>
BODY { color: black}
</STYLE>
```

2. Use the `background-color` property to change text background color.

```
<STYLE>
BODY { color: black; background-color: white; }
</STYLE>
```

3. Use pseudo-classes to select special types of selector.

```
<STYLE>
BODY { color: black; background-color: white; }
A:link { color: blue; }
```

```
A:visited { color: purple; }
A:active { color: red; }
</STYLE>
```

Table 13.2 provides a list of font color properties and their values.

TABLE 13.2 **Table of font color properties**

Property	Values
`color`	`<color>`
`background-color`	`<color>`, `transparent`
Table of pseudo-classes	`A:link` (an unvisited link)
	`A:visited` (a visited link)
	`A:active` (a link in the process of being selected)

Okay. Now how do we make sure that the contrast is good when the page is displayed? We argue a high-contrast black on white display.

```
BODY { font-family: verdana, garamond, palatino, times
roman, serif; font-size: 12pt; color: black; background-
color: white; }
```

Next we want to make hyperlinks stand out but look like the default colors used in most browsers, so we use *pseudo-classes* to modify the link selector.

```
BODY { font-family: verdana, garamond, palatino, times
roman, serif; font-size: 12pt; color: black; background-
color: white; }
A:link { color: blue; }
A:visited { color: purple; }
A:active { color: red; }
```

That's actually all we need; the browser will supply automatic font-size changes for headings. If the Fayne family wants to change those defaults, they could argue anything they like, selecting from the entire range of properties available under CSS1. We won't bother deciding whether to make this an external or an embedded style sheet, because the choices are described clearly in the previous section.

This style sheet results in the display shown in Figure 13.2.

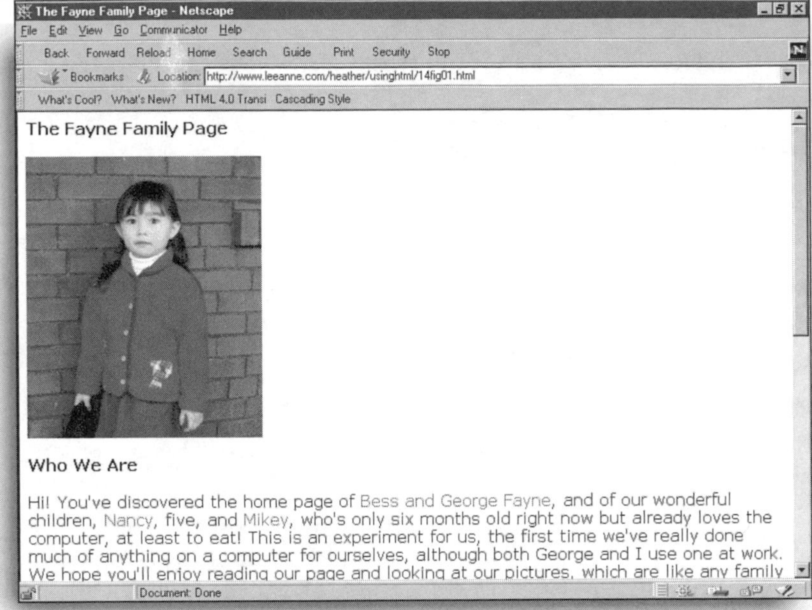

FIGURE 13.2
The Fayne Family page with a unique style of its own.

Different Displays for Different Media

Choosing style sheets based on the type of display they'll be used on

Use the `media` attribute on style and link elements to define the purpose of the style. Set up different style sheets for different display devices.

```
<LINK href="als-style.css" rel="stylesheet"
type="text/css" media="Screen" title="ALS Basic
Stylesheet">
<LINK href="als-braille-style.css" rel="stylesheet"
type="text/dss" media="Braille" title="ALS Braille
Stylesheet">
```

One of the most exciting things available with style sheets and HTML 4.0 is the ability to define different styles associated with different output media. This means that you can define one style sheet for display on a computer screen, another for printing on a laser printer, another for a simple text printer, and yet another for a handheld device with a tiny screen.

All this power is accessed through the `media` attribute of the style and link tags, so a browser can decide which style sheet to use based on what medium the display is intended for. Cool. Table 13.3 lists various media types and their common uses.

TABLE 13.3 **Table of media types**

Media type	Intended Use
`Screen`	Computer screens
`TTY`	Terminals using a fixed-pitch character grid, such as teletypes, terminals, or portable devices with limited display capabilities
`TV`	Television-type devices (low-resolution, limited-colors, limited scrolling ability)
`Projection`	Projectors
`Handheld`	Hand-held devices (small screen, monochrome, bitmapped graphics, limited bandwidth)
`Print`	Paged, opaque material (paper) and for documents viewed onscreen in Print Preview mode
`Braille`	Braille tactile feedback devices
`Aural`	Speech synthesizers
`All`	Suitable for all devices

We'll use a `<LINK>` tag to link to two external style sheets, one for a screen display and one designed for Braille output devices. Of course a corporation would probably take the time to design styles for all available media types, since a uniform appearance is important in presenting the company in a consistent and professional way across all possible media.

```
<HTML>
  <HEAD>
    <TITLE>Aristotelian Logical Systems, Ltd.</TITLE>
    <META http-equiv="Content-Style-Type"
    content="text/css">
    <LINK href="als-style.css" rel="stylesheet"
    type="text/css" media="Screen" title="ALS Basic
    Stylesheet">
```

```
<LINK href="als-braille-style.css" rel="stylesheet"
type= "text/dss" media="Braille" title="ALS Braille
Stylesheet">
</HEAD>
<BODY>
  <A href="developers.html"><IMG src="alslogo.gif"
  alt="[ALS Logo]" longdesc="als-description.html"
  border="0"height="100" width="100" align="left"></A>
  <H1>Aristotelian Logical Systems, Ltd.</H1>
    <BR clear="left">
    <BR>
    <P>
      <STRONG>ALS</STRONG> is a world leader in machine
      translation software and offers the most
      comprehensive suite of translation engines with
      the best recognition of idiomatic constructs in the
      known universe.
    <P>
      We want to help you, our present customers, as well
      as others interested in seeing how ALS products can
      power up international businesses as well as
      improve communications between the far-flung offices
      of global and trans-nationalbusinesses.
    <P>
      Explore our site:
    <DL>
      <DT><DD><A href="alsfaq.html">Company Fact Sheet</A>
      <DT><DD><A href="alsprods.html">Product
      Information</A>
      <DT><DD><A href="alssales.html">Contact Sales and
        Marketing</A>
      <DT><DD><A href="alsitpstatus.html">Intelligent
        Translation Prototype Product Status</A>
      <DT><DD><A href="alssupport.html">24-hour by 7-day
        Customer Support</A>
      <DT><DD><A href="alshistory.html">The History of
      Machine Translation</A>
    </DL>
    <ADDRESS>
      Contact the Webmaster:
        <Ahref="mailto:Webmaster@ALSLtd.com">
        <STRONG>Webmaster
        @ALSLtd.com</STRONG></A>
```

```
        </ADDRESS>
    </BODY>
</HTML>
```

This code results in the display shown in Figure 13.3. Though this figure doesn't appear to be different from a regular onscreen view, the Braille browser will generate printed pages that translate the letters into Braille or print the onscreen text with raised letters.

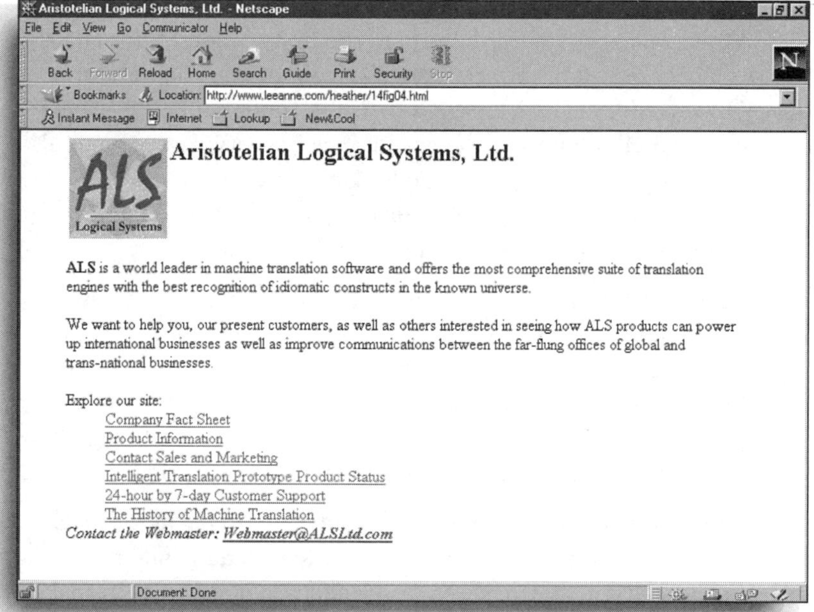

FIGURE 13.3
The Workgroup page displayed as it would be for a Braille browser.

Creating a Uniform Look and Feel for an Entire Site

Using external style sheets to make the most important style decisions in one place

1. Use the <META> and <LINK> tags to link to an external style sheet.

```
<HEAD>
    <META>
    <LINK>
</HEAD>
```

2. Define the external style sheets location with the `href` attribute.

```
<HEAD>
     <META http-equiv="Content-Style-Type"
     content="text/css">
     <LINK type="text/css" rel="stylesheet" href="als-
     style.css">
</HEAD>
```

We've talked about this before, in the first section of this chapter, but the rest of the sections talked about one page at a time. Once you've made one page look right, though, one style sheet can be used to improve the appearance of every page. You don't have to go through every page looking for opportunities to improve the look of this page or that; make one decision for all pages and then test to see if anything looks odd.

Fortunately there's a better way. HTML 4.0 allows you to use a single repository of style sheet information in the form of a link to an external style sheet. Simply put, that means that you can make one style sheet that covers an entire site, linking to it from every page. This way, if you decide to change anything, you change it in one place and it automatically propagates to every page.

The technique is really simple, just put a `<LINK>` tag in the head section of your page pointing to the style file and telling the browser that it's a style sheet. You could also import an external style sheet into an embedded style. Since external links are not as well-supported as they might be, you may also decide to include the external style as an embedded style and then import it again at the end, which is a bit more of a hassle to change but does cover more bases and will allow some changes to be made globally.

CHAPTER

14

Controlling Layout with Cascading Style Sheets

Using style sheets to control the layout of your page

Using layout styles to give pages a unique appearance

Understanding the space surrounding elements

Pros and Cons of Using Style Sheets

Style sheets are good for so many things they feel like ginseng tea or Mesmerism or other miracle cures. Not only can you use style sheets to control the appearance of your text in the ordinary way, but you can also use style sheets to affect the layout of your page directly, without terrorist invisible images and all the other tricks and tweaks that HTML writers have been struggling with for years. So there's got to be a catch, right?

Right. Unfortunately, none of the browser manufacturers have managed to put out a complete or bug-free version of Cascading Style Sheets, no matter what they claim or imply. While style sheets show tremendous promise, that promise has been compromised by uneven and uncertain implementations.

We'll just use some examples in this chapter, with the understanding that you should keep a thumb in Appendix B, "CSS Quick Reference." If you look at it, you'll notice that a few elements are entered in boldface. Boldface elements are those that are widely supported across multiple platforms. The depressing lack of large sections of boldface is a sad testimony to how poorly style sheets have penetrated the market, in spite of user demand.

By the time you read this, however, there should be better support in Netscape. This is one of the primary reasons that more properties and values in Appendix B aren't in bold, but you can take a yellow highlighter or a pencil and mark new property/ value pairs as you discover they're more widely supported. Netscape's Web site (`www.netscape.com`) will announce improvements in this area, or you could check the URL listed in the adjacent sidenote.

Keeping track of style sheets

There are several places on the Web that track compatibility between the different implementations of style sheets. One of the best is Web Review's Style Sheet Reference Guide at `http://style.webreview.com/`.

It has a feature-by-feature comparison of properties broken down into "safe" and "dangerous" lists, which will save you loads of time when browser updates come out later this year.

Controlling Margins and Other White Space

Controlling margins using style sheets

1. Use `BODY {margin-left: 3%; margin-right: 3%;}` to control the margins of an entire document.
2. By selecting other HTML elements, you can control vertical and horizontal spacing, depending on the context of an individual element.

```
H1 {clear: left; margin-top: 2em; text-align: center;}
```

Quick usage tips: Tag syntax

```
<STYLE type="mimetype" media="mediatype" title="title">
...style
selectors and {property/value pairs}... </STYLE>
```

where *mimetype* is the MIME type of the style "text/css"; *mediatype* is the media the style is designed for; and *title* is the title of the style element.

```
<LINK href="linkurl" rel="linktype" type="mimetype"
media="mediatype" title="title"> ...style selectors and
{property/value pairs}... </STYLE>
```

where *linkurl* is the location of the external stylesheet; *linktype* is the type of link, "stylesheet"; *mimetype* is the MIME type of the style "text/css"; *mediatype* is the media the style is designed for; and *title* is the title of the link element.

```
<htmltag style= "style property: value; pairs" ... >
```

The amount of power style sheets give you over the whitespace surrounding each element of HTML is enormous. You can select by individual HTML tag and by tags in context. Style sheet commands, as you can see in the following example, consist of simple text strings with each command consisting of an HTML element, special pseudo-element, or subclass of elements followed by a curly bracketed list of properties and values. If there is more than one property and value pair listed, they should be separated by semicolons. Styles can be further refined by declaring what context they would apply to by listing elements in order or by applying pseudo-elements or attributes to modify the HTML element.

For our first trick, we'll take the Hypatia page and put in some left and right margins, but we'll show only the actual style to save space. The result is shown in Figure 14.1.

```
<HTML>
  <HEAD>
    ...
    <STYLE><!--
       BODY { margin-left: 3%; margin-right: 3%; }
    -->
    </STYLE>
  </HEAD>
    ...
</HTML>
```

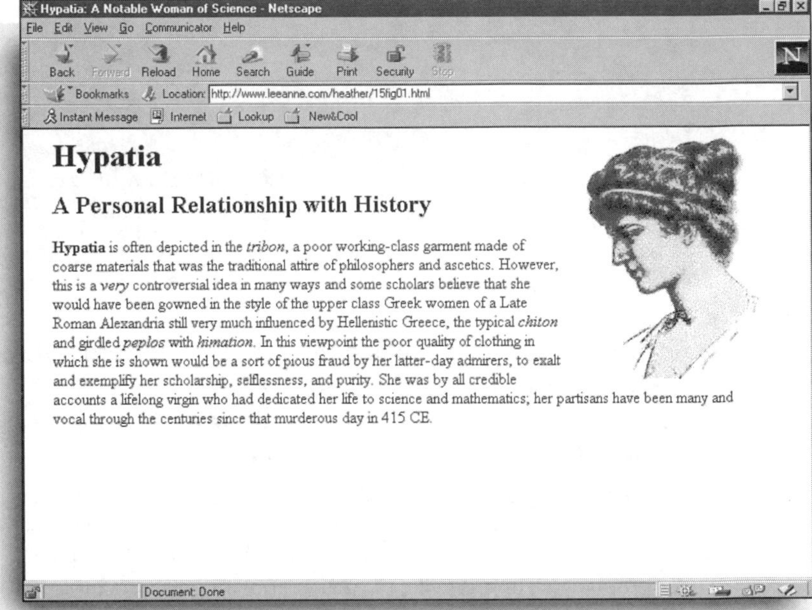

FIGURE 14.1
The Hypatia page with styled margins.

Placing Text Where You Want It

Defining text placement for individual elements

1. Use the <STYLE> tags placed within the head section, along with comment marks, to hide them from browsers that don't support CSS:

```
<STYLE><!--
     -->
     </STYLE>
```

2. Define the text placement for each style within the <STYLE> tags:

```
<STYLE><!--
        BODY { margin-left: 15%; margin-right: 5%; }
        H1 { margin-left: -11%; }
        H2 { margin-left: -7%; }
        H3 { margin-left: -3%; }
     -->
     </STYLE>
```

Each element can have an individual placement in relation to the margins, so if you want hanging headings, for example, it's a simple matter to argue different margin widths for your elements:

```
<HTML>
  <HEAD>
    ...
    <STYLE><!--
       BODY { margin-left: 15%; margin-right: 5%; }
       H1 { margin-left: -11%; }
       H2 { margin-left: -7%; }
       H3 { margin-left: -3%; }
    -->
    </STYLE>
  </HEAD>
    ...
</HTML>
```

This code results in the display shown in Figure 14.2.

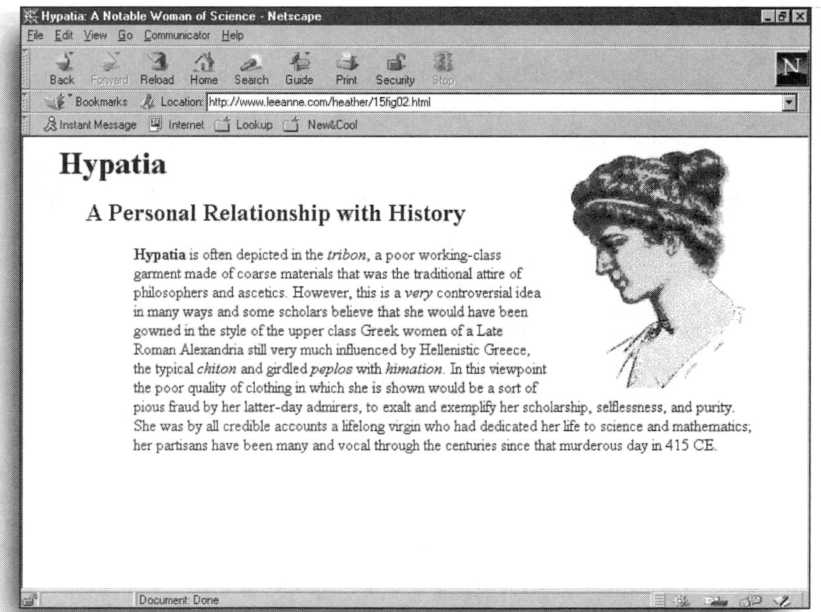

FIGURE 14.2
The Hypatia page with hanging headings.

Spot Color with CSS Attributes

Use margin and background color commands to control placement and help set off text and graphics with spot color

1. Set the size of the box surrounding an object with `padding` properties:

```
<STYLE>
     <!--
       H1 { padding: 5 }
     -->
     </STYLE>
```

2. Set the size of the transparent margin surrounding an element with `margin` properties:

```
<STYLE>
     <!--
       H1 { padding: 5; margin 15% }
     -->
     </STYLE>
```

3. Set the visibility and width of the border with `border` properties:

```
<STYLE>
     <!--
       H1 { padding: 5; margin 15%; border-width: thin;}
     -->
     </STYLE>
```

4. Set the foreground and background color with the `color` and `background-color` properties:

```
<STYLE>
     <!--
       H1 { padding: 5; margin 15%; border-width: thin;
       color: black; background-color: aqua }
     -->
     </STYLE>
```

Spot color is a great way to set off your text from the page or to highlight an important feature by treating it differently from other text. Because most graphical Web browsers are capable of coloring almost any element, the use of spot color is no longer the economically significant decision it once was, and it's easy to go too far, coloring almost everything in a crazy-quilt of color and contrast.

Used with restraint, though, a little color can make your words stand out from the page and enliven your text without intruding on the reader. There are several areas you'll have to understand before you can use background colors effectively with style sheets. Table 14.1 provides a list of `margin` and `padding` properties.

TABLE 14.1 Margin and padding properties

Attributes	Properties
`margin-top`	`length, percentage, auto` Specify the exterior top margin or gutter of an element.
`margin-right`	`length, percentage, auto` Specify the exterior right margin or gutter of an element.
`margin-bottom`	`length, percentage, auto` Specify the exterior bottom margin or gutter of an element.
`margin-left`	`length, percentage, auto` Specify left exterior margin or gutter of an element.
`margin`	`length, percentage, auto` Specify one or more exterior margins or gutters of an element. If four length values are specified they apply to top, right, bottom, and left respectively. If there is only one value, it applies to all sides; if there are two or three, the missing values are taken from the opposite side.
`padding-top`	`length, percentage, auto` Specify the top interior margin or gutter of an element. It sets the amount of space between one "invisible" border of an element and the element itself.
`padding-right`	`length, percentage, auto` Specify the right interior margin or gutter of an element. It sets the amount of space between one "invisible" border of an element and the element itself.
`padding-bottom`	`length, percentage, auto` Specify the bottom interior margin or gutter of an element. It sets the amount of space between one "invisible" border of an element and the element itself.
`padding-left`	`length, percentage, auto` Specify the left interior margin or gutter of an element. It sets the amount of space between one "invisible" border of an element and the element itself.

continues...

Style sheet measurements

There are five options for specifying values that include points, pixels, inches, centimeters, and percentage. These are designated by following the value with a suffix to denote the measurement type. To specify a measurement in points, use `pt`; for pixels, use `px`; for inches, use `in`; for centimeters, use `cm`; and for percentage, use `%`. The `auto` value will set the value to whatever is needed, depending on the size of the browser window.

TABLE 14.1 Continued

Attributes	Properties
padding	length, percentage, auto
	Specify one or more interior margins or gutters of an element. They set the amount of space between the "invisible" borders of an element and the element itself. If four length values are specified, they apply to top, right, bottom, and left respectively. If there is only one value, it applies to all sides; if there are two or three, the missing values are taken from the opposite side.
border-top-width	thin, medium, thick, length
	Specify the thickness (and visibility) of the top border of an element.
border-right-width	thin, medium, thick, length
	Specify the thickness (and visibility) of the right border of an element.
border-bottom-width	thin, medium, thick, length
	Specify the thickness (and visibility) of the bottom border of an element.
border-left-width	thin, medium, thick, length
	Specify the thickness (and visibility) of the left border of an element.
border-width	thin, medium, thick, length
	Specify the thickness (and visibility) of one or more borders of an element. This property is a shorthand property for setting border-width-top, border-width-right, border-width-bottom, and border-width-left in one fell swoop. There can be from one to four values, with the following interpretation: one value: all four border widths are set to that value; two values: top and bottom border widths are set to the first value, right and left are set to the second; three values: top is set to the first, right and left are set to the second, bottom is set to the third; four values: top, right, bottom, and left, respectively.
border-style	none, dotted [adv], dashed [adv], solid, double [adv], groove [adv], ridge [adv], inset [adv], offset [adv]

Attributes	Properties
	Specify the rule style of one or more borders of an element. There can be from one to four values, with the following interpretation: one value: all four border rules are set to that value; two values: top and bottom border rules are set to the first value, right and left are set to the second; three values: top is set to the first, right and left are set to the second, bottom is set to the third; four values: top, right, bottom, and left, respectively.
`border-top`	`border-top-width`, `border-style`, `color` Set the width, color, and rule styles of the top border (only) at one time.
`border-right`	`border-right-width`, `border-style`, `color` Set the width, color, and rule styles of the right border (only) at one time.
`border-bottom`	`border-right-width`, `border-style`, `color` Set the width, color, and rule styles of the bottom border (only) at one time.
`border-left`	`border-right-width`, `border-style`, `color` Set the width, color, and rule styles of the left border (only) at one time.
`border`	`border-right-width`, `border-style`, `color` Set the width, color, and rule styles of all borders at one time and to the same values. You can't use multiple values to set different values for the four sides.

Every visible HTML element is surrounded with a border that is invisible by default. Between the border and the page background is the always transparent margin, and between the border and the element is the padding, which is always the same color as the element itself. The border can be made visible and the size of the margin, border, and padding may be varied as fancy dictates.

That's as far as we'll go now, but we'll continue making our spot color background in the next section.

Use Style Sheet Color and Placement to Decorate Your Page Without Graphics

Now that you know how to position and size the elements surrounding each HTML element, you can use them to decorate the page with little bits of color without also introducing graphic elements. Table 14.2 lists text and element and color properties.

TABLE 14.2 Text and element color properties

Attributes	Properties
`border-color`	`color` Specify the color of one or more borders of an element. There can be from one to four values, with the following interpretation: one value: all four border colors are set to that value; two values: top and bottom border colors are set to the first value, right and left are set to the second; three values: top is set to the first, right and left are set to the second, bottom is set to the third; four values: top, right, bottom, and left, respectively.
`color`	`color`
`background-color`	`color, transparent`

By manipulating margins and padding, you can vary the size of the invisible box surrounding an element, whether it's a heading, a paragraph, or an arbitrary span or division in the text.

Background colors nest without limit

Each element can have a background color, so a particular element may be located within the background box of another element. You'll have to take this into account when designing your styles if you want to achieve complex effects with color.

To set off spot color all you have to do is set the background to a different color than the background of the page or of an enclosing element.

```
<HTML>
  <HEAD>
    <TITLE>The Fayne Family Page</TITLE>
    <STYLE>
    <!--
      BODY { margin-left: 15%; margin-right: 5%; color:
      black; background-color: white; }
```

```
        H1 { margin-left: -11%; padding: 5; background-color:
        lime; }
        H2 { margin-left: -7%; padding: 5; background-color:
        yellow; }
        H3 { margin-left: -3%; padding: 5; background-color:
        aqua; }
        A;link { color: blue; }
        A;visited { color: purple; }
        A;active { color: red; }
      -->
      </STYLE>
    </HEAD>
    <BODY bgcolor="FFFFFF" text="000000" link="0000FF"
  alink="FF0000" vlink="800080">
      <H1>The Fayne Family Page</H1>
        <IMG align="center" src="fanyne-ani.gif" height="280"
             width="235" alt="[Slide show of Nancy, Mikey,
             Bess &amp;
                  Mikey]">
        <H2>Who We Are</H2>
          <P>
           Hi! You've discovered the home page of <A
           href="marriage.html">Bess and George Fayne</A>,
           and of our wonderful children,
           <A href="nancy.html">Nancy</A>,
           five, and <A href="mikey.html">Mikey</A>, who's
           only six months old right now but already loves
           the computer, at least to eat! This is an
           experiment for us, the first time we've really
           done much of anything on a computer for ourselves,
           although both George and I use one at work. We
           hope you'll enjoy reading our page and looking at
           our pictures, which are like any family photo
           albums, except that you can set them aside as soon
           as you want without hurting our feelings!
        <H2>Where We Live</H2>
          <P>
           We're both natives of the <A
           href="backhome.html">Midwest </A>, born in a
           little suburb of Chicago, "hog butcher to the
           nation," but moved to California shortly after we
           were married.  Both our children were born here
           and this is home for us now, although we both
```

```
            enjoy going "back home" to visit the folks on
            holidays. Right now we're living in <A href="wal
            nutcreek.html">Walnut Creek </A>, California, which
            is right over the hills from the beautiful San
            Francisco Bay Area. We love our adopted home and
            really enjoy being only a few hours drive from the
            ocean to the west and not so very far to some of
            the most <A href="yosemite.html">spectacular
            mountains </A> in the world to the east.
        <H2>Our Special Interests</H2>
          <P>
            I'm a gourmet chef and George is a budding <A
            href="toys.html">helicopter</A> pilot (at least the
            model airplane variety) so our weekends are often
            spent out at the local model airfield, where
            George can tell "war stories" to all the other ace
            pilots over an ice cold soft drink or two. Nancy's
            favorite hobby right now is her bicycle (the
            training wheels came off last week!) and her
            stuffed animal collection while Mikey's favorite
            activity is still eating the computer!
        <H2>Fun Places We've Been</H2>
          <P>
            Since we've been living in California, we just had
            to go to <A href="disneytrip.html">Disneyland</A>
            (especially since Nancy discovered that it was
            only 450 miles south of us), although it seemed
            like a lot longer with a five year old and a
            nursing infant all piled into one little car.
            We've also been to the simply spectacular <A href=
            "reyes.html">Point Reyes National Seashore</A> and,
            of course, <A href="sfmemories.html">San
            Francisco!</A>
    </BODY>
</HTML>
```

This code results in the display shown in Figure 14.3.

Warning: Bugs are common in style sheet implementations

Although I carefully set the `padding` value in the code, Netscape ignores it as far as the background color is concerned. This is a flaw in the current Navigator 4.0 browser. Luckily it doesn't really hurt anything other than to change the appearance of the spot color boxes slightly.

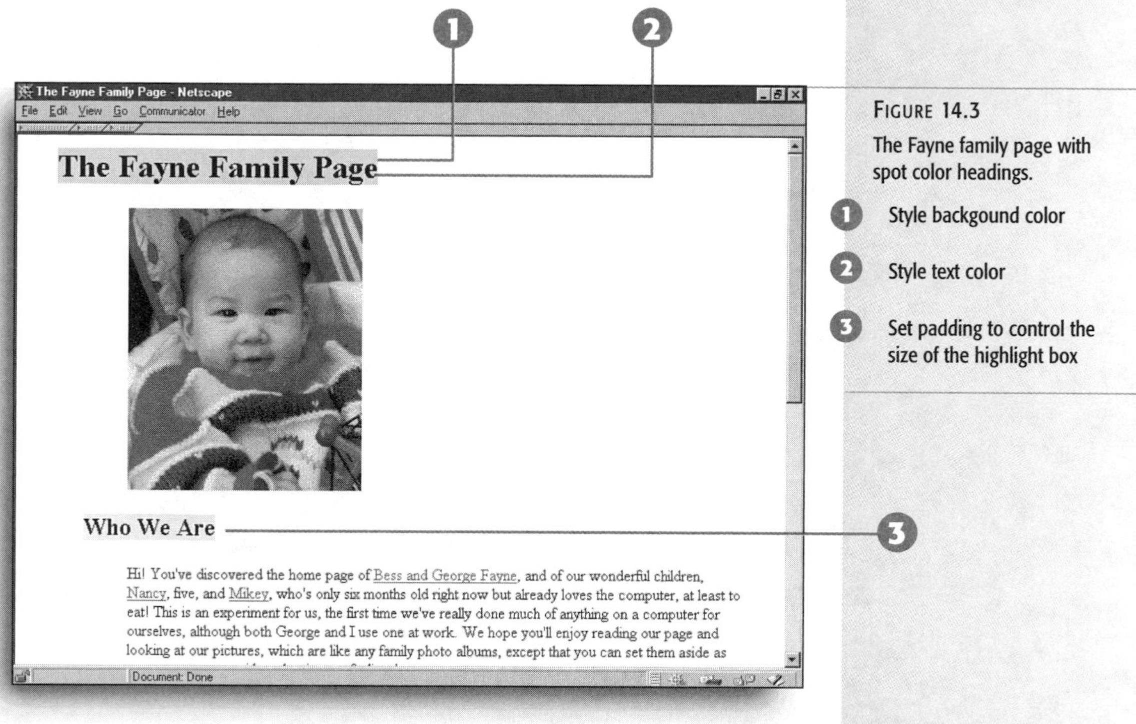

FIGURE 14.3

The Fayne family page with spot color headings.

1. Style backgound color
2. Style text color
3. Set padding to control the size of the highlight box

CHAPTER

15

Creating Tables for Data

Using tables to organize data

Grouping columns and rows

Identifying columns and rows with headers

Visual Organization

Neat little arrays of facts, set in a nice and square manner, attract many of us, and there's no better way to organize things in rows and columns than a table. Tables are simple to use and fairly easy to do right, especially if you follow a logical plan when first creating your data.

Making a Simple Table

Tables are basically simple

1. Add a simple table to your page with the <TABLE> tag.

   Quick usage tip: Tag syntax

   ```
   <TABLE summary="summary" align="alignment"
   frame="frametype" border="bordertype" rules="rulestype"
   width="colwidth" cellspacing="gutter"
   cellpadding="gutter">
   ```

   where *summary* is a short description of the table; *alignment* is the default alignment of the table; *frametype* is void, above, below, hsides, lhs, rhs, vsides, box, or border; *bordertype* is a value in pixels for the border width; *rulestype* is none, groups, rows, cols, or all; *colwidth* is the default width of column elements; and *gutter* is the amount of space within and outside cells, respectively.

2. Define rows with the <TR> tag.

   Quick usage tip: Tag syntax

   ```
   <TR align="alignment" valign="verticalalignment"
   char="decimalcharacter" charoff="decimaloffset">
   ```

   where *alignment* is left, center, right, justify, or char; *verticalalignment* is top, middle, bottom, or baseline; *decimalcharacter* is the decimal character used to align data; and *decimaloffset* is the offset in pixels to the decimal position.

3. Define header cells with the <TH> tag.

   Quick usage tip: Tag syntax

   ```
   <TH abbr="abbreviation" axis="relatedheaders"
   headers="headerids" scope="scope" rowspan="span"
   ```

```
colspan="span" align="alignment" valign=
"verticalalignment" char="decimalcharacter"
charoff="decimaloffset">
```

where *abbreviation* is an abbreviation for the header cell; *relatedheaders* is a list of groups of related headers; *headerids* is a list of header cell IDs; *scope* is the scope covered by header cells; *span* is the number of rows or columns spanned by a cell; *alignment* is `left`, `center`, `right`, `justify`, or `char`; *verticalalignment* is `top`, `middle`, `bottom`, or `baseline`; *decimalcharacter* is the decimal character used to align data; and *decimaloffset* is the offset in pixels to the decimal position.

4. Define data cells with the `<TD>` tag.

Quick usage tip: Tag syntax

```
<TD abbr="abbreviation" axis="relatedheaders"
headers="headerids" scope="scope" rowspan="span"
colspan="span" align="alignment" valign=
"verticalalignment" char="decimalcharacter"
charoff="decimaloffset">
```

where *abbreviation* is an abbreviation for the header cell; *relatedheaders* is a list of groups of related headers; *headerids* is a list of header cell IDs; *scope* is the scope covered by header cells; *span* is the number of rows or columns spanned by a cell; *alignment* is `left`, `center`, `right`, `justify`, or `char`; *verticalalignment* is `top`, `middle`, `bottom`, or `baseline`; *decimalcharacter* is the decimal character used to align data; and *decimaloffset* is the offset in pixels to the decimal position.

Tables are absolutely great for organizing your data in columns and rows, and they don't require a great deal of fiddling if you start out on the right foot. The secret of error- and hassle-free editing of tables is that old standby, create the data first and then add tags to turn it into a table.

We'll start by creating a table for the ALS corporate page, detailing languages the product handles and cross translations available.

```
ALS Aristotelian Logical Systems Cross Language Translation
          Chinese Dutch English French German Japanese Spanish
Chinese     N/A     X      X       X      X                X
Dutch        X     N/A     X       X      X       X        X
English      X      X     N/A      X      X       X        X
French       X      X      X      N/A     X       X        X
German       X      X      X       X     N/A      X        X
Japanese            X      X       X      X      N/A       X
Spanish      X      X      X       X      X       X       N/A
Translation between Japanese and Chinese is not currently
possible
```

Notice that the table is already arranged as it should be, making our job of adding tags easy. First we surround the table with the <TABLE> tag, separating it from the rest of the text on the page.

Then we identify the title with a <CAPTION> tag.

Then we insert a <TR> tag at the beginning of each row.

```
<TABLE>
  <TR>Language Chinese Dutch English French German Japanese Spanish
  <TR>Chinese     N/A     X      X       X      X                X
  <TR>Dutch        X     N/A     X       X      X       X        X
  <TR>English      X      X     N/A      X      X       X        X
  <TR>French       X      X      X      N/A     X       X        X
  <TR>German       X      X      X       X     N/A      X        X
  <TR>Japanese            X      X       X      X      N/A       X
  <TR>Spanish      X      X      X       X      X       X       N/A
  <TR>Translation between Japanese and Chinese is not currently
  possible
</TABLE>
```

Then we label each header cell with the <TH> tag. Since we discover that the table lines can become very long during this maneuver, break each line into separate lines for each column during this phase, to allow you to line up elements easily.

Finally, we tag the legend at the bottom of the table with a <TD> tag with the colspan attribute to ensure that the note is displayed across the bottom of the data properly.

```
<TABLE>
  <TR>
      <TH>Language</TH>
          <TH>Chinese</TH>
              <TH>Dutch</TH>
                 <TH>English</TH>
                     <TH>French</TH>
                         <TH>German</TH>
                             <TH>Japanese</TH>
                                 <TH>Spanish</TH>
  </TR>
  <TR>
      <TH>Chinese
          <TD>N/A
              <TD>X
                  <TD>X
                      <TD>X
                          <TD>X
                              <TD>
                                  <TD>X
  <TR>
      <TH>Dutch
          <TD>X
              <TD>N/A
                  <TD>X
                      <TD>X
                          <TD>X
                              <TD>X
                                  <TD>X
  <TR>
      <TH>English
          <TD>X
              <TD>X
                  <TD>N/A
                      <TD>X
                          <TD>X
                              <TD>X
                                  <TD>X
```

```
<TR>
    <TH>French
        <TD>X
            <TD>X
                <TD>X
                    <TD>N/A
                        <TD>X
                            <TD>X
                                <TD>X
<TR>
    <TH>German
        <TD>X
            <TD>X
                <TD>X
                    <TD>X
                        <TD>N/A
                            <TD>X
                                <TD>X
<TR>
    <TH>Japanese
        <TD>
            <TD>X
                <TD>X
                    <TD>X
                        <TD>X
                            <TD>N/A
                                <TD>X
<TR>
    <TH>Spanish
        <TD>X
            <TD>X
                <TD>X
                    <TD>X
                        <TD>X
                            <TD>X
                                <TD>N/A
<TR>
    <TD>
        <TD colspan="7">Translation between Japanese
         and Chinese is not currently possible
</TABLE>
```

The result is shown in Figure 15.1.

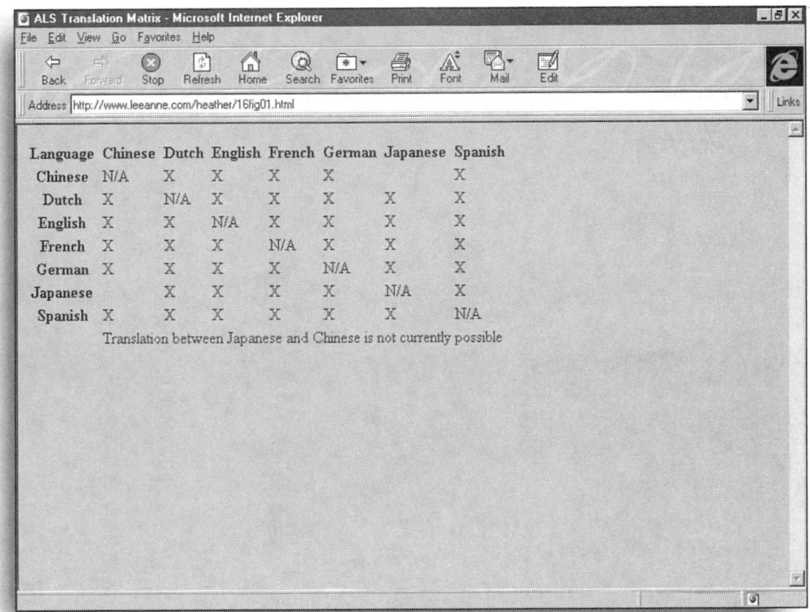

Language	Chinese	Dutch	English	French	German	Japanese	Spanish
Chinese	N/A	X	X	X	X		X
Dutch	X	N/A	X	X	X	X	X
English	X	X	N/A	X	X	X	X
French	X	X	X	N/A	X	X	X
German	X	X	X	X	N/A	X	X
Japanese		X	X	X	X	N/A	X
Spanish	X	X	X	X	X	X	N/A

Translation between Japanese and Chinese is not currently possible

FIGURE 15.1
The ALS Cross-Language Translation Matrix.

Creating Complex Tables

Control the size of images on the page with simple attributes

1. Nest tables by including an entire table inside a table data cell.
2. Eliminate the boundaries between cells by using the `colspan` and `rowspan` attributes.

Tables can be nested and cells can span both rows and columns to allow you almost complete control over the size and alignment of data in tables. For the ALS page, we'll add an internal matrix to the cells that represent Chinese/Japanese translation. showing that certain types of translation are possible after all but only between Romanized transliterations of the actual Chinese and Japanese texts. The use of Chinese characters in Japanese isn't ideal, because it makes unambiguous translation difficult.

We'll start by defining the matrix and then placing it into the existing code.

```
            Romanized  Chinese
Romanized       X
Japanese
```

which turns into

```
<TABLE>
  <TR>
       <TD>Language
           <TD>Romanized
               <TD>Chinese
  <TR>
        <TD>Romanized
            <TD>     X
                <TD>
  <TR>
        <TD>Japanese
            <TD>
                <TD>
</TABLE>
```

when we insert tags, and results in the display shown in Figure 15.2 when inserted into the existing code.

This still leaves a little something to be desired, since the alignment of the Xs is a little confusing. We'll address this problem in the "Grouping Common Table Elements" section.

Dividing the Table into Sections

Use *<THEAD>*, *<TBODY>*, and *<TFOOT>* sections to group rows together

1. Use the `<THEAD>` tag to define a header section that can remain constantly visible even as the table body scrolls.

   Quick usage tip: Tag syntax

   ```
   <THEAD align="alignment" valign="verticalalignment"
   char="decimalcharacter" charoff="decimaloffset">
   ```

where *alignment* is `left`, `center`, `right`, `justify`, or `char`; *verticalalignment* is `top`, `middle`, `bottom`, or `baseline`; *decimalcharacter* is the decimal character used to align data; and *decimaloffset* is the offset in pixels to the decimal position.

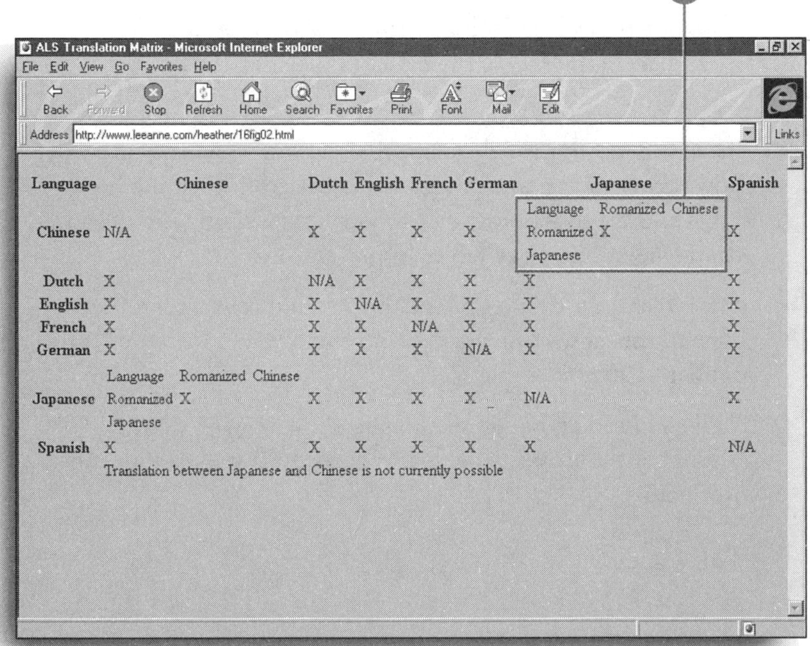

FIGURE 15.2
The ALS table with a nested table.

1 nested table

2. Use the <TBODY> tag to define one or more body sections containing actual data.

   Quick usage tip: Tag syntax

```
<TBODY align="alignment" valign="verticalalignment"
char="decimalcharacter" charoff="decimaloffset">
```

   where *alignment* is `left`, `center`, `right`, `justify`, or `char`; *verticalalignment* is `top`, `middle`, `bottom`, or `baseline`; *decimalcharacter* is the decimal character used to align data; and *decimaloffset* is the offset in pixels to the decimal position.

3. Use the <TFOOT> tag to define a footer section that can remain constantly visible as the table body scrolls.

   Quick usage tip: Tag syntax

   ```
   <TFOOT align="alignment" valign="verticalalignment"
   char="decimalcharacter" charoff="decimaloffset">
   ```

   where *alignment* is `left`, `center`, `right`, `justify`, or `char`; *verticalalignment* is `top`, `middle`, `bottom`, or `baseline`; *decimalcharacter* is the decimal character used to align data; and *decimaloffset* is the offset in pixels to the decimal position.

These tags are not widely supported yet but when they are will allow browsers to perform sophisticated scrolling of the body data while keeping header and footer information visible, an irritation when using large tables in present browsers.

Precedence of attributes is undefined

Choose which tag to define attributes carefully and use only one, because different browsers do different things when faced with a choice. Some choose the lowest level element as taking priority and some the exact opposite.

The `alignment` attributes affect all rows and cells within the scope of the tags, so they are a convenient way to enter a large number of attributes at once.

We'll add head and body sections to show how it's done, although most browsers currently don't do anything with this information.

```
<TABLE>
<THEAD>
  <TR>
      <TH>Language
          <TH>Chinese
              <TH>Dutch
                 <TH>English
                     <TH>French
                         <TH>German
                             <TH>Japanese
                                 <TH>Spanish
<TBODY>
  <TR>
      ...
```

Figure 15.3 shows the effect of using the <THEAD> and <TBODY> tags in a current browser.

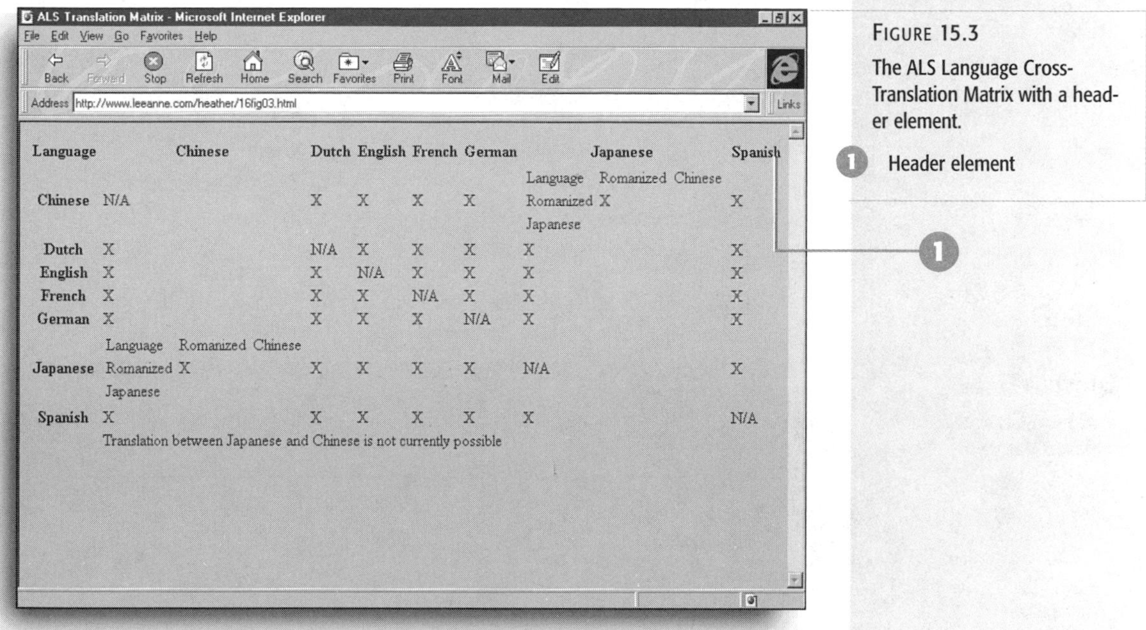

FIGURE 15.3

The ALS Language Cross-Translation Matrix with a header element.

1 Header element

Grouping Common Table Elements

Save typing and ease maintenance by grouping common elements together. Use the `<COLGROUP>` tag to group columns.

If we wanted to center text in all the cells of the ALS table, we'd have to enter the same alignment data in each cell, a painful chore, especially if you try to anticipate the things you might want to change later. Using the `<COL>` and `<COLGROUP>` tags, you can set attributes that follow each of the cells in that column, simplifying adding alignment or other information.

We'll add centering to the ALS table because it looks nice, and the table headers are already centered. We'll show just the code fragment and the first few lines of the table to save space.

```
<TABLE>
  <COLGROUP> <COLGROUP span="7" align="center">
<THEAD>
  <TR>
      <TH>Language
          <TH>Chinese
```

```
                        <TH>Dutch
                           <TH>English
                              <TH>French
                                 <TH>German
                                    <TH>Japanese
                                       <TH>Spanish
      <TBODY>
        <TR>
```

This code results in the display shown in Figure 15.4.

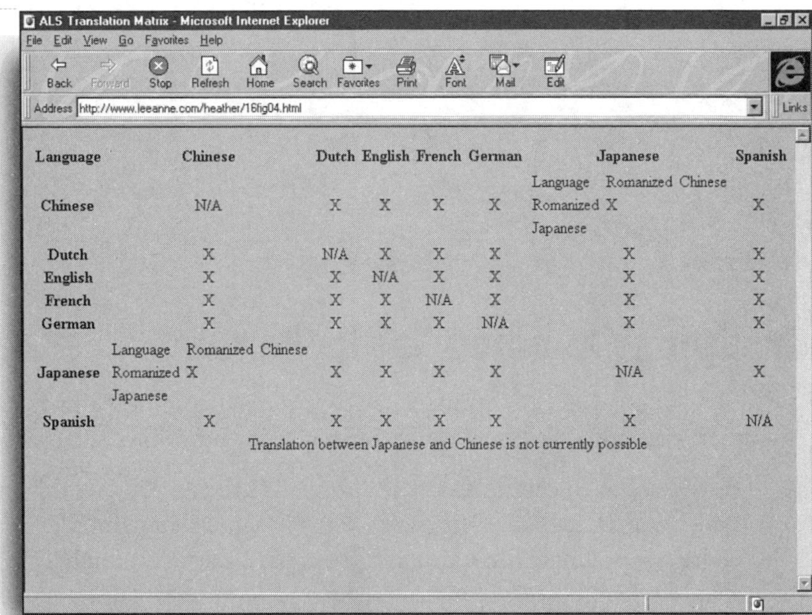

Language	Chinese	Dutch	English	French	German	Japanese	Spanish
Chinese	N/A	X	X	X	X	Language Romanized Chinese Romanized X Japanese	X
Dutch	X	N/A	X	X	X	X	X
English	X	X	N/A	X	X	X	X
French	X	X	X	N/A	X	X	X
German	X	X	X	X	N/A	X	X
Japanese	Language Romanized Chinese Romanized X Japanese	X	X	X	X	N/A	X
Spanish	X	X	X	X	X	X	N/A

Translation between Japanese and Chinese is not currently possible

FIGURE 15.4
The ALS Cross-Language Translation Matrix.

Providing a Table Caption

Use the <CAPTION> tag to provide a title for your table

1. Insert a `<CAPTION>` tag immediately after the `<TABLE>` tag to provide a title for the table.
2. The caption can be placed at the top or bottom of the table with the `align` attribute.

   Quick usage tip: Tag syntax

   ```
   <CAPTION align="alignment">
   ```

   where *`alignment`* is `top` or `bottom`.

Adding a caption is so simple that we'll just show the code.

```
<CAPTION>ALS Aristotelian Logical Systems Cross
 Language Translation
```

This code results in the display shown in Figure 15.5.

You could also place a caption at the bottom of the table if you prefer table titles at the bottom.

```
<CAPTION align="bottom">ALS Aristotelian Logical
 Systems Cross Language Translation
```

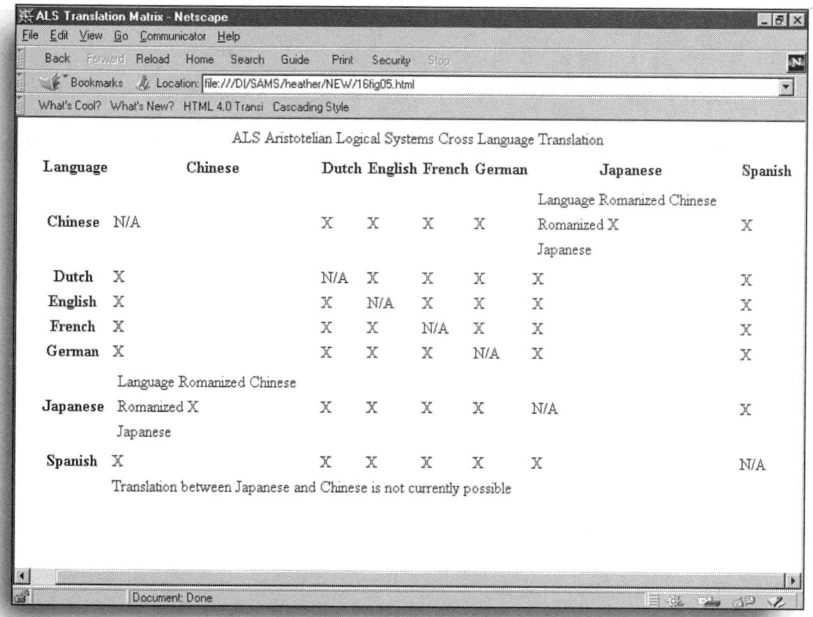

ALS Aristotelian Logical Systems Cross Language Translation

Language	Chinese	Dutch	English	French	German	Japanese	Spanish
Chinese	N/A	X	X	X	X	Language Romanized Chinese Romanized X Japanese	X
Dutch	X	N/A	X	X	X	X	X
English	X	X	N/A	X	X	X	X
French	X	X	X	N/A	X	X	X
German	X	X	X	X	N/A	X	X
Japanese	Language Romanized Chinese Romanized X Japanese	X	X	X	X	N/A	X
Spanish	X	X	X	X	X	X	N/A

Translation between Japanese and Chinese is not currently possible

FIGURE 15.5
The ALS table with a caption.

CHAPTER

16

Using Tables for Page Layout

- Use tables to lay out your page invisibly
- Place company logos in a table cell
- Add whitespace to your pages with empty cells

Why Use Tables for Page Layout?

Neat little rows and columns of data might be one way to describe a newspaper, a book, or almost anything printed. Our writing system depends on putting text in rows and the rows into columns, or we have great difficulty deciphering it.

Use both transitional attributes and style sheets

Until style sheets become more widely supported, you'll have to use both to account for the many browsers that don't support the standard fully. As of this writing that was practically all of them, but the situation may improve by the time you read this. The only browser supporting almost the entire recommendation is emacs-W3 (Gnuscape Navigator), a freely available browser that few people use in comparison with the mainstream competitors.

Tables allow you to exploit this regularity by placing text in tables created especially for the purpose of organizing a page. Usually this means explicit descriptions of height and width, allowing the data to flow into the space provided, but sometimes the data is allowed to dictate the size of the table, which guarantees long load times unless the table is very short.

HTML was designed for displaying rather prosaic documents, basically dull research papers with a few illustrations thrown in. The default format was linear and the structures available were few, some heading levels and a few block-level elements that were formatted slightly in from the left margin.

If that were all there was, we wouldn't have nearly as much fun with design as we do. The same tables that were introduced to make entering columnar data easy were soon pressed into service to get text off the dreaded left margin and out into the page.

Tables are best at horizontal and vertical placement of text, so the avant garde effects you see in some of the radical 'zines are not part of the table cuisine. Plain and fairly simple is our byword here, the plainer and simpler the better. Diagonal text and bleeds are pretty much restricted to the printed page, because there's simply no mechanism available in HTML to rotate your text or carry an image off the left or right margin.

For an ordinary layout, tables can format your text precisely and efficiently without resorting to exotic techniques that are not supported by most browsers. Layouts similar to those created by using tables can be found in books, magazines, and newspapers.

When combined with Cascading Style Sheets (see Chapter 14, "Controlling Layout with Cascading Style Sheets") and Dynamic HTML, tables can achieve extraordinary and complex effects. Almost every major corporate site on the Web is designed with tables as the basic formatting mechanism, so they must be pretty neat gadgets.

Creating a Left-Margin Navigation Bar

Use a table to design a corporate page with a navigation bar

1. Fill the page with the <TABLE> tag.

```
<TABLE>
</TABLE>
```

Quick usage tip: Tag syntax

```
<TABLE summary="summary" align="alignment"
frame="frametype" border="bordertype" rules="rulestype"
width="colwidth" cellspacing="gutter"
cellpadding="gutter">
```

where `summary` is a short description of the table; `alignment` is the default alignment of the table; `frametype` is `void`, `above`, `below`, `hsides`, `lhs`, `rhs`, `vsides`, `box`, or `border`; `bordertype` is a value in pixels for the border width; `rulestype` is `none`, `groups`, `rows`, `cols`, `all`; `colwidth` is the default width of column elements; and `gutter` is the amount of space within and outside cells.

2. Define columns with the column tag <COL>.

```
<TABLE border="0" width="100%" cellspacing="3">
      <COL width="100"><COL="*">
</TABLE>
```

Quick usage tip: Tag syntax

```
<COL width="widthvalue">
```

where `widthvalue` is either an absolute measurement in pixels, a percentage, or a relative width.

3. Define rows with the table row tag (<TR>).

```
<TABLE border="0" width="100%" cellspacing="3">
      <COL width="100"><COL="*">
      <TR height="150">
      <TR>
    </TABLE>
```

Quick usage tip: Tag syntax

```
<TR align="alignment" valign="verticalalignment"
char="decimalcharacter" charoff="decimaloffset">
```

where *alignment* is `left`, `center`, `right`, `justify`, or `char`; *verticalalignment* is `top`, `middle`, `bottom`, or `baseline`; *decimalcharacter* is the decimal character used to align data; and *decimaloffset* is the offset in pixels to the decimal position.

4. Define layout columns with the table data tag (`<TD>`).

```
<TABLE border="0" width="100%" cellspacing="3">
        <COL width="100"><COL="*">
        <TR height="150">
             <TD width="100">
             <TD>
        <TR>
             <TD>
             <TD>
</TABLE>
```

Quick usage tip: Tag syntax

```
<TD abbr="abbreviation" axis="relatedheaders"
headers="headerids" scope="scope" rowspan="span"
colspan="span" align="alignment" valign="verticalalign-
ment" char="decimalcharacter" charoff="decimaloffset">
```

where *abbreviation* is an abbreviation for the header cell; *relatedheaders* is a list of groups of related headers; *headerids* is a list of header cell IDs; *scope* is the scope covered by header cells; *span* is the number of rows or columns spanned by a cell; *alignment* is `left`, `center`, `right`, `justify`, or `char`; *verticalalignment* is `top`, `middle`, `bottom`, or `baseline`; *decimalcharacter* is the decimal character used to align data; and *decimaloffset* is the offset in pixels to the decimal position.

Start your design on paper

Just as you should start entering HTML pages with the raw text, you should always start tables with a paper sketch and then enter that table without anything inside. Turn on rules temporarily to make it easier to see what's going on while you refine the shape, and then start moving text and graphics into the cells.

For our layout problem, we'll update the ALS Web site with a simple framework made of one table and see how it changes the visual dynamic of the page.

First, take a piece of paper and follow along as we draft our layout on paper before trying to put it into our code. Draw a big rectangle about the shape of your computer screen. That's the area we have to play with really, although we can extend the page downward slightly. The best designs minimize scrolling, though, especially on the first page. We want the corporate logo to sit in the top-left corner, just as it does now, and the full name of the company to form a masthead immediately to its right. The first thing we can draw in is a long skinny horizontal rectangle with a squarish box sectioned off on the left end at the top of our screen box. It's starting to look like a table already.

Hmmm...The title box will be mostly empty space, so let's plan on partially filling it with an image toned down toward pastel colors that capture the dynamic urban environment in which ALS staffers live and work. It's a Toronto corporation and proud of its cosmopolitan heritage, so it's a very apt background for the corporate name. We won't worry too much about how to tone down and lighten the image because we know that we can do it in almost any graphics tool, including all the ones discussed in this book.

We definitely want a menu or navigation bar down the left margin of the page, so continue the vertical line that sections off the logo down the page to form a menu box. The rest of the page will be used to carry the text and another picture. Let's show the staff hard at work, thinking of new and better ways to communicate across language boundaries. We can throw the picture onto the right margin with basic HTML commands, so we won't divide the space any more.

What we've come up with is a two-by-two table asymmetrically skewed toward the upper-left corner. Simple to lay out with a table. We're going to go a little backward from our usual process here, since we have to move elements of our existing page around to make them fit into the new layout. We'll make the table at the top of the page and then move the pieces in one at a time, splitting off the logo information from the ALS name, for example, and adding graphic elements as we go along.

Here's the result so far. Notice that we've argued a width that will be overridden because the data fills more width than we left available, but we'll be changing the page more in chapters to come and it will do for now.

Organization is important

The browser will usually override your arguments if it discovers that a better arrangement is possible, but it's important to try and organize the table properly from the start. If the browser has to figure out how big the cells should be, it won't display any of the table until the entire table is loaded, causing long delays if the table is large or contains many graphics.

```
<HTML>
  <HEAD>
    <TITLE>Aristotelian Logical Systems, Ltd.</TITLE>
  </HEAD>
  <BODY>
    <TABLE border="0" width="100%" cellspacing="3">
      <COL width="100"><COL="*">
      <TR height="150">
          <TD width="100">
            <A href="developers.html"><IMGsrc="alslogo.gif"
            alt="[ALS Logo]"
               longdesc="als-description.html" border="0"
               height="100" width="100" align="left"></A>
              <TD background="toronto.jpeg">
                <H1>Aristotelian Logical Systems, Ltd.</H1>
                <BR clear="left">
                <BR>
      <TR>
          <TD>
             Explore our site:
             <DL>
               <DT><DD><A href="alsfaq.html">Company Fact
               Sheet</A>
               <DT><DD><A href="alsprods.html">Product
               Information</A>
               <DT><DD><A href="alssales.html">Contact
               Sales and Marketing</A>
               <DT><DD><A href="alsitpstatus.html">
               Intelligent
                 Translation Prototype Product Status</A>
               <DT><DD><A href="alssupport.html">24-hour by
               7-day
                 Customer Support</A>
               <DT><DD><A href="alshistory.html">The
               History of Machine Translation</A>
             </DL>
            <TD>

              <P>
                <STRONG>ALS</STRONG> is a world leader in
machine translation software and offers the most
comprehensive suite of translation engines with the best
recognition of idiomatic constructs in the known universe.
```

```
                <P>
                  We want to help you, our present customers,
as well as others interested in seeing how ALS products can
power up international businesses as well as improve commu-
nications between the far-flung offices of global and trans-
national businesses.
     </TABLE>
              <P>
       <ADDRESS>
         Contact the Webmaster:
           <A href="mailto;Webmaster@ALSLtd.com"><STRONG>
           Webmaster @ALSLtd.com</STRONG></A>
       </ADDRESS>
   </BODY>
</HTML>
```

This code results in the display shown in Figure 16.1.

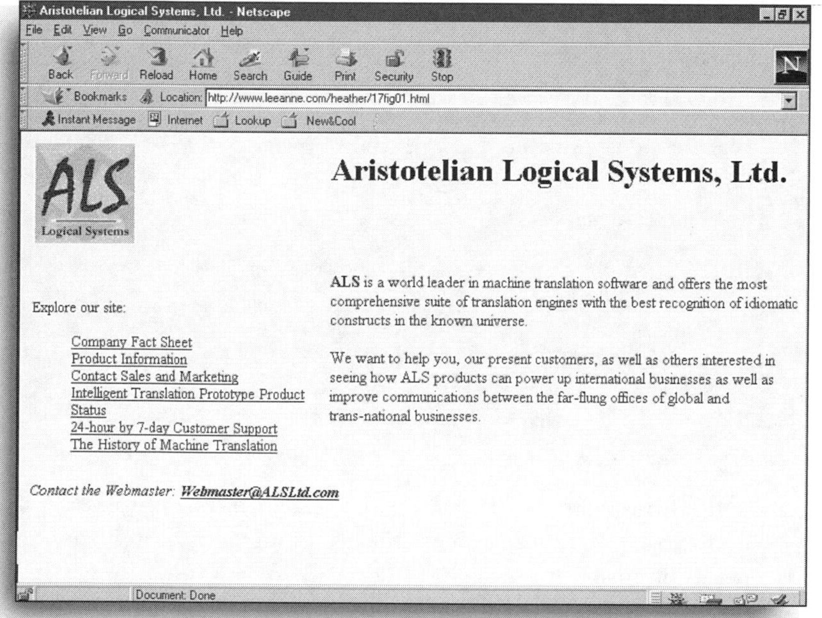

FIGURE 16.1
The ALS page spruced up in formal table cells.

Adding Whitespace with Table Cells

Adding whitespace to make your page easier to read

1. Fill the screen with the <TABLE> tag.

```
<TABLE>
</TABLE>
```

2. Define rows with the <TR> tag.

```
<TABLE>
        <TR>
    </TABLE>
```

3. Define columns with the <COL> tag. Insert some additional tags to add more white space to your page.

```
<TABLE>
        <COL>
        <COL>
        <COL>
        <TR>
</TABLE>
```

4. Define layout columns with the <TD> tag.

```
<TABLE>
        <COL>
        <COL>
        <COL>
        <TR>
             <TD>
             <TD>
             <TD>
</TABLE>
```

The ALS page in the previous section uses whitespace to break up the page slightly, but sometimes you want even more than is readily available at the edges of boxes filled with other things. In that case you can simply add empty cells in your table to correspond to the places you want to remain blank.

We'll use the Fayne family page to demonstrate layout using empty cells.

```
<HTML>
  <HEAD>
    <TITLE>The Fayne Family Page</TITLE>
  </HEAD>
  <BODY bgcolor="FFFFFF" text="000000" link="0000FF"
  alink="FF0000" vlink="800080">
    <TABLE>
      <COL>
      <COL>
      <COL>
      <TR>
          <TH colspan="3">
            <H1>The Fayne Family Page</H1>
      <TR>
           <TD>
                <TD>
                   <IMG align="center" src="Bess-Mikey.gif"
                   height="280" width="235" alt="[Picture of
                   Bess &amp; Mikey]">
                    <TD>
      <TR align="top">
           <TD>
             <H2>Who We Are</H2>
                <TD colspan="2">
                  <P>
                  Hi! You've discovered the home page of
                  <A href="marriage.html">Bess and George
                  Fayne</A>, and of our wonderful children,
                  <A href="nancy.html">Nancy</A>, five, and
                  <A href="mikey.html">Mikey</A>, who's only
                  six months old right now but already loves
                  the computer, at least to eat! This is an
                  experiment for us, the first time we've
                  really done much of anything on a computer
                  for ourselves, although both George and I
                  use one at work. We hope you'll enjoy
                  reading our page and looking at our
                  pictures, which are like any family photo
                  albums, except that you can set them aside
                  as soon as you want without hurting our
                  feelings!
```

```
<TR align="top">
    <TD>
      <H2>Where We Live</H2>
        <TD colspan="2">
         <P>
         We're both natives of the <A href=
         "backhome.html"> Midwest</A>, born in a
         little suburb of Chicago, "hog butcher to
         the nation," but moved to California shortly
         after we were married.  Both our children
         were born here and this is home for us now,
         although we both enjoy going "back home" to
         visit the folks on holidays. Right now we're
         living in <A href="walnutcreek.html">Walnut
         Creek </A>, California, which is right over
         the hills from the beautiful San Francisco
         Bay Area. We love our adopted home and
         really enjoy being only a few hours drive
         from the ocean to the west and not so very
         far to some of the most <A
         href="yosemite.html">spectacular
         mountains</A> in the world to the east.
<TR align="top">
    <TD>
      <H2>Our Special Interests</H2>
        <TD colspan="2">
         <P>
         I'm a gourmet chef and George is a budding
         <A href="toys.html">helicopter</A> pilot (at
         least the model airplane variety) so our
         weekends are often spent out at the local
         model airfield, where George can tell "war
         stories" to all the other ace pilots over an
         ice cold soft drink or two. Nancy's favorite
         hobby right now is her bicycle (the training
         wheels came off last week!) and her stuffed
         animal collection while Mikey's favorite
         activity is still eating the computer!
<TR align="top">
    <TD>
      <H2>Fun Places We've Been</H2>
        <TD colspan="2">
         <P>
          Since we've been living in California, we
          just had to go to <A href="disneytrip.html">
          Disneyland</A> (especially since Nancy
          discovered that it was only 450 miles south
          of us), although it seemed like a lot
```

```
                    longer with a five year old and a nursing
                    infant all piled into one little car. We've
                    also been to the simply spectacular <A
                    href="reyes.html">Point Reyes National
                    Seashore</A> and, of course, <A
                    href="sfmemories.html">San Francisco!
                    </A>
    </TABLE>
  </BODY>
</HTML>
```

Figure 16.2 shows the Fayne family page with lots of whitespace added.

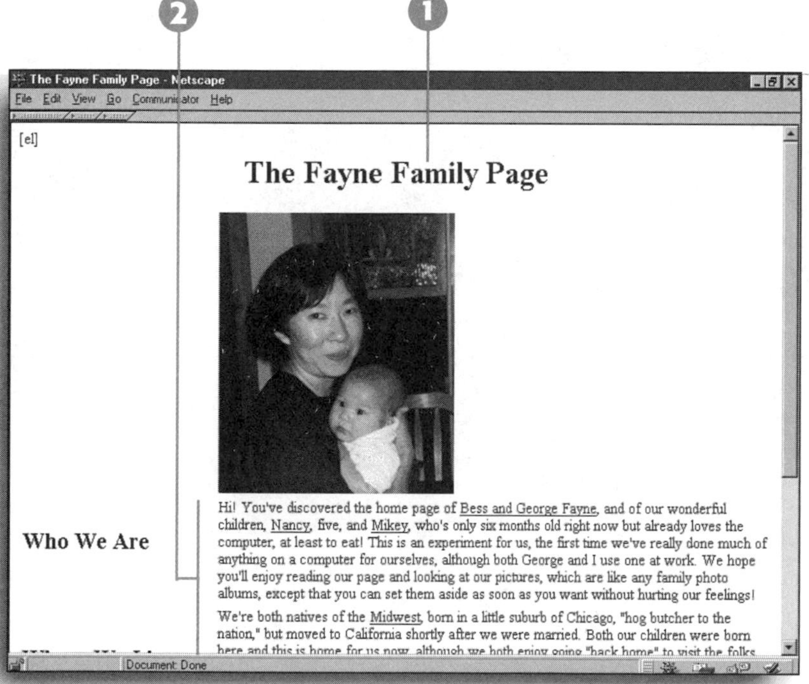

FIGURE 16.2
The Fayne family page using tables to create whitespace.

1. `Colspan` used to combine table cells into one
2. Alignment attributes used to control text placement

CHAPTER

17

Creating Frames

Understand what frames are and how they are used

Create simple layout frames

Control the appearance of frame borders and margins

Create complex frames with nested framesets

Creating a Frame

Frames were introduced as an HTML extension by Netscape in their Navigator 2 browser, and the feature caught on to such an extent that frames are now part of the official HTML specification. They are supported by Microsoft Internet Explorer 3 and 4 and by all versions of Netscape Navigator since version 2, inclusive. Frames are very powerful layout and navigation tools, though they do harbor some pitfalls for the unwary Web designer.

Understanding Frames and Their Use

Framing is simply a method of placing two or more windows on the screen at the same time, giving the viewer control of some, none, or all of the content of these windows. A page within a frame can reference other pages, independent of the behavior of the rest of the display. This gives a Web designer great flexibility in organizing and presenting graphical, textual, or multimedia content.

Frames can be conveniently divided into two types. First, there are *static* frames. A static frame remains visible to the user, no matter what he or she does, and its content does not change. Static frames are often used to display navigational tools, which normally should be visible at all times.

Second are *dynamic* frames. The content of a dynamic frame will change in response to what the user does, such as clicking a hyperlink. You can see an example of a static/dynamic frame pair at the Netscape Web site, as shown in Figure 17.1.

When you are deciding how (or even if) to use a framed environment for your site, you should keep the following in mind:

- Use frames only if they contribute to the user-friendliness of your site. Don't employ them just because you can.
- Don't crowd too many frames into one browser window. The more frames you display, the smaller they are, and the more confusing the relationships between them can become.

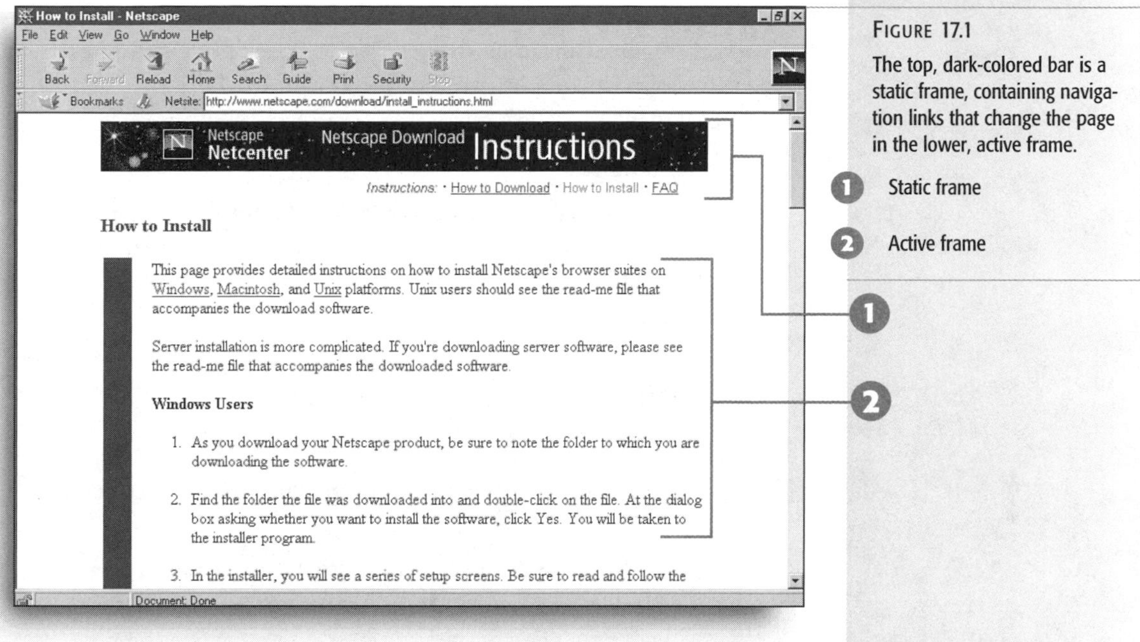

FIGURE 17.1

The top, dark-colored bar is a static frame, containing navigation links that change the page in the lower, active frame.

1 Static frame

2 Active frame

- Use static frames sparingly, for things like tables of contents, navigational tools, and site identification.
- Dynamic frames are most important to the viewer because that's where he or she makes things happen. Commit most of the display's real estate to dynamic frames.
- Remember that most people use 14" or 15" monitors. Frames that look good on a 17" or larger display may look terrible on the smaller ones. Keep this in mind when you're laying out your frames.

Setting Up a Simple Frameset of Two Frames

The collection of frames that organizes a framed environment (that is, what the user sees in his monitor) is called the *frameset*. A frameset all by itself does not contain any information for the user. To be useful, it needs content, and the content of a frame is simply an HTML page. You can think of the frameset as the scaffolding that arranges HTML pages, and relates them to each other. A frameset itself is contained in an HTML page—in fact, a frameset is just a text file, like any HTML page.

A frameset is defined within the <FRAMESET> and </FRAMESET> tags, which together make up the <FRAMESET> container. All framesets, even the most complex, are produced with the following general steps.

Creating a frameset

1. Create the HTML page to contain the frameset, using the following code. (Note that there is no <BODY> container. This is intentional.)

```
<HTML>
<HEAD>
</HEAD>
</HTML>
```

2. Add any <HEAD> elements you want, such as a <TITLE> container.
3. Immediately after the closing </HEAD> tag, create the main frameset container, using the <FRAMESET> and </FRAMESET> tag pair:

```
<FRAMESET>
</FRAMESET>
```

4. Insert rows and/or cols attributes into the <FRAMESET> tag. You can also insert other optional frameset attributes as needed (not shown in the following example).

```
<FRAMESET cols = "50%,50%">
```

5. Into the main frameset container, insert a <FRAME src> statement to specify the URL of each page that initially appears in the frameset. You must have one such <FRAME> statement for each frame of the frameset.

```
<FRAME src = "url">
```

6. Add optional attributes as desired to the <FRAME> tag.
7. If needed, insert further frameset containers into the main frameset container. These are called *nested frames*, and are used to produce complex framed environments. These will be covered later in this chapter. The complete code for the

simplest possible frameset, which creates two frames that each contain an HTML page, looks like this:

```
<HTML>
<HEAD>
</HEAD>
    <FRAMESET cols = "50%,50%">
        <FRAME src="page01.htm">
        <FRAME src="page02.htm">
    </FRAMESET>
</HTML>
```

You can produce any frameset you want with the above procedure. In this chapter and the next, we'll explore the many variations on this theme.

As mentioned above, the simplest frameset displays two frames, either side-by-side or one above the other—two columns, or two rows, respectively. The following code shows you how to make a frameset page that produces two side-by-side frames—two columns, in other words. Once you've had a chance to look at the code and what it does, we'll go into more detail about how it works.

```
<HTML>
<HEAD>
</HEAD>
    <FRAMESET cols = "15%,85%">
        <FRAME src="page01.htm">
        <FRAME src="page02.htm">
    </FRAMESET>
</HTML>
```

You can see what the results look like in Figure 17.2.

The HTML pages that appear in the two frames are PAGE01.HTM and PAGE02.HTM. Any frameset must call upon an existing HTML page to appear in each of its displayed frames. If these pages don't exist, the frameset won't work. In the example, the HTML pages are referenced by the two `<FRAME src>` attribute lines, which we'll discuss a little later in this chapter.

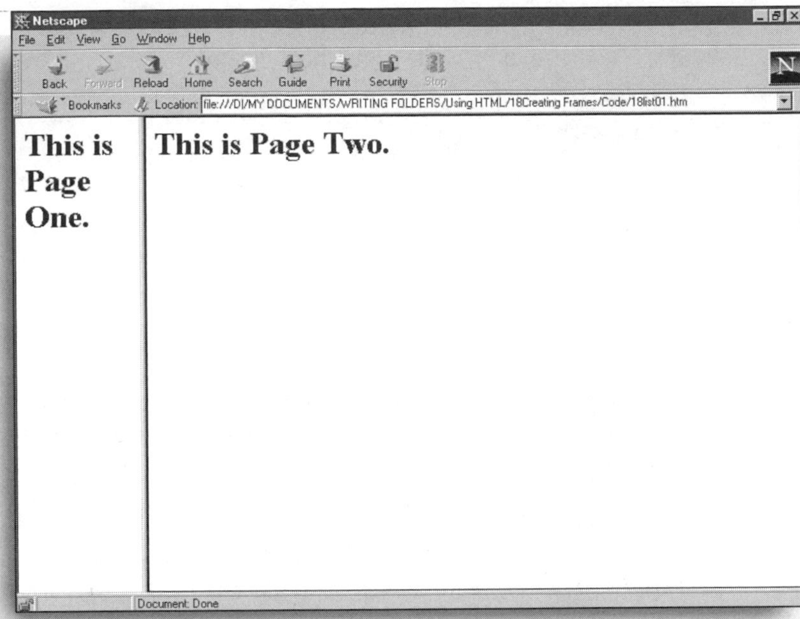

FIGURE 17.2
A two-column frameset displaying two different HTML pages.

Problems with the <BODY> tag

If your frameset doesn't work, check the HTML for the frameset page and make sure there is no `<BODY> </BODY>` tag pair. Frameset pages are not permitted to use the `<BODY>` container. A consequence is that you can't use any of the body attributes, such as `backgrounds`, on a frameset page. If you want `backgrounds`, you have to put them into the regular pages that appear within the frames.

As you may have figured out, the `cols` attribute of the `<FRAMESET>` tag defines the number and width of the side-by-side frames. In the previous example, the left frame got 15% of the width of the browser's display, and the right frame got the rest. If the `cols` attribute had been `30%, 30%, 40%`, there would have been three frames of the appropriate percentage widths.

If you want rows instead of columns, you would substitute the attribute `rows` for `cols`. For example, to split the browser window into two equal rows, the opening `<FRAMESET>` tag in our earlier example would be

```
<FRAMESET rows = "50%,50%">
```

If you accidentally put in two percentages that add up to less or more than 100%, nothing dire happens—the browser tries to approximate the proportions suggested by the incorrect values. If you're getting odd frame sizes, check the percentages to see if they add up to 100%.

If you're wondering how to create framesets with both rows and columns, we'll get to it a little later in this chapter.

Defining Frames Proportionally or by Pixel Value

The sample code for our two-column frameset defines the frame sizes by setting percentage widths. There's a more flexible way to define frame widths or heights, however, which is to use proportional value.

Suppose you want the left frame to be one-third of the browser window width, and the right frame to be two-thirds of it. You would write:

```
<FRAMESET cols = "*,2*">
```

An asterisk represents one slice of the window. To figure out how many slices the window has in total, add up all the asterisks specified by the numbers beside them. In the previous code line, there are three slices—the first asterisk (a "1" is understood to be beside it) plus the two asterisks defined by the `2*`. If you wrote `"2*,3*,5*"` for the `cols` value, the browser window would have a total of 10 slices: the left column would get two of them, the middle column three, and the right column five.

You can also specify the width or height of a frame by giving its size in pixels. To do this, you use numbers as the values. To specify two frames, one 80 pixels high and the other 120 pixels high, you would write:

```
<FRAMESET rows = "80,120">
```

Using pixel definitions is usually not a good idea. This is because you don't know for sure what type of monitor your viewers are using. If you define frames so that they are 800 pixels wide, and the viewer is using a 640×480 display, your frames won't fit his or her screen. Proportional or percentage definitions are usually much safer.

However, specifying pixels for frame dimensions is very useful in certain cases. For instance, if you have a logo that you know is 70 pixels high, you may want to reserve a frame of 80 pixels height for it. This ensures that it will appear exactly as you want it to, no matter what screen resolution the user's monitor is displaying.

Using at least one row or column

If you define a frameset with one column or one row (for example, `<FRAMESET cols= "100%">`), a browser will display a blank page. You must define at least two columns or two rows.

What's a pixel?

Pixel stands for picture element. A pixel is the smallest part of the fine-grained mosaic that makes up a monitor display. A standard VGA display is 640 pixels wide by 480 pixels high. An SVGA (Super VGA) display is 800 pixels wide by 600 pixels high.

You can also mix definitions, if you need to. Suppose you want the left half of the browser window for one frame, while the right half is to be divided into two frames. One of these two frames takes up a third of the right half of the screen, and the other, the remaining two thirds. You would write

```
<FRAMESET cols = "50%,*,2*">
```

The `50%` is allocated first, and the proportional values are applied to whatever space is left over—in this case, another 50%.

Defining the Content of Frames

Since we defined two frames in our example earlier, the frameset needs to call on two HTML pages to fill them. The page that provides the content of a frame is referenced by the attribute `src`. The generic form of the `src` attribute is

```
<FRAME src = "url">
```

where `"url"`, of course, is the location of the HTML page to be displayed. This location can be any valid URL, as well as paths to local HTML files. If you wanted to show the Netscape home page in a frame, for example, the attribute would read

```
<FRAME src = "http://www.home.netscape.com">
```

There must be exactly one `src` attribute for each frame in the frameset, as you can see in the previous two-frame code example—two frames, two `<FRAME src>` statements.

Note that you must reference only HTML files or URLs in the `SRC` attribute, and no other element. You can't write a line like `<FRAME src = "my_image.gif">`. If you do, the browser will ignore the entire frameset.

As you know, the page displayed in a frame can be changed, usually by the user clicking a link to another page. We'll cover this subject in Chapter 18, "Naming and Navigating Frames."

Using the <*NOFRAME*> Container

While later versions of Microsoft Internet Explorer and Netscape Navigator support frames, not everyone (even now) is using a frames-capable browser. To deal with this, you use the

<NOFRAME> container and put a normal HTML page within it. People using nonframe browsers will see the page defined inside the <NOFRAME> container; the frameset code surrounding the container will be ignored. To do this with our two-frame example, perform the following steps.

Hiding frames from nonframe browsers

1. Create the frameset as needed.
2. Insert the <NOFRAME></NOFRAME> container into the frameset container. If you have another frameset nested inside the main frameset, make sure the <NOFRAME> container appears in the main frameset, before the code for the nested frameset.
3. Within the <NOFRAME> container, create the HTML code for the alternate page that will be seen by people using nonframe browsers. This page is a normal HTML page, and can contain any HTML elements.

A general example of such code looks like this.

```
<HTML>
<HEAD>
</HEAD>
    <FRAMESET cols = "50%,50%">
        <FRAME src="page01.htm">
        <FRAME src="page02.htm">
            <NOFRAME>
                <HEAD>
                <TITLE>Your Home Page</TITLE>
                </HEAD>
                <BODY> . . .</BODY>
                </HTML>
            </NOFRAME>
    </FRAMESET>
</HTML>
```

Note that this is the only case where you can have the <BODY> container on the same page as the <FRAMESET> container. <BODY> is inside the <NOFRAME> container, so the frameset code ignores it.

Providing a nonframe alternative

A large number of people simply do not like frames and try to avoid Web sites that use them. To ensure that you keep such people from moving on, consider giving them a set of alternate pages that don't use frames, and make sure that this option is prominently displayed on all pages that may be entry points for your site. Running such parallel sites requires more work and organization than doing just one, but the results in terms of satisfied visitors may be worth it.

Using Frames for Page Layout

Creating a framed environment can be an effective and efficient way of controlling page layout in a browser display, especially if you need the control capabilities of a frameset. Not only can you create a layout grid, you can manage its appearance and behavior.

Creating a Layout Grid Using Frames

Suppose you want a page that is laid out in a grid that is two rows high and three columns across. Use the following code to produce such a page.

```
<HTML>
<HEAD>
</HEAD>
    <FRAMESET rows = "50%,50%" cols = "*,*,*">
        <FRAME src="test.htm">
        <FRAME src="test.htm">
        <FRAME src="test.htm">
        <FRAME src="test.htm">
        <FRAME src="test.htm">
        <FRAME src="test.htm">
    </FRAMESET>
</HTML>
```

Some points worth noting about this code are

- Because the frameset has six frames, there must be six HTML pages assigned to them, or the frameset will not display properly. Accordingly, there are six `<FRAME src>` lines in the code.
- For testing purposes, you can use a dummy HTML file, like the test.htm file used in the code.
- The row and column proportions have been assigned using percentage and proportional values, respectively. This is an arbitrary decision on the Web author's part. You can mix the ways of assigning the frame sizes to your own liking.

This frameset produces the browser display shown in Figure 17.3.

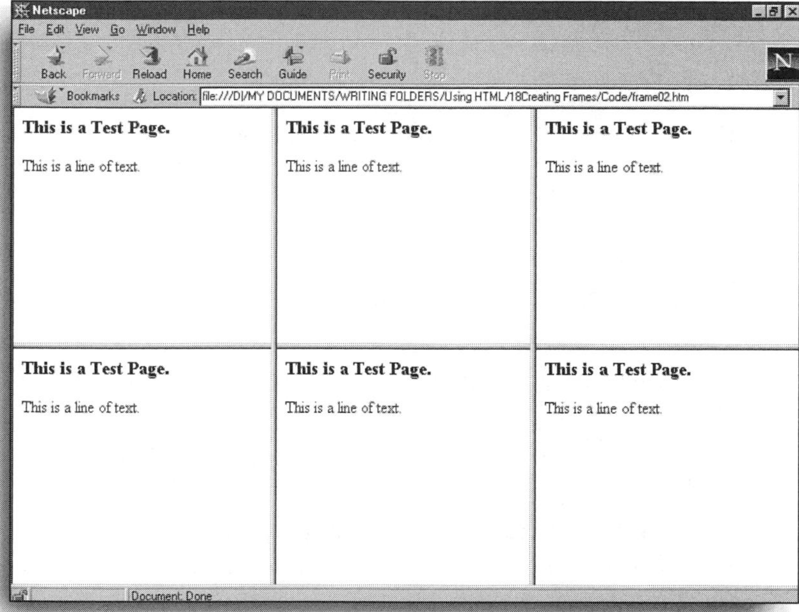

FIGURE 17.3
Framesets can be used to create a layout grid.

Using *<FRAME>* Attributes

You can control the look and behavior of the layout frameset by using certain `<FRAME>` attributes. These attributes are

- `scrolling="yes|no|auto"` The optional `scrolling` attribute is used to determine whether the frame should have scrollbars. `Yes` makes scrollbars always visible on that frame. `No` results in scrollbars never being visible. `Auto` instructs the browser to decide whether scrollbars are needed and place them where necessary. The default value is `auto`.
- `noresize` The optional `noresize` attribute has no value. It indicates that the frame is not resizable by the user. Users typically resize frames by dragging a frame edge to a new position. By default, all frames are resizable.
- `marginwidth="value"` The optional `marginwidth` attribute is used when you want to control the margins of the text or images within the frame. If specified, the *`value`* for `marginwidth` is in pixels. Margins cannot be less than one pixel. By default, the browser decides an appropriate margin width.

Should I use frames or tables for layout?

Frames can indeed help you in laying out the look of a browser display. However, if you need more than two or three rows and/or columns, consider using a table. This is especially true if you don't need the control features offered by the framed environment. For simple layout and formatting of static information, tables are usually the better choice.

- `marginheight="value"` The optional `marginheight` attribute behaves like `marginwidth` above, except it controls the upper and lower margins of the frame.

The following code demonstrates no resizing, scroll bars set to be always visible, and margins of 50 pixels (in the lower frame).

```
<HTML>
<HEAD>
</HEAD>
    <FRAMESET cols = "*,*">
        <FRAME src = "page01.htm">
        <FRAME scrolling="YES" noresize marginwidth="50"
        marginheight="50" src="test02.htm">
    </FRAMESET>
</HTML>
```

You can see the results of this code in Figure 17.4. (Some generic text has been provided on the right frame). Note that even though all the text in the right frame is visible, the scroll bars are present, though they are grayed out. This is the result of setting `scrolling = "YES"`. Note also the 50-pixel margins set by the `marginheight` and `marginwidth` attributes.

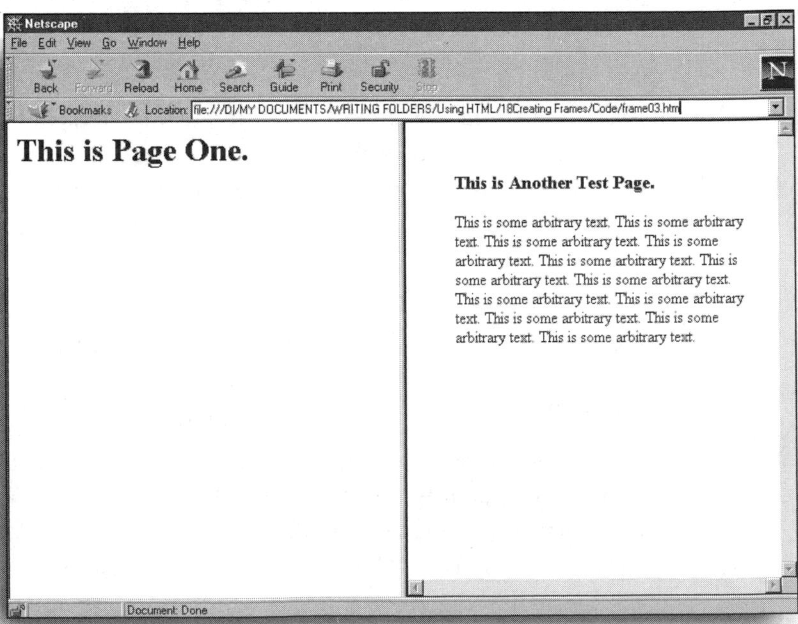

FIGURE 17.4
You control margins, resizing, and scrolling with optional <FRAME> attributes.

Using Frame Border Attributes

One of these two attributes, `frameborder`, is supported by Internet Explorer 3 and 4 and by Netscape 3 and Netscape Communicator. The other attribute, `framespacing`, is supported by only the Microsoft browsers. They are attributes of the `<FRAMESET>` tag.

- `frameborder = "0"` removes the 3D border from all frames in the frameset. If scroll bars for a frame are needed or are required, they will remain visible even though the frame border cannot be seen. `frameborder="1"` sets the borders to the visible state (deleting the `frameborder` attribute has the same effect).
- `framespacing = "value"`, where *value* is in pixels, sets the thickness of the 3D border (use only with Internet Explorer 3 and later; Netscape browsers will always display the default border thickness).

The next little chunk of code produces the borderless framed display shown in Figure 17.5.

```
HTML>
<HEAD>
</HEAD>
    <FRAMESET frameborder="0" rows = "50%,50%"
    cols = "*,*,*">
        <FRAME src="test.htm">
        <FRAME src="test.htm">
        <FRAME src="test.htm">
        <FRAME src="test.htm">
        <FRAME src="test.htm">
        <FRAME src="test.htm">
    </FRAMESET>
</HTML>
```

Incidentally, if you set `scrolling = "YES"` with borderless frames, the scroll bars are still displayed.

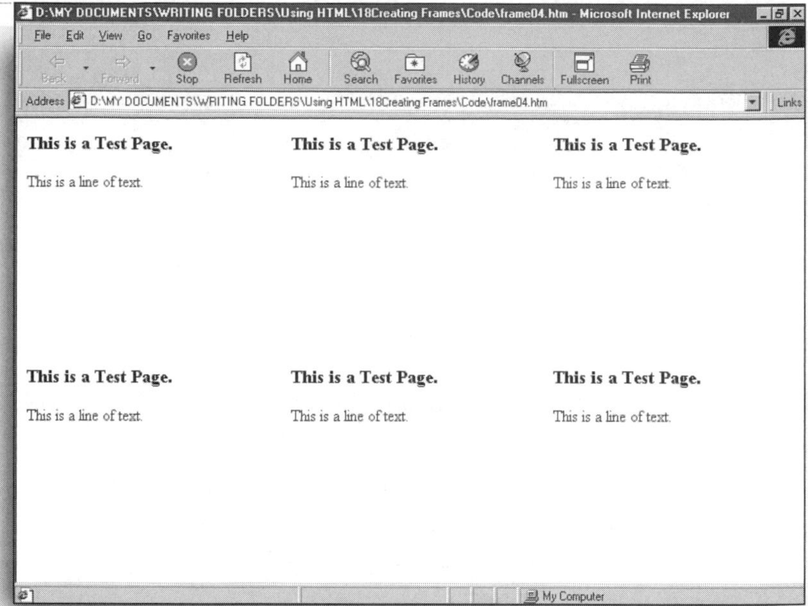

FIGURE 17.5
A borderless display as seen in Internet Explorer 4. Netscape Navigator 3 and Netscape Communicator also support borderless frames.

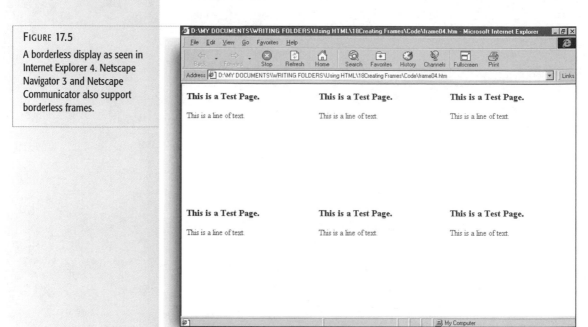

Creating Complex Frames

You may have noticed that the examples so far have set up a strictly rectangular grid. You may also have noticed that dragging the vertical border of an upper frame in our 2×6 grid also dragged the vertical border of the frame beneath it. What do you do if you want something other than a regular grid of frames—for example, a row the width of the display, with two columns under it? Or if you want some frames to be resizable independently of others?

The answer: you put one frameset inside another frameset. This technique is called *nested framesets*.

Creating Nested Framesets

Suppose, as was previously suggested, you want to create a browser display that has a single frame running across the top of the browser window and two columns of unequal width beneath this upper frame. Perform the following steps.

Set up a nested frameset

1. Begin by writing the main frameset code to create the row structure:

```
<FRAMESET rows = "20%,80%">
    <FRAME src = "top.htm">
</FRAMESET>
```

   This wouldn't work properly, of course, since there's no HTML file to populate the lower row. We'll fix that in step 2.

2. Type the code for the nested frameset into the main frameset, immediately after the `<FRAME src>` line that specifies the HTML file for the top row. The completed code looks like this:

```
<FRAMESET rows = "20%,80%">
    <FRAME src = "top.htm">
        <FRAMESET cols = "20%, 80%">
            <FRAME src = "left.htm">
            <FRAME src = "right.htm">
        </FRAMESET>
</FRAMESET>
```

When the browser reads this frameset code, this is what happens: It sees the row definition, sees the `src` line giving the HTML file for the top row, and displays that file in the upper frame. But next, instead of seeing an `src` line for the lower row (the one defined by the **80%**), it instead sees another frameset definition. This is the nested frameset. This new frameset defines columns, so the browser obediently cuts the lower row into two columns of the designated widths. Only then does it look for the `src` lines that will fill the two columns with HTML files. When it finds them, it displays them in the appropriate columns. After that, it sees the two closing tags of the framesets, so it's finished. You can see the results of the finished code in Figure 17.6.

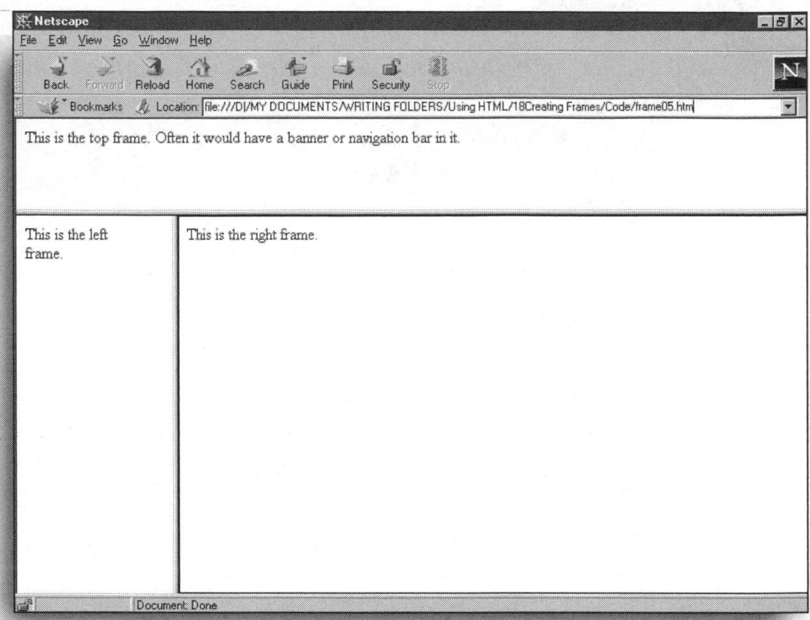

FIGURE 17.6
This more complex layout uses nested frames. The two lower columns can be resized independently of the upper row.

Creating Independent Columns

Frames can get complicated, so let's look at another example to clarify things further. Suppose you want a browser display of two rows, and each row will have two columns. However, the columns of the top row will be different widths than the columns in the bottom row, so you can't simply create a 2×2 grid. The code for such a display looks like this.

```
<FRAMESET rows = "30%,70%">
        <FRAMESET cols = "20%, 80%">
            <FRAME src = "left.htm">
            <FRAME src = "right.htm">
        </FRAMESET>

        <FRAMESET cols = "40%, 60%">
            <FRAME src = "test.htm">
            <FRAME src = "test02.htm">
        </FRAMESET>
</FRAMESET>
```

This code first establishes a frameset of two rows, the upper of 30% height, the lower of 70%. When the browser sees this, it first expects to get something to fill in the top row. What it does get is another frameset, which specifies two columns of 10% width and 90% width. The browser creates the two columns, looks for something to go into them, and finds the two HTML files in the `src` lines.

After it displays them, it goes on to look for something to fill the lower row of the main frameset. It finds another frameset, this one defining two columns of 40% width and 60% width. It creates the columns and then fills them according to the following `src` lines. It then encounters the two closing tags, and finishes. The result looks like the display in Figure 17.7.

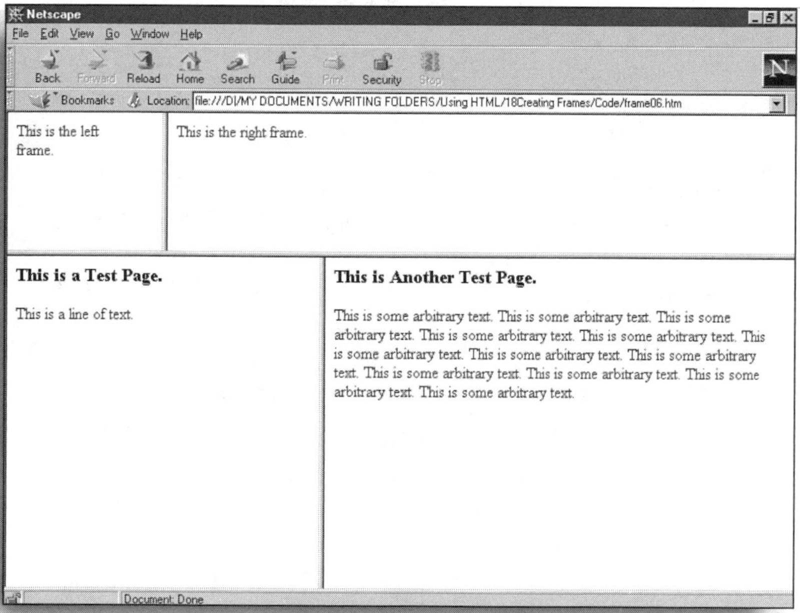

FIGURE 17.7
You can make columns that are independent of other columns by nesting framesets.

Creating Common Types of Framesets

The first complex frameset we created—the one with the single top row and two columns under it—is a common type. Often the top row is a banner, with a table of contents in the left column and a main display frame in the right. There are some other common types, and we'll look at three of them in the next few sections.

Creating a Table of Contents with Top and Bottom Bars

This is an elaboration of the table of contents frameset described immediately above. The code is as follows.

```
<HTML>
<HEAD>
<TITLE>TOC WITH TWO BARS</TITLE>
</HEAD>
    <FRAMESET rows="15%,70%,15%">
        <FRAME src="top.htm" noresize>
        <FRAMESET cols="20%,80%">
            <FRAME src="content.htm">
            <FRAME src="main01.htm">
        </FRAMESET>
    <FRAME src="bottom.htm" noresize>
    </FRAMESET>
</HTML>
```

Of course, you can use it for things other than tables of contents—the only limit is your imagination. Note that the top and bottom bars have the `noresize` attribute. This is to ensure that the navigation tools and banners are always visible to the user. You can see what it looks like in Figure 17.8.

Creating a Top-Down, Three-Level Hierarchy

This is useful for sites whose structure reflects a flow from the general to the specific. It has three frames, set up as superimposed rows. The top frame contains the most general divisions of your Web; the middle frame is often used to display the documents called for by the user; and the bottom frame can be site identification or further navigation tools. Alternatively, if you are presenting data that flows from a very general level (for example, birds) to a subdivision of that (songbirds) to a third subdivision (thrushes), you could make the three frames reflect this, from top to bottom.

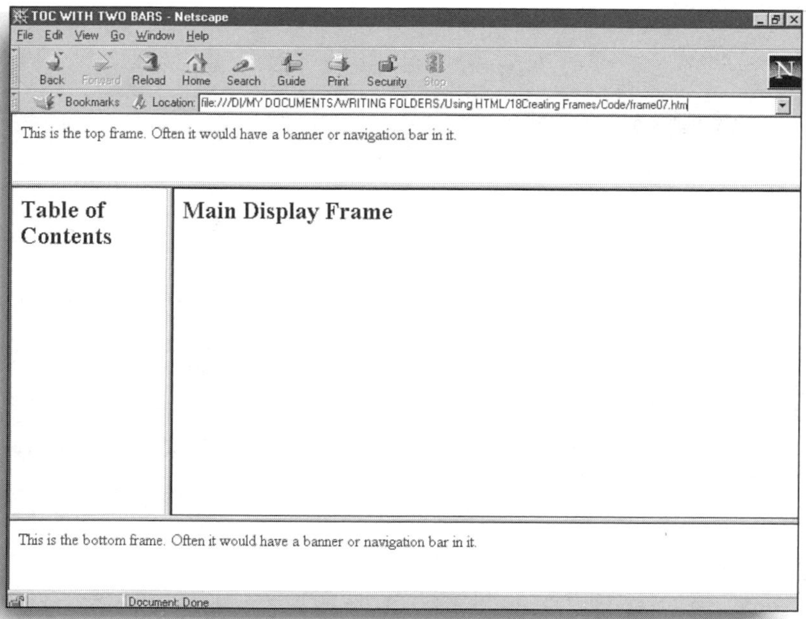

FIGURE 17.8
The four-frame structure is extremely flexible, and you can put it to dozens of uses.

The code is as follows:

```
<HTML>
<HEAD>
<TITLE>Top-Down, Three-Level Hierarchy</TITLE>
</HEAD>
    <FRAMESET rows="15%,65%,20%">
        <FRAME src="top01.htm">
        <FRAME src="middle.htm">
        <FRAME src="bottom01.htm">
    </FRAMESET>
</HTML>
```

You can see the results in Figure 17.9.

Creating a Nested Three-Level Hierarchy

This frameset is also hierarchical, but the hierarchy works from top-left to top-right and then down. The left frame is the most general, the top-right is a middle category, and the bottom-right is the most specific. Using the bird example mentioned above, birds would be in the left frame, songbirds in the top-right frame, and thrushes in the bottom-right frame.

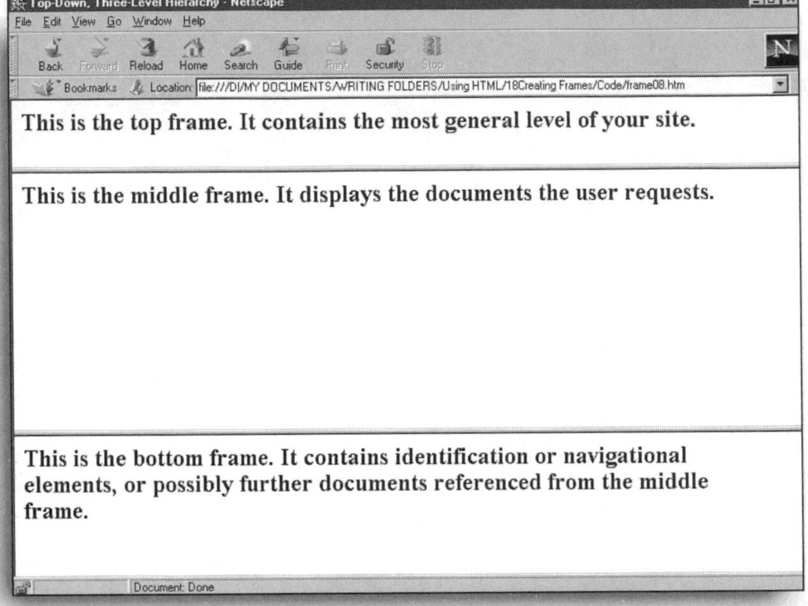

FIGURE 17.9
A hierarchical structure gives a cascade effect, from the general to the specific.

The code for such a frameset is as follows.

```
<HTML>
<HEAD>
<TITLE>Nested Three-Level Hierarchy</TITLE>
</HEAD>
    <FRAMESET cols="20%,80%">
        <FRAME src="left02.htm">
            FRAMESET rows = "30%,70%">
                <FRAME src="tright.htm">
                <FRAME src="bright.htm">
            </FRAMESET>
    </FRAMESET>
</HTML>
```

The results in a browser screen would look like Figure 17.10.

Putting Frames to Basic Uses

We'll examine advanced usage of frames in Chapter 18. For the moment, we'll explore two very simple applications.

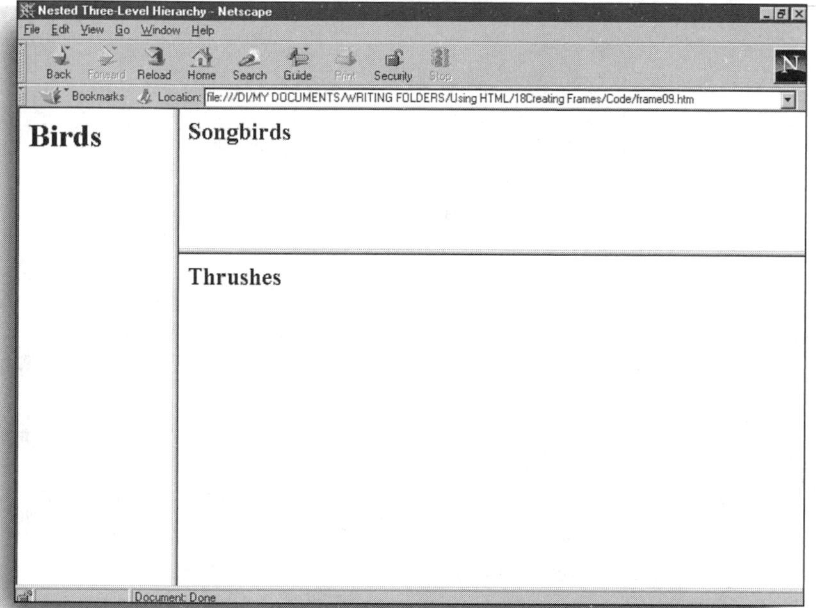

FIGURE 17.10
A nested hierarchy gives a different organization than a vertically organized hierarchy.

Branding Your Site with a Logo

This is very straightforward. Begin by creating a logo for your organization or company, or by locating the existing graphics file that contains the logo. Once you've created or identified it, place the logo in the top-left corner of an ordinary HTML page. The code for such a page might look like this.

```
<HTML>
<HEAD>
<TITLE>Company Logo</TITLE>
</HEAD>
<BODY>
    <IMG alt = "Company Logo" src = "comlogo.gif">
</BODY>
</HTML>
```

Note the use of an `alt` attribute in the `IMG` line to provide alternative text that will show up if the user is running a browser with images turned off.

Now create the frameset. It would look something like this.

```
<HTML>
<HEAD>
<TITLE>Drama Supply Home Page</TITLE>
</HEAD>
    <FRAMESET frameborder="0" noresize rows = "100,*">
        <FRAME src="comlogo.htm">
        <FRAME src="drama.htm">
    </FRAMESET>
</HTML>
```

There are three points to notice about the attributes for `<FRAMESET>` here.

- The `frameborder` attribute is set to zero, so that the logo will appear in a borderless frame.
- `noresize` is used to prevent viewers from moving the frame border. It's invisible, but inquisitive people would find it and move it if they could.
- The upper frame is sized in pixels—100 pixels to be exact—and not by percentage or by proportion. This ensures that the logo always appears in a frame of this height, so that the lower frame gets as much of the display area as possible. If you used proportional or percentage heights in this case, the upper frame would vary in height, at the expense of the lower frame. Of course, it's useful to know the height of the logo in pixels. If you don't, you can change the pixel number until you get the frame boundary just below the lower edge of the logo graphic. Make sure the pixel value is big enough so that no scroll bar appears.

You can see the results of the code in Figure 17.11. The advantage of this approach is that if you change the logo, you only have to change the graphic of one page (`comlogo.htm` in the example) to update the entire site.

Create an Advertising Billboard

Here is a somewhat more complex example. It's an advertising billboard that has four frames. The top frame is a logo, and each of the three frames below it displays a category of goods. This is how the implementation of such a framed environment would begin; when it is complete, the images in the three lower frames will be links to other pages.

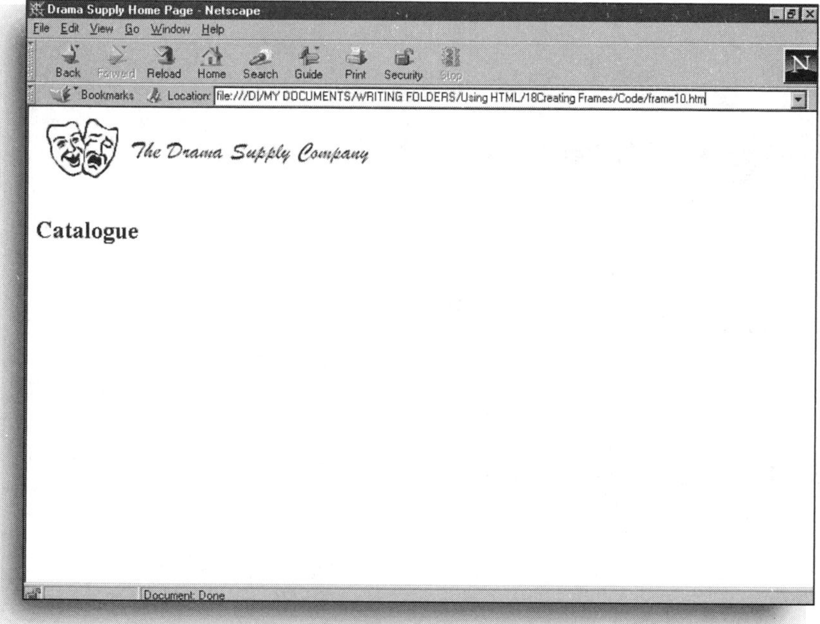

FIGURE 17.11
The logo here sits in a borderless frame with a height specified in pixels.

Here's the code:

```
<HTML>
<HEAD>
<TITLE>Drama Supply Home Page</TITLE>
</HEAD>
    <FRAMESET frameborder="0" noresize rows = "140,*">
    <FRAME src="billtop.htm">
        <FRAMESET frameborder="0" noresize cols = "*,*,*">
            <FRAME src="billleft.htm">
            <FRAME src="billmid.htm">
            <FRAME src="billrt.htm">
        </FRAMESET>
    </FRAMESET>
</HTML>
```

Again, the frame containing the logo is set to 140 pixels to ensure that the logo always has enough room to display but will not encroach on the lower frames. The `noresize` attribute is also used, and the frames in the lower row are sized with proportional values. Finally, the frames are borderless.

The results might look something like the display in Figure 17.12.

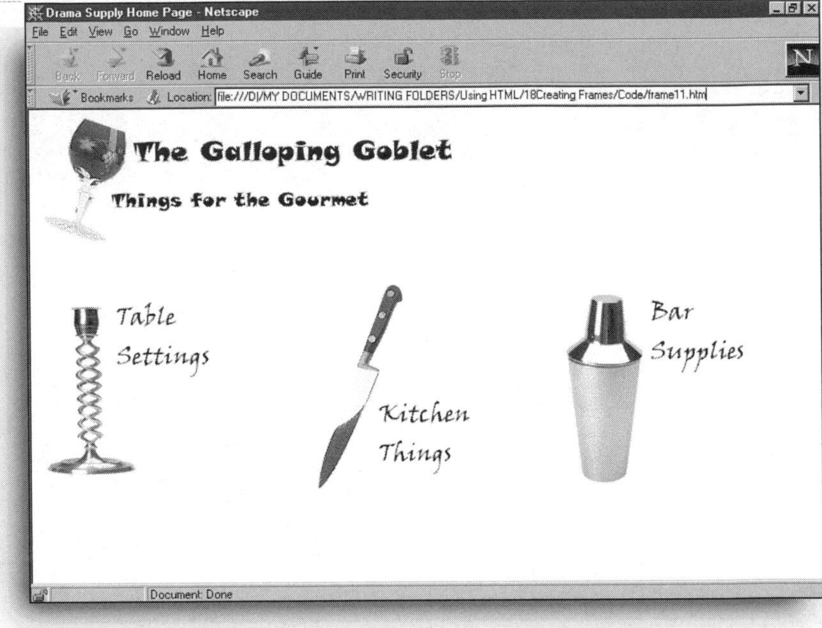

FIGURE 17.12
An advertising billboard with a logo frame and three frames containing categories of merchandise.

CHAPTER

18

Naming and Navigating Frames

- Make frames user friendly
- Load content into existing windows
- Load content into new windows
- Make navigation bars
- Use floating frames with Internet Explorer browsers

Making Frames Easy to Use

A great advantage of the framed environment is the way in which the relationships between its windows and their content can work to keep viewers oriented to the site's structure. The most common approach among Web authors is to use a static frame to keep a map of the site (or part of it) in sight all the time, while one or more dynamic frames display the information desired by the visitor. This simplifies the navigation of a complicated site. (If the site is not complicated, consider whether you need frames at all).

One of the major characteristics of "unfriendly" Web sites is that they are difficult to navigate. This problem is not restricted to sites created by amateurs—there are plenty of major and corporate sites, whose designers should have known better, that are confusing to move around in.

But adding frames to a site that is hard to navigate is not the answer to such a fundamental flaw. A poorly organized site, even without frames, is bad enough; adding frames will only make it worse. This means, obviously, that you must do some detailed site planning on paper, before you write the first `<FRAMESET>` tag.

You might consider using a storyboard approach to sketch out what the viewer should experience as he or she negotiates your site. (A storyboard is just a succession of small sketches, showing the sequence of windows the viewer will see as he or she clicks the links in the various frames.) This is useful for identifying lapses in continuity and spotting unnecessary switches between frames. It will also, very importantly, remind you to give the user a way to return to where he or she came from. That prevents him or her from landing in a blind alley, one that can't escape unless he or she leaves the site altogether.

To sum up, plan ahead. This is sometimes hard to do; most programmers like to get down to writing code right away to see what the results look like (and whether the code works!). But you must resist the temptation to plunge right in. Frameset code is picky to write; if you produce hundreds of lines of it, and it confuses and repels your visitors, the overhaul and debugging process will tie you in knots. You'd be better off scrapping all the code and starting over, this time with a plan.

Loading Content into Existing Windows

The framesets we worked on in the previous chapter, "Creating Frames," were very static indeed—their windows contained HTML pages, but gave the user no hyperlinks that would change the content of these windows. Making such changes, at the basic level, is quite simple.

Loading Content into the Current Window

The least complicated example of changing frame content is when the user clicks a link in a window and the content of that window is replaced with new content.

Let's examine this in detail. Assume you have a two-column frameset, like the following one:

```
<HTML>
<HEAD>
</HEAD>
    <FRAMESET COLS = "50%,50%">
        <FRAME SRC = "page01.htm">
        <FRAME SRC = "page02.htm">
    </FRAMESET>
</HTML>
```

As you remember from the previous chapter, the SRC attribute defines the default page that appears in each window of the frameset; in this case, the pages are the HTML files page01.htm and page02.htm.

To change the content of the left window, you'd simply insert a hyperlink into the HTML for page01.htm, which is specified in the frameset as the default page for the left window. This link is just a normal `<A=HREF "url">`*`Link Text`*`</A>` construction that you learned about in Chapter 7, "Adding Links."

Now, when a visitor clicks the link in the left window of the frameset, a new page (the target page of the hyperlink) will appear in that window.

A framed environment with such a structure, and two hyperlinks, might resemble the one shown in Figure 18.1.

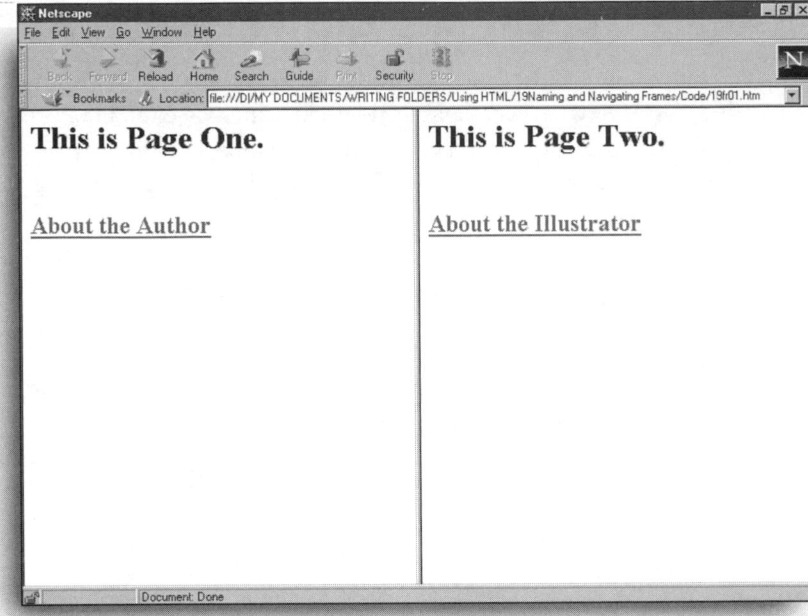

FIGURE 18.1
This two-window frameset has a hyperlink in each frame.

Keeping hyperlinks out of the frameset

Note that you never insert the hyperlink into the HTML for the frameset page itself. The only time you put an URL into the <FRAMESET> container is when you specify the initial page for each window of the frameset, using the SRC attribute.

Loading Content into a Different Window

However, you've likely noticed a serious flaw in this technique—once the user has clicked the link, the link vanishes as its page is replaced with the new content. But what if the earlier page had other, unused links on it, or it had content the viewer needed to look at again? You could, of course, put a back link on the new page, or you could expect the viewer to rely on the browser's methods of returning to a previous window. Neither of these solutions is a very good one.

The usual, and much better, technique is to force the content to appear in a different window, so that the original page remains visible. A sample procedure for doing this, with a simple two-window frameset, works as follows.

Load content into a different window

1. Begin by creating a two-window frameset, like the one below. Note the new NAME attribute that has been added within the <FRAME> tag. This NAME attribute assigns a name to each frame of the frameset; or putting it another way, each window of the frameset has its very own name. In the

following example, the name of the left window is `left` and the name of the right window is `right`. You can use such frame names to specify the windows in which new content appears.

```
<HTML>
<HEAD>
</HEAD>
    <FRAMESET COLS = "50%,50%">
        <FRAME SRC="pageleft.htm" NAME = "left">
        <FRAME SRC="pagert.htm" NAME = "right">
    </FRAMESET>
</HTML>
```

2. Now modify the HTML of the page that contains the hyperlinks (not the HTML of the frameset) so that these hyperlinks will send their pages to the proper window. To do this, add the `TARGET` attribute to the HTML page's hyperlink code. `TARGET` and its value, which is a frame name, go within the hyperlink. An example of such code, in a page called pageleft.htm (which belongs to the frameset example immediately previous) looks like this:

```
HTML>
<HEAD>
</HEAD>
<BODY>
<H1>Today's Reviews</H1>
<BR>
<BR>
<A HREF = "pagert.htm" TARGET = "right" >Review of
"Silicon Alley"</A>
<BR>
<A HREF = "Author.htm" TARGET = "right" >About the
Author</A>
<BR>
<A HREF = "Illustr.htm" TARGET = "right" >About the
Illustrator </A>
<BR>
</BODY>
</HTML>
```

As you can see, the TARGET attribute specifies the name of the window where the hyperlinked HTML page will appear. You can see the browser display that results from this code in Figure 18.2.

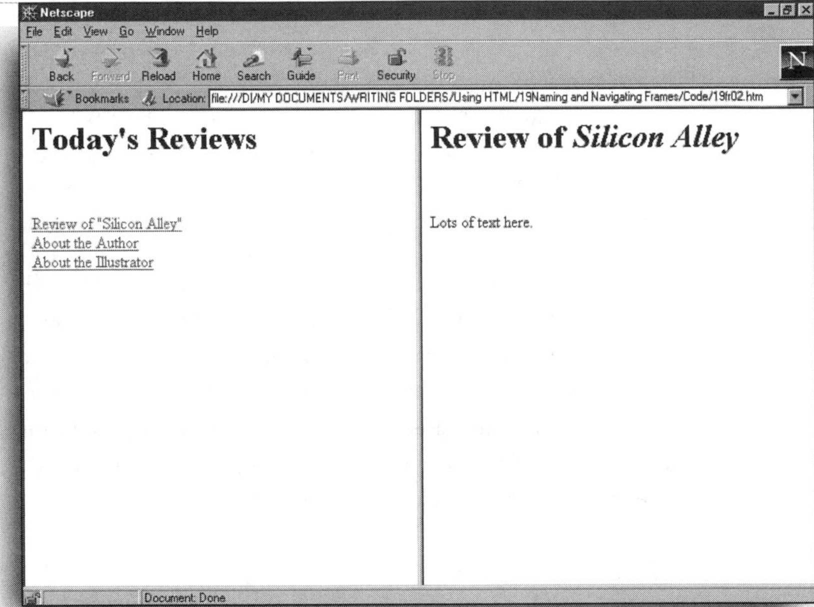

FIGURE 18.2
The links in the left window of this frameset force their destination pages to appear in the right window.

More about frame names

By default, all frames are unnamed. If you want your frames to have names, you have to assign them. Frame names also have to begin with an alphanumeric character. The exception to this rule is the four special target names, explored later in this chapter.

To extend the idea: If you had three or more windows in the frameset, you could send the content pages to any of them, depending on how you set the value of the TARGET attribute for each link.

Using the <*BASE*> Tag with *TARGET*

Sometimes you want all or most of the links in an HTML page to appear in the same window. If there were many such pages, you'd have to specify the TARGET attribute in the link for each page. To avoid this extra typing, and the errors it invites, you can use the <BASE> tag with the TARGET attribute.

Suppose you have a four-window frameset (top and bottom bars, and two columns between them) that is produced by the following HTML:

```
<HTML>
<HEAD>
<TITLE>TOC WITH TWO BARS</TITLE>
</HEAD>
    <FRAMESET ROWS="15%,70%,15%">
        <FRAME SRC="top.htm" NAME ="top">
        <FRAMESET COLS="20%,80%">
            <FRAME SRC="content.htm" NAME = "left">
            <FRAME SRC="main01.htm" NAME = "right">
        </FRAMESET>
    <FRAME SRC="bottom.htm" NAME = "bottom">
    </FRAMESET>
</HTML>
```

As you can see, the individual frames (windows) have been named: `top`, `left`, `right`, and `bottom`.

Now suppose that the page content.htm, which appears in the left window when the frameset loads, has a lot of links on it. You want all the pages referred to by these links to appear in the right window, the one named `right`. However, you don't need to type the `TARGET` attribute into each of these links. Just put the targeting information into the `<BASE>` tag, in the `<HEAD>` section of the page where the links are. The HTML for content.htm, for example, will look like this:

```
<HTML>
<HEAD>
<BASE TARGET = "right">
</HEAD>
<BODY>
<h2>Table of Contents</h2>
<BR>
<BR>
<A HREF = "chap01.htm">Chapter 1</A>
<BR>
<A HREF = "chap02.htm">Chapter 2</A>
</BODY>
</HTML>
```

The `<BASE TARGET = "right">` line specifies that all the links on this page will load into the window with the name `right`; this name was defined, of course, in the HTML of the frameset.

If you want one or more of the links to appear in a window other than `right`, you need merely specify a `TARGET` attribute for that particular link. This overrides the `<BASE>` tag's effects for that link.

Using the `<BASE>` tag has another advantage: If you want to change the window where the linked pages appear, you need only change the `TARGET` attribute in the `<BASE>` line. This is a lot easier than editing every link on the page to have the new window name.

Figure 18.3 shows a framed environment produced partly by the frameset HTML and the content.htm HTML given in this section.

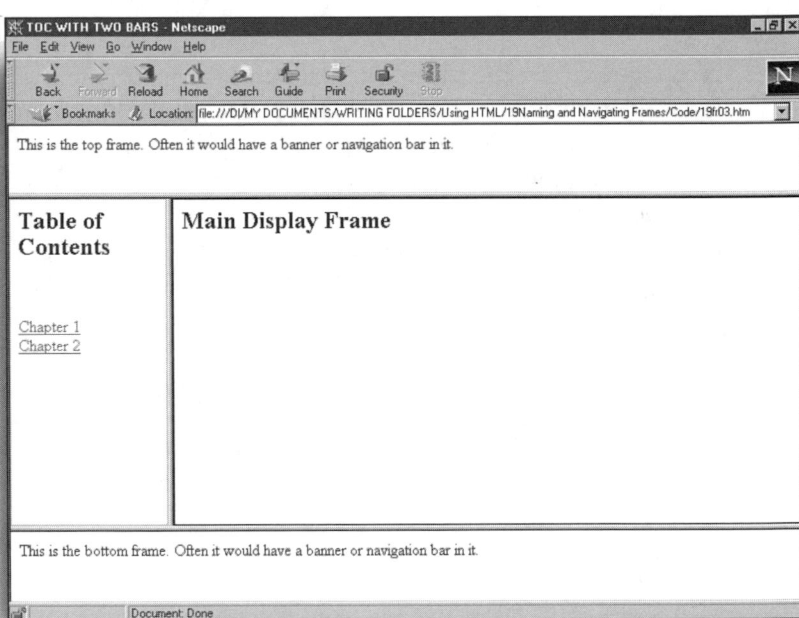

FIGURE 18.3
In this frameset, the left-middle window displays all its linked pages in the right-middle window.

Loading Content into a New Window

You don't need to be using a frameset to employ the techniques described in the next section. However, you may find them handy in enhancing a framed environment. We'll begin by examining how new windows are created.

Creating a New Window

With this technique, clicking a link doesn't make the new page appear in the current browser window. Clicking a link actually opens a new browser window, in which the linked page appears. This new window is the "child" window, and the window containing the original link is the "parent" window. When the user closes the child window, the page containing the links remains onscreen in the parent browser window.

To get this effect, you put a target name into the HTML of the link. In the following example, the page isn't part of a frameset; however, its linked pages appear in a new window when clicked.

```
<HTML>
<HEAD>
</HEAD>
<BODY>
<H1>Loading in New Windows</H1>
<BR>
<BR>
<H2><A HREF = "chap01.htm" TARGET = "any_window">Chapter
One</A> </H2>
<BR>
<H2><A HREF = "chap02.htm" TARGET = "any_window">Chapter
Two</A> <H2>
</BODY>
</HTML>
```

Note that the window name `"any_window"` has never been defined until now—to repeat, this page is not part of a frameset. Merely writing `TARGET = "any_window"` creates the window. If this page is opened in a browser, and the Chapter One link is clicked, the result is shown in Figure 18.4. If the Chapter Two link is clicked, the new page is loaded into the same window, replacing the Chapter One content.

Vanishing windows

If the old (parent) window seems to vanish, it's actually just covered up. What's happened is that the new (child) window is hiding the parent window. Resize or move the child window, and you'll find the parent lurking behind it.

If you create a named child window in this way, you can display other pages in it. For example, if the page displayed in the new window has a link, the linked page will be displayed in the child window (assuming this link has no `TARGET` attribute that specifies a different window).

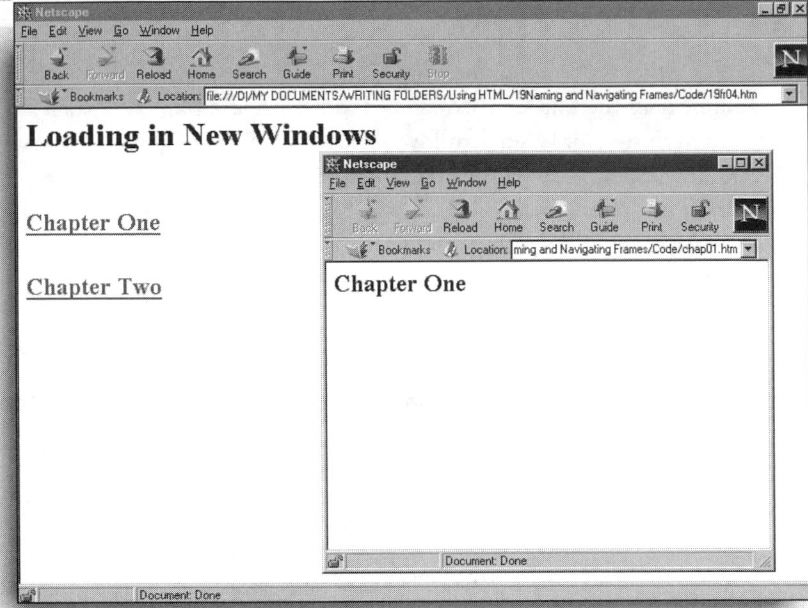

FIGURE 18.4
Opening a link that has a newly defined target window opens a new browser window.

Using Special Target Names

It was mentioned earlier that frame names (which we're also referring to as window names) can begin with any alphanumeric character except an underscore. There are four exceptions to this: a set of pre-defined target names you can use for special purposes. They are included in the hyperlink tag in the same way that normal `TARGET` attributes are.

Using *TARGET = "_blank"*

Using this target forces the linked page to be loaded into a new browser window. Functionally it's the same as creating a child window by naming that window in a link. The difference is that with `_blank`, the new window has no name associated with it. You can also use `_blank` to override a `TARGET` attribute specified in the page's `BASE TARGET` line, if this line is present.

Using *TARGET = "_self"*

Using this target forces the linked page to be loaded into the window or frame that contains the link itself. In effect, you are overriding any `TARGET` attribute contained in the link, or in the page's `BASE TARGET` line, if this line is present. You can use `TARGET = "_self"` in a frameset, to make a linked page open in the same frame as its link.

Using *TARGET = "_parent"*

Using this target forces the linked page to be loaded into the window or frame that contains the link itself and resets the browser window.

This target works like `_self`, except for the bit about resetting the browser window. The practical effect of this takes a little explanation. If the link (with the `_parent` target) resides in a frame of a frameset, clicking the link first removes all the frames from the browser display. They are replaced by a single, unframed window. This replacement action is called *resetting the browser window*. The linked page is then loaded into this full-browser window. There is no child window opened in this case.

Why would you want to use this? The answer is: when you have placed a link in a frame, and that link opens a frameset. Using `_parent` as the target with such a link prevents the new frameset from being opened inside the current frame. Instead, the new frameset opens in a reset browser window, giving the user a completely fresh start.

A common example of using `_parent` is the following. If your home page is a frameset, and you place a link to that home page inside one of its own frames, you should use the `_parent` target with this link. If you don't, you get the unwanted result shown in Figure 18.5. The home page frameset is sitting inside itself, so to speak.

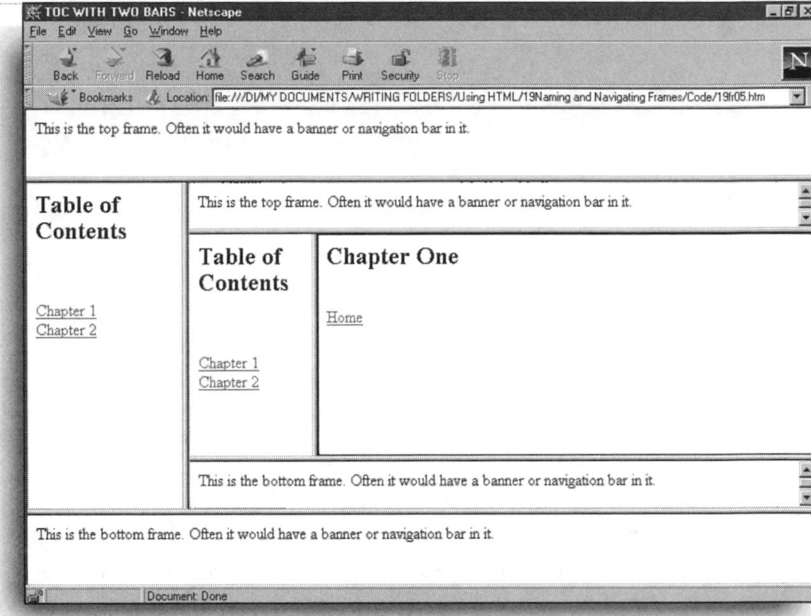

FIGURE 18.5
An effect you probably don't want–the home page frameset squashed into one of its own frames!

One final note—if you use `_parent` in a link in a window, and the window is not part of a frameset, `_parent` behaves exactly like `_self`.

Using *TARGET = "_top"* to Break Out of the Frameset

Sometimes you want a link to load in its own browser window, but you don't want to produce a child window, as happens with the `_blank` target or with a window newly named inside the link. The simplest way of achieving this is to use the `_top` target within the link. No matter how deeply your visitor has gone into child frames or framesets, `_top` will break him out of them into the topmost level of the window hierarchy.

Creating a Navigation Bar

As a representative example of what you can do with frames, we'll create a navigation bar, along with a frameset and its essential pages. We'll keep everything very plain and simple, with the understanding that a real-world version would be much more elaborate.

A common layout is the three-frame one with a banner across the top, and under it the navigation bar in the left column and the content frame in the right. The pages in the content frame may also have links to other pages, but such pages will appear in the content frame.

Begin by writing the frameset code, like this:

```
<HTML>
<HEAD>
<TITLE>A Simple Navigation Environment</TITLE>
</HEAD>
<FRAMESET FRAMEBORDER = "1" ROWS = "90,*">
<FRAME SRC = "banner.htm" NORESIZE NAME = "banner">
    <FRAMESET FRAMEBORDER = "1" COLS = "*, 7*">
        <FRAME SRC = "navbar.htm" NORESIZE NAME = "navbar">
        <FRAME SRC = "pages.htm" NAME = "pages" MARGINWIDTH
        = "40">
    </FRAMESET>
</FRAMESET>
</HTML>
```

You might want to note some points about this code:

- While developing the look of the page, it's useful to leave borders turned on, so you can judge proportions while you're laying things out. After the frameset is adjusted to your liking, you can turn borders off by setting `FRAMEBORDER = "0"` (assuming you want borderless frames). Be sure to catch all occurrences of the attribute—there are two in the previous code, one for each frameset.
- The height of the banner frame is set to 90 pixels. This is to reserve exactly enough room for the banner graphic.
- The banner window and the navigation bar's window are set to `NORESIZE`. This prevents users from losing them.
- The `NAME` attribute has been employed to give names to the three windows. You don't have to use the names, but they'll be there if you want them. In this example, the `pages` name will be used to set up a default target frame, using the `<BASE>` tag.

- The MARGINWIDTH attribute has been set to 40 pixels, to supply spacing for content appearing in the right column of the frameset.

Next, create the page that will hold the navigation bar (navbar.htm in the example). The HTML for such a page might look something like this:

```
<HTML>
<HEAD>
<TITLE>Navigation</TITLE>
<BASE TARGET = "pages">
</HEAD>
<BODY>
<A HREF = "sales.htm">Sales</A>
<BR>
<BR>
<A HREF = "products.htm">Products</A>
<BR>
<BR>
<A HREF = "support.htm">Support</A>
<BR>
<BR>
<A HREF = "contacts.htm">Contacts</A>
<BR>
<BR>
</BODY>
</HTML>
```

Here is where the <BASE> tag is used, as mentioned earlier. This ensures that all linked pages will appear in the right window, unless the link is customized to do otherwise, with its own TARGET attribute.

The HTML for banner.htm looks like this:

```
<HTML>
<HEAD>
</HEAD>
<BODY>
<CENTER>
<IMG SRC = "banner.gif">
</CENTER>
</BODY>
</HTML>
```

And finally, the HTML for pages.htm is

```
<HTML>
<HEAD>
</HEAD>
<BODY>
<CENTER>
<BR>
<BR>
<BR>
<BR>
<H1>ABC ENTERPRISES</H1>
</CENTER>
<BR>
<BR>
<BR>
<P>Text saying something about the site.</P>
</BODY>
</HTML>
```

The result, when it is all put together, is shown in Figure 18.6. The FRAMEBORDER attributes in the frameset file have been set to zero to produce borderless frames.

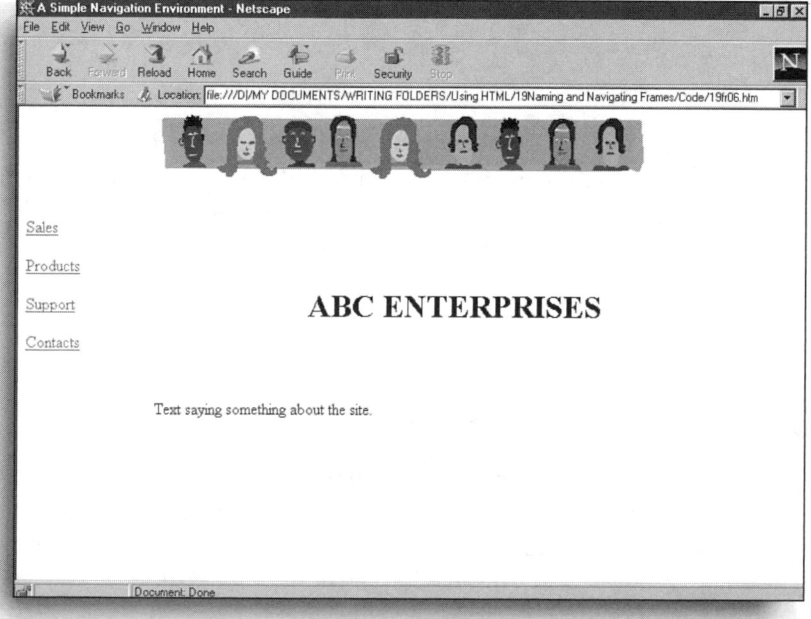

FIGURE 18.6
The links of a navigation bar (left frame) open various pages in the right frame.

Creating a Floating Navigation Bar

A floating navigation bar is one the user can drag around the screen and resize to suit himself or herself. If you want to make one, all you need to do is create and save the page that contains the navigation bar. Its HTML might look like this.

```
<HTML>
<HEAD>
<TITLE>Navigation</TITLE>
<BASE TARGET = "a_window">
</HEAD>
<BODY>
<A HREF = "sales.htm" >Sales</A>
<BR>
<BR>
<A HREF = "products.htm" >Products</A>
<BR>
<BR>
<A HREF = "support.htm" >Support</A>
<BR>
<BR>
<A HREF = "contacts.htm" >Contacts</A>
<BR>
<BR>
</BODY>
</HTML>
```

When the user clicks a link, the linked page appears in its own window, which is defined by the `<BASE TARGET = "a_window">` line. Each time a link is clicked, the new page appears in the a_window window, replacing the previous page. The results might look like the screen in Figure 18.7. Usually the browsers must be resized to make all the windows visible.

Using Floating Frames

Floating frames provide an interesting effect; unfortunately, only the Microsoft browsers 3.0 and later support them—Netscape Navigator and Communicator do not. So, if you want to use them, be sure to provide an alternative page for visitors who aren't using Internet Explorer to look around your site.

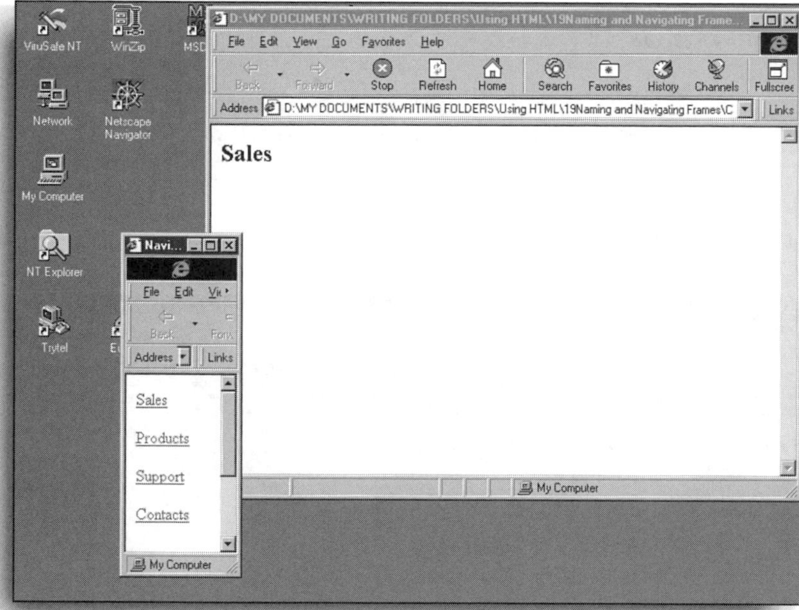

FIGURE 18.7
You can create a floating navigation bar with the use of targeted and named windows.

Creating a Floating Frame

A floating frame is like a cutout in the browser window; through this cutout, another page is visible. To make such a frame, perform the following steps.

Create a floating frame

1. Create the page that will show through the cutout.
2. Insert the <IFRAME> container into the page that actually has the cutout. Include in the <IFRAME> tag any required or optional attributes of the floating frame.
3. Into the <IFRAME> container, type the <FRAME> statement that specifies the URL of the page that shows through the cutout. The HTML for the example page (shown in Figure 18.8) looks like this:

```
<HTML>
<HEAD>
<TITLE>Floating Frames</TITLE>
</HEAD>
<BODY>
```

```
<H2>This page has a floating frame in it!<H2>
<BR>
<BR>
<IFRAME  WIDTH=40% HEIGHT=40% SRC="navbar.htm">
   <FRAME  WIDTH=40% HEIGHT=40% SRC="navbar.htm">
</IFRAME>
</BODY>
</HTML>
```

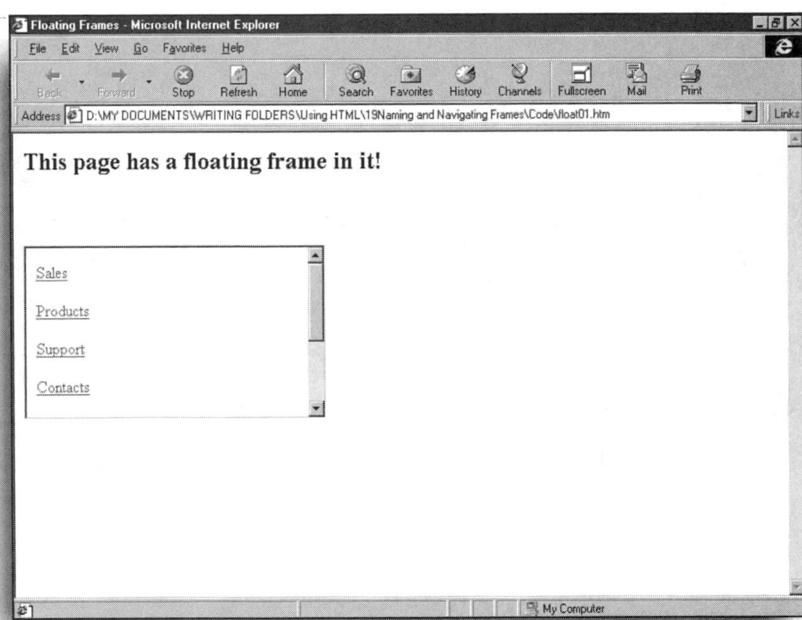

FIGURE 18.8
Internet Explorer browsers let you use floating frames, so a different page (like this link menu) can be seen as a cutout in the main page.

The SRC attribute, of course, specifies the URL or HTML file that is to appear in the floating frame. The <IFRAME> container does look a little peculiar, because of the repeated SRC reference. Despite its oddity, however, this is how it's done.

The floating frame can be treated exactly like a floating image. That is, you can use the ALIGN attributes to position it on the page. For more information about floating images, see Chapter 8, "Adding Images to a Web Page." To put the frame at the right side of the page, you'd use this HTML:

```
<IFRAME WIDTH=20% HEIGHT=20% ALIGN=RIGHT SRC="navbar.htm">
    <FRAME WIDTH=20% HEIGHT=20% ALIGN=RIGHT
    SRC="navbar.htm">
</IFRAME>
```

Using Other Floating Frame Attributes

You can use other attributes with the <IFRAME> tag. If several of these look familiar, it's because you've seen them in connection with sizing and positioning images.

- FRAMEBORDER=1 or 0 creates a 3D edge border around the frame. 1 (default) inserts a border. 0 displays no border.
- HEIGHT and WIDTH control the size of the floating frame. The values can be in pixels or percentage of the browser window.
- HSPACE and VSPACE set the margins, in pixels, around the content displayed in the frame.
- SCROLLING can be set to Yes or No. If it's absent, a scrollbar will appear if needed. If it's Yes, the scrollbar will always be present, needed or not. If No, the scrollbar will always be absent, even if it's needed.
- The NAME attribute is supported. It's examined in more detail in the next section.

Using Frame Names with Floating Frames

Suppose you've created a page that contains a floating frame, as well as some links to other pages. Now you want those pages to appear within the floating frame when the user clicks their links.

In fact, it's easy. Supply a window name in the <IFRAME> code, as in this example:

```
<IFRAME WIDTH=50% HEIGHT=50% SRC="page.htm"
NAME="A_Frame">[sr]
<FRAME WIDTH=50% HEIGHT=50% SRC="page.htm"
NAME="A_Frame">[sr]
</IFRAME>
```

Then edit the links on the main page according to this pattern:

```
<A HREF="Start.htm" TARGET="A_Frame">Start Page</A>
```

Now the linked pages will appear in the floating frame when the links in the main page are clicked. Remember, if there are a lot of such links, you can add a <BASE TARGET="A_Frame"> line to the <HEAD> section.

PART

IV

Adding Interactivity

CHAPTER

19

Creating HTML Forms

Using forms to gather information

Setting up your first online form

Adding more functions to your form with check boxes and radio buttons

Uploading files to a Web server from a form

Forms Collect Information

HTML forms, just like their hardcopy counterparts, are mainly used to collect information from the user. That's a really boring way to say that forms offer visitors to your Web site a simple way to either provide you with usable information, allow them to interact with your site, or both.

Unlike some of the other tags covered in this book, the form tags have been a standard since back in the days of HTML 2.0. With this in mind, you can easily assume that nearly every viewer of your pages will be able to use your forms.

Use Forms to Organize User Input Logically

Just like building any other Web page, it helps to start out with a plan. First, figure out what information you need to collect from the user. If you are converting a hardcopy form to use on the Web, most of this work is done. Otherwise, I'd start with a sheet of paper and list the information you want.

Is this going to be a feedback form? They'll need space to type in their comments, and maybe a name and email address for your response. Are they ordering something from you? You'll want to provide them with a list of items, sizes, colors, prices, and so on.

Organize your material

1. Consider what you want your form to do. Having a clear purpose in mind will help immensely when laying out your form.
2. List all the information you will require from the user.
3. Decide what you will do with the information once it is gathered. Asking the user to fill out a form and then doing nothing with some of the information is a waste of everyone's time.

What is this form supposed to accomplish? In the simplest state, the form is generally used to email information back to the Web site's administrator or to a person who will respond to the user. For more complex uses, it will actively interface with a back-end database.

Assuming that you've already organized your thoughts and information for your form, let's move on to the next step—building the HTML.

Creating Your First Form

The HTML used to build form pages is the same used for any other page. With these pages, you add tags that are specific to forms, just like certain tags are used with tables and others are used with frames.

These form-specific tags allow you to add all types of features to your form page, like buttons, check boxes, drop-down lists, password areas, and text boxes to name a few. These items provide a quick and efficient way for your user to interact with you or your site, and just about everyone knows how to use a checkbook.

The *<FORM>* Tag

To build a table you use a `<TABLE>` tag. To build a form you use the `<FORM>` tag.

To demonstrate how forms are created, we'll begin by building a simple feedback form for your Web site. Your form will be part of a normal HTML page, so we'll start out with some simple code to introduce the page.

```
<html>
<head>
<title>Feedback Form</title>
</head>
<body bgcolor="#ffffff">
<font size=+1>MyCompany's Feedback Form</font>
<hr>
```

Looks like a fairly simple page at this point. Let's start adding the code for our feedback form. The form starts with the `<FORM>` tag—seems appropriate. Between the opening and closing `<FORM>` tags lie the form elements as well as the structure tags that make up the form layout. You can place as many forms on a page as you need, however you can notnest forms—meaning you can't place one form inside another one.

The opening tag of the form element usually includes two attributes: `METHOD` and `ACTION`. The `METHOD` attribute can be either `GET` or `POST`, which determines how your form data is sent to the script to process it.

Quick usage tip: Tag syntax

```
<FORM action="action" method="method" enctype="enctype"
accept-charset="charset">
```

where *`action`* specifies a form processing agent; *`method`* specifies which HTTP method will be used to submit the form data set; *`enctype`* specifies the content type used to submit the form to the server; and *`charset`* specifies the list of character encodings for input data.

The `ACTION` attribute is a pointer to the script that processes the form on the server side. The action can be indicated by a relative path or by a full URL to a script on your server or somewhere else. For example, the following snippet of code would call a script called feedback.cgi in the cgi-bin directory on the current Web server.

```
<html>
<head>
<title>Feedback Form</title>
</head>
<body bgcolor="#ffffff">
<font size=+1>MyCompany's Feedback Form</font>
<hr>

<form method="post" action="/cgi-bin/feedback.cgi">
...
</form>
```

Adding Text Fields with the <*INPUT*> Tag

Check with your service provider

Check with your Internet service provider (ISP) to see if they offer any special feedback form programs that can make receiving information from forms easier. Many ISPs provide scripts to their subscribers that will parse form submissions into email messages.

Now that we've got the form started, we need to use the `<INPUT>` tag to place some text boxes or areas on the screen. These will give the user space to type in his or her name, email address, and so on.

The elements for use within a form are simple enough for the basic developer but include enough variety to fit almost any situation you may encounter when designing a form. The base tag for defining each element in an online form is the `<INPUT>` tag, which is used to add buttons, images, check boxes, radio buttons, passwords, and text fields.

Text fields are the most basic of form elements. A text field can accept virtually any type of input, and is one of the most versatile elements.

In our example, we need to give the user some space to type in his or her name, so we'll create a Name field.

```
<b>Name:</b>
<input type="text" name="employee_name">
```

This creates a bolded label (**Name:**) and a text box. The name of the text box (`employee_name`) will be passed to the CGI program, along with whatever the user types into the field.

Quick usage tip: Tag syntax

```
<INPUT TYPE="type" NAME="name" VALUE="value" CHECKED
SIZE="size"MAXLENGTH="maxlength">
```

where *`type`* specifies either `text`, `password`, `hidden`, `checkbox`, `radio`, `submit`, `reset`, `button`, `file`, or `image`; *`name`* specifies the name label; *`value`* specifies the initial value; *`size`* tells the user agent the initial width of the control; and *`maxlength`* specifies the maximum number of characters the user may enter.

There are other types of text fields that we won't be using in this example, but you might want to use them in your development, namely the `password` field and the `hidden` field.

The `password` field was specially designed for entering passwords. These text fields are very similar to normal text fields except that the characters entered appear as asterisks to mask the input.

Anything typed into a `password` field is hidden from view to protect passwords, account numbers, or other guarded information. Although the display is masked on the screen, the server receives the original text.

```
<input type="password" name="pswd">
```

Another type of text field is the `hidden` option. Using this field, nothing is displayed on the screen; however, it provides a way to send additional information to the CGI script that cannot be changed by the user.

```
<input type="hidden" name="survey" value="Employee Survey
#2">
```

The `<INPUT>` tag is the most widely used, maybe because it is the easiest to create. There are a lot of things you can't do with a text field, or maybe you don't want to give your user the total freedom to type whatever they want. Maybe you just want to give them a choice. Next, we'll see what options you have as a developer.

Creating Radio Buttons

Radio buttons indicate a list of items, only one of which can be chosen, similar to a question that can only have one response. If one radio button in a list is selected, all the other radio buttons in the same list are deselected. Make sense? You can only make one selection when using a radio button. This is very important to consider when developing your form.

Using the `radio=TYPE` attribute of the `<INPUT>` tag creates radio buttons. You can create groups of radio buttons by using the same name for each button in the group. However, each radio button in the group must have a unique `value` attribute.

Quick usage tip: Tag syntax

```
<INPUT TYPE="RADIO" NAME="name" VALUE="value" CHECKED>
```

where *`name`* is the name of the group for this button; *`value`* is the value of the button passed to the CGI script; and `CHECKED` is present for pre-selected buttons.

Here's a quick example of using radio buttons, and Figure 19.1 shows an example of radio button in practice.

```
Where do you want to go on vacation:<br>
<input type="radio" name="Vacation" value="Aruba">Aruba<br>
<input type="radio" name="Vacation" value="Paris">Paris<br>
<input type="radio" name="Vacation" value="Seattle">Seattle
<br><input type="radio" name="Vacation"
value="Houston">Houston<br>
```

You can just as easily use multiple, independent groups of radio buttons by using different names for each group. We'll make it easier to make the selection by organizing the form a little bit. Figure 19.2 shows the changes this code makes in the look of the screen.

```
Where do you want to go on vacation:
<ol>

    <li><input type="radio" name="Vacation"
    value="Aruba">Aruba<br>
        <ul>
            <li><input type="radio" name="Location1" value="
            Beachfront">Beach-front<br>
            <li><input type="radio" name="Location1" value="
    Inland">Inland<br>
        </ul>
    <li><input type="radio" name="Vacation"
    value="Paris">Paris<br>
    <li><input type="radio" name="Vacation"
    value="Seattle">Seattle
    <br><li><input type="radio" name="Vacation"
    value="Houston">
    Houston<br>
</ol>
```

By default, all radio buttons are unselected. A default button can be preselected. You can specify the default button in a group by using the `CHECKED` attribute.

```
Where do you want to go on vacation:<br>
<input type="radio" name="Vacation" value="Aruba"
CHECKED>Aruba<br>
<input type="radio" name="Vacation" value="Paris">Paris<br>
<input type="radio" name="Vacation"
value="Seattle">Seattle<br>
<input type="radio" name="Vacation"
value="Houston">Houston<br>
```

When the form is finally submitted to the server, the browser passes a single name/value pair for the entire group of buttons to the CGI script. That pair includes the NAME attribute for each group of radio buttons and the VALUE attribute of the button that is currently selected.

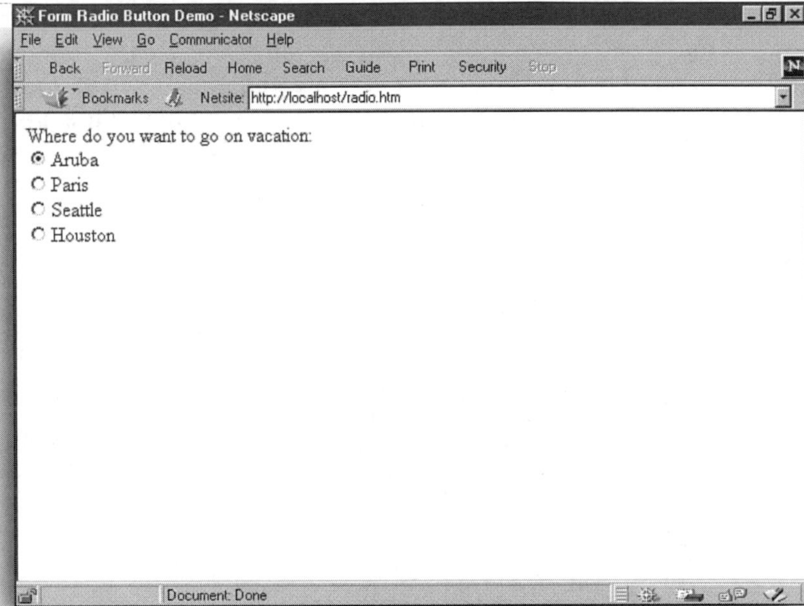

FIGURE 19.1
Choosing your next vacation using radio buttons.

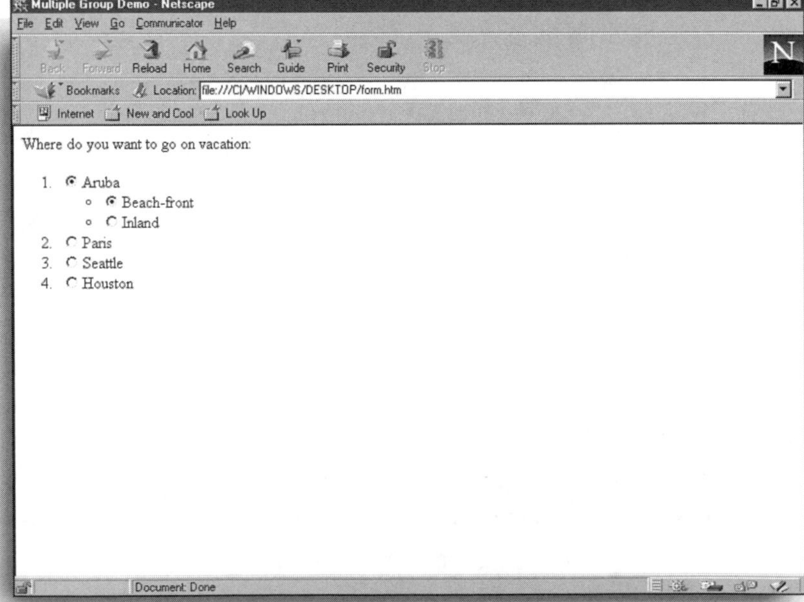

FIGURE 19.2
Using multiple groups to fine-tune your vacation choices.

For our Company feedback form example, we'll use a set of radio buttons to find out what department an employee is from.

```
<b>Department:</b>
<input type="radio" name="dept" value="Sales">Sales
<input type="radio" name="dept" value="HR">HR
<input type="radio" name="dept" value="PR">PR
<input type="radio" name="dept" value="R&D">R&D
```

This will give the user the choice of one of the four departments in our company. Because we are using radio buttons, he or she can only choose one.

Adding Check Boxes

When multiple selections are required you'll need to use check boxes. Many questions simply don't have one answer, so that's where check boxes come into play. Check boxes, as with radio buttons, are placed in groups. Each check box can either be checked or unchecked; by default they're unchecked.

Quick usage tip: Tag syntax

```
<INPUT TYPE="CHECKBOX" NAME="name" VALUE="value" CHECKED>
```

where *name* is the name of the group for this button; *value* is the value of the button passed to the CGI script; and CHECKED is present for pre-selected buttons.

We'll continue with our vacation selection form example, this time asking the user for more than one answer. Figure 19.3 shows the result of this code.

```
Where would you like to go on vacation:<br>
<input type="checkbox" name="Vacation"
value="Aruba">Aruba<br>
<input type="checkbox" name="Vacation"
value="Paris">Paris<br>
<input type="checkbox" name="Vacation"
value="Seattle">Seattle<br>
<input type="checkbox" name="Vacation"
value="Houston">Houston<br>
```

Up to this point, the VALUE attribute has always matched with the text displayed in the browser. If you would rather pass some other value to the CGI script, simply place it as the VALUE.

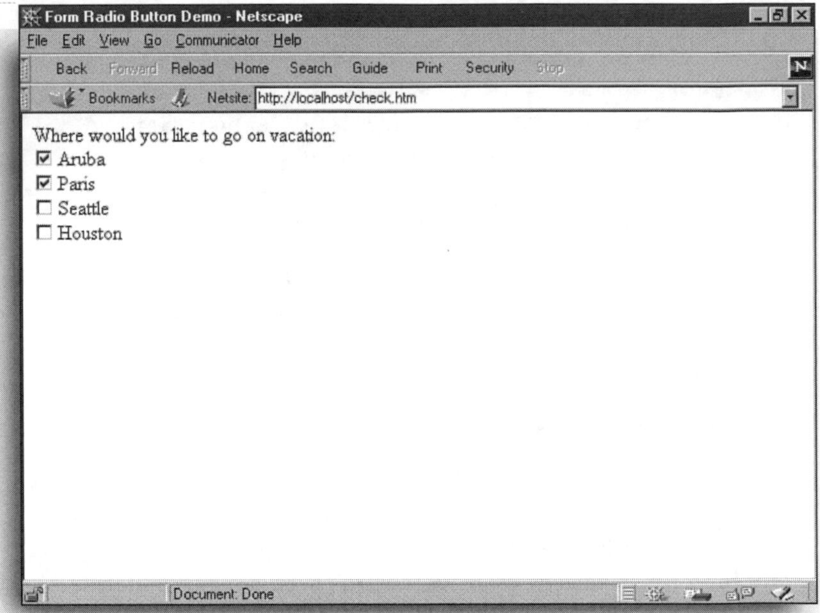

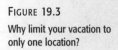

FIGURE 19.3
Why limit your vacation to only one location?

Check boxes can also be preselected by using the `CHECKED` attribute in the `<INPUT>` tag, just like radio buttons.

Back to the company feedback form, we'll use check boxes to survey the surfing habits of the employee. Here's a snippet of the code.

```
<b>Which Internet sites have you visited:</b><br>
<input type="checkbox" name="sites" value="company" checked>
MyCompany's Web site<br>
<input type="checkbox" name="sites" value="Excite">Excite
Search Engine<br>
<input type="checkbox" name="sites" value="Lycos">Lycos
Search Engine<br>
<input type="checkbox" name="sites" value="CNN">CNN Cable
News<br>
<input type="checkbox" name="sites" value="ESPN">ESPN
Sports<br>
<input type="checkbox" name="sites" value="Dow Jones">Dow
Jones Report<br>
<input type="checkbox" name="sites" value="WSJ">Wall Street
Journal
```

Since I would assume they have seen my company's Web site, I have pre-checked it for them. Really, that's just the nice guy showing through. But we could just as easily use that feature to save the user some of the effort needed to fill out the form—and the main focus is still to get them to the end of the form.

The Making of a Drop-Down List

Selections enable the reader to select one or more items from a menu or a scrollable list. They're similar in functionality to radio buttons or check boxes, but they're displayed differently onscreen.

Selections are created by using the `<SELECT>` tag, and the individual options within the selection are indicated by the `<OPTION>` tag. This seems way too simple, doesn't it? The `<SELECT>` tag also contains a `NAME` attribute to hold its value when the form is submitted.

Quick usage tip: Tag syntax

```
<SELECT NAME="name" SIZE="size" MULTIPLE SELECTED>
```

Where *`name`* is the element's name; *`size`* specifies the number of rows in the list that should be visible at one time; `MULTIPLE` is a Boolean attribute that allows multiple selections; and `SELECTED` is present for the initial value.

`<SELECT>` and `<OPTION>` work much like ordered and unordered lists do, with the entire selection surrounded by the opening and closing `<SELECT>` tags. Each option begins with a single-sided `<OPTION>`, like the following code. Figure 19.4 shows the onscreen result.

```
Please select an appliance type:<br>
<select name="appliance">
<option>Dish washer
<option>Stove
<option>Refrigerator
<option>Freezer
</select>
```

Usually, the first option in the list is the one that is selected and displayed as the initial value. You can set the default item to be initially selected by using the `SELECTED` attribute.

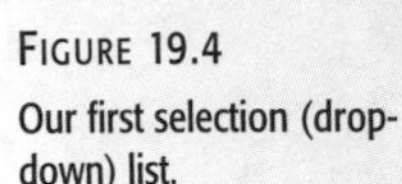

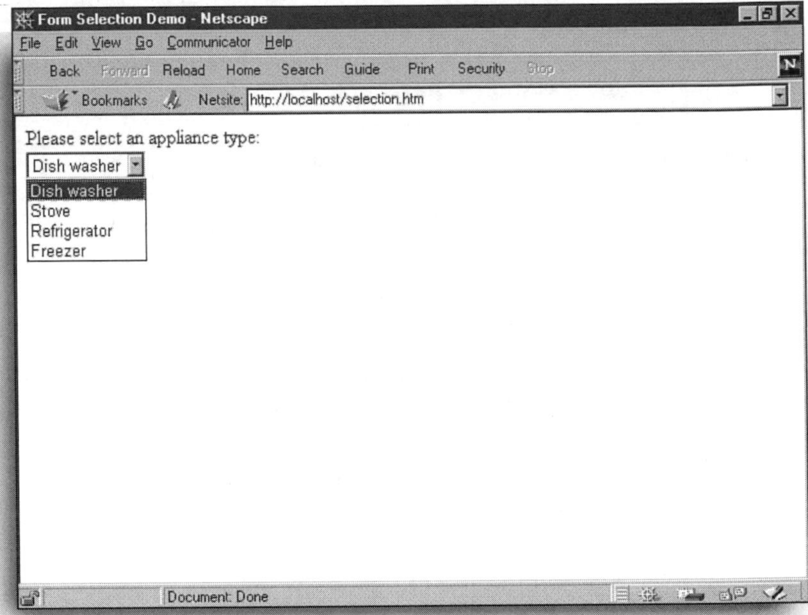

FIGURE 19.4
Our first selection (drop-down) list.

By default, selections act like radio buttons; that is, only one item can be selected at a time. You can change the behavior of selections to allow multiple options to be selected by using the `MULTIPLE` attribute, part of the `<SELECT>` tag.

The optional `SIZE` attribute usually displays the selection as a scrolling list in graphical browsers, with the number of elements in the `SIZE` attribute visible on the form itself, as shown in the following code. Figure 19.5 shows the result.

```
What are your favorite colors:
<select name="color" multiple size="5">
<option>Red
<option>Green
<option>Blue
<option>Orange
<option>Yellow
<option>Brown
<option>White
<option>Black
</select>
```

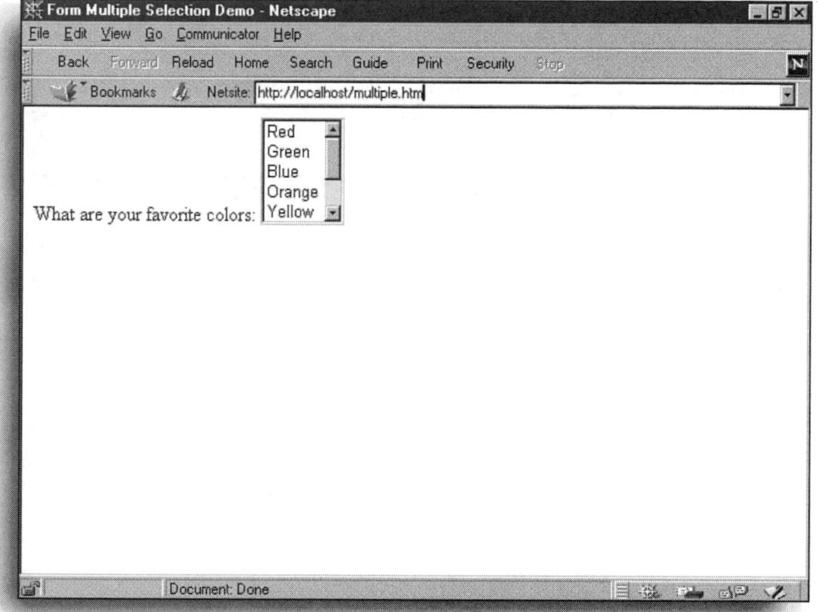

FIGURE 19.5
A multiple select list using the SIZE attribute.

Free-Form Text Input

When the single line approach of a regular text-input field (`<INPUT TYPE="text">`) isn't enough room for your form, you can use a text area input field for your users. Text areas are great to use when you want to provide your user with ample room to type as much as they need. This is usually a good match for comment or suggestion fields, where you want to encourage the user to type until their fingers fall off.

As with many other tags, the `<TEXTAREA>` tag must be used with an ending tag, `</TEXTAREA>`. The text you place between the beginning and ending tags will be default text placed inside the text field.

Quick usage tip: Tag syntax

```
<TEXTAREA NAME="name" ROWS="rows" COLS="cols"WRAP="wrap">
```

where *name* is the element's name; *rows* specifies the number of visible text lines; *cols* specifies the visible width in average character widths; and *wrap* specifies the display format (soft/virtual, hard/physical).

Figure 19.6 displays the result of the following use of the <TEXTAREA> tag.

```
<textarea name="mytext" rows="10" cols="50">Replace this
text with your own.</textarea>
```

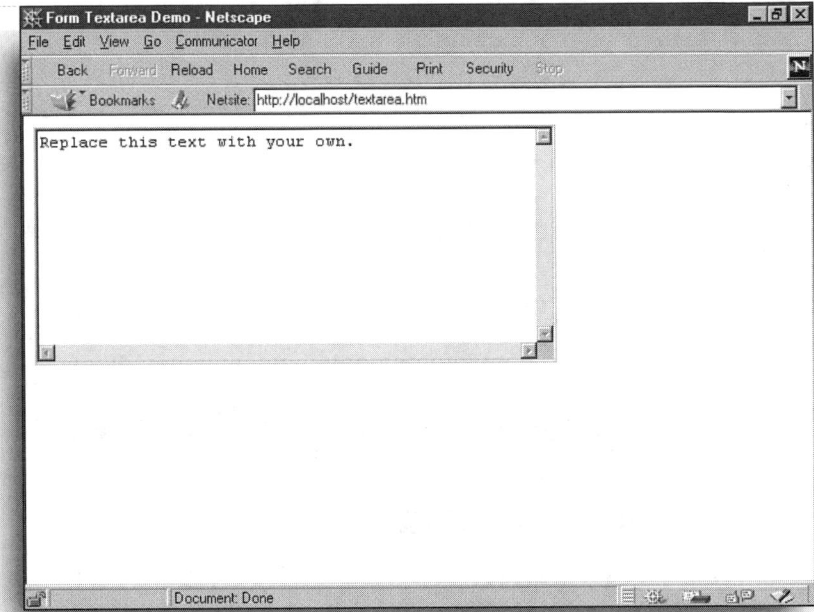

FIGURE 19.6
An example of using the <TEXTAREA> tag.

The text within the text area is generally formatted in a fixed-width font such as Courier, the same as appears when using the preformat tag, <PRE>. Some browsers will allow text wrapping in text areas, others will scroll to the right.

To specify how the browser wraps text, add the `WRAP` attribute to the <TEXTAREA> tag.

`WRAP=off`	Defaulted; text will be on one line, scrolling to the right, until the reader presses Enter to begin a new line.
`WRAP=soft` (or virtual)	Causes the text to wrap automatically in the browser window, but is sent to the server as all on one line.

`WRAP=hard` (or physical)	Causes the text to wrap automatically in the browser window. That text is also sent to the server with new-line characters at each point where the text is wrapped.

In our feedback example, we really like to get comments and feedback about the company, so we'll give the user ample room to type away. We even make it easy for them to read along as they type by turning on the physical wrap.

```
<b>Comments:</b><br>
<textarea name="comments" cols="30" rows="7" wrap="
physical">
</textarea>
```

Browser note

Microsoft Internet Explorer 4.0, by default, sets the `WRAP` attribute to `soft` (or virtual).

After this there's only one thing left to do—in fact that the most important thing out of this whole form—submit the form.

The Submit and Reset Buttons

One last thing to do in order to use all this valuable information is to get the data from your form to your backend CGI script. To do this you will need to use a Submit button. Although it is included with input types, the `SUBMIT` type results in a button that, when clicked sends the contents of the form to the CGI script specified in the `ACTION` attribute of the `<FORM>` tag.

The default label on a Submit button is simply `"Submit"`. You can customize this label by using the `VALUE` attribute for the Submit button.

```
<input type="submit" value="Submit Form">
```

On the flip-side, every form should have a way to clear all the selections and bring the form back to its original state. This is done using the `RESET` attribute of the `<INPUT>` tag.

As with the `SUBMIT` attribute, the `RESET` attribute will also create a button on the form. Clicking the Reset button clears the form and restores any default values specified in the individual form elements. If a default value is not defined, any content within the element is erased.

Like the Submit button, you can also change the name of the Reset button by using the `VALUE` attribute for that tag.

Uploading a Document Through a Form

Although we won't need to upload any files with our current example of the company feedback form, there is the possibility that you will need to implement this feature with some of your forms. Along with submitting information from the user back to a server, the current specifications for HTML include the ability for forms to upload whole files to the Web server.

If you are going to use form-based file upload, you'll need to make two simple changes to the HTML code in your form. The first is to include the `ENCTYPE="multipart/form-data"` attribute inside your `<FORM>` tag.

```
<form method="post" enctype="multipart/form-data"
action="http://www.myserver.com/cgi-bin/form_upload">
```

The second change will be to the `<INPUT>` tag on your Web page. A new value for the `TYPE` attribute, `TYPE="file"`, inserts a file-upload element (a text field and a button labeled Browse that lets you browse your own local hard-drive or network). Figure 19.7 shows the result of the following code.

```
<form enctype="multipart/form-data" action=http://
www.myserver. com/cgi-bin/upload method="post"> Put this
file on the server: <input name="myfile" type="file">
<input type="submit" value="Send File">
</form>
```

Our Finished Feedback Form

We've managed to incorporate a lot of the different elements of form design into the feedback page. The following is the finished code, and Figure 19.8 shows our final feedback form screen.

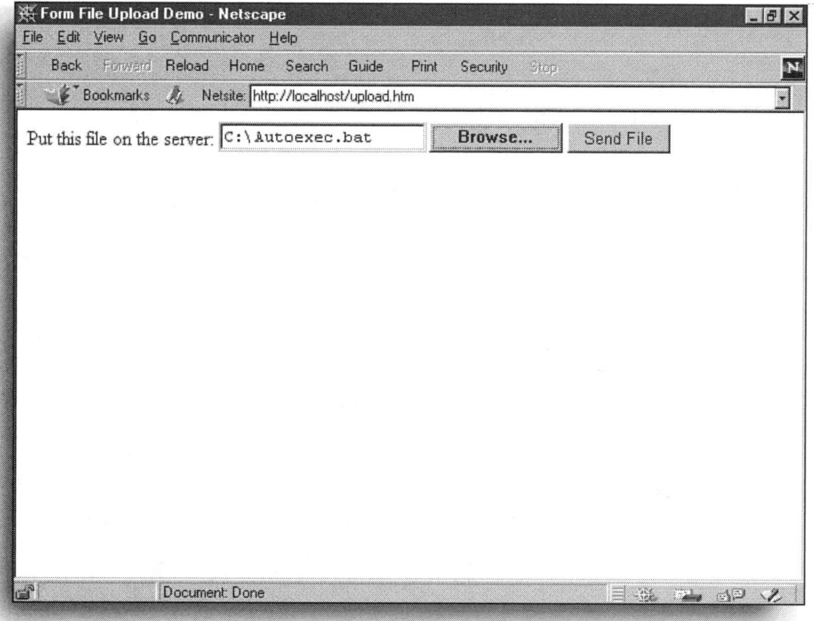

FIGURE 19.7
Uploading a file via a form page.

```
Our workgroup feedback form<html>
<head>
<title>Feedback Form</title>
</head>
<body bgcolor="#ffffff">
<font size=+1>MyCompany's Feedback Form</font>
<hr>

<form method="post" action="/cgi-bin/feedback.cgi">
<table width=100%>
<tr><td>
<b>Name:</b>
<input type="text" name="employee_name">

</td><td>

<b>Department:</b>
<input type="radio" name="dept" value="Sales">Sales
<input type="radio" name="dept" value="HR">HR
<input type="radio" name="dept" value="PR">PR
```

```
<input type="radio" name="dept" value="R&D">R&D

</td></tr>
<tr><td valign=top>
<br>
<b>Which Internet sites have you visited:</b><br>
<input type="checkbox" name="sites" value="company" checked>
MyCompany's Web site<br>
<input type="checkbox" name="sites" value="Excite">Excite
Search Engine<br>
<input type="checkbox" name="sites" value="Lycos">Lycos
Search Engine<br>
<input type="checkbox" name="sites" value="CNN">CNN Cable
News<br>
<input type="checkbox" name="sites" value="ESPN">ESPN
Sports<br>
<input type="checkbox" name="sites" value="Dow Jones">Dow
Jones Report<br>
<input type="checkbox" name="sites" value="WSJ">Wall Street
Journal

</td><td valign=top>
<br>
<b>Comments:</b><br>
<textarea name="comments" cols="30" rows="7"></textarea>

</td></tr>
</table>

<P>

<input type="submit" value="Submit Form"> <input
type="reset" value="Reset Form">

</form>
</body>
</html>
```

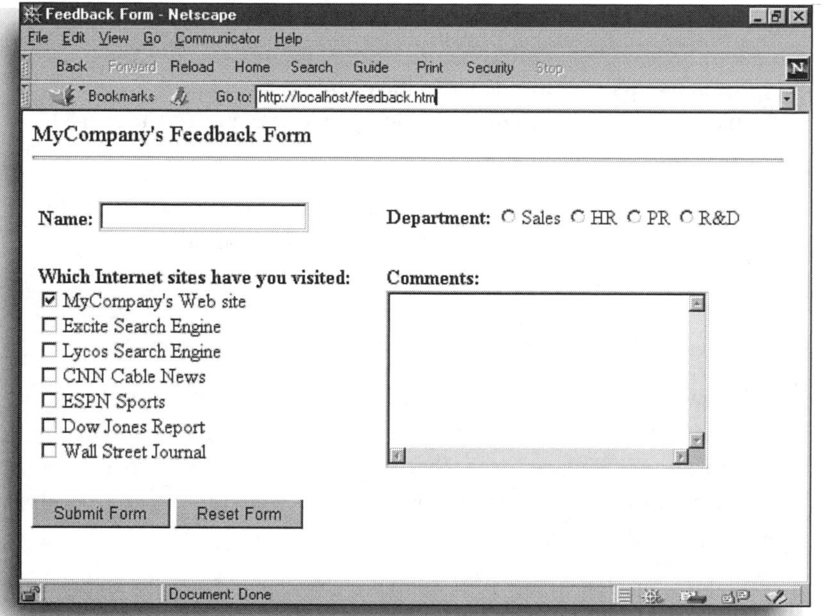

FIGURE 19.8
A company feedback form.

Making Forms Self-Explanatory

You should follow a few simple rules with any form you put on your Web site. Actually, I wouldn't say they are rules, these are merely just some suggestions to make your life easier and hopefully have more people filling out your forms.

First, make the form as short and simple as possible. A form that stretches for more than a couple of pages or screens is very cumbersome and wears down users before they reach the end. The more questions you ask, the more users won't hang around to complete the form. If you do need to ask a lot of questions, be sure to tell your users before they start filling out the form. Also, it's nice to let them know where they are in the process (for example, 2 of 4 pages completed).

Second, plan, plan, plan. Know what information you want from the user and why you want it. Be careful not to offend any of your users with questions that are irrelevant or too invasive.

Sketch your form on paper the way it should appear on the user's screen. You don't have to be an artist at this point. A good outline works wonders. There should be some kind of flow to the form. One element should lead to the next, so the user doesn't skip anything. If users have to guess where to go next, chances are higher that they won't get to the end of the form to press the Submit button.

It's always a good idea to tell the user why you're asking for the information. Is this to register software or to be on a mailing list? Is it to sign a guest book or provide an opinion? There are a lot of reasons for people not to trust what they see on their browsers. Give them a reason to trust your request.

Know your environment. Look at your form from the user's point of view. Are you asking for trusted information in a public environment? Place forms that request confidential information, like credit card numbers, income, Social Security numbers, and so on, on a secured server.

Make it easy for your users to make changes. Always give them a Reset button to clear the information, and a link to more information about the form. Place Submit and Reset buttons at intuitive locations—normally at the end of the form—or at least make them highly visible.

Always remember that you are requesting information from your users. They probably don't HAVE to be there, filling out your form. Be sure to keep that mindset and your forms will be successful.

CHAPTER

20

Using a Scripting Language

- Make script code available within an HTML document or from a separate file
- Place time, date, and user information into a document without using server-side programming
- Make a page come alive and interact with a user
- Animate menu items on your page

Inserting Scripts into HTML

The advent of scripting languages has made it possible for content providers to go beyond the traditional static Web page and provide a browsing experience that is rich with interactivity. Embedded script code is transferred to a browser, along with HTML code, where both are interpreted by the browser. The interpreted HTML produces the static or unchanging content you see in the browser's display. The interpreted script code, when executed, produces some kind of dynamic effect on the page like a scrolling banner or an animated graphic. It is these kinds of effects that enrich a reader's visit to your page.

Since you are a conscientious content provider, you want visitors to your site to have the same enriched experience as well. An important first step to using scripts is learning how to embed script code in your documents. This section of the chapter demonstrates the two techniques you can use to include scripts in your publications. These techniques are

- Placing the script code in the same file as your HTML code
- Placing the script code in its own file and having that file read in by the browser.

You accomplish either of these approaches by using the HTML `<SCRIPT>` tag and its different attributes.

Placing Script Code into an HTML File

Suppose you want to have a scrolling text message appear in a visitor's browser status bar, like the one shown in Figure 20.1. The following code, widely available from one of the public-domain JavaScript libraries on the Web, creates the desired banner. By changing the values of the variables `m1`, `m2`, `m3`, and `m4`, you can alter the code to produce whatever scrolling message you want.

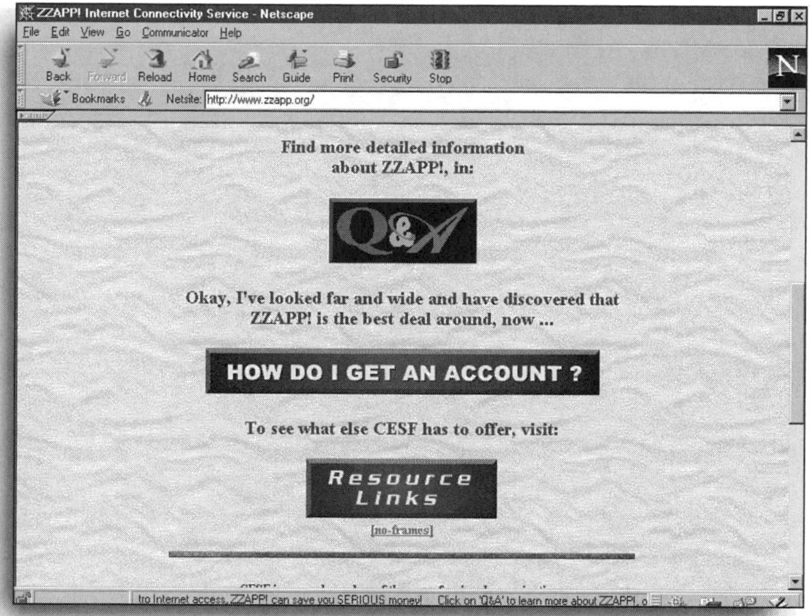

FIGURE 20.1
Scrolling status bar messages inform users about the highlights of your site.

```
function scrollit_r2l(seed)
{
        var m1  = "Welcome to my Family Genealogy page!";
        var m2  = "    Using the techniques shown here, you
";
        var m3  = "can investigate your own family's
heritage.";
        var m4  = "    Click the 'Getting Started' menu
option to
          begin.";

        var msg=m1+m2+m3+m4;
        var out = " ";
        var c   = 1;
        if (seed > 135) {
                seed--;
                var cmd="scrollit_r2l(" + seed + ")";
                timerTwo=window.setTimeout(cmd,135);
        }
        else if (seed <= 135 && seed > 0) {
                for (c=0 ; c < seed ; c++) {
```

```
                        out+=" ";
                }
                out+=msg;
                seed--;
                var cmd="scrollit_r21(" + seed + ")";
                    window.status=out;
                timerTwo=window.setTimeout(cmd,135);
        }
        else if (seed <= 0) {
                if (-seed < msg.length) {
                        out+=msg.substring(-
seed,msg.length);
                        seed--;
                        var cmd="scrollit_r21(" + seed +
")";
                        window.status=out;

timerTwo=window.setTimeout(cmd,135);
                }
                else {
                        window.status=" ";
                        timerTwo=window.setTimeout
("scrollit_r21
                          (135)",75);}
        }
}
```

To place this code directly into the document file, you need to do two things.

Place JavaScript code in an HTML file

1. Place the code between the HTML comment tags: `<!--` and `-->`.
2. Place the script code and the comment tags within the HTML `<SCRIPT>` and `</SCRIPT>` tags.

The first step, which contains the script code with comment tags, is technically not required. However, it is useful for those occasions when a user is viewing your document with a browser that cannot process a script. These script-challenged browsers often display the script code onscreen, rather than ignore it. By placing the code in comment tags, you instruct a script-challenged browser to disregard the code. When you place the

Scripting languages

JavaScript is just one example of a scripting language you can use to write client-side scripts. JavaScript was invented by Netscape Communications Corporation as part of its LiveWire development environment. Most browsers that can process a script can handle JavaScript.

The other two major scripting languages were created by Microsoft. JScript is a language that is very similar to JavaScript. VBScript is derived from Microsoft's popular Visual Basic application development language. Both of these scripting languages can only be processed by the Microsoft Internet Explorer browser.

closing comment tag `-->`, make sure you also put two slashes (`//`) in front of it. This tell the JavaScript interpreter to treat the line that the `-->` tag appears on as a comment line and prevents the `-->` tag from being erroneously processed by the interpreter. If you're using VBScript, you should use a single quote (`'`) instead of the two slashes.

Using the `<SCRIPT>` tag is a necessary step though. The `<SCRIPT>` tag has a required `type` attribute that is set equal to the MIME type of the script code. In most instances, the MIME type is the word `text`, followed by a slash (`/`), followed by the name of the scripting language. For example, the `<SCRIPT>` tag to embed the code in the preceding code listing into an HTML file would be

```
<SCRIPT TYPE="text/javascript">
```

Once you've inserted the code into your HTML file, the finished product should look like the following:

```
<SCRIPT type="text/javascript">
<!--
function scrollit_r2l(seed)
{
        var m1  = "Welcome to my Family Genealogy page!";
        var m2  = "    Using the techniques shown here, you
";
        var m3  = "can investigate your own family's her-
itage.";
        var m4  = "    Click the 'Getting Started' menu
option to
          begin.";
...
else {
                        window.status=" ";
                        timerTwo=window.setTimeout("scrol-
lit_r2l
                          (135)",75);
                }
        }
}
// -->
</SCRIPT>
```

What happened to the `language` attribute?

If you've used the `<SCRIPT>` tag before, you may have also used the `language` attribute of the tag to specify the scripting language. In HTML 4.0, however, the `language` attribute has been deprecated in favor of using the `type` attribute.

Where should I place the script code in the HTML file?

It used to be that all script code had to go into the document head–that is, between the <HEAD> and </HEAD> tags. Under the HTML 4.0 specification, you are free to place script code anywhere in the document head or body (between the <BODY> and </BODY> tags) that you like.

Reading in Script Code from a Separate File

If you have a script you want to use in several different documents, it is a good idea to store the script code in a single file and reference the file from within your HTML documents. One advantage to this is that when you need to change the script, you only have to change it once in the source file, rather than having to make the same changes in all of your individual HTML files. Another advantage is that you don't have to worry about enclosing your script code in comment tags because browsers that can't process the code will ignore the HTML you use to reference the file that contains the code.

To read in script from an external file, perform the following steps.

Place script code in an external file

1. Save your script in a text file. For example, you might save the previous code example in a file named banner.js. The .js extension stands for JavaScript.
2. Use the `<SCRIPT>` tag in your HTML file with the `type` attribute set to the appropriate MIME type and with the `src` attribute set equal to the URL of the file containing the script code.
3. Place the `</SCRIPT>` tag immediately after the `<SCRIPT>` tag.

If you store your script files in a common directory named scripts, the resulting HTML code would look like the following:

```
<SCRIPT type="text/javascript" src="/scripts/banner.js">
</SCRIPT>
```

When using the `src` attribute of the `<SCRIPT>` tag, you are not limited to referring to files placed on your own Web server. You are free to reference script files on other servers as well. For example, the following `<SCRIPT>` tag would read the file animate.vbs from the vbscript directory on the Web server named `www.scriptlibrary.com/`.

```
<SCRIPT type="text/vbscript"
src="http://www.scriptlibrary.com/vbscript/animate.vbs">
</SCRIPT>
```

Providing an Alternative to Script Content

Since there are some browsers that do not come with built-in script interpreters, HTML has to provide a way for document authors to specify what should happen if a script can't execute. In HTML 4.0, the <NOSCRIPT> and </NOSCRIPT> tags contain the content that should be displayed if a script does not run. To include this kind of alternate content, perform the following steps.

Place alternative to script content in an HTML file

1. Place your script code into the HTML file or set it up to be read in from an external file as per the instructions earlier in the chapter.
2. Put a <NOSCRIPT> tag on the line after the </SCRIPT> tag.
3. Place your alternate content after the <NOSCRIPT> tag.
4. Place the </NOSCRIPT> tag after the alternate content.

In the event that your document is requested by a browser that cannot process the script code, the content between the <NOSCRIPT> and </NOSCRIPT> tags will be rendered. Browsers that know how to process scripts also know that they should ignore anything found between <NOSCRIPT> and </NOSCRIPT> tags, so there's no chance of the alternate content being presented.

Using the <NOSCRIPT> and </NOSCRIPT> tags is also a good idea when you're reading in script code from an external file. If the code should fail to load, the browser will be able to render the alternate content instead.

Adding Date and Time Information to a Page

It is often useful to be able to put a time and date stamp on a Web page. For example, an online commerce site might want to include time and date information on the "receipt" page issued to consumers after they complete their shopping. Because these users may be in a different time zone than the server, it makes more sense to use the date and time information from the users' computers, rather than stamping everything with the server's date and time information.

JavaScript is object oriented

If the terms "object" and "methods" don't make a lot of sense to you, you may want to look into a beginning reference on the subject of object-oriented programming. JavaScript, JScript, and VBScript are all object-oriented languages.

For the purposes of this chapter, you can just keep the following in mind: An object is merely a collection of information and the functions that can be performed on that information. The individual pieces of information are called the *properties* of the object and the different functions that can act upon the object are called *methods*.

Some simple JavaScript commands let you read time and date information from a user's PC with ease. This information is available through the JavaScript `Date` object. You can use one of the `Date` object's many methods to extract the information you want to present onscreen.

The JavaScript `Date` object contains the pieces of information shown in the following list. Or, stated another way, the following are the properties of the `Date` object:

- `Month`
- `Day` (day of the week)
- `Date` (day of the month)
- `Year`
- `Hours`
- `Minutes`
- `Seconds`

Each of these properties has an associated `get` method that extracts the property from the `Date` object. For example, to extract the `Year` property from the `Date` object, you would apply the `getYear` method to the `Date` object. Knowing this, it now becomes fairly easy to set up a time and date stamp in an HTML document.

Place time and date information on a page

1. Begin your script at the point in HTML file where you want to insert the time and date. You do this with the `<SCRIPT>` tag as follows:

   ```
   <SCRIPT type="text/javascript">
   <!--
   ```

2. Capture the current time and date information from the user's machine. This is accomplished by setting a variable equal to the current value of the `Date` object.

   ```
   var rightnow = new Date();
   ```

3. Use the `getHours`, `getMinutes`, and `getSeconds` methods on the variable `rightnow` to extract hour, minute, and second information. This can be done in the same line that you use to print the time. The `document.writeln` method is what you use to write a line of output to the HTML document itself:

```
document.writeln("<B>Time:</B> " + rightnow.getHours()
+ ":" +
rightnow.getMinutes() + ":" + rightnow.getSeconds());
```

4. Put a line break between the time and date.

```
document.writeln("<BR>");
```

5. The `getMonth` method will return a numerical value between `0` (for January) and `11` (for December). Since these month values are not intuitive to your end user, you need to extract the month information and then add 1 to it.

```
month = rightnow.getMonth() + 1;
```

6. With the proper numerical value for the month now stored in the variable `month`, you can print the date information in much the same way as you did the time information:

```
document.writeln("<B>Date:</B> " + month + "/" + right-
now.
  getDate() +
"/" + rightnow.getYear());
```

7. Close out the script.

```
// -->
</SCRIPT>
```

The script built in the previous steps is presented in its entirety next. The output from the script is shown in Figure 20.2.

```
<SCRIPT type="text/javascript">
<!--
var rightnow = new Date();
document.writeln("<B>Time:</B> " + rightnow.getHours() + ":"
+ rightnow.getMinutes() + ":" + rightnow.getSeconds());
document.writeln("<BR>");
month = rightnow.getMonth() + 1;
```

```
document.writeln("<B>Date:</B> " + month + "/" +
rightnow.getDate()
+ "/" + rightnow.getYear());
// -->
</SCRIPT>
```

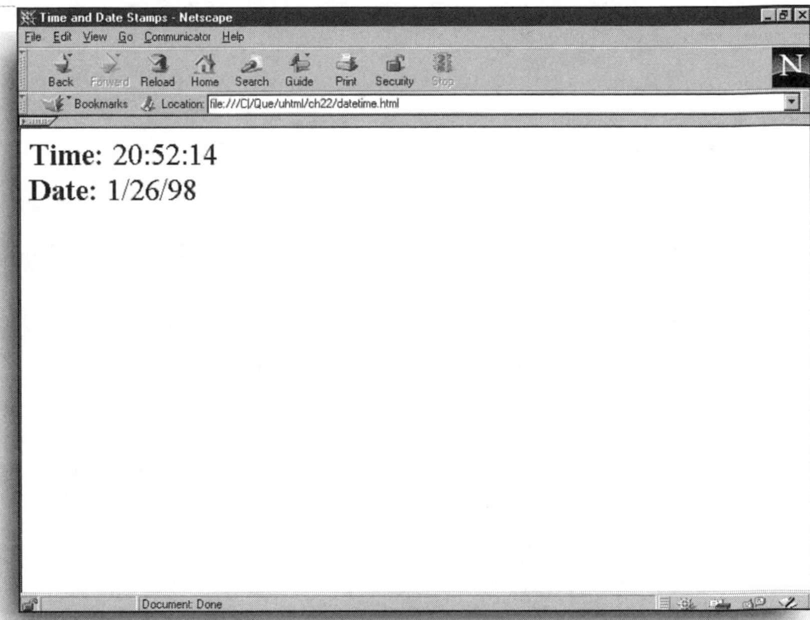

FIGURE 20.2
Time and date information can be taken right from a user's computer and displayed on a Web page.

Adding User Information to a Page

Sometimes it's fun to show users just how much you know about them when they hit one of your pages. Prior to JavaScript, you could only do this using environment variables and CGI scripts running on the server. But now JavaScript lets you peek at some basic user information and present it back to the user without any server involvement.

The two main objects you can use for extracting user information are the `navigator` and `window` objects. To a lesser extent, you can also use the `document` object to extract user information. The `navigator` object has properties that describe the browser in use. These properties are summarized in Table 20.1.

TABLE 20.1 **Properties of the *navigator* object**

Property	Information
`appCodeName`	The code name for the browser (for example, `Mozilla` for a Netscape browser)
`appName`	The regular name of the browser (for example, `Microsoft` for Internet Explorer)
`appVersion`	The version number of the browser in use
`language`	What language is supported by the browser
`mimeTypes`	A list of MIME types that the browser is able to process
`platform`	The operating system on which the browser is running
`plugins`	A list of all plug-ins available to the browser
`userAgent`	The value of the user agent header (summary information about the browser)

The `window` object contains information about the browser window. This includes things like the size of the screen (`screen`), the URLs the user has visited previously (`history`), whether the browser window has been broken up into frames (`frame`), and the current URL (`location`).

The `document` object has many properties, but the only one related to user information is the `referrer` property. This property is set equal to the URL of the document that the user was looking at previously.

You can use combinations of these properties to present users with information about their browsers, their screens, and the pages they have visited prior to yours.

Place *user* information in a document

1. Write a routine that will present the user information you want. For this example, we'll use the JavaScript `alert` instruction, which will present the information in a pop-up dialog box.

```
<SCRIPT type="text/javascript">
<!--
function bigBrother() {
```

```
   alert('Are you really using ' + navigator.appName +
' and did
   you enjoy your visit to ' + document.referrer +
'?');
}
// -->
</SCRIPT>
```

2. Use the `onLoad` event handler in the `<BODY>` tag to launch the script when the document body is loaded into the browser window.

```
<BODY bgcolor="#FFFFFF" onLoad="bigBrother()">
```

The following code is a complete file to present the user information used in the example. Figure 20.3 shows what the JavaScript alert box will look like once the page is loaded.

```
<HTML>
<HEAD>
<TITLE>User Information</TITLE>
<SCRIPT type="text/javascript">
<!--
function bigBrother() {
   alert('Are you really using ' + navigator.appName + ' and
 did you enjoy your visit to ' + document.referrer + '?');
}
// -->
</SCRIPT>
</HEAD>
<BODY bgcolor="#FFFFFF" onLoad="bigBrother()">
<H1>Welcome to my Special Interests Page</H1>
...
</BODY>
</HTML>
```

Event handlers

Sometimes you don't want a script to execute when a document is loaded. Instead, you may want the script triggered by a specific event that takes place during the user's stay on the page. JavaScript comes with several different event handlers that capture the instances of many browser-related events and launch a script in response to the event. The `onLoad` event was set equal to the `bigBrother` function so that the function would run once the page was loaded.

Some other JavaScript event handlers include

- `onChange` When a form field has been modified
- `onClick` When an object on a form has been clicked
- `onError` When there is an error loading a document
- `onKeyDown` When the user presses a key
- `onKeyUp` When the user releases a key
- `onMouseOver` When the user's mouse point passes over an object
- `onSubmit` When a user submits a form
- `onUnload` When the user exits a document

Using Scripts to Interact with the User

Scripts let you do more than just surprise users with information about their browsers. You can write scripts that actually respond to user input. This is a very popular approach with online forms to make sure that users don't miss filling out a required form field or that the form data submitted is in an appropriate format.

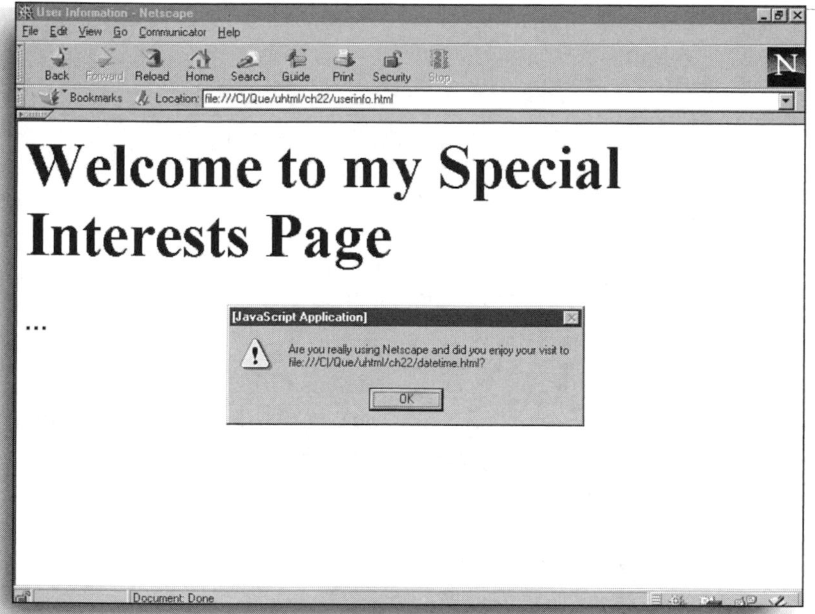

FIGURE 20.3
You can capture information about users' browsers and their browsing histories and present that information back to them.

Checking for a Mandatory Form Field

Suppose you have an online form on your site with one field that is required to be filled in. It used to be that all of the form data had to be passed back to the Web server before you could check to make sure that the required field was filled in. With JavaScript, you can now perform this check before the data is sent to the server. This is advantageous because it reduces the processing load on your server.

The following code shows the HTML code for the form. Note that the text field named `MANDATORY` is the one that needs to be filled out.

```
<HTML>
<HEAD>
<TITLE>Form with a Required Field</TITLE>
</HEAD>
<BODY bgcolor="#FFFFFF">
Please fill in the information requested below.  Note that
the Name field <B>must</B> be filled in.
```

```
<FORM action="process_it.cgi" method="POST">
...
<B>Name:</B> <INPUT type="TEXT" length=20 name="MANDATORY">
...
<INPUT type="BUTTON" value="Submit">
</FORM>
</BODY>
</HTML>
```

You can verify that the mandatory field was filled out before the form data is submitted by performing the following steps:

1. Create a function that checks to see if the required input field was left blank and, if it was, notify the user. You can do this with just a few lines of JavaScript.

```
<SCRIPT>
<!--
function emptyField() {
tmp=document.form.mandatory.value;
if (tmp.length<1) {
alert("You forgot to fill in your name!");
}
// Place cursor back into mandatory field
document.form.manadatory.focus();
}
//-->
</SCRIPT>
```

Blur and `focus`

The `focus` method you see used in this code refers to the action of placing the cursor into a form field. Usually a form field is given focus by the user clicking it or tabbing the cursor to it. With JavaScript, you can give a `form field` object focus by applying the `focus` method to it.

When the cursor leaves a form field, the field is said to be *blurred*.

2. Use the `onClick` event handler with your Submit button so that the `emptyField` function is called whenever the Submit button is clicked.

```
<INPUT type="BUTTON" value="Submit"
onClick="emptyField()">
```

Putting it all together gives you the code you see next. The resulting alert box that is displayed in the event of an empty field appears in Figure 20.4.

```
<HTML>
<HEAD>
<TITLE>Form with a Required Field</TITLE>
<SCRIPT>
<!--
function emptyField() {
```

```
tmp=document.example.mandatory.value;
if (tmp.length<1) {
alert("You forgot to fill in your name!");
}
// Place cursor back into mandatory field
document.example.mandatory.focus();
}
// -->
</SCRIPT>
</HEAD>
<BODY bgcolor="#FFFFFF">
Please fill in the information requested below.<P>Note that
the Name field <B>must</B> be filled in.
<FORM action="process_it.cgi" method="POST">
...<P>
<B>Name:</B> <INPUT type="TEXT" length=20 name="MANDATORY"
value=""><P>
...<P>
<INPUT type="BUTTON" value="Submit" onClick="emptyField()">
</FORM>
</BODY>
</HTML>
```

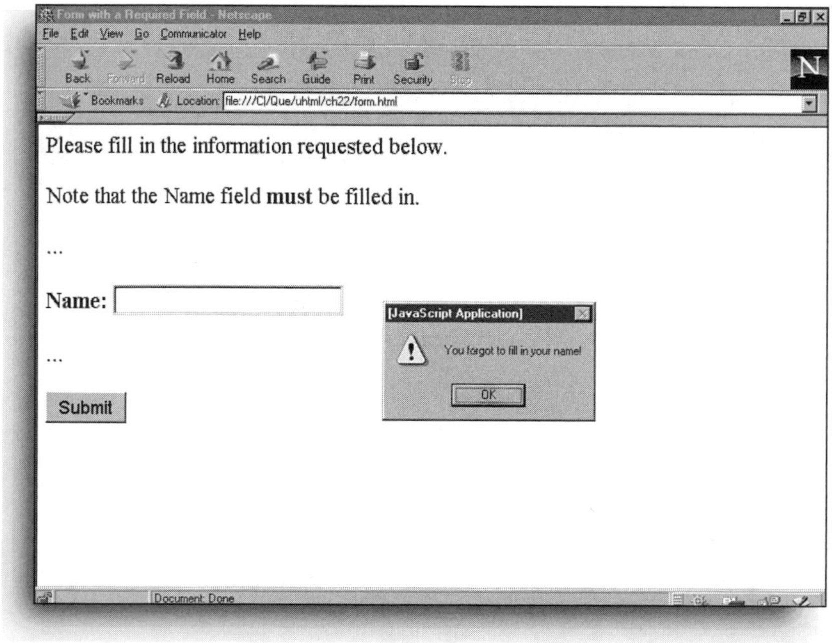

Form with a Required Field - Netscape
File Edit View Go Communicator Help
Back Forward Reload Home Search Guide Print Security Stop
Bookmarks Location: file:///C|/Que/uhtml/ch22/form.html

Please fill in the information requested below.

Note that the Name field **must** be filled in.

...

Name:

[JavaScript Application]
You forgot to fill in your name!
OK

...

Submit

Document: Done

FIGURE 20.4
Client-side scripts are great for checking over a user's form submissions before sending them on to the server.

It's easy to expand the `emptyField` function to accommodate other mandatory form fields. You simply add another `if` statement for each one to check for an empty field. If you have to give feedback to the user about more than one empty field, you may want to return a single message listing all of the empty fields rather than displaying an alert box for each one.

Creating an Interactive Game

It doesn't have to be all business with client-side script—you can have some fun, too! Many people have coded very enjoyable games in JavaScript that are no more than a few kilobytes in size. That's pretty respectable when you consider that many computer games these days need to be distributed on CD-ROM.

The following code is for a browser-based number guessing game. First, the user provides a range of numbers and the computer chooses a number somewhere in the range. The user then tries to guess the number the computer selected, receiving feedback on whether the guess is too low or too high. When the user guesses the number exactly, an alert box displays the total number of guesses.

JavaScript libraries

The code for the number guessing game is a modified version of a game available through the public JavaScript library found at `http://www.javascript-source.com/`. This excellent site has freely available scripts that you can download and use on your Web pages.

There are many other JavaScript repositories out on the Web in addition to the JavaScript Source. For a listing, check out `http://www.yahoo.com/Computers_and_Internet/Programming_Languages/JavaScript/`.

```
<HTML>
<HEAD>
<TITLE>Number Guessing Game</TITLE>
<SCRIPT type="text/javascript">
<!--
var my_no,count;
// Set up the initial screen
function load() {
window.defaultStatus="JavaScript Guess-a-Number Game";
document.game.help.value="Please set range of numbers and
press the Start button.";document.game.from.focus();
}
// Pick a random seed
function rnd(scale) {
var dd=new Date();
return((Math.round(Math.abs(Math.sin(dd.getTime()))*8.71*
scale)%
```

```
scale));
}
// Come up with the target number
function range() {
var to=1+1*document.game.to.value;
count=0;
my_no=rnd(to);
while(my_no<document.game.from.value) {
my_no=rnd(to); }
document.game.help.value="Please guess a number, enter it,
and press Guess.";
 }
// Process the user's guess
function guess() {
var no=document.game.number.value;
count++;
if(no<my_no) document.game.help.value="My number is greater
 than "+no+".";
else if(no>my_no) document.game.help.value="My number is
less than "+no+".";
else alert("It takes you "+count+" attempts to guess this
number");
}
//  -->
</SCRIPT>
</HEAD>
<!-- run the set up function when the document loads -->
<BODY onLoad="load()">
<CENTER>
<FORM name=game>
<TABLE border=3>
<TR>
<!-- Prompt for the range of numbers and use it to determine
 the target number. -->
<TD align=center colspan=2>Range of numbers</TD>
<TD align=center rowspan=2><input type=button value=" Start "
 onclick="range()"></TD>
</TR>
<TR>
```

```
<TD align=center>From:<br><input type=text name=from
size=10></TD>
<TD align=center>To:<br><input type=text name=to
size=10></TD>
</TD>
<TR>
<TD></TD>
</TR>
<TR>
<!-- Use a text field for presenting feedback messages. -->
<TD align=center colspan=3><input type=text name=help
size=70></TD>
</TR>
<TR>
<TD></TD>
</TR>
<!-- Prompt for a guess and process it. -->
<tr><td align=right colspan=3><input type=text name=number
size=10>
<input type=button value=" Guess " onclick="guess()"></TD>
</TR>
</TABLE>
</FORM>
</CENTER>
</BODY>
</HTML>
```

Figure 20.5 shows the number guessing game in action.

Highlighting Menu Items with Special Graphics

A very useful application of JavaScript is making a menu item "light up" when a user's mouse is over it. Doing this provides important visual feedback to the user about the menu option he or she is about to select.

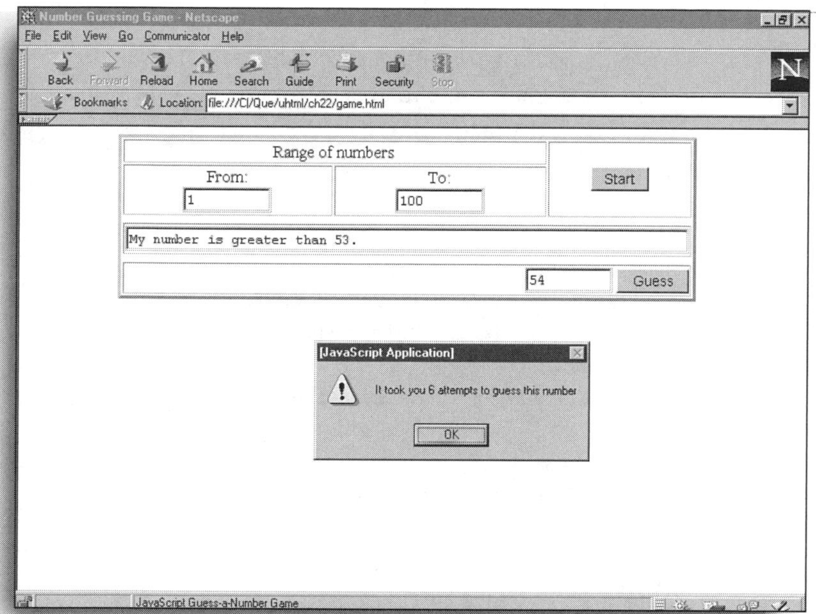

FIGURE 20.5
You can build small games into your pages with just a few lines of JavaScript.

When you use graphics to represent your menu items, it's a fairly easy matter to build in some JavaScript that will animate the graphics when the user's mouse is over them. The key here is to treat each image as an object that's part of the document. Each `image` object has a property `src` that specifies the URL of the image. By changing the value of `src` when a user's mouse is over a linked image, you can read in and display a completely different image in its place.

For this example, we'll consider the simple case of using graphics as bullets in front of each menu option. The bullet graphic will be a downward-pointing triangle when a user's mouse is not over it. When the mouse does pass over the graphic, we'll replace the downward-pointing triangle with one that points to the menu option itself. When the graphic changes, it creates the illusion of the downward-pointing triangle rotating to point at the selected menu option.

To set up animated bullets in front of your menu options, perform the following steps:

1. Set up the HTML to display your menu items with the downward-pointing triangle in front of each. This is best done in an HTML table to ensure good alignment of the graphics with the text.

```
<HTML>
<HEAD>
<TITLE>Genealogy Page</TITLE>
<BODY bgcolor="#FFFFFF">
<H1>Welcome to my Family Genealogy Page</H1>
Please select one of the options below:
<P><HR noshade>
<TABLE cellpadding=12 cellspacing=4>
<TR>
<TD>
<A href="father.html"><IMG src="graphics/tridown.gif"
border=0>
</A>
</TD>
<TD><B>My Father's Heritage</B></TD>
</TR>
<TR>
<TD>
<A href="mother.html"><IMG src="graphics/tridown.gif"
border=0>
</A>
</TD>
<TD><B>My Mother's Heritage</B></TD>
</TR>
<TR>
<TD>
<A href="doyourown.html"><IMG src="graphics/
tridown.gif" border=0>
</A>
</TD>
<TD><B>Trace Your Own Roots</B></TD>
</TR>
<TR>
<TD>
<A href="links.html"><IMG src="graphics/tridown.gif"
border=0></A>
</TD>
<TD><B>Other Genealogy Sites on the Web</B></TD>
```

```
</TR>
</TABLE>
<P><HR noshade><P>
</BODY>
</HTML>
```

2. Make the downward-pointing and right-pointing triangle graphics into objects and define their `src` properties. The following `if` statement says to execute the `loadImages` function if the `document.images` object is empty (which it is when the file is loaded):

```
function loadImages() {
    this[1] = new Image();
    this[1].src = "graphics/tridown.gif";
    this[2] = new Image();
    this[2].src = "graphics/triright.gif";
}
if (document.images) {
    loadImages();
}
```

3. Write a function that switches the two graphics. Because you can switch from downward-pointing to right-pointing and vice versa, it's easiest to write this function with an `if` statement that handles both cases.

```
function switchTri(i,flag) {
// i = the number of the bullet graphic you want to
change
// flag = 0 means switch to the downward pointing image
// flag = 1 means switch to the right pointing image
    if (document.images) {
        if (flag == 1) {
            document.images[i].src =
            "graphics/triright.gif";
        }
        else {
            document.images[i].src =
            "graphics/tridown.gif";
        }
    }
}
```

4. Modify your <A> tags to include `onMouseOver` and `onMouseOut` events that call the `switchTri` function. When the mouse is over the linked graphic, it should switch to the right-pointing triangle. When the mouse is no longer over the graphic, it should switch to the downward-pointing triangle.

```
<TABLE cellpadding=12 cellspacing=4>
<TR>
<TD>
<A onMouseOver="switchTri(0,1)"
onMouseOut="switchTri(0,0)"
 href="father.html"><IMG src="graphics/tridown.gif"
 border=0></A>
</TD>
<TD><B>My Father's Heritage</B></TD>
</TR>
<TR>
<TD>
<A onMouseOver="switchTri(1,1)"
onMouseOut="switchTri(1,0)"
 href="mother.html"><IMG src="graphics/tridown.gif"
 border=0></A>
</TD>
<TD><B>My Mother's Heritage</B></TD>
</TR>
<TR>
<TD>
<A onMouseOver="switchTri(2,1)"
onMouseOut="switchTri(2,0)"
 href="doyourown.html"><IMG src="graphics/tridown.gif"
 border=0>
</A>
</TD>
<TD><B>Trace Your Own Roots</B></TD>
</TR>
<TR>
<TD>
<A onMouseOver="switchTri(3,1)"
onMouseOut="switchTri(3,0)"
 href="links.html"><IMG src="graphics/tridown.gif"
 border=0></A>
</TD>
<TD><B>Other Genealogy Sites on the Web</B></TD>
</TR>
</TABLE>
```

The following code shows you the finished HTML and JavaScript code, while Figures 20.6 and 20.7 show you how the triangles change when the mouse passes over one of them.

```
<HTML>
<HEAD>
<TITLE>Family Genealogy Page</TITLE>
<SCRIPT type="text/javascript">
<!--
function loadImages() {
   this[1] = new Image();
   this[1].src = "graphics/tridown.gif";
   this[2] = new Image();
   this[2].src = "graphics/triright.gif";
}
if (document.images) {
   loadImages();
}
function switchTri(i,flag) {
   if (document.images) {
      if (flag == 1) {
         document.images[i].src = "graphics/triright.gif";
      }
      else {
         document.images[i].src = "graphics/tridown.gif";
      }
   }
}
// -->
</SCRIPT>
</HEAD>
<BODY bgcolor="#FFFFFF">
<H1>Welcome to my Family Genealogy Page</H1>
Please select one of the options below:
<P><HR noshade>
<TABLE cellpadding=12 cellspacing=4>
<TR>
<TD>
<A onMouseOver="switchTri(0,1)" onMouseOut="switchTri(0,0)"
 href="father.html"><IMG src="graphics/tridown.gif"
 border=0></A>
```

Arrays in JavaScript

Notice in this script that the first image in the `document.images` array is indexed by the number **0** (zero) rather than **1** (one). This is true for all JavaScript arrays and can be confusing for many first-time script authors.

```
</TD>
<TD><B>My Father's Heritage</B></TD>
</TR>
<TR>
<TD>
<A onMouseOver="switchTri(1,1)" onMouseOut="switchTri(1,0)"
 href="mother.html"><IMG SRC="graphics/tridown.gif"
 border=0></A>
</TD>
<TD><B>My Mother's Heritage</B></TD>
</TR>
<TR>
<TD>
<A onMouseOver="switchTri(2,1)" onMouseOut="switchTri(2,0)"
 href="doyourown.html"><IMG SRC="graphics/tridown.gif"
 border=0>
</A>
</TD>
<TD><B>Trace Your Own Roots</B></TD>
</TR>
<TR>
<TD>
<A onMouseOver="switchTri(3,1)" onMouseOut="switchTri(3,0)"
 href="links.html"><IMG SRC="graphics/tridown.gif"
 border=0></A>
</TD>
<TD><B>Other Genealogy Sites on the Web</B></TD>
</TR>
</TABLE>
<P><HR noshade><P>
</BODY>
</HTML>
```

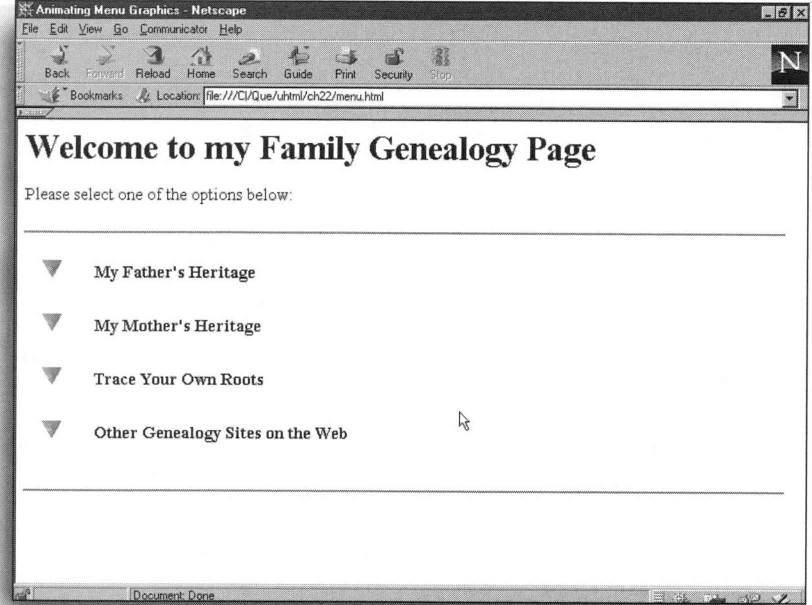

FIGURE 20.6
When the mouse pointer is not over any of the menu items, all of the triangles point downward.

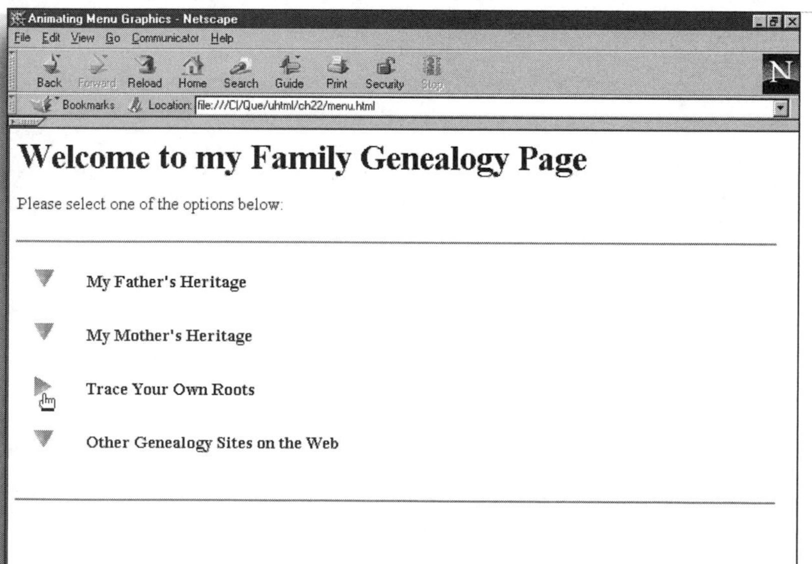

FIGURE 20.7
When the user moves the mouse pointer over one of the bullets, the graphic changes so that the triangle now points to the right.

CHAPTER 21

Adding Layers

- Learn about layers and their role in Netscape's concept of Dynamic HTML
- Create layers for both absolute and relative positioning of content
- Make pop-up help windows that users can call up for additional information
- Animate different objects on your pages
- Simulate layers on browsers that aren't layer enabled

What Are Layers?

If you've been keeping up with recent trends in Web publishing, you've probably at least heard of Dynamic HTML. One of the biggest challenges of Dynamic HTML is reaching agreement on what the term means. Both Netscape Communications Corporation and the Microsoft Corporation touted the version 4 releases of their browsers as supporting Dynamic HTML. But while both companies were using the same term, there were some substantial differences in what each company meant when it used the term.

If you stay focused on the similarities though, you'll find that implementations of Dynamic HTML in the two major browsers have some things in common. These include the following:

- Use of style sheets for controlling content presentation
- Precise positioning of content in the browser window
- Downloading of fonts for the browser to use when rendering text

In spite of these features being common to both browsers, the ways each went about supporting each feature were not the same. The most glaring case of this is with the content positioning. Microsoft programmed Internet Explorer 4.0 to use the Cascading Style Sheet (CSS) approach to doing content positioning. (To learn more about how to insert style information using this technique, see Chapter 13, "Using Cascading Style Sheets to Define Appearance.") This chapter focuses on how Netscape implemented content positioning in Navigator 4.0—an approach that involves the concept of a *layer* and the extended HTML tags used to create layers.

Layers rejected by the W3C

Netscape's concept of a layer was proposed to the World Wide Web Consortium (W3C) for inclusion in the HTML standard, but the W3C rejected Netscape's proposal on the grounds that CSS could already do just about everything that layers could. Once this happened, Netscape modified its browser so that it would correctly process the CSS approach to content positioning.

You can think of a Netscape layer as being like an overhead transparency sheet that contains some portion of your content. When laying out content on these transparent sheets, a number of compelling possibilities arise.

- When placing content on a transparent sheet, you are free to put it anywhere on the sheet that you want. This freedom is what is meant by content positioning—you can specify the exact x and y coordinates of where you want the content to go.

- By overlaying the various transparent sheets, you can piece together the entire page. With this layering approach, it's also possible to have some content that overlaps other content. This means there is also a z coordinate to consider because these layers are somehow "stacked," and content at the top of the stack can obscure content below it.
- Finally, consider that you can remove any transparent sheet from the stack, thereby hiding the content on that sheet completely. You could reinsert the sheet later on, perhaps higher or lower in the stack, to create an entirely new effect.

If you've done a lot of two-dimensional Web page layout, these situations probably have left you eager to know how you can break out of the 2D rut and into this new world. The balance of this chapter is devoted to showing you the way. To begin, you'll learn the basics of how to create a layer, and then you'll move on to look at some of the interesting applications of layers.

Creating a Layer

One important thing to know before creating a layer is which kind of layer you want to create. Netscape supports two types of positioning within a layer.

- Absolute positioning—With absolute positioning, content in the layer is placed with respect to the upper-left corner of the Web browser window. The (x,y) coordinates of this point are taken to be (0,0). The x coordinate increases as you move to the right and the y coordinate increases as you move down.
- Relative positioning—If you use relative content positioning within a layer, you are placing the content with respect to the position that the content would normally occupy if you weren't moving it elsewhere. Thus, if a piece of content would normally appear in the very center of the browser window, relative positioning of the content would position it relative to the window's center point.

What is an inline layer?

When reading documentation about layers and the HTML tags that support them, you might see a reference to an inline layer. Put simply, an inline layer is one that uses relative positioning. The "I" in the <ILAYER> tag stands for inline—this makes for an easy mnemonic for keeping the two tags straight in your mind.

Netscape introduced two different tags to handle these types of positioning. The <LAYER> tag is used to set up layers with absolutely positioned content and the <ILAYER> tag defines layers with relatively positioned content.

Setting Up a Layer with Absolute Positioning

When you're setting up a document that uses layers, you don't use the HTML <BODY> tag as you normally would. Rather, you just start placing layer tags right after the document header section. Each layer can contain content or it can be used to contain other layers (also called *nested layers*). The <LAYER> tag is a container tag, so you should always use a </LAYER> tag for each <LAYER> tag you introduce.

The <LAYER> tag also has a long list of attributes. By varying the values of these attributes, you can create some pretty spectacular effects on your Web pages. The attributes of the <LAYER> tag include the following:

- `background` The `background` attribute is set equal to the URL of an image to tile in the background of the layer. In the absence of a background image or background color (see `bgcolor` next), the layer background is transparent and will let any layers stacked beneath it show through.
- `bgcolor` You can set `bgcolor` equal to a reserved English-language color name, an RGB triplet, or a hexadecimal triplet that specifies a background color for the layer. Otherwise, the layer's background is transparent.
- `src` There are two ways to place content in layer. You can place the content between the <LAYER> and </LAYER> tags, or you can import the content from another file by using the `src` attribute. `src` is set equal to the URL of the document you want to import.
- `id` The `id` attribute is used to assign a unique name to a layer so that it can be referenced in other <LAYER> tags or in JavaScript code.
- `left` and `top` `left` and `top` are set equal to the number of pixels from the upper-left corner of the browser screen where the layer should begin. These two attributes permit exact positioning of the layer on the screen.

- `z-index`, `above`, and `below` These three attributes all help to specify how the layers stack up along the z axis (the axis coming out of the browser screen toward the user). `z-index` is set equal to a positive integer and a layer with a larger `z-index` value will appear stacked on top of layers that have lower `z-index` values. You can place a new layer above or below an existing, named layer by setting `above` or `below` equal to the named layer's name. In the absence of `z-index`, `above`, or `below` attributes, new layers will be stacked on top of old layers.
- `visibility` `visibility` can take on one of the following three values: `SHOW`, `HIDE`, or `INHERIT`. If a layer's `visibility` attribute is set to `SHOW`, the content of the layer will be displayed. Setting `SHOW` to `HIDE` conceals the layer content. A `SHOW` value of `INHERIT` means the layer will have the same `SHOW` behavior as its *parent layer*.
- `clip` The clipping region of a layer is a rectangular area that defines how much of the layer content is visible. You can control the size of the clipping region using the `CLIP` attribute. `clip` is set equal to a comma-delimited list of four numbers that represent the coordinates of the upper-left and lower-right corners of the clipping region. Measurements for clipping region coordinates are taken with respect to the upper-left corner of the layer. By default, the clipping region is large enough to display all of the contents of the layer.
- `height` In the absence of a `clip` attribute, `height` controls the height of the clipping region. `height` may be set equal to a number of pixels or to a percentage of the layer's height.
- `width` The `width` attribute specifies the width at which layer contents begin to wrap to new lines. Like `height`, `width` can be set equal to a number of pixels or to a percentage of the layer width.
- `pagex` and `pagey` Because it's possible to nest layers inside of layers, you may end up in a situation where you want to position a layer with respect to the entire browser screen and not its parent element (the layer that contains it). In this case you can use the `pagex` and `pagey` attributes to specify where the layer should begin with respect to the upper-left corner of the browser screen.

The <LAYER> tag's extensive set of attributes make many interesting effects possible. For example, by changing the size of the clipping region, you can show or hide different parts of the layer's content. Or you can change the z-index of a layer to make it rise above or drop below other layers. You could even adjust the top and left attributes to make a layer move to a new position. All of these changes are possible thanks to the ability to use JavaScript to modify layer properties. You'll see some examples of that in later sections, but to complete the discussion of the <LAYER> tag's syntax, here is a list of JavaScript event handlers you can use with the <LAYER> tag.

- `OnMouseOver` The `OnMouseOver` event is invoked when a user's mouse pointer enters the layer.
- `OnMouseOut` When the mouse pointer leaves a layer, the `OnMouseOut` event is fired.
- `OnFocus` If the layer acquires keyboard focus (for example, a user clicks a form field in a layer so as to be able to type in it), an `OnFocus` event is triggered.
- `OnBlur` Blurring refers to the loss of focus. When a layer blurs, Navigator will invoke an `OnBlur` event.
- `OnLoad` The `OnLoad` event is triggered when the layer is initially loaded.

Using these event handlers is the first step in making your positioned content dynamic. Depending on what JavaScript code you execute upon an event firing, you can change a layer's content or move it to a new position to create an animation effect.

Now that you know the basic syntax of the <LAYER> tag and its attributes, you can begin to look at how to set up layered pages.

Placing Content in a Single Layer

The simplest example of a layered document is one with a single layer that contains all of the content. To set up such a layer, follow these instructions.

Creating a single-layer document

1. Begin your document with the <HTML> tag and create a header section so that the document has a title.

```
<HTML>
<HEAD>
<TITLE>A Simple Layer</TITLE>
</HEAD>
```

2. Create the layer using the <LAYER> tag. Make use of the attributes previously listed to handle backgrounds, positioning of the content, and other presentation characteristics.

```
<HTML>
<HEAD>
<TITLE>A Simple Layer</TITLE>
</HEAD>
<LAYER left=107 top=83 bgcolor="WHITE">
```

3. Place the content of the layer into the file and then close the layer with the </LAYER> tag.

```
<HTML>
<HEAD>
<TITLE>A Simple Layer</TITLE>
</HEAD>
<LAYER left=107 top=83 bgcolor="WHITE">
<H1>All of the content you see in on a single layer</H1>
<IMG src="layers.gif width=120 height=72 border=0>
<HR>
</LAYER>
```

4. Complete the file with the </HTML> tag.

```
<HTML>
<HEAD>
<TITLE>A Simple Layer</TITLE>
</HEAD>
<LAYER left=107 top=83 bgcolor="WHITE">
<H1>All of the content you see in on a single layer</H1>
<IMG src="layers.gif width=120 height=72 border=0>
<HR>
</LAYER>
</HTML>
```

A single-layer document usually isn't very interesting unless you animate it by dynamically changing colors or by resizing the clipping region to show or hide various parts of the content. You'll see how to do these things later in this chapter.

Placing Content in Multiple Layers

A more likely situation is the one in which you need to place content across multiple layers. In this case, you simply create as many layers as you need by introducing more `<LAYER>` tags into your document file. Suppose, for example, you have two images you want to overlap to create a certain effect. You can place each one on its own layer, positioned so that they overlap on this screen. To accomplish this, follow these instructions.

Overlapping two images

1. Begin your document with the `<HTML>` tag and create a header section so that the document has a title.

```
<HTML>
<HEAD>
<TITLE>Content on Multiple Layers</TITLE>
</HEAD>
```

2. Next place the image that will be partially obscured into its own layer.

```
<HTML>
<HEAD>
<TITLE>Content on Multiple Layers</TITLE>
</HEAD>
<LAYER left=25 top=48>
<IMG src="lower.gif" width=200 height=180 border=0>
</LAYER>
```

3. Now place the image that will be completely visible into its own layer. Since new layers automatically go on top of old layers, you are assured that this new layer will produce the effect you want without having to use the `visibility` attribute.

```
<HTML>
<HEAD>
<TITLE>Content on Multiple Layers</TITLE>
</HEAD>
<LAYER left=25 top=48>
```

```
<IMG SRC="lower.gif" width=200 height=180 border=0>
</LAYER>
<LAYER left=135 top=98>
<IMG src="upper.gif" width=210 height=117 border=0>
</LAYER>
```

4. Complete the file with the </HTML> tag.

```
<HTML>
<HEAD>
<TITLE>Content on Multiple Layers</TITLE>
</HEAD>
<LAYER LEFT=25 TOP=48>
<IMG src="lower.gif" width=200 height=180 border=0>
</LAYER>
<LAYER left=135 top=98>
<IMG src="upper.gif" width=210 height=117 border=0>
</LAYER>
</HTML>
```

Figure 21.1 shows a page with overlapping images. Note that doing this previously would require reading both images into an image editing program like Photoshop and combining them into a single image.

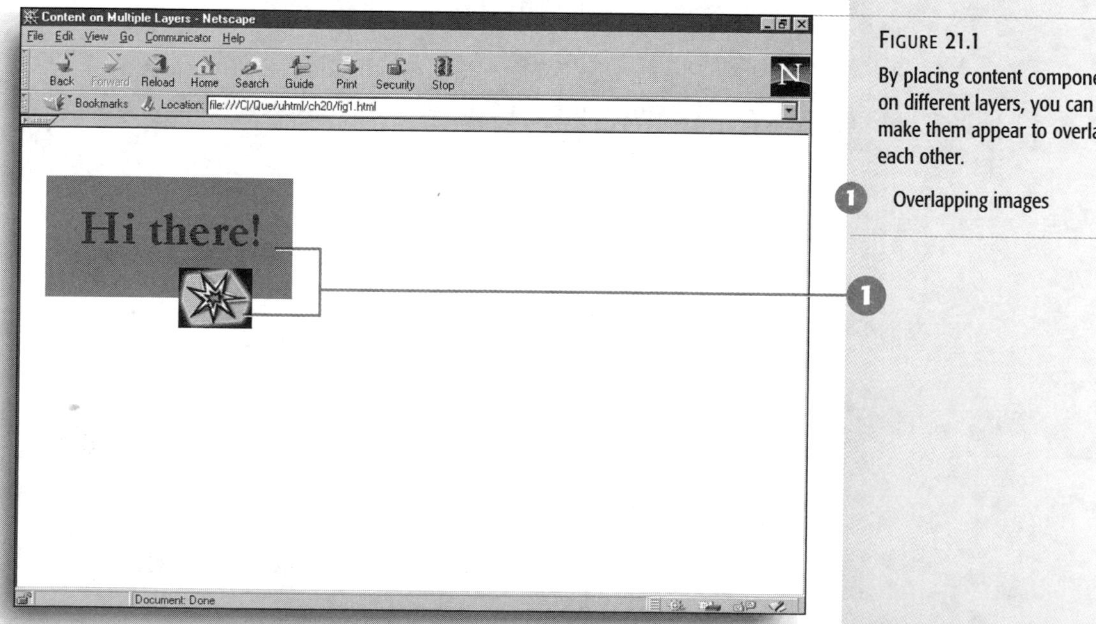

FIGURE 21.1
By placing content components on different layers, you can make them appear to overlap each other.

1 Overlapping images

Creating Nested Layers

A more advanced application of layers is to use a layer to contain other layers. In this case, the containing layer is called the parent layer. Any layers that the parent layer contains are called *child layers*.

Why nested layers?

Content developers use nested layers when they want individual chunks of content (what's placed in the child layers) and the object containing all of the content (the parent layer) to have the properties of a layer. That is, they want to modify the different layer properties (like `background`, `z-index`, and `visibility`) by using JavaScript. When you place content in individual layers, like you saw in the previous section's example, you can modify the properties of each individual layer, but you can do something that affects all of the layers simultaneously. By gathering all of the layers inside a parent layer, you can change the properties of the parent layer, thereby changing how the child layers are presented.

Setting up nested layers is a fairly easy thing to do. You simply place the `<LAYER>` and `</LAYER>` tags for each child layer between the `<LAYER>` and `</LAYER>` tags for the parent layer.

Creating nested layers

1. Begin your document with the `<HTML>` tag and create a header section so that the document has a title.

```
<HTML>
<HEAD>
<TITLE>Nested Layers</TITLE>
</HEAD>
```

2. Start the parent layer by placing its `<LAYER>` tag.

```
<HTML>
<HEAD>
<TITLE>Nested Layers</TITLE>
</HEAD>
<LAYER left=20 top=20 id="parent">
```

3. Place each of the child layers inside the parent layer. Indenting the HTML for the child layers makes it easier to read and edit later.

```
<HTML>
<HEAD>
<TITLE>Nested Layers</TITLE>
</HEAD>
<LAYER left=20 top=20 id="parent">
    <LAYER left=38 top=44 id="child1" src="child1.html">
    </LAYER>
    <LAYER left=38 top=44 id="child2" src="child2.html">
    </LAYER>
    <LAYER left=38 top=44 id="child3" src="child3.html">
    </LAYER>
...
    <LAYER left=38 top=44 id="childx" src="childx.html">
    </LAYER>
```

4. Close out the parent layer with the </LAYER> tag and then finish the document with the </HTML> tag.

```
<HTML>
<HEAD>
<TITLE>Nested Layers</TITLE>
</HEAD>
<LAYER left=20 top=20 id="parent">
   <LAYER left=38 top=44 id="child1" src="child1.html">
   </LAYER>
   <LAYER left=38 top=44 id="child2" src="child2.html">
   </LAYER>
   <LAYER left=38 top=44 id="child3" src="child3.html">
   </LAYER>
...
   <LAYER left=38 top=44 id="childx" src="childx.html">
   </LAYER>
</LAYER>
</HTML>
```

Setting Up a Layer with Relative Positioning

Creating layers that use relative positioning is no more difficult than creating them with absolute positioning. You have to use the <ILAYER> tag to create a layer with relative positioning, but since <ILAYER> takes the same attributes as <LAYER>, there's not much new to learn. Just keep in mind these few extra rules when using <ILAYER>.

- `left` and `top` specify displacement from the left of and below the point where the layer would ordinarily start, rather than from the upper-left of the browser screen.
- When using relative positioning, you can set `left` and `top` equal to negative values.

The second rule—that you can use negative values for specifying content position—usually takes some getting used to. All it really means is that you can move the content of a layer back toward the left or top edges of the browser window rather than being stuck always moving content down and to the right. The steps in the next example illustrate how to use these negative values.

Creating an inline layer

1. Begin your document with the <HTML> tag and create a header section so that the document has a title.

```
<HTML>
<HEAD>
<TITLE>An Inline Layer</TITLE>
</HEAD>
```

2. Create an absolutely positioned layer so that you can place other layers with respect to it.

```
<HTML>
<HEAD>
<TITLE>An Inline Layer</TITLE>
</HEAD>
<LAYER top=25 left=40>
<IMG src="layer1.jpg" width=222 height=136 border=0>
</LAYER>
```

3. Place the content you want positioned relative to the first layer. Remember that with relative positioning, you are computing displacement from the point where the layer would ordinarily be placed—in this case, from the point just to the right of the absolutely positioned layer and aligned with the bottom of the layer. For example, suppose you wanted the content in the relatively positioned layer to 100 pixels to the left of the reference point and 28 pixels above it. Then you would use the following:

```
<HTML>
<HEAD>
<TITLE>An Inline Layer</TITLE>
</HEAD>
<LAYER top=25 left=40>
<IMG src="layer1.jpg" width=222 height=136 border=0>
</LAYER>
<ILAYER top=-28 left=-100>
<H2>Heading positioned relative to the first layer, not
the upper left of the browser window</H2>
</ILAYER>
```

4. Finish the document with the </HTML> tag.

```
<HTML>
<HEAD>
<TITLE>An Inline Layer</TITLE>
</HEAD>
<LAYER top=25 left=40>
<IMG src="layer1.jpg" width=222 height=136 border=0>
</LAYER>
<ILAYER top=-28 left=-100>
<H2>Heading positioned relative to the first layer, not
the upper left of the browser window</H2>
</ILAYER>
</HTML>
```

Relative positioning lets you achieve an overlapping effect like the one shown in Figure 21.2.

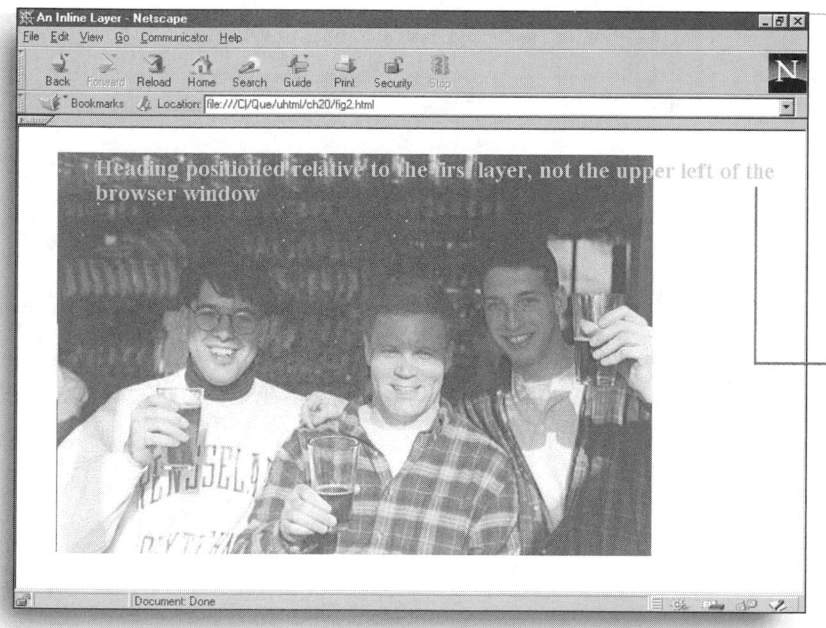

FIGURE 21.2

By positioning with respect to other layers, you can move back up and to the left on the page to place new content.

1 Text positioned with negative `top` and `left` values

Providing Alternative Content

Netscape knew it was creating proprietary tags when it introduced <LAYER> and <ILAYER>, so it also included a <NOLAYER> element for specifying non-layered versions of layered content. Netscape Navigator ignores anything between <NOLAYER> and </NOLAYER>, so it will render the previous example just fine. A browser that does not understand the layer-related tags will ignore the two <LAYER> elements and the <NOLAYER> element, and will display the HTML between the <NOLAYER> and </NOLAYER> tags.

What should you place inside the <NOLAYER> tag?

Most users of the <NOLAYER> tag will place all of the content from their layered document between the <NOLAYER> and </NOLAYER> tags. In these cases, the <NOLAYER> tag is usually followed with a <BODY> tag and then all of the necessary content. Once the content is down, you can close the alternative document with the </BODY> and </NOLAYER> tags.

To include non-layered content in your document, follow these steps.

Providing alternative content

1. Complete the layered version of your document.

```
<HTML>
<HEAD>
<TITLE>Including Non-Layered Content</TITLE>
</HEAD>
<LAYER top=12 left=24>
...
</LAYER>
...
<LAYER top=187 left=213>
...
</LAYER>
```

2. Immediately after your last </LAYER> tag, put in a <NOLAYER> tag, followed by the non-layered content.

```
<HTML>
<HEAD>
<TITLE>Including Non-Layered Content</TITLE>
</HEAD>
<LAYER top=12 left=24>
...
</LAYER>
...
<LAYER top=187 left=213>
...
```

```
</LAYER>
<NOLAYER>
<BODY bgcolor="#FFFFFF">
<H1>You're not using Netscape Navigator!</H1>
<P>This document is composed with layers.  Since you
 don't have a browser that's capable of processing
 layer, you might be interested in the<A href="nonlayer/
 index.html">non-layered version of this site</A>.</P>
```

3. Complete the document with the </NOLAYER> and </HTML> tags.

```
<HTML>
<HEAD>
<TITLE>Including Non-Layered Content</TITLE>
</HEAD>
<LAYER top=12 left=24>
...
</LAYER>
...
<LAYER top=187 left=213>
...
</LAYER>
<NOLAYER>
<BODY bgcolor="#FFFFFF">
<H1>You're not using Netscape Navigator!</H1>
<P>This document is composed with layers.  Since you
 don't have a browser that's capable of processing
 layer, you might be interested in the<A href="nonlayer/
 index.html">non-layered version of this site</A>.</P>
</NOLAYER>
</HTML>
```

Balloon Help

So far you've seen some very basic examples showing you how to set up different kinds of layers. Now it's time to put that knowledge to use and create some interesting effects on your pages.

One very popular kind of effect is a balloon help box. This kind of box pops up to explain a term or concept when a user places a mouse pointer over the text describing the term or concept. The idea is similar to that of hypertext, except that with balloon help, you don't have to click the text. You simply hold the mouse pointer over some highlighted text and the balloon help text appears.

The idea behind balloon help is fairly simple. All balloon help text is loaded into layers that are initially hidden. Then, when a user's mouse moves over some highlighted text, a JavaScript function is triggered that reveals the layer containing the balloon help for the highlighted term. When the mouse arrow no longer points to the highlighted text, the balloon help layer gets hidden again.

You can add balloon help to your pages by adapting the steps in the following example.

Adding balloon help to a page

1. Set up layers that contain the body text of the document and the balloon help text. Initially, the body text should be visible and the balloon help text should be hidden. The balloon help text layer is positioned relative to the body text layer so that the balloon will pop up close to the highlighted keyword.

```
<HTML>
<HEAD>
<TITLE>Balloon Help Text</TITLE>
</HEAD>
<LAYER visibility="SHOW">
Netscape introduced the concept of a layer with its
Netscape  Navigator 4.0 product.  Special HTML tags
allow you to create  layered Web documents.
</LAYER>
<ILAYER visibility="HIDE" top=-50 left=5>
<FONT size=-1>A layer is like a transparent sheet on
which you<BR> place your content.  Stacking these sheets
allows you to create<BR>overlapping and animation
effects.</FONT>
</ILAYER>
</HTML>
```

2. Set up the highlighted text with a visual cue, such as boldface or italics, and place it in its own layer so that you can use mouse-related event handlers with it. This layer is positioned relatively so that the words it contains will end up on the same line as the body text. Note also that the layer is given an ID so that it can be referenced later by JavaScript functions.

```
<HTML>
<HEAD>
<TITLE>Balloon Help Text</TITLE>
</HEAD>
<LAYER visibility="SHOW">
Netscape introduced the concept of a
<ILAYER id="help1">
<B><I>layer</I></B>
</ILAYER>
with its Netscape Navigator 4.0 product.  Special HTML
tags allow you to create layered Web documents.
</LAYER>
<ILAYER visibility="HIDE" top=-50 left=5>
<FONT SIZE=-1>A layer is like a transparent sheet on
which you <BR> place your content.  Stacking these
sheets allows you to create <BR> overlapping and anima-
tion effects.</FONT>
</ILAYER>
</HTML>
```

3. Set up a JavaScript routine that will reveal the balloon help text layer when the mouse pointer enters the relatively positioned layer containing the highlighted keyword.

```
<HTML>
<HEAD>
<TITLE>Balloon Help Text</TITLE>
<SCRIPT type="text/javascript">
<!--
function revealText();  {
   document.top.document.help1.visibility = "SHOW";
}
 // -->
 </SCRIPT>
```

```
</HEAD>
<LAYER visibility="SHOW" id="top">
Netscape introduced the concept of a
<ILAYER id="help1" onMouseOver="revealText();">
<B><I>layer</I></B>
</ILAYER>
with its Netscape Navigator 4.0 product.  Special HTML
tags allow you to create layered Web documents.
</LAYER>
<ILAYER visibility="HIDE" top=-50 left=5>
<FONT size=-1>A layer is like a transparent sheet on
which you<BR> place your content.  Stacking these
sheets allows you to create <BR>overlapping and
animation effects.</FONT>
</ILAYER>
</HTML>
```

4. Finally, set up a JavaScript function that will hide the balloon text layer when the mouse pointer leaves the layer containing the keyword.

```
<HTML>
<HEAD>
<TITLE>Balloon Help Text</TITLE>
<SCRIPT type="text/javascript">
<!--
function revealText();  {
   document.top.document.help1.visibility = "SHOW";
}
function hideText();  {
   document.top.document.help1.visibility = "HIDE";
}
// -->
</SCRIPT>
</HEAD>
<LAYER visibility="SHOW" id="top">
Netscape introduced the concept of a
<ILAYER id="help1" onMouseOver="revealText();"
onMouseOut= "hideText();">
```

```
<B><I>layer</I></B>
</ILAYER">
with its Netscape Navigator 4.0 product.  Special HTML
tags allow you to create layered Web documents.
</LAYER>
<ILAYER visibility="HIDE" top=-50 left=5>
<FONT size=-1>A layer is like a transparent sheet on
which you <BR> place your content.  Stacking these
sheets allows you to create <BR> overlapping and
animation effects.</FONT>
</ILAYER>
</HTML>
```

Figures 21.3 and 21.4 show the two states described in this code.

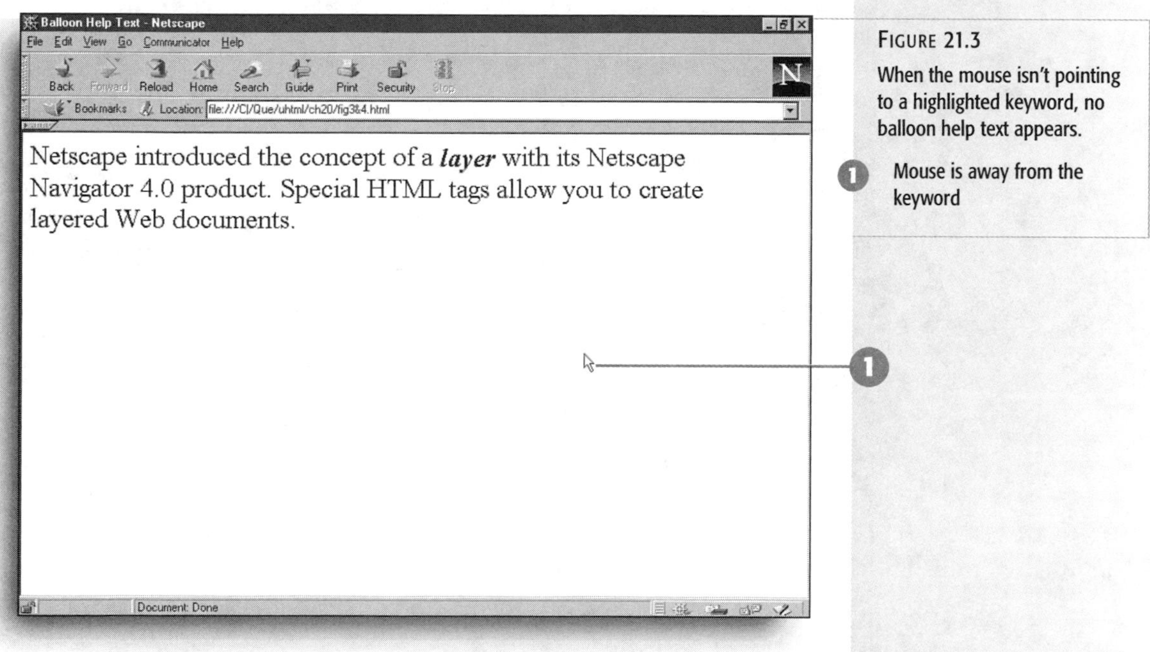

FIGURE 21.3
When the mouse isn't pointing to a highlighted keyword, no balloon help text appears.

1. Mouse is away from the keyword

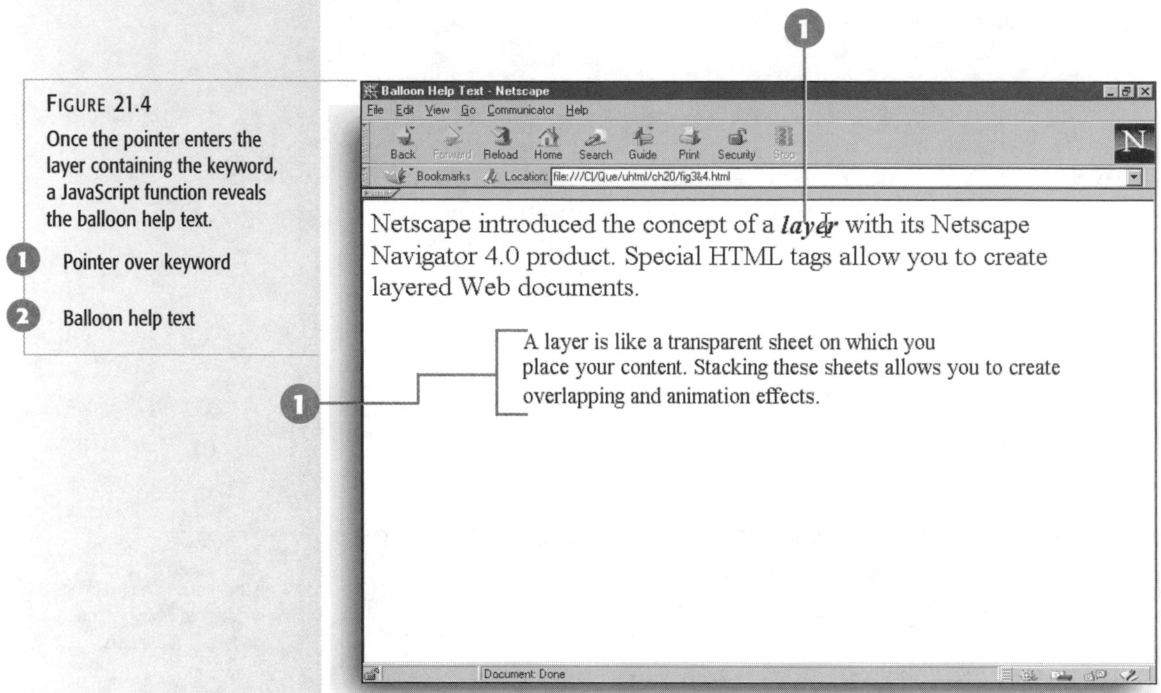

FIGURE 21.4
Once the pointer enters the layer containing the keyword, a JavaScript function reveals the balloon help text.

1. Pointer over keyword
2. Balloon help text

Animating the Page and Other Special Effects

Layers give you a number of different ways to animate content. Some approaches include the following:

- Changing the `left` or `top` property of a layer to move it around the browser screen.
- Changing the `visibility` property to selectively show and hide layers.
- Adjusting the size of the clipping region to show various parts of an entire layer.

A simple application of the first approach is detailed in the following example. By performing the steps given, you will create a layer that moves to the right across the screen.

Animating a layer

1. Set up the layer with the content that you want to animate.

```
<HTML>
<HEAD>
<TITLE>An Animated Layer</TITLE>
</HEAD>
<LAYER src="train.gif" name="train" top=10 left=0>
```

2. Write a script that will increase the `left` property of the layer after a short delay. The delay is handled by the `setTimeout` method used in a function that calls itself `layerWait`. `layerWait` continues to call itself as long as the value of the layer's `left` property is less than 600 (at which point you're getting pretty close to the right side of the screen where the animation should stop).

```
<HTML>
<HEAD>
<TITLE>An Animated Layer</TITLE>
</HEAD>
<LAYER src="train.gif" name="train" top=10 left=0>
<SCRIPT type="text/javascript">
<!--
function shiftRight() {
   document.train.left = document.train.left + 10;
}
function layerWait() {
   shiftRight();
   if (document.train.left > 600) {
      setTimeout("layerWait();",100);
   }
}
layerWait();
```

3. Be sure to complete your document by including the appropriate closing comment, `</SCRIPT>`, and `</HTML>` tags.

```
<HTML>
<HEAD>
<TITLE>An Animated Layer</TITLE>
</HEAD>
<LAYER src="train.gif" name="train" top=10 left=0>
<SCRIPT type="text/javascript">
```

```
<!--
function shiftRight() {
   document.train.left = document.train.left + 10;
}
function layerWait() {
   shiftRight();
   if (document.train.left > 600) {
      setTimeout("layerWait();",100);
   }
}
layerWait();
//  -->
</SCRIPT>
</HTML>
```

You could easily tweak these scripts to include changes to the layer's `top` property as well. This would allow you to animate in both the horizontal and vertical directions.

JavaScript has some special functions that can be very useful when creating an animation. These include the following:

- `moveTo()` Moves a layer to a new position
- `offset()` Changes the position of a layer in either the horizontal or vertical direction
- `resizeTo()` Changes the size of the clipping region

For example, you could repeatedly apply the `resizeTo()` method to gradually open up a clipping region until the entire layer is revealed.

Simulating Layers with Inline Frames and Dynamic HTML

By now, you may have created many layered documents for your site, but all of your hard work will be lost on users who aren't using Netscape Navigator 4.0 to view your pages. It's true that the `<NOLAYER>` tag lets you provide alternate content for browsers that can't process layers, but that content is not likely to be as interactive and engaging as what you placed in the layered version of your document.

In these instances, what you can do is simulate a layered document using other HTML constructs. In particular, frames used together with CSS content positioning instructions (what Microsoft calls Dynamic HTML) can come pretty close to emulating many of the effects you can create with layers. In the example in this section, you'll replicate the balloon help text feature you created with layers earlier in the chapter.

Creating balloon help text using frames and Dynamic HTML

1. Create a frameset with two frames—one that is 75% of the screen width and the another that is 25% of the screen width.

```
<HTML>
<HEAD>
<TITLE>Simulating Layers</TITLE>
</HEAD>
<FRAMESET cols="75%,25%>
</FRAMESET>
</HTML>
```

2. Populate the wider frame with the body text of the document and leave the narrower frame empty for now. Since the narrower frame will be referenced later with JavaScript, it will be important to give the frame a name.

```
<HTML>
<HEAD>
<TITLE>Simulating Layers</TITLE>
</HEAD>
<FRAMESET cols="75%,25%>
   <FRAME name="main" src="main.html" noresize>
   <FRAME name="help" src="blank.html" noresize>
</FRAMESET>
</HTML>
```

3. In the file main.html, set up keywords that are to have balloon help with `<A>` tags, using the `nohref` attribute to indicate that they aren't really linked to anything. You need to set them up with this tag so that they are accessible by the JavaScript `onMouseOver` and on `MouseOut` event handlers.

```
<P>The idea of <A nohref>frames</A> has been embraced by
 the World Wide Web Consortium and the frame tags are
 now part of standard HTML.</P>
```

4. Write a JavaScript function that will populate the frame named "help" with the appropriate balloon text when the user's mouse passes over the keyword linked in the previous step.

```
...
<SCRIPT type="text/javascript">
<!--
function showHelp(); {
   document.frames[help].src = "frame.html";
}
//  -->
</SCRIPT>
...
<P>The idea of <A nohref
 onMouseOver="showHelp():">frames</A>
 has been embraced by the World Wide Web Consortium and
 the frame tags are now part of standard HTML.</P>
```

5. Write a JavaScript function that will change the content of the frame named "help" when the user's mouse is no longer over the keyword.

```
...
<SCRIPT type="text/javascript">
<!--
function showHelp(); {
   document.frames[help].src = "frame.html";
}
function hideHelp(); {
   document.frames[help].src = "blank.html";
}
//  -->
</SCRIPT>
...
<P>The idea of <A nohref onMouseOver="showHelp():"
 onMouseOut="hideHelp();">frames</A> has been embraced
 by the World Wide Web Consortium and the frame tags
 are now part of standard HTML.</P>
```

The document object model (DOM)

The use of frames and Dynamic HTML to simulate the effects created by layers is possible because of the browser document object model (DOM), which allows you to access various parts of a document and treat them as objects. This means you can alter their properties or apply methods to them so that they change.

The World Wide Web Consortium is working to standardize the DOM. You can read more about this effort at their Web site `http://www.w3c.org/`.

CHAPTER 22

Dynamically Changing Style

- Choose what you want to accomplish first
- Learn to create the basic document with HTML
- Add style elements to your Web page
- How to use scripts to modify style
- How to handle browser differences
- Make style decisions at load time
- Use interactive style controls to accommodate user preferences

Choosing What You Want to Accomplish

HTML 4 includes features that enable dynamic interaction in Web pages. You can dramatically change a Web page when your readers interact with the page. There are infinite possibilities made available to you. So you must choose what you want to accomplish through creating dynamic content. Ask yourself, "Why do I want to change a Web page after delivery?" Here are some reasons for your consideration:

- To provide feedback to a reader
- To add emphasis to a specific area in the Web page
- To animate the Web page
- To show content in a specific order
- To keep a reader's interest
- To allow for reader customization

All these reasons are valid. Sometimes a simple style change is all you need to add to your Web page to make it more aesthetically pleasing. This chapter is about dynamic style changes. You can quickly apply style changes to content you created a year ago when following the HTML 3 specification. Just follow three easy steps:

1. Create the basic document with HTML.
2. Add style elements to your text elements.
3. Add scripts that change style dynamically.

Creating the Basic Document with HTML

Starting with a basic HTML document

1. Start with the following simple example that demonstrates adding dynamic style change to a stale, static Web page. Create a simple Web page that places two words in a table: Yes and No.

```
<HTML>
<HEAD>
<TITLE>A simple dynamic style change</TITLE>
```

```
</HEAD>
<BODY>
<TABLE>
<TR><TD>Yes</TD></TR>
<TR><TD>No</TD></TR>
</TABLE>
</BODY>
</HTML>
```

2. This code shows the simple Web page with no frills.
3. You are now ready to add additional attributes.

Identifying tags for dynamism

1. In order to change the style of some text on a Web page, you add `id` attributes to the text elements you want to dynamically change. In the case of the previous code, both table cells contain text you might want to dynamically change. Add `id` attributes to the opening `<TD>` tags of each table cell to make the cells available for dynamic change. `id` attributes expect text strings as values. Use values that make sense. Try the following:

```
<HTML>
<HEAD>
<TITLE>A simple dynamic style change</TITLE>
</HEAD>
<BODY>
<TABLE>
<TR><TD id="C1">Yes</TD></TR>
<TR><TD id="C2">No</TD></TR>
</TABLE>
</BODY>
</HTML>
```

2. In this code, you have created two document objects: a table cell named `C1` and a table cell named `C2`. In official HTML 4 talk, you have "named" two text "elements." Naming the text elements you want to change is an important first step.
3. Next, you apply style to your two text elements.

Adding Style Elements

There exist two popular ways to add styles to your text elements. You can create a <STYLE></STYLE> tag pair near the top of your HTML document and define your styles within that tag pair. Alternatively, for a simple style change, you can add styles directly within your existing tags through the use of the `style` attribute.

Adding style elements

1. Try the second approach here. To create a red, 12-point, italicized style for the table cell named `C1`, you add a

```
style="font-size:12pt; color:rgb(0,255,0);
font-style:italic;"
```

   attribute within the `<TD id="C1">` tag. To create a blue, 12-point, italicized style for the table cell named `C2`, you add a

```
style="font-size:12pt; color:rgb(255,0,0); font-
style:italic;"
```

   attribute within the `<TD id="C2">` tag. Your simple style change should look like the following code. Figure 22.1 shows your Web page created from this code.

```
<HTML>
<HEAD>
<TITLE>A simple dynamic style change</TITLE>
</HEAD>
<BODY>
<TABLE>
<TR><TD id="C1" style="font-size:12pt; color:rgb
(0,255,0); font-style:italic;" >Yes</TD></TR>
<TR><TD id="C2" style="font-size:12pt; color:rgb
(255,0,0); font-style:italic;" >No</TD></TR>
</TABLE>
</BODY>
</HTML>
```

2. You could attain the exact same results by using a <STYLE></STYLE> tag pair in your code. In that case, your Web page would appear as the following code:

```
<HTML>
<HEAD>
<TITLE>A simple dynamic style change</TITLE>
</HEAD>
```

```
<BODY>
<STYLE type="text/css">
.greensmall  {color:rgb(0,255,0);
               font-size:12pt;
               font-style:italic;}
.redsmall     {color:rgb(255,0,0);
               font-size:12pt;
               font-style:italic;}
</STYLE>
<TABLE>
<TR><TD id="C1" class="greensmall" >Yes</TD></TR>
<TR><TD id="C2" class="redsmall" >No</TD></TR>
</TABLE>
</BODY>
</HTML>
```

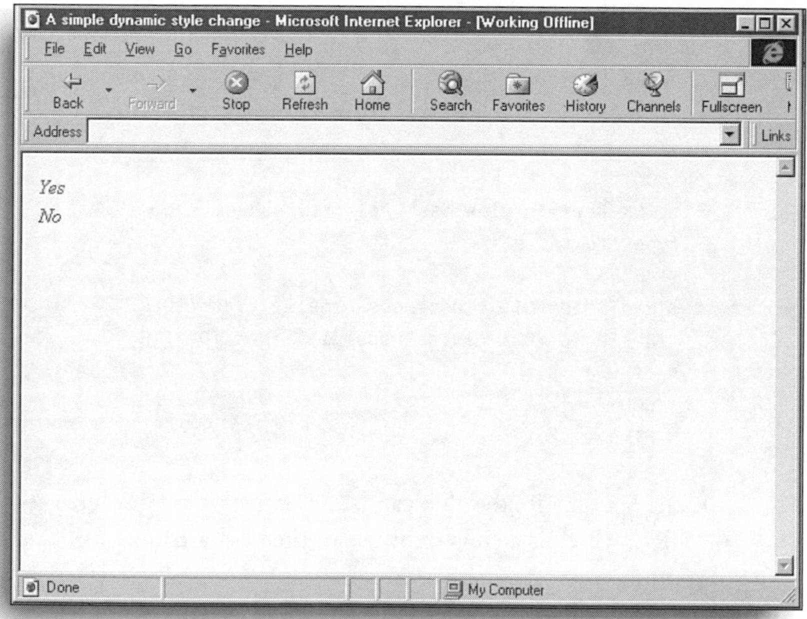

FIGURE 22.1
A simple Yes/No Web page.

You can assign a class name to each unique style defined in the `<STYLE></STYLE>` tag pair throughout your HTML documents. In the previous code, you created a class named `greensmall` by putting a period in front of the class name you wanted to use. You also created a class named `redsmall`.

Within the table data open tag, you used the class attribute and specified the appropriate class name as its value. The style for each table cell was then derived from the appropriate class definition in the STYLE element. Note that in this chapter, your style syntax follows the Cascading Style Sheet syntax introduced in Chapter 13, "Using Cascading Style Sheets to Define Appearance."

3. There is a third way you can add styles to your Web page. You can use a style sheet. With a style sheet, you can easily reuse the same styles for multiple Web pages. If you were to take the STYLE element from the previous code example and place it in a file you name styles.css (without the <STYLE> </STYLE> tags), you could then apply that style sheet to any HTML file through the <LINK> tag. The following demonstrates the use of the <LINK> tag:

```
<HTML>
<HEAD>
<TITLE>A simple dynamic style change</TITLE>
</HEAD>
<BODY>
<LINK href="styles.css" rel="stylesheet"
type="text/css">
<TABLE>
<TR><TD id="C1" class="greensmall" >Yes</TD></TR>
<TR><TD id="C2" class="redsmall" >No</TD></TR>
</TABLE>
</BODY>
</HTML>
```

The href attribute value can be a relative or an absolute URL, which is a consistent use of the href attribute as within your <IMG> tags.

The code examples in this chapter use the Cascading Style Sheet (CSS) standard, which is very popular. Other style sheet standards can be used similarly, but the value of the type attribute should reflect the standard you use.

Other examples of defining styles

1. Before dynamically changing the styles in the previous examples, try defining some different styles following the CSS

standard. Try creating a white text paragraph named `PG1` with a blue background, 20-point font, and justified alignment. Such a style should would look like the following:

```
<P id="PG1" style="color:rgb(255,255,255);
     background:rgb(0,0,255);
     font-size:12pt;
     text-align: justify">
```

as a `style` attribute within the `<P>` tag for a paragraph named `PG1`, or as a `STYLE` element like the following:

```
<STYLE>
P {"color:rgb(255,255,255);
     background:rgb(0,0,255);
     font-size:12pt;
     text-align: justify }
</STYLE>
```

In this case, your style would be applied to all paragraphs since you put the `P` identifier in front of the style instead of class name preceded by a period. Try another one. Create a style for a division named `DIV6` that contains purple text that is centered, boldfaced, and uses a small caps font variant. Such a style would look like

```
<DIV id="DIV6" style="color:rgb(80,0,80);font-variant:
small-caps; text-align: center;font-style:bold;">
```

as a `style` attribute within the `<P>` tag for a paragraph named `PG1`, or as a `STYLE` element like the following:

```
<STYLE>
DIV.purple {"color:rgb(80,0,80);
     font-variant: small-caps;
     text-align: center;
     font-style:bold }
</STYLE>
```

2. In this case, your style would be applied to all `DIV` elements that include a `class=purple` attribute. The style would not be applied to any other element types.
3. Now you are ready to add scripts to your Web pages.

Using Scripts to Modify Style

With your styles properly defined within the contents of your HTML file, you can turn to adding dynamic style changes by writing appropriate scripts. A script is a sequential list of lines of code that a computer runs from top to bottom (and occasionally loops around or skips lines conditionally). The scripts you write in this chapter are specific to changing elements within an HTML document. Scripts can also calculate mathematical formulas, interface to other sources of information, or respond only at certain times on certain dates.

A very popular scripting language on the Web is JavaScript. JavaScript was created to be a reliable, cross-platform, computer language—ideal for the Web. You will write JavaScript scripts in this chapter, but you can consider other scripting languages in other situations. The scripts you write take advantage of the names and attributes you establish within the confines of your HTML tags. The HTML 4 specification located at the World Wide Web Consortium's Web site (`http://www.w3c.org/MarkUp/`) identifies 18 events you can use to initiate dynamic style changes. The following examples use just a few popular ones.

Browsers are different

Note that the dynamic style changes in most of the following examples in this chapter closely follow the HTML 4 recommendation. The latest version of Internet Explorer available from Microsoft at press time includes the functionality necessary to see the intended effect. Netscape Communicator 4.04, the latest version available from Netscape at press time, does not include the functionality necessary to see the intended effect. Later in the chapter, however, there is an example that shows an alternate method for providing dynamic style changes as promoted by Netscape.

Adding scripts that modify style

1. Start with a minimal example. Write a script that changes the `C1` table cell style from red to blue when a reader clicks the contents of the cell. Your scripts will always appear within a `<SCRIPT></SCRIPT>` tag pair. Add a `type` attribute to the open `<SCRIPT>` tag to identify the scripting language you are using for the script. You can include multiple functions in the same `SCRIPT` element. The following is your first script:

```
<HTML>
<HEAD>
<TITLE>A simple dynamic style change</TITLE>
</HEAD>
<BODY>
<TABLE>
<TR><TD id="C1" style="font-size:12pt; color:rgb
```

```
(0,255,0); font-style:italic;" >Yes</TD></TR>
<TR><TD id="C2" style="font-size:12pt; color:rgb
(255,0,0); font-style:italic;" onclick=
"RedToBlue();">No</TD></TR>
</TABLE>
<SCRIPT type="text/javascript" >
function RedToBlue() {
     C2.style.color= "rgb(0,0,255)";
}
</SCRIPT>
</BODY>
</HTML>
```

This code sets up the `onclick` event for table cell `C2` by adding an `onclick="RedToBlue();"` attribute within its `<TD>` tag. Pay close attention to the syntax. The attribute name must be the same as one of the 18 standard events identified by the HTML specification. The attribute value is for you to decide. You will use the attribute value as a function name in one of your scripts.

2. The previous code also contains a single script function within a `<SCRIPT></SCRIPT>` tag pair. Notice that the name of the function, `RedToBlue()`, is the exact same as the `onclick` attribute value in the `<TD>` tag for `C2` table cell. Remember to refer back to Chapter 20, "Using a Scripting Language," for more information on scripting languages.

You are now ready to try a second scripting example.

A second style modifying script

1. Now try adding a second script function named `GreenToBlue()`, which enables a double-click event for table cell `C1`. The double-click event changes the cell contents from the color green to blue. The following is a possible solution:

```
<HTML>
<HEAD>
<TITLE>A simple dynamic style change</TITLE>
</HEAD>
```

```
<BODY>
<TABLE>
<TR><TD id="C1" style="font-size:12pt; color:
rgb(0,255,0); font-style:italic;" ondblclick=
"GreenToBlue();">Yes</TD></TR>
<TR><TD id="C2" style="font-size:12pt; color:
rgb(255,0,0); font-style:italic;" onclick=
"RedToBlue();">No</TD></TR>
</TABLE>
<SCRIPT type="text/javascript" >
function GreenToBlue() {
      C1.style.color= "rgb(0,0,255)";
}
function RedToBlue() {
      C2.style.color= "rgb(0,0,255)";
}
</SCRIPT>
</BODY>
</HTML>
```

2. Note how similar the `GreenToBlue()` function appears to the `RedToBlue()` function. The difference is that table cell `C1` enables an `ondblclick` event instead of the `onclick` event and the object name in the script functions differ as `C1` and `C2` respectively.

Now it's time to consider some of the terminology related to scripting.

The details of how a computer program treats components of an object is called an object model. The HTML 4 object model is much more robust than the HTML 3 model when considering the treatment of the document object. You often will see references to the DOM, Document Object Model, when you read the online HTML 4 specification provided at `http://www.w3c.org/MarkUp/`. The details of how a computer program responds to input from attached devices (keyboards, mice, and so on) is called an event model. An *event model* specifies how input signals should be treated relative to the underlying document model. HTML 4 Web browsers specify both the source of the event (mouse click, key press, mouse double-click, and so on) and the object focus of the event when running a process that responds to the event.

You can take advantage of the fact that your scripts have access to the object focus of the event. You saw in the previous example that both script functions turn text to red. Through having access to the object that is the source of the event, you can write a single function that turns the event's source object red. The following example uses the event object source technique:

```
<HTML>
<HEAD>
<TITLE>A simple dynamic style change</TITLE>
</HEAD>
<BODY>
<TABLE>
<TR><TD id="C1" style="font-size:12pt; color:rgb(0,255,0);
font-style:italic;" ondblclick="ToBlue();">Yes</TD></TR>
<TR><TD id="C2" style="font-size:12pt; color:rgb(255,0,0);
font-
style:italic;" onclick="ToBlue();">No</TD></TR>
</TABLE>
<SCRIPT type="text/javascript" >
var src
function ToBlue() {
     src = window.event.srcElement;
     src.style.color= "rgb(0,0,255)";
}
</SCRIPT>
</BODY>
</HTML>
```

Creating another scripting example

1. Go ahead and try another example. Create a Web page with dynamic style changes. Your page should contain the word DYNAMIC, where each letter in the word is enclosed within a `<SPAN></SPAN>` tag pair. Add `onmouseover` events to each letter that dynamically italicize the letter. Add an `onclick` event to the letter D that resets the word to normal font.

```
<HTML>
<HEAD>
<TITLE>A simple dynamic style change</TITLE>
</HEAD>
<BODY>
<SPAN id="D" style="font-size:48pt; font-style:normal;"
 onmouseover="Italicize();" onclick="Reset();">D</SPAN>
<SPAN id="Y" style="font-size:48pt; font-style:normal;"
onmouseover="Italicize();">Y</SPAN>
<SPAN id="N" style="font-size:48pt; font-style:normal;"
onmouseover="Italicize();">N</SPAN>
<SPAN id="A" style="font-size:48pt; font-style:normal;"
onmouseover="Italicize();">A</SPAN>
<SPAN id="M" style="font-size:48pt; font-style:normal;"
onmouseover="Italicize();">M</SPAN>
<SPAN id="I" style="font-size:48pt; font-style:normal;"
onmouseover="Italicize();">I</SPAN>
<SPAN id="C" style="font-size:48pt; font-style:normal;"
onmouseover="Italicize();">C</SPAN>
<SCRIPT type="text/javascript" >
var src
function Italicize() {
      src = window.event.srcElement;
      src.style.fontStyle= "italic";
}
function Reset() {
      D.style.fontStyle= "normal";
      Y.style.fontStyle= "normal";
      A.style.fontStyle= "normal";
      N.style.fontStyle= "normal";
      M.style.fontStyle= "normal";
      I.style.fontStyle= "normal";
      C.style.fontStyle= "normal";
}
</SCRIPT>
</BODY>
</HTML>
```

2. Figure 22.2 shows your Web page when it initially loads in the Web browser or after a reader clicks the letter D. Figure 23.3 shows the same page after a reader has passed the mouse over the letters D, N, A, and C.

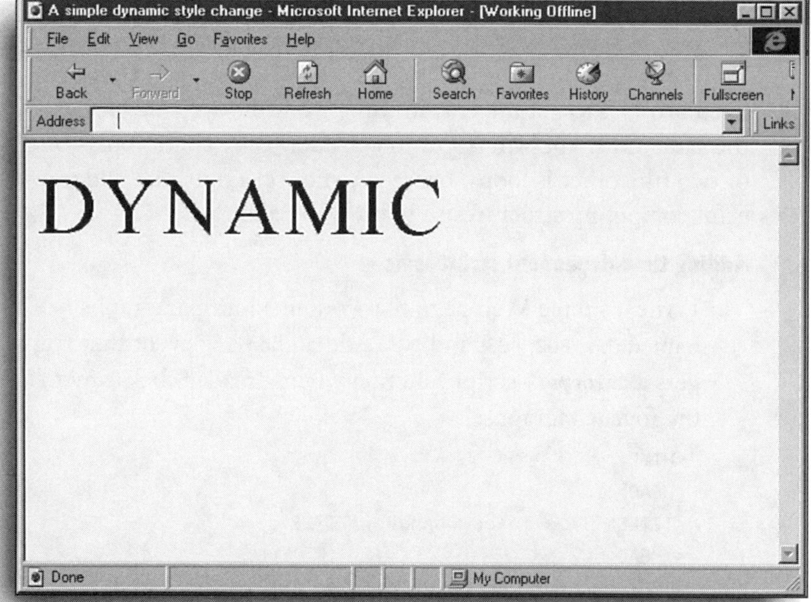

FIGURE 22.2
Your DYNAMIC Web page at load time.

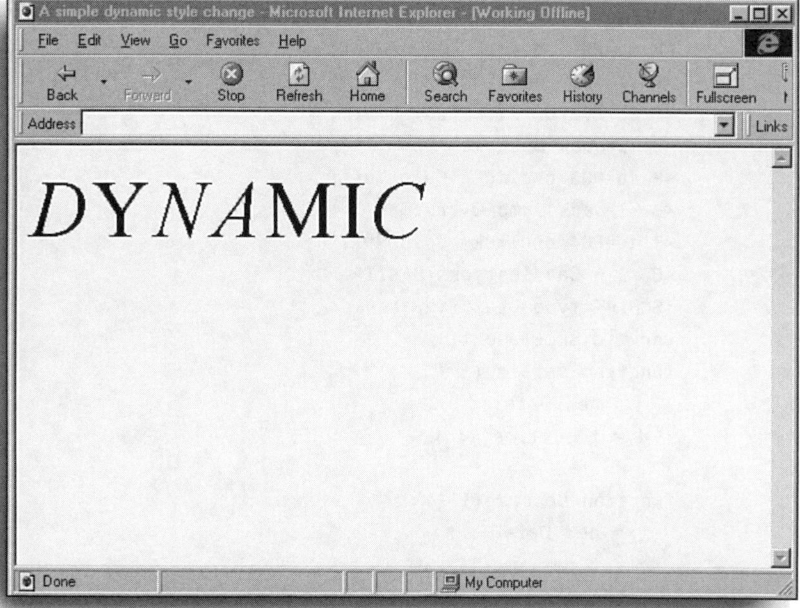

FIGURE 22.3
Your DYNAMIC Web page after reader interaction.

Your scripts have access to all kinds of interesting Web browser features. For your next style change, you will take advantage of a Web browser's time service. A time service allows you to ask the Web browser to get the current time from the system clock. At the same time, you will begin to consider using conditions—one of two (the other is loops) characteristics of scripts that add powerful computing structures to your Web pages.

Adding time-dependent script logic

1. Write a simple Web page that contains four paragraphs named `PG1`, `PG2`, `PG3`, and `PG4`. Add an `onclick` event that triggers a `ColorMe()` script function when a reader clicks any of the four paragraphs:

```
<HTML>
<HEAD>
<TITLE> Time Based Changes</TITLE>
</HEAD>
<BODY bgcolor="#FFFFFF" onload="setTime();">
<H2>Time Based Changes</H2>
<HR>
<BR>
<P id=PG1 onclick="ColorMe();">
<B><I>Jack Be Nimble</B></I>
<P id=PG2 onclick="ColorMe();">
<B><I>Jack Be Quick</B></I>
<P id=PG3 onclick="ColorMe();">
<B><I>Jack Jump Over</B></I>
<P id=PG4 onclick="ColorMe();">
<B><I>A Candlestick</B></I>
<SCRIPT type="text/javascript" >
var t,d,srcElement;
function setTime() {
  t = new Date();
  d = t.getTime();
}
function ColorMe() {
  t = new Date();
  d = t.getTime() - d;
  srcElement = window.event.srcElement;
  if (d<4000) {
     srcElement.style.color= "rgb(200,0,0)";
  } else if (d<8000){
```

```
      srcElement.style.color= "rgb(0.200,0)";
   } else if (d<12000){
      srcElement.style.color= "rgb(0,0,200)";
   } else if (d<16000){
      srcElement.style.color= "rgb(0,200,200)";
   } else {
      srcElement.style.color= "rgb(100,0,100)";
   }
   d = t.getTime();
}
</SCRIPT>
<HR>
</BODY>
</HTML>
```

2. To access a computer's system clock within a script, you create a `Date` object and access the current time from that `Date` object's `getTime()` method. A method is a function that belongs to a specific object. The script in the previous code measures the time between a reader's mouse clicks and then changes the color of the text the reader has clicked, based on the amount of time that has passed. The variable `d` holds the amount of time that passes between mouse clicks. The `getTime()` method returns the current time in milliseconds, so `d` also uses milliseconds as its unit of measure. A millisecond is one-thousandth of a second.

   If you want to respond to a reader's first mouse click and measure the time that has passed since the Web page finished loading, you can set the current time through an `onload` event. The `onload` event becomes active when the Web page finishes loading completely. In the previous code example, the `onload="setTime();"` attribute on the opening `<BODY>` tag does the job of setting up the timing for the first mouse click.

3. Figure 22.4 shows your time-aware Web page after a reader has clicked the second and fourth lines, and the color has changed in response to the time that passed between mouse clicks.

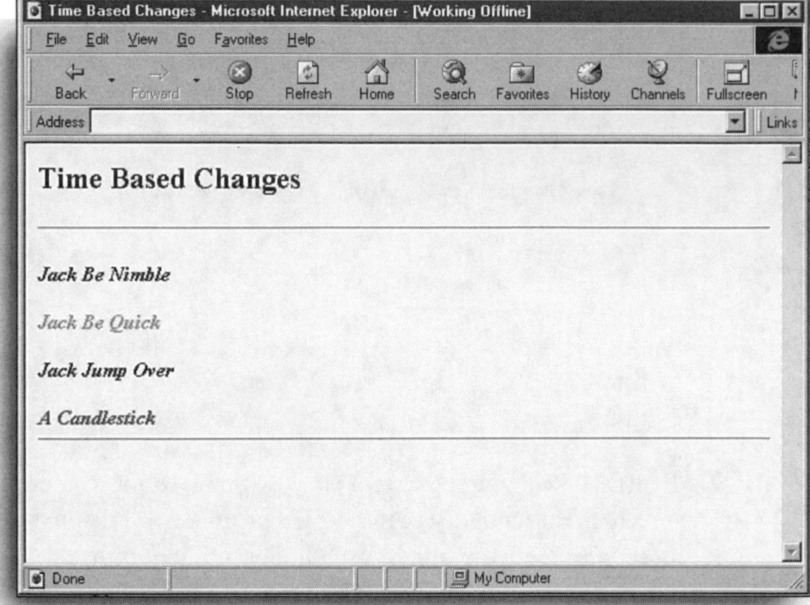

FIGURE 22.4
Your time-aware Web page.

You can use conditions (`if` statements) to provide many interesting effects on your Web pages. Web pages can check the current state of one element on the page and respond differently depending on its condition. Consider the following snippet of code:

```
if (C1.style.fontSize=16) {
      C2.style.fontSize=16;
  } else if (d<8000){
      C2.style.fontSize=24;
  }
```

In this case, you check the current state of the element named `C1`. If `C1` currently has a font size of 16 points, you set the element named `C2` to a 16-point font as well. If `C1` is not 16 points, `C2`'s font becomes 24-points. Using a conditional statement, you can check to see if a reader has chosen the right answer to a multiple choice question and respond with a style change that rewards the reader only if he or she has answered correctly.

You will use loops in your scripts to provide dynamic movement of items on the Web page. Loops can appear as in the following script function snippet.

```
while(C1.style.fontSize<16) {
      -- do something interesting ---
}
```

Loops and conditions in unison extend a script's potential. You may notice that loops include a condition that determines when the loop should end. In this case, the loop would continue until element `C1` increased its font size to more than 16 points.

Handling Browser Differences

The scripts you write can take advantage of whatever objects and services are available from the Web browsers your readers use to surf the Web. Not all browsers support the same services, although the basic HTML 4 services should eventually (hopefully soon) appear in the most popular browsers. If the past 18 months are any indication, you can expect Microsoft to keep adding new features to their Internet Explorer browser that stay ahead of the standard setting process. Microsoft realizes that many of the features of their Visual Basic development platform are appropriate for Web pages as well as applications. Re-engineering Visual Basic tools in order to generate Web page scripts would appear not to be very difficult.

Since Netscape is not as active in the HTML 4 specification setting process, many of its features may continue to be unique to the Communicator Web browsing package. Consider the unique opportunities provided by Netscape and Microsoft carefully, and try your best to make sure that using features in one browser does no harm to the presentation of that Web page in another browser.

Special Netscape Features

As introduced in Chapter 20, Netscape provides some very interesting features centered around its `<LAYER></LAYER>` tag pair, which is available for use with Netscape's Communicator 4.x Web browser. The `LAYER` element allows you to embed standard HTML tags within its tags. By including multiple layers on a Web page, you can provide style changes similar to the examples you created in the last five examples in this chapter. Try creating a simple layer by embedding a simple P element within a <LAYER></LAYER> tag pair. Make the text in your paragraph 24 points and red colored.

Your layer should look similar to the following LAYER element.

```
<LAYER>
<P><FONT size=24 color=#ff0000>
This is my favorite color
</FONT></P>
</LAYER>
```

This LAYER element creates a simple paragraph with 24-point green font, and the text `This is my favorite color`. Just by using a LAYER element, you have registered the layer as an object to Netscape Communicator's document model. By including scripts in the same Web page in which this layer resides, you can dynamically change the attributes of the layer. A layer has a TOP attribute that you can set to position a layer relative to the top of the current browser window. A layer has a `left` attribute you can set to position a layer relative to the left of the current browser window. A layer also has a `visibility` attribute you can use to hide and show the layer at different times and under different conditions.

Of interest in Netscape's LAYER element implementation is the fact that the Web page's document object automatically knows so much about the layers contained in its document without you, the author, having to explicitly tell the browser what is happening. For example, if you contain two layers in the same Web page, Netscape's browser will register the first layer it encounters while reading the HTML file from top-to-bottom, left-to-right, as layer `0`, and the next it encounters as layer `1`. The fact that the Web browser already has a way to distinguish the layers is very helpful when you write scripts to move the layers around.

Using layers for dynamic style changes

1. Try using layers in a dynamic style change Web page. To create dynamic style changes with layers that appear similar to the HTML 4 specification's method, you create two layers with different styles and alternate their visibility in response to a reader's actions. The following code shows an example of using layers to provide dynamic style change:

```
<HTML>
<HEAD>
<TITLE>Netscape's Layers</TITLE>
</HEAD>
<SCRIPT type="text/javascript" >
function showLayer() {
   if(document.layers[0].visibility=="show") {
      document.layers[0].visibility = "hide";
      document.layers[1].visibility = "show";
   } else {
      document.layers[1].visibility = "hide";
      document.layers[0].visibility = "show";
   }
}
function initializeLayers () {
   document.layers[0].visibility = "show";
   document.layers[1].visibility = "hide";
}
</SCRIPT>
<BODY onLoad="initializeLayers()">
<LAYER>
<P><FONT size=24 color=#ff0000>
This is my favorite color
</FONT></P>
</LAYER>
<LAYER>
<P><I><FONT size=36 color=#00ff00>
This is my favorite color
</FONT></I></P>
</LAYER>
<LAYER top=200 left=0>
<FORM>
<INPUT type="button" value="Change"
onClick="showLayer()">
</FORM>
</LAYER>
</BODY>
</HTML>
```

In this example, you create two layers, each of which contains a simple paragraph. One paragraph is red with 24-point font. The other is green, 36-point, and italic. When the Web page finishes loading, the `onLoad` event runs the `initializeLayers()`

script function which makes the red paragraph (contained in layer `0`) visible but hides the green paragraph. Figure 22.5 shows the Web page when it initially loads.

FIGURE 22.5
Your Web page with layers.

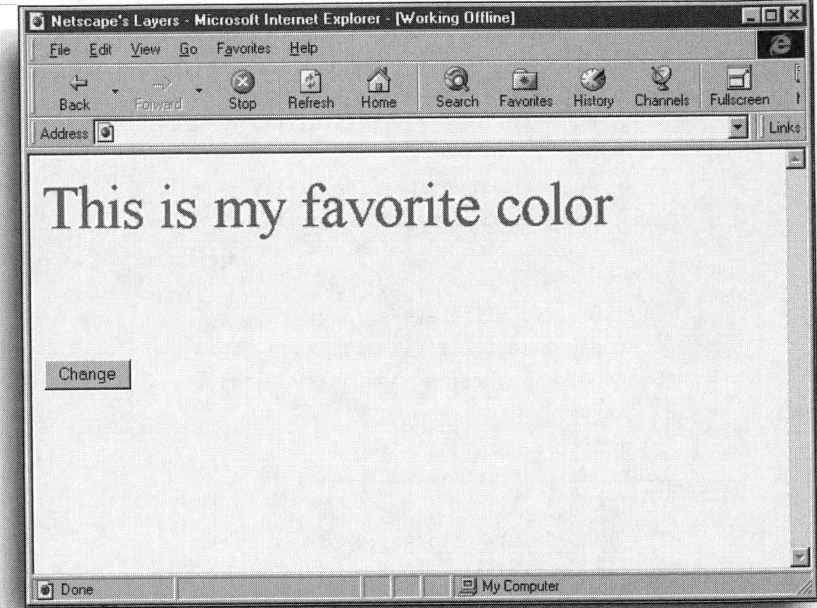

2. When a reader clicks on the **Change** button, the `showLayer()` script function runs. The `showLayer()` function changes the visible layer, depending on which layer is currently visible. Note that the button is part of a `FORM` element that is inside a third layer. You can use a layer solely to place certain Web page components in a specific location on the Web page through a `LAYER` element's `top` and `left` attributes. In this case, the form is placed at location (0,200) relative to the upper-left corner of the Web browser window.

You can think of layers as actors that come and go (and move around) on a stage called a visible Web page. With layers, you become the choreographer as well as the author of Web page content.

Special Internet Explorer Features

Most of the methods for providing dynamic style changes included in Microsoft's Internet Explorer 4.0 Web browser are also incorporated into the HTML 4 specification maintained by the World Wide Web Consortium (W3C). Layers are not included in the HTML 4 specification, nor are they included in the Internet Explorer 4.0 Web browser. Microsoft's list of implemented events goes beyond the 18 events specified in the HTML 4 specification, but many of those events are only significant when working with an external data source such as a relational database within an HTML form.

If you believe that the W3C should have the authority to specify Web page standards through the HTML specification, you won't consider Internet Explorer's dynamic style features "special" since they comply with the current recommendation for HTML 4. They are special in the fact that the current Netscape Web browser does not follow the HTML 4 recommendation and will not show Microsoft's dynamic style change content. All the examples you created in this chapter, except for the layers example, work as intended in the Internet Explorer 4.0 final release Web browser. The layers example works as intended only in Netscape Communicator 4.x.

Making Style Decisions at Load Time

The dynamic style change examples you have created up to this point have defined styles within the `style` attribute of a text element. Remember that you could have just as easily defined your styles within `<STYLE></STYLE>` tag pairs or in external style sheets. If you use external style sheets to define your styles, an interesting situation develops. The styles used in a Web page are dependent on information from outside that Web page's HTML file. If you think that through, you will realize that you lose a lot of control if someone else controls the style sheet file's contents.

The W3C has high hopes for external style sheets. It hopes readers with sight impairments will be able to create their own style sheets for use with all Web pages. Sounds like a caring idea, right? But if someone else controls the style sheet (a coworker, editor, reader, and so on), your dynamic style changes might not work for your intended effect.

To do the best job of providing attractive style changes, you may have to make certain style decisions at load time based on what styles a reader is using with the current page. You have the `onload` event at your disposal for starting your load time scripts. Consider an example of making a style decision at load time. You have an inkling that some readers may want to read your page in black and white and want to check if that is the case. Your external style sheet defines a style class named `dark` which looks like

```
.dark  {color:rgb(0,255,0);
        font-size:12pt;
        font-style:italic;}
```

with green color and 12-point italic font. In your Web page, you have a paragraph that starts with a `<P id=PG4 class=standout>` tag that you want to change to dark red dynamically. But you don't want to change its color if your reader is using an external style sheet that sets the color for class `dark` to black. No problem. You add an `onload=checkDark()` attribute to your opening `<BODY>` tag and provide a `SCRIPT` element that appears as

```
<SCRIPT>
function checkDark() {
     if(PG1.style.color=="rgb(0,0,0)") {
          PG4.style.color="rgb(0,0,0)";
     }
}
</SCRIPT>
```

assuming that `PG1` includes a `class="dark"` attribute. In this case, paragraph `PG4` will not stand out compared to any other `P` elements that contain the `class=dark` attribute.

You probably realize how cumbersome load time decisions can become if you needed to check for all possible conditions. You can minimize much of the work by putting all the styles into the external style sheet and placing the responsibility for style coordination on whomever changes the styles. Perhaps you might want to have control of a couple of the style decisions within your Web page scripts. You can then code for just the most important conditions (such as making sure you don't end up with text that has the same text color and background color).

There are other load time decisions you may want to investigate that have nothing to do with styles but involve going out on the Web to get dynamic data for inclusion in your Web page. Current stock prices would be one example. You could set up a dynamic script that gets a stock quote from a stock server and then colors the quote red if the price has been falling and green if it has been rising.

Using Interactive Style Controls to Handle User Preferences

Allowing for external style sheets is one way you could pass style decision control to the reader of your Web page. You can also provide a more explicit interface through which a user could select styles. Why not use HTML form component elements to allow a reader to click style choices at any time after a Web page finishes loading? You can create a style interface through check boxes, radio buttons, text boxes, or drop-down lists.

Adding interactive style controls

1. Try including a simple interface of two drop-down list boxes that allow a reader to determine the color and size of the text in a document. Remember that you create a drop-down list box with the `<SELECT></SELECT>` tag pair by creating `OBJECT` elements for each choice in the list box. The following code shows a possible implementation of a simple interactive style interface:

```
<HTML>
<HEAD>
<TITLE>Style Interface Controls</TITLE>
</HEAD>
<BODY bgcolor="#FFFFFF">
<H2>Style Interface Controls</H2>
<FORM>
<SELECT name="colors" onchange="Change();">
<OPTION value="Black">Black
<OPTION value="Red">Red
```

```
<OPTION value="Green">Green
<OPTION value="Blue">Blue
</SELECT>
<SELECT name="size" onchange="Change();">
<OPTION value="16">16
<OPTION value="24">24
<OPTION value="36">36
</SELECT>
</FORM>
<HR>
<P ID=PG1><B><I>This is the text of my document.
You can change it by changing the current contents
of the list-boxes above, etc.
</B></I></P>
<SCRIPT type="text/javascript" >
function Change() {
    PG1.style.color= colors.value;
    PG1.style.fontSize = size.value;
}
</SCRIPT>
<HR>
</BODY>
</HTML>
```

This example contains two drop-down list controls. The first, named colors with a `name="colors"` attribute, allows a reader to choose the color of the document text. The second list-box control, named size with a `name="size"` attribute, allows a reader to choose the size of the document text. Each `OPTION` element contains a `value` attribute that defines the necessary value that the style change script needs to create the desired effect. For example, your `Red` option provides the value `"Red"` to the style changing script.

Both `SELECT` elements contain an `onchange="Change();"` attribute. The `Change()` script function will run whenever a reader changes the active choice in either drop-down list. The `Change()` script sets the color and size of the text based on the reader's choices.

2. Figure 22.6 shows the interface controls in action. The user selects a 24-point font and the font dynamically changes.

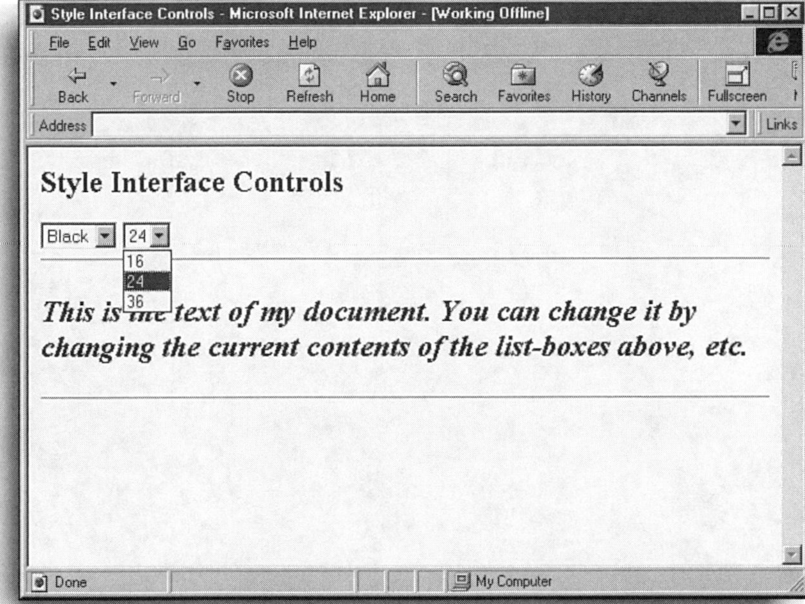

FIGURE 22.6
Your drop-down control in action.

3. Consider that you could even create a simple style interface without a single form component. You could just use the text for each option within a `SPAN` element with an `onclick` attribute that starts the `Change()` script function. For example, you could use a `<SPAN onclick="Change();">Red</SPAN>` element that changes the document text to red whenever a reader clicks on the word `Red`.

CHAPTER 23

Dynamically Changing Page Content

- Decide what content to change and how to do it
- Create a basic document with HTML
- Add the change elements to your document
- Use scripts to modify your content
- Handling browser differences

Deciding What Content Should Change and How

Start this chapter with a review of the reasons why you might consider creating dynamic Web page content.

- To provide feedback to a reader
- To add emphasis to a specific area in the Web page
- To animate the Web page
- To show content in a specific order
- To keep a reader's interest
- To allow for reader customization

Sometimes a simple dynamic style change is appropriate. Other times you want to make more dramatic changes in response to your reader's actions. Dynamic content change features let you completely replace one or more Web page elements with completely new content—new words, new graphics, and new attributes for any new elements.

There is an additional reason why you might want to consider dynamic content replacement versus static HTML 3.2 format Web pages: to take advantage of a new delivery strategy.

When you deliver content via HTML 3.2 Web pages, you add hyperlinks to your pages that allow a user to get additional information with a mouse click. Each time a reader clicks one of your hyperlinks, his or her computer connects to a Web server, requests a specific document, and waits for the document to be delivered before showing the entire document.

With HTML 4 Web pages, you can package all your content into a single .html file and dynamically present information over time in response to mouse clicks (or other HTML 4 events). Much HTML 4 content can be delivered with a single Web server connection and a single document request. Your reader only waits for a single download. No more download interruptions after the initial waiting period.

If the new HTML 4 delivery model makes sense to you, start thinking about your .html files as multiple Web pages bundled in a single file. Otherwise, think of dynamic content change as one step beyond dynamic style change—with a similar implementation.

Start with a simple dynamic content change. The following are the general steps to create a simple dynamic content change.

- Create the basic document with HTML.
- Specify the objects you want to dynamically change.
- Add scripts that change element contents dynamically.

Creating the Basic Document

Creating a basic HTML document

1. Start with a simple HTML Web page. Add a couple of elements to your home page: your picture and a caption. Make the caption reflect the emotion you express in the picture. The following code shows a possible solution for a happy emotion. Figure 23.1 shows the result of this code in a Web browser.

```
<HTML>
<HEAD>
<TITLE>A Simple Dynamic Content Change</TITLE>
</HEAD>
<BODY>
<IMG SRC="myphoto.jpg">
<H2>Me Feeling Happy<H2>
</BODY>
</HTML>
```

FIGURE 23.1
A basic HTML document.

2. Study the simplicity of the previous code.
3. You are ready to add attributes that will allow you to dynamically change either your text or your images.

Adding the Change Elements

Adding the necessary attributes

1. Now that you have created your simple Web page, add the appropriate attributes to your HTML tags in preparation for making content changes. Set up your Web page so both the photo image and the caption can change dynamically. Add an `ID=photo` attribute to your `<IMG>` tag. Place the last word of your caption within a `<SPAN></SPAN>` tag pair. Identify your emotion by adding an `ID=emotion` attribute within the opening `<SPAN>` tag.

   You have set up both your image and your caption in preparation for dynamic content change. The code should appear as the following:

```
<HTML>
<HEAD>
<TITLE>A simple dynamic content change</TITLE>
</HEAD>
<BODY>
<IMG ID=photo SRC="myphoto.jpg">
<H2>Me Feeling <SPAN ID=emotion>Happy</SPAN></H2>
</BODY>
</HTML>
```

2. You will refer to the contents of the `<IMG>` tags through the `photo` identifier. You will refer to the text representing your emotion through the `emotion` identifier.
3. You are now ready to add the scripts that make your content change.

Using Scripts to Modify Content

Adding scripts to your Web page

1. You are ready to write a script that dynamically changes the content of your Web page. Remember that your scripts are enabled through events. Choose an appropriate event. How

about a reader's mouse click? A mouse click event is enabled through the `onclick` event of the HTML 4 recommendation. Add an `onclick="Change();"` attribute to your `<IMG>` tag. Whenever a reader clicks on your photo image, the Web browser will run a script function named `Change()`.

All your dynamic content change functions belong inside of a `<SCRIPT></SCRIPT>` tag pair. In the case of your `Change()` function, you want the function to determine the current emotion being displayed in the Web browser and change the emotion appropriately. The specifics of how you determine the current state of your Web page depend on the document object model (DOM) you are using.

Microsoft's implementation of dynamic content changes allows you to check the current contents of any element through the `innerHTML` attribute of the element. To check the current HTML contents of a `SPAN` element, you investigate the current value of the `SPAN` element's `innerHTML` attribute. Netscape's implementation relies on layers, which are covered later in this chapter in a section entitled "Simulating Dynamic Content with Layers." The effect of both methods is identical.

You can use the `SRC` attribute of `IMG` elements to change the current image shown on a Web page. Use the `innerHTML` attribute to change tags that intermix images and text together.

Try creating your `Change()` script function by comparing the current `emotion.innerHTML` to a `Happy` emotion. If the `emotion.innerHTML` attribute's value is equal to `Happy`, change the photo image to a sad photo and change the caption text to `Sad`. On the other hand, if the `emotion. innerHTML` attribute's value is not equal to `Happy`, change the photo image to a happy photo and change the caption text to `Happy`. The following code shows the appropriate script as part of your dynamic content change Web page.

```
<HTML>
<HEAD>
<TITLE>A simple dynamic content change</TITLE>
</HEAD>
<BODY BGCOLOR=#ffffff>
```

```
<H2>Me Feeling <SPAN ID=emotion>Happy</SPAN></H2>
<IMG ID=photo SRC="myphoto.jpg" onclick="Change();">
<SCRIPT TYPE="text/javascript" >
function Change() {
    if (emotion.innerHTML=="Happy") {
        photo.src="myphoto1.jpg";
        emotion.innerHTML="Sad";
    } else {
        photo.src="myphoto.jpg";
        emotion.innerHTML="Happy";
    }
}
</SCRIPT>
</BODY>
</HTML>
```

2. Now, when your reader clicks on a happy photo image on your home page, the Web page dynamically changes to the screen shown in Figure 23.2.

FIGURE 23.2
A sad Web page.

3. When the reader clicks again on the photo image, the Web page dynamically changes back to the happy face seen in Figure 23.1.

To recap, the steps you follow to create dynamically changing content include:

- Creating the basic HTML document using the `ID` attribute to name your elements.
- Adding event attributes to HTML tags for the events that will trigger your content changes.
- Using scripts to dynamically change the current visible Web page content.

Try dynamically changing content for different effects through the next few sections' examples.

Handling Mouse Actions

Your readers are probably quite used to clicking on Web pages, since earlier HTML specifications relied on the mouse click for action. With HTML 4, you no longer require a reader to click on a Web page for something to happen in response. The HTML 4 specification provides you with the `onmouseover` and `onmouseout` events, which you can use to provide dynamic content changes that only require the mouse to move over and off a visible HTML element. No clicks are necessary.

Adding rollovers to your Web page

1. Try creating a simple rollover effect using the same happy face and sad face images you used in the last code example. Your page should load with a happy face that becomes sad when a reader moves the mouse over the happy face.

   You can place your script elements wherever you find them most convenient. To prove that your scripts will work in the head element as well as in the body element, place your script in the head element. Also, you can place your script functions within HTML comment delimiters to be compatible with Web browsers that do not support the JavaScript scripting language. For older browsers, your script will not work, but because you place it inside of a comment, the script's text will not appear in the Web page's body text.

The following code provides a solution that works in both Netscape Communicator 4.x and Internet Explorer 4.x.

```
<HTML>
<HEAD>
<TITLE>Image Rollover</TITLE>
<SCRIPT TYPE="text/javascript">
<!-- hide from Browsers without JavaScript support
Image1= new Image(124,156)
Image1.src = "myphoto.jpg"
Image2 = new Image(124,156)
Image2.src = "myphoto1.jpg"
function Sad() {
document.Face.src = Image2.src; return true;
}
function Happy() {
document.Face.src = Image1.src; return true;
}
// - stop the comment -->
</SCRIPT>
</HEAD>
<BODY BGCOLOR="#FFFFFF">
<CENTER>
<P>
<A HREF="http://www.mcp.com"
onmouseover="Sad()"
onmouseout="Happy()">
<IMG NAME="Face" SRC="myphoto.jpg"
WIDTH=124 HEIGHT=156 BORDER=0>
</A>
</P>
</CENTER>
</BODY>
</HTML>
```

2. The script in this code is straightforward. You initialize two variables named `Image1` and `Image2` and initialize them to the two images you use in the rollover. Your `Sad()` function

shows the sad image. Your `Happy()` function shows the happy image. You tie the two script functions to event attributes of the `A` element. You set up the `onmouseover` event attribute to trigger the `Sad()` script function and set up the `onmouseout` event attribute to trigger the `Happy()` script function.

3. Your rollover is complete and functional.

Adding a Pull-Down Menu

The following code example adds two pull-down (also known as drop-down) list boxes to a Web page in order to let a reader change styles while reading your content. You can also add a pull-down list box to let a reader select content. Your Web page can present a reader's requests dynamically without having to return to the Web for additional information.

To review, you create pull-down list boxes with `SELECT` and `OPTION` elements. The `OPTIONs` elements nest inside of the `<SELECT></SELECT>` tag pair.

Using pull-downs and dynamic content change

1. Try creating a pull-down list box that lets a reader select from the five Pacific Northwest States: Alaska, Idaho, Montana, Oregon, and Washington. Your pull-down list box should appear as follows:

```
<SELECT>
<OPTION VALUE="Alaska">Alaska
<OPTION VALUE="Idaho">Idaho
<OPTION VALUE="Montana">Montana
<OPTION VALUE="Oregon">Oregon
<OPTION VALUE="Washington">Washington
</SELECT>
```

When a reader chooses a state from the list, you want to show him or her census information for that state, along with a state image. This information is shown in Table 23.1. Create a simple Web page for the state of Alaska using the following information and the state image contained in file Alaska.jpg.

TABLE 23.1 **State census information**

State	Population	Rank	Birth Rate	% > 84 years
Alaska	550,043	5	.23	1.78
Idaho	1,006,749	3	1.13	1.41
Montana	799,065	4	1.34	1.28
Oregon	2,842,321	2	1.37	1.24
Washington	4,866,692	1	1.16	1.32

As a separate Web page, your Alaskan Web page might look like the following:

```
<HTML>
<HEAD>
<TITLE>Alaskan Web Page</TITLE>
</HEAD>
<BODY BGCOLOR="#FFFFFF">
<H2>1990 Alaskan Census Facts</H2>
<IMG SRC=alaska.jpg ALIGN=LEFT HEIGHT=128 WIDTH=128>
<P>Alaska is the 5th largest state in population in the
Pacific Northwest with 550,043 people reported in the
1990 US Census.
<P>Alaska had a birth rate of .23 percent in 1990 and
had 1.78 percent of its population over 84 years of
age.
</BODY>
</HTML>
```

Instead of creating a separate page for each state, with HTML 4 you can present your Alaska Web page along with the other four states' information in a single .html file using dynamic content changes. The following presents a possible implementation.

```
<HTML>
<HEAD>
<TITLE>Pull-down List Box Content Changes</TITLE>
</HEAD>
<BODY BGCOLOR="#FFFFFF">
```

```
<H2>Pull-down List Box Content Changes</H2>
<SELECT NAME="states" onchange="Change();">
<OPTION VALUE="Alaska">Alaska
<OPTION VALUE="Idaho">Idaho
<OPTION VALUE="Montana">Montana
<OPTION VALUE="Oregon">Oregon
<OPTION VALUE="Washington">Washington
</SELECT>
<HR>
<DIV ID=div1><B><I>Choose a state from the list above.
</B></I></P>
<SCRIPT TYPE="text/javascript">
function Change() {
    if(states.value=="Alaska") {
          div1.innerHTML="<IMG SRC=alaska.jpg
 ALIGN=LEFT HEIGHT=128 WIDTH=128>
<P>Alaska is the 5th largest state in population in the
Pacific Northwest with 550,043 people reported in the
1990 US Census.
 <P>Alaska had a birth rate of .23 percent
in 1990 and had 1.78 percent of its population over 84
years of age.";
    } else if(states.value=="Idaho") {
          div1.innerHTML="<IMG SRC=idaho.jpg
ALIGN=LEFT HEIGHT=128 WIDTH=128>
<P>Idaho is the 3rd largest state in population in the
Pacific Northwest with 1,006,749 people
reported in the 1990 US Census.
<P>Idaho had a birth rate of 1.13 percent in 1990 and
had 1.41 percent of its population over 84 years of
age.";
    } else if(states.value=="Montana") {
          div1.innerHTML="<IMG SRC=montana.jpg
ALIGN=LEFT HEIGHT=128 WIDTH=128><P>Montana is the 4th
largest state in population in the Pacific Northwest
with 799,065 people reported in the 1990 US
Census.<P>Montana had a birthrate of 1.34 percent in
1990 and had 1.28  percent of its population over 84
years of age";
    } else if(states.value=="Oregon") {
          div1.innerHTML="<IMG SRC=oregon.jpg ALIGN=LEFT
```

```
HEIGHT=128 WIDTH=128><P>Oregon is the 2nd
largest state in population in the
Pacific Northwest with 2,842,321 people reported in
the 1990 US Census.<P>Oregon had a birth
rate of 1.37 percent in 1990 and had
1.24 percent of its population over 84 years of age.";
    } else if(states.value=="Washington") {
         div1.innerHTML="<IMG SRC=washingt.jpg
ALIGN=LEFT HEIGHT=128 WIDTH=128><P>Washington is the
1st largest state in populationin the Pacific Northwest
with 4,866,692 people reported in the 1990 US
Census.<P>Washington had a birth rate of 1.16 percent
in 1990 and had 1.32 percent of its population over 84
years of age.";
    }
}
</SCRIPT>
</BODY>
</HTML>
```

2. Each state's information appears as a separate content chunk within a `SCRIPT` element. The `Change()` script function changes the state content whenever an event triggers the function to run.

   Your `SELECT` element contains an `onchange="Change();"` attribute. The `Change()` script function will run whenever a reader changes the active choice in the pull-down list box. The `Change()` script sets the visible contents based on the selection of the reader. Note in this case, the content for each state consists of an image and two paragraphs. There is no inherent limit to the size of your content chunks.

3. Figure 23.3 shows your pull-down list box control in action. The reader selects Washington and the page contents change to be Washington specific.

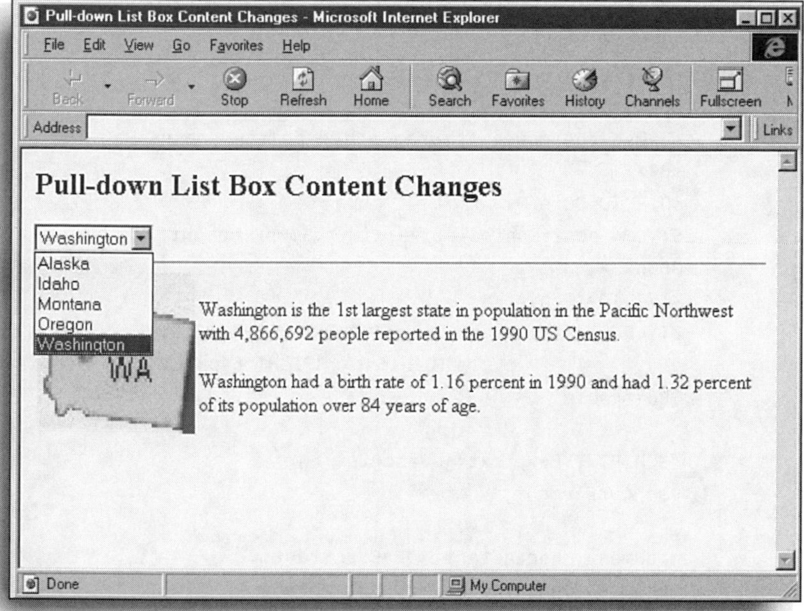

FIGURE 23.3
A pull-down list box with dynamic content change.

Installing Drag-and-Drop Controls

Microsoft's dynamic features also allow you to enable drag-and-drop controls for your Web content. With drag and drop, readers can move Web page content within an area defined by you, the author.

Adding drag-and-drop controls to a Web page

1. To enable drag-and-drop content, you first create a `DIV` element to define the drag region.
2. Create the element you want to drag within the drag region.
3. Add the appropriate `ondragstart`, `onmousedown`, `onmouseup`, and `onmousemove` functions for the Web page.
4. Register your functions from step 3 to the respective document attributes.

   The following code shows the results of following the right steps to create a drag-and-drop robin.

```
<HTML>
<HEAD>
```

```
<TITLE>Drag and Drop The Robin</TITLE>
</HEAD>
<BODY BGCOLOR="#FFFFFF">
<H2>Drag and Drop The Robin</H2>
<B>Use the mouse to drag and drop the robin</B>
<BR>
<DIV ID=OuterDiv
STYLE="position:relative;width:300px;height:
300px">
<IMG ID="robin"
STYLE="position:absolute;TOP:90px;LEFT:90px;
                WIDTH:64px;HEIGHT:64px;ZINDEX:-4;"
SRC="robin.
                jpg">
<SCRIPT TYPE="text/javascript">
var curElement;

document.ondragstart = doDragStart;
document.onmousedown = doMouseDown;
document.onmousemove = doMouseMove;
document.onmouseup = new Function("curElement=null")

function doDragStart() {
    // Don't do default drag operation.
    if ("IMG"==event.srcElement.tagName)
      event.returnValue=false;
}

function doMouseDown() {
    if ((event.button==1) &&
(event.srcElement.tagName=="IMG"))
      tx = window.event.x -
event.srcElement.style.pixelLeft;
      ty = window.event.y -
event.srcElement.style.pixelTop;
        curElement = event.srcElement;
}

function doMouseMove() {
    var newleft=0, newTop = 0
```

```
    if ((event.button==1) && (curElement!=null)) {
        // position the robin
        newleft=window.event.x - tx
        if (newleft<0) newleft=0;
        if (newleft+curElement.width >
document.all.OuterDiv.
             offsetWidth)newleft =
document.all.OuterDiv.
             offsetWidth - curElement.offsetWidth
        curElement.style.pixelLeft= newleft
        newtop=event.clientY-
document.all.OuterDiv.offsetTop-
        (curElement.offsetHeight/2)
        if (newtop<0) newtop=0;
        if (newtop+curElement.height >
document.all.OuterDiv.
        offsetHeight)newtop = window.event.y - ty
        curElement.style.pixelTop= newtop
    }
}
</SCRIPT>
</BODY>
</HTML>
```

5. Your `DIV` element named `OuterDiv` creates the area on the Web page in which your reader can drag the robin. The area will fall within the flow of the Web page and appear 300 pixels high and 300 pixels wide. The reader can drag the `IMG` element named robin within the `OuterDiv` area.

   The `doMouseDown()` script function registers where the mouse appears relative to the draggable object when the reader first presses the mouse button. The `doMouseMove()` script function checks the move relative to the allowable area. Then, upon release of the mouse, the current element is reset to `null`.

6. Figure 23.4 shows the Web page from this code after the reader drags the robin to the upper-right corner of the draggable area.

FIGURE 23.4
A drag-and-drop robin.

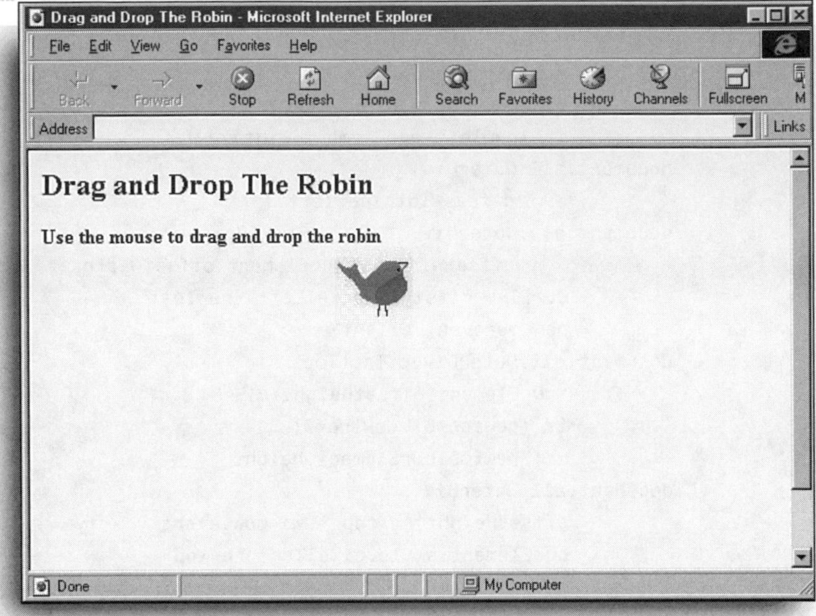

Reflow Text Based on User Choices

When you dynamically change content between two chunks of HTML tags that occupy different area sizes, the Web browser reflows the Web page to dynamically fit the content. You should test your pages to make sure the flow looks attractive no matter what combination of content a reader chooses.

You can use the Web browser's reflow feature to your advantage with a properly planned design. As a reader moves the mouse closer to an area on the page you want to give extra attention to, you can make tag and attribute decisions that grow that area. The area of focus can fill the page and cause the reflow of content around that area to move off the visible region, yet allow the reader to scroll freely to see the content later.

Animating Page Elements

You can also animate elements on a Web page by dynamically changing their position over time. Try animating three robins by changing their positions over time.

You can move images on a Web page by changing their `posTop` and `posLeft` style attributes over time. A popular animation technique is linear interpolation, where you specify key coordinates in the movement of each image and then define intermediate coordinates by adding a piece of the line between the key coordinates for each animation loop cycle.

Adding Animation

Create three `IMG` elements, each of which uses the robin.jpg bitmap file. Name the elements `robin1`, `robin2`, and `robin3`. Set the initial location of each robin image through the `TOP` and `LEFT` style attribute components. Then, by using the script function format proposed by Microsoft, create two arrays for each image, fill the arrays with your key coordinates, and then change the `posLeft` and `posTop` style attributes dynamically through a `moverobins()` script function.

The following code contains a working robins animation Web page. All the script functions listed are necessary to make animation work in the Internet Explorer 4.x Web browser. Figure 23.5 shows your robins as they near completion of the animation.

```
<HTML>
<HEAD>
<TITLE>Animating Robins</TITLE>
</HEAD>
<BODY>
<H2 ID=sg STYLE="color:Black;">Animating Robins</H2>
<IMG SRC="robin.jpg" ID=robin1 BORDER=0
STYLE="container:positioned;position:absolute;
TOP:50pt;LEFT:0px;WIDTH:64px;HEIGHT:64px;ZINDEX:1;">
<IMG SRC="robin.jpg" ID=robin2 BORDER=0
STYLE="container:positioned;position:absolute;
TOP:50pt;LEFT:142px;WIDTH:64px;HEIGHT:64px;ZINDEX:2;">
<IMG SRC="robin.jpg" ID=robin3 BORDER=0
STYLE="container:positioned;position:absolute;
TOP:50pt;LEFT:284px;WIDTH:64px;HEIGHT:64px;ZINDEX:3;">

<SCRIPT LANGUAGE=VBScript>
function window_onload()
     initialize()
```

```
end function
</SCRIPT>

<SCRIPT TYPE="text/javascript">
count = 1;
loopcount = 0;
robin1x = new Array();
robin1y = new Array();
robin2x = new Array();
robin2y = new Array();
robin3x = new Array();
robin3y = new Array();

robin1x[1] = 0;   robin1y[1] = 50;
robin1x[2] = 126; robin1y[2] = 126;
robin1x[3] = 0;   robin1y[3] = 50;
robin1x[4] = 284; robin1y[4] = 136;
robin1x[5] = 0;   robin1y[5] = 50;
robin1x[6] = 142; robin1y[6] = 146;
robin1x[7] = 284; robin1y[7] = 50;
robin1x[8] = 142; robin1y[8] = 156;
robin1x[9] = 0;   robin1y[9] = 50;

robin2x[1] = 12;  robin2y[1] = 70;
robin2x[2] = 142; robin2y[2] = 100;
robin2x[3] = 12;  robin2y[3] = 150;
robin2x[4] = 142; robin2y[4] = 76;
robin2x[5] = 204; robin2y[5] = 150;
robin2x[6] = 0;   robin2y[6] = 76;
robin2x[7] = 60;  robin2y[7] = 150;
robin2x[8] = 0;   robin2y[8] = 136;
robin2x[9] = 208; robin2y[9] = 80;

robin3x[1] = 214; robin3y[1] = 50;
robin3x[2] = 24;  robin3y[2] = 90;
robin3x[3] = 284; robin3y[3] = 100;
robin3x[4] = 0;   robin3y[4] = 176;
robin3x[5] = 142; robin3y[5] = 50;
robin3x[6] = 284; robin3y[6] = 176;
robin3x[7] = 142; robin3y[7] = 50;
robin3x[8] = 284; robin3y[8] = 176;
robin3x[9] = 142; robin3y[9] = 50;
```

```
tickTimeout = 1;
at_end = false;

function tick() {
      doTick();
      window.setTimeout("tick();", tickTimeout,
"JavaScript");
}

function doTick() {
      moverobins();
}

function initialize() {
      // really initialize
      robin1.style.visibility="visible"
      robin2.style.visibility="visible"
      robin3.style.visibility="visible"
      tick();
}

function moverobins() {
  if(!at_end){
      robin1.style.posLeft = robin1x[count] +
      ((robin1x[count+1]-robin1x[count])*loopcount/40);
      robin1.style.posTop = robin1y[count] +
      ((robin1y[count+1]-robin1y[count])*loopcount/40);
      robin2.style.posLeft = robin2x[count] +
      ((robin2x[count+1]-robin2x[count])*loopcount/40);
      robin2.style.posTop = robin2y[count] +
      ((robin2y[count+1]-robin2y[count])*loopcount/40);
      robin3.style.posLeft = robin3x[count] +
      ((robin3x[count+1]-robin3x[count])*loopcount/40);
      robin3.style.posTop = robin3y[count] +
      ((robin3y[count+1]-robin3y[count])*loopcount/40);
      if(loopcount<40) {
           loopcount=loopcount+1;
      } else {
           loopcount=0;
           if(count<8) {
                count=count+1;
           } else {
                at_end=true;
```

```
                    }
                }
            }
        }
        </SCRIPT>
        </BODY>
        </HTML>
```

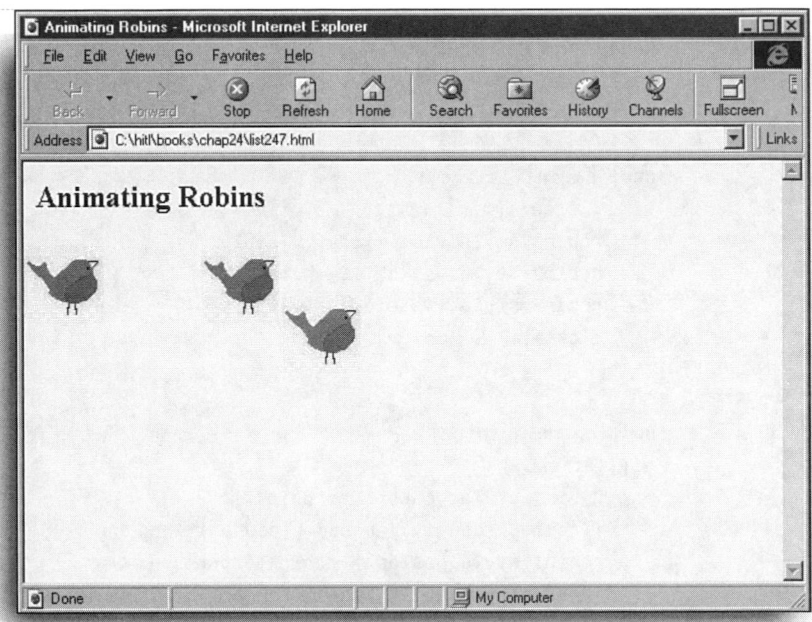

FIGURE 23.5
The three robins animation.

Rearrange a Table on Demand

Dynamic table expansion and sorting is a feature of a data presentation tool that enables variable-length data sources to automatically be presented in a table of any length. For Web browser presentation, dynamic table expansion means that you, the Web author, must identify only the first row of the table with the appropriate headers and then identify which column from the data source belongs with which header field in your table. The Web browser does the rest, dynamically creating the necessary table tags to show the complete contents of the data source.

When to use animation

Consider using animation when a Web page first loads to draw your readers' attention to the most important content of the page. Once the animation stops, you can make the animated content invisible or replace it with new content. Most readers do not like being bothered by an animation that continues running over and over again. Perhaps you see the opportunity animation offers to commercial advertisers for presenting marketing slogans and animated logos. You can use the same technique for informational purposes.

Dynamic tables are implemented in Microsoft's Internet Explorer 4.x Web browser. The dynamic table expansion feature works especially well with variable-length data sources that change over time. You do not have to change the Web page, because the Web browser does all the work in creating the appropriate tags depending on the number of records in the data source. Only the data source changes to present more recent data.

Adding a dynamic table

1. Try creating a dynamic table to present the latest standings for a fictitious baseball league. On the Web server, you would daily replace each data source's file with a file of the same name. The data source contains the latest standings for each team. Dynamic table expansion means that each league's standings are already expanded and visible on the page when the Web browser finishes loading the Web page. You give your readers the capability to dynamically sort data in a dynamically generated table.

   The Web browser reads the definition of the first table row from the <TABLE>, <TR>, and <TD> HTML tags that define the row. Then, through the attributes associated with a second row of table tags, the Web browser associates the appropriate columns from the data source with the different cells in the table. After that, the browser reads through all the data and expands the table to make room for each row of data in the data source.

   Use the data source in the following code as a representative team standings data file.

   ```
   Team,Wins:INT,Losses:INT,BA:FLOAT,ERA:FLOAT
   Tigers,16,6,.292,2.67
   Bears,14,8,.244,2.87
   Robins,13,8,.267,2.67
   Lions,11,10,.282,4.07
   Rhinos,10,10,.255,3.55
   Frogs,9,12,.264,3.88
   Sharks,8,12,.251,4.15
   Spiders,4,14,.212,3.86
   ```

2. To add dynamic table generation and sorting to your Web pages, you insert into your HTML file an <OBJECT></OBJECT> tag that enables the appropriate data binding control. The data binding control is an ActiveX control that is a part of the standard Internet Explorer 4.0 Web browser release.

Assuming you name your data source teamlist and save your data in a file named wblteam.txt, your OBJECT element should look like the following:

```
<OBJECT ID="teamlist"
        CLASSID="clsid:333C7BC4-460F-11D0-BC04-
0080C7055A83"
        BORDER="0" WIDTH="0" HEIGHT="0">
  <PARAM NAME="DataURL" VALUE="wblteam.txt">
  <PARAM NAME="UseHeader" VALUE="True">
</OBJECT>
```

3. You then create the first row of the table using a <THEAD></THEAD> tag pair. You nest the table header within a <TABLE></TABLE> tag pair. The opening <TABLE> tag needs a few attributes like where an ID attribute gives the table the name mytable and a DATASRC attribute associates the appropriate data source object with the table.

```
<TABLE BORDER="1" ID="mytable" DATASRC="#mydata">
```

The BORDER attribute defines the thickness of the border to be used between cells in the table.

4. You then create three lines after the opening <TABLE> tag to look like the following, which begins the table head with a <THEAD> tag, begins the first row with a <TR> tag, and begins the first column header cell with a <TD> tag.

```
<THEAD>
<TR>
<TD><FONT COLOR="#0000FF"><B><U><DIV
ID=col1>Name</DIV></U></B></FONT></TD>
```

Of all the tags nested within the <TD></TD> table cell tag pair, the <DIV ID=col1>Name</DIV> sequence is the most critical. The division creates an object with the name col1. Remember that a division is just another word for a section, but a division is a section that can be much smaller than a typical word processing section. You can reference col1 from any script function in order to modify the appearance or contents of the division.

The text `Name` actually appears within the table cell on the Web page. In this case, the table headings are colored blue and are boldfaced and underlined. Add some form of text formatting to the header row to make it stand out from the rest of the table.

5. For each column in your data source, add an additional `<TD></TD>` tag pair similar to the preceding example. After you declare all the column headers, close off the first table row with a `</TR>` tag, and close off the table head with a `</THEAD>` tag.

6. After the table head, you create a table body identifier by using a `<TBODY></TBODY>` tag pair. In a table with four columns, the table body identifier might look like the following:

```
<TBODY>
<TR>
<TD><DIV DATAFLD="Col1"></DIV></TD>
<TD><DIV DATAFLD="Col2"></DIV></TD>
<TD><DIV DATAFLD="Col3"></DIV></TD>
<TD><DIV DATAFLD="Col4"></DIV></TD>
</TR>
</TBODY>
```

7. Each cell in the table body identifier contains a division with a `DATAFLD` attribute. The value of the `DATAFLD` attribute is the column name as specified in your data source that you identified in the opening `<TABLE>` tag. In this case, you are using the `mydata` data source.

8. That is all you need to do to add dynamically expanding tables to a Web page that follow Microsoft's approach. The Web browser does the rest.

To enable dynamic sorting, you create a simple sorting script function for each column. For example, to sort your table by the team wins column, you add the following script function.

```
function winsClick() {
  teamlist.Sort = "Wins";
  teamlist.Reset();
```

```
}
wins.onclick = winsClick;
```

Your complete dynamic league standings example should look similar to the following code. Figure 23.6 shows the Web page as you present your page to a reader.

```
<HTML>
<HEAD><TITLE>WBL Current Standings</TITLE></HEAD>
<BODY BGCOLOR= "#FFFFFF">
<H2>WBL Current Standings</H2>
<HR>
<P>
<OBJECT ID="teamlist"
      CLASSID="clsid:333C7BC4-460F-11D0-BC04-0080C7055A83"
      ALIGN="baseline" BORDER="0" WIDTH="0" HEIGHT="0">
      <PARAM NAME="DataURL" VALUE="wblteam.txt">
      <PARAM NAME="UseHeader" VALUE="True">
</OBJECT>

This Table is Sortable By Clicking on the Column Header<P>
<TABLE BORDER="1" ID="elemtbl" DATASRC="#teamlist">
<THEAD>
<TR>
<TD><FONT COLOR="#0000FF"><B><U><DIV
     ID=team>Team</DIV></U></B></FONT></TD>
<TD><FONT COLOR="#0000FF"><B><U><DIV
     ID=wins>Wins</DIV></U></B></FONT></TD>
<TD><FONT COLOR="#0000FF"><B><U><DIV
     ID=losses>Losses</DIV></U></B></FONT></TD>
<TD><FONT COLOR="#0000FF"><B><U><DIV ID=BA>
     Batting Avg</DIV></U></B></FONT></TD>
<TD><FONT COLOR="#0000FF"><B><U><DIV ID=ERA>
     ERA</DIV></U></B></FONT></TD>
</TR>
</THEAD>
<TBODY>
<TR>
<TD><SPAN DATAFLD="Team"></SPAN></TD>
<TD><DIV DATAFLD="Wins"></DIV></TD>
<TD><SPAN DATAFLD="Losses"></SPAN></TD>
<TD><DIV DATAFLD="BA"></DIV></TD>
<TD><DIV DATAFLD="ERA"></DIV></TD>
</TR>
```

```
</TBODY></TABLE>
<SCRIPT TYPE="text/javascript">
function teamClick() {
  teamlist.Sort = "Team";
  teamlist.Reset();
}

team.onclick = teamClick;

function winsClick() {
  teamlist.Sort = "Wins";
  teamlist.Reset();
}

wins.onclick = winsClick;

function lossesClick() {
  teamlist.Sort = "Losses";
  teamlist.Reset();
}

losses.onclick = lossesClick;

function BAClick() {
  teamlist.Sort = "BA";
  teamlist.Reset();
}

BA.onclick = BAClick;

function ERAClick() {
  teamlist.Sort = "ERA";
  teamlist.Reset();
}

ERA.onclick = ERAClick;

</SCRIPT>
<HR>
</FONT>
</BODY>
</HTML>
```

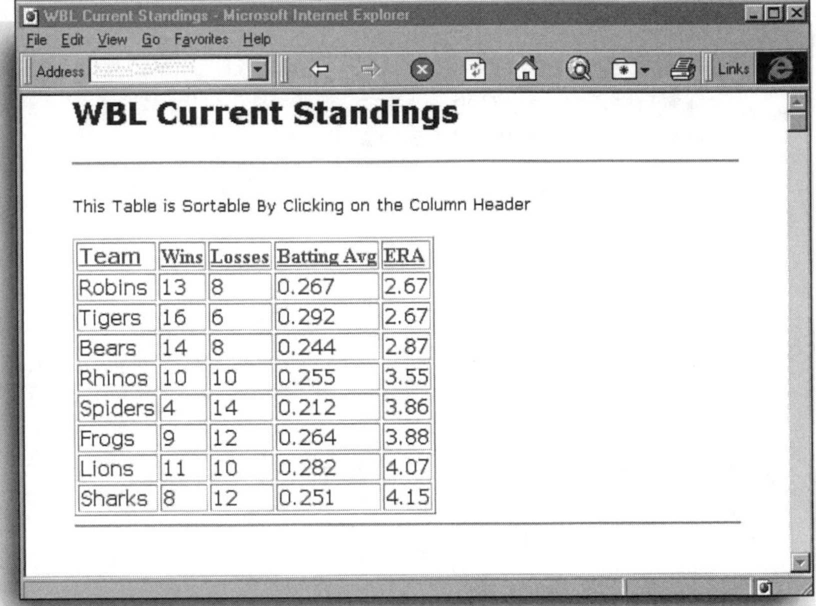

FIGURE 23.6
The sortable dynamic standings table.

Handling Browser Differences

Many of the features presented in this chapter are specific to the Internet Explorer 4.x Web browser. You can write Web pages that include multiple HTML tag sets and scripts in order to make a feature work for multiple Web browsers. If you believe in the ability of the World Wide Consortium's authority to influence Web browser development, the HTML 4 recommendation (see `http://www.w3c.org/MarkUp/`) should help bring common dynamic content features to both Microsoft's and Netscape's Web browser. The HTML 4 recommendation just recently became official in late 1997, so you should not be surprised that existing Web browsers handle dynamic effects differently.

Special Netscape Features

Netscape's browser allows you to create dynamic content through layers. You can also add animation to your Web pages by using Netscape's animation model. Netscape Communicator 4.0 does not include dynamic tables, but there are many plug-in technologies available that you can use to connect data sources to HTML forms. Investigate Netscape Communicator's features online at `http://www.netscape.com`.

Simulating Dynamic Content with Layers

As you explored in Chapter 21, "Adding Layers," Netscape provides some very interesting features centered around their `<LAYER></LAYER>` tag pair that is available for use with Netscape's Communicator 4.x Web browser. The `LAYER` element allows you to embed standard HTML tags within its tags. By including multiple layers on a Web page, you can provide dynamic content changes that appear similar to the Web page you created with the happy and sad face page earlier.

Using layers and dynamic content change

1. Try creating your photo and caption Web page with simple layers. Embed your happy photo and happy caption within a `<LAYER></LAYER>` tag pair. (The `<LAYER>` tag is covered in detail in Chapter 21.) Embed your sad photo and sad caption within a second `<LAYER></LAYER>` tag pair.

   Your two layers should look like the following `LAYER` elements:

   ```
   <LAYER NAME="happy">
   <H2>Me Feeling Happy</H2>
   <IMG ID=photo SRC="myphoto.jpg">
   </LAYER>

   <LAYER NAME="sad">
   <H2>Me Feeling Sad</H2>
   <IMG ID=photo SRC="myphoto1.jpg">
   </LAYER>
   ```

   Remember that when you contain two layers in the same Web page, Netscape's browser registers the first layer it encounters while reading the HTML file from top-to-bottom, left-to-right, as layer `0`, and the next it encounters as layer `1`. The fact that the Web browser already has a way to distinguish the layers is very helpful when you write scripts to move the layers around.

To create dynamic content changes using your two layers, you alternate which layer is visible and which is hidden. The following code shows your Web page as it should appear to provide dynamic style change.

```
<HTML>
<HEAD>
<TITLE>Netscape's Layers</TITLE>
</HEAD>
<SCRIPT TYPE="text/javascript">
function showLayer() {
   if(document.layers[0].visibility=="show") {
      document.layers[0].visibility = "hide";
      document.layers[1].visibility = "show";
   } else {
      document.layers[1].visibility = "hide";
      document.layers[0].visibility = "show";
   }
}
function initializeLayers () {
   document.layers[1].visibility = "hide";
   document.layers[0].visibility = "show";
}
</SCRIPT>
<BODY onLoad="initializeLayers()">
<LAYER NAME="happy">
<H2>Me Feeling Happy</H2>
<IMG ID=photo SRC="myphoto.jpg">
</LAYER>
<LAYER NAME="sad">
<H2>Me Feeling Sad</H2>
<IMG ID=photo SRC="myphoto1.jpg">
</LAYER>
<LAYER name="form" top=300>
<FORM>
<INPUT type="button" value="Change"
onClick="showLayer()">
</FORM>
</LAYER>
</BODY>
</HTML>
```

2. When your Web page finishes loading in Netscape's Web browser, the `onLoad` event runs the `initializeLayers()` script function, which makes the happy layer (contained in layer `0`) visible but hides the sad layer.
3. Whenever a reader clicks the **Change** button, the layers swap and the visible layer becomes hidden while the hidden layer becomes visible. The visible effect again alternates between Figure 23.1 and Figure 23.2.

Special Internet Explorer Features

Remember that the drag-and-drop and dynamic table features presented earlier are specific to Internet Explorer 4.x only. Expect Microsoft to continue to push new features aggressively. Investigate the latest Internet Explorer features online at `http://www.microsoft.com`.

CHAPTER

24

Using CGI

Increase the interactivity of your Web site by using common CGI applications: Web-based email, guest books, and message boards

Improve the sales cycle by processing client orders over the Web

Obtain valuable marketing information by monitoring the activity of site visitors

Make use of passwords to create member areas in your site

CGI on the Web

CGI has very little to do with HTML, except of course that it can be used to produce HTML-on-the-fly documents—it creates an HTML document based on the instructions in a CGI application and sends that document back to the user. In addition, a CGI application can be fired from an HTML document using the `<FORM>` tag.

```
<FORM method="post" action="script.pl">
```

Dynamic HTML

Until recent changes in the object model for IE and NN browsers, this HTML-on-the-fly effect of CGI applications was termed Dynamic HTML. In order to prevent any confusion that may arise from using the term here, I won't. We will stick with the old and well-established term, HTML on-the-fly.

The many tongues of CGI

CGI applications and scripts can be written with Visual Basic, C/C++, Perl, and AppleScript. All are common languages for developing CGI applications. The language you use is not very important, and your platform may even determine the language (for developing).

But no HTML reference book would be complete without a chapter on this extremely diverse technology. CGI is an acronym for Common Gateway Interface; it permits data sharing between a client and server application by establishing an interface between the two systems, even if those systems reside on completely different hardware or software platforms.

Essentially, the Internet's greatest asset, its ability to share information over a networked environment—regardless of the operating system or hardware being used, would have been the biggest hurdle for developers to overcome, were it not for CGI. You can concentrate on developing interactive applications for your Web project on any system, and feel confident it will work for all users, regardless of the system they are using to access your site.

The following list contains URLs for information and other resources about programming languages often used for CGI applications.

- Perl `ftp://ftp.sedl.org/pub/mirrors/CPAN/doc/refguide`
- C/C++ `http://www.boutell.com`
- Java `http://www.javasoft.com`
- Visual Basic `http://www.microsoft.com/visualbasic/`
- TCL `http://www.tcltk.com/`

Can't or Don't Want to Write Your Own CGI Applications?

If you shudder at the thought of programming, relax; there is another way. For many of you, using a CGI application on your Web site is almost impossible. Either the server administrator will not allow you to run CGI applications, or, for whatever reason, you simply do not want to bother with it on your own. In both cases there is relief on the Internet.

A number of service providers have made available their server for form processing and other services; hitch a ride with them. Be aware that you're probably going to have to pay for this service. If this option interests you, you can find out more at the site for QuickTools, `www.quicktools.com`, or you can check out the script archives at `www.shareware.com` and search for `web&mail&services`.

Form processing services

It is possible to have the work of processing your form farmed out to another server. This is an especially useful option if you do not have the capabilities to process the form from your server's system.

There are a few sites on the net that allow you to use their servers for free. You will have to try to track them down if interested; which is not an easy task since they don't go out of their way to advertise. The biggest single concern is that the server that is permitting you to use its resources could, at any time and without any notice, stop allowing offsite CGI processing. For this reason you should know the URL of at least one alternative CGI processing site. The other concern is that the script that is processing your form may be used for data mining purposes; the script operator could be collecting name and email address information and selling it to commercial e-lists.

If offsite CGI processing is your only choice, there are a few things to keep in mind. You will be required to provide information into hidden fields of your HTML form, so that the application can process your form properly. This includes things like your email address and any special processing instructions. Each CGI processing service will have its own requirements; be sure to read the information at its Web site so that your forms are properly processed. That's about all there is to it.

You will need to design your HTML forms according to the guidelines provided by the application author, and there may be other usage criteria you will have to meet in order to qualify for using the application.

Each Language Will Have Its Own Programming Rules

Rules must be adhered to when developing the CGI application. But the CGI standards identify certain elements that facilitate data sharing by using information in the HTTP header. Actually, the HTTP header has a set of valid data fields for request and response actions. Usually the request header is passed to the server from the client application, and the response header is passed to the client application from the server. Data items, known as environment variables, are used by CGI to identify the initiator, and determine other conditions that may be present. (`REMOTE_HOST` identifies the host computer of the site user. For example, `206.190.91.x` is the IP address of my server and would therefore be considered the `remote_host` for any CGI-powered forms I happened to complete.)

More about CGI

There is a limited CGI reference section–a couple of tables and lists–at the end of this chapter.

If you intend to write your own CGI applications, you are advised to purchase a book that is dedicated to CGI and learn a programming language (unless you already know how to program and need only to learn the intricacies of the common gateway interface). If you will not be writing your own CGI applications, you have two options: get the CGI application you need from some shareware site and customize your form to the CGI applications requirements, or find a site that allows you to borrow its CGI application and server resources for processing your form.

CGI applications are used to facilitate Web-based email, guest books, message boards, and commercial order forms. They provide a mechanism for securing portions of a Web site, and they can gather information based on CGI searches and visitor logging.

The remainder of this chapter provides detailed information about some of your CGI options. The CGI examples are all written in Perl because it's the language I use. I think we have spent enough time talking about what CGI is. Let's get to the meat and potatoes of this chapter—how to use CGI on your Web site.

Web-Based Email

Communicating with users

Examples of how one would communicate with users include Web email, message boards, and guest books. Each of these options gives you the opportunity to communicate interactively with your site's visitors.

As recently as six months ago, I would have thought Web-based email to be a waste of time. A number of things have happened recently to change my outlook on this particular use of CGI though. Web TV and hand-held Web browsers have proven to be quite the commercial success; the hand-held market recently reported that over three million units are in use already.

By ignoring these segments of the market, you will be crippling your site before you even have the chance to get it going.

The Form

A Web-based email form need not be complicated, only a few data fields and a couple of buttons required; anything else is optional. Figure 24.1 shows a simple email form.

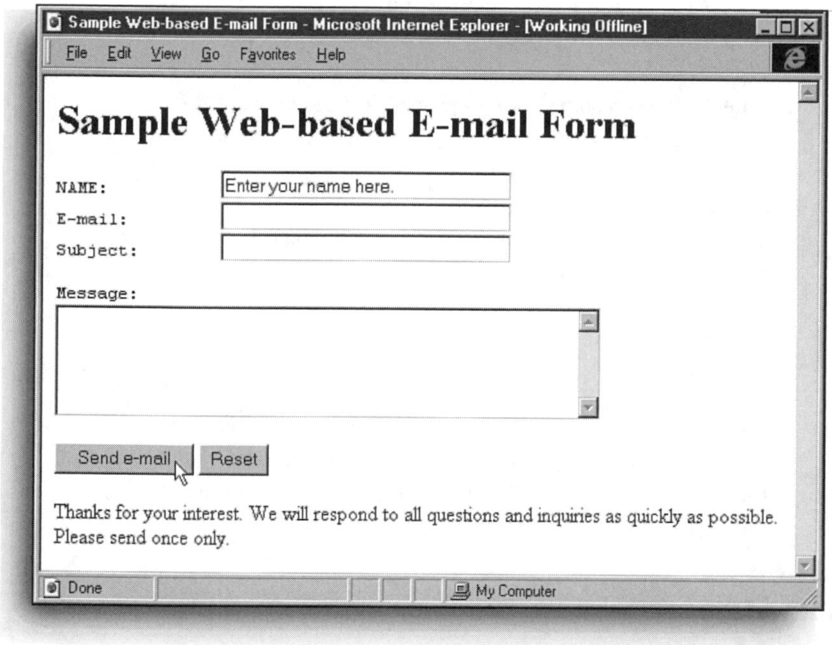

FIGURE 24.1
Name, email address, subject, and message—all that's required for a simple Web-based email form.

This form represents the absolute minimum that any Web-based email form should contain. You may want to gather additional information about the user, such as a telephone number, a Web page URL, or anything else, but that is all extra.

```
<HTML>
<HEAD>
    <TITLE>Sample Web-based E-mail Form</TITLE>
</HEAD>
<BODY>
<H1> Sample Web-based E-mail Form</H1>
<FORM METHOD="post" ACTION="/cgi-bin/webmail.pl">
```

Reading the HTML

The code identifies a portion of the page as an HTML form and identifies a CGI application to use for processing the form. Pay particular attention to the `name` attribute (`$name`) of the various form elements, because it plays an important role in the Perl script.

```
<PRE>
NAME:          <INPUT TYPE="text" NAME="sender" SIZE=30
maxlength=60
value="Enter your name here.">
E-mail:          <INPUT TYPE="text" NAME="addr" SIZE=30
maxlength=60 >
Subject:     <INPUT TYPE="text" NAME="about" SIZE=30
maxlength=60 ><BR>
Message:
<TEXTAREA NAME="msg2u" rows=5 cols=50
wrap=physical></TEXTAREA>
</pre>
<INPUT TYPE="submit" value="Send e-mail"> <INPUT
TYPE="reset">
</FORM>
<P>Thanks for your interest.  We will respond to all
questions and inquiries as quickly as possible. Please
send once only.</P>
</BODY>
</HTML>
```

Designing forms

The simple layout of the form used for Figure 24.1 should not be considered as indicative of what you can do; the thrust of this chapter is CGI. Chapter 19, "Creating HTML Forms," provides many excellent examples of well-designed HTML forms.

There's no need to present a forms tutorial of any sort here. The `ACTION` attribute of the `<FORM>` tag directs the form to the CGI application for processing when the user clicks the submit button. When the CGI application runs, it will read the form and process it.

The Script

The CGI application for this simple Web-based email form is written in Perl 4.

```
#!/usr/local/bin/perl
# Initialize the message
 $owner = "webman/@netroute.net";
```

The `$owner` variable is where you put your email address. The variable could be called anything: `$myaddress`, `$hereiam`, `$hithere`, or anything else. As with most variable names, it's just something you make up that will be fairly easy to remember when it's needed for other parts of the application.

```
 $hostname = "www.netroute.net";
```

Where is the application being served from? This is the URL of your ISP.

```
$from = $ENV{'HTTP_FROM'};
$byway = $ENV{'REMOTE_HOST'};
```

The `HTTP_FROM` environment variable, although not supported by all browsers, will tell you the email address of the person submitting the form. The `REMOTE_HOST` environment variable tells you the name of the user's host (ISP). This information is useful later in the application for confirming the email address, or at least the `@host.net` portion of the email address, provided by the user—especially if the browser being used doesn't support the `HTTP_FROM` variable.

```
$sendmail = "/usr/local/lib/sendmail";
&parse_now (*INFO);
```

Tell the server where it can find the sendmail application. The `&parse_now(*INFO)` operator tells the application to run the `parse_now` subroutine and to place the incoming data into an associative array called $info.

```
# check the form for missing information
 $info('sender") = "Unknown" if !$info('sender');
 $info('addr") = $from if !$info('addr');
 $info('about') = "Subject Unknown" if !$info('about');
 $info('msg2u") = "Another Test Document" if
!$info('msg2u');
# send the e-mail message - run the send_mail subroutine;
 &send_mail();
# send the confirmation document - run the confirm
subroutine;
 &confirm_send();
# this is the end of the application;
# what follows after the exit statement are the subroutines;
# the subroutines are kind of like mini-scripts;
exit(0);
# Sub Routines;
# prepare the e-mail message;
sub send_mail {
    open (MAIL, "¦ $sendmail");
```

Create a new file called MAIL and pipe its output to the sendmail application.

```
    print MAIL <<Mail_Here;
```

Print everything between here and the next instance of the phrase `Mail_Here`. This is the email header.

```
From: $info('addr');
        To: $owner;
        Reply-To: $info('addr');
        Subject: $info('about');
        X-Remote-Host: $byway;
    Mail_Here;
```

Now we can format the body of the email message.

```
    Print MAIL <<EOMail
        $info('sender') \n
        at $from \n
        $info('addr') \n
        Has this to say. \n
        \n $info('msg2u') \n
    EOMail;
    Close (MAIL);
}
# prepare the HTML confirmation document;
sub confirm_send{
```

This subroutine creates an HTML page that confirms that the email was sent. It extracts information contained in the $info associative array to fill in the personalized portions of the response form.

```
    print "Content-type: text/html", "\n\n";
    print <<confirmed;
        <HTML>
        <HEAD><TITLE>Web-Mail Sent</TITLE></HEAD>
        <BODY>
        <H1>Your Message has been sent</H1>
        <P>$sender from $from at $byway sent the following
        message to $owner.</P>
        <P>$info('msg2u')</P>
        <P>Return to our
        <A
HREF="http://www.netroute.net/~webman">Homepage</A>.</P>
        </BODY></HTML>
    confirmed;
```

Syntax tip

The << operator indicates that everything following the end of that line and the next instance of the phrase immediately following the << operator, is to be processed as if the command–in this case `print`–were used for each line. The identifier MAIL is simply a reference to the temporary file that was created in the previous step. Everything is sent to the temporary file MAIL, which is sent to the user as an email when an expected event occurs.

```
}
# decode form data;
sub parse_now {
```

Here we decode the data from the form and check it out to make sure that only alphanumeric characters are being used. This is known as parsing the data.

```
    local (%info, $post_info, $info_data,
            @info_data, $key, $data);
    read (STDIN, $post_info, $ENV{'CONTENT_LENGTH'});
    $post_info =~ s/\+/ /g;
    @info_data = split(/&/, $post_info);
    foreach $info_data (@info_data) {
        ($key, $data) = split (/=/, $info_data);
        $key =~ s/%([a-fA-F0-9][a-fA-F0-9])/pack("c",
        hex($1))/eg;
        $data =~ s/%([a-fA-F0-9][a-fA-F0-9])/pack("c",
        hex($1))/eg;
        $info{$key} = $value;
        }
    return %info;
}
```

The script reads the incoming data and decodes it into human-readable language. Then it takes the decoded form information and places it into an email message. The email is sent to the site owner and the application creates an HTML document for the user confirming that the email was sent.

Require (`require "filename.pl";`)

Any additional CGI examples will make use of `require`, a command that shortens the length of the file by attaching other files to the application when it is executed. These supporting files will typically contain many of the subroutines needed for your CGI applications. Instead of writing out the subroutines for each CGI script you create, simply write out a single file with all the subroutines you will need and attach it to the application.

How to Do Web-Mail

You want people using Web TV or hand browsers, as well as everyone else on the Internet, to be able to communicate with you. There is a problem though; you don't know how to write CGI scripts, or your server will not allow you to use CGI scripts. Don't worry, that is a minor problem with several possible solutions.

Processing without a server

If your site is hosted from a server other than your dial-up ISP, it may not be very easy to arrange form processing. Fortunately there are several servers that offer form processing for sites off their servers.

If you cannot use CGI scripts from your server:

- Pay someone else to take care of your form processing needs. This could mean having your entire Web site hosted from another server, as is the case with the QuickTools™

resource mentioned earlier in this chapter. (Research a few service providers and select the one that best meets your requirements. `Yahoo.com` is a good starting point for your research.)

- Search the Net until you find someone generous enough to let you use server resources strictly for processing your form. You will probably have to pay for this service.

If you have the server resources:

- There are many well-designed freeware CGI applications available on the Internet. For example, mailto.cgi, webmail, and web2mail are available at `scriptsearch.com`. You may also want to check out `shareware.com` and `twocows.com`.
- Pay someone to write the script for you. If you can't find the right script in the freeware or shareware domain, or if you have specific requirements that absolutely must be met, hire a programmer to develop the script for you. While none of the scripts you already looked at will do exactly what you need, they will give you an idea about the abilities of their authors, who would probably be very happy to help you develop your business solutions.

If you have decided to use a freeware script, there are a few steps that must be taken before you can start using it.

Data comes in pairs

The information from the HTML form is passed to the CGI application as data pairs: a variable name and a value for that name. Where the response reads "`$sender from $from`", the application will insert the values associated with those variable names into the HTML response document.

Customizing CGI applications

1. Review the code. Open the CGI file into any text editor and read through the entire document once, looking for all commented sections. A commented section is indicated by the presence of the pound character (`#`) at the beginning of the line of code.

   ```
   # This is a comment;
   ```

   A well-commented CGI application will give you a good idea about what each line of code is for—which lines can be edited and which should be left unchanged.

2. Customize the code according to your specifications. Now you will begin modifying all the portions of the code that must be changed. For example, each installation must clearly

indicate the location of the Perl application on that system. The first line of code, which starts with the #! key combination, is used to indicate that Perl is located in the directory path indicated.

```
#!/usr/local/bin/perl
```

In this case, /usr/local/bin/perl is the directory path to the Perl program files. Chances are that your system will look slightly different. Discuss the matter with your ISP, who will be able to provide you not only with the exact path for the Perl program files, but also with the procedures for installing new CGI applications. These procedures will probably include information such as the directory in which CGI applications must be placed and any security testing requirements they may have in place for new CGI scripts.

Finding Perl

If you have shell access try: `whereis perl` at the prompt. Other than that, you will need to ask your sysadmin.

Other variables that must be changed include the reference to the site owner and host name, as well as the location of sendmail or any other supporting programs that the script may be using.

```
$owner = "webman@netroute.net";
$hostname = "www.netroute.net";
$sendmail = "/usr/local/lib/sendmail";
```

These variables will probably use different names, but figuring them out is usually pretty straightforward. This should give you an idea about the importance of reading through the document first. By reading it through you can identify all these elements. Printing the document, and reading from a hard copy is also helpful because you can mark off the elements on the paper and refer to it when making the changes.

3. Match all value names. The names assigned to data fields in your HTML form will probably not be the same as those used in the CGI application. You have two choices: change the names in your HTML document or change the names in the CGI application.

4. Change or add to the functionality. If the application does exactly what you want, great. It will probably require some modifications though, to do what you really want. A couple of examples of these modifications include:

   - Change the HTML reply page:

     Add or remove information from that page. Instead of having the page include a complete copy of the message sent, you may want it to simply provide a generic thank you message. For example, the following HTML reply page

```
print "Content-type: text/html", "\n\n";
print <<confirmed;
     <HTML>
     <HEAD><TITLE>Web-Mail Sent</TITLE></HEAD>
     <BODY>
     <H1>Your Message has been sent</H1>
     <P>$sender from $from at $byway sent the
     following message to $owner.</P>
     <P>$info('msg2u')</P>
     <P>Return to our
     <A HREF="http://www.netroute.net/~webman">
     Homepage</A>.</P>
     </BODY></HTML>
confirmed;
```

     can be simplified and made into a more generic reply, such as:

```
print "Content-type: text/html", "\n\n";
print <<confirmed;
     <HTML>
     <HEAD><TITLE>Web-Mail Sent</TITLE></HEAD>
     <BODY>
     <H1>Your Message has been sent</H1>
     <A HREF="http://www.netroute.net/~webman">Back
     to Homepage</A>
     </BODY></HTML>
confirmed;
```

     It is also possible to add extra items to the reply, depending on the information gathered in the form itself.

- Add more functions and features to the application:

  You may decide to email a response to the message sender as well, something indicating that the message was received and will be acted upon as soon as possible, or whatever you feel is appropriate for your needs.

5. Testing and Installation. All the required modifications have been made and the necessary variables changed, and the paths are all correct. Now you need to give the application, and any supporting library files, to your ISP for testing. If the ISP approves the CGI script, it will likely become active within a few days, depending on the schedule.

That's about it. Your Web-Mail application should now be up and running.

Message Boards

Message boards give you an opportunity to tell your customers about some new and exciting product or service, the latest addition to the company, or just about anything you want. If your messages are going to be few and infrequent, you may not even want to use a CGI application; writing the HTML page the old way may be better suited to your needs. Figure 24.2 shows an example of a message board page.

Get the message out

Used properly, message boards are a great way to keep visitors coming back to a site. Keep the content fresh and relevant. A message of the day, or even message of the week, would do the trick.

If you want people to keep coming back to your site though, a message of the day (MOD) section is definitely an option that deserves serious consideration. The message doesn't have to be anything significant—it can be a simple quote—either way, people will come back, if for no other reason than to see what it says on their next visit.

There are a few ways to design and use a message board.

- A completely automated application selects a message, at random or by some preconceived method, from a list of choices and adds it to the page, one per day for an entire week, month, or any other period.
- An operator interface could be utilized, allowing the site owner to add a new message each day. (The visitor sees only the MOD page.)

- Allow anyone on the network to add a message, listing all the messages by date posted and subject given (this option is bordering on another type of CGI application, the CGI Chat application).
- Finally, the MOD page could be a combination of any of the previously mentioned options.

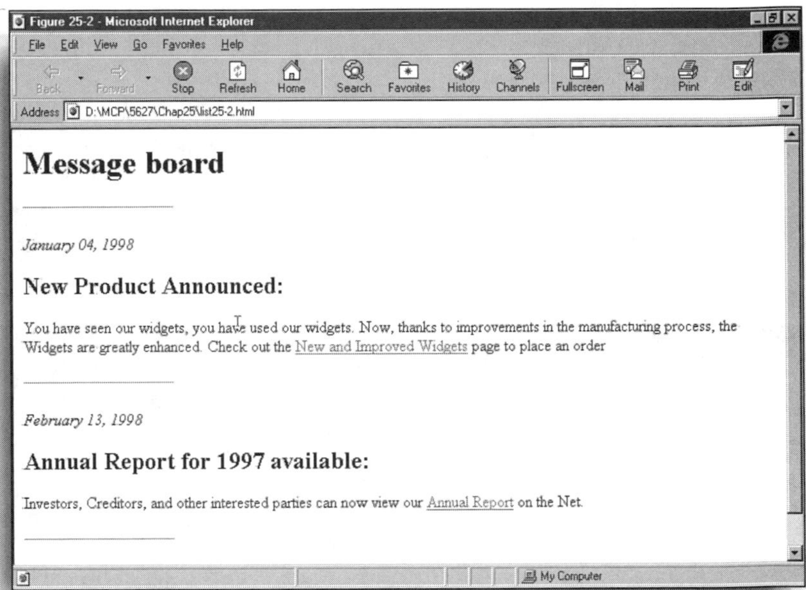

FIGURE 24.2
The message board gives the site owner the opportunity to let the user know about any current issues without writing a new HTML page for it.

Who wants a message board?

Companies may use a message board to brag about new products or services. The government might utilize one to explain why they are raising the taxes yet again. A community organization will use a message board to tell you about upcoming events, and finally, your ISP likely uses a message board to inform you about any policy changes.

I'm sure that there are many other ways to implement a message board, but this list should give you a general idea of its application. It is important to get an understanding of who may want to use a message board, and how they would use it.

- Corporate Web site—A business should use a message board to introduce new products or services, make announcements about any current products or services, or anything else that it may want its customers to know about.
- Internet service provider—The message boards I have seen at various ISP sites are typically used as community announcement services. If a local school or church is planning a bake sale, if a politician is speaking at the community center, if someone lost a pet, tell it to your neighbors on the

Net. There are messages posted about almost everything you can imagine on local ISP message boards.

- Government entity—Changes in the mill rate, a suspension of service, key position openings, any matter of public interest can—and I would say, should—quickly be passed on to the public by way of a message board.
- Community organization—When certain organizations begin their fundraising campaigns, they make use of the Internet to inform the public about the campaign, why they need the money, specifics of their programming objectives, and the amount they hope to raise. The message board provides these organizations with an easy method for posting current standing results. That way people know how much is still required for their favorite organization to meet its fundraising goals.

You will have no trouble implementing your message board if you follow a few simple instructions.

Implementing your message board

1. Determine your needs. The type of message board you use will depend entirely on your expectations. You should write out your specifications—for example, "The message board will..."—and fill in the statement. You should clearly identify the objectives a message board will fulfill. Who can post to the message board? How often will its message be changed? Answer all of these questions before you attempt to design or acquire the application.
2. Design the application. Design the application from scratch or download a pre-made script from one of the many Internet resources. (Recall from our discussion about Web mail that you'll probably have to make some minor modifications to the script so that it does exactly what you need. The same is true for any CGI script that you download.)
3. Install it onto the server computer. This step will also require the assistance of your ISP. In addition to testing for possible security threats, the ISP can instruct you on how your public_html directory should be structured for the files created by the CGI application.

Why do you need a message board?

Do you fit any of the groups already identified? If not, that's okay; there is no rule saying that only specific types of sites can use a message board. In fact, it could be fun having a message board on a personal site; use it to tell your friends about an upcoming party... or anything else.

4. Test the application. I can't overemphasize the importance of giving your CGI application a test run. Remember Murphy's Law. (Who is this Murphy anyway? And why is he there whenever things go wrong?)

Sign in, please...

Get your visitors involved. When surfing, the question that comes to mind is usually something along the lines of "What is here for me?" If there is a guest book, the answer is, "Hey! I can leave my mark here," or so the line of thought goes.

Guest Books

Everyone who visits your site is given an opportunity to leave his or her mark behind. Giving the visitor a chance to interact with your site is one way to ensure a relative amount of repeat visits. Figure 24.3 shows an example of a guest book.

FIGURE 24.3
A guest book page.

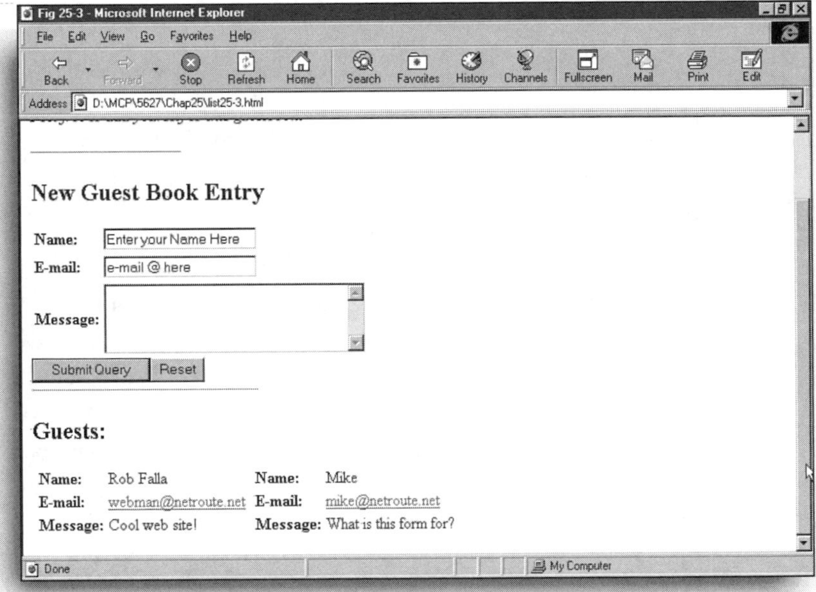

We all know why someone would want a guest book on his or her site, but what you may not yet know is what's involved in creating one. I am going to go through the process of putting a guest book together. We will discuss everything from planning to implementation. And once again, I am going on the assumption that you will download a guest book application from the net.

Implementing your guest book

1. Design the Specifications for the guest book application. Often, guest books end up being rather large files that, eventually, become too large to work. The reason this happens is that people often don't plan for the guest book properly. Therefore, the first step must be to develop a plan for the guest book. A simple subroutine to split the guest book into as many files as is necessary—after 10 or even 20 entries—would be an easy fix to the problem of the page becoming too large. If you don't plan the application in advance, you will probably overlook such things. Your plan should also indicate the type of data you want to collect from the people who submit an entry to the guest book. This is an excellent opportunity to gather specific information from your customers, such as their names and email addresses. By associating a visitor log with a particular guest book entry, you will be better able to determine which entries are from people actually interested in your products or services and eliminate the ones that were just surfing, thus concentrating more of your effort to improving your site for actual consumers. Beware, though, that you don't give the impression that surfers are not welcome. All data filtering will be done quietly and in the background of the CGI application.
2. Write the code. Put your plan into action. This means that you will begin the process of writing the application or looking into other guest book applications that are available on the Internet. A good place to start is `www.worldwidemart.com/scripts/guestbook.shtml`, written by Matt Wright. This script is easy to read, thanks to the level of commenting inserted into the source code. You will notice that this code differs from the Web-based email application in several ways. One of the biggest differences is that it actually opens and appends an HTML file when a new guest book entry is submitted. The HTML file must be locked when the application is run, so that only one copy of it is open and active at a time. If you were to allow multiple access to the guest book file, only the last instance to completely run through the application would

be saved. The others would be overwritten as soon as the last one was completed. For that reason, only one instance of the file can be active at a time. Remember, though, that the application is completed so fast that the user is not likely to even notice that the file has been locked. As soon as it is unlocked by the first activation, the next user in line will get his or her crack at it.

3. Install it onto the ISP's server computer. Get assistance from the ISP at this stage. Testing will probably be required (by the ISP operator) to determine if the application poses a security threat of any sort.
4. Test the application's usability. To properly test, you should submit several test entries until you surpass the split-file count and the new file is created. If a new guest book file is created and the contents of the original are saved into an archive file of sorts, you know that the application passed the test.

Restricting Site/Page Access

Stop right there!

Well, okay, you can keep reading. But I bet the heading got your attention. If you are sharing sensitive information over the Internet, you owe a certain responsibility to control access to that information.

From time to time, it becomes necessary to limit access to your site or portions thereof. You need look no further than the message board we talked about earlier to see that. The page for entering new messages into the message board is password protected so only the site administrator can add new messages. Figure 24.4 shows a secure access login screen.

Here is a partial list of types of sites that may need some form of CGI security.

- Fees for information sites—These sites offer services for their customers that include information gathering and presentation. To keep their services valuable, they will want to incorporate a system that requires user authorization before someone can access any information.
- Content that is user sensitive—If a site makes sensitive information, like pictures, available over the Internet, it will probably want to use some sort of password system so that only those who want to see those items will, and others will not happen across them accidentally.

- Government or corporate sites—These organizations may want to take advantage of the Internet's ability to share information over vast geographical areas at a relatively inexpensive cost. For example, many companies are now having their sales staffs file daily reports over the Internet when they are on the road.

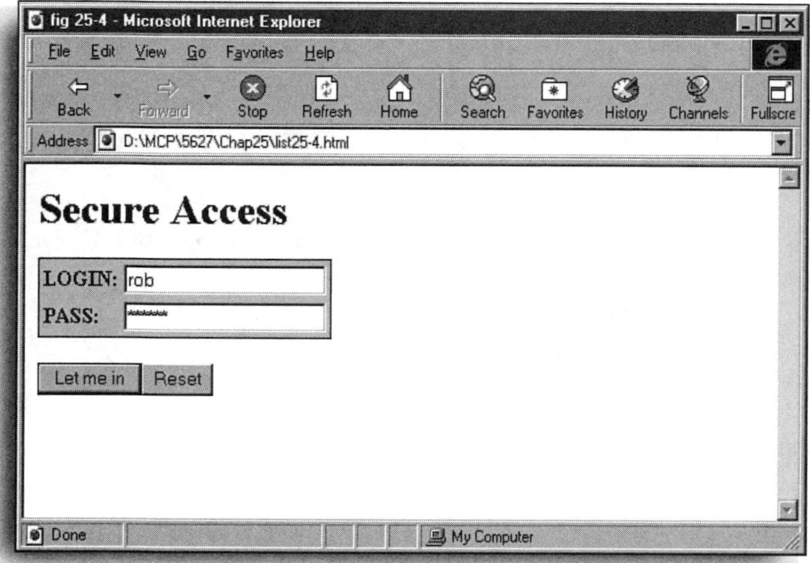

FIGURE 24.4
Enforcing security restrictions.

There are three methods of securing site access.

How can a page be protected?

There are a few common methods for securing your information on the Internet using a Perl script. Permit access to specific domains, or alternatively, restrict specific domains. Have users complete a login form that asks for a userID, or check both the userID and the domain.

- Restricted domains—Uses a list of domains that are either granted or denied access. If the purpose of the list is to specify that only users from the domains specified are allowed access, it will deny all others. If it specifies only a listing of banned domains, all others will be granted access.

```
$auth_host = $ENV{'REMOTE_HOST'};
if ($auth_host eq "hishost.net"){
# let the user in if he is from the right domain;
}
else {
     print "\n I'm sorry, the site you are attempting
to access
     is reserved. \n";
}
```

- User authentication—A file is written that contains a listing of usernames and passwords. When someone attempts to access the site, it checks the identity information provided, either in a form or with a prompt box, and grants access only if he or she is found on the list.

```
$auth_user = $info($user_name);
if ($auth_user eq "roger")&&($pas_word eq "$ropas"){
# let the user in if he is who he says he is;
}
else {
     print "\n I'm sorry, you need to provide a valid
      userID and Password to access this site. \n";
}
```

- User and domain checking—This method combines the other two methods to give you the best protection against unauthorized access. The steps to create an extra strong authorization routine are indicated next.

```
$auth_user = $info($user_name);
$auth_host = $ENV{'REMOTE_HOST'};
if ($auth_user eq "roger")&&($pas_word eq
"$ropas")&&($auth_host
eq "hishost.net"){
# let the user in if he is who he says he is;
}
else {
     print "\n I'm sorry, you need to provide a valid
      userID and Password to access this site. \n";
     print "If you have a valid ID and Password but
      are using a new server please contact the systems
      administrator. \n"
}
```

Implementing your extra-fort secure connection with CGI

1. Who can use your site? Compile a list of all your users/customers who are authorized for access to the site/page.
2. Assign a userID and password to each authorized user. Create a separate file, with appropriate access restrictions, containing a list of userIDs and passwords.

3. Verify authorized users with CGI. Include a subroutine that verifies that a user is logging on from the expected host. If the `REMOTE_HOST` matches the `$hostname` identified in the login script and the password is correct, access is granted. If either condition is not met, the user is denied access. If a user needs to access the site from more than one server, like from home and from work, this script may present a bit of a problem for that user. The solution is rather simple, though. Either limit the user to accessing the site from a single location, assign a different account for each server the user will be using, or let the script choose from a list of possible domains, and, as long as the user is accessing the site from one of the domains listed and all other requirements (password and userID) are met, grant access.

You can also use the HTTP header

The NCSA server provides a method for creating a list of authorized users of a site or page. This method does not require the use of a CGI application. It does, however, require that you understand how the server authorization routine works. For beginners, the CGI application is probably much easier to learn and implement.

Even with all these precautions, there is no guarantee that the pages are completely secure. Other methods of securing your directories include using secure servers, firewalls, and server configuration settings that enforce your access limits. Unless you are using secure server software like Netscape's Commerce Server, you should never request information like credit card numbers. Secure servers allow the data to be encrypted.

Processing Orders

Commonly known as Shopping Cart Applications, these CGI scripts take the information from an order form, process it, and send copies to the person placing the order as well as to the company. Figure 24.5 shows an example of a commercial order form. You should expect a few things from your Shopping Cart Application.

Internet commerce

The amount of money changing hands, or accounts, on the Internet is mind numbing. Ten years ago, electronic commerce was a creature of financial institutions alone. Ten years from now I can't imagine any business or professional surviving without it.

- It will perform computations on the order and provide the purchaser with an HTML and email invoice that includes all costs. Some of the costs to include in the application include taxes, duty, shipping, insurance, and any other incidental costs.
- The site owner will most likely want a copy of the order formatted and emailed so that it can be printed and filed.

- A page should also be created that allows the company to find out if any new orders have been submitted over the Net, and, if so, to see an exact copy of the order or orders for that day or week. This page should also allow additional data to be entered by the company, such as when the order was processed, billed, and shipped. The entire order can be piped to a database application, allowing even greater automation of the order-to-ship process.

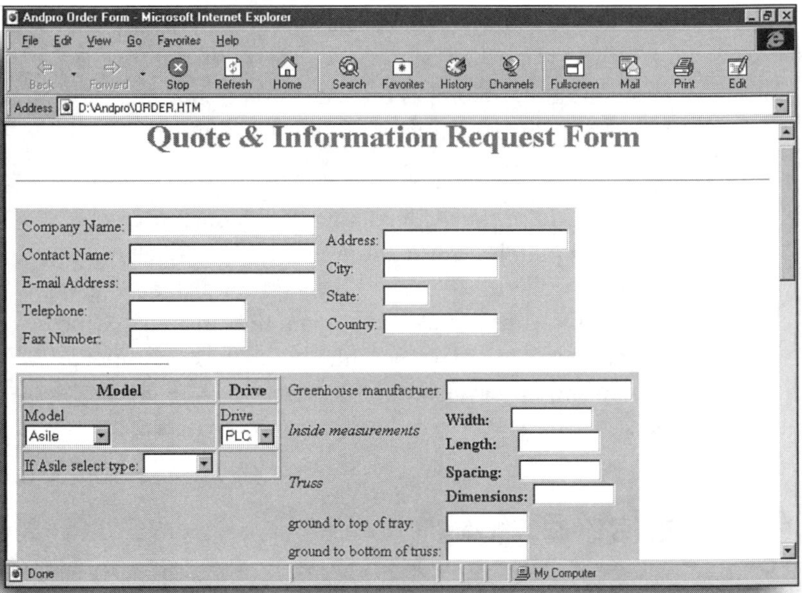

FIGURE 24.5
A typical commercial order form.

There are really only two types of commercial order processing applications. We have already mentioned one by name, the Shopping Cart Application.

Shopping online

Already you can log on to the Net and buy most anything: beer, flowers, a car, a house, what's next? What are you going to sell online?

This type assigns a shopping cart ID to a user as soon as he or she begins browsing the products and services section of the site. The user is given the opportunity to add an item to the shopping cart from any product or service page. If you want to see an example of this type of application, check out the `Amazon.com` online book store.

The other type is a straight order form where all the products or services are presented on a single HTML order form page. The user completes the order form and clicks the **Submit** button, causing the CGI application to jump into action. It will process the order and send a copy to all concerned parties, as well as append the daily/weekly orders page with the new order.

If you want users to pay for their orders online with a credit card, be sure to provide them with a secure connection using a Secure Server software package. Go to `www.scriptsearch.com` or `www.shareware.com` for sample shopping cart and order processing applications.

Data Mining

Search tools provide a benefit for both user and site owner. The user benefits from the ease with which he or she can find information from a site; the owner benefits from the ability to learn more about user behavior (what users expect to find on your site). Another source of data, which can be used for evaluating the effectiveness of your site and all its components, is hit counters.

Gathering useful data

By collecting and analyzing information about your customers preferences, you can learn to predict what they need and thus keep them happy. A happy customer will spend a lot more money than a customer who is merely interested.

Searching the Site

Providing keyword searching is of benefit to users with regard to ease of navigation on your Web presence.

Keyword searching

Letting people search your site by keyword gives them a much better chance of finding information that may be on your site, especially when it is not indexed in a way that would make it easily accessible to them.

For instance, someone comes to your site looking for information about a particular product or service. They enter their search keyword and click the **Search** button. Your application reads the keyword, searches all the documents on the site, and gives the user a list of all pages that meet the search criteria. They don't waste time surfing through the site one page at a time, and they don't leave your site in search of another site that may be easier to navigate.

You, the site owner, also benefit from making site-wide searches possible. People are more likely to stay at your site long enough to find what they were looking for, and, in the process learn more about your company and possibly become customers.

But that is all a side effect of the real reason you should have search capabilities on your site. Search logs indicate the kinds of information people are looking for. If there are a lot of requests for something that you don't yet offer but were considering adding, the log may give you the justification for going ahead with the changes. If there are a lot of requests for something that you thought should be easy to find without using the search tool, it could be possible that a re-evaluation of the layout of the site is needed. You can learn a lot about your site and your customers by evaluating the log files.

A CGI search is quite different from a guest book, a shopping cart, or even a message board application in one very important way—the other application types all opened predetermined files and used them as part of the application in some way or another. The search application uses a pipe and the `fgrep` command to open and have a quick look at all the HTML documents within a specified scope. It then searches them for any occurrences of the query string and, if any matches are found, it sends the location of that file in the form of a hyperlink to the user in the search results page. Let's look at the code.

```
#!/usr/local/bin/perl
# Initialize the message
 $owner = "webman@netroute.net";
 $hostname = "www.netroute.net";
# information for the log file;
 $from = $ENV{'HTTP_FROM'};
 $byway = $ENV{'REMOTE_HOST'};
```

Here we are telling the CGI program to look in another file for additional information and processing instructions for the current script.

```
 require (mycgi-lib.pl);
```

The fgrep application reads and grabs data from files that are found within the scope of the current document root. The document root is the directory from which the page that initiated the CGI application originates.

```
 $fgrep = "usr/local/bin/fgrep";
 $doc_root = $ENV{'DOCUMENT_ROOT'};
 &parse_now (*INFO);
```

The search string is parsed, the parse_now subroutine is found in the mycgi-lib.pl file (not shown, but if you're curious, it's the same subroutine that was used in the Web-Mail example). Once the data is parsed, we can create a variable for the search string; $search represents the phrase that we are looking for.

```
$search = $info{'search'}
# check the form for missing information
 if ($search eq "") {
   &return_error(500, "Error", "Did you enter a search
phrase?");
}
else {
 print "content type;text/html", "\n\n";
   print <<DOC_HEAD;
     "<HTML>" \n;
     "<HEAD><TITLE>SEARCH RESULTS</TITLE></HEAD>";
     "<BODY>" "\n";
     "<H1>Search For:", $search, "</H1>";
     "<HR>";
     DOC_HEAD;
    Open (SEARCH, "$fgrep -i -s $search $doc_root/* ¦");
```

In plain English, that line of code is telling the application to create an associative array named search. It will use the fgrep application to search all files and subdirectories of $doc_root for the phrase indicated by the $search string. When a match is found, the fgrep program will send the particulars about the match, such as the filename and the line number on which the match was found, back to the application for further processing instructions.

```
    $found = 0;
    %files = ();
while (<SEARCH>){
```

While fgrep is searching the files and subdirectories, it will constantly be feeding data to this application for processing. The following routines instruct the application to create a list of all files that meet the search criteria and prepare to send it back to the person who made the search request.

```
  if ($file, $type, $line) = m¦^(/\s+)([\-:])\d+\2(.*)¦){
    unless ($count) {
```

```
        if(defined ($files{$file})){
           next;
        }
        else {
          $files{$file} = 1;
        }
        $file =~ s/^$docroot\/(.*)/$1/;
        $found++;
        pring qq¦<UL><LI><A
HREF="/$file">$file</A></LI></UL>¦;
```

The list is created here.

```
      }
      $count++;
      $line =~ s/<(([^>][\n)*)>//g;
      }
      if ($count) {
        print "<HR>";
        $count=0;
       }
     }
  }
  print <<END;
```

Now the HTML document is completed, and the user is informed of the total number of matches found at the site. Once the final footer processing is complete, the HTML page is sent back to the user.

```
"<P>";
"Found " , $found, "files matching your search.";
"</P>";
"<A HREF=\"http://yourco.com\">Back to homepage</A>;
"</BODY></HTML>", "\n";
END;
Close(SEARCH);
}
exit(0);
```

Other types of visitor logging could include logging the pages that the user visits while at your site, and where the user goes when he or she leaves your site (if they follow one of your links).

A Few Notes About CGI

These are only a few notes; if you need more specific information, get a book devoted to CGI. The information in this section is included to help you understand the code used throughout the chapter. It will also prove very useful when you download a CGI application from the net and want to customize it.

Okay, admittedly this section covers a very narrow topic focus—working with supporting files—but as you will see, it covers the topic well. And, aside from basic programming techniques, which you must at least attempt to learn before trying to write your own CGI application, this is one of the most important topics for the CGI newcomer.

Geek stuff!

I admit it, I'm a geek. Or so I am told by my friends whenever they come over and I'm at the computer working on a script or some other project. The stuff in this section will help you to make the transition to geek a little faster. Yes! It's true, you too can become an Internet Geek.

Exclusive File Access—Working with Supporting Files

One way that a message board, and many other CGI applications, differs from the Web-based email example we looked at earlier is that it opens, writes to, and saves a file on the server while performing its intended tasks. If this file is accessed by several users at once, it will only save the changes posted last. To prevent this from happening, you will open the file and place an exclusive-use lock on it so that no one else can open it until you are finished.

```
flock (filehandle, 2)
```

The values associated with the file-lock command are listed in Table 24.1.

TABLE 24.1 **Flock values for CGI applications**

Value	Means	Definition
1	shared	Allows multiple instances of file to run simultaneously.
2	exclusive	Locks file until current instance is complete.
4	non-blocking	The file is not blocked.
8	unlock	Releases any locks on the file, allowing the next user to access it.

In addition to locking the file, you will also have to open and close it. The syntax for opening and closing files is

```
OPEN (filehandle, [file]¦
["<".file]¦
[">".file]¦
[">>".file]¦
["+>".file]¦
["¦cmd".file]
CLOSE filehandle
```

The entire command should be on a single line; I have split it only to highlight the different options available. These options are explained in Table 24.2.

TABLE 24.2 Optional *OPEN* command operators

Operator	Means	Definition
file	input to file	Opens file for data input.
<	same as file	Opens file for data input.
>	output from file	Opens a file to generate necessary output. If the file does not exist, it will be created.
>>	append current file	Opens the file and appends the new data to the end of the file.
+>	read/write access	Opens the file with the read/write access set to true, allows you to edit an entry.
| cmd	pipe to cmd	A pipe is opened to a cmd command.

PART V

Advanced Topics

CHAPTER

25

Using Meta Information to Describe Your Document

- Present suggested keywords to search engines
- Summarize page content
- Describe document relationships
- Assert ownership rights

Information About Information

Although computers can't really understand what they read, we can help them by adding very structured information about the information to the page. This sort of information about other information is called meta information, and the tag that helps you to create meta content is called, logically enough, a `<META>` tag.

Make Page Descriptions Visible to Search Engines

Using meta information to deliver your own text to search engines and spiders

1. Use the `<META>` tag to encode keyword and description information. It should be positioned in the HEAD section.

```
<META>
```

2. Use the `http-equiv` and `content` attributes to add keywords that will be searched and indexed.

```
<META http-equiv="keywords" content="machine computer-
assisted translation translate translator interpreter
interpretation foreign language">
```

Quick usage tip: Tag syntax

```
_<META http-equiv="http-response-header-name"
name="meta-information-name" content="response-header-
or-name-content" scheme="response-header-or-name-
context" lang="language-code" dir="text-direction">
```

where *http-response-header-name* is the header name of a response passed directly to a requesting HTTP server; *meta-information-name* is an equivalent name not passed directly; *response-header-or-name-content* is the content passed under either name; *response-header-or-name-context* is the context in which a name is defined; *language-code* is the official code identifying a human language; and *text-direction* is the default direction that language is written in.

We'll use one <META> tag entry to code keyword information about the ALS corporate site so people looking for companies specializing in machine translation can easily find them. We'll use another <META> tag entry to present a short paragraph describing the company to control the text that many search engines use to show a summary of a site's content. While not all search engines use this information, enough do that you should always add these tags to any site intended for the public.

Start out by deciding what keywords you'll use to give people some idea of what the site contains; ALS does machine translation, sometimes known as computer-assisted translation, so we'll start out with a list of words that broadly refer to these subjects. Be generous, but avoid duplication, and especially avoid extraneous words that have little to do with the site.

```
machine computer-assisted translation translate translator
interpreter interpretation foreign language
```

To use these words for ALS, we'll place them in a <META> tag like this:

```
<META http-equiv="keywords" content="machine computer-
assisted translation translate translator interpreter
interpretation foreign language">
```

We used the `http-equiv` attribute instead of a `name` attribute because we're almost always talking to an HTTP server or, indirectly, to a spider requesting information about a site from an HTTP server. The `name` attribute is usually used with custom-coded CGI scripts whose use is beyond the scope of this book. The `scheme` attribute is not currently used but can be used to add important information about the context of a name.

An example might be an identifier named, let's say, ID. A robot searching won't know what sort of ID is meant unless you also specify a context like SSI, ISBN, CADL, or LOC. If the application knows that these stand for Social Security ID, International Standard Book Number, California Driver's License, and Library of Congress, respectively, it will be able to make better decisions about what to do with the information.

Search engines and meta tags

You can make it easy for search engines to describe and index your site by providing description and keyword information in <META> tags. Although not all search engines pay attention, enough do that it's very worthwhile. Especially use a <META> tag description when your head section contains a script; otherwise, the description may well be the first few lines of your script.

The next thing we want to do for the ASL page is to add a real description, more than the simple keywords used for the first tag. To do that we'll want to put on our public relations hat and create something that summarizes the site and the business in a very short but evocative sentence or two. Let's try it for ASL.

```
Aristotelian Logical Systems is the premier creator and ven-
dor of machine translation and computer-aided interpretation
services in the world. ALS is ready with answers to your
most difficult computer-assisted translation requirements.
```

We'll show both of these in a fragment, as usual, to avoid cluttering the text with needless duplications and combine it with the tag already presented.

```
<HTML>
  <HEAD>
    <META http-equiv="description" content="Aristotelian
          Logical Systems is the premier creator and vendor
          of machine translation and computer-aided
          interpretation services in the world. ALS is
          ready with answers to your most difficult
          computer-assisted translation requirements.">
    <META http-equiv="keywords" content="machine computer-
          assisted translation translate translator
          interpreter interpretation foreign language">
  </HEAD>
  <BODY>
    ...
  </BODY>
</HTML>
```

By placing this information where the spiders can see and understand it easily, you can gain some control over the manner in which many search engines describe your site in response to a search.

Rate Your Site to Attract a Preferred Audience

Rating your site to help people who don't want to see it avoid it in the first place

1. Use the `<META>` tag to encode an RSACI PICS or other rating system.

2. Go to the RSACI site at `http://www.rsac.org/homepage.asp` to fill out the rating information using their form to ensure accuracy.
3. Alternative sites are SafeSurf at `http://www.safesurf.com/` or Vancouver Web Pages at `http://vancouver-webpages.com/VWP1.0/`. All use the same general scheme of filling out a form that describes your site and then generating a well-formed `<META>` tag that can be placed in your document head.
4. The Safe for Kids site, at `http://www.weburbia.com/safe/`, is very simple. If you certify that your site is free of content about which a reasonably responsible parent might be concerned, place the following tag in your head section:

```
<META http-equiv="PICS-Label" content='(PICS-1.1
http://www.weburbia.com/safe/ratings.htm" l r (s 0))'>
```

If your site has things that may be suitable for children but should probably have parental guidance available, replace the last `0` with a `1`, like this:

```
<META http-equiv="PICS-Label" content='(PICS-1.1
"http://www.weburbia.com/safe/ratings.htm" l r (s 1))'>
```

If your site is for adults only, replace the `0` with a `2`, like this:

```
<META http-equiv="PICS-Label" content='(PICS-1.1
"http://www.weburbia.com/safe/ratings.htm" l r (s 2))'>
```

Rating your site for content makes the most sense if you have a site containing things that would interest children. Since many filter programs rate sites as "adults only" by default, the actual rating often works as a safe-entry sign rather than "keep away." If, for example, you want to put your wholesale plumbing supply catalog online, you're probably not all that interested in whether kids come visit it or not (since few of them are plumbers) and can skip the minimal effort required to rate the site.

Here are a few sample ratings from the major ratings sites so you can see what they look like, but I won't show you a page since they're all invisible in use.

```
<HTML>
  <HEAD>
```

Make sure your rating system makes sense

The only widely known rating system that filters anything but sex and violence is the Canadian Vancouver Web Pages system, with ratings covering a slew of topics including environmentalism, Canadian content, animal rights, violence, sexuality, and other controversial topics that might interest a broad range of parents, and not just those with a morbid fixation on a few particular activities. Many people, for example, might become just as agitated by a site advocating vivisection of animal subjects without benefit of anesthesia as by a site featuring nude models, if not more.

```
    <META http-equiv="PICS-Label" content='(PICS-1.1
      "http://vancouver-webpages.com/VWP1.0/"
       l gen true comment "VWP1.0" by "leeanne@leeanne.com"
       on "1998.01.16T11:03-0800" for
       "http://www.igc.apc.org/women/bookstores/"
       r (P 0 S 0 SF 0 V 0 Tol 0 Com 0 Env 0 MC 0 Gam -1
       Can -1
         Edu -1 ))'>
    <META http-equiv="PICS-Label" content='(PICS-1.1
      "http://www.weburbia.com/safe/ratings.htm" l r
      (s 0))'>
    <META http-equiv="PICS-Label" content='(PICS-1.1
      "http://www.classify.org/safesurf/"
       l by "leeanne@leeanne.com" r (SS~~000 1))'>
    <META http-equiv="PICS-Label" content='(PICS-1.1
      "http://www.rsac.org/ratingsv01.html"
       l gen true comment "RSACi North America Server"
       by "leeanne@leeanne.com" for
      "http://www.igc.apc.org/women/bookstores/"
       on "1998.01.16T09:34-0800" r (n 0 s 0 v 0 l 0))'>
  </HEAD>
  ...
```

Define an Expiration Date to Keep Content Fresh

Defining expiration dates

1. Set an `expires` value for the `http-equiv` attribute to override caching on your computer or on an intermediate server.

   ```
   <META http-equiv="expires" >
   ```

2. Next, add the date and time using the `content` attribute.

   ```
   <META http-equiv="expires" content="Tue, 20 Aug 1996
   14:25:27 GMT">
   ```

Quick usage tip: Tag syntax

```
<META http-equiv="expires" content="expiration-date">
```

where `expires` is the actual value of the header name passed directly to a requesting HTTP server, and *`expiration-date`* is the ISO expiration date and time.

Many browsers cache the pages they load so that they load more quickly on a second visit. This is usually a good idea, but if your page changes daily, or even hourly, you may want to encourage visitors to reload the fresh page on every visit. In addition, some firewall servers maintain a separate cache of recently-used pages, making it even more complicated to provide fresh content.

To force some browsers and firewall servers to reload automatically, a special `expires` value for the `http-equiv` attribute allows you to set an expiration date for the page. Unfortunately, most browsers and servers ignore this value right now, but more browsers may support it in future, so what the heck. It can't hurt and it may help, like much else in the HTML world, so it's worth doing for time-sensitive content.

New developments in Dynamic HTML have largely superseded the `expires` value, allowing the designer to have complete control over the timeliness of the information presented on the page, but only for some browsers. Until all browsers support the same version of Dynamic HTML, the more primitive expiration methods will have a continuing place.

Warning: Always provide alternative ways to guarantee fresh content

Expiration dates are only as good as the browsers that support them. Since most browsers ignore expiration dates, you should have a backup plan in place to enforce reloading pages that change. The simplest scheme is merely to create a new named page at intervals, so anyone bookmarking the old page will see it disappear when the new page comes online. This encourages bookmarking a stable base page instead of transient updated ones and solves the problem without depending on expiration dates. For more information, see Chapter 23, "Dynamically Changing Page Content."

Document Relationships Between Your Pages and Other Content Information

Using standard names to describe the structure and content of your site without ambiguity

1. Use the `<META>` tag to document basic information about each page, including relationships between the page and parent or related URLs.

```
<META scheme="URL" http-equiv="Relation"
content="index.html" scheme="Rev">
```

2. Use the `<LINK>` tag as an alternative or supplemental way to specify exact relationships between pages, including the location of style sheets or scripts that affect the rendering of the page.

```
<LINK href="index.html" rev="previous">
```

Quick usage tip: Tag syntax

```
<LINK href="resourceURL" rel="rellinktype" rev="revlink-
type" type="mimetype" media="mediatype" charset="charen-
coding" hreflang="hreflanguage">
```

where *resourceURL* is the URL of the linked resource; *rellinktype* is the forward link type, including style sheet or script; *revlinktype* is the reverse link type, including parent page(s); *mimetype* is the MIME type of the resource; *mediatype* is the type of media for which this resource is designed; *charencoding* is the character encoding of the linked resource; and *hreflanguage* is the language of the linked resource.

Standard meta labels

The Dublin Core, and other standard meta label names, allows you to specify quite a lot about the content of your page. As your page development process becomes more formal, and less unstructured as your site grows, they become more and more important to maintaining inline documentation about who created what and what goes where.

The meta element can be used for a wide variety of relationships, and although the exact format these will take is still in flux, an experimental set of attributes is widely used on the Web. These are sometimes known as the Dublin Core elements, for reasons that have nothing to do with Ireland. Other values are commonly seen as well, and most are currently useful for encoding text that would otherwise be included as a comment but with slightly more structure. Table 25.1 lists Dublin Core elements and their descriptions. Other commonly seen keywords are shown in Table 25.2.

TABLE 25.1 Dublin Core element descriptions

Element	Keyword	Description
Title	`title`	The name given to the resource
Author or Creator	`creator`	The person or organization responsible for creating the resource
Subject and Keywords	`subject`	The subject of the resource in the form of keywords
Description	`description`	A text description of the resource
Publisher	`publisher`	The organization making the resource available

Element	Keyword	Description
Other Contributor	`contributor`	A person or organization not specified as a creator who is responsible for adding significant content, such as an editor, a translator, or an illustrator
Date	`date`	The publication date in ISO 8601 format
Resource Type	`type`	The general category of the resource, such as `Text`, `Image`, `Sound`, `Software`, or `Data`
Format	`format`	The data format of the resource as a MIME type or other descriptive text
Resource Identifier	`identifier`	A character string or number used to uniquely identify the resource
Source	`source`	A character string or number used to uniquely identify the work from which this resource was derived, such as a URL or an ISBN number
Language	`language`	The language(s) the resource uses in RFC 1766 format
Relation	`relation`	The relationship of this resource to other resources
Coverage	`coverage`	The range of applicability of the resource
Rights Management	`rights`	A link to a copyright notice or other description of rights

TABLE 25.2 **Other Dublin Core keywords commonly seen**

Element	Keyword	Description
Author or Creator	`author`	The person or organization responsible for creating the resource
Creation Method	`generator`	The method used to generate the page

continues...

TABLE 25.2 Continued

Element	Keyword	Description
Rights Management	`copyright`	An inline copyright notice
Keyword List	`keywords`	The subject of the resource in the form of keywords
Distribution	`distribution`	How widely the information is disseminated
Content Type	`content-type`	The data format of the resource as a MIME type and/or other descriptive text (for example, `text/html; charset=iso-8859-1`
Resource Type	`resource-type`	The general category of the resource, such as `Document`, `Text`, `Image`, `Sound`, `Software`, or `Data`

These elements can be used freely for the time being, using your own logical relationships until the structure of these attributes becomes more stable. They can be very useful for encoding all sorts of information about the page that can be used by humans inspecting the code, say to determine which page is the logical parent or child of this one, as well as the specific tasks listed in the sections immediately preceding this one.

```
<HTML>
  <HEAD>
    <TITLE>Aristotelian Logical Systems, Ltd. Sub-
    page</TITLE>
    <META scheme="URL" http-equiv="Relation"
    content="index.html" scheme="Rev">
  </HEAD>
  <BODY>
    ...
  </BODY>
</HTML>
```

In many cases you could also encode relationship information in a link element as well, and many designers prefer this method. Some browsers will even pull out certain named relationship information and create a navigation bar at the top of the page. The following code describes the same general relationship as the previous <META> tag:

```
<HTML>
  <HEAD>
    <TITLE>Aristotelian Logical Systems, Ltd.
    Sub-page</TITLE>
    <LINK href="index.html" rev="previous">
  </HEAD>
  <BODY>
    ...
  </BODY>
</HTML>
```

Using Client-Pull Pages to Control a Slide Show

Using proprietary meta elements to load or reload a page periodically

1. Use the proprietary `refresh` keyword in a <META> tag to control loading or reloading a page after a fixed interval:

   ```
   <META http-equiv="refresh" >
   ```

2. Use the `content` attribute to specify the time in seconds and the URL to load next.

   ```
   <META http-equiv="refresh" content="5,http://www.
   als-translation.com/">
   ```

   Quick usage tip: Tag syntax

   ```
   <META http-equiv="refresh" content="timeout-value-and
   destination">
   ```

   where `refresh` is the actual header name value passed directly to a requesting HTTP server, and *`timeout-value-and-destination`* is the length of time to pause before continuing to the page URL identified in the content.

Client pull allows a page to affect its own destiny

Client pull allows a primitive form of Dynamic HTML to refresh content on the page periodically and can be valuable for reloading pages with content that quickly grows stale. As Dynamic HTML support becomes more widespread, you can expect to see client pull gradually disappear, except perhaps in referral pages notifying visitors of site changes. For more information, see Chapter 23, "Dynamically Changing Page Content."

In Chapter 10, "Animating Graphics," we saw one way of creating a slide show using an animation. If you want differently sized images to appear in your show, you'll need to use another method, client pull.

Many people like to show an introductory page that leads people into their site with a slide show effect using successive pages. When a page moves to another location, it's also thoughtful to include a "we've moved" page to direct visitors to the new location. Using the redirection mechanism listed here is a popular way to help visitors on their way.

On the other hand, many browsers don't support this sort of redirection, so you have to include explicit navigation elements anyway, and the timeout value is often so short that the message can't be read or the page is not loaded completely before the next one appears. Because the algorithm doesn't take into account how fast the connection is, either the visitor is left staring at the screen for a while or the screen is snatched away too soon. Because the whole transaction is handled automatically, it actually encourages people not to update their bookmarks for a relocated site with the new location but just let the browser handle it. Assuming that the transitional message will eventually disappear, you could be left with visitors who don't know how to find you anymore. If the slide show effect is an important element of your site, you can rest assured that it will annoy some by taking too long and be lost on others because they never see the effect.

```
<HTML>
  <HEAD>
    <META http-equiv="refresh" content="5,http://www.als-
      translation.com/">
  </HEAD>
  <BODY>
    ...
  </BODY>
</HTML>
```

CHAPTER

26

Creating Widely Accessible Web Pages

Making pages that work on different browsers

Making pages more accessible

Handling language differences

Who is using your site?

Have you ever thought about the people that are using your site? Chances are, unless the HTML documents are accessible to a select group of individuals only, visitors will be viewing your site using a variety of platforms and browsers.

Accessibility Is Being Ignored

There are several styles or methods of creating or designing HTML documents that allow anyone, regardless of the browser or platform, to use the site. If it looks great in Internet Explorer 4.0 or Nestscape Navigator 4.0, it should be at the very least functional in Lynx; and it should look good for everything in between. The attitude that, "They have the WRONG browser, and it's their fault that the page isn't working properly," will turn a lot of people off of your site altogether—a customer lost forever. While it is true that there are several ways to write good HTML, there is only one way to write bad HTML documents.

Out of curiosity, I logged into my UNIX shell account to try out a few well known Web sites with the Lynx browser. I was shocked to find that so many were completely unreadable in a text-only browser. And there is no excuse for not supporting it. Even with sites that are "best experienced with (I hate that line) a frames-capable browser." The page developer can still provide a plain version using the `<NOFRAMES>` tag.

Making Pages That Work on Different Browsers

Is your site user friendly?

By that I don't mean to ask if your site offers a warm and friendly hug to its guests. For the purposes of this discussion, user-friendly means can anyone, regardless of their system or browser, view and use your site?

Even if you wanted to use all the new Web technologies, like DHTML, CSS, Java, Movies, and Live Audio, your site should be reverse compatible with any browser under it in the evolutionary browser chain. There is a term, graceful degradation, which means that although the site loses much of its functionality in down-level browsers, its appearance remains graceful; it has a structured look that is appropriate for the material being presented.

In this section we will look at a few methods for ensuring that your Web site is available to all. Also, there are several ways to use these new technologies to get the most from your HTML document without having to surrender functionality.

First, let's consider the obstacles to an "anybrowser" Web site. There are the obvious, sites that use frames, browser-dependent tags, and platform differences. These so-called obstacles are very easy to work around. Let's talk about each for a minute.

Using Frames

Frames are a very common way to control the layout of a site. There are, however, problems associated with using frames incorrectly, rendering entire sites useless for non-framed browsers.

Framed sites that work

1. De-frame the site. Copy all the information from each of the frames and add it to the <NOFRAMES> section. The <NOFRAMES> tag, along with the <FRAMES> tag, is completely ignored when the site is being viewed from a browser that does not support frames. But when viewed with a frames-capable browser, the <NOFRAMES> tag tells the HTML interpreter to ignore everything within its scope. That is why you must remember to use the <FRAMESET> tag first, and then the <NOFRAMES> alternative HTML can follow.
2. Save the new document. Once the information from the various framed pages of the site is added into the main page in its logical order, you will save the file as the index.html page.
3. Upload the new index.html. Having made and saved the new version of the index page, you will need to replace the old one—if this is a fix-it job—that is already available on the Net.

The problem with frames

Many framed sites are not supported by non-frames browsers. Site visitors are finding blank pages at these sites. Instead of sending an email complaint, they usually just don't return to the site. A customer lost forever.

Browser-Dependent Tags

It's the curse of the "isms." Web site designers that have a preference to a particular browser may opt to use tags or tag attributes that are useful for one browser only, or worse yet… for one version of one browser.

Table 26.1 identifies several "isms" (tags or attributes) by browser and indicates if they were added to the HTML standards and, if so, at which level.

Are you using "isms"?

When one of these "ism" tags is used, like the <MULTICOLS> and <LAYERS> tags for Netscape, or the <MARQUEE> tag (or mouse-event attributes) for Internet Explorer, everyone not using the "right browser" ends up seeing something that's not quite perfect.

TABLE 26.1 Browser-specific tags

HTML Tag	NN	IE	HTML 4	HTML 3.2	HTML 2	Deprecated
ALINK	✔	✔		✔		✔
BASE TARGET	✔	✔	✔			
BGCOLOR	✔	✔				
BGPROPERTIES		✔				
BGSOUND		✔				✔
BIG	✔	✔	✔			
COLS	✔	✔	✔			
FRAMES	✔	✔	✔			
GUTTER	✔					
LOOP	✔	✔				
MAP	✔	✔	✔	✔		
MARQUEE		✔				
MULTICOLS	✔					
OBJECT	✔	✔	✔			
RECT	✔	✔	✔			
SMALL	✔	✔	✔	✔		
VLINK	✔	✔				✔
WHITESPACE	✔		✔			

Things really start to get confusing when you consider that HTML 4.0 has added several tags to the standards and deprecated others.

By using only standard tags, the layout and appearance of your site will be pretty much the same, regardless of the browser or platform.

That being said, it is not very likely that you will shy away from using the tags suggested by your favorite browser's manufacturer. Instead of trying to convince you to not use those tags, some of which I use, let's concentrate on making it all work.

There is nothing wrong with making two or more versions of a Web site. My site, at `www.netroute.net/~webman`, uses a JavaScript forwarding function built into the HEAD of the index.html page. When you call up my URL, the JavaScript scripplet checks out the browser being used to view the site and changes the `document.location()` object to the URL for a version of the site specific to that browser. So far the site offers browser-specific versions for Internet Explorer 3, Internet Explorer 4, Netscape Navigator 4, and a generic HTML 3.2 version. I use CGI, CSS, DHTML, JAVA, and ActiveX on my site. Instead of worrying about frustrated visitors thinking I don't know what I'm doing because of a JavaScript error, they get a perfect version of the site for their browser. We will have a closer look at this option later in the chapter.

Multi-browser compatible

Your site is multibrowser compatible if the HTML is of the kind that all browsers will recognize and properly render, or if it contains those ingredients plus uses some method for making other versions of the same information available. These other versions could be a framed version, a generic JavaScript version, an Internet Explorer and Netscape Navigator version, and so on.

Platform Issues (Visual Rendering)

The most common platform issues involve rendering differences. This has to do with which platform you used when developing the site. In fact, the majority of PC users have no idea how (sizing and alignment) a Macintosh renders Web pages, and neither group understands the rendering of Web TV.

Page designers often take advantage of `width` and `height` attributes to make the page look a specific way. For example, suppose you are using tables to control the layout; chances are, you will want to assign a specific width to embedded tables. Nothing special, this is in fact a very common way to control your page's layout. Problems arise when you determine the sizing of the page as an absolute size, for example, `<TABLE width="800">`, telling the browser to stretch the table across 800 pixels. If everyone had their computer display setting set at 800×600, that would be just fine. But they don't; PC display settings are, by default, 640×480. The two other somewhat common display settings—800×600 and 1024×768—are specified as user preferences; if users want the bigger canvas, they will change their settings. It gets even more complicated when you consider the screen settings for Macintoshes, Web TV, and hand-held Web browsers, all of which have different display setting schemes.

Common layout problems

Specifying the size of an element has its obvious benefits. But did you know that the method you use for determining the size of an element can cause major layout problems?

Tables are but one source of the problem; font size and border size properties, which can be set in a CSS style sheet (or with the `<FONT>` tag for older browsers), can also mess up a page's appearance when viewed with the "wrong" browser or platform. By specifying the font size as an absolute value, such as 12pt., you are forcing all users to view it at that setting, regardless of how their systems render pixels as a font.

Suggesting an element's size

A great layout tool. The ability to access an element's sizing properties greatly improved HTML designers' control over the appearance of the documents they were making.

In the case of the table, instead of saying that it's 800 pixels, specify the size as a percentage of the canvas size. For example, `<TABLE width="95%">`. Regardless of the screen settings, the table will be stretched out across 95% of the browser's window. Be sure to express any embedded tables as a percentage (of the table in which they reside) as well.

You have even more flexibility with the sizeable elements (see Table 26.2). You can express an element's size as `em`, `ex`, `pc`, `pt`, `px`, `cm`, `mm`, or `in`.

Improve your site's accessibility with relative units

1. Open the HTML document. If you have used an absolute sizing method for any HTML document you created, open and edit that document.
2. Find all elements that use an absolute size. You are looking for any instances where an element's size is stated as pixels or some other absolute value. If the element uses a percentage, such as `<TABLE WIDTH=95%>`, it can be left as is and you can feel confident that it will be properly displayed in almost any browser that supports tables.
3. Save the document and put it back on the Net.

TABLE 26.2 **Units of measurement**

Units	Meaning	Description
`em`	The width of "m"	This unit of measurement draws an element at a size relative to the parent element. Personally, I think the browser's default settings make a good starting point. Any element sizing you do will be expressed as a percentage of the default setting. In other words, it will work on any platform.

Units	Meaning	Description
`ex`	The height of "x"	This is basically the same as an `em` space, except, of course, that it references a different letter, and in a different way, for determining sizing.
`pc`	Picas = 12 pt	One `pc` is 12 points or 12/72 of an inch. In other words, this is an absolute size.
`pt`	Points 1pt=1/72in	Another absolute size.
`px`	Pixels of canvas	Relative to the display setting for the monitor.
`cm`	Centimeters	Absolute size.
`mm`	Millimeters	Absolute size.
`in`	Inches	Absolute size.

Measurement units are easy to use. For example, to make an element slightly smaller or larger than its parent element, use the `em` (relates to parent "m") or `ex` (relates to parent "x") units. The `pc` and `pt` units are also useful with text, but should be used cautiously because they are absolute sizes, relative to an inch. But some measuring units, although great for a PC, are very problematic on other systems. For example, `px`, the measurement of pixels, is not recommended for pages that will be viewed on a Macintosh; the text would possibly be too small to read. For measuring things like borders and margins, `em` and `ex` can be used as well, but `pc` and `px` work great for this purpose. My recommendation is to stick to using the units that will be supported for the largest audience, unless the browser and platform of the user are known with a relative amount of certainty.

The Object Model

It was once thought that, as the HTML standards progressed, the way browsers handled that HTML would be pretty much the same. In fact, the opposite is true. With HTML 4.0, DOM, and CSS, each browser has decided to treat the elements and properties of those elements differently.

Consider the differences in the browser object models—that part of the browser program that decides which elements are accessible to scripting and to what degree. For example, both browsers

Accessible properties

An object model provides a mechanism for accessing the properties of an HTML element programmatically. This access is permitted either when the document is parsed by the browser, known as static element access, or anytime during and after the browser parses the document, known as dynamic access.

support a mechanism for capturing mouse events, but NetScape Navigator allows mouse events on the `<A ...>` and `<INPUT ...>` elements only. The Internet Explorer object model allows you to attach a mouse event to any HTML element.

When I design a site for Internet Explorer, it's a pretty safe bet that Netscape Navigator will only support part of the site's functionality. Internet Explorer has given the HTML developer about the same level of element control as a Windows application programmer has over the program he or she creates.

On the flip side, if I develop a site according to the Netscape Navigator object model, chances are good that none of the functionality will be lost by using the site in Internet Explorer (with the exception of the `<LAYER>` tag). Obviously, this is a major advantage for developers who aren't really interested in using all the advanced features of Internet Explorer.

One version or several?

Basically, for sites that do not use frames, ActiveX, Dynamic HTML, CSS, or any other HTML enhancements, the single version site is appropriate. Otherwise, if you are going to use the enhancements, give serious thought to versioning the site according to the browser that supports the enhancements used.

If your goal is to design a really cool Web site using DHTML and CSS, but you only want to write a single version of the site, you are probably better off with Netscape Navigator. Providing you stay away from the Netscapisms like `<LAYER>`, the site should work just fine in both browsers.

But if you really like the `accesskey` property and can't seem to stop yourself from putting filter effects onto HTML elements that do not support them when viewed in Netscape Navigator, you should give serious thought to creating that second version of the site, and using JavaScript to forward the user to the version for his browser.

There is a third option. (It's a little messy, and makes HTML file sizes much larger than they really need to be.) Web browsers have a knack for ignoring tags and attributes they do not know. Therefore, it's possible to create a single version of the site and incorporate the intended features and functionality of both browsers into the code. Should you decided to go this route, the first time you open the HTML file to make some changes you will see what is meant by "a little messy." With all the extra HTML elements—tags and properties—the code has a tendency to get somewhat cluttered and finding anything becomes a mission.

CSS

Using style sheets gives you the opportunity to specify exactly how most elements of your HTML document should look. In addition to defining such basic features as the color and size of the elements, you can also specify the element's position on the document. With newer features coming down the unending line of browser enhancements (read version 4.0 of Netscape Navigator and Internet Explorer), the possibilities within the medium would appear almost limitless.

Although the concept of using style sheets for HTML documents has been around for quite some time, nothing definitive, in terms of implementation recommendations (the standards), was available until the second half of 1996. Internet Explorer 3.01 offered partial support for the early version of CSS, but it wasn't until version 4.0 that we began to see CSS become an important part of the browser's overall performance and functionality. Netscape Navigator 4.0 also offers a mostly complete implementation of CSS. There are some differences in the way each treats specific elements, but both browsers are CSS compliant according to the requirements of the W3C.

CSS will not mess up the appearance

Since the **<STYLE>** tag is ignored by all browsers that do not support CSS, you can add this enhancement to a single version site without having to worry about its effect on non-compliant browsers. Just remember to design the site without this enhancement first, getting the look you want. Then you can move on to adding the CSS style sheet for further appearance enhancements.

It has already been stated in this chapter, and you've probably heard it from others, that browsers will ignore anything that they don't understand. This is a very important piece of information because it means that if you are designing several versions of your Web site, you can still include the CSS style rules in the version for HTML 3.2-compliant browsers. On the off chance that someone using a CSS-compliant browser—other than one of the browsers in your navigator.appversion list—decides to look at your site, they will benefit from the style sheet rules. If you are just going to design one version of the site, the same argument holds true. When viewed with browsers that support CSS it will work, when viewed with older browsers it will be ignored.

Browser-Independent Pages

To make your site browser independent (browser neutral, or whatever else you want to call it), you will have to use various workaround techniques that allow incompatible tags to be ignored but still keep the structure of the page intact. For example, wrapping a JavaScript `document.write` command into an Internet Explorer 4 dynamic—ticking—clock ensures that the visitor will see a clock on his page, whether he is using Internet Explorer or Netscape Navigator.

There are a few "rules of the road" for designing Web documents that will work on all browsers.

- Never use frames. Never! I don't care how much you like the look of frames. There are alternate methods for controlling the layout of your site, methods for emulating the look of frames without having to worry about creating that noframes section we discussed earlier. (This section is about creating a single version of the site.)
- Remember to keep your source code as readable as possible. This means inserting comments to remind yourself about things in the HTML that may be confusing at a later date. This could include such things as why a particular paragraph—or any other element of the document—has been coded three different ways (an extreme example, but entirely possible).
- Develop the functionality of the site for one browser first, then the other. Work backwards when finished, to make sure nothing is broken as a result of adding the features of the other browser. To make the process run more smoothly, you should keep records of the development process so you can refer back to them whenever a problem does arise—maybe you had already encountered the problem and fixed it—the records will help to eliminate the process of having to reinvent the wheel.

A well-developed plan makes all the difference

All too often, new Web developers are scared to attempt to include specific layout instructions in their site; they are probably worried that learning would take too much time. But when you see a site that is obviously using layout techniques, its benefits are clear to you. Instead of waiting to regret the first attempt, when writing the sites plan, be sure to include sufficient time to learn how to manipulate document layout.

Once you have put the plan on paper, identified the vision for the Web site, and started a formal process for keeping track of the site, you can get down to the business of creating the HTML pages. Or, you can skip all the planning and just dive into the HTML. The following will be used as the content for the all-browser HTML document.

Who Knew?

©1998 By, JRF—Used by permission of the author.

When they sent the crew of the Space Station America up for their three-year mission, no one could have guessed they were never to set foot on the Earth again.

Captain Spencer was to retire upon his return home. Jenny, his wife and life long companion had already picked out their retirement cottage, a nice two-bedroom bungalow in the Fingers Lakes region of upper New York State.

But Spencer wasn't thinking about the cottage, or even his wife, at that moment it finally occurred to him that he would never again go fishing with his grandson, Charles.

Now that we have written out the script for the page, put it into an HTML editor and begin adding the tags needed to make it HTML 3.2 compatible.

Create an HTML document

1. Determine the contents of the site. Write out the script for your site. This step requires you to first imagine, then write out, a storyboard of sorts, to become a person and a writer. Once you have determined the approximate shape and depth of the site (how many pages, what is each page about), you can get to work writing the script for each page. Alternatively, you can hire professionals in both the advertising field (to plan the look and layout) and a scribe (to write out the script for the site).
2. HTMLize your document. Copy and paste, or enter the text directly into an HTML editor. If you are using a WYSIWYG editor, most of the coding is handled for you automatically. If you are using a text-based HTML editor, you will have to code all the elements by hand. It is also possible to use both types of editors; the WYSIWYG editor inserts all the basic code into the document. You can then shut it down and open the document in a text editor to fine-tune the code.

3. Test the results. To ensure that the site will indeed work on several browsers and platforms, publish the plain HTML documents onto the Net and ask friends and associates to check it out for you. Be sure to find out which platform they are running (Windows 3.x, Windows 95, OS2, UNIX, and so on) and which browser(s) they use. Remember to ask them specific questions about the site's appearance, such as what color the embedded table on the third page was.

```
<HTML>
<HEAD>
<TITLE>Who Knew? By, JRF</TITLE>
</HEAD>
<BODY bgcolor="white" alink="brown">
<H1><FONT color="red">Who Knew?</FONT></H1>
<P><SMALL>©1998 - By, JRF - Used by permission of the
author.
</SMALL></P>
<P>When they sent the crew of the <A href="#1">Space
Station America</A> up for their three-year mission, no
one could have guessed they were never to set foot on
the Earth again.</P>
<P><A href="#2">Captain Spencer</A> was to retire upon
his return home. Jenny, his wife and life long companion
had already picked out their retirement cottage, a nice
two-bedroom bungalow in the Fingers Lakes region of
upper New York State.</P>
<P>But Spencer wasn't thinking about the cottage, or
even his wife, at that moment it finally occurred to him
that he would never again go fishing with his grandson,
Charles.</P>
<A name="1">
<IMG src="a01.jpg" alt="The cottage" width=200
height=250></A>
<A name="2">
<IMG src="a02.jpg" alt="A portrait of the Captain"
width=200 height=250></A>
</BODY>
</HTML>
```

The result of this code is shown in Figure 26.1.

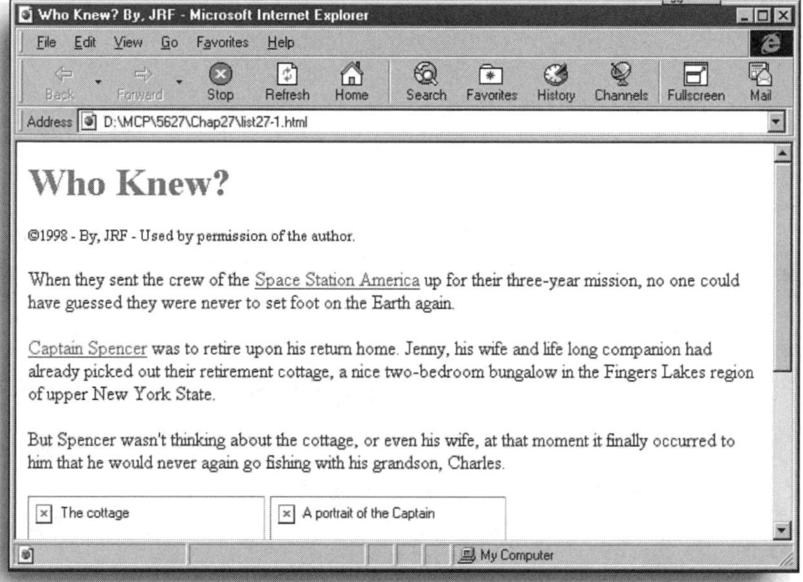

FIGURE 26.1
Our example uses HTML 3.2 code as the absolute lowest level of support.

We will add CSS and DHTML to the page now, but since this is the only version of the document we have, we need to be careful about how we do it. Some of the DHTML features that we add are meant to be used with Internet Explorer 4.x only and therefore will be ignored by all other browsers. The following includes everything for HTML 3.2, plus the Internet Explorer 4.x enhancements. Figure 26.2 shows the result of the following code.

Create an HTML document with Internet Explorer 4.x enhancements

1. Open the document for editing. The document you created earlier will now need to be re-opened.
2. Add the new features. The `<STYLE>` and `<SCRIPT>` elements can now be added to the site.
3. Save, publish, test. Replace the HTML documents that you had previously put on the Net and ask the same group of friends and associates to test the site again. You should get mixed results this time. Not all the testers will see the same results, and some will probably report a few unexpected problems.

```
<HTML>
<HEAD>
<TITLE>Who Knew? By, JRF</TITLE>
```

```
<STYLE type="text/css">
/* lets have fun, I'm going to change the colors for CSS
compliant browsers */
BODY {background;black; color;white;}
A {text-decoration;none; color;gold; font-family;arial;
font-size:1.1em;}
P {text-indent:2.5ex;}
H1 {font-family;arial; font-size:1.5em;}
.cool {font-family;impact; font-size:1.3em;}
</STYLE>
<SCRIPT language="JavaScript">
function show1() {
document.all.div1.style.display='block';
}
function show2() {
document.all.div2.style.display='block'
}
function hide1() {
document.all.div1.style.display='none'
}
function hide2() {
document.all.div2.style.display='none'
}
</SCRIPT
</HEAD>
<BODY bgcolor="white" alink="brown">
<H1><FONT color="red">Who Knew?</FONT></H1>
<P><SMALL>&copy;1998 - By, JRF - Used by permission of
the author.
</SMALL></P>
<P><B class=cool>W</B>hen they sent the crew of the
<A href="#1" onClick="show1(); ">Space Station
America</A> up for their three-year mission, no one
could have guessed they were never to set foot on the
Earth again.</P>
<P><A href="#2" onclick="show2()"><B
class=cool>C</B>aptain Spencer</A>was to retire upon his
return home. Jenny, his wife and life long companion had
already picked out their retirement cottage, a nice two-
bedroom bungalow in the Fingers Lakes region of upper
New York State.</P>
```

```
<P><B class=cool>B</B>ut Spencer wasn't thinking about
the cottage,or even his wife, at that moment it finally
occurred to him that he would never again go fishing
with his grandson, Charles.</P>
<A name="1" onclick="hide1()">
<DIV   id=div1 style="display;none;">
<IMG SRC="a01.jpg" alt="The cottage" width=200
height=250></A>
</DIV></A>
<A name="2"  onclick="hide2()">
<DIV id=div2 style="display;none;">
<IMG src="a02.jpg" alt="A portrait of the Captain"
width=200 height=250>
</DIV></A>
</BODY>
</HTML>
```

This code will return an error

If viewed in Netscape Navigator 4.x, the previous code will return a JavaScript error message that document.all is not an object. Adding the layers and the corresponding JavaScript to the code will correct that problem.

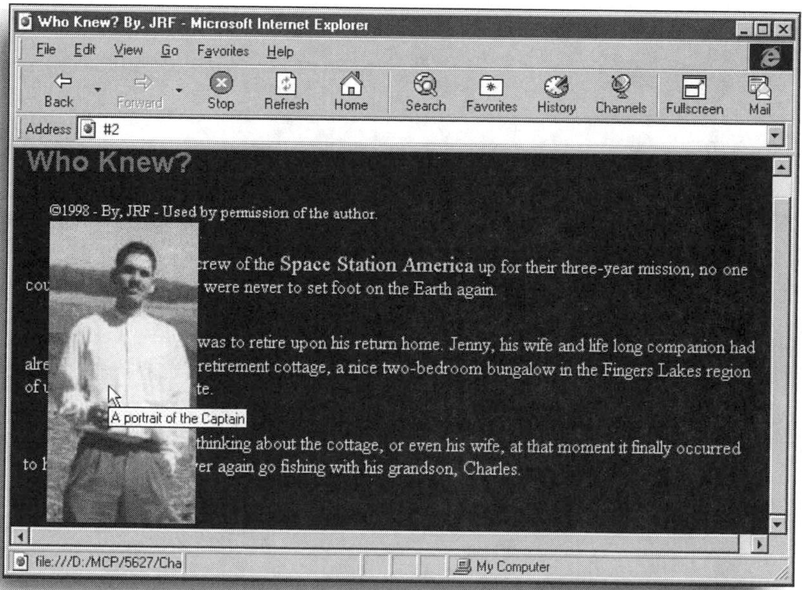

FIGURE 26.2

Now that we've added some CSS and DHTML for Internet Explorer 4, the images use CSS absolute positioning and a DHTML script tells the image to pop up or to hide.

The page has the following advanced features so far:

- JavaScript to control the DHTML functionality
- CSS to specify how the results of the DHTML script will look
- An event handler that tells the script to show or hide the images

All that with only three new tags: the <SCRIPT>, <STYLE>, and <DIV> tags.

To make this example work in Netscape Navigator with the same degree of functionality, we need only to add a <LAYER> tag for the two pictures.

```
<A name="1" onclick="hide1()">
<DIV   id=div1 style="display;none;">
<LAYER visibility=hide name="lay1">
<IMG src="a01.jpg" alt="The cottage" width=200
height=250></A>
</LAYER>
</DIV></A>
<A name="2"  onclick="hide2()">
<DIV id=div2 style="display;none;">
<LAYER visibility=hide name="lay2">
<IMG src="a02.jpg" alt="A portrait of the Captain" width=200
height=250>
</LAYER>
</DIV></A>
```

Because Netscape Navigator does not support a method for dynamically resized DIVs, the layers need to wrap around the images. It is also possible, however, to eliminate the <DIV> and <LAYER> tags and simply stick the CSS `display;none` property onto the image, letting the code handle showing the images.

Anyway, here is the code for displaying hidden layers; notice that the code identifies a routine for an Internet Explorer and a Netscape Navigator version.

```
<SCRIPT language="JavaScript">
function show1() {
if (navigator.appname == "MSIE" ){
document.all.div1.style.display='block';
} else {
document.layers["lay1"].visibility="show";
```

```
} }
function show2() {
if (navigator.appname == "MSIE" ){
document.all.div2.style.display='block';
} else {
document.layers["lay2"].visibility="show"
} }
function hide1() {
if (navigator.appname == "MSIE" ){
document.all.div1.style.display='hide';
} else {
document.layers["lay1"].visibility='hide'
} }
function hide2() {
if (navigator.appname == "MSIE" ){
document.all.div2.style.display='none';
} else {
document.layers["lay2"].visibility='hide'
} }
</SCRIPT>
```

There is going to be a lot of testing and tuning to make the page work in several different browsers. The fact that something can be done shouldn't be considered reason enough to do it. The better option is to write out as many versions of the document as needed to ensure that you can take full advantage of the features of the more advanced browsers, while still supporting even the oldest text-based browsers.

Multiversion Solution

Making a multiversion site is very easy. Take your script for the page and create a new document in an HTML editor for each version you need. Code each one according to the requirements of that browser or version, and add a JavaScript forwarding function to the page that supports the low-end browsers.

Enhance usability

By creating several versions of your site, you enable more users to enjoy the best possible rendering of the site.

Create a multiversion site

1. Create a plain HTML version.
2. Create other versions. Using the features and functionality of the most popular browsers and platforms, create at least three versions: one for generic HTML, one for Internet Explorer flavors of HTML, and a Netscape Navigator version.

3. Create an appropriate directory structure. With multiversion sites, maintenance is improved if you can quickly access all the documents of each version, one version at a time.
4. Publish the site on the Net and test it.

The following code (freeware JavaScript) comes from my Web site at `http://www.netroute.net/~webman/`. Feel free to use and modify it as required.

```
<SCRIPT language="JavaScript">
var browser, version
browser = navigator.appName;
version = navigator.appVersion
if (browser.indexOf("Explorer") >= 0){
    if (version.indexOf('4.0') >=0 ){
        alert(
    "                                    __________________ \n \n"
+
    "                                    Please enjoy your Visit!
\n" +
    "                                    __________________ \n \n"
+
    "You are using Internet Explorer ver.4.x,. \n\n" +
    "I have provided a comments and questions section for
your convenience.\n" +
    "Please let me know about any problems with this
site.\n\n" +
    "                                                  Thanks!\n"
    );
    location='newdoc.html';
    }
    else
// Here we know that the browser is IE; //
// if its not IE4, but it understands JS;
// it must be IE3.  So load the IE3 version //
    location='someotherdoc.html'
}
// If the browser is not IE check if its NN //
else if (browser.indexOf("Netscape") >= 0){
    if (version.indexOf('4.0') >=0){
    alert(
```

```
     "                                    __________________ \n \n"
+
     "                                    Please enjoy your Visit!
\n" +
     "                                    __________________ \n \n"
+
     "You are using Netscape ver.4.x,. \n\n" +
     "I have provided a comments and questions section for
your convenience.\n" +
     "Please let me know about any problems with this
site.\n\n" +
     "                                             Thanks!\n"
);
     location='nn4newdoc';
     }
     else
     alert("Please enjoy your Visit! Your browser is not
recognized. This is a generic version of the site.  Please
tell me which browser you are using by completing the com-
ments form. ");
}
else
// Not IE or NN but supports JavaScript //
alert("Please enjoy your Visit. Your browser is not recog-
nized. This is a generic version of the site.  Please tell
me which browser you are using by completing the comments
form. ");
</SCRIPT>
```

Making Pages More Accessible

There are already browsers for the blind; they read the document, ignoring the HTML tags when possible, and read the contents of the page out loud. These browsers usually read the contents in a top-to-bottom order. You should consider this fact when writing your code. Try to ensure that it is written in such a way that if all the HTML tags were stripped out and it was read aloud to you, it would still make sense.

Accessible to people with disabilities

The Internet is one place that people can conduct business without having to worry about the limitations of any physical disability. Hearing-impaired persons simply rely upon the printed word in the HTML documents. Sight-impaired persons (if not blind) can simply opt to increase the text display size. But blind persons have to rely on audio interpreters, browsers that are specially designed to read the document aloud.

Audio control

Most present audio browsers simply read the entire document in a very monotonous tone—never changing pitch, voice, or volume, nothing to indicate any sort of difference in the content at all. Obviously it is better to be able to emulate these changes, when appropriate.

CSS Aural Style Sheets

An aural style sheet lets you specify speech styles, pace, pause, relative volume, and many other audio properties. The specification is available for reference from the W3C site.

They will also have information about the browsers currently supporting aural style sheets and which ones plan to support it in the future.

Handling Language Differences

Have you ever considered publishing an HTML document in a language other than English? If you have a large customer base in Germany, for example, it would probably be in your best interest to have a version of your site, or at least part of it, translated into the German language.

As you may or may not be aware, the German alphabet—although mostly similar to the English alphabet—has a few additional letter characters, as well as the accent, umlaut, and other features that distinguish it from English.

A common workaround when writing German is to substitute and omit. Distinctive German characters, called compound consonants, like the scharfes ess (β), are commonly substituted by using ss. Accents and umlauts are simply dropped from the text. This kind of workaround is suitable in a pinch, but there is no reason the document can't be properly formatted for the language in which it is written, using the language libraries available for Web browsers.

You can get more information on using different languages either by searching Help in Internet Explorer or Netscape Navigator or from their Web sites. The W3C (`http://www.w3.org/`) is working on the language and accessibility standards for the Internet. If this is an important part of your overall Web site, you will benefit from checking their information and resources.

PART

VI

HTML Publishing

CHAPTER

27

Validating Your HTML

Use a Web-based HTML validator for checking your documents online

Use local desktop tools to check documents before putting them on the Net

Ensuring Valid HTML

Validating an HTML document means checking that the HTML is valid according to a DTD (Document Type Definition) as defined by the HTML standards. There are several DTDs from which an HTML document may be validated. They are:

- HTML 2.0
- HTML 3.0
- HTML 3.2—Standard (W3C)
- HTML 4.0—Standard (W3C)
- HTML 4.0—Netscape Navigator or Internet Explorer (both use W3C proposed DOM extensions)
- Plus browser-specific HTML extensions

The most common HTML error is probably the omission of the `<DOCTYPE>` tag that identifies the HTML flavor for which the document was written. Without it, an HTML document will still render correctly, but the browser will not know which DTD it uses. This may seem a minor problem, but if you consider that HTML validation services require this information to properly check the document, it becomes clear that it's worth taking a few seconds to add this simple tag.

Table 27.1 identifies the `<DOCTYPE>` tag syntax available for most HTML validation services.

TABLE 27.1 Document type definition

DTD	HTML Syntax
HTML 2.0	`<!DOCTYPE HTML PUBLIC "-//IETF//DTD HTML 2.0//EN">`
HTML 3.0	`<!DOCTYPE HTML PUBLIC "-//IETF//DTD HTML 3.0//EN">`
HTML 3.2	`<!DOCTYPE HTML PUBLIC "-//W3C//DTD HTML 3.2//EN">`
Netscape Navigator Extensions	`<!DOCTYPE HTML PUBLIC "-//Mozilla//DTD HTML x.0//EN">`

DTD	HTML Syntax
Internet Explorer Extensions	`<!DOCTYPE HTML PUBLIC "-//MSIE//DTD HTML x.0//EN">`
HTML 4.0	`<!DOCTYPE HTML PUBLIC "-//W3C//DTD HTML 4.0//EN">`

Using a Web-Based Validator

There are several HTML validation services available on the Internet. Some are free, some aren't. You will find five of them in this chapter. The entry for each includes instructions on using its services and tips for getting the most out of the experience.

Online validation

The easiest way to find online HTML validators is to do a search at Yahoo!. The validation services found in this chapter are accessible from a Yahoo! search.

WebTechs HTML Validation Service

WebTechs checks your HTML document against the DTD for the HTML version you indicate. WebTechs' home page is shown in Figure 27.1.

Lots of options

The WebTechs HTML validation service lets you select from a list of validation options.

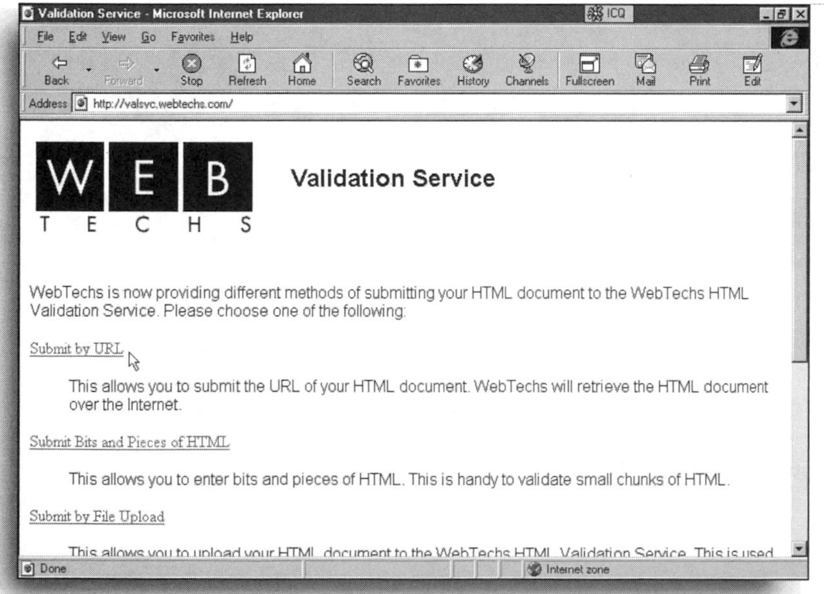

FIGURE 27.1
The WebTechs validation service lets you specify the method for testing the HTML document.

How to use the WebTechs validation service

1. Go to `http://valsvc.webtechs.com/`.
2. Select the validation method. This is the method you want to use for validating your HTML document. Table 27.2 shows the optional validation methods available.

   If you want to use the second or third option, follow the link from the validation service page, follow the onscreen instructions, skip step 3, and go on to step 4 now.
3. If you decided to use the online method, fill out the form (see Figure 27.2), indicating the URL of the page to be checked. There are four steps to be considered when completing the form.

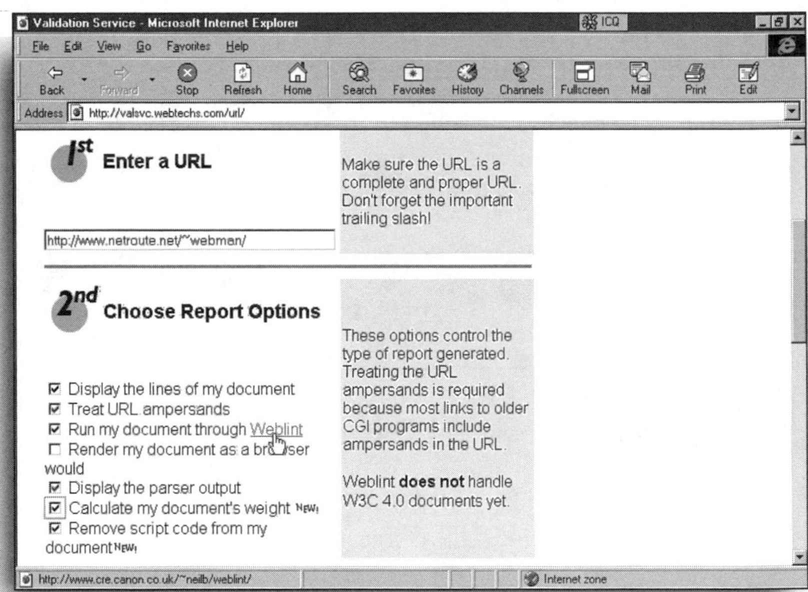

FIGURE 27.2
Submit by URL.

3.1. Enter the URL.

3.2. Choose the report options you want. Table 27.3 identifies all the options.

3.3. Choose a Formal Public Identifier (an FPI is really an SGML DTD) only if you didn't specify a DTD to use in the `<DOCTYPE>` tag, or if you want to see how the page compares to another DTD for compatibility.

3.4. Click **Submit**.

4. Analyze the response page (see Figure 27.3). It may take a couple of minutes to get back to you; this is a very popular service. Once you get the response, check to see if there were any errors.

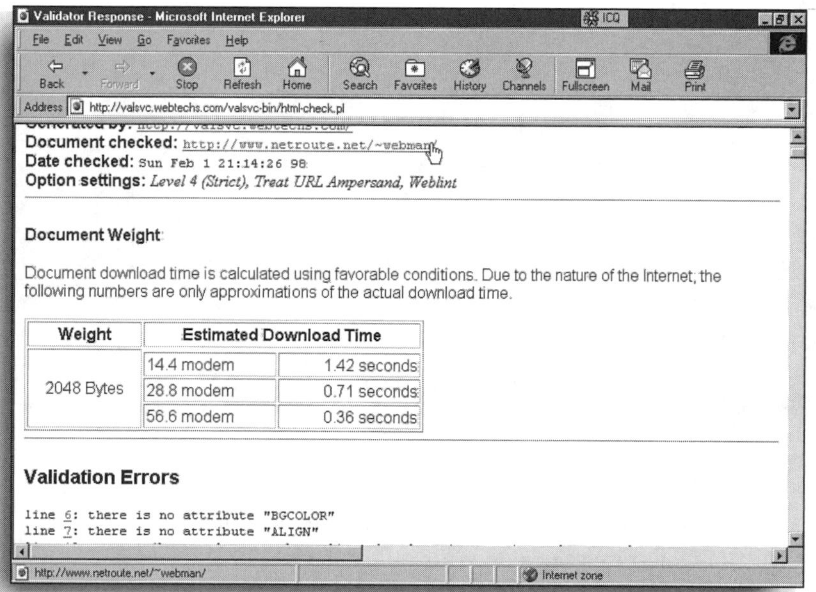

FIGURE 27.3
Errors are reported in the HTML validation service response.

Depending on the options you selected, you may also have to analyze additional sections of the response (see Figures 27.3 and 27.4). These sections may be difficult to understand, but that's perfectly all right; just check out the WebTechs FAQ page if you have any real problems deciphering the report.

The errors may at first seem confusing: Properties that you thought were proper attributes of an HTML tag turn out to be wrong, attributes that should be included are missing, and so on. Table 27.4 describes some of the error messages you are likely to see.

5. Correct any errors. If there are any errors or omissions in the site's HTML source code, you will fix them now. When the editing is finished, replace the current networked document with the new one. Now go back to step 1 and start the process again, continuing until the site is clean and pure HTML.

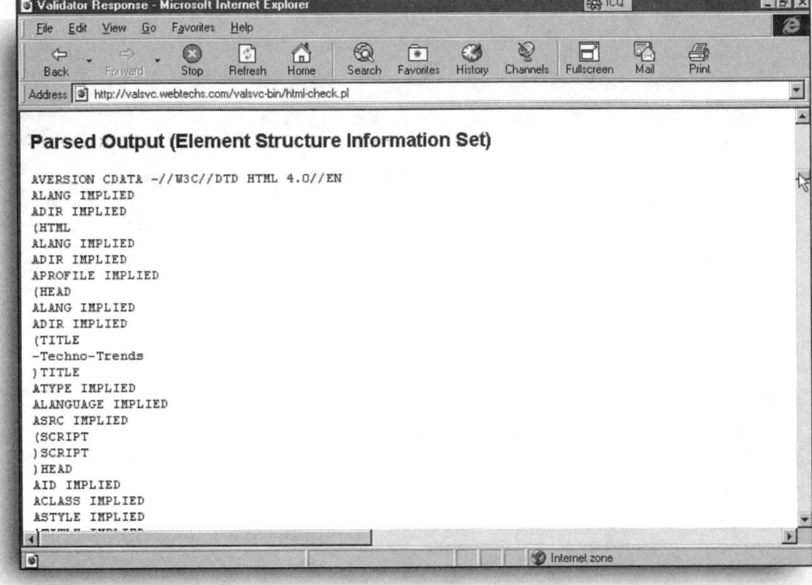

FIGURE 27.4
Parse output for the validated document.

Multiple validation services

You can validate your HTML online, bit-by-bit, or by uploading the site.

6. If your site gets through the WebTechs validation service, you can place an image on your site claiming as much. Congratulations on your valid "Pure HTML" site.

TABLE 27.2 WebTechs validation options

Option	Description
Submit by URL	The document is retrieved by WebTechs from the URL provided.
Submit Bits and Pieces of HTML	Check portions of the code while developing the document. This is handy if you are unsure about the proper use of a tag but don't want to read through the specs.
Submit by File Upload	This option allows you to validate your HTML documents before putting them on the Web.

TABLE 27.3 WebTechs reporting options

Option	Description	Recommendation
Display the lines of my document	Tells you where the error can be located in the HTML code.	Use this option always; it makes locating and fixing code errors much easier a task.

Option	Description	Recommendation
Treat URL ampersands	For testing links to CGI programs.	Only those pages that include a link to a CGI application should include this option.
Run my document through Weblint	See the entry later in this section for WebLint.	Use it always.
Render my document as a browser would	After WebTechs validation service checks out your document, you can confirm that it looked at the right page by selecting this option. It gives you a link to a copy of the document as served from the WebTechs server. The copy is discarded when the application finishes its job.	This is a neat feature, but not necessary. You can confirm that the right document was tested by checking the parse information.
Display the parser output	Shows you how the document would be parsed by a browser. Each DTD will parse the document differently.	Use always; it gives you an idea of how the various elements are parsed and can provide valuable planning information; once you understand how a parser works you can better layout the document.
Remove script code from my document	Apparently some scripts can cause unforeseen problems when being validated.	It's up to you. The error messages may not be correct with the script tag still intact.
Calculate my document's weight	Calculates the estimated download time for the page and all images at 14400, 28800, and 56000 modem speeds.	Yes, use this option. A page that loads in 10 seconds on a 56K modem may take four minutes on a 14.4K modem.

TABLE 27.4 Reading the WebTechs validation report

Message	Possible solution
`Missing DOCTYPE definition line x.`	The WebTech validation service relies on you including this tag, so the solution is to add the tag to your code.
`Missing ALT attribute from IMG`	The `Missing ALT attribute` error message is generated because, although not required, including it is considered good design.
`Extra quotation (") mark at line x.`	You somehow inserted an extra quotation mark in one of the tags. Go to the line and take the extra character out of the code.
`Missing opening/ closing quotation mark. At line x.`	Go to the line and insert the character where it is needed.
`Closing Tag missing from line x.`	This error arises quite often for those new to HTML. If you're not sure whether the element requires a closing tag, use one. There are only a few HTML elements that really can't have a closing tag: `IMG`, `OPTION`, `INPUT`, and a few others.

Kinder, Gentler HTML Validator

KGV is easier

Since there are fewer service options to consider, the KGV service is easier for those who want only a fast and effective validation of their online HTML documents.

The kinder, gentler HTML validator (shown in Figure 27.5) has only six options from which to choose. These are listed in Table 27.5.

TABLE 27.5 Kinder, gentler test options

Option	Description
Include Weblint results	Runs the WebLint line checker. (see Figure 27.8)
run Weblint in "pedantic" mode	There are three WebLint modes available.
Show source input	Displays the HTML source code so you can see the error in your code without having to switch applications.
Show an outline of this document	Creates an H1–H6 outline and comments on your use of the various H-level outlining tags.
Show parse tree	Shows you how the HTML parser read the document.
don't show attributes in the parse tree	Hides the HTML attributes from the parse tree you see.

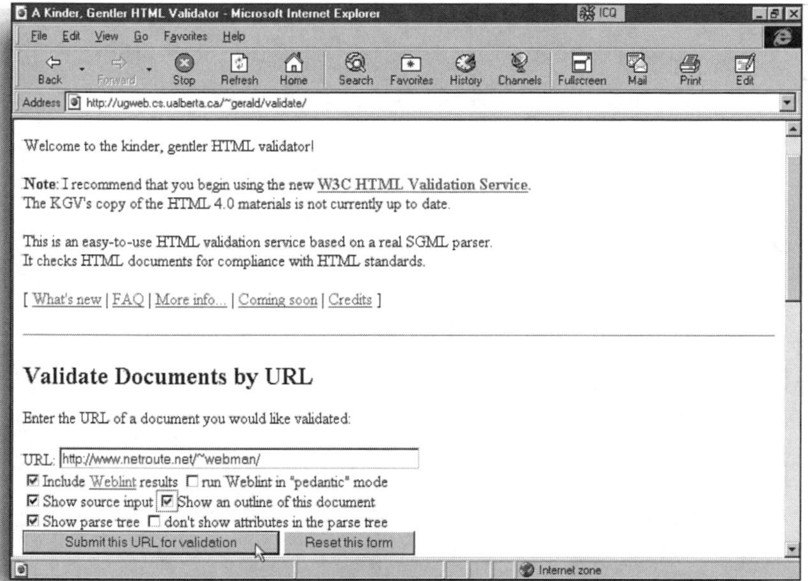

FIGURE 27.5
A kinder, gentler HTML validation service.

There is no option for telling the program to check your document against a specific DTD. If you do not include a `<DOCTYPE>` tag, the kinder, gentler HTML validator checks HTML level 2.0 by default.

A kinder, gentler, HTML validation

1. Go to `http://ugweb.cs.ualberta.ca/~gerald/validate/`.
2. Fill out the form, indicating the URL of the page to be checked and the options you want to be included in the check.
3. Analyze the response page (see Figure 27.6). It may take a couple of minutes to get back to you; this is a very popular service. Once you get the response, check to see if there were any errors.
4. Correct any errors or omissions in the source code and go back to step 1, start the process again, continuing until the site is pure HTML.

Figure 27.7 shows what must be meant by "kinder, gentler HTML validator." You can actually read the output with very little effort. Compare this output to Figure 27.4, which is not all that readable.

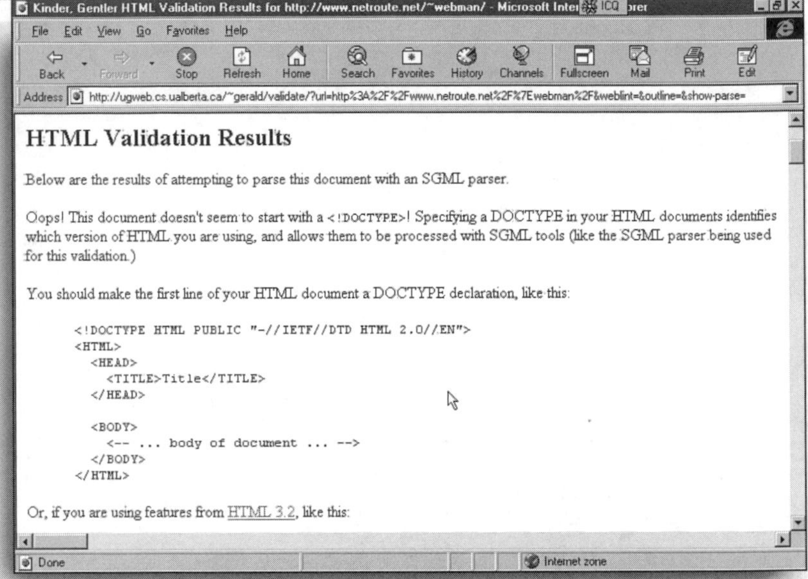

Kinder, Gentler HTML Validation Results for http://www.netroute.net/~webman/ - Microsoft Internet Explorer
File Edit View Go Favorites Help
Back Forward Stop Refresh Home Search Favorites History Channels Fullscreen Mail Print Edit
Address http://ugweb.cs.ualberta.ca/~gerald/validate/?url=http%3A%2F%2Fwww.netroute.net%2F%7Ewebman%2F&weblint=&outline=&show-parse=
HTML Validation Results
Below are the results of attempting to parse this document with an SGML parser.
Oops! This document doesn't seem to start with a <!DOCTYPE>! Specifying a DOCTYPE in your HTML documents identifies which version of HTML you are using, and allows them to be processed with SGML tools (like the SGML parser being used for this validation.)
You should make the first line of your HTML document a DOCTYPE declaration, like this:
<!DOCTYPE HTML PUBLIC "-//IETF//DTD HTML 2.0//EN">
<HTML>
<HEAD>
<TITLE>Title</TITLE>
</HEAD>
<BODY>
<-- ... body of document ... -->
</BODY>
</HTML>
Or, if you are using features from HTML 3.2, like this:
Done
Internet zone

FIGURE 27.6
I forgot to use a <DOCTYPE> tag; the validation response page suggests that I do so.

FIGURE 27.7
The parse tree from a kinder, gentler HTML validator.

Kinder, Gentler HTML Validation Results for http://www.netroute.net/~webman/ - Microsoft Internet Explorer

File Edit View Go Favorites Help

Back Forward Stop Refresh Home Search Favorites History Channels Fullscreen Mail Print Edit

Address http://ugweb.cs.ualberta.ca/~gerald/validate/?url=http%3A%2F%2Fwww.netroute.net%2F%7Ewebman%2F&weblint=&outline=&show-parse=

Parse Tree

Below is the parse tree for this document. *Note: this feature is still under construction! I'm trying to make this easier to read somehow, with little success. It helps a bit if you select the "don't show attributes" option on the form.*

```
AVERSION CDATA -//IETF//DTD HTML 2.0//EN
<HTML>

  <HEAD>

    <TITLE>
      Techno-Trends
    </TITLE>
    ALANGUAGE CDATA javascript
    <SCRIPT>
      var browser, version browser = navigator.appName; version = navigator.appVersion if (b
    </SCRIPT>
  </HEAD>
  ABGCOLOR CDATA #ffff80
  <BODY>

    AALIGN CDATA center
```

Internet zone

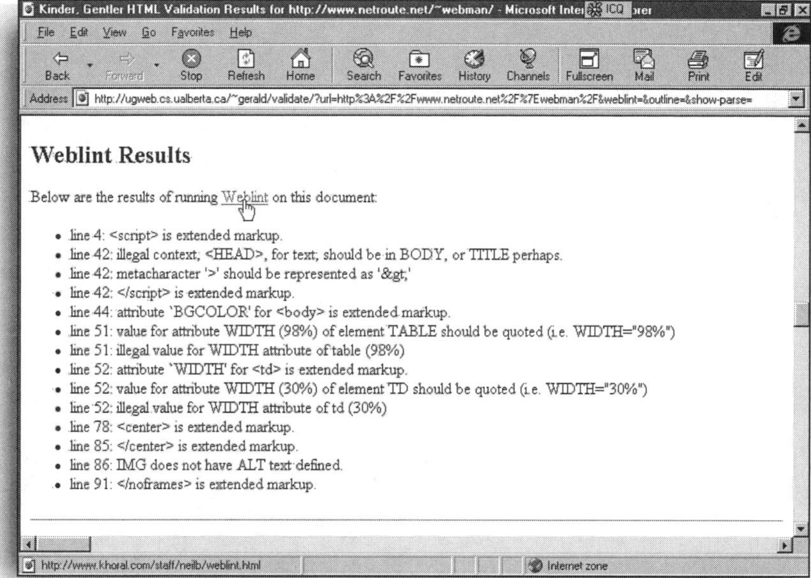

FIGURE 27.8
Weblint Results from a kinder, gentler HTML validator.

You can see the effect of omitting a `<DOCTYPE>` tag. Many of the errors reported are only errors when checked against the wrong version of HTML.

Pick a flavor

Rather than worry about a page showing errors in the validation results, simply specify the HTML and extensions used. The validator will consider those extensions as valid HTML for the purposes of the test.

Dr. Watson

Dr. Watson (shown in Figure 27.9) lets you pick the browser extensions and the level of HTML to test for, as well as a few other optional tests. Select the options you want to include in the test from the list in Table 27.6.

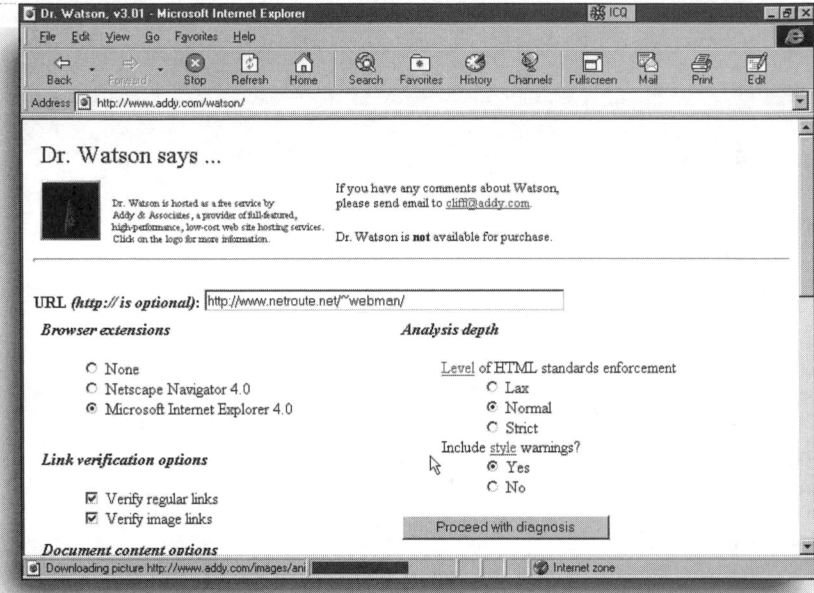

FIGURE 27.9
Dr. Watson's validator.

TABLE 27.6 Dr. Watson validation options

Feature	Choices...		
Browser extensions	None	Netscape Navigator 4.0	Microsoft Internet Explorer 4.0
Link verification options	Verify regular links	Verify image links	Choose one, both, or neither.
Level of HTML standards enforcement	Lax	Normal	Strict
Include style warnings?	Yes	No	
Spell Check the content	This option is either checked on or not.		

Check your HTML with the doctor

1. Go to `http://www.addy.com/watson/`.

2. Fill out the form indicating the URL of the page to be checked and the other features you want to be included in the check. When the form is complete, submit it.
3. Analyze the response page (see Figure 27.10) for errors.

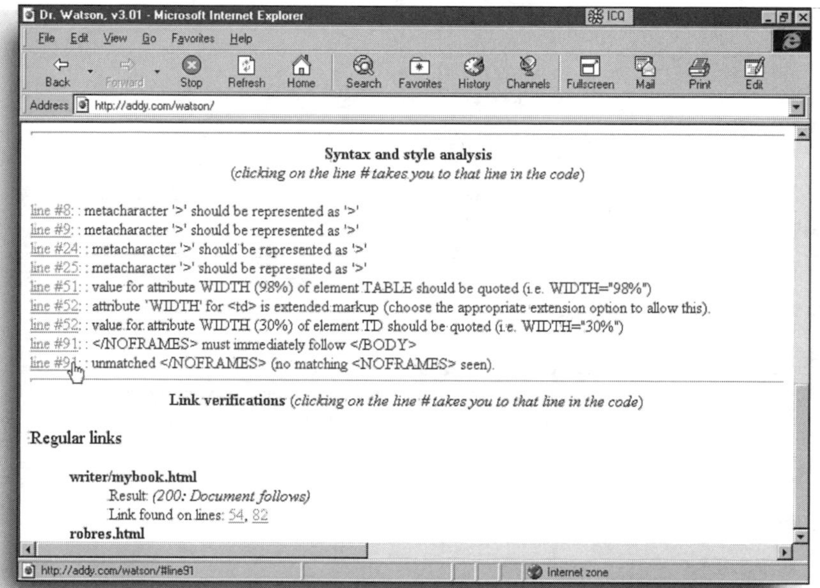

FIGURE 27.10
Dr. Watson's report on the condition of my page.

4. Correct any errors or omissions in the site's HTML source code. When the editing is finished, replace the current networked document with the new one. Now go back to step 1 and start the process again, continuing until the site is clean and pure HTML.

WebLint

There is a good reason so many other HTML validation services use WebLint (see Figure 27.11); it performs a pretty good test of your HTML code and returns an easy-to-read list of errors by line. Table 27.7 lists the options available in WebLint.

Line checking

Forget about checking the logical structure or any other extras. WebLint will check for valid HTML syntax, ensuring that all "required" attributes are present and that end tags are properly used.

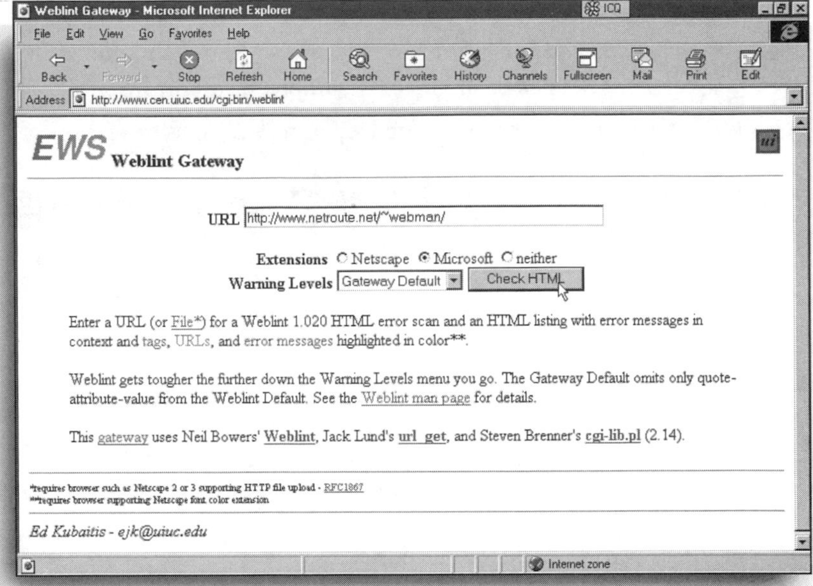

FIGURE 27.11
EWS Weblint Gateway.

TABLE 27.7 EWS validation options

Option	Choices...(pick one from each row)		
Extensions	Netscape Navigator	Microsoft Internet Explorer	None
Warning Level	Weblint Default	GateWay Default	Pendantic Mode

Using WebLint at the EWS gateway

1. Go to `http://www.cen.uiuc.edu/cgi-bin/weblint/`. Or you can go to one of the many other WebLint gateways.
2. Fill out the form indicating the URL of the page to be checked and the other features you want to be included in the check. When the form is complete, submit it.
3. Analyze the response page (see Figure 27.12). The errors are shown in a list and indicate the line in the document where you can find them.

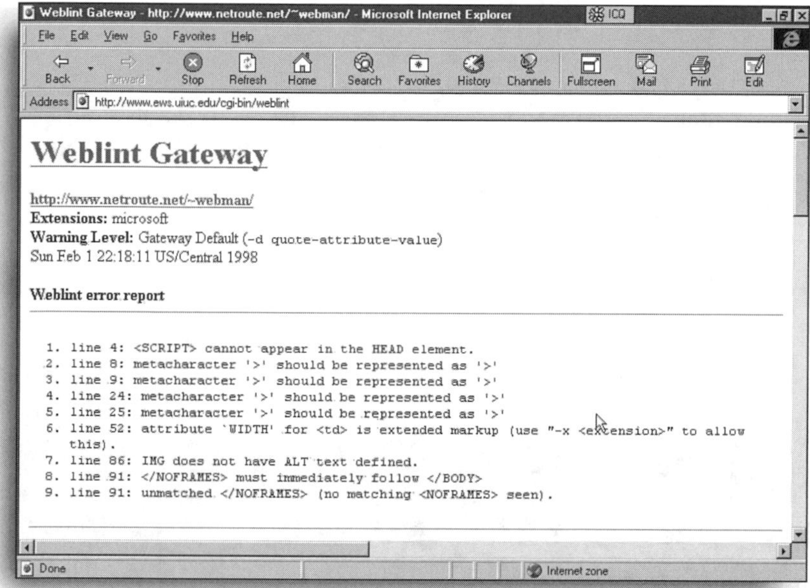

FIGURE 27.12
WebLint results.

5. Correct any errors or omissions in the site's HTML source code. When the editing is finished, replace the current networked document with the new one. Now go back to step 1 and start the process again, continuing until the site is clean HTML.

Validating a Site with Local Tools

If you would rather check your site from your own computer, there are a few programs available. You can use the programs discussed here by downloading them from their home page, or if they don't quite meet your needs, you can go to the Yahoo! HTML validators category page at `http://www.yahoo.com/Computers_and_Internet/Information_and_Documentation/Data_Formats/HTML/Validation_and_Checkers/` and pick another program to use instead.

Check first

Rather than risk putting a badly designed HTML document on the Net, where anyone can access it, check it out while it's still on your hard drive.

CSE 3310 HTML Validator

Validate as you write

After each HTML document is completed, spend a few minutes running it through the CSE 3310 HTML Validator. Checking the documents immediately, while their content and layout are still fresh in your memory, ensures that you will not forget your "intentions" at a later date.

This is a nice little program that runs from your desktop on a Window 95 or Windows NT system. It has many features for customizing the validation, including adding new HTML tags to the library and customizing error messages.

You can get your own copy of CSE 3310 HTML Validator (see Figure 27.13) from `http://www.htmlvalidator.com/`. The shareware license allows you to perform 150 document validations before requiring you to purchase a licensed copy. That's quite an evaluation period.

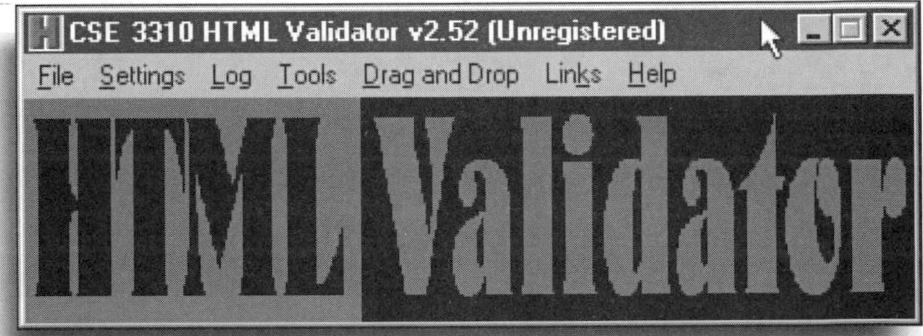

FIGURE 27.13
The CSE 3310 HTML Validator doesn't use up much space on your screen.

Using CSE 3310 HTML Validator is very straightforward

1. From the HTML Validator window, select **Validate HTML Document** from the **File** menu (see Figure 27.14), or press **F2**.

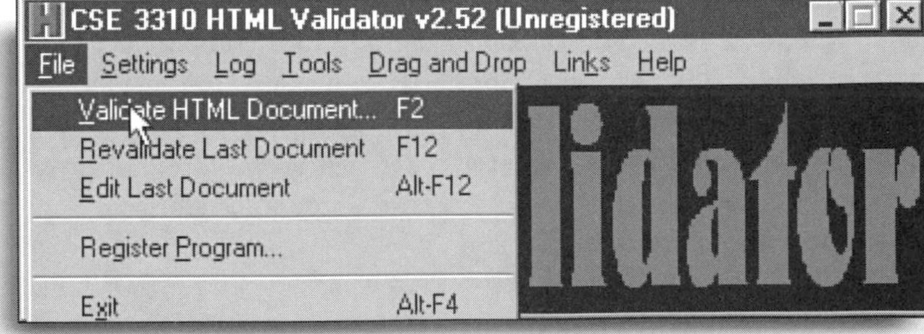

FIGURE 27.14
Starting a validation session with the CSE 3310 HTML Validator.

2. This will open a file select window (see Figure 27.15) that allows you to browse your hard drive and choose a file to validate. Select your file by highlighting the file or typing its name into the **File name** field. Press the **Open** button.

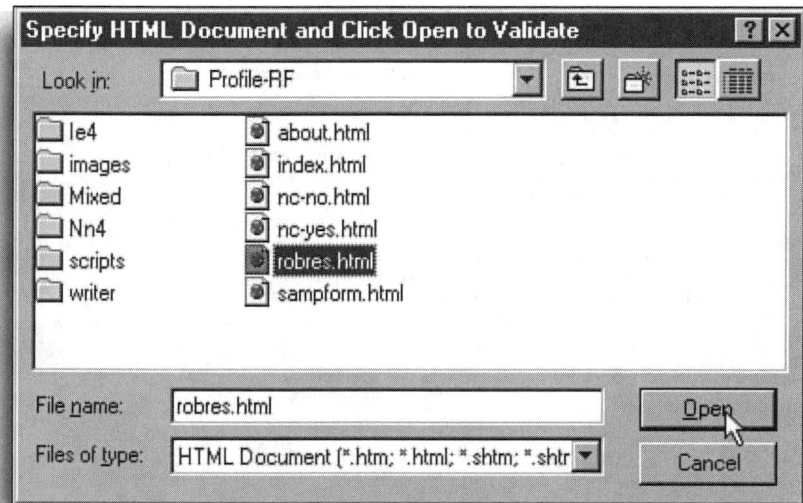

FIGURE 27.15
Choose an HTML document.

3. Review the results (see Figure 27.16). When you clicked the **Open** button in step 2, the validation ran instantly, providing you the feedback in a temporary file called output.txt. Saving this output file with a distinctive name allows you to compare it with your next validation.

There are several ways to use this application beyond simple validation. You can customize the configuration, set logging options, change the case of HTML tags, or modify the validator or program options. Table 27.8 lists the options in the CSE 3310 HTML Validator opening menu, and Table 27.9 lists the settings options.

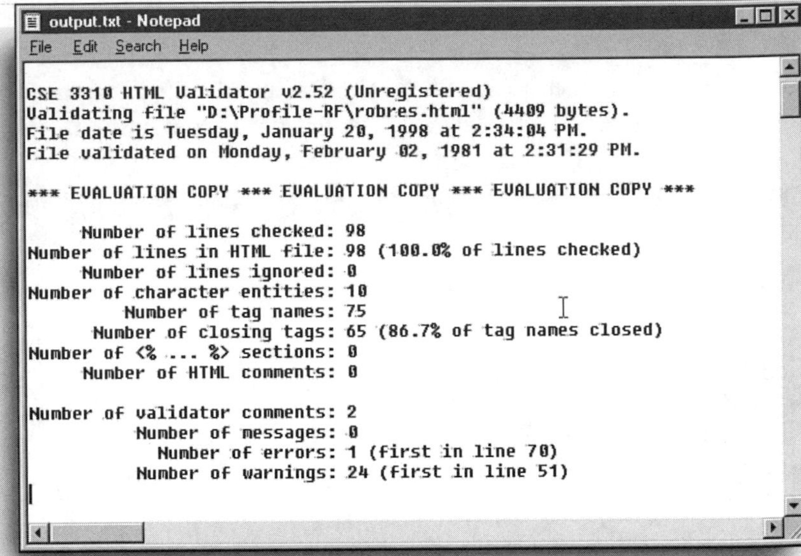

output.txt - Notepad
File Edit Search Help
CSE 3310 HTML Validator v2.52 (Unregistered)
Validating file "D:\Profile-RF\robres.html" (4409 bytes).
File date is Tuesday, January 20, 1998 at 2:34:04 PM.
File validated on Monday, February 02, 1981 at 2:31:29 PM.
*** EVALUATION COPY *** EVALUATION COPY *** EVALUATION COPY ***
Number of lines checked: 98
Number of lines in HTML file: 98 (100.0% of lines checked)
Number of lines ignored: 0
Number of character entities: 10
Number of tag names: 75
Number of closing tags: 65 (86.7% of tag names closed)
Number of <% ... %> sections: 0
Number of HTML comments: 0
Number of validator comments: 2
Number of messages: 0
Number of errors: 1 (first in line 70)
Number of warnings: 24 (first in line 51)

FIGURE 27.16
Reading the results.

TABLE 27.8 CSE 3310 HTML validator file menu options

Menu Item	Description	Shortcut Key
Validate HTML Document	Runs the validator.	F2
Revalidate Last Document	Opens last validation report.	F12
Edit Last Document	Edits last document validated.	Alt+F12
Register Program	Online registration application.	
Exit	Closes CSE 3310 HTML validator.	Alt+F4

TABLE 27.9 CSE 3310 HTML validator settings

Menu Item	Description	Shortcut Key
Program Options	Set optional features such as format for the "Convert File to" tool. (See Figure 27.17.)	F4

Menu Item	Description	Shortcut Key
Validator Options	Set validation options such as types of errors to report and types to ignore. (See Figure 27.18.)	Ctrl+F4
HTML Configuration Editor	Allows you to modify the HTML tag and attribute library that the program uses to check your document. (See Figure 27.19.)	F5
Clean Configuration	For removing non-built-in categories from the HTML configuration.	
Reset Configuration	Reset the default configuration.	
Load Configuration	Load a custom configuration designed with the HTML configuration editor.	
Save Configuration	Save a custom configuration.	
Save Configuration As	Save a configuration with a distinctive name.	

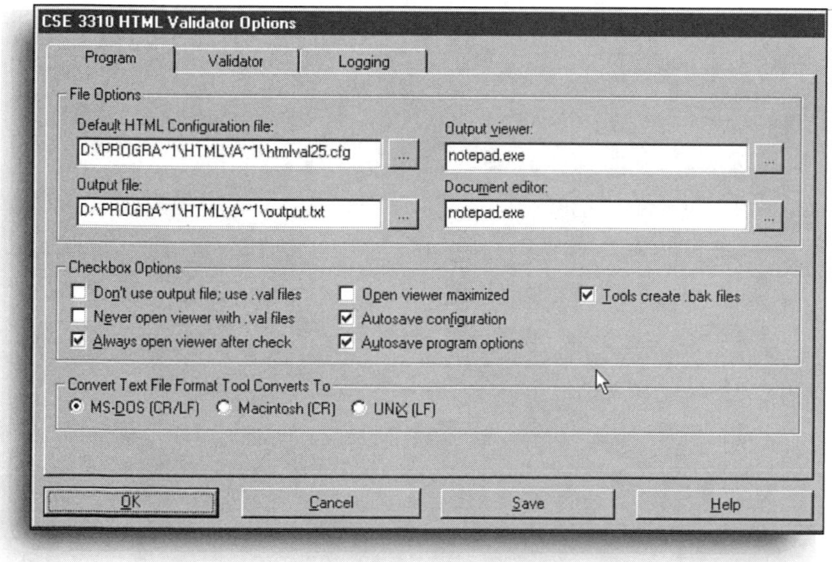

FIGURE 27.17

Program Options lets you pick the support programs and the default configuration file. It is also where you enter the file format for conversions.

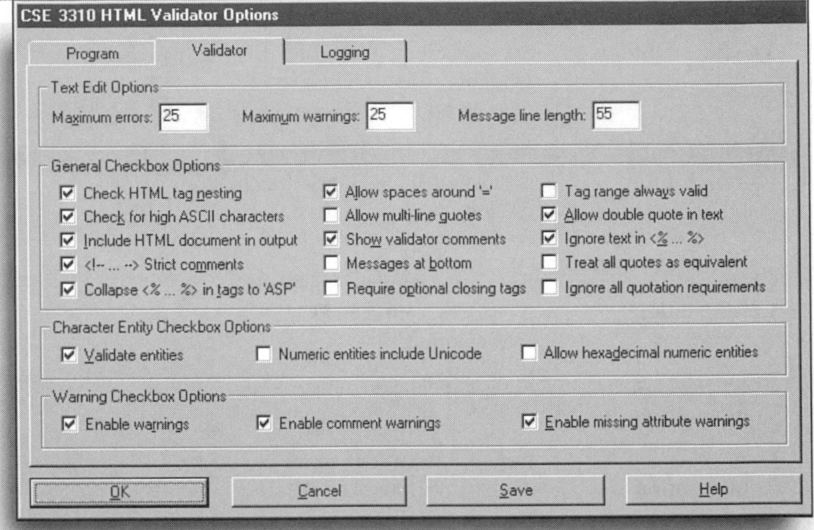

FIGURE 27.18

Validator Options includes options like whether or not nested HTML elements should be checked, or if a copy of the HTML document should be included into the output file.

You control the Edit, General, Character Entity, and Warning options here.

Tables 27.10 through 27.14 list CSE 3310's log setting options, tools, drag-and-drop options, links, and Help options, respectively.

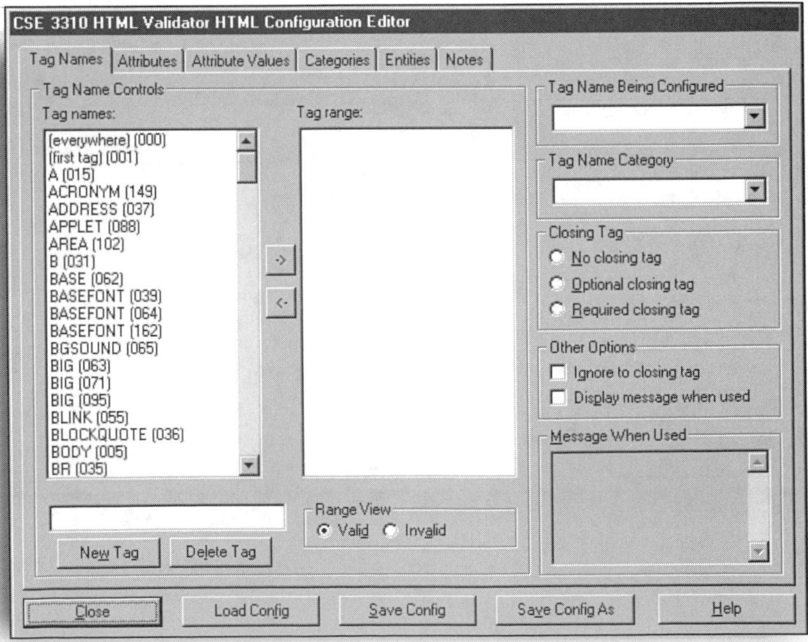

FIGURE 27.19

HTML Configuration Editor allows you to customize the validator's test criteria.

TABLE 27.10 **CSE 3310 log settings**

Menu Item	Description	Shortcut Key
Enable Logging	Start logging.	Alt+F5
Logging Options	What events are logged?	
View Log	Open the log file.	Alt+F6
Delete Log	Remove the log from the hard drive.	Alt+F7

TABLE 27.11 **CSE 3310 tools**

Menu Item	Description	Shortcut Key
Lowercase	Convert HTML tags to lowercase	F6
Uppercase	Convert to UPPERCASE	F7
Strip HTML Tags	Remove HTML tags	F8
Template	Specifies a template to use	F9
Convert Text File Format	Converts file to format specified in the program options dialog box	F10
Help with Tools	Provides help on using these tools	

TABLE 27.12 **CSE 3310 drag-and-drop options**

Menu Item	Description	Shortcut Key
Use Default Tool on Dropped files	Automatically applies one of the tools to the results of a drag and drop	Alt+F1
Use Validator on Dropped files	Default setting	Alt+F2
Set Default Drag and Drop Tool	Select the tools to use	Alt+F3

TABLE 27.13 **CSE 3310 links**

Menu Item	Description	Shortcut Key
CSE 3310 HTML Validator Home Page	Home page	
Download Page	HTML validator and supporting files	
Ordering Information Page	Register your program	
Support Page	For registered users only	
Download Latest HTML Configuration	New HTML tags and attributes	

TABLE 27.14 **CSE 3310 Help options**

Menu Item	Description	Shortcut Key
Help Contents	Get Help using HTML Validator	**F1**
Online Help Contents	Information that is not included in the help files	
Ordering Information	Print out an order form	
About	About CSE 3310 HTML Validator	**F3**

InfoLink

Fresh links count

Have you attempted to check all the links on your site? A manual link check can be very time consuming. Rather than spend your time following all the links on your site, let InfoLink do the work for you (see Figure 27.20). You can then go through and manually check on any probable trouble spots.

Ensure that all links are working, verify that your images are working, and maintain the site map whenever changes are posted. InfoLink will not check the validity of your HTML code, but it will determine if your site is working properly. Table 27.15 lists InfoLink's features.

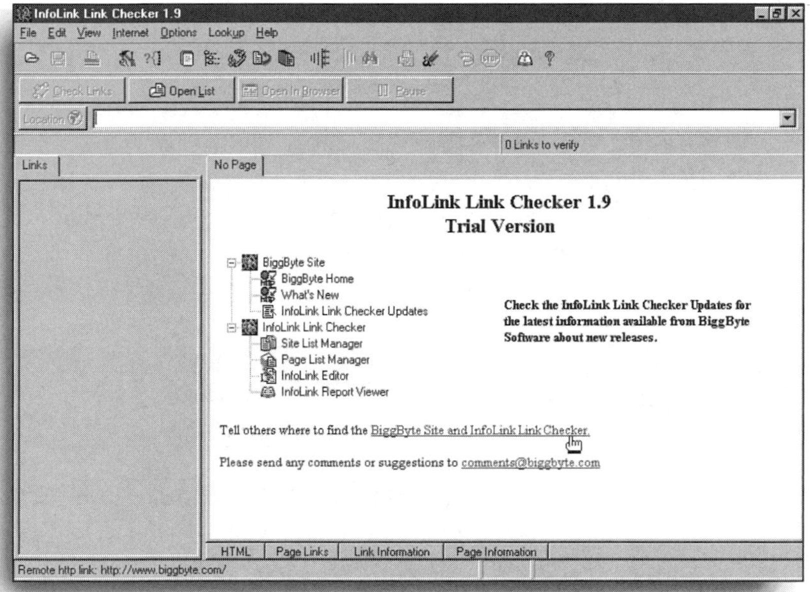

FIGURE 27.20
InfoLink application window.

TABLE 27.15 InfoLink features

Feature	Description
Page List Manager	Allows you to verify that individual pages or groups of pages are still working. This is handy for checking on pages that you commonly visit, but are not actually a part of your site.
Site List Manager	Allows you to verify every single link within the scope of a particular site. You can have one or several sites in your site list manager.
InfoLink Editor	Corrects broken links.
InfoLink Report Viewer	A complete report is prepared outlining the size of the site, the number of links and images found, the status of those links and images, and any problems found.

InfoLink is available as shareware, and can be downloaded from BiggByte's Web site at `www.biggbyte.com/`. The shareware license allows you to perform 50 link checks before requiring that the program be registered.

The following steps are necessary to set up the InfoLink Site Manager, which allows for checking on your site links as often as you want (keeping the license restriction in mind).

Setting up the InfoLink Site Manager

1. Open the Site List. This is done either by clicking the **Open List** button and selecting **Open Site List** or selecting **Open Site List** from the **Internet** menu. This will open the Site List Manager window. (See Figure 27.21.)

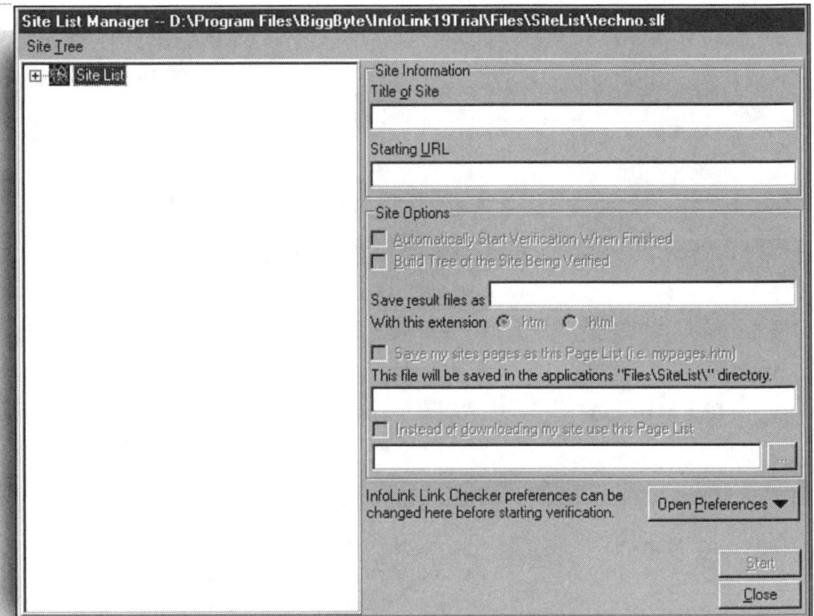

FIGURE 27.21
The Site List Manager window is split into two frames. The left frame contains the tree view, and the right frame is where you enter the information to identify the site.

2. Select **Add New Site** from **Site Tree** from the **Site List Manager** menu. This will expand the tree to include a blank branch for the new site. (See Figure 27.22.)
3. On the right side of the Site Manager window are data areas. Use these fields to identify your site to the program, and change any of the default options. You need to enter the **Site Information** first, consisting of a **Title of Site** and **Starting URL**.

   You can then either change the **Site Options** or just use the default settings. Site options are shown in Table 27.16.

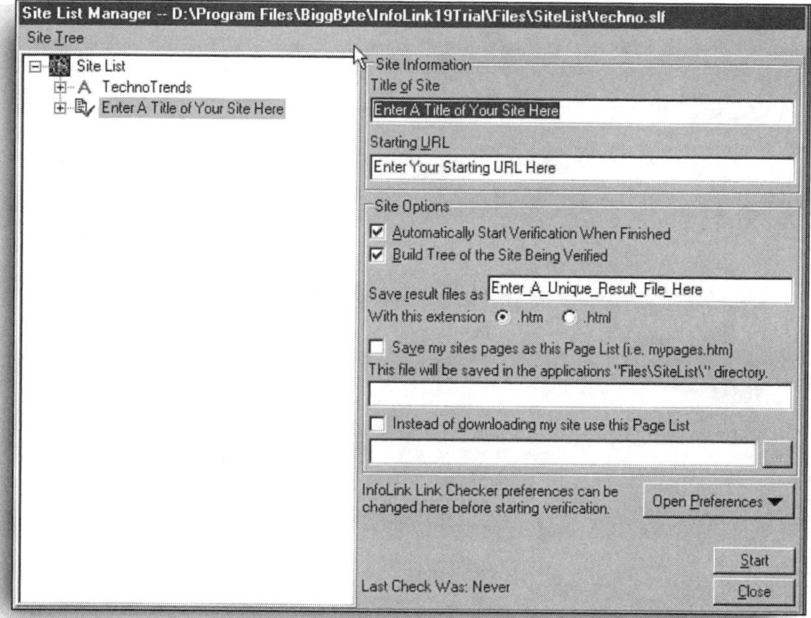

FIGURE 27.22

A new branch is added to the Site Managers tree view with the words `Enter A Title of Your Site Here`.

4. Set the InfoLink Link Checker Preferences by clicking the **Open Preferences** button and selecting the preferences group you want to modify. You can select any or all of the following: **Verification Preferences** (see Figure 27.24 and Table 27.17), **General Preferences** (see Figure 27.25 and Table 27.18), or **Network Preferences** (see Figure 27.26 and Table 27.19).

5. Click the **Start** button to run the Link Checker. The results are presented in the reports window. Figure 27.23 gives you a pretty good example of what you can expect to see in your own site reports window.

6. Evaluate the results of the InfoLink Link Check by reading through the reports. Select **Show HTML Reports** from the **Reports** menu. The reports created by the application are listed in Table 27.20.

That's all Folks! If you have any broken links, go and fix them. Use this application as often as is necessary to maintain a reasonable amount of certainty that your site is working properly.

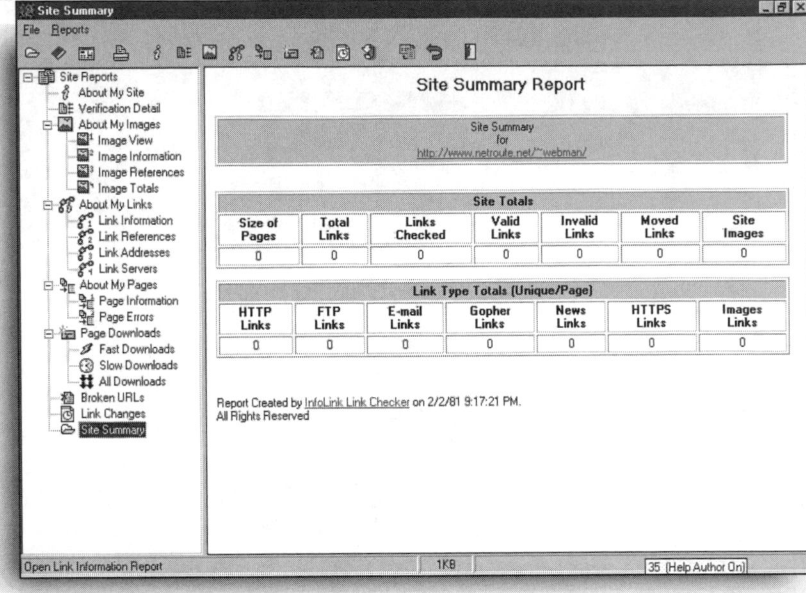

FIGURE 27.23
Site Manager Reports Viewer—click a report item to see the report.

TABLE 27.16 **InfoLink Site Manager site options**

Option	Description or choices
Automatically Start Verification When Finished	Check to start automatically.
Build Tree of the Site Being Verified	Check to build a site map tree.
Save result files as	Enter the name to be used as a group name prefix.
With this extension	Check either `.htm` or `.html`.

TABLE 27.17 **InfoLink Link Checker's verification preferences**

Option	Description
Verify These Links (list of options)	**All Links, Local Links Only, Remote Links Only**
Verify These Link Types	**http, https, Graphic, ftp gopher, mailto, news**
View as HTML Files	A list of file types to be checked

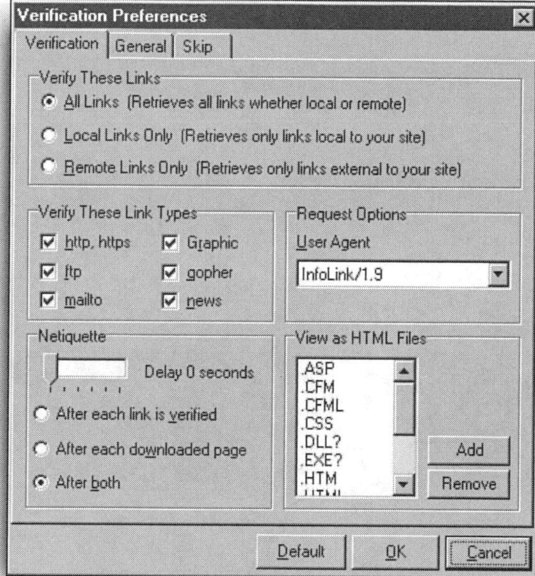

FIGURE 27.24
Verification Preferences.

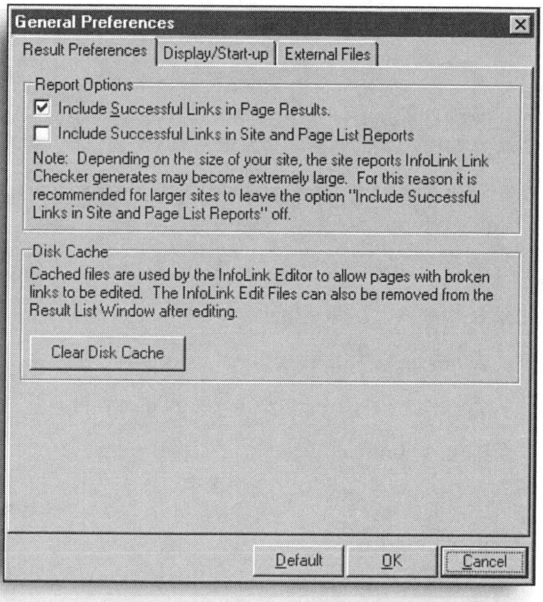

FIGURE 27.25
General Preferences.

TABLE 27.18 **InfoLink Link Checker's General preferences**

Option	Description
Include Successful Links in Page Results	Links for page verification.
Include Successful Links in Site and Page List Reports	Links for page or site verification.
Disk Cache	This button allows you to dump the cache.

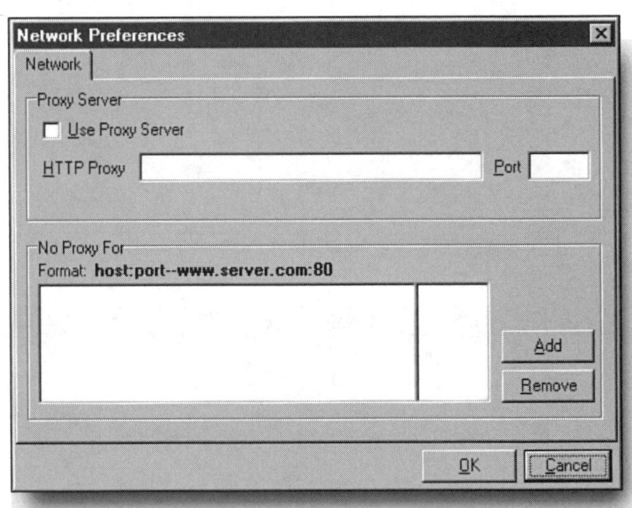

FIGURE 27.26
Network Preferences.

TABLE 27.19 **InfoLink Link Checker's Network preferences**

Option	Description
Proxy Server	Proxy Server address
No Proxy For	Exceptions to the proxy server requirements

TABLE 27.20 **InfoLink Site Reports Viewer's report options.**

Report	Description
About My Site	URL domain and address information for the site checked
Verification Detail	Verification that the site was found and checked
About My Images	List of images
About My Links	List of links
About My Pages	Listing of links and images on all pages
Page Downloads	Times for page downloads
Broken URLs	A list of all broken URLs
Link Changes	A list of all changed links
Site Summary	A summary of all the other reports

CHAPTER

28

Publishing Your Web Pages

Finding a home for your pages

Using publishing power tools

Behind the scenes on your server

A Web Site Needs a Home

Now that you've built your shiny new Web site, what do you do next? Assuming that you've been checking the Web pages on your own computer, you'll have to *upload* them to their Web home. You may already have a place to put them, as most Internet service providers give you an allowance of space for your pages. If you've made a site for your company, it probably has a server of its own on its local network; uploading your Web pages may be simply a matter of copying them to a particular location on the network.

Regardless, there are a lot of issues about publishing besides just loading onto the server—people have to know the Web site is there. You may have to know a little bit about special methods of uploading your Web pages or getting around in the world of servers, and you may want to consider other options besides paying for the space yourself. This chapter is all about publishing.

Finding a Web Home

Determining your basic needs

1. Look at your Web site plan and decide whether you need CGI service for your pages.
2. Consider other special needs such as
   - The amount of space your site will take on the server
   - Expected bandwidth your visitors will be using
   - If you need secure online ordering
   - If you will use Cold Fusion, Microsoft FrontPage extensions, server-side JavaScript, Java servlets, or other external features.
3. Classify the pages as personal, public service, or commercial.
4. Ask your present provider if your intended use lies within its terms of service.
5. If your provider doesn't meet your needs, shop around on the Web for a Web hosting service that will.

One of the most important questions is whether you'll need access to the Common Gateway Interface (CGI) to run custom programs on your site. You'll need this especially for online ordering, index searches, and for most other sorts of form input. Be aware that many providers offer different levels of access, with more offering a small selection of "canned scripts" than those allowing you to put up your own scripts.

Kick all the tires and look under the hood

Finding a Web home can be the most important decision you make about your page. It's worth spending some time investigating your present provider's offerings and comparing it to those of other local or even national companies.

Whether the former option is feasible depends entirely on what you want to do and should be discussed thoroughly with your provider before signing anything or spending a lot of time designing something that may not be possible at an existing site.

If CGI scripts are not on your horizon, you might be able to use any one of the several canned script alternatives, Cold Fusion and Web Objects. Either product offers rapid application development of CGI-style applications by stringing together predefined building blocks. Of the two, Cold Fusion is easier for non-programmers to use, but both require some level of expertise and may require hiring a programmer or highly skilled HTML coder with specialized knowledge to make the best use of their advanced technologies. Similar products include LiveWire, Domino, Net Objects, and Sapphire Web.

CGI alternatives

Many alternatives to CGI have easy-to-use development techniques or even drag-and-drop graphical interfaces, so it's possible to use some of them without programming skills or knowledge. Be aware, though, that your chosen provider has to support the particular technology you think you might like to use, so you may need to compromise or find another provider.

Related to Cold Fusion and Web Objects only by the level of power they give the Web site developer, Java servlets also provide the ability to access databases, interact with the user, and other useful things without going through the CGI.

All of these technologies have the advantage over CGI of being less expensive. The reasons for this are rather technical, but basically it's because the CGI interface is a "Whoops! I got a request! Now what do I do?!!" kind of thing that has to drop everything and start fresh with each request, while all the others are more narrowly defined. Their response to a request is "Another one of those? I'll put it on my stack of work to be done." In programming terms this is known as a lightweight (or threaded) protocol, but I'm not going to define that or even go into it here. I'll just throw out that hint if you want to research this topic further. Table 28.1 lists some of the technologies available for Web development and where they can be located on the Web.

TABLE 28.1 Table of rapid Web-development technologies

Name	Location
Cold Fusion	`http://www.allaire.com/`
Web Objects	`http://www.stepwise.com/`
	`http://enterprise.apple.com/`
LiveWire	`http://oem.netscape.com/comprod/server_central/product/livewire/index.html`
Domino	`http://www2.lotus.com/`
NetObjects Fusion	`http://www.netobjects.com/`
Sapphire Web	`http://www.bluestone.com/`
Java servlets	`http://www.javasoft.com/`

What Kind of Numbers Are We Talking About?

Visitor number, "hit count" in the industry, translates directly into cost and profit potential

Your Web site will cost more if it generates thousands of visitors an hour, less if it generates tens or hundreds per day. Most providers will step up your charges if you start costing them money, so it's just as well to start out small and let your provider tell you when the numbers get big rather than pay for a level of service you never reach. On the other hand, you ought to feel secure about the ability of your provider to meet higher levels of service on demand and bill you for them rather than throttling your service just as it starts to become popular. Find out what happens when your service limits are met. Some providers don't bill you for higher hit rates, so look around if you're not satisfied.

Next, think realistically about how many visitors you can reasonably expect every month. Don't be wildly optimistic, but don't be overly pessimistic either. If a page is well done and informative it will find an audience, no matter how esoteric the subject matter. I have one site of interest primarily to women that attracts a few thousand visitors every month, a small blip on the charts as far as high-traffic sites go, but a respectable number for a noncommercial site with no advertising budget. Figure 28.1 shows a typical hit count report.

Many providers who offer Web space do so with the understanding that your site won't swamp their server. So if you manage to land exclusive rights to the first interviews with the newly discovered inhabitants of the planet Mars, don't be surprised if your provider wants a little more money for the site. If your site is devoted to the taxonomy and anatomical structures of Caribbean snails, you can probably get by with less bandwidth and less money overall.

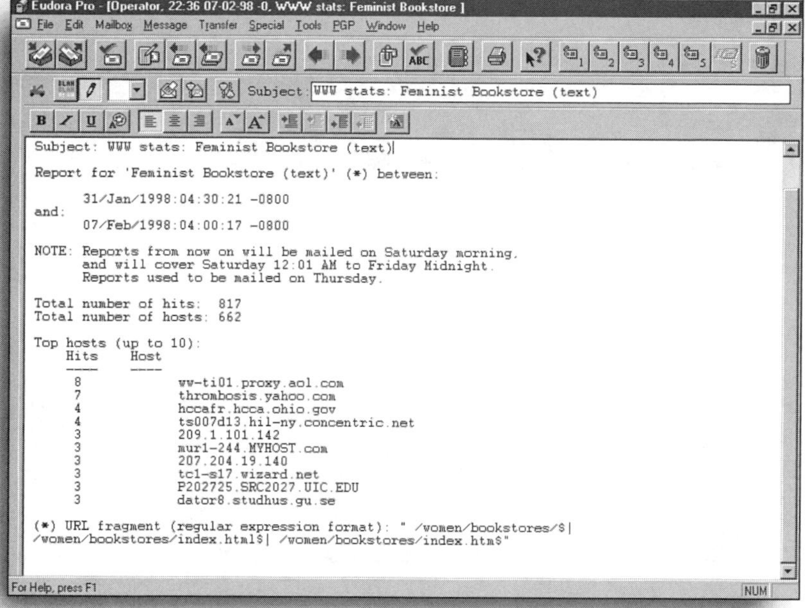

FIGURE 28.1
A typical hit count report.

Related to bandwidth is the question of disk capacity. Many sites set limits on disk storage for their customers that range from a few megabytes to twenty-five megabytes. While this is enough space to store a good-sized encyclopedia, your plans may include more—much more. Either talk to a database expert or keep track of your total size as you grow (remember that notebook?) so you can forecast what your eventual size may be. At some point it may start to make sense to dedicate a server to your site.

What Sort of Page Is It?

You should also think about what sort of page you're doing. Is it personal, commercial, or public service? For personal pages you might consider locating on a public server like GeoCities, `http://www.geocities.com/` (see Figure 28.2), which offers free personal pages if you don't have a space already. For a commercial site you'll almost certainly want a site of your own, and your provider may want you to pay commercial rates. But there are other options available for sites that could legitimately be called a public service.

FIGURE 28.2
GeoCities main page.

Public services are valuable properties, not burdens

You shouldn't have to pay much to provide a public service, assuming that other people also find it useful. It may be only a matter of finding a willing host to cut your server costs to little or nothing.

Many sites on the Web are anxious to find more content to distinguish themselves from the competition. If your site is worthwhile and is a true public service, you may be able to cut a deal with a provider to host your pages for free or at very reduced cost. You may even wind up on staff. Think about it. A newspaper pays its reporters a salary; it doesn't depend on volunteers to produce copy every day. Your Web "hobby" may eventually turn into a career. If so, you should expect to be paid in some way.

Along the same lines, make sure your provider will permit you to operate the sort of page you're thinking about. Don't waste time developing a commercial site if your provider won't permit it. Your own imagination can probably come up with other instances where it would be thoughtful to ask your provider if your use might violate their terms of service. Never heard of such a thing? Ask your provider to tell you what their terms of service are or where they can be found so you can read them carefully. Most providers prohibit mass mailings and certain types of content of questionable taste, which of course you wouldn't dream of, but there may be quirky restrictions you weren't aware of, or prohibitive increases in price for a commercial site that may force you to alter your plans to accommodate your provider's reality.

From this short discussion, you can see that you have many options for publishing your site, from how to find resources to what sorts of resources you might need. Consider your options carefully before you plunge in and you may save yourself time and energy.

And when you do find your new home, take time to settle in, invite all your friends to come look and make themselves at home, and congratulate yourself on a job well done. Welcome Home!

Do I Need a Dedicated Domain?

Obtaining a dedicated domain

1. First, you need to see if the domain name you want is taken. Many Web hosting providers offer a simple form to check domain names, or you can look at `http://internic.net/cgi-bin/whois`.
2. Type in the domain name you wish to check and submit the form. If the name is registered, a page will return that tells you who registered it (see Figure 28.3).
3. If the name is not registered, check with your Web hosting provider about registering the name. Most providers are set up to take care of this for you. They may charge a small fee for the service.
4. The bill for domain name registration will come directly from the InterNIC, the agency that regulates domain names.

There's a big difference between a Web address like `http://www.random-isp.com/~fredsplace/` and `http://www.fredsplace.com/`. For one thing, a shorter address is easier to remember and type correctly. For another, it means that you've made a commitment to the Web as a place to do business and to work. The cost of registering your own domain is really minimal, $100 for two years and $50 per-year thereafter. Your provider may charge you something extra every month for performing the magic that points your domain to a location on their server, but this is usually on the order of $10 a month on top of your regular service agreement.

So it's up to you.

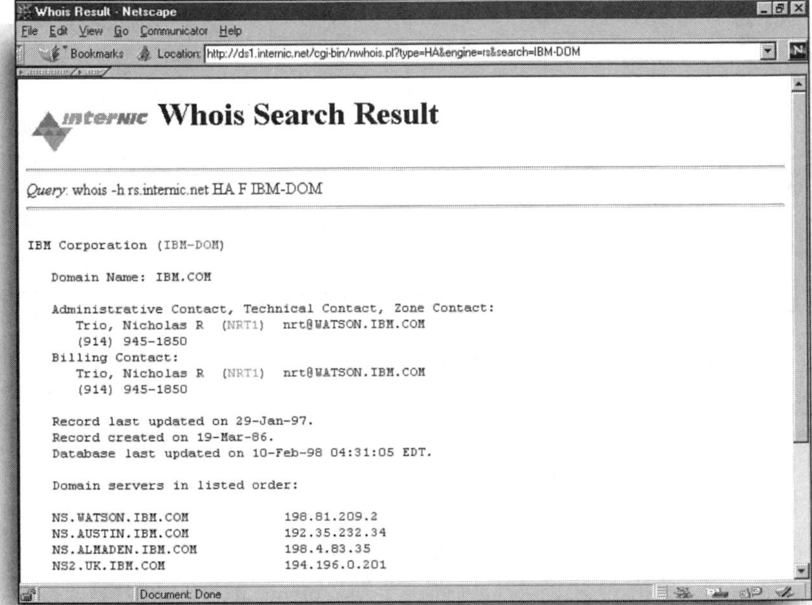

Whois Result - Netscape
File Edit View Go Communicator Help
Bookmarks Location: http://ds1.internic.net/cgi-bin/nwhois.pl?type=HA&engine=rs&search=IBM-DOM
internic Whois Search Result
Query: whois -h rs.internic.net HA F IBM-DOM
IBM Corporation (IBM-DOM)
Domain Name: IBM.COM
Administrative Contact, Technical Contact, Zone Contact:
Trio, Nicholas R (NRT1) nrt@WATSON.IBM.COM
(914) 945-1850
Billing Contact:
Trio, Nicholas R (NRT1) nrt@WATSON.IBM.COM
(914) 945-1850
Record last updated on 29-Jan-97.
Record created on 19-Mar-86.
Database last updated on 10-Feb-98 04:31:05 EDT.
Domain servers in listed order:
NS.WATSON.IBM.COM 198.81.209.2
NS.AUSTIN.IBM.COM 192.35.232.34
NS.ALMADEN.IBM.COM 198.4.83.35
NS2.UK.IBM.COM 194.196.0.201
Document: Done

FIGURE 28.3
Whois search result.

Table 28.2 lists some North American English-language sites that let you search to see if your dream name is already taken. Don't give up and don't be afraid to try simple things that "would have been taken long ago." I got my own name as a domain with no problem at all, and found several other things I probably would have liked just as well if my name hadn't been available.

Domain names are the postal addresses of the Web

An individual domain name says a lot about a company or even an individual. It says you're serious about the Web as a place of business and committed for the long haul. While a sub-address off a larger site is perfectly adequate for some smaller businesses or for an individual, such addresses are the Web equivalent of a Post Office Box number.

TABLE 28.2 **Table of North American domain name providers and search pages**

Name	Location
InterNIC	`http://internic.net/`
	`http://internic.net/cgi-bin/whois`
Canadian Registrar	`http://www.cdnnet.ca/`
	`http://www.cdnnet.ca/search/index.html`

Note that the Canadian Registrar listed supplies only Canadian businesses with registration services. There is no annual maintenance fee for Canadian registrations, but there may be a setup fee. The qualifications are very strict in comparison with U.S. registrations, but closely map the actual structure and name of the company. In other words, if you see a company site called www.companyname.ca, you can be assured that the company is named companyname, is nationally chartered, or has offices in at least two provinces or territories.

Every country in the world has a domain of its own, so there are literally hundreds of registrars that may be applicable to your business or personal Web space. Contact a local Internet service provider for information on how to contact these organizations or see the Norwegian global registrar list at `http://www.uninett.no/navn/domreg.html`.

There are even more registrars in the wings waiting for a chance at center stage. They will offer new domain names ending in .firm, .shop, .web, .arts, .info, .rec, and .nom. These are meant to stand for large firms, retail stores, Web-related businesses, fine arts-related sites, information providers, recreational businesses, and personal names, respectively.

You may have heard about these new top-level domains opening up. Well, they aren't here quite yet, but they will be soon, probably by the time you read this book. The downside is that the big corporations are colonizing that space as well with every trademark they own, and if they happen to forget or overlook one, you really don't want to get into a fight with one. They have lawyers who bite nails and spit out paper clips, so don't mess with trademarks if you value your pocketbook. Even if your name happens to be Ronald McDonald, I wouldn't count on getting that as a domain name if I were you. To help ensure that you don't conflict with an existing domain, Table 28.3 provides more domain name providers and search pages. Being extra thorough with your research now may save you time, and court costs, later.

TABLE 28.3 Table of alternative domain name providers and search pages

Name	Location
Domain Direct	`http://www.domaindirect.com/`
NetNames	`http://www.netnames.com/`

Most of these provide similar services, and this short list is by no means exhaustive, just a random sampling of new registrars I happen to know about.

What About Bandwidth?

Bandwidth is one of those esoteric terms that describes a very common experience. If you've ever seen your high-speed connection slow to a trickle, you've experienced what happens when you don't have enough bandwidth. The term is actually from an arm of science called information theory and refers to the fact that signals of any sort take up room. How much room they take depends on how much information is being presented.

As a simple example, when you're driving, a stop sign is a one bit piece of information. Whenever you come to one you have to stop and then proceed with caution. That simple system is good enough when there isn't much traffic. It isn't nearly good enough when there are more cars on the road, so new inventions were required.

When traffic engineers decided to add more information to stop signs, so that they could change the condition from stop to go to help eliminate traffic jams that resulted from people trying to proceed when it wasn't their turn, they discovered that they needed two bits of information and a way to change the state of the information. Their invention was the traffic semaphore, which had two arms that popped up in turn to indicate stop and go. As traffic speed increased, however, they found that they needed a third state, to make the transition from stop to go harder to miss because traffic jams (and accidents) developed anyway. And so the familiar traffic light was born with three signals, green, yellow, and red, with a complex mechanism to change from one state to another.

Life on the Internet has followed a similar path; as speeds have increased, more and more sophisticated signaling systems have been required to pump the information through the wires that form the pipeline that carries information to your home or office. The most artfully designed systems can be overwhelmed by too much traffic though, and your provider can be bogged down if it sells too many connections with too little available signaling space. Since all lines are shared with other users, providers can easily sell more space than they actually have (and often do).

Providers may restrict your line speed to share what's available equitably, they may disconnect users who haven't been active for a while (sometimes a very short while), or they may just give you a busy signal during peak traffic hours, typically the early evening. Their argument, of course, is essentially that they have plenty of bandwidth, if only those darned users would arrange their lives so they could surf the Web at three in the wee small hours of the morning.

Make sure your provider has enough capacity to handle your traffic during normal business and evening surfing hours before putting money on the table. Ask to see records of how many busy signals and disconnects are experienced by a typical user and try dialing their access lines on your own, just for a sanity check.

Use FTP to Upload and Download Pages

Uploading files with FTP

1. Locate and install an FTP program.
2. When the program starts, input the domain you are accessing, your username, and password. Then, click **OK** to connect to the FTP site.
3. The FTP program will show two areas. One area displays the files on your local system and the other will show the files on the FTP site. Use the program to move the files between the two windows.
4. Disconnect when you are finished.

Moving files via raw FTP is so arcane and prone to errors that there are many commercial vendors who specialize in replacements for the ungainly but effective original. Among the best are seven companies (see Table 28.4), three for the Macintosh and four for the Windows 95 PC. In each of these it's possible to enter the FTP address information once and then just point and click for every future file transfer. Cool!

TABLE 28.4 FTP clients

Name	Platform	Location
WS-FTP	PC	`http://www.ipswitch.com/Products/WS_FTP/index.html`
CuteFTP	PC	`http://www.cuteftp.com`
FTP Voyager	PC	`http://www.rhinosoft.com/RhinoSoft/index.htm`
AbsoluteFTP	PC	`http://www.vandyke.com`
Fetch	Macintosh	`http://www.dartmouth.edu/pages/softdev/fetch.html`
NetFinder	Macintosh	`http://www.ozemail.com.au/~pli/netfinder/`
Anarchie	Macintosh	`http://www.share.com/peterlewis/`

All these tools share many features and typically allow you to set up a site once and then choose from a list of sites to automatically take you to the site via FTP and upload or download files by clicking them in some way.

For those times when you can't use one of these products, Table 28.5 is a capsule summary of how to use raw FTP.

TABLE 28.5 FTP commands

Command	Action
`FTP ftp.anysite.com`	Invokes FTP and connects to an FTP site
`open ftp.anysite.com`	Opens an FTP site from within FTP
`help`	Asks for a short list of commands
`help` *`commandname`*	Explains how to use a command
`ls`	Lists filenames in current directory
`dir`	Lists filenames in current directory
`get` *`filename`*	Downloads a file from a remote site
`put` *`filename`*	Uploads a file to a remote site
`pwd`	Shows the current remote directory
`cd`	Changes the remote directory
`binary`	Changes the transfer mode from ASCII (text) to Binary (graphics or other non-text information)
`ascii`	Changes the transfer mode from Binary (graphics or non-text information) to ASCII (text)
`mget` *`file-expression`*	Downloads all files specified by the expression from a remote site
`mput` *`file-expression`*	Uploads all files specified by the expression to the remote site
`close`	Closes the session with a particular host
`quit`	Closes the session if any and exits FTP

Using FTP is pretty simple, even if cryptic and confusing until you get familiar with it. You simply log into the remote system using your own ID and password, change to the correct directory, and then start transferring files in either direction. When you're done, you type `quit` and the session is over. There is a special anonymous login ID that takes an email address as the password and allows downloads only. You use FTP exactly the same way whether downloading anonymously or using a full account. Try an anonymous login at `ftp.apple.com` or `ftp.microsoft.com`.

The main way you can get into trouble is by transferring files in the wrong mode. It's surprisingly easy to forget what mode you are in when you download or upload a file. If you do ASCII files the wrong way, it just takes twice as long, and some conversions may not be made. If you transfer a binary file as ASCII, it simply won't work correctly ever after.

Telnet and Other Power-User Tools

Maintaining your site with Telnet

1. Locate your Telnet client on your local machine.
2. From a command line (such as the Windows Run dialog box), type `telnet` and the domain address, for example, `telnet mysite.com`.
3. Log on by entering your username and password.
4. Use the standard Telnet commands to work on your site.
5. Log out when you are finished.

Just like FTP, Telnet so flusters some people that there is a large base of commercial programs that hide the "hard stuff" and make life lots easier for everyone involved. They allow you to pick and choose from a menu of Web servers so you only have to enter login IDs, passwords, and such once if it bothers you. Table 28.6 lists Telnet clients, their platforms, and their locations on the Web.

TABLE 28.6 Telnet clients

Name	Platform	Location
CRT	PC	`http://www.vandyke.com/`
NetTerm	PC	`http://starbase.neosoft.com/~zkrr01/`
ZOC	PC	`http://www.emtec.com/`

Name	Platform	Location
Better Telnet	Macintosh	`http://www.cstone.net/~rbraun/mac/telnet/`
Data Comet	Macintosh	`http://www.databeast.com/`
Proterm	Macintosh	`http://www.intrec.com`

To use Telnet, type `telnet` *`anysite.com`*, where *anysite.com* is the domain name.

That's it. Once you're connected, you simply type in UNIX commands to the server (assuming that it's a UNIX machine) to do whatever you have to do and then type `exit` when you're done.

Using Dedicated Publishing Environments

One thing a lot of the dedicated publishing environments have is a very good handle on publishing the pages to the Web. In many cases you simply press a menu button and you're done. The tool will automatically FTP to your site and replace old files with new ones.

HotDog Pro, Adobe PageMill/SiteMill, FrontPage, and many others all have this or a similar feature. Read the instructions for your own package to see what publishing services are available.

Publicizing Your New Web Site

Attracting visitors by listing your site in major search engines and other lists

1. Identify major search engines and find the page that allows you to submit your site.
2. Submit your site by following their guidelines.
3. Locate the sites with submission engines that let you submit to several sites at once.

4. Tour the Web searching for sites similar to your site. Ask the owners of these sites if you can share links so people who find one may be able to explore related sites easily.
5. Join a Web ring.

Publicizing your new site is actually pretty simple, although the purveyors of those "submit your site to more than a few hundreds search engines" would have you believe that it's time consuming and difficult. All you have to do is go to the sites you use and submit your site using their forms. They'll do the rest. For more detailed information about ways to do this most effectively, see Chapter 25, "Using Meta Information to Describe Your Document."

Table 28.7 lists a selection of major sites. Like minor telephone directories, the smaller sites usually aren't worth doing unless they are specialized and relate directly to your site. If the submission information isn't immediately apparent, try their Help screen for better directions.

TABLE 28.7 Major search engines

Name	Location
AltaVista	`http://www.altavista.digital.com/`
Yahoo!	`http://www.yahoo.com/`
Excite!	`http://www.excite.com/`
Infoseek	`http://www.infoseek.com/`
Lycos	`http://www.lycos.com/`
Magellan	`http://www.mckinley.com/`

There are a few sites that specialize in submitting to many sites at once (see Table 28.8). A few of them offer a "free trial" that submits to a handful of sites and then asks whether you want to submit to all of them in exchange for a fee, or shows you all of them and suggests that you feel free to spend oodles of time submitting to 400 sites. Well, do it if you must, but I think you're better off figuring out what's happening on your own and then doing it on your own as well. You really don't save all that much time if you eliminate all the tiny search engines that hardly anyone ever uses, and many of the large sites have special things you can check off to categorize your site more closely than the submission engines allow.

TABLE 28.8 Web site submittal firms

Name	Location
Submit It!	`http://www.submit-it.com/`
Add-It	`http://www.tradewind1.com/websitepromotion/addit.html`
Launchpad	`http://www.creativeworlds.com/launchpad/`
SubmitSpider	`http://www.suzton.com/`

After that you should try touring the Web using the previously mentioned search engines to find related sites on your own. Many of these sites will link to you for free in exchange for a link back to them. This can make even small sites useful as part of a larger network of sites. If you see that the field is pretty well covered except for a few things, cover those well and link to the sites that cover the rest. There's no sense redoing something if it's already been done, although it may pay to contact the owners of other sites in any case, even if they don't offer links. Sometimes they can point you to other sites or offer suggestions that you'd spend many hours discovering on your own.

And finally, join a Web ring! This is a free service that puts you into a group of related sites who share links with each other in a circular way. The main URL is `http://www.webring.com/`, but there are many others. While you're exploring the Web, make note of any rings you see and investigate them to be sure there aren't too many broken links or unrelated sites in the loop. There are literally thousands of rings ranging from specific women's rings (see Figure 28.4), to artists' rings, to mermaids. Dive in and see what's available!

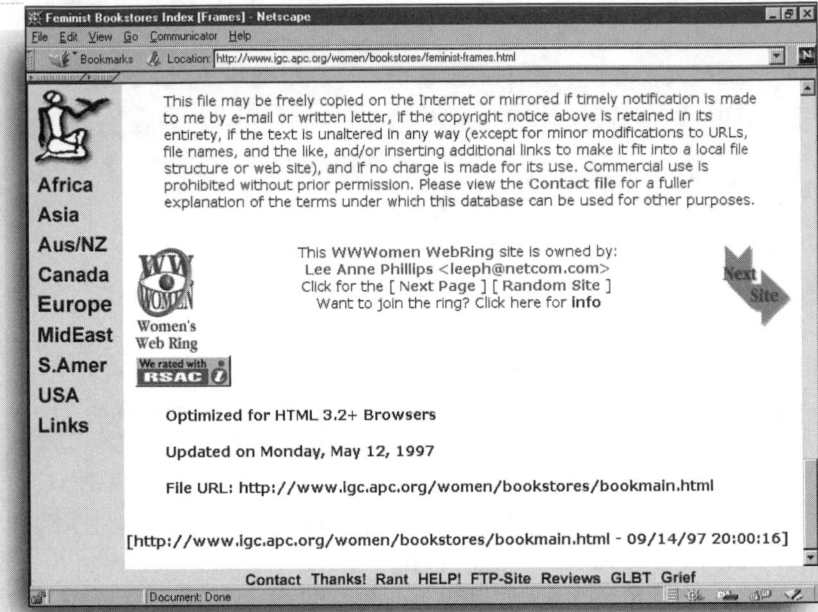
Feminist Bookstores Index [Frames] - Netscape
File Edit View Go Communicator Help
Bookmarks Location: http://www.igc.apc.org/women/bookstores/feminist-frames.html
This file may be freely copied on the Internet or mirrored if timely notification is made to me by e-mail or written letter, if the copyright notice above is retained in its entirety, if the text is unaltered in any way (except for minor modifications to URLs, file names, and the like, and/or inserting additional links to make it fit into a local file structure or web site), and if no charge is made for its use. Commercial use is prohibited without prior permission. Please view the Contact file for a fuller explanation of the terms under which this database can be used for other purposes.
Africa
Asia
Aus/NZ
Canada
Europe
MidEast
S.Amer
USA
Links
This WWWomen WebRing site is owned by:
Lee Anne Phillips <leeph@netcom.com>
Click for the [Next Page] [Random Site]
Want to join the ring? Click here for info
Women's Web Ring
Next Site
We rated with RSAC
Optimized for HTML 3.2+ Browsers
Updated on Monday, May 12, 1997
File URL: http://www.igc.apc.org/women/bookstores/bookmain.html
[http://www.igc.apc.org/women/bookstores/bookmain.html - 09/14/97 20:00:16]
Contact Thanks! Rant HELP! FTP-Site Reviews GLBT Grief
Document: Done

FIGURE 28.4
A site affiliated with The WWWomen WebRing.

CHAPTER

29

Maintaining Your Web Site

- Keep your page current and timely
- Eliminate broken links
- Measure your market

Keeping Your Site Fresh and Updated Is Important

Now that your site is visible on the Web, you're going to be having visitors. Make sure your Web home is always ready to receive them graciously. That means taking care of housekeeping tasks to ensure that your guests have a nice time and want to call again soon.

The most important task is to make sure that any time-sensitive content is updated on a regular basis. Even unchanging content should be touched up or improved regularly so that your site is worth a repeat visit every once in a while to see what's new.

At one extreme, a site featuring daily news updates might redo its front page content every day or even hourly (by means of a script). While a site with basically static resources can make sure it's up to date, adding a new section or article from time to time, adding or changing links as related external sites come online or move, and adding some topical content should be considered so that there's always a reason to refer to the page, even if your visitor has been there before.

Dealing with Changes: Project Management

Keeping track of your Web site

1. Manage small sites with a notebook and careful planning.
2. Use HTML editor functions and add-ons for medium-size projects.
3. Control large sites with dedicated tools.
4. Use site mapping to get an overview of your site.

Managing a site can range from a few simple housekeeping tasks once every month or so to a job requiring the full-time services of professional Web maintenance personnel. I'll assume that your site is toward the low-maintenance end of that spectrum for now. But, hey, every large site has to start somewhere, so I'll talk a little bit about the more sophisticated tools required by a major site as well.

For the smallest sites, all you really need is a little notebook in which you can jot down ideas and changes as they occur to you. I use my mail program to mail myself notes that are automatically filtered into special work files based on the subject header. But then I'm on the computer a lot and it's handy. Depending on your work habits, the exact form your "notebook" takes can vary, depending on what you're comfortable with, but it's a really good idea to have some system. Even small sites quickly become large and complex enough that you forget from one day to the next what you were going to do that struck you as such a good idea at the time.

When it comes time to update, just go through your notes (or email messages) taking care of them one at a time until you're done. Simple and effective. Why waste time learning how to use a great honking maintenance program for a few minutes, or even hours, worth of work every month?

When your site grows larger, though, those great honking maintenance programs are worth their weight in gold.

There are many different Web management tools to choose from. Some of the best are:

- Net Objects Fusion, `http://www.netobjects.com`. Controls all aspects of a site with a central repository of design decisions and features other centralized management tools.
- HotDog Pro, `http://www.sausage.com`. Makes it fairly easy to keep track of projects by filename and does link checking as well, but has no central repository of design decisions and is still a little buggy after more than a year (see Figure 29.1).
- Adobe Page Mill and Site Mill, `http://www.adobe.com`. A marvelous package fully available for the Macintosh and partially for Windows 95 PCs.
- Microsoft's FrontPage 98, `http://www.microsoft.com/sitebuilder`. Has the problem of encouraging use of Microsoft-specific tags and features without telling what it's doing, but does have good publishing features as well.

Size your management effort to the minimum required

Management isn't much fun sometimes. Instead of actually doing things, you're performing meta-tasks and making meta-decisions about what to do and how you're going to do it. Every minute spent on managing is a minute you're not doing productive work. On the other hand, when a site gets large, those minutes translate directly into hours saved redoing work done incorrectly or undoing work that shouldn't have been done in the first place. So, although it is not fun, it is necessary.

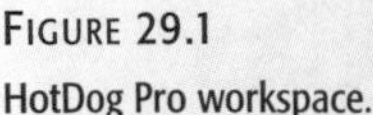

FIGURE 29.1
HotDog Pro workspace.

You should also use a site mapping tool periodically to get some idea of what the actual relationship between your pages is. Links can turn into spaghetti very quickly, and a site mapping tool will automatically follow each one and show you where in the file hierarchy they all fit (see Figure 29.2). Table 29.1 lists some popular site mapping tools and their Web locations.

TABLE 29.1 Site mapping tools

Name	Location
MapXsite	`http://www.mapxsite.com/`
ClearWeb	`http://www.clearweb.com/`
WebAnalyzer	`http://www.incontext.com/`
HotSauce	`http://hotsauce.apple.com/`
Site Map	`http://junior.apk.net/~jbarta/`
Governor	`http://www.governor.co.uk/`

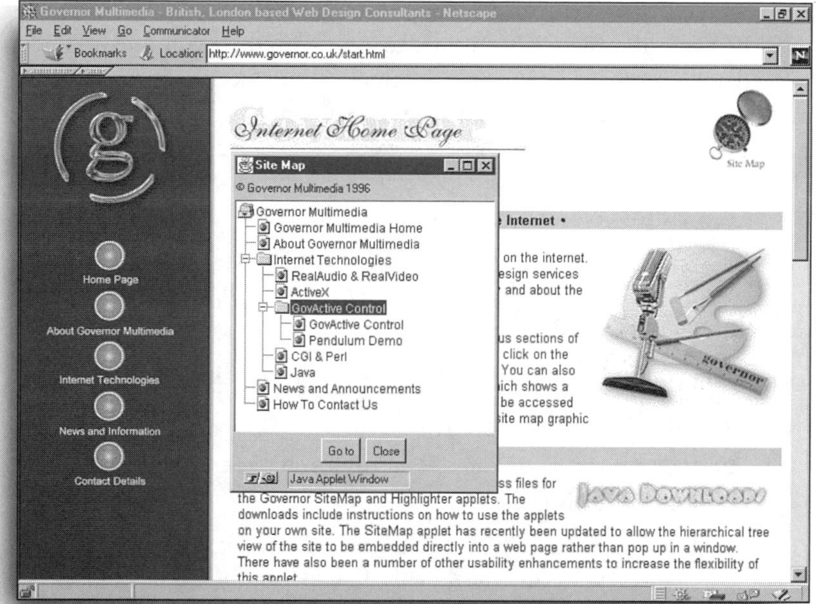

FIGURE 29.2
The Governor site mapping tool in action.

Keeping Up with the Times: Making Sure Content Is Current

Dewey Wins By A Landslide! It's a famous mistaken newspaper headline from years gone by. Of course he didn't, and few people actually remember who he was nowadays. I was far too young to remember, of course, and only heard about it in my high school American History class. The point is that they relied on outdated information and wound up looking foolish.

You don't want to look foolish, of course, unless your site discusses the methods and art of clownology. So your content should always be fresh and as current as you can make it. If you read a headline or see something on the news or in a magazine that belongs on your page instead of or in addition to what's already there, the time to do the update is now. Don't wait for the end of the month or when you have some free time. Visitors get tired of seeing last month's (or last year's) magazine "buzz" when fresher content is just a click away.

The only way to be really sure your site is fresh is to open it in a browser and read it from time to time. Anytime you find an outdated bit of information, make note of it or change it right then so you stay on top of the maintenance before it becomes drudgery. A few changes every week or so is far better than facing a more-or-less complete rewrite every few months and will keep visitors coming back in the meantime.

Keeping Track of Links

Taking care of your visitors by giving them good directions

1. Check your links regularly!
2. If you move your site, leave a referral page in place for a while after it moves.
2. Use automated link checkers for basic maintenance (see Figure 29.3), but always supplement automatic tools with manual inspection from time to time. Most automated link checkers won't tell you if the only data on the page is "We've moved!" and an address.
3. If external links truly disappear, wait a month or two and then see if you can find them with a Web search. Chances are that they only moved and will show up again somewhere.

Keep links current!

Nothing dates a page more quickly than a collection of links that generate those tiresome `Not Found` messages. If you check from time to time, you'll usually be able to update the link simply. If you wait until people complain, you may have a time-consuming job ahead of you trying to find where the site moved.

Maintaining a link list can be a real pain if you go about it the wrong way. The first and most wrong thing you can do is to collect links about subjects that don't interest you. If you're not interested, the links won't be of the highest quality (because you really don't care) and it will be a tiresome chore to check on them. So just because you helped your daughter collect a list of Web sites about Hello Kitty merchandise doesn't mean you have to publish it on the Web. The Hello Kitty stage only lasts a year or so; sooner or later you'll get tired of keeping it current, and your daughter won't care either because she's moved on to knock-knock jokes and Sailor Moon.

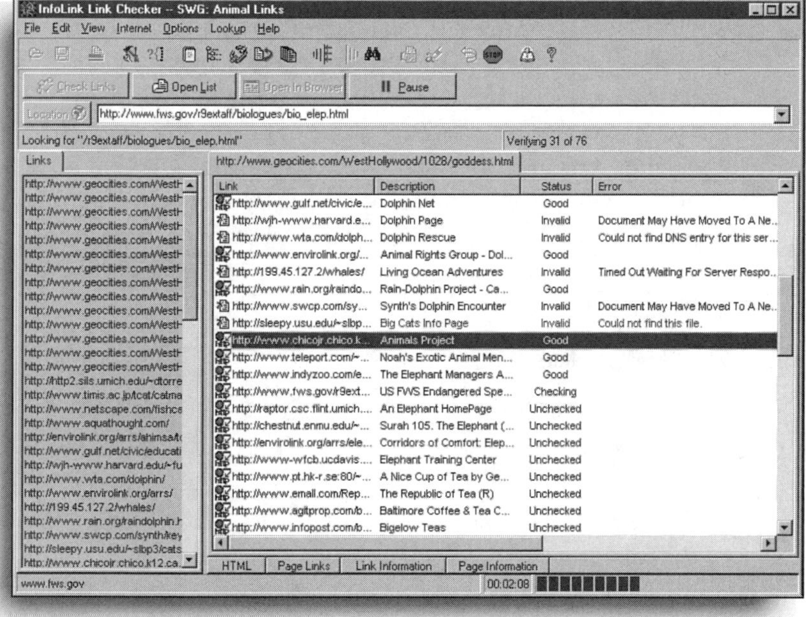

FIGURE 29.3
Using the InfoLink link checker.

When a subject interests you, though, things look different. You'll probably know enough to be able to judge whether a site is worth listing, and checking on sites is a pleasure because you might find new updates or links to new sites in the process. Link lists are like gardens; they have to be planted and weeded from time to time or they go to seed.

It's such a common problem that many browsers and development tools have link checkers built in. Netscape has an **Update Bookmarks** option on the **View** menu item that marks bookmarks with a check mark if they've been changed since the bookmark was created. HotDog Pro has a link checker built in that will check every link on a page or project, and others have similar utilities included.

Take the time to look through the menus or documentation of your own Web-related programs to see if you might have something already before spending money on a separate package.

When the list of links becomes large, or when you're compiling lists from several sources, a link checker can be a good adjunct to the manual process by keeping track of which sites have changed or moved and might therefore be worth a short visit. Table 29.2 lists programs that handle some phase of link maintenance, from organizing your links to actually converting your link lists into HTML so you can drop them into your pages. These are similar to the site mapping tools covered earlier, but these packages will help identify and fix bad links.

TABLE 29.2 Link checkers

Tool	Organize	Check	Publish	Platform
QuickLink	✓			Windows 95
Autobot		✓		Windows 95
WebWizard			✓	Windows 95
WebTabs	✓	✓	✓	Windows 95
Web Squirrel	✓		✓	Macintosh
Big Brother		✓		Macintosh

QuickLink Explorer, Autobot, and WebWizard are a complete set of Windows 95 packages that lets you organize your links across multiple browsers, check them for currency, and publish them to a page at low cost. See the QuickLink Software Web site at `http://www.quicklinks.com/`.

WebTabs is a single Windows 95 program that also lets you organize links across multiple browsers, check them, and publish them. See the Robert Ballance & Associates Web site at `http://www.swcp.com/products/`.

On the Macintosh, a combination of tools supports the same functionality. Web Squirrel organizes your data, while Big Brother checks on timeliness and accuracy and even automatically updates bookmarks to pages that have moved. See the Web Squirrel Web site at `http://www.eastgate.com/squirrel/` and the Big Brother Web site at `http://pauillac.inria.fr/~fpottier/brother.html.en`.

Using Traffic Reports to Fine-Tune Your Web Site

Keeping track of visitors gives you a handle on how popular your site is

1. Your visitor count is your scorecard in the Web popularity contest. It pays to know the score! Check first with your provider to see if they offer this feature.
2. You could also use an off-site hit counter to get a rough measure of traffic. Even small sites can build up impressive numbers over time.
3. Many Web advertising programs provide traffic measurements, as well as an occasional check if your site receives many hits.

When a site gets large, or even when you're deciding if it's big enough to warrant more space or bandwidth, a detailed traffic report can be a valuable tool that lets you know which pages get the most hits and which are not so popular. There are several ways to do this, from a simple page counter that you periodically check manually to sophisticated log file utilities that access server logs directly and generate reports limited only by the range of your imagination.

Your Internet service provider (ISP) may provide a counter utility and may even provide access to the server logs. If you're concerned about this, you should make it one of the questions you ask before you sign up.

You can also use the hit counter statistics provided by some Web advertising or link exchange programs.

PART VII

Appendixes

APPENDIX

HTML Quick Reference

A

HTML Background

HTML is a markup language meant to be applied to text after it's written in order to help format and present the text in a meaningful way. All the tags have a long history and reason for being there so it's important to at least be familiar with what's available.

I've heard some well-meaning people say that you shouldn't bother learning things like the address tag, or the emphasis tag, because they're "just the same" as the italics tag. Nothing could be farther from the truth! Both these tags have meanings distinct from the italics tag and allow automated searches by Web spiders as well as special handling by current or future browsers that few of us are aware of.

Most HTML tags are containers that require a matching closing tag—the same tag name preceded by a forward slash—to delimit their content. A few are empty by design or occur in situations where the browser can always figure out where the closing tag should be placed. In those instances the closing tag may be omitted.

The opening tag usually has a number of attributes that modify the tag in some way. These can be quite complex but one usually needs only a few in day-to-day work. Most HTML coders keep a reference list handy while working so they can look up the right way to use tags and attributes that they don't use every day, so don't be embarrassed about it if you rely on this list from time to time.

In general, [in] inline (or text-level) elements can be freely placed inside [st] block (or structural) elements. The reverse is not true, and a block element by definition will break the flow of text and start a new paragraph or section. Block elements can usually be contained within other block elements as well. There are several special cases that follow different rules, but they're really common sense sorts of things for the most part. So insertions and deletions can contain almost anything, although you might think of them as text treatments at first.

Quick Reference

HTML Tag	Explanation
`<!-- -->`	
`<!-- comment -->`	SGML Comment—The comment tag allows you to insert comments in your text that are invisible in the browser.
`<!DOCTYPE>`	SGML Document Type—This tag defines the type of document and the document type definition used to create it.
`<A>...</A>` [in]	Anchor—The anchor tag allows a link to another document or location, or furnishes a way for other documents or locations to link to the tag itself.
	`accesskey=`, `charset=`, `class=`, `coords=`, `dir=`, `href=`, `hreflang=`, `id=`, `lang=`, `name=`, `rel=`, `rev=`, `shape=`, `style=`, `tabindex=`, `target=`, `title=`, `type=`, `onfocus=`, `onblur=` {event}=
`<ABBR>...</ABBR>` [in]	Abbreviation—Identifies an abbreviation or acronym so it can be treated specially in audio browsers, and potentially allows the browser to let the user see what it stands for with a pointing device selection.
	`class=`, `dir=`, `id=`, `lang=`, `style=`, `title=`, {event}=
`<ACRONYM>...</ACRONYM>` [in]	Acronym—A tag that identifies an acronym or abbreviation so it can be treated specially in audio browsers and potentially allows the browser to let the user see what it stands for with a pointing device selection.

HTML Tag	Explanation
	class=, dir=, id=, lang=, style=, title=, {event}=
<ADDRESS>...</ADDRESS> [st]	Address—Either a physical address or an email address. Usually rendered in an italic font. Causes a break in the text flow.
	class=, dir=, id=, lang=, style=, title=, {event}=
<APPLET>...</APPLET> [in]	Applet—Calls a Java applet.
	align=left | center | right | top | middle | bottom, alt=, archive=, class=, code=, codebase=, height=, hspace=, id=, name=, object=, style=, title=, vspace=, width=
<AREA>...</AREA> [in]	Area—Describes the layout of an imagemap.
	accesskey=, alt=, dir=, class=, coords=, href=, id=, lang=, name=, nohref=, shape=circ | circle | poly | polygon | rect | rectangle, style=, tabindex=, target=, title=, {event}=, onfocus=, onblur=
<B>...</B> [in]	Bold—Bold text.
	class=, dir=, id=, lang=, style=, title=, {event}=
<BASE>...</BASE> [st]	Base—Changes the assumed base of URL references.
	href=, target=
<BASEFONT> [in] ...</BASEFONT>	Changes the base font of a document. This is not usually a good idea because it messes up browsers that don't use standard fonts by blithely overriding user choices. Examples are audio browsers that render large fonts more loudly, foreign language browsers that don't use English fonts at all, and any per son for whom font choice is important for legibility or comprehension and has carefully set up his or her browser to use a particular font.
	color=, face=, size=

HTML Tag	Explanation
<BDO>...</BDO> [in]	Bi-Directional Override—Changes the default direction and language rendering of included text. dir=, lang=
<BGSOUND> [in]	Background Sound—Obsolete tag used to play a background sound on a page. A primitive multimedia device. loop=, src=, id=, title=
<BIG>...</BIG> [in]	Big Text—Big text. class=, dir=, id=, lang=, style=, title=, {event}=
<BLINK>...</BLINK> [in]	Blinks the contents. This effect is hated and despised by many with a passion usually reserved for infernal spirits and axe-murderers.
<BLOCKQUOTE>...</BLOCKQUOTE> [st]	Block Quote—A block quotation. Usually rendered indented on both margins. cite=, class=, dir=, id=, lang=, style=, title=, {event}=
<BODY>...</BODY> [st]	Body—HTML body. Always assumed to be present even if the tag is missing. align=center ¦ left ¦ right, alink=, background=, bgcolor=, class=, dir=, id=, lang=, link=, style=, text=, title=, vlink=, {event}=
  [st][in]	Break—Break the flow of the line without causing the text flow to stop. class=, clear=left ¦ right ¦ all ¦ none, id=, style=, title=
<BUTTON>...</BUTTON> [st]	Button—Create a button in a form. accesskey=, class=, dir=, disabled, id=, lang=, name=, style=, tabindex=, title=, type=button ¦ submit ¦ reset, value=, {event}=, onfocus=, onblur=

HTML Tag	Explanation
<CAPTION>...</CAPTION> [st]	Caption—Create a caption for a table. `align=center ¦ left ¦ right ¦ top ¦ bottom, class=, dir=, id=, lang, style=, title=, valign=top ¦ bottom,` {event}=
<CENTER>...</CENTER> [st]	Center—Shorthand for `<DIV align="center">...</DIV>`. This tag is often supported when other alignment options are not and is far more foolproof for pages with wide readership. `class=, dir=, id=, lang=, style=, title=,` {event}=
<CITE>...</CITE> [in]	Cite—Identify a citation. Usually rendered in an italic font. `class=, dir=, id=, lang=, style=, title=,` {event}=
<CODE>...</CODE> [in]	Code Text—Program or HTML code of any sort. Usually rendered in a fixed-width font. `class=, dir=, id=, lang=, style=, title=,` {event}=
<COL>...</COL> [st]	Column—A column in a table. `align=center ¦ left ¦ right ¦ justify ¦ char, char=, charoff=, class=, dir=, id=, repeat=, span=, style=, title=, valign=baseline ¦ bottom ¦ center ¦ top, width=,` {event}=
<COLGROUP>...</COLGROUP> [st]	Column Group—A group of columns in a table. `align=center ¦ left ¦ right ¦ justify ¦ char, char=, charoff=, class=, id=, span=, style=, title=, valign=baseline ¦ bottom ¦ center ¦ top, width=`
<DD>...</DD> [st]	Definition—A definition in a definition list. `class=, dir=, id=, lang=, style=, title=,` {event}=

HTML Tag	Explanation
<DEL>...</DEL> [in][st]	Deleted Text—Mark text as deleted.
	cite=, class=, datetime=, dir=, id=, lang=, style=, title=, {event}=
<DFN>...</DFN> [in]	Definition or Defining Instance—Identify a defining instance of a term.
	class=, dir=, id=, lang=, style=, title=, {event}=
<DIR>...</DIR> [st]	Directory—Create a directory list. Usually represented as an unordered list.
	class=, compact, dir=, id=, lang=, style=, title=, {event}=
<DIV>...</DIV> [st]	Division—A generic block or structural tag used to create a division in the text.
	align=center ¦ left ¦ right ¦ justify, charset=, class=, dir=, href=, hreflang=, id=, lang=, media=, rel=, rev=, style=, target=, title=, type=, {event}=
<DL>...</DL> [st]	Definition List—Create a definition list of terms and definitions.
	align=, center ¦ left ¦ right, class=, clear=, left ¦ right ¦ all, compact, dir=, id=, lang=, style=, title=, {event}=
<DT>...</DT> [st]	Definition Term—A term in a definition list.
	align=center ¦ left ¦ right, class=, dir=, id=, lang=, style=, title=, {event}=
<EM>...</EM> [in]	Emphasis—Regular emphasis. Usually rendered as italics.
	class=, dir=, id=, lang=, style=, title=, {event}=
<EMBED>...</EMBED> [in]	Embedded Content—An obsolete tag used to embed multimedia or other content in an HTML page. A slightly less primitive multimedia device. Object will eventually replace it.

HTML Tag	Explanation
	accesskey=, align=, absbottom ¦ absmiddle ¦ baseline ¦ bottom ¦ left ¦ middle ¦ right ¦ texttop ¦ top, height=, hidden=, id=, palette=, pluginspage=, src=, style=, title=, width=, {event}=
<FIELDSET>...</FIELDSET> [st]	Fieldset—Group together fields in a form for easier navigation and understandability. class=, dir=, id=, lang=, style=, title=, {event}=
<FONT>...</FONT> [in]	Font—Change font characteristics. This is not the best of ideas, although widely used on the Web. Still, it beats using heading tags to change font size. Face or color should be changed rarely if at all because, like the basefont tag, this can cause unforeseen problems for many users. Style sheets are far safer, even though they're not widely supported yet. color=, face=, id=, size=, style=, title=, {event}=
<FORM>...</FORM> [st]	Form—Create a form for user input. acceptcharset=, action=, class=, dir=, enctype=, id=, lang=, method=get ¦ post, name=, script=, style=, target=, title=, {event}=
<FRAME>...</FRAME> [st]	Frame—Identify the location of a frame for inclusion in a page frameset. class=, dir=, frameborder=, id=, longdesc=, marginheight=, marginwidth=, method=, name=window _name ¦ _blank ¦ _parent ¦ _self ¦ _top, noresize=noresize ¦ resize, scrolling=auto ¦ no ¦ yes, src=, style=, target=, title=
<FRAMESET>...</FRAMESET> [st]	class=, cols=, id=, rows=, style=, title=, onload=, onunload=
<HEAD>...</HEAD> [st]	Head Section—The head section in an HTML document. Always assumed to be present even if the tag is not. dir=, lang=, profile=

HTML Tag	Explanation
<H1>...</H1> [st]	Heading—A level 1 heading. align=left ¦ center ¦ right ¦ justify, class=, clear=left ¦ right ¦ all, dir=, id=, lang=, style=, title=, {event}=
<H2>, <H2>, <H3>, <H4>, <H5>, <H6> [st]	Headings—Level 2 through level 6 headings. Same as <H1>
<HR> [st]	Horizontal Rule—Insert a horizontal rule in the body of the page. align=center ¦ left ¦ right ¦ justify, class=, clear=left ¦ right ¦ all, color=, id=, md=, noshade=, size=, style=, title=, width=, {event}=
<HTML>...</HTML> [st]	HTML—Originally used to identify HTML content as opposed to other text on the Web. It's always assumed to be present even if the tag itself is missing as its function has been largely replaced by MIME types passed from the server and by the .htm or .html suffix on files. Some browsers do pay attention to the tag in the absence of any other clue, so it should probably be used. The closing tag, although also optional, makes an easy way to check if a file transfer was interrupted before downloading was complete. dir=, lang=, version=
<I>...</I> [in]	Italic Text—Italic text. class=, dir=, id=, lang=, style=, title=, {event}=
<IFRAME>...</IFRAME> [st]	Inline Frame—An inline subwindow. align=absbottom ¦ absmiddle ¦ baseline ¦ bottom ¦ left ¦ middle ¦ right ¦ texttop ¦ top, border=, bordercolor=, frameborder=, framespacing=, height=, hspace=, id=, marginheight=, marginwidth=, name=window_name ¦ _blank ¦ _parent ¦ _self ¦ _top, noresize=noresize ¦ resize, scrolling=auto ¦ no ¦ yes, src=, style=, title=, vspace=, width=, {event}=

HTML Tag	Explanation
<ILAYER>...</ILAYER> [st]	Inline Layer—An inline layer.
<IMG> [in]	Image—A link to an external image that will be replaced by the image itself during rendering of the page. align=bottom ¦ left ¦ middle ¦ right ¦ top, alt=, border=, class=, controls=, dir=, datafld=, datasrc=, dynsrc=, height=, hspace=, id=, ismap=, lang=, loop=, lowsrc=, md=, name=, src=, style=, title=, usemap=, vrml=, vspace=, width=, {event}=
<INPUT>...</INPUT> [st]	Input—An input element in a form. accesskey=, accept=, align=bottom ¦ left ¦ middle ¦ right ¦ top, alt=, checked, class=, datafld=, datasrc=, dir=, disabled, error, id=, lang=, language=javascript ¦ vbscript, max=, maxlength=, md=, min=, name=, readonly=, size=, src=, style=, tabindex=, title=, type=button ¦ checkbox ¦ hidden ¦ image ¦ password ¦ radio ¦ reset ¦ selectmultiple ¦ selectone ¦ submit ¦ text ¦ textarea, usemap=, value=, {event}=
<INS>...</INS> [in][st]	Inserted Text—Mark text as inserted. cite=, class=, datetime=, dir=, id=, lang=, style=, title=, {event}=
<ISINDEX> [in]	Isindex—An obsolete tag indicating that the document is a searchable index. This tag should be replaced by a form on a modern page, although you still see them occasionally on the Web. action=, class=, dir=, id=, lang=, prompt=, style=, title=
<KBD>...</KBD> [in]	Keyboard Text—Keyboard input text; what a user is expected to type in response to program output. class=, dir=, id=, lang=, style=, title=, {event}=

Note

Use <FORM> instead, if possible.

HTML Tag	Explanation
<LABEL>...</LABEL> [in]	Label—Provide a label for a form element.
	accesskey=, class=, dir=, for=, id=, lang=, style=, title=, {event}=, onfocus=, onblur=
<LAYER>...</LAYER> [st]	Layer—An obsolescent means of defining objects on the page. They are easier to use than objects for most people and are capable of providing quite a few interesting effects on the page.
<LEGEND>...</LEGEND> [st]	Legend—Provide a legend for a form fieldset.
	accesskey=, align=, class=, dir=, id=, lang=, style=, title=, {event}=
<LI>...</LI> [st]	List Item—A list item in any list other than a definition list.
	align=center ¦ left ¦ right, class=, dir=, id=, lang=, style=, title=, type=1 ¦ a ¦ A ¦ i ¦ I ¦ disk ¦ circle ¦ square, value=, {event}=
<LINK>...</LINK> [st]	Link—Define the relationship between pages on a site.
	class=, dir=, href=, hreflang=, id=, lang=, media=, methods=, name=, rel=Contents ¦Home ¦ Toc ¦ Index ¦ Glossary ¦ Copyright ¦ Up ¦ Next ¦ Previous ¦ Start ¦ Help ¦ Bookmark ¦ Banner ¦ StyleSheet ¦ Alternate, rev=, style=, target=, title=, type=, urn=
<LISTING>...</LISTING> [in]	Listing Text—An obsolete tag representing a computer listing or printout.
	align=center ¦ left ¦ right, class=, id=, lang=, style=, title=, {event}=
<MAP>...</MAP> [in]	Map—The outer container for the areas defined in an imagemap.
	class=, id=, name=, style=, title=, {event}=

HTML Tag	Explanation
`<MENU>...</MENU>` [st]	Menu List—Create a menu list. Usually represented as an unordered list. `compact=, dir=, id=, lang=, style=, title=,` {event}=
`<META>` [st]	Meta-information—Pass information to the HTTP server or an external program on the server. `content=, dir=, httpequiv=, lang=, name=, scheme=, title=, url=`
`<NOEMBED>...</NOEMBED>` [in]	Noembed Content—Provide alternative content for browsers that don't support the embed tag. Actually, this tag tells browsers that do support the embed tag to ignore the contents.
`<NOFRAMES>...</NOFRAMES>` [st]	Noframes Content—Provide alternative content for browsers that don't support the frame tag. Actually, this tag tells browsers that do support the frame tag to ignore the contents. `id=, style=, title=`
`<NOLAYER>...</NOLAYER>` [st]	Nolayer Content—Provide alternative content for browsers that don't support the layer tag. Actually, this tag tells browsers that do support the layer tag to ignore the contents.
`<NOSCRIPT>...</NOSCRIPT>` [in]	Noscript Content—Provide alternative content for browsers that don't support the script tag. Actually, this tag tells browsers that do support the script tag to ignore the contents. `title=`
`<OBJECT>...</OBJECT>` [in]	Object Content—Provide a generic way to include information from outside the page in the body of the page. Theoretically, this tag can subsume images, applets, and other multimedia workarounds.

HTML Tag	Explanation
	accesskey=, align=absbottom ¦ absmiddle ¦ baseline ¦ bottom ¦ left ¦ middle ¦ right ¦ texttop ¦ top, border=, class=, classid=, code=, codebase=, codetype=, data=, datafld=, datasrc=, declare=, dir=, disabled, height=, hspace=, id=, lang=, name=, shapes=, standby=, style=, tabindex=, title=, type=, usemap=, vspace=, width=, {event}=
<OL>...</OL> [st]	Ordered List—An ordered or numbered list. Many browsers allow you to select the style of numbering, including roman numerals and letters as well as numbers.
	align=center ¦ left ¦ right, class=, clear=left ¦ right ¦ all, compact, continue, dir=, id=, lang=, seqnum=, start=, style=, title=, type=1 ¦ a ¦ A ¦ i ¦ I, {event}=
<OPTION>...</OPTION> [st]	Option—A selectable option in a form.
	class=, dir=, disabled, id=, label=, lang=, name=, selected=, style=, title=, value=, {event}=
<OPTGROUP>...</OPTGROUP> [st]	Option Group—Provide a hierarchy of choices in a form.
	class=, dir=, disabled, id=, label=, lang=, name=, style=, title=, value=, {event}=
<P>...</P> [st]	Paragraph—Identifies the following text as a paragraph. The closing tag is optional and usually left off, although a bug in some versions of Microsoft Internet Explorer causes difficulty with style sheets if the closing tag is omitted.
	align=center ¦ left ¦ right ¦ justify, class=, clear=left ¦ right ¦ all, dir=, id=, lang=, style=, title=, width=, {event}=
<PARAM>...</PARAM> [in]	Parameter—A parameter passed to an object or applet as data.
	data=, datafld=, datasrc=, name=, object=, ref=, title=, type=, value=, valuetype=data ¦ ref ¦ object

HTML Tag	Explanation
<PERSON>...</PERSON> [in]	Person—An obsolete tag still used by some to identify personal names. It has no direct function, but it can be useful to robots or other automated tools for searching HTML pages. class=, id=, lang=
<PLAINTEXT> [st]	Plaintext—An obsolete tag used to tell the browser to render everything following as plain, preformatted text. The tag turned off interpretation of HTML tags so the browser would also print HTML without interpretation.
<PRE>...</PRE> [st]	Preformatted Text—Text that has been preformatted so whitespace is significant. Useful for laying out forms precisely and other layout work, although it typically uses a typewriter fixed-width font that's less than beautiful in many contexts. class=, clear=left ¦ right ¦ all, dir=, id=, lang=, style=, title=, width=, {event}=
<Q>...</Q> [in]	Quote—An inline quote. cite=, class=, dir=, id=, lang=, style=, title=, {event}=
<S>...</S> [in]	Strikeout—Strikeout text. class=, dir=, id=, lang=, style=, title=, {event}=
<SAMP>...</SAMP> [in]	Sample Text—Sample output from a program. class=, dir=, id=, lang=, style=, title=, {event}=
<SCRIPT>...</SCRIPT> [in]	Script—Insert an inline script into HTML code. Scripts should be escaped with a surrounding SGML comment tag. charset=, defer, language=javascript ¦ vbscript, src=, type=

HTML Tag	Explanation
<SELECT>...</SELECT> [st]	Select—Option selector element in a form.
	class=, dir=, disabled, id=, lang=, multiple, name=, size=, style=, tabindex=, title=, {event}=
<SMALL>...</SMALL> [in]	Small—Small text.
	class=, dir=, id=, lang=, style=, title=, {event}=
<SPAN>...</SPAN> [in]	Span—A generic inline (text-level) tag to surround content to be rendered inline.
	align=, class=, datafld=, dataformats=, datasrc=, dir=, id=, style=, title=, {event}=
	ID=
<STRIKE>...</STRIKE> [in]	Strikeout—Strikeout text.
	class=, dir=, id=, lang=, style=, title=, {event}=
<STRONG>...</STRONG> [in]	Strong Emphasis—Strongly emphasize text, usually with a bold font.
	class=, dir=, id=, lang=, style=, title=, {event}=
<STYLE>...</STYLE> [in]	Style Sheet Definition—Define a style sheet. Contents should be escaped by enclosing them in an SGML comment.
	dir=, lang=, media=, title=, type=
_{...} [in]	Subscript—Subscript text.
	class=, dir=, id=, lang=, style=, title=, {event}=
^{...} [in]	Superscript—Superscript text.
	class=, dir=, id=, lang=, style=, title=, {event}=
<TABLE>...</TABLE> [st]	Table—A rectangular array of rows and columns used to organize data neatly or sometimes used as a page layout device.

HTML Tag	Explanation
	align=left ¦center ¦ right, class=, background=, bgcolor=, border=, cellpadding=, cellspacing=, class=, cols=, dir=, frame= above ¦ below ¦ border ¦ box ¦ insides ¦ lhs ¦ rhs ¦ void ¦ vsides, height=, id=, lang=, rules=all ¦ cols ¦ groups ¦ none ¦ rows, style=, summary=, title=, units=, width=, {event}=
<TBODY>...</TBODY>	Table Body Section—The body section of a table. Assumed present if not labeled.
	align=center ¦ left ¦ right, bgcolor=, char=, charoff=, class=, dir=, id=, lang=, style=, title=, valign=baseline ¦ bottom ¦ center ¦ top, {event}=
<TD>...</TD> [st]	Table Data—An individual cell in a table used to contain data.
	abbr=, align=center ¦ left ¦ right ¦ decimal ¦ justify, axis=, background=, bgcolor=, char=, charoff=, class=, colspan=, dir=, height=, id=, lang=, nowrap, rowspan=, style=, title=, valign=baseline ¦ bottom ¦ center ¦ top, width=, {event}=
<TEXTAREA>...</TEXTAREA> [st]	Text Area—A freeform text entry field in a form.
	accesskey=, align=, bottom ¦ left ¦ middle ¦ right ¦ top, class=, cols=, datafld=, datasrc=, dir=, disabled, error=, id=, lang=, name=, readonly=, rows=, style=, tabindex=, title=, wrap=virtual ¦ physical ¦ none, {event}=
<TFOOT>...</TFOOT> [st]	Table Footer Section—The footer section of a table. Not required.
	align=center ¦ left ¦ right, bgcolor=, char=, charoff=, dir=, id=, lang=, style=, title=, valign=baseline ¦ bottom ¦ center ¦ top, {event}=

HTML Tag	Explanation
<TH>...</TH> [st]	Table Heading—An individual cell in a table used to contain a heading. Usually centered in boldface. abbr=, align=center ¦ left ¦ right ¦ decimal ¦ justify, axis=, background=, bgcolor=, char=, charoff=, class=, colspan=, dir=, height=, id=, lang=, nowrap, rowspan=, style=, title=, valign=baseline ¦ bottom ¦ center ¦ top, width=, {event}=
<THEAD>...</THEAD> [st]	Table Header Section—The head section of a table. Not required. align=center ¦ left ¦ right, bgcolor=, char=, charoff=, class=, dir=, id=, lang=, style=, title=, valign=baseline ¦ bottom ¦ center ¦ top, {event}=
<TITLE>...</TITLE> [st]	Title—Displayed in the title bar of most browsers. One and only one is required in every document. dir=, lang=
<TR>...</TR> [st]	Table Row—Starts every row in a table. align=center ¦ left ¦ right ¦ justify, bgcolor=, char=, charoff=, class=, dir=, height=, id=, lang=, style=, title=, valign=baseline ¦ bottom ¦ center ¦ top, vspace=, {event}=
<TT>...</TT> [in]	Teletype or Typewriter Text—A fixed-width font like an old-fashioned typewriter. class=, dir=, id=, lang=, style=, title=, {event}=
<U>...</U> [in]	Underline—Underline the enclosed text. class=, dir=, id=, lang=, style=, title=, {event}=
<UL>...</UL> [st]	Unordered List—A bulleted list. Many browsers allow you to select the bullet type and automatically select a different bullet for nested lists.

HTML Tag	Explanation
	align=center ¦ left ¦ right, class=, clear=left ¦ right ¦ all, compact, dingbat=, dir=, id=, lang=, md=, plain, src=, style=, title=, type=disk ¦ square ¦ circle, wrap=vert ¦ horiz, {event}=
<VAR>...</VAR> [in]	Variable—A program variable.
	class=, dir=, id=, lang=, style=, title=, {event}=
<XMP>...</XMP> [st]	Example—An obsolete tag used to show an example and not clearly distinguished from the sample tag.
	id=, style=, title=, {event}=

Attributes

Attribute	Definition
abbr	Abbreviation for header cell.
accept-charset	List of supported character sets.
accept	List of MIME types for file upload.
accesskey	Accessibility key character.
action	Server-side form handler.
align	Alignment relative to table or fieldset, vertical or horizontal alignment, or other relationship between logical elements.
alink	Set the color of active links.
alt	A short description for accessibility.
archive	A space-delimited archive list.
axis	Identify a group of related headers.
background	Graphic image for tiling the background of a page.
bgcolor	Set a background color.
border	Set border width.
cellpadding	Set cell interior gutter.

Attribute	Definition
cellspacing	Set cell exterior gutter.
char	Set the alignment character.
charoff	Set the offset for the alignment character.
charset	Define the expected character encoding of a resource.
checked	Define radio buttons or check boxes on a form as checked.
cite	Location to examine for further information.
class	Space-delimited list of classes.
classid	Identifies an object implementation.
clear	Break text flow down to margin.
code	Reference an applet class file.
codebase	Base URL for applets and objects.
codetype	Predefine a MIME content type for code.
color	Either a color name or a hex pair definition of a color, #RRGGBB.
cols	Set the size or relative size of a column.
colspan	Set the number of columns a cell spans.
compact	Display a list in compact form.
content	Define the information content of a <META> tag.
coords	Define the coordinates of an imagemap area.
data	Reference an object's data.
datetime	Define the time and date for a change.
declare	Tell the browser to declare an object but not do anything with it.
defer	Tell the browser to defer execution of a script.
dir	Define the direction in which the enclosed text should be rendered.
disabled	Form item is unavailable.
enctype	MIME content type.
export	Export imagemap shapes to a parent object.
face	Comma-delimited list of font names.

Attribute	Definition
`for`	Identify the field ID target of a label tag.
`frame`	Set the appearance of the border around a table.
`frameborder`	Set frame borders to be visible.
`headers`	A list of IDs for header cells.
`height`	Set or override the height of an object or element.
`href`	Define the URL of a linked resource.
`hreflang`	Define the language code of a linked resource.
`hspace`	Horizontal gutter.
`http-equiv`	Define the name used to pass data to the server in a `<META>` tag.
`id`	Define a unique ID for an element.
`ismap`	Use a server-side imagemap.
`label`	Define a label for use in a menu on a form.
`lang`	Define an expected language code.
`language`	Declare the script language.
`link`	Set the color of unvisited links.
`longdesc`	Link to a long description.
`marginheight`	Set the margin height in pixels.
`marginwidth`	Set the margin width in pixels.
`media`	Define the media with which this element is designed to work.
`method`	Declare the HTTP method used to submit form data.
`multiple`	Declare that multiple selections are possible from a form selection list.
`name`	Declare a name so things can find each other.
`nohref`	Identify an area as having no action on an imagemap.
`noresize`	Don't let users resize a frame.
`noshade`	Alter the appearance of a horizontal rule.
`nowrap`	Suppress word wrapping in a table.
`object`	Reference an applet file.
`onblur`	Intrinsic event that occurs when an element loses focus.

Attribute	Definition
`onchange`	Intrinsic event that occurs when an element changes.
`onclick`	Intrinsic event that occurs when an element is clicked.
`ondblclick`	Intrinsic event that occurs when an element is double-clicked.
`onfocus`	Intrinsic event that occurs when an element gains focus.
`onkeydown`	Intrinsic event that occurs when a key is pressed.
`onkeypress`	Intrinsic event that occurs when a key is pressed and released.
`onkeyup`	Intrinsic event that occurs when a key is released.
`onload`	Intrinsic event that occurs when an element.
`onmousedown`	Intrinsic event that occurs when a mouse button is pressed.
`onmousemove`	Intrinsic event that occurs when the mouse pointer is moved.
`onmouseout`	Intrinsic event that occurs when the mouse pointer is moved away from an element.
`onmouseover`	Intrinsic event that occurs when the mouse pointer is moved into an element.
`onmouseup`	Intrinsic event that occurs when a mouse button is released.
`onreset`	Intrinsic event that occurs when a form is reset.
`onselect`	Intrinsic event that occurs when text is selected.
`onsubmit`	Intrinsic event that occurs when a form is submitted.
`onunload`	Intrinsic event that occurs when all pages or frames have been unloaded.
`profile`	Declare a dictionary of meta information.
`prompt`	Set a prompt message.
`readonly`	Text cannot be altered.
`rel`	Forward link type.
`repeat`	Repeat count for COL in a table.
`rev`	Reverse link type.
`rows`	Declare a list of lengths for a frameset or the vertical size of a textarea.

Attribute	Definition
rowspan	Set the number of rows spanned by a cell.
rules	Define the appearance of rules in the interior of a table.
scheme	Declare the form of the content of a <META> tag.
scope	Declare the scope of header cells.
scrolling	Set the presence or absence of a scrollbar.
selected	Predefine a form item as selected.
shape	Declare the shape of an area on an imagemap.
shapes	Declare the existence of shaped hypertext links in an object.
size	Declare the size of an element in some logical way.
span	Set the number of columns in a group.
src	Reference an exterior resource.
standby	Define a message to display while loading an object.
start	Declare the starting sequence number of an ordered list.
style	Set style information associated with a particular tag.
summary	Declare a purpose or structure for a table.
tabindex	Alter the default tabbing order for an element.
target	Identify the target frame where an element should be rendered.
text	Set the document text color.
title	Set an advisory title.
type	Set an advisory content type.
usemap	Use a client-side imagemap.
valign	Vertical alignment in the cells of a table.
value	Declare the value of an element.
valuetype	Define the type of the value passed in a parameter tag.
version	A constant identifying a particular version of HTML.
vlink	Set the color of visited links.
vspace	Set vertical gutter.
width	Set or override the width of a frame or element.

Intrinsic Events

The following events are identified as {event} in the quick reference table above.

`onclick, ondblclick, onmousedown, onmouseup, onmouseover, onmousemove, onmouseout, onkeypress, onkeydown, onkeyup`

APPENDIX

CSS Quick Reference

Style Sheet Example

All style sheets follow roughly the same pattern so here's a sample showing how you might set up your own page with an inline style sheet, as well as override some default values with the style attribute on a tag.

```
<HTML>
  <HEAD>
    <STYLE type="text/css">
      <--
      BODY { margin-left: 3%; margin-right: 3%;
      color: black;
             font-family: serif; background: #def url
(background.jpg); }
      A:link { color: blue }
      A:visited { color: purple }
      A:active { color: red }
      DIV.block { margin-left: 9%; }
      DIV.block H2, DIV.block H3 { margin-left: -9%; }
      H1 { clear: left; margin-top: 2em;
      text-align: center; }
      PRE { font-family: monospace; }
      IMG { border: 0; }
      -->
    </STYLE>
  </HEAD>
  <BODY text="black" bgcolor="#ddeeff" background="back-
ground.jpg"
```

```
        link="blue" vlink="purple" alink="red">
    <H1 style="color:red background-color:yellow">Main
Heading</H1>
```

This style sheet sets up standard margins of 3% of the browser window, sets text color to black, chooses a serif font without specifying a particular one, and sets the background color to `#ddeeff` using a shorthand three hexadecimal digit notation. Each single digit is doubled to make the final number. It also loads an image into the background, after the color is set to a close match, so the transition from blank page to background is smooth. Multiple property and value pairs are separated by semicolons so the browser can keep them straight in its tiny brain.

Note that I've argued pretty much the same effects in the `<BODY>` tag. Because the implementation of style sheets is uneven at best, as a general rule you should always argue the old styles as well as the new during the transition between the two different ways of doing things.

The margin changes may or may not take place, depending on the browser. Right margins are less commonly implemented than left margins, but the page will be readable without margin information so we can let that slide. If they appear, we're happy. If not, we truck on with our lives.

The rest of the style commands are also niceties that we'd prefer to see, and some of them can be argued in the body as a fall-back position. You can see what the effect of each should be by looking up the keywords in the reference list below.

Quick Reference

Boldface entries are safe to use

In the following table, selectors and properties that seem to be supported across all browsers and platforms are listed in boldface. As you can see, there aren't too many of them. Lightface entries may not work in all browsers or across all platforms, even those that theoretically support style sheets.

The numbers below refer to the actual section headings in the Cascading Style Sheets, Level 1 (CSS1) style sheet recommendation of the World Wide Web Consortium (W3C). Some numbers are skipped because they discuss issues that have no properties.

Each entry consists of a selector, usually an HTML element followed by a property/value pair enclosed in curly braces, followed by an optional example, description, or explanation. The value can be a list of values that the property can take.

I left out examples for all the properties after font-family because they're all the same and it not only gets boring but fills up space that could be better spent on other things. The initial (and more complex) items all have examples to help you figure out what's going on.

I've shown ellipses (...) after the property and value pairs to show that you could add more properties if you wanted to, always remembering to separate the pairs with a semicolon, as shown in the earlier example.

The text of the CSS1 recommendation is surprisingly readable, and if you want a more technical explanation and don't mind reading documents on your computer, you can look it up on the Web at `http://www.w3.org/Style/css/`.

They also have online tutorials and background information to make life easier for the budding style sheet *maven*. (That's *guru* to those whose metaphors for expertise are more influenced by the Far East than by Middle Europe.)

The conventions used in this appendix are:

Heading numbers	Refers to paragraphs in the W3C Style Sheet Recommendation
Boldface	Style properties and values safe across all browsers
Lightface	Style properties and values not supported across all browsers
Italics	Comments and explanations
[adv]	Marks advanced features that are not required to claim CSS compliance and are not supported on most browsers
element1...	Refers to HTML elements (tags)
classid	Refers to a value entered in a class attribute in the HTML tag
id	Refers to a value entered in an ID attribute in the HTML tag

Angle brackets < >	Surround HTML elements but are also used to surround a property value to indicate that the entire element, including the brackets, should be replaced by a single word
Curly braces { }	Surround property/value pairs and are mandatory
property	Refers to CSS properties found in front of the colon
value	Refers to CSS values found after the colon

Reminder: Numbers in the following table

The numbers below refer to the actual section headings in the Cascading Style Sheets, Level 1 (CSS1) style sheet recommendation of the World Wide Web Consortium (W3C). Some numbers are skipped because they discuss issues that have no properties.

Most entries consist of a selector followed by the property/value pair enclosed in curly braces ({}). The selector defines the scope of the following property/value pair while the property/value pair defines how the browser will render text selected by the selector used. In a few cases the description also shows inline styles.

1–Basic Concepts

1.1 Containment in HTML

```
<LINK rel="stylesheet" type="text/css" href="imported-stylesheet" ... >
```

External style sheet.

```
@import importedstylesheet
```

External style sheet imported into an inline style element.

```
<STYLE type="text/css" ... ><-- style sheet commands -->
</STYLE>
```

Inline style sheet with style commands contained within SGML comments.

```
<STYLE><-- commands --></STYLE>
```

```
<XXX style=" ... ">
```

Style commands added directly to an HTML element.

1.2 Grouping

```
element1, element2, element3 { property: value }
```

Save space in style sheets by grouping elements that will be treated in the same fashion in a comma-separated list.

1.3 Inheritance

```
element1 { property: value ... }
<element1> <element2> (same as outer) </element2>
</element1>
```

If an element is not otherwise declared, it takes on the values of an enclosing element.

1.4 Class as selector

```
element1.classid { property: value ... }
<element1 class="classid">
```

Elements can be grouped and selected according to class attributes on the HTML tags themselves.

1.5 ID as selector

```
#xxx { property: value ... }
element1#xxx { property: value ... }
<element1 id=#xxx>
```

Elements can be addressed directly by means of a unique id attribute on the individual HTML tag.

1.6 Contextual selectors

```
element1 element2 { property: value ... }
<element1> <element2>this text is affected</element2>
</element1>
<element2>this text is not</element2>
```

Commands can be limited in scope to elements within the scope of a containing tag.

1.7 Comments

```
/* comment */
```

Comments can be inserted in the style sheet to explain the code.

2—Pseudo-Classes and Pseudo-Elements

2.1 anchor pseudo-classes

```
A:link { property: value ... }
A:active { property: value ... }
A:visited { property: value ... }
```

Anchors can be styled based on their browser status.

2.2 Typographical pseudo-elements

2.3 first-line [adv]

```
first-line { property: value ... }
```

The first line of any element can be selected directly.

2.4 first-letter [adv]

```
first-letter { property: value ... }
```

The first letter of any element can be selected directly.

2.5 Pseudo-elements in selectors

```
element1 element2:pseudo-element { property: value ... }
```

Pseudo-elements must be last in a contextual list of selectors.

2.6 Multiple pseudo-elements

```
element1 { property: value ... }
element1:pseudo-element1 { property: value ... }
element1:pseudo-element2 { property: value ... }
```

Several pseudo-elements that have overlapping effects can be defined.

3.1—Important

```
element1 { ! important property: value ... }
```

Add weight to a style command, promoting it over conflicting commands that would otherwise override it. There are few times that you'd be justified in using this command, because it's one method whereby persons with special visual needs can override your style sheet with a high contrast or large print alternative rendering.

3.2 Cascading Order

Weight sorting

! Important commands are more important than unmarked ones.

Origin sorting

Author style sheets are more important than the reader's style sheets, which are more important than the default style sheet for the browser.

Specificity sorting

Resolve conflicts by means of a complex algorithm that attempts to discover how "specific" a command is.

Order sorting

Resolve remaining conflicts by means of a last-seen algorithm. If two commands are otherwise equal, the last seen takes precedence.

5.2—Font Properties

5.2.2 font-family

`element1 { font-family: value ... }`

`<family-name>`

Specify a font family name like Garamond or Beppo.

`<generic-family>`

`serif`

`sans-serif`

`cursive`

`fantasy`

`monospace`

Specify a font family by generic characteristics.

5.2.3 font-style

`normal`

`italic`

`oblique`

Specify a text treatment. Oblique is similar to italic but only slants the characters. True italic also alters the shape of the characters.

5.2.4 font-variant

`normal`

`small-caps`

Specify a text treatment. Small caps are required in the core functionality but may turn into regular caps in text-based browsers, and browsers may ignore the command in non-Western European alphabets for which capital letters are not defined or whose techniques for emphasizing words are different.

5.2.5 font-weight

`normal`

`bold`

`bolder`

`lighter`

`100-900`

Specify a text treatment. The language allows for nine weights, but if there are fewer available, they may be mapped onto the missing weights in some logical way.

5.2.6 font-size

<absolute-size>

`xx-small`

`x-small`

`small`

`medium`

`large`

`x-large`

`xx-large`

<relative-size>

`larger`

`smaller`

`<length>`

`<percentage>`

Specify a text treatment. Font size may be specified in absolute terms or relative to the current size, whichever is convenient.

5.2.7 font

`<font-family>`

`<font-style>`

`<font-variant>`

`<font-weight>`

`<font-size>`

`<font-height>`

Specify several text treatments. This property is a shorthand notation for `<font-style>`, `<font-variant>`, `<font-weight>`, `<font-size>`, `<line-height>`, and `<font- family>`. The values each can take can be entered after this property without worrying about which goes with which. The browser will figure it out.

5.3–Color and Background Properties

5.3.1 color

`<color>`

Specify a foreground (text) color on an element.

5.3.2 background-color

`color`

`transparent`

Specify a background color on an element. Unlike traditional HTML, style sheets allow you to add "spot color" behind any visible element. This can be either wonderful or annoying, depending on how well one uses the capability.

5.3.3 background-image

<url>

`none`

Specify a background image on an element.

5.3.4 background-repeat

`repeat`

`repeat-x`

`repeat-y`

`no-repeat`

Specify a repeat value and method. `repeat` tiles the available area both horizontally and vertically. `repeat-x` tiles horizontally only. `repeat-y` tiles vertically only.

5.3.5 background-attachment

`scroll`

`fixed` [adv]

Specify how the background moves while scrolling. The default is to scroll with the text, but you can specify that a logo, for example, remains centered and immovable on the page while the rest of the page scrolls over it.

5.3.6 background-position

<percentage>

<length>

`top`

`center`

`left`

`bottom`

`right`

Specify an initial position for a background image. Values can be combined, and if two numeric values are present, the horizontal value is presumed to be first.

5.3.7 background

<background-color>

<background-image>

<background-repeat>

<background-attachment>

<background-position>

Specify several background values at once. This property is a shorthand notation for `<background- color>`, `<background-image>`, `<background-repeat>`, `<background-attachment>`, and `<background-position>`. The values each can take can be entered after this property without worrying about which goes with which. The browser will figure it out.

5.4—Text Properties

5.4.1 word-spacing

`normal`

<length> [adv]

Specify the default whitespace between words.

5.4.2 letter-spacing

`normal`

<length> [adv]

Specify the default whitespace between letters. This is useful in old-style German Fraktur fonts, where emphasis is usually made by spacing out the letters more widely than normal.

5.4.3 text-decoration

`none`

`underline`

`overline`

`line-through`

`blink`

Specify a text treatment. Line-through text is what we would ordinarily call strikeout or strike-through. This is useful for turning off link underlining globally, among other things.

5.4.4 vertical-align

`baseline`

`sub`

`super`

`top`

`text-top`

`middle`

`bottom`

`text-bottom`

`<percentage>`

Specify the vertical alignment of an element in relation to the surrounding text.

5.4.5 text-transform

`capitalize`

`uppercase`

`lowercase`

`none`

Specify a text transformation treatment. Transformations are required in the core functionality but may be ignored by browsers in the case of non-Western European alphabets, for which capital letters are not defined, or whose techniques for emphasizing words are substantially different.

5.4.6 text-align

`left`

`right`

`center`

`justify` [adv]

Specify a text treatment. Justification refers to spacing out the text to precisely fit within the left and right margins, which browser makers hate to do because it's complicated and difficult.

5.4.7 text-indent

`<length>`

`<percentage>`

Specify a text treatment that occurs at the beginning of an element. This is useful for indenting (or outdenting) the first line of a paragraph, for one example. Hanging (outdented) paragraphs are quite common in technical materials.

5.4.8 line-height

`normal`

`<number>`

`<length>`

`<percentage>`

Specify the line height in relation to the font. In typographical terms this is called the body of the text. So you could set a 12-point font on a 14-point body to achieve a set separation between lines. Or you could set the same font on a 12-point body to jam them together rather tightly. Ordinarily the browser will set the text with a reasonably loose fit to allow easy legibility, but you can use this property to gain complete control, as when you want to bring the top of a following line up to meet the bottom of the current one to achieve a special typographic effect in a logo or headline.

5.5—Box Properties

All the following properties specify how the “invisible” boxes that surround each element are treated, including being made visible by means of rules or changing the color of the background. Using spot background color to emphasize a headline, for example, looks rather ill-done unless you also expand the “invisible” border box the headline sits in to allow the background to make a nice border around it.

Margins are the outermost piece of the nested puzzle. They affect the whitespace gutter around an element and are always transparent to allow the background to show through. Borders come next. They affect the “elbow room” inside the box and take on the characteristics of the background set for the element itself. The border values affect whether the “invisible” box is made visible by the addition of a visible border. They appear between the margin and the border boxes if present.

5.5.01 margin-top

<length>

<percentage>

`auto`

Specify the exterior top margin or gutter of an element.

5.5.02 margin-right

<length>

<percentage>

`auto`

Specify the exterior right margin or gutter of an element.

5.5.03 margin-bottom

<length>

<percentage>

`auto`

Specify the exterior bottom margin or gutter of an element.

5.5.04 margin-left

<length>

<percentage>

`auto`

Specify left exterior margin or gutter of an element.

5.5.05 margin

<length>

<percentage>

`auto`

Specify one or more exterior margins or gutters of an element. If four length values are specified, they apply to top, right, bottom, and left, respectively. If there is only one value, it applies to all sides, if there are two or three, the missing values are taken from the opposite sides.

5.5.06 padding-top

<length>

<percentage>

`auto`

Specify the top interior margin or gutter of an element. It sets the amount of space between one "invisible" border of an element and the element itself.

5.5.07 padding-right

<length>

<percentage>

`auto`

Specify the right interior margin or gutter of an element. It sets the amount of space between one "invisible" border of an element and the element itself.

5.5.08 padding-bottom

<length>

<percentage>

`auto`

Specify the bottom interior margin or gutter of an element. It sets the amount of space between one "invisible" border of an element and the element itself.

5.5.09 padding-left

<length>

<percentage>

`auto`

Specify the left interior margin or gutter of an element. It sets the amount of space between one "invisible" border of an element and the element itself.

5.5.10 padding

<length>

<percentage>

`auto`

Specify one or more interior margins or gutters of an element. They set the amount of space between the "invisible" borders of an element and the element itself. If four length values are specified, they apply to top, right, bottom and left respectively. If there is only one value, it applies to all sides, if there are two or three, the missing values are taken from the opposite side.

5.5.11 border-top-width

`thin`

`medium`

`thick`

`<length>`

Specify the thickness (and visibility) of the top border of an element.

5.5.12 border-right-width

`thin`

`medium`

`thick`

`<length>`

Specify the thickness (and visibility) of the right border of an element.

5.5.13 border-bottom-width

`thin`

`medium`

`thick`

`<length>`

Specify the thickness (and visibility) of the bottom border of an element.

5.5.14 border-left-width

`thin`

`medium`

`thick`

`<length>`

Specify the thickness (and visibility) of the left border of an element.

5.5.15 border-width

`thin`

`medium`

`thick`

<length>

Specify the thickness (and visibility) of one or more borders of an element. This property is a shorthand property for setting border-width-top, border-width right, border-width-bottom, and border-width-left in one fell swoop. There can be from one to four values, with the following interpretation: one value—all four border widths are set to that value; two values—top and bottom border widths are set to the first value, right and left are set to the second; three values—top is set to the first, right and left are set to the second, bottom is set to the third; four values—top, right, bottom, and left, respectively.

5.5.16 border-color

<color>

Specify the color of one or more borders of an element. There can be from one to four values, with the following interpretation: one value—all four border colors are set to that value; two values—top and bottom border colors are set to the first value, right and left are set to the second; three values—top is set to the first, right and left are set to the second, bottom is set to the third; four values—top, right, bottom, and left, respectively.

5.5.17 border-style

`none`

`dotted` [adv]

`dashed` [adv]

`solid`

`double` [adv]

`groove` [adv]

`ridge` [adv]

`inset` [adv]

`offset` [adv]

Specify the rule style of one or more borders of an element. There can be from one to four values, with the following interpretation: one value—all four border rules are set to that value; two values—top and bottom border rules are set to the first value, right and left are set to the second; three values—top is set to the first, right and left are set to the second, bottom is set to the third; four values—top, right, bottom, and left, respectively.

5.5.18 border-top

`<border-top-width>`

`<border-style>`

`<color>`

Set the width, rule styles, and color of the top border (only) at one time.

5.5.19 border-right

`<border-right-width>`

`<border-style>`

`<color>`

Set the width, rule styles, and color of the right border (only) at one time.

5.5.20 border-bottom

`<border-bottom-width>`

`<border-style>`

`<color>`

Set the width, rule styles, and color of the bottom border (only) at one time.

5.5.21 border-left

`<border-left-width>`

`<border-style>`

`<color>`

Set the width, rule styles, and color of the left border (only) at one time.

5.5.22 border

<border-width>

<border-style>

<color>

Set the width, rule styles, and color of all borders at one time and to the same values. You can't use multiple values to set different values for the four sides.

5.5.23 width

<length>

<percentage>

`auto`

Override the default width of an element.

5.5.24 height

<length>

`auto`

Override the default height of an element.

5.5.25 float

`left`

`right`

`none`

Override the default behavior of an element to cause text to flow around it as if it were a bump on the left or right margin. It also overrides the display property and causes the element to behave as a block element regardless of type.

5.5.26 clear

`left`

`right`

`both`

`none`

Fix the behavior of an element in relation to floating elements by listing sides on which the element will refuse to float. `none` says the element will float on either side. `both` says it will always clear down to the next available free space on both margins. `left` says it will clear down to the left margin but ignore the right, and vice versa for `right`.

5.6—Classification Properties

5.6.1 display [adv]

`block`

`inline`

`list-item`

`none`

Override the default behavior of an element to make it behave however one wants. Very cool. Unfortunately only Netscape Navigator for Windows 95 does much about it so far.

5.6.2 white-space [adv]

`normal`

`pre`

`nowrap`

Override the default whitespace behavior of an element to make whitespace behave however you want. This is very cool because it lets you typeset poetry and other text requiring exact placement of whitespace without fooling around with non-break spaces and breaks while retaining the ability to control the look of the font. Unfortunately, only Netscape Navigator for Windows 95 and Mac does much about it so far.

5.6.3 list-style-type

`disc`

`circle`

`square`

`decimal`

`lower-roman`

`upper-roman`

`lower-alpha`

`upper-alpha`

`none`

This sets the default numeration type of a list element, similar to the way the type attribute can be used on a list tag.

5.6.4 list-style-image

<url>

`none`

Override the numeration type of a list element by picking up an image to be used as a bullet.

5.6.5 list-style-position

`inside`

`outside`

Override the default display of list elements by specifying whether the bullet or number will be displayed as a hanging indent (outdent), as usual, or inline, as if it were part of the text.

5.6.6 list-style

<keyword>

<position>

<url>

A shorthand notation for setting all list style values at once.

6—Units

6.1 Length Units

`em` `em-quad`, the point size of the current font.

`ex` `x-height`, the height of the letter x in the current font.

`px` pixels

`in` inches

`cm` centimeters

`mm` millimeters

`pc` percent

`pt` points, a typographical measure equal to $^1/_{72}$ of an inch. In other words, there are 72 points to the inch.

6.2 Percentage Units

<percentage>

Percentage values are not inherited. The result of a percentage calculation is inherited.

6.3 Color Units

`#000`

`#000000`

(`RRR,GGG,BBB`)

(`R%,G%,B%`)

`keyword`

Style sheet colors do not affect images.

6.4 URLs

<url>

URLs are always enclosed in parentheses and may be surrounded by optional single or double quote marks. Parentheses, commas, whitespace characters, single quotes (`'`) and double quotes (`"`) appearing in a URL must be escaped with a backslash (\). Partial URLs are interpreted relative to the source of the style sheet, not relative to the document.

Background

Cascading style sheets are the wave of the future on the Web. Designers are pushing hard for the ability to control all variables on the page, from typeface to line spacing and exact layout and control of whitespace, just as they're used to in print media.

They're not quite there yet, but they're getting closer with each new browser release.

The theory behind style sheets is simple. You can create a master style sheet for an entire site and then override or extend the style sheet on any particular page while not altering global settings not specifically addressed.

Likewise, a user can create a style sheet that overrides the default style sheet the browser uses to display pages, while allowing the page designer to override those settings to format a particular page.

For the designer, this means that you should usually specify sizes in terms of relative size and not force a user to accept your idea of what's "big enough." For the most part you're free to play around with whatever you want, though, and you can really do quite stunning things with fairly simple commands.

The style sheet commands consist of simple text strings, with each command consisting of an HTML element, special pseudo-element, or subclass of elements followed by a curly bracketed list of properties and values. If there is more than one property and value pair listed, they should be separated by semicolons. Styles can be further refined by declaring what context they would apply to by listing elements in order or by applying pseudo-elements or attributes to modify the HTML element.

So a style referring to anchor elements might be modified by saying this style applies only to anchor elements that are also links, `A:link { color:blue }`, have been visited, `A:visited { color:red }`, or occur within the scope of a paragraph, `P A { color:green }`.

The commands can be placed in a separate file, which is very convenient for controlling an entire site from one uniform location, in the head section of a file, or inline, attached to an individual tag. In the case of an inline style, there can be no need of an element description, since the style affects the element to which it is attached. Likewise, you don't bracket the style with curly braces but just list the style commands in a comma-separated list within quotation marks.

Browser Support

Quite frankly, support for CSS1 has so far been a dismal failure. The few things available across multiple platforms are almost not worth doing. We can only hope the situation will improve over time, and there is every reason to hope that it will if the browser makers will only get behind existing standards and concentrate on getting *at least* the defined syntax and commands right before haring off after quirky or non-standard "features" and "extensions" to attain some hoped-for Nirvana of product differentiation.

You'll note that I put those two terms, much bandied-about by both major manufacturers, in wry quotes. It's my considered opinion that you can't make an extension to a standard until you've done it right to begin with, and an extension without a stable and agreed-upon base is merely a fancy and disingenuous name for a bug.

Overall, the best cross-platform support in a main-stream browser is with Netscape Navigator/Communicator 4.0. Their coverage of Windows platforms and the Macintosh is even-handed for the most part, and what works in one will pretty much work in the other. They also support UNIX rather well, which accounts for pretty much all the major platforms. Since they still have the largest market share and people with Macintoshes are known to be, shall we say, easily distressed regarding page design issues and matters of typographical taste, this might be a good platform to concentrate on as the most common denominator.

On the other hand, if you're only interested in Windows 95, Microsoft's Internet Explorer 4.0 has very good coverage for Windows and Intel PCs. Unfortunately their implementation of CSS1 on the Macintosh is terrible, and their UNIX support is an afterthought at best and a slight at worst.

If you're willing to go against the mainstream, the GNU version of Emacs-W3 (GnuScape Navigator) is probably the most complete and up-to-date implementation of CSS1 available. Although configuring GNU Emacs-W3 is not for the faint of heart, it being assumed that you have not one, but two shirt pockets with many colored pens and pencils safely ensconced in unmatched pocket protectors, it's easily the most powerful and extensible Web browser around. It has many features built in, including out-of-the-box integration with Emacspeak, a marvelous audio browser package by T.V. Raman entirely suitable for surfing the Web without the assistance of vision.

Since Emacs-W3 is built around an editor, importing information from the Web and incorporating it into documents is a trivial task. Since it's Emacs, you can do sophisticated filtering and rearranging of the data you get off the Web without fighting what the designers thought you *should* be doing every step of the way.

GNU Emacs-W3 can be found at

`http://www.cs.indiana.edu/elisp/w3/docs.html`

T.V. Raman's Emacspeak can be found at

`http://www.research.digital.com/CRL/personal/raman/emacspeak/emacspeak.html`

Handling Bugs Gracefully

I'm of two minds about this. On the one hand it's not right for the designers of Web pages to spend countless hours trying to account for the vagaries and oversights of the manufacturers.

In that frame of mind, I tend to think that we should code for the way it *ought* to work and let people see just how bad most browsers are. Let the chips fall where they may.

On the other hand, people will judge your page based on how well you use the tools at hand, and using features that break some browsers just makes your pages look bad. Few people are sophisticated enough to realize that the terrible-looking page they're trying to read is due to the failure of the maker of the browser they're reading it with and not the errors of the page's creator. Just as people who need new glasses tend to think that print is getting smaller, people who need new browsers tend to think that pages are looking sloppier.

In practice this means that you have to do the best job you can with traditional tags first and then apply a style sheet after the fact. This makes sense because there are still lots of browsers out there for whom your style sheet is so much gobbledegook, and you should probably try to account for them as well.

That can mean arguing typographical elements several times, calling for a background color and image and link colors in the `<BODY>` tag as well as the body selector, and so on.

It can also mean asking for things that don't really affect the look of the page drastically. Calling for a particular font, for example, is a nice touch, but failure to actually *use* the font is unlikely to affect readability unless it's Russian Cyrillic or something like that.

Reference

Although the information in this appendix is current as of this writing, the most up-to-date source for information is the World Wide Web Consortium at `http://www.w3.org/Style/`.

This directory contains both the latest thinking on cascading style sheets and research projects showing where they may be headed over time.

In addition, browser capabilities change rapidly and both major manufacturers are committed to supporting style sheets. This means we can expect that some of the features marked as questionable for actual use may be less undependable in the future. My own recommendation is to take a yellow highlighter to those elements that you've personally tested and found to be safe or that have been recommended as safe to you by some credible resource. In most cases, failure to honor a style sheet command won't result in any harm other than to mess up your formatting a bit. But in the worst cases, the formatting will be trashed and the document will be rendered unreadable.

In short, style sheets are not quite ready for prime time unless you have lots of spare time on your hands to fiddle and tweak your pages as new and possibly less buggy implementations appear.

Notes on CSS2, the Next Generation of Style Sheets

CSS2, the next version of style sheets, takes some of the characteristics of the existing specification and extends them to include many more pseudo-elements to allow even finer control of the document, as well as providing specific properties for affecting the rendering of audio browsers.

These changes track the increasing importance of network information retrieval in daily life. As Web browsers become ubiquitous, appearing everywhere from luxury cars to home theater systems, the possible *best* renderings for information multiply far beyond the simple tricks we ask of them now.

If you're under the car trying to fix some doohickey according to instructions on the manufacturer's Web site, you probably want the text to be spoken and the pictures to be as large as possible so you can see them with your neck at an awkward angle peering around a wheel.

In the car tooling down the road at high speed, you don't want anything to distract you at all. Perhaps the car, itself, will apply a style sheet while in motion that restricts output to spoken material, but lets you look at maps and text descriptions while at a full stop.

For a surgeon accessing medical records in the midst of an operation, perhaps a very telegraphic and rapid-fire aural rendering might be needed to keep up with the exigencies of the medical moment.

We can only guess at what the future may look like once we get more than a few years out, but I think it's safe to say that the Web will still be around in some form, and that it will be integrated into our daily lives in ways we can only dimly imagine today.

APPENDIX

Colors

Making Sense of Color

Specifying color names on the Web is simple, though not intuitive for the most part, because the most universal method is by using hexadecimal digits to separately say how much red, green, and blue are mixed to create a given color. The trouble lies in how those numbers are rendered on every machine. If you want to make your colors work on the widest variety of machines and monitors, choose from the browser-safe palette described in "Browser-Safe Colors" in this appendix. If you want to understand the reasons why, I've included a short and fairly non-technical explanation below.

Using Color on the World Wide Web

Color is one of the most difficult things to get right on the Web because there are so many different types of display monitors in use on the desktops of your readers. They can range from text-only monochrome through 16-color and 256-color through thousands or even millions of colors, use different standard colors (Macintoshes versus PCs versus UNIX), and generally make life difficult. The problem lies in something called *dithering* and a related defect called *banding*.

Dithering is not a bad thing, in fact every color monitor or TV uses tiny dots of red, green, and blue (RGB) to make up the colors we think we see. The dots are so close together that our eyes can't really see them, so they blend together and appear like one color unless you look at them through a magnifying glass. The trouble starts because the software and hardware that make the monitor work on a computer use digital descriptions to display colors instead of the analog commands we're used to on TV.

Figure C.1 shows the effects of dithering and banding on a black-and-white image at two color depths. Notice how the image looks muddy in the image on the left although it's clear on the right.

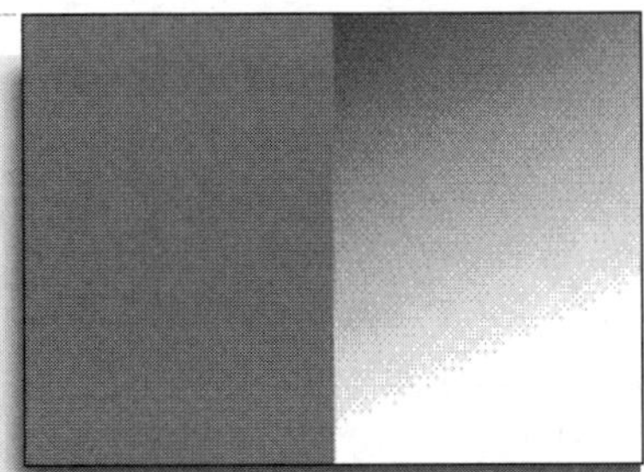

FIGURE C.1
A Paint Shop Pro screen shot showing two versions of the same image, one dithered and showing banding and one without.

We all tend to think of *digital* as a good thing, due to shrewd marketing by the makers of digital devices, and there *are* advantages. But there are disadvantages as well; digital basically means counting on your fingers, and just as it's hard to do fractions on your fingers, the little color dots on a digital display can only take a few of the possible colors. If the number of possible values is small, the jumps between values become noticeable. It's like the difference between the household dimmers with a knob or slide, which can adjust a light to any level, and those "one touch" dimmers that cycle through three levels, from dim to fully bright, and then off again. A "one touch" dimmer is digital, with four discrete levels; a dimmer with a knob is analog and can theoretically take any of billions and jillions of values.

Of course we can't actually *see* the difference between a billion and a jillion and one, so compromises can be made. Since most people, until the advent of Web browsers and CD-ROM games, didn't look at photographs on their computers, many computer makers scrimped on space and expense by keeping only two or four values per primary color, which translated into 16 or 256 colors on the screen. This made a lot of sense then because computers with the graphics capabilities we take almost for granted today would have been terribly expensive and out of reach for anyone without a Pentagon-style budget.

And that's where we are today, with very many 256-color monitors out there on users' desks, a smaller number of workstations supporting thousands or even millions of colors, and a small but significant number of monochrome, grayscale, text-only, and 16-color monitors that refuse to go away for very good reasons.

Dithering takes place whenever you specify colors from one standard that don't exist in the standard in use on a target machine; instead of rendering a pure color, the color is approximated by using a pattern of relatively large dots. Some dithering patterns look just awful and so we try to avoid dithering completely by using colors that are the same on every machine.

In the case of photographs, usually kept as JPEG files on the Web, we don't have to worry too much because the browser usually does a good job of dithering the photo so it looks as good as possible at a given resolution. GIF files are the problem, and the new PNG files as well, because they're usually used for line art and dithering can really hurt the way they look.

By using colors that are common to as many platforms as possible, we can minimize the chances that an image will look bad and, by following the browser-safe "best practices" of professional graphic artists, we can at least ensure that our pictures don't look any worse than most of the others a user will see on a nonstandard platform.

As more and more people upgrade to machines capable of thousands or millions of colors, dithering and banding are becoming less important to consider, but for several years to come I think we'll have to take it into account on every project.

This appendix lists several of the standard ways of talking about color on the Web and offers immediate Web access to examples of each color type.

HTML 4.0 Named Colors

The colors in Table C.1 are approximations of the standard Windows colors as displayed on a 16-color monitor, a sort of lowest common denominator. The full gamut of colors available on your display are available through the hex pair syntax to specify the named color. Note that these may or may not be browser safe, depending on your monitor and operating system.

I've also added the process color (print) names often used to refer to the pure *subtractive* colors (CYMK) as well as the *additive* (monitor) primary colors (RGB) in the USA. However, they aren't official names in the standard; in fact, they partially conflict with it. Because of the confusing different naming spaces for colors used by browser manufacturers, it's probably best to use the unambiguous numeric values rather than the superficially more self-explanatory names.

TABLE C.1 HTML 4.0 named colors

Color Name	Hex Pair Value	Process Color
Black	= #000000	K = (Black)
Navy	= #000080	
Blue	= #0000FF	B = (Blue)
Green	= #008000	
Teal	= #008080	
Lime	= #00FF00	G = (Green)
Aqua	= #00FFFF	C = (Cyan)
Maroon	= #800000	
Purple	= #800080	
Olive	= #808000	
Gray	= #808080	
Silver	= #C0C0C0	
Red	= #FF0000	
Fuchsia	= #FF00FF	M = (Magenta)

Color Name	Hex Pair Value	Process Color
Yellow	= #FFFF00	Y = (Yellow)
White	= #FFFFFF	

Netscape Named Colors

The colors in Table C.2 are basically thousands or millions of colors standard borrowed from UNIX systems by Netscape and later adopted by Microsoft, supplemented by the HTML 4.0 named colors from the list above in **boldface**. Many browsers don't support color names, and most support a completely different set of colors on 256-color monitors, so your pages should always use the hex pairs and not names if you're designing for the widest audience. You shouldn't use these colors at all if you're designing for the 256-color default, lowest common denominator standard because most of them dither badly at lower color depths. The named colors are very handy for initial design, though, since they're a lot easier to remember than the weird hex numbers, and, if your audience is exclusively (as on a corporate intranet) on machines with at least thousands-of-color monitors, you can use them freely. Just remember to convert them to the nearest browser-safe equivalent if you need to.

TABLE C.2 Netscape named colors

Color Name	Hex Pair Value
aliceblue	#F0F8FF
antiquewhite	#FAEBD7
aqua	**#00FFFF**
aquamarine	#7FFFD4
azure	#F0FFFF
beige	#F5F5DC
bisque	#FFE4C4
black	**#000000**

continues…

TABLE C.2 **Continued**

Color Name	Hex Pair Value
blanchedalmond	#FFEBCD
blue	**#0000FF**
blueviolet	#8A2BE2
brown	#A52A2A
burlywood	#DEB887
cadetblue	#5F9EA0
chartreuse	#7FFF00
chocolate	#D2691E
coral	#FF7F50
cornflowerblue	#6495ED
cornsilk	#FFF8DC
crimson	#DC1436
cyan	#00FFFF (same as aqua)
darkblue	#00008B
darkcyan	#008B8B
darkgoldenrod	#B8860B
darkgrey	#A9A9A9
darkgreen	#006400
darkkhaki	#BDB76B
darkmagenta	#8B008B
darkolivegreen	#556B2F
darkorange	#FF8C00
darkorchid	#9932CC
darkred	#8B0000
darksalmon	#E9967A
darkseagreen	#8FBC8F
darkslateblue	#483D8B

Color Name	Hex Pair Value
darkslategray	#2F4F4F
darkturquoise	#00CED1
darkviolet	#9400D3
deeppink	#FF1493
deepskyblue	#00BFFF
dimgray	#696969
dodgerblue	#1E90FF
firebrick	#B22222
floralwhite	#FFFAF0
forestgreen	#228B22
fuchsia	**#FF00FF**
gainsboro	#DCDCDC
ghostwhite	#F8F8FF
gold	#FFD700
goldenrod	#DAA520
gray	**#808080**
green	**#008000**
greenyellow	#ADFF2F
honeydew	#F0FFF0
hotpink	#FF69B4
indianred	#CD5C5C
indigo	#4B0082
ivory	#FFFFF0
khaki	#F0E68C
lavender	#E6E6FA
lavenderblush	#FFF0F5
lawngreen	#7CFC00

continues…

TABLE C.2 **Continued**

Color Name	Hex Pair Value
lemonchiffon	#FFFACD
lightblue	#ADD8E6
lightcoral	#F08080
lightcyan	#E0FFFF
lightgoldenrodyellow	#FAFAD2
lightgreen	#90EE90
lightgrey	#D3D3D3
lightpink	#FFB6C1
lightsalmon	#FFA07A
lightseagreen	#20B2AA
lightskyblue	#87CEFA
lightslategray	#778899
lightsteelblue	#B0C4DE
lightyellow	#FFFFE0
lime	**#00FF00**
limegreen	#32CD32
linen	#FAF0E6
magenta	#FF00FF (same as fuschia)
maroon	**#800000**
mediumaquamarine	#66CDAA
mediumblue	#0000CD
mediumorchid	#BA55D3
mediumpurple	#9370DB
mediumseagreen	#3CB371
mediumslateblue	#7B68EE
mediumspringgreen	#00FA9A
mediumturquoise	#48D1CC
mediumvioletred	#C71585
midnightblue	#191970

Color Name	Hex Pair Value
mintcream	#F5FFFA
mistyrose	#FFE4E1
moccasin	#FFE4B5
navajowhite	#FFDEAD
navy	**#000080**
oldlace	#FDF5E6
olive	**#808000**
olivedrab	#6B8E23
orange	#FFA500
orangered	#FF4500
orchid	#DA70D6
palegoldenrod	#EEE8AA
palegreen	#98FB98
paleturquoise	#AFEEEE
palevioletred	#DB7093
papayawhip	#FFEFD5
peachpuff	#FFDAB9
peru	#CD853F
pink	#FFC0CB
plum	#DDA0DD
powderblue	#B0E0E6
purple	**#800080**
red	**#FF0000**
rosybrown	#BC8F8F
royalblue	#4169E1
saddlebrown	#8B4513
salmon	#FA8072
sandybrown	#F4A460
seagreen	#2E8B57

continues…

TABLE C.2 **Continued**

Color Name	Hex Pair Value
seashell	#FFF5EE
sienna	#A0522D
silver	**#C0C0C0**
skyblue	#87CEEB
slateblue	#6A5ACD
slategray	#708090
snow	#FFFAFA
springgreen	#00FF7F
steelblue	#4682B4
tan	#D2B48C
teal	**#008080**
thistle	#D8BFD8
tomato	#FF6347
turquoise	#40E0D0
violet	#EE82EE
wheat	#F5DEB3
white	**#FFFFFF**
whitesmoke	#F5F5F5
yellow	**#FFFF00**
yellowgreen	#9ACD32

Browser-Safe Colors

If this were the best of all possible worlds, every operating system would have the same very large number of colors to choose from and we wouldn't have to worry about our great page turning into a dark brown mess on a different machine from the one we used to design it. But it's not.

Every manufacturer chooses its own standard without talking to anyone else, and there are quite a few different standards to choose from. Most of the standards share a subset of 216 different colors that are the same, or similar, across many platforms. This means that if you use these colors exclusively, you have a good chance of having your picture rendered the same way on both a Macintosh and a PC, as well as most UNIX systems.

Unfortunately, the browser-safe colors can't easily be described in words and have no standard descriptive names, so we've done the next best thing by making available on the World Wide Web a list of browser-safe colors—those that display correctly and without dithering on the widest possible range of computers—where you can see the colors as well as the hex codes that create them. This list uses HTML itself to display the colors, so you know that the color you see is exactly what was intended.

Looking at the table on the Web, you'll notice an unfortunate characteristic of the browser-safe colors; they were created by a programmer and not by an artist or anyone with an understanding of how human vision works and are distributed evenly across the color space. We don't see well in the blue and green regions though, so many of the blue and green combinations are indecipherable and unusable mud.

On the other hand, we see yellow and red very well so there are big jumps in value between many of those colors. One day in the far distant future, it may be that a programmer will ask whether it's *sensible* to do things "logically." On that happy day I'm sure there will be general rejoicing and quite possibly dancing in the streets.

You can also tell whether a particular color is browser-safe by looking at the values of the hex RBG pairs, or even the RGB decimal values if you're working in a graphics editor.

In hex RBG, each value must be one of `00`, `33`, `66`, `99`, `CC`, or `FF`. Hex RBG values are usually used in HTML because the programmers who coded the browsers paid little or no attention to the fact that few people understand hexadecimal notation or arithmetic.

In decimal RGB, each value must be one of `0`, `51`, `102`, `153`, `204`, or `255`. RGB decimal values are usually used in graphics editors because graphics artists are rarely computer programmers and everybody knows what they mean.

In an HTML color description, the hex values are typically run together and preceded by a pound (crosshatch) sign, so a color with a red value of `33`, a blue value of `66`, and a green value of `99` looks like this: `#336699`.

Using colors by name and by value

1. Ordinarily, you should specify colors by the hex pair method. Every color is defined by a single number specifying how much red, green, and blue are contained in the target color ranging from none, `00`, to as much as possible, `FF`, pronounced "Fox Fox." Quick Usage Tip: `color="#RRGGBB"` where *RR* stands for the two digits reserved for red, *GG* stands for the two digits reserved for green, and *BB* stands for the two digits reserved for blue. Hex numbers are usually spoken aloud by naming the letters by a naming scheme, of which there are almost as many as there are people who use them. A common sequence is Able, Baker, Charlie, Dog, Easy, Fox. So the hex number `5F9EA0`, which codes for cadetblue, would be pronounced "five, fox; nine, easy; able, zero."
2. You can also use the 16 HTML 4.0 named colors, which are a very small number of colors that are usually very stable across platforms and are also browser-safe on almost every color and grayscale monitor.
3. You can use browser-safe colors, which are 216 colors defined by hexadecimal pairs for the most part, although the HTML 4.0 named colors are part of, or in addition to, the 216.
4. Finally, you can use the Netscape named colors if you're designing for thousands or millions of colors. Most of the Netscape named colors are not browser-safe on either 16- or 256-color monitors.

APPENDIX

Entities and Characters

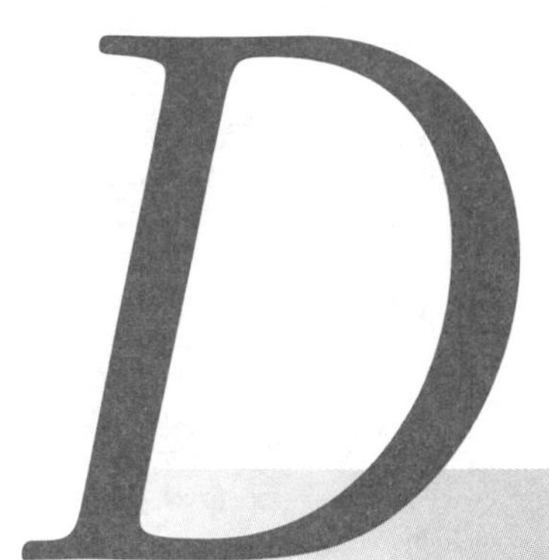

Characters Not on Your Keyboard

You may have noticed that your keyboard doesn't have all the characters you might want to type at one time or another. The cent character is missing, the copyright symbol, and many characters used in foreign languages. The people at the World Wide Web Consortium missed those characters too, and more that other people thought of. They were all added to the HTML 4.0 specification as Named Entities, which is a fancy way of saying that they've been given names that you can type in and browsers are supposed to figure out how to display them. They all follow the same pattern, an ampersand followed by the name followed by a semicolon. So the first one on the list, capital A with an acute accent over, Aacute, would be written in your code as `Á`, and the browser would display it as Á.

You can also type them in as numbers, which are harder to remember but have the slight advantage that some browsers handle numeric Named Entities better than they do the named versions. The previous capital A with an acute accent could be written as `Á` and the browser would handle it exactly the same way, displaying it as Á.

HTML 4.0 Character Entities

The following tables offer the same data in two different ways: in alphabetical order (see Table D.1) and in numerical order (see Table D.2). The reason for doing so is that if you know or can guess the name of the character, you can find the numeric equivalent that matches easily. Conversely, if you know the number, you can figure out what it does by looking at the description.

Tip

The general rule in HTML is that letter case doesn't matter, but character names are exceptions because they belong to another standard—ISO. Few browsers support all the characters, however, so if you have your heart set on one particular but obscure glyph, it's probably safer to use the numeric value and test it in many browsers before passing it onto the Web.

Note

Portions ® International Standards Organization, 1986.

Permission to copy in any form is granted for use with conforming SGML systems and applications as defined in ISO 8879, provided this notice is included in all copies.

TABLE D.1 **HTML 4.0 character entities in alphabetical order**

Name	Value	Description
Á	Á	capital A, acute accent
á	á	small a, acute accent
Â	Â	capital A, circumflex accent
â	â	small a, circumflex accent
´	´	acute accent
Æ	Æ	capital AE diphthong (ligature)
æ	æ	small ae diphthong (ligature)
À	À	capital A, grave accent
à	à	small a, grave accent
ℵ	ℵ	alef symbol, first transfinite cardinal, Unicode: 2135
Α	Α	Greek capital letter alpha, Unicode: 0391
α	α	Greek small letter alpha, Unicode: 03B1
&	&	ampersand, Unicode: 0026
∧	⊥	logical and, wedge, Unicode: 2227
∠	∠	angle, Unicode: 2220
Å	Å	capital A, ring
å	å	small a, ring
≈	≈	almost equal to, asymptotic to, Unicode: 2248
Ã	Ã	capital A, tilde
ã	ã	small a, tilde
Ä	Ä	capital A, dieresis or umlaut mark

Name	Value	Description
ä	ä	small a, dieresis or umlaut mark
„	„	double low-9 quotation mark, Unicode: 201E
Β	Β	Greek capital letter beta, Unicode: 0392
β	β	Greek small letter beta, Unicode: 03B2
¦	¦	broken (vertical) bar
•	•	bullet, black small circle, Unicode: 2022
∩	∩	intersection, cap, Unicode: 2229
Ç	Ç	capital C, cedilla
ç	ç	small c, cedilla
¸	¸	cedilla
¢	¢	cent sign
Χ	Χ	Greek capital letter chi, Unicode: 03A7
χ	χ	Greek small letter chi, Unicode: 03C7
ˆ	ˆ	modifier letter circumflex accent, Unicode: 02C6
♣	♣	black club suit, shamrock, Unicode: 2663
≅	≅	approximately equal to, Unicode: 2245
©	©	copyright sign
↵	↵	downwards arrow with corner leftwards, carriage return, Unicode: 21B5
∪	∪	union, cup, Unicode: 222A
¤	¤	general currency sign
⇓	⇓	downwards double arrow, Unicode: 21D3
‡	‡	double dagger, Unicode: 2021
†	†	dagger, Unicode: 2020
↓	↓	downwards arrow, Unicode: 2193
°	°	degree sign
Δ	Δ	Greek capital letter delta, Unicode: 0394
δ	δ	Greek small letter delta, Unicode: 03B4
♦	♦	black diamond suit, Unicode: 2666

continues...

TABLE D.1 Continued

Name	Value	Description
`÷`	`÷`	division sign
`É`	`É`	capital E, acute accent
`é`	`é`	small e, acute accent
`Ê`	`Ê`	capital E, circumflex accent
`ê`	`ê`	small e, circumflex accent
`È`	`È`	capital E, grave accent
`è`	`è`	small e, grave accent
`∅`	`∅`	empty set, null set, diameter, Unicode: 2205
` `	` `	em space, Unicode: 2003
` `	` `	en space, Unicode: 2002
`Ε`	`Ε`	Greek capital letter epsilon, Unicode: 0395
`ε`	`ε`	Greek small letter epsilon, Unicode: 03B5
`≡`	`≡`	identical to, Unicode: 2261
`Η`	`Η`	Greek capital letter eta, Unicode: 0397
`η`	`η`	Greek small letter eta, Unicode: 03B7
`Ð`	`Ð`	capital Eth, Icelandic
`ð`	`ð`	small eth, Icelandic
`Ë`	`Ë`	capital E, dieresis or umlaut mark
`ë`	`ë`	small e, dieresis or umlaut mark
`∃`	`∃`	there exists, Unicode: 2203
`ƒ`	`ƒ`	Latin small f with hook, function, florin, Unicode: 0192
`∀`	`∀`	for all, Unicode: 2200
`½`	`½`	fraction one-half
`¼`	`¼`	fraction one-quarter
`¾`	`¾`	fraction three-quarters
`⁄`	`⁄`	fraction slash, Unicode: 2044
`Γ`	`Γ`	Greek capital letter gamma, Unicode: 0393
`γ`	`γ`	Greek small letter gamma, Unicode: 03B3

Name	Value	Description
`≥`	`≥`	greater-than or equal to, Unicode: 2265
`>`	`>`	greater-than sign, Unicode: 003E
`⇔`	`⇔`	left right double arrow, Unicode: 21D4
`↔`	`↔`	left right arrow, Unicode: 2194
`♥`	`♥`	black heart suit, valentine, Unicode: 2665
`…`	`…`	horizontal ellipsis, three dot leader, Unicode: 2026
`Í`	`Í`	capital I, acute accent
`í`	`í`	small i, acute accent
`Î`	`Î`	capital I, circumflex accent
`î`	`î`	small i, circumflex accent
`¡`	`¡`	inverted exclamation mark
`Ì`	`Ì`	capital I, grave accent
`ì`	`ì`	small i, grave accent
`ℑ`	`ℑ`	blackletter capital I, imaginary part, Unicode: 2111
`∞`	`∞`	infinity, Unicode: 221E
`∫`	`∫`	integral, Unicode: 222B
`Ι`	`Ι`	Greek capital letter iota, Unicode: 0399
`ι`	`ι`	Greek small letter iota, Unicode: 03B9
`¿`	`¿`	inverted question mark
`∈`	`∈`	element of, Unicode: 2208
`Ï`	`Ï`	capital I, dieresis or umlaut mark
`ï`	`ï`	small i, dieresis or umlaut mark
`Κ`	`Κ`	Greek capital letter kappa, Unicode: 039A
`κ`	`κ`	Greek small letter kappa, Unicode: 03BA
`⇐`	`⇐`	leftwards double arrow, Unicode: 21D0
`Λ`	`Λ`	Greek capital letter lambda, Unicode: 039B
`λ`	`λ`	Greek small letter lambda, Unicode: 03BB
`⟨`	`〈`	left-pointing angle bracket, Unicode: 2329

continues…

TABLE D.1 Continued

Name	Value	Description
«	«	angle quotation mark, left
←	←	leftwards arrow, Unicode: 2190
⌈	⌈	left ceiling, apl upstile, Unicode: 2308
“	“	left double quotation mark, Unicode: 201C
≤	≤	less-than or equal to, Unicode: 2264
⌊	⌊	left floor, apl downstile, Unicode: 230A
∗	∗	asterisk operator, Unicode: 2217
◊	◊	lozenge, Unicode: 25CA
‎	‎	left-to-right mark, Unicode: 200E RFC 2070
‹	‹	single left-pointing angle quotation mark, Unicode: 2039
‘	‘	left single quotation mark, Unicode: 2018
<	<	less-than sign, Unicode: 003C
¯	¯	macron
—	—	em dash, Unicode: 2014
µ	µ	micro sign
·	·	middle dot
−	−	minus sign, Unicode: 2212
Μ	Μ	Greek capital letter mu, Unicode: 039C
μ	μ	Greek small letter mu, Unicode: 03BC
∇	∇	nabla, backward difference, Unicode: 2207
		no-break space
–	–	en dash, Unicode: 2013
≠	≠	not equal to, Unicode: 2260
∋	∋	contains as member, Unicode: 220B
¬	¬	not sign
∉	∉	not an element of, Unicode: 2209
⊄	⊄	not a subset of, Unicode: 2284
Ñ	Ñ	capital N, tilde

Name	Value	Description
ñ	ñ	small n, tilde
Ν	Ν	Greek capital letter nu, Unicode: 039D
ν	ν	Greek small letter nu, Unicode: 03BD
Ó	Ó	capital O, acute accent
ó	ó	small o, acute accent
Ô	Ô	capital O, circumflex accent
ô	ô	small o, circumflex accent
Œ	Œ	Latin capital ligature oe, Unicode: 0152
œ	œ	Latin small ligature oe, Unicode: 0153
Ò	Ò	capital O, grave accent
ò	ò	small o, grave accent
‾	‾	overline, spacing overscore, Unicode: 203E
Ω	Ω	Greek capital letter omega, Unicode: 03A9
ω	ω	Greek small letter omega, Unicode: 03C9
Ο	Ο	Greek capital letter omicron, Unicode: 039F
ο	ο	Greek small letter omicron, Unicode: 03BF
⊕	⊕	circled plus, direct sum, Unicode: 2295
∨	⊦	logical or, vee, Unicode: 2228
ª	ª	ordinal indicator, feminine
º	º	ordinal indicator, masculine
Ø	Ø	capital O, slash
ø	ø	small o, slash
Õ	Õ	capital O, tilde
õ	õ	small o, tilde
⊗	⊗	circled times, vector product, Unicode: 2297
Ö	Ö	capital O, dieresis or umlaut mark
ö	ö	small o, dieresis or umlaut mark
¶	¶	pilcrow (paragraph sign)
∂	∂	partial differential, Unicode: 2202

continues…

TABLE D.1 Continued

Name	Value	Description
‰	‰	per mille sign, Unicode: 2030
⊥	⊥	up tack, orthogonal to, perpendicular, Unicode: 22A5
Φ	Φ	Greek capital letter phi, Unicode: 03A6
φ	φ	Greek small letter phi, Unicode: 03C6
Π	Π	Greek capital letter pi, Unicode: 03A0
π	π	Greek small letter pi, Unicode: 03C0
ϖ	ϖ	Greek pi symbol, Unicode: 03D6
±	±	plus-or-minus sign
£	£	pound sterling sign
″	″	double prime, seconds, inches, Unicode: 2033
′	′	prime, minutes, feet, Unicode: 2032
∏	∏	n-ary product, product sign, Unicode: 220F
∝	∝	proportional to, Unicode: 221D
Ψ	Ψ	Greek capital letter psi, Unicode: 03A8
ψ	ψ	Greek small letter psi, Unicode: 03C8
"	"	quotation mark, apl quote, Unicode: 0022
⇒	⇒	rightwards double arrow, Unicode: 21D2
√	√	square root, radical sign, Unicode: 221A
⟩	〉	right-pointing angle bracket, ket, Unicode: 232A
»	»	angle quotation mark, right
→	→	rightwards arrow, Unicode: 2192
⌉	⌉	right ceiling, Unicode: 2309
”	”	right double quotation mark, Unicode: 201D
ℜ	ℜ	blackletter capital R, real part symbol, Unicode: 211C
®	®	registered sign
⌋	⌋	right floor, Unicode: 230B,
Ρ	Ρ	Greek capital letter rho, Unicode: 03A1

Name	Value	Description
ρ	ρ	Greek small letter rho, Unicode: 03C1
‏	‏	right-to-left mark, Unicode: 200F RFC 2070
›	›	single right-pointing angle quotation mark, Unicode: 203A
’	’	right single quotation mark, Unicode: 2019
‚	‚	single low-9 quotation mark, Unicode: 201A
Š	Š	Latin capital letter s with caron, Unicode: 0160
š	š	Latin small letter s with caron, Unicode: 0161
⋅	⋅	dot operator, Unicode: 22C5
§	§	section sign
		soft hyphen
Σ	Σ	Greek capital letter sigma, Unicode: 03A3
σ	σ	Greek small letter sigma, Unicode: 03C3
ς	ς	Greek small letter final sigma, Unicode: 03C2
∼	∼	tilde operator, varies with, similar to, Unicode: 223C
♠	♠	black spade suit, Unicode: 2660
⊂	⊂	subset of, Unicode: 2282
⊆	⊆	subset of or equal to, Unicode: 2286
∑	∑	n-ary summation, Unicode: 2211
⊃	⊃	superset of, Unicode: 2283
¹	¹	superscript 1
²	²	superscript 2
³	³	superscript 3
⊇	⊇	superset of or equal to, Unicode: 2287
ß	ß	small sharp s, German (sz ligature)
Τ	Τ	Greek capital letter tau, Unicode: 03A4
τ	τ	Greek small letter tau, Unicode: 03C4
∴	∴	therefore, Unicode: 2234
Θ	Θ	Greek capital letter theta, Unicode: 0398

continues...

TABLE D.1 Continued

Name	Value	Description
θ	θ	Greek small letter theta, Unicode: 03B8
ϑ	ϑ	Greek small letter theta symbol, Unicode: 03D1
		thin space, Unicode: 2009
Þ	Þ	capital THORN, Icelandic
þ	þ	small thorn, Icelandic
˜	˜	small tilde, Unicode: 02DC
×	×	multiply sign
™	™	trade mark sign, Unicode: 2122
⇑	⇑	upwards double arrow, Unicode: 21D1
Ú	Ú	capital U, acute accent
ú	ú	small u, acute accent
↑	↑	upwards arrow, Unicode: 2191
Û	Û	capital U, circumflex accent
û	û	small u, circumflex accent
Ù	Ù	capital U, grave accent
ù	ù	small u, grave accent
¨	¨	umlaut (dieresis)
ϒ	ϒ	Greek upsilon with hook symbol, Unicode: 03D2
Υ	Υ	Greek capital letter upsilon, Unicode: 03A5
υ	υ	Greek small letter upsilon, Unicode: 03C5
Ü	Ü	capital U, dieresis or umlaut mark
ü	ü	small u, dieresis or umlaut mark
℘	℘	script capital P, power set, Weierstrass p, Unicode: 2118
Ξ	Ξ	Greek capital letter xi, Unicode: 039E
ξ	ξ	Greek small letter xi, Unicode: 03BE
Ý	Ý	capital Y, acute accent
ý	ý	small y, acute accent

Name	Value	Description
¥	¥	yen sign
Ÿ	Ÿ	Latin capital letter Y with dieresis, Unicode: 0178
ÿ	ÿ	small y, dieresis or umlaut mark
Ζ	Ζ	Greek capital letter zeta, Unicode: 0396
ζ	ζ	Greek small letter zeta, Unicode: 03B6
‍	‍	zero width joiner, Unicode: 200D
‌	‌	zero width non-joiner, Unicode: 200C

TABLE D.2 HTML 4.0 character entities in numerical order

Name	Value	Description
"	"	quotation mark, apl quote, Unicode: 0022
&	&	ampersand, Unicode: 0026
<	<	less-than sign, Unicode: 003C
>	>	greater-than sign, Unicode: 003E
		no-break space
¡	¡	inverted exclamation mark
¢	¢	cent sign
£	£	pound sterling sign
¤	¤	general currency sign
¥	¥	yen sign
¦	¦	broken (vertical) bar
§	§	section sign
¨	¨	umlaut (dieresis)
©	©	copyright sign
ª	ª	ordinal indicator, feminine
«	«	angle quotation mark, left
¬	¬	not sign
		soft hyphen
®	®	registered sign

continues…

TABLE D.2 **Continued**

Name	Value	Description
`¯`	`¯`	macron
`°`	`°`	degree sign
`±`	`±`	plus-or-minus sign
`²`	`²`	superscript 2
`³`	`³`	superscript 3
`´`	`´`	acute accent
`µ`	`µ`	micro sign
`¶`	`¶`	pilcrow (paragraph sign)
`·`	`·`	middle dot
`¸`	`¸`	cedilla
`¹`	`¹`	superscript one
`º`	`º`	ordinal indicator, masculine
`»`	`»`	angle quotation mark, right
`¼`	`¼`	fraction one-quarter
`½`	`½`	fraction one-half
`¾`	`¾`	fraction three-quarters
`¿`	`¿`	inverted question mark
`À`	`À`	capital A, grave accent
`Á`	`Á`	capital A, acute accent
`Â`	`Â`	capital A, circumflex accent
`Ã`	`Ã`	capital A, tilde
`Ä`	`Ä`	capital A, dieresis or umlaut mark
`Å`	`Å`	capital A, ring
`Æ`	`Æ`	capital AE diphthong (ligature)
`Ç`	`Ç`	capital C, cedilla
`È`	`È`	capital E, grave accent
`É`	`É`	capital E, acute accent
`Ê`	`Ê`	capital E, circumflex accent
`Ë`	`Ë`	capital E, dieresis or umlaut mark

Name	Value	Description
Ì	Ì	capital I, grave accent
Í	Í	capital I, acute accent
Î	Î	capital I, circumflex accent
Ï	Ï	capital I, dieresis or umlaut mark
Ð	Ð	capital Eth, Icelandic
Ñ	Ñ	capital N, tilde
Ò	Ò	capital O, grave accent
Ó	Ó	capital O, acute accent
Ô	Ô	capital O, circumflex accent
Õ	Õ	capital O, tilde
Ö	Ö	capital O, dieresis or umlaut mark
×	×	multiply sign
Ø	Ø	capital O, slash
Ù	Ù	capital U, grave accent
Ú	Ú	capital U, acute accent
Û	Û	capital U, circumflex accent
Ü	Ü	capital U, dieresis or umlaut mark
Ý	Ý	capital Y, acute accent
Þ	Þ	capital THORN, Icelandic
ß	ß	small sharp s, German (sz ligature)
à	à	small a, grave accent
á	á	small a, acute accent
â	â	small a, circumflex accent
ã	ã	small a, tilde
ä	ä	small a, dieresis or umlaut mark
å	å	small a, ring
æ	æ	small ae diphthong (ligature)
ç	ç	small c, cedilla
è	è	small e, grave accent

continues...

TABLE D.2 **Continued**

Name	Value	Description
`é`	`é`	small e, acute accent
`ê`	`ê`	small e, circumflex accent
`ë`	`ë`	small e, dieresis or umlaut mark
`ì`	`ì`	small i, grave accent
`í`	`í`	small i, acute accent
`î`	`î`	small i, circumflex accent
`ï`	`ï`	small i, dieresis or umlaut mark
`ð`	`ð`	small eth, Icelandic
`ñ`	`ñ`	small n, tilde
`ò`	`ò`	small o, grave accent
`ó`	`ó`	small o, acute accent
`ô`	`ô`	small o, circumflex accent
`õ`	`õ`	small o, tilde
`ö`	`ö`	small o, dieresis or umlaut mark
`÷`	`÷`	divide sign
`ø`	`ø`	small o, slash
`ù`	`ù`	small u, grave accent
`ú`	`ú`	small u, acute accent
`û`	`û`	small u, circumflex accent
`ü`	`ü`	small u, dieresis or umlaut mark
`ý`	`ý`	small y, acute accent
`þ`	`þ`	small thorn, Icelandic
`ÿ`	`ÿ`	small y, dieresis or umlaut mark
`Œ`	`Œ`	Latin capital ligature oe, Unicode: `0152`
`œ`	`œ`	Latin small ligature oe, Unicode: `0153`
`Š`	`Š`	Latin capital letter S with caron, Unicode: `0160`
`š`	`š`	Latin small letter s with caron, Unicode: `0161`
`Ÿ`	`Ÿ`	Latin capital letter Y with dieresis, Unicode: `0178`

Name	Value	Description
ƒ	ƒ	Latin small f with hook, function, florin, Unicode: 0192
ˆ	ˆ	modifier letter circumflex accent, Unicode: 02C6
˜	˜	small tilde, Unicode: 02DC
Α	Α	Greek capital letter alpha, Unicode: 0391
Β	Β	Greek capital letter beta, Unicode: 0392
Γ	Γ	Greek capital letter gamma, Unicode: 0393
Δ	Δ	Greek capital letter delta, Unicode: 0394
Ε	Ε	Greek capital letter epsilon, Unicode: 0395
Ζ	Ζ	Greek capital letter zeta, Unicode: 0396
Η	Η	Greek capital letter eta, Unicode: 0397
Θ	Θ	Greek capital letter theta, Unicode: 0398
Ι	Ι	Greek capital letter iota, Unicode: 0399
Κ	Κ	Greek capital letter kappa, Unicode: 039A
Λ	Λ	Greek capital letter lambda, Unicode: 039B
Μ	Μ	Greek capital letter mu, Unicode: 039C
Ν	Ν	Greek capital letter nu, Unicode: 039D
Ξ	Ξ	Greek capital letter xi, Unicode: 039E
Ο	Ο	Greek capital letter omicron, Unicode: 039F
Π	Π	Greek capital letter pi, Unicode: 03A0
Ρ	Ρ	Greek capital letter rho, Unicode: 03A1
Σ	Σ	Greek capital letter sigma, Unicode: 03A3
Τ	Τ	Greek capital letter tau, Unicode: 03A4
Υ	Υ	Greek capital letter upsilon, Unicode: 03A5
Φ	Φ	Greek capital letter phi, Unicode: 03A6
Χ	Χ	Greek capital letter chi, Unicode: 03A7
Ψ	Ψ	Greek capital letter psi, Unicode: 03A8
Ω	Ω	Greek capital letter omega, Unicode: 03A9
α	α	Greek small letter alpha, Unicode: 03B1

continues…

TABLE D.2 **Continued**

Name	Value	Description
β	β	Greek small letter beta, Unicode: 03B2
γ	γ	Greek small letter gamma, Unicode: 03B3
δ	δ	Greek small letter delta, Unicode: 03B4
ε	ε	Greek small letter epsilon, Unicode: 03B5
ζ	ζ	Greek small letter zeta, Unicode: 03B6
η	η	Greek small letter eta, Unicode: 03B7
θ	θ	Greek small letter theta, Unicode: 03B8
ι	ι	Greek small letter iota, Unicode: 03B9
κ	κ	Greek small letter kappa, Unicode: 03BA
λ	λ	Greek small letter lambda, Unicode: 03BB
μ	μ	Greek small letter mu, Unicode: 03BC
ν	ν	Greek small letter nu, Unicode: 03BD
ξ	ξ	Greek small letter xi, Unicode: 03BE
ο	ο	Greek small letter omicron, Unicode: 03BF
π	π	Greek small letter pi, Unicode: 03C0
ρ	ρ	Greek small letter rho, Unicode: 03C1
ς	ς	Greek small letter final sigma, Unicode: 03C2
σ	σ	Greek small letter sigma, Unicode: 03C3
τ	τ	Greek small letter tau, Unicode: 03C4
υ	υ	Greek small letter upsilon, Unicode: 03C5
φ	φ	Greek small letter phi, Unicode: 03C6
χ	χ	Greek small letter chi, Unicode: 03C7
ψ	ψ	Greek small letter psi, Unicode: 03C8
ω	ω	Greek small letter omega, Unicode: 03C9
ϑ	ϑ	Greek small letter theta symbol, Unicode: 03D1
ϒ	ϒ	Greek upsilon with hook symbol, Unicode: 03D2
ϖ	ϖ	Greek pi symbol, Unicode: 03D6
		en space, Unicode: 2002

Name	Value	Description
		em space, Unicode: 2003
		thin space, Unicode: 2009
‌	‌	zero width non-joiner, Unicode: 200C
‍	‍	zero width joiner, Unicode: 200D
‎	‎	left-to-right mark, Unicode: 200E RFC 2070
‏	‏	right-to-left mark, Unicode: 200F RFC 2070
–	–	en dash, Unicode: 2013
—	—	em dash, Unicode: 2014
‘	‘	left single quotation mark, Unicode: 2018
’	’	right single quotation mark, Unicode: 2019
‚	‚	single low-9 quotation mark, Unicode: 201A
“	“	left double quotation mark, Unicode: 201C
”	”	right double quotation mark, Unicode: 201D
„	„	double low-9 quotation mark, Unicode: 201E
†	†	dagger, Unicode: 2020
‡	‡	double dagger, Unicode: 2021
•	•	bullet, black small circle, Unicode: 2022
…	…	horizontal ellipsis, three dot leader, Unicode: 2026
‰	‰	per mille sign, Unicode: 2030
′	′	prime, minutes, feet, Unicode: 2032
″	″	double prime, seconds, inches, Unicode: 2033
‹	‹	single left-pointing angle quotation mark, Unicode: 2039
›	›	single right-pointing angle quotation mark, Unicode: 203A
‾	‾	overline, spacing overscore, Unicode: 203E
⁄	⁄	fraction slash, Unicode: 2044
ℑ	ℑ	blackletter capital I, imaginary part, Unicode: 2111

continues...

TABLE D.2 **Continued**

Name	Value	Description
℘	℘	script capital P, power set, Weierstrass p, Unicode: 2118
ℜ	ℜ	blackletter capital R, real part symbol, Unicode: 211C
™	™	trade mark sign, Unicode: 2122
ℵ	ℵ	alef symbol, first transfinite cardinal, Unicode: 2135
←	←	leftwards arrow, Unicode: 2190
↑	↑	upwards arrow, Unicode: 2191
→	→	rightwards arrow, Unicode: 2192
↓	↓	downwards arrow, Unicode: 2193
↔	↔	left right arrow, Unicode: 2194
↵	↵	downwards arrow with corner leftwards, carriage return, Unicode: 21B5
⇐	⇐	leftwards double arrow, Unicode: 21D0
⇑	⇑	upwards double arrow, Unicode: 21D1
⇒	⇒	rightwards double arrow, Unicode: 21D2
⇓	⇓	downwards double arrow, Unicode: 21D3
⇔	⇔	left right double arrow, Unicode: 21D4
∀	∀	for all, Unicode: 2200
∂	∂	partial differential, Unicode: 2202
∃	∃	there exists, Unicode: 2203
∅	∅	empty set, null set, diameter, Unicode: 2205
∇	∇	nabla, backward difference, Unicode: 2207
∈	∈	element of, Unicode: 2208
∉	∉	not an element of, Unicode: 2209
∋	∋	contains as member, Unicode: 220B
∏	∏	n-ary product, product sign, Unicode: 220F
∑	∑	n-ary summation, Unicode: 2211
−	−	minus sign, Unicode: 2212

Name	Value	Description
∗	∗	asterisk operator, Unicode: 2217
√	√	square root, radical sign, Unicode: 221A
∝	∝	proportional to, Unicode: 221D
∞	∞	infinity, Unicode: 221E
∠	∠	angle, Unicode: 2220
∩	∩	intersection, cap, Unicode: 2229
∪	∪	union, cup, Unicode: 222A
∫	∫	integral, Unicode: 222B
∴	∴	therefore, Unicode: 2234
∼	∼	tilde operator, varies with, similar to, Unicode: 223C
≅	≅	approximately equal to, Unicode: 2245
≈	≈	almost equal to, asymptotic to, Unicode: 2248
≠	≠	not equal to, Unicode: 2260
≡	≡	identical to, Unicode: 2261
≤	≤	less-than or equal to, Unicode: 2264
≥	≥	greater-than or equal to, Unicode: 2265
⊂	⊂	subset of, Unicode: 2282
⊃	⊃	superset of, Unicode: 2283
⊄	⊄	not a subset of, Unicode: 2284
⊆	⊆	subset of or equal to, Unicode: 2286
⊇	⊇	superset of or equal to, Unicode: 2287
⊕	⊕	circled plus, direct sum, Unicode: 2295
⊗	⊗	circled times, vector product, Unicode: 2297
∧	⊥	logical and, wedge, Unicode: 2227
⊥	⊥	up tack, orthogonal to, perpendicular, Unicode: 22A5
∨	⊦	logical or, vee, Unicode: 2228
⋅	⋅	dot operator, Unicode: 22C5
⌈	⌈	left ceiling, apl upstile, Unicode: 2308

continues...

TABLE D.2 **Continued**

Name	Value	Description
`⌉`	`⌉`	right ceiling, Unicode: 2309
`⌊`	`⌊`	left floor, apl downstile, Unicode: 230A
`⌋`	`⌋`	right floor, Unicode: 230B
`⟨`	`〈`	left-pointing angle bracket, bra, Unicode: 2329
`⟩`	`〉`	right-pointing angle bracket, ket, Unicode: 232A
`◊`	`◊`	lozenge, Unicode: 25CA
`♠`	`♠`	black spade suit, Unicode: 2660
`♣`	`♣`	black club suit, shamrock, Unicode: 2663
`♥`	`♥`	black heart suit, valentine, Unicode: 2665
`♦`	`♦`	black diamond suit, Unicode: 2666

Glossary

abbreviation A shorthand way of writing a longer phrase or word. Bldg. is an abbreviation for building and should be pronounced as the full word rather than bulldig. We may chuckle about this, but it's a real problem for foreign speakers of English, audio browsers, and anyone not familiar with the word being abbreviated. Quick, do you really know what DNA stands for? Or MAD? (Hint: Deoxyribonucleic Acid and Mutually Assured Destruction)

acronym A shortened phrase or word combination identified by its initials rather than the full phrase for convenience in speaking or writing. Most people just say FBI (Eff Bee Eye), rather than Federal Bureau of Investigation, because the full phrase sounds stilted in American English since we're very familiar with the agency here. In India or Scotland the acronym might not be so clear so there is a special acronym tag to explain further without annoying the many who do understand.

additive color A color formed by combinations of colored lights that create the appearance of a pure color by adding certain wavelengths to the transmitted light. Adding all three of the additive colors together makes white: a combination of red, green, and blue.

algorithm A sequence of steps or program routines that carry out a particular task. The algorithm for ordering a delivered pizza is look up the pizza number, call, order the pizza, hang up, and wait for delivery. It's basically a fancy way of describing a recipe or procedure.

animation An image composed of several consecutive images that are loaded by the browser one after the other, creating the illusion of movement, a slide show, or both. Most are GIF images, although other formats are possible, including video and three-dimensional formats that allow the user to look around inside the image. Making these latter sorts of animated images is beyond the scope of this book, because they require special hardware or very expensive software. When we talk about animations, we mean GIF files unless otherwise specified.

attributes Keywords and associated values that modify or extend a basic HTML tag in some way. Attributes are always included in the opening tag like this: `<TAG attribute1="value1" attribute2="value2">your text</TAG>`.

banding A noticeable jump in value between areas of what should be a smooth gradient or wash in a photograph or illustration.

bandwidth The speed at which you access the Internet is often called bandwidth because it's a complex interaction between the speed at which your provider can access the Net and your own access speed. If your provider is trying to share relatively low-speed access with too many customers, even an ISDN line may not get you much real speed.

binary file A program code, document, spreadsheet, graphic, sound, or other multimedia or structured file that can't be read as ordinary text. In general, if you have to use a program to decipher the file, it's a binary file. Even text files can be binary files if they allow you to insert formatted text like boldface or italics into them. It usually doesn't hurt to err by treating a file as binary. Ignoring its binary characteristics can break the file and prevent you from using it in the future, but it will soon become obvious which is which. Check destination files before deleting the originals if you have any doubts.

body section The main visible part of an HTML page, after the head section that contains housekeeping and setup information.

Browser Wars A lighthearted term for a spiteful conflict between the commercial browser makers conducted in deadly earnest. Basically, the "war" consists of including non-standard or quirky extensions to HTML so that pages designed to take advantage of them appear messy in competing browsers, or worse, display partial text or none. To say that this is destructive is an understatement, although they call it marketing. In the real world, it would be like driving into a gas station for a fill-up and having the gas company install a device on your car that caused it to stall or run badly if you used any other brand of gasoline.

Cascading Style Sheets Style sheets allow you to control almost every typographical element on the page. The "Cascading" part of the name means that you can have levels of style sheets defined, with the values specified in higher layers cascading or spilling over into lower layers. You could have a corporate style sheet that defined an overall look for an organization, but which could be extended or overridden for a particular department or publication; the lower-level style could, in turn, be overridden by individual style attributes on tags, or by a user style sheet on an individual browser. The current specification is CSS1 but there is already a CSS2 in the works.

child layer A layer (the child) that is contained by another layer (the parent). *See* **layer**.

client pull Actions that a browser takes on its own to reload a page or load a different page after a fixed interval. Client pull puts the cost of updating a session and keeping track of timing directly on the browser and is more popular today than the earlier server push. *See* **server push**.

closing tag Most HTML tags occur in pairs, an opening tag and a closing tag that duplicates the opening tag with the addition of a forward slash in front of the tag name. So the opening HTML tag is `<HTML>` while the closing HTML tag is `</HTML>`. Tag pairs like these are used like quotation marks or parentheses, almost always in pairs and surrounding some text in between.

coordinates For two dimensional figures, a number pair representing distances along the horizontal and vertical axes. In an image, the values are measured from the upper-left corner and the horizontal value comes first, so 0, 0 is the upper-left corner itself. 100, 50 is 100 pixels to the right of the left edge and 50 pixels down from the top.

dedicated access line A connection to the Internet that is always "on," requiring no dial-up or connection to be made. They usually come in 56Kbps or 64Kbps increments up to T1 and T3 capacities.

definition A way of making more information about a word or phrase available to visitors without being obtrusive. Related to abbreviations and acronyms but more widely supported right now. A definition allows you to use a phrase as if people would understand it, which is flattering, while at the same time providing a full explanation, which is tedious at times.

dithering A technique used to approximate colors that can't be displayed on a given monitor by using speckles of other colors in a sort of pointillist impression of the color if seen from a distance.

Document Type Definition (DTD) A language grammar in which all elements of a markup language are defined and their possible syntax and values are limited by rule.

download Copying files off the network (by which we mean another computer) and onto your own local machine. *See* **upload**.

element Loosely, an HTML tag. More precisely, the grammatical rule and indivisible portion of HTML that the tag embodies. This distinction is all very platonic and philosophical, and real people usually just call them tags unless they're speaking with great precision.

File Transfer Protocol A command line interface that allows you to select files for transfer to or from a remote machine using commands like `put` and `get`. There are other commands for changing directories on either end and choosing whether the file is a "binary" (code or graphics) file or contains ordinary ASCII text. *See* **FTP**.

frameset The collection of frames that organizes a framed environment (that is, what the user sees in his monitor). A frameset all by itself does not contain any information for the user. To be useful, it needs content, and the content of a frame is simply an HTML page.

FTP The File Transfer Protocol (FTP) is loosely any program that uses the FTP command protocol to transfer files. The actual commands of the interface are slightly quirky and obscure, and it is much easier to use with a graphical interface that hides the messy details from you. *See* **File Transfer Protocol**.

head section The first part of an HTML page that contains housekeeping and setup information.

hexadecimal A base-16 number system that uses digits that run from 0 through F, 0 1 2 3 4 5 6 7 8 9 A B C D E F. Because of the way computers are made, this is very convenient for machines and very difficult for people. If you think of ordinary decimal numbers as counting on your fingers, you could think of hexadecimal numbers as counting on your fingers plus the toes of one foot—if you had six toes.

hexadecimal pairs A series of three two-digit hexadecimal numbers, grouped together as one six-digit number preceded by a pound sign or hatch mark (#). Often shortened to the more casual *hex pairs*, they are used in HTML to identify colors without any possibility of confusion.

hexadecimal triplet A series of three hexadecimal numbers grouped together as one number, preceded by a pound sign or hatch mark.

HTML Hypertext Markup Language, the overall name for the tags you use to mark up your Web pages so they display and link to other pages correctly. HTML is the official standard endorsed by the World Wide Web Consortium (W3C), but is also a hodgepodge assortment of proprietary extensions and kludges invented more by marketeers than by any standards body.

imagemap An image with clickable areas that can link to other pages or locations within a file.

interim Literally, something used as a stopgap or temporary measure. The intent of the HTML 4.0 Recommendation is to replace the countless proprietary browser extensions with a single standard. Interim support for the most popular of these proprietary or badly-engineered schemes ensures that Web sites remain viewable through the majority of the browsers in service until browser technology catches up with the standard.

interlacing Structuring an image file so that an initial low resolution sample is transmitted first with more pixels being filled in at each successive pass over the image. The effect is of big blocky superpixels gradually resolving to finer and finer detail, almost as if the image were coming into focus in a telescope.

Internet service provider (ISP) A business that makes dial-up or dedicated connections to the Internet available to subscribers. Your local phone company undoubtedly offers ISP services and there are many others available, from national companies with thousands of access points in almost every major city or town to small, local businesses offering only local service. If you travel, you'll probably want a nationwide or even worldwide service, but you can sometimes get better deals and service through a local company if being able to dial in while on the road is not an issue.

Java A programming language that provides platform independence for Web applications and other user applications.

kludge A hastily thrown-together or slapdash code or page design that is unpleasant to look at or work on, and embarrassing to sign your name to.

layer An element whose position can be assigned above or below other elements within an HTML document, much like an overhead transparency sheet. This is implemented in Microsoft Internet Explorer through Cascading Style Sheets, while Netscape Navigator uses the <LAYER> tag.

markup language A language designed for the purpose of tagging raw text with inline formatting information that affects the display without changing the underlying text.

meta information Information that describes information itself, rather than being directly usable by an end user or process.

metaphor In programming terms, an underlying concept or physical task that allows a user to visualize the operation of a program or Web site in terms of a more familiar object.

MIME Type (multipart Internet mail extensions) A way of labeling files to tell programs, like mailers and browsers, what the file is so the application knows what to do with the files.

modem A device for connecting your computer to the Internet over ordinary phone lines. The name stands for MOdulator-DEModulator because it converts (modulates) electrical signals into sounds for transmission over phone lines and back again.

modem speed Modems are measured (roughly speaking) by how many tiny bits of information they can transmit every second. The means by which they do this is incredibly complex in today's modems but the bottom line is that the more bits-per-second they can transmit, the faster your browser seems to download pages.

navigation Generally, the activity of choosing and following hyperlinked destinations on the Web. Specifically, the elements that allow a visitor to find his way around in a Web site.

nested layer Layers contained within other layers. *See* **layer**.

optimize the color palette Many programs allow you to minimize the number of colors available in a color image on the Web. This may make it possible to compress the file and make downloading the file quicker.

outline A structured list of ideas and concepts organized so that main topic headings have sub-topic headings under them and are usually indented so that sub-topics get farther away from the margin. The HTML heading tags, `<H1>` through `<H6>`, correspond directly to outline topic headings, and some browsers allow you to view a page in outline form.

parent layer A layer (the parent) that contains other layers (a child or children). *See* **layer**.

PICS A voluntary rating system that can be placed on a page to help describe page content in a simple way. Most are used to rate sites based on violence and sexual content, so parents can control the sites their children are permitted to see. At least one, the Vancouver Web Pages system, also rates the page for things like ecological sensitivity and Canadian content.

pixel A pixel is the smallest part of the fine-grained mosaic that makes up a monitor display. A standard VGA display is 640 pixels wide by 480 pixels high. An SVGA (Super VGA) display is 800 pixels wide by 600 pixels high.

polygon Any geometric figure enclosed by a continuous path of straight line segments. Typically the word is reserved for figures that can't be described more simply as either rectangles or circles.

PPP Point-to-Point Protocol. A way of accessing the Internet that allows graphical information to be transmitted over a regular telephone line as if you were on a real network. PPP is a more modern and flexible protocol than SLIP but either will work.

property A style sheet term referring to the typographical characteristic being applied to a selector. A property might be font-size and the value applied to it might be 18pt. This would be written out as `{ font-size: 18pt; }`. *See* **value** and **selector**.

pseudo-class A modifier that acts to limit the scope of a selector to certain instances or to special states of the HTML element. Pseudo-classes are typically used to modify the anchor tag to distinguish visited, active, and unvisited links.

RSACI A PICS rating system describing sites in terms of sexual and violent content. Parents can control exactly which levels of any of the rated parameters they will allow their children to see, always assuming that the children aren't more skilled on the computer than their parents are. Most such schemes can be defeated rather simply by downloading a different browser and using it instead of the one filtered, or by tweaking a file located in a directory on disk.

scan To convert a physical image into machine-readable form by using a scanner that converts tiny bits of light and dark into bits. You can buy an inexpensive scanner for your own machine or "borrow" one from a commercial business that offers them by the hour. Many print and copy shops have scanners available.

search engine An indexing site that allows a visitor to search for sites that mention particular words or don't mention particular words. Most allow visitors to combine words and phrases to narrow down the number of sites returned to a manageable number. *See* **spider**.

selector A style sheet term referring to the series of elements that define the scope of a style sheet command. They are usually the name of an HTML tag, but may be combined to limit the scope of a command to tags in certain contexts or with certain modifiers. The selector might be H2 and the property value pair given to this tag might be a font size of 18 points. This would be written out in full as `H2 { font-size: 18pt; }`. *See* **value** and **property**.

server A machine dedicated to servicing requests from other computers. On the Web, this usually means delivering Web pages and their supporting files but also includes FTP servers and other specialized services like ICQ, a program that allows you to see if friends or colleagues are currently online.

server push Actions that the Web server takes on its own to force new content onto a page. Server push is not widely used any more because it's more expensive to keep track of sessions on the server end. *See* **client pull**.

shell account A UNIX account that allows direct access to a command line interface to a UNIX machine. If you get really serious about the Internet, you'll probably have one of these eventually, but this is really beyond the scope of this book.

SLIP Serial Line Interface Protocol. A way of accessing the Internet that allows graphical information to be transmitted over a regular telephone line as if you were on a real network. SLIP is an older and slightly less flexible protocol than PPP but either will work.

specifications HTML is theoretically defined by Document Type Definitions (DTDs) that define exactly what the syntax of the markup language should be. Unfortunately, none of the commercial browser manufacturers follows a DTD in reality, compromising on adherence to standards in favor of not breaking existing badly written pages and making their product different from the others by adding the browser equivalent of the Edsel automobile's tailfins and front grille.

spider A spider, or Web spider, is a program that automatically searches the Web for information. General-purpose spiders can be used to make indexes of many Web sites that form the raw material that a search engine can use to return a list of sites in response to a search request. Sometimes called a Web crawler or robot. *See* **search engine**.

spot color An area with a differently-colored background or text color, meant to highlight or set off a block of text or graphics from the rest of the page.

subtractive color A color formed by combinations of dyes or inks that creates the appearance of a pure color by subtracting certain wavelengths from the reflected light. Adding all three subtractive colors together makes black: a combination of cyan, magenta, and yellow.

T1 line A dedicated digital access line capable of transmitting one and a half megabits (millions of bits) per second. The equivalent of 24 ISDN lines.

T3 line A dedicated digital access line capable of transmitting forty-five megabits (millions of bits) per second. The equivalent of thirty T1 lines or seven hundred and twenty ISDN lines.

tag An HTML element, loosely speaking. A tag is a left angle bracket followed by an element keyword and zero or more optional attributes or a left angle bracket followed by a forward slash followed by an element keyword.

typography The science and art of arranging words on paper in ways that are both esthetically pleasing and maximally legible. The field encompasses type design, page layout, physical media selection, printing and display techniques, selecting the fonts used for different elements in the overall design, and designing and preparing the overall packaging of the work.

upload Copying the files on your computer to a Web server so other people can see them besides yourself. The server is presumed to be at a "higher" level than you are, which is why you load "up." In fact, the Internet is a peer-to-peer sort of place, very egalitarian, but the term originated in mainframe days and has stuck with us long after mainframes lost their cachet of holy superiority. *See* **download**.

value A style sheet term referring to the exact value being applied to a property. A value of `18pt` could be given to the property `font-size`. This would be written out as `{ font-size: 18pt; }`. *See* **property** and **selector**.

whitespace Extra spaces and carriage returns in the text. Unless specifically told otherwise by a tag, all browsers collapse all whitespace to a single space on output.

zip A type of file compression used to make files download faster over the Web. Basically, the program squeezes the extra space out of the files in such a way that it knows how to put all the extra space back later.

Index

Symbols

A

D

E

I

N

O

P

Q

R

T

U

V

W

X-Y-Z